GRE®

Graduate
Record
Examination

PREP 2022

Our 80 years' expertise = Your competitive advantage

2 PRACTICE TESTS + PROVEN STRATEGIES + ONLINE

GRE® is a registered trademark of the Educational Testing Service. Kaplan is neither

Acknowledgments

Editor, 2022 Edition
Craig Harman

Special thanks to our faculty authors and reviewers
Harry Broome, James Carney, Chris Cosci, Elisa Davis, Boris Dvorkin, Hannah Gist, Jack Hayes, Rebecca Houck, Jo L'Abbate, Jennifer Land, Heather Maigur, Robert Reiss, Gail Rivers, Jason Selzer, Gordon Spector, Gene Suhir, Ethan A. Weber

Additional special thanks to
Matthew Belinkie; Kim Bowers; M. Dominic Eggert; Paula L. Fleming, MA, MBA; Robin Garmise; Rita Garthaffner; Joanna Graham; Adam Grey; Rebecca Knauer; Mandy Luk; Jennifer Moore; Camellia Mukherjee; Monica Ostolaza; Michele Sandifer; Carly Schnur; Sascha Strelka, MA; Jay Thomas; Michael Wolff; Amy Zarkos; and the countless others who have contributed to this and past editions.

GRE® is a registered trademark of the Educational Testing Service. Kaplan materials do not contain actual GRE items and are neither endorsed by nor affiliated in any way with ETS.

Published by Kaplan Publishing
750 Third Avenue
New York, NY 10017

ISBN: 978-1-5062-7716-5

10 9 8 7 6 5 4 3 2 1

Kaplan Publishing books are available at special quantity discounts to use for sales promotions, employee premiums, or educational purposes. For more information or to order books, please call the Simon & Schuster special sales department at 1-866-506-1949.

TABLE OF CONTENTS

HOW TO USE THIS BOOK xi

PART ONE GETTING STARTED 1

   CHAPTER 1: INTRODUCTION TO THE GRE 3

      Understanding the GRE 3

      How the GRE is Organized 5

      Scoring 6

      Cancellation and Multiple-Scores Policy. 7

      Test Registration 8

      GRE Checklist 8

      GRE Subject Tests. 9

   CHAPTER 2: MULTI-STAGE TEST MECHANICS 11

      How the MST Works 11

      Navigating the GRE MST Interface 12

      MST Section Management Techniques. 14

      MST: The Upside 15

      MST: The Downside 15

      Paper-Based GRE Strategies 16

PART TWO VERBAL REASONING. 19

   CHAPTER 3: INTRODUCTION TO VERBAL REASONING 21

      Overview 21

      Verbal Reasoning Question Types. 22

      Pacing Strategy 22

      Navigating the Verbal Reasoning Section of This Book 23

   CHAPTER 4: VERBAL FOUNDATIONS AND CONTENT REVIEW. 25

      Introduction to Verbal Foundations and Content Review 25

      The Kaplan Guide to Improving Your Vocabulary 26

      Text Completion and Sentence Equivalence Practice Set 39

      Text Completion and Sentence Equivalence
      Practice Set Answer Key. 42

GO ONLINE

kaptest.com/moreonline

Text Completion and Sentence Equivalence Practice Set
Answers and Explanations 42

The Kaplan Guide to Improving Your Reading Comprehension Skills. . . . 45

Reading Comprehension Practice Set 49

Reading Comprehension Practice Set Answer Key. 54

Reading Comprehension Practice Set Answers and Explanations 54

CHAPTER 5: TEXT COMPLETION 57

Introduction to Text Completion 57

Kaplan's Additional Tips for Text Completion Questions 66

Text Completion Practice Set. 67

Text Completion Practice Set Answer Key. 70

Text Completion Practice Set Answers and Explanations 70

CHAPTER 6: SENTENCE EQUIVALENCE 73

Introduction to Sentence Equivalence 73

Kaplan's Additional Tips for Sentence Equivalence 78

Sentence Equivalence Practice Set 79

Sentence Equivalence Practice Set Answer Key 82

Sentence Equivalence Practice Set Answers and Explanations 82

CHAPTER 7: READING COMPREHENSION 85

Introduction to Reading Comprehension 85

How to Approach Reasoning Questions 119

Reading Comprehension Practice Set 123

Reading Comprehension Practice Set Answer Key. 126

Reading Comprehension Practice Set Answers and Explanations 126

CHAPTER 8: VERBAL REASONING PRACTICE SETS 129

Review of the Kaplan Methods for Verbal Reasoning 129

Verbal Reasoning Practice Set 1 130

Verbal Reasoning Practice Set 1 Answer Key 138

Verbal Reasoning Practice Set 1 Answers and Explanations. 140

Verbal Reasoning Practice Set 2 145

Verbal Reasoning Practice Set 2 Answer Key 152

Verbal Reasoning Practice Set 2 Answers and Explanations. 153

Verbal Reasoning Practice Set 3 158

Verbal Reasoning Practice Set 3 Answer Key 166

Verbal Reasoning Practice Set 3 Answers and Explanations. 167

PART THREE QUANTITATIVE REASONING 173

CHAPTER 9: INTRODUCTION TO QUANTITATIVE REASONING 175

    Overview 175

    Quantitative Reasoning Question Types 176

    What the GRE Quantitative Section is Testing 176

    Pacing Strategy 177

    Navigating the Quantitative Reasoning Section of This Book 178

**CHAPTER 10: MATH FOUNDATIONS—ARITHMETIC AND NUMBER
PROPERTIES REVIEW** 179

    Introduction to Arithmetic and Number Properties Review 179

    Arithmetic 180

    Number Properties 184

    Arithmetic and Number Properties Practice Set 196

    Arithmetic and Number Properties Practice Set Answer Key 198

    Arithmetic and Number Properties Practice Set
    Answers and Explanations 198

CHAPTER 11: MATH FOUNDATIONS—RATIOS AND MATH FORMULAS REVIEW 201

    Introduction to Ratios and Math Formulas Review 201

    Ratios 201

    Math Formulas 219

    Ratios and Math Formulas Practice Set 228

    Ratios and Math Formulas Practice Set Answer Key 230

    Ratios and Math Formulas Practice Set Answers
    and Explanations 230

CHAPTER 12: MATH FOUNDATIONS—ALGEBRA REVIEW 233

    Introduction to Algebra Review 233

    Algebraic Terms 233

    Basic Operations 234

    Advanced Operations 235

    Polynomials and Quadratics 241

    Alternative Strategies for Multiple-Choice Algebra 243

    Dealing with Word Problems 247

    Dealing with Logic Problems 250

    Algebra Practice Set 251

    Algebra Practice Set Answer Key 254

    Algebra Practice Set Answers and Explanations 254

CHAPTER 13: MATH FOUNDATIONS—STATISTICS REVIEW 257

Introduction to Statistics Review 257

Median, Mode, and Range 257

Quartiles 259

Standard Deviation. 261

Frequency Distributions 263

Graphs and Tables 267

Statistics Practice Set 274

Statistics Practice Set Answer Key. 280

Statistics Practice Set Answers and Explanations 280

**CHAPTER 14: MATH FOUNDATIONS—COUNTING METHODS AND
PROBABILITY REVIEW** 283

Introduction to Counting Methods and Probability Review 283

Counting Methods 283

Probability 288

Counting Methods and Probability Practice Set 291

Counting Methods and Probability Practice Set Answer Key 294

Counting Methods and Probability Practice Set
Answers and Explanations 294

CHAPTER 15: MATH FOUNDATIONS—GEOMETRY REVIEW 297

Introduction to Geometry Review. 297

Lines and Angles 297

Polygons 301

Triangles 302

Quadrilaterals 308

Circles. 311

Coordinate Geometry 314

Graphing Functions and Circles. 318

Solids 321

Multiple Figures. 323

Geometry Practice Set 326

Geometry Practice Set Answer Key 330

Geometry Practice Set Answers and Explanations. 330

CHAPTER 16: QUANTITATIVE COMPARISON 333

Introduction to Quantitative Comparison. 333

Kaplan's Additional Tips for Quantitative Comparison Questions 337

Quantitative Comparison Practice Set 339

Quantitative Comparison Practice Set Answer Key 342

Quantitative Comparison Practice Set Answers and Explanations 342

CHAPTER 17: PROBLEM SOLVING 345

Introduction to Problem Solving 345

Kaplan's Additional Tips for Problem Solving 352

Problem Solving Practice Set 354

Problem Solving Practice Set Answer Key 358

Problem Solving Practice Set Answers and Explanations. 358

CHAPTER 18: DATA INTERPRETATION 361

Introduction to Data Interpretation Questions 361

Kaplan's Additional Tips for Data Interpretation Questions 368

Data Interpretation Practice Set 370

Data Interpretation Practice Set Answer Key 374

Data Interpretation Practice Set Answers and Explanations. 374

CHAPTER 19: QUANTITATIVE REASONING PRACTICE SETS 377

Review of the Kaplan Methods for Quantitative Reasoning 377

Quantitative Reasoning Practice Set 1 378

Quantitative Reasoning Practice Set 1 Answer Key 384

Quantitative Reasoning Practice Set 1 Answers and Explanations 386

Quantitative Reasoning Practice Set 2 390

Quantitative Reasoning Practice Set 2 Answer Key 396

Quantitative Reasoning Practice Set 2 Answers and Explanations 397

Quantitative Reasoning Practice Set 3 401

Quantitative Reasoning Practice Set 3 Answer Key 406

Quantitative Reasoning Practice Set 3 Answers and Explanations 407

PART FOUR ANALYTICAL WRITING 411

CHAPTER 20: INTRODUCTION TO ANALYTICAL WRITING 413

Overview 413

Analytical Writing Essay Types 414

Scoring 414

Pacing Strategy 417

Navigating the Analytical Writing Section of This Book 418

CHAPTER 21: ANALYTICAL WRITING FOUNDATIONS AND CONTENT REVIEW 419

Introduction to Analytical Writing Foundations and Content Review . . . 419

Writing Correctly 420

Writing Clearly 433

Writing Concisely 437

Kaplan's Additional Tips for Writing Foundations 443

CHAPTER 22: THE ISSUE ESSAY 447

Introduction to the Issue Essay 447

How the Kaplan Method for Analytical Writing Works 449

Kaplan's Additional Tips for the Issue Essay 459

Issue Essay Practice Set 461

Issue Essay Practice Set Answers and Explanations 463

CHAPTER 23: THE ARGUMENT ESSAY 467

Introduction to the Argument Essay 467

Kaplan's Additional Tips for the Argument Essay 479

Argument Essay Practice Set 481

Argument Essay Practice Set Answers and Explanations 483

CHAPTER 24: ANALYTICAL WRITING PRACTICE SETS 487

Review of the Kaplan Method for Analytical Writing 487

Analytical Writing Practice Set 1 489

Analytical Writing Practice Set 2 491

Analytical Writing Practice Set 1 Answers and Explanations 493

Analytical Writing Practice Set 2 Answers and Explanations 498

PART FIVE PRACTICE TEST 503

CHAPTER 25: PRACTICE TEST 505

Analytical Writing 1: Analyze an Issue 506

Analytical Writing 2: Analyze an Argument 507

Verbal Reasoning 1 509

Quantitative Reasoning 1 518

Verbal Reasoning 2 525

Quantitative Reasoning 2 534

CHAPTER 26: PRACTICE TEST ANSWERS 541

Verbal Reasoning 1 541

Quantitative Reasoning 1 541

Verbal Reasoning 2 541

Quantitative Reasoning 2 541

Analytical Writing 1: Analyze an Issue Answers and Explanations 545

Analytical Writing 2: Analyze an Argument Answers and Explanations . 547

Analytical Writing Scoring Rubric 549

Verbal Reasoning 1 Answers and Explanations 551

Quantitative Reasoning 1 Answers and Explanations 555

Verbal Reasoning 2 Answers and Explanations 560

Quantitative Reasoning 2 Answers and Explanations 565

PART SIX TEST DAY AND BEYOND 571

CHAPTER 27: TAKE CONTROL OF THE TEST 573

Kaplan's Four Basic Principles of Good Test Mentality 573

The Kaplan Stress-Management System 575

Test Day 576

CHAPTER 28: WHERE AND WHEN TO APPLY 579

What Programs You Should Consider 579

Where You Can Get In 585

When to Apply 586

CHAPTER 29: HOW TO APPLY TO GRADUATE SCHOOL 589

How Schools Evaluate Applicants 589

Who Evaluates Applicants 592

Preparing Your Application 593

Maximizing the Various Parts of Your Application 593

Before You Submit Your Application 597

Putting It All Together 598

Congratulations! 598

A Special Note for International Students 598

PART SEVEN GRE RESOURCES. 601

    APPENDIX A: KAPLAN'S WORD GROUPS 603

    APPENDIX B: KAPLAN'S ROOT LIST 609

    APPENDIX C: COMMON GRE-LEVEL WORDS IN CONTEXT 639

    APPENDIX D: MATH REFERENCE 651

HOW TO USE THIS BOOK

Welcome to Kaplan GRE Prep 2022

Congratulations on your decision to pursue a graduate degree, and thank you for choosing Kaplan for your GRE preparation. You've made the right choice in acquiring this book—you're now armed with a comprehensive GRE program that is the result of decades of researching the GRE and teaching many thousands of students the skills they need to succeed. You have everything you need to score higher, so let's start by walking through what you need to know to take advantage of this book and the online resources.

Your Book

There are two main components to your *Kaplan GRE Prep* study package: your book and your online resources. This book contains the following:

- Detailed instruction covering the essential Verbal Reasoning, Quantitative Reasoning, and Analytical Writing concepts
- Time-tested and effective Kaplan Methods and strategies for every question type
- One full-length practice test and chapter-end practice questions with detailed answer explanations

Your Online Resources

Your online resources let you access additional instruction and practice materials to reinforce key concepts and sharpen your GRE skills. They include the following:

- A full-length practice test
- Videos, guided practice, and practice sets to help you master the various GRE question types

Getting Started

1. Register your online resources.
2. Take a GRE practice test to identify your strengths and weaknesses.
3. Create a study plan.
4. Learn and practice using this book and your online resources.

Step 1: Register Your Online Resources

Register your online resources using these simple steps:

1. Go to **kaptest.com/moreonline**.
2. Follow the onscreen instructions. Please have a copy of your book available.

Access to the online resources is limited to the original owner of this book and is nontransferable. Kaplan is not responsible for providing access to the online resources for customers who purchase or borrow used copies of this book. Access to the online resources expires one year after you register.

Step 2: Take a GRE Practice Test

It's essential to take a practice test early on. Doing so will give you the initial feedback and diagnostic information that you need to achieve your maximum score.

Your diagnostic test is Practice Test 1, which is found in your online resources. Like all of Kaplan's online full-length tests, this multi-stage test (MST) is in the same format as the actual GRE. The multi-stage test format feels different from a paper-based test and scores differently, so if you only have time to take a single practice test before you sit for the real GRE, this is the one you should use. However, for your convenience, we've also included a paper-based practice test in this book. The practice test in this book, which includes full-length Analytical Writing, Verbal, and Quantitative sections, will give you a chance to familiarize yourself with the various question types. It will also allow you to gauge the content you know and identify areas for practice and review.

After any practice test that you take, we recommend that you fully review the detailed answer explanations to better understand your performance. Look for patterns in the questions you answered correctly and incorrectly. Were you stronger in some areas than others? This thorough analysis will help you target your practice time to specific concepts.

Step 3: Create a Study Plan

Use what you've learned from your practice test to identify areas for closer study. Take time to familiarize yourself with the key components of your book and online resources. Think about how many hours you can consistently devote to GRE study. We have found that most students have success with about three months of committed preparation before Test Day. Schedule time for study, practice, and review. One of the most frequent mistakes in approaching study is to take practice tests and not review them thoroughly— review time is your best chance to gain points. It works best for many people to block out short, frequent periods of study time throughout the week. Check in with yourself frequently to make sure you're not falling behind your plan or forgetting about any of your resources.

Step 4: Learn and Practice

Your book and online resources come with many opportunities to develop the skills you'll need on Test Day. Read each chapter of this book and complete the practice questions. Depending on how much time you have to study, you can do this work methodically, covering every chapter, or you can focus your study on those question types and content areas that are most challenging for you. You will inevitably need more work in some areas than in others, but know that the more thoroughly you prepare, the better your score will be. Remember also to take advantage of the additional material in your online resources.

As always, review the explanations closely. Initially, your practice should focus on mastering the needed skills and not on timing. Add timing to your practice as you improve fundamental proficiency.

Thanks for choosing Kaplan. We wish you the best of luck on your journey to graduate school.

http://kaptest.com/publishing

The material in this book is up-to-date at the time of publication. However, the Educational Testing Service may have instituted changes in the tests or test registration process after this book was published. Be sure to read carefully the materials you receive when you register for the test.

If there are any important late-breaking developments—or changes or corrections to the Kaplan test preparation materials in this book—we will post that information online at **http://kaptest.com/publishing**. Check to see if any information is posted there regarding this book.

PART ONE

GETTING STARTED

CHAPTER 1

INTRODUCTION TO THE GRE

This book will prepare you for everything that you are likely to encounter on the GRE. Between the book and its companion online resources, you'll see lots of individual questions and their explanations. But more than that, we explain the underlying principles behind *all* of the questions on the GRE. We give you the big picture so you can take charge of this test.

Understanding the GRE

Let's take a look at how the GRE is constructed. The GRE, or Graduate Record Examination, is a computer-based exam required by many graduate schools for admission to a wide variety of programs. In this section, you will learn about the purposes of the GRE and ways you can learn to be successful on it.

The Purposes of the GRE

The ways in which graduate schools use GRE scores vary. Scores are often required as part of the application for entrance into a program, but they also can be used to grant fellowships or financial aid. Each section of the GRE is designed to assess general skills necessary for graduate school. Some of these skills include the ability to read complex informational text and understand high-level vocabulary words in the Verbal Reasoning section, respond to a prompt in written form in the Analytical Writing section, and apply general mathematical concepts to a variety of problem types in the Quantitative Reasoning section. Graduate school admissions officers often view the GRE score as an important indicator of readiness for graduate-level studies. In addition, graduate school admissions officers are comparing hundreds or even thousands of applications, and having a quantitative factor, such as a GRE score, makes the job of comparing so many applicants much easier. Just by having this book and making a commitment to yourself to be as well prepared as possible for this exam, you've already taken the crucial first step toward making your graduate school application as competitive as possible.

The Secret Code

Doing well on the GRE requires breaking down the "secret code" upon which each and every test is constructed. Like all of the tests created by the Educational Testing Service (ETS), the GRE is based on psychometrics, the science of creating "standardized" tests. For a test to be standardized, it must successfully do three things. First, the test must be reliable. In other words, a person who takes the GRE should get approximately the same score if she takes the GRE a second time (assuming, of course, that she doesn't study during the intervening period). Second—and this is closely related to the first point—it must test the same concepts on each test. Third, it must create a "bell curve" when a pool of test takers' scores are plotted; in other words, some people will do very well on the test and some will do very poorly, but the great majority will score somewhere in the middle.

What all this boils down to is that to be a standardized test, the GRE has to be predictable. And this is what makes the GRE and other standardized tests coachable. Because ETS has to test the same concepts in each and every test, certain Reading Comprehension question types appear over and over again, as do certain math patterns. Moreover, the GRE has to create some questions that most test takers will get wrong—otherwise, it wouldn't be able to create its bell curve. This means that hard questions will usually contain "traps"—wrong answer choices that will be more appealing than the correct answer to a large percentage of test takers. Fortunately, these traps are predictable, and we can teach you how to recognize and avoid them. The goal of this book is to help you break the code of the test.

Acquiring the Skills

If all of that above sounds too good to be true, or if you feel like you are just not a naturally gifted test taker, then take heart: none of the GRE experts who work at Kaplan were *born* knowing how to ace the GRE. No one is. That's because these tests do not measure innate skills; they measure *acquired* skills. People who are good at standardized tests aren't necessarily smarter or more clever than anybody else—they've just developed the skills appropriate for the test they are taking. Maybe they acquired those skills years ago in a math class, or while reading lots of books and academic articles. Or maybe they simply learned how to defeat the test by preparing with a book, a class, or a tutor. If you haven't yet acquired those skills, don't worry. It's simply time to acquire them now.

Same Problems—But Different

As we noted, the testmakers use some of the same problems on every GRE. We know it sounds incredible, but it's true—only the words and numbers change. Here's an example:

$$2x^2 = 32$$

Quantity A	Quantity B
x	4

This is a type of math problem known as a Quantitative Comparison. Your job is to examine the relationship and pick (A) if Quantity A is bigger, (B) if Quantity B is bigger, (C) if they're equal, or (D) if not enough information is given to solve the problem.

Most people answer (C), that the quantities are equal. They divide both sides of the centered equation by 2 and then take the square root of both sides to get $x = 4$. However, this is incorrect because x doesn't *have* to be 4. It could be 4 *or* -4; that is, the quantities could be equal *or* Quantity B could be bigger. Both work, so the answer is **(D)** because the answer cannot be determined from the information given. If you just solve for 4, you'll get this problem—and every one like it—wrong. ETS figures that if you get burned here, you'll get burned again next time. Only next time, it won't be $2x^2 = 32$; it will be $y^2 = 36$ or $s^4 = 81$.

The concepts tested on any particular GRE—right triangles, logical deductions, word relationships, and so forth—are the underlying concepts at the heart of *every* GRE. ETS makes changes only after testing them exhaustively. This process is called *norming*, which means taking a normal test and a changed test and administering them to a random group of students. As long as the group is large enough for the purposes of statistical validity and the students get consistent scores from one test to the next, then the revised test is just as valid and consistent as any other GRE.

How the GRE is Organized

The Graduate Record Examination (GRE) is administered on computer and is approximately four hours long, including breaks. The exam consists of six sections, with different amounts of time allotted for you to complete each section.

BASICS OF THE GRE	
Exam Length	About 4 hours, including breaks
Scoring Scale	130–170 (1-point increments) for Verbal and Quantitative; 0–6 for Analytical Writing
Format	Multi-stage test (MST), a computer-based format that allows students to navigate forward and backward within each section of the test
Number of Test Sections	6 sections, including an experimental or research section
Breaks	One 10-minute break after your third section; 1-minute breaks between all other sections
Analytical Writing	One section with two 30-minute tasks: analyze an issue and analyze an argument
Verbal Reasoning	Two 30-minute sections with approximately 20 questions each
Quantitative Reasoning	Two 35-minute sections with approximately 20 questions each; onscreen calculator available

Your test will also contain an experimental section—an additional Verbal Reasoning or Quantitative Reasoning section that ETS puts on the test so that ETS can norm the new questions it creates for use on future GREs. That means that if you could identify the experimental section, you could doodle for half an hour, guess in a random pattern, or daydream and still get exactly the same score on the GRE. However, the experimental section is disguised to look like a real section—there is no way to identify it. All you will really know on the day of the test is that one of the subject areas will have three sections instead of two. Naturally, many people try to figure out which section is experimental. But because ETS really wants you to try hard on it, it does its best to keep you guessing. If you guess wrong, you could blow the whole test, so we urge you to treat all sections as scored unless you are told otherwise.

Lastly, instead of an experimental section, your test could contain a research section. This section is unscored and will be indicated as such. If you have a research section on the test, it will be the last section. Pay careful attention to the directions at the beginning of the section.

Scoring

The Analytical Writing section is scored on a scale of 0–6 in half-point increments. (See Chapter 20: Introduction to Analytical Writing, for details on this scoring rubric.) The Verbal Reasoning and Quantitative Reasoning sections each yield a scaled score within a range of 130–170 in one-point increments. You cannot score higher than 170 for either the Verbal Reasoning or the Quantitative Reasoning sections, no matter how hard you try. Similarly, it's impossible to score lower than 130 for Verbal Reasoning or Quantitative Reasoning.

But you don't receive *only* scaled scores; you also receive a percentile rank, which rates your performance relative to that of a large sample population of other GRE takers. Percentile scores tell graduate schools just what your scaled scores are worth. For instance, even if everyone got very high scaled scores, universities would still be able to differentiate candidates by their percentile scores. The following tables give a cross section of the percentile ranks that correspond with certain scaled scores on each section of the GRE, based on test takers between July 1, 2016, and June 30, 2019. For the full percentile-to-score conversion tables, see **www.ets.org/s/gre/pdf/gre_guide_table1a.pdf**.

VERBAL REASONING		QUANTITATIVE REASONING		ANALYTICAL WRITING	
PERCENTILE RANKING	**SCALED SCORE**	**PERCENTILE RANKING**	**SCALED SCORE**	**PERCENTILE RANKING**	**SCORE**
99	169–170	96	170	99	6.0
96	165	92	168	98	5.5
88	161	80	163	92	5.0
79	158	72	160	80	4.5
63	154	59	156	55	4.0
50	151	48	153	38	3.5
36	148	33	149	14	3.0
22	144	18	145	6	2.5
11	140	9	141	1	2.0

Universities pay great attention to percentile rank. It's important that you do some research into the programs you're thinking about. Admissions officers from many top graduate school programs consider the GRE the most important factor in graduate school admissions. Some schools have cutoff scores below which they don't even consider applicants. But be careful! If a school tells you it looks for applicants scoring an average of 150 per section, that doesn't mean those scores are good enough for immediate acceptance. Some students will be accepted with scores below that average, and some students may be denied admission even with scores that are higher. Consider the score of 150 per section an initial target score but also be sure the rest of your application is strong. You owe it to yourself to find out what kinds of scores *impress* the schools you're interested in and to work hard until you get those scores. Every day we see students achieve their target scores. Study diligently and you can be among them.

A final note about percentile rank: the sample population to which you are compared to determine your percentile is not the group of people who take the test on the same day you do. ETS doesn't want to penalize an unlucky candidate who takes the GRE on a date when everyone else happens to be a rocket scientist. Instead, it compares your performance with that of test takers from the past three years. Don't worry about how other people do—strive for your best score. We often tell our students, "Your only competition in this classroom is yourself."

Cancellation and Multiple-Scores Policy

Unlike many things in life, the GRE allows you a second chance. If at the end of the test, you feel that you've definitely not done as well as you could have, you have the option to cancel your score. Although score cancellation is available, the option to use *ScoreSelect®* means there's rarely a good reason to cancel scores. (See below for a description of the *ScoreSelect®* feature.) If you cancel, your scores will be disregarded—but you also won't get to see them. Canceling a score means that it won't count; however, you will not receive any refund for your test fee.

Two legitimate reasons to cancel your score are illness and personal circumstances that may have caused you to perform unusually poorly on that particular day.

But keep in mind that test takers historically underestimate their performance, especially immediately following the test. They tend to forget about all of the things that went right and focus on everything that went wrong. So unless your performance has been terribly marred by unforeseen circumstances, don't cancel your score. Even if you do cancel your score, it is possible to reinstate it within 60 days for a fee. (See **www.ets.org/gre/revised_general/test_day/policies** for details.)

Also, ETS now offers test takers more choices in determining which scores to report to schools. The *ScoreSelect®* option allows GRE test takers to choose—*after* viewing their scores on Test Day—to report their scores from only the most recent test they took or from all of the GRE tests they have taken in the past five years. Additionally, if a student sends score reports after Test Day, the student can have full freedom to report scores from any testing administration(s), not just the most recent. However, test takers cannot report only Quantitative Reasoning scores or only Verbal Reasoning scores from a given test—results from any testing administration must be reported in full. For more on the *ScoreSelect®* option, go to **www.ets.org/gre/revised_general/about/scoreselect**.

Requested score reports are sent to schools 10–15 days after the exam. All GRE testing administrations will remain valid (and usable) in your ETS record for five years. If you choose to report multiple scores, many grad schools will consider the highest score you have for each section, but check with the schools to which you plan to apply for their policies on multiple scores.

Lastly, know that schools receiving your scores will have access to photos taken of you at the test center, plus your Analytical Writing essays from each test administration whose scores you choose to report.

Test Registration

The computer-based GRE General Test is offered year-round. To register for and schedule your GRE, visit **www.ets.org/gre/revised_general/register/how** where you'll find information on scheduling, pricing, repeat testing, cancellation policies, and more. (If you live outside the United States, Canada, Guam, the U.S. Virgin Islands, or Puerto Rico, visit **www.ets.org/gre** for instructions on how to register.)

Registering earlier is strongly recommended because spaces often fill quickly.

As of the writing of this book, the GRE also offers students the ability to take the test at home instead of in a testing center. The computer that you use must meet certain requirements, and the test is administered and monitored by an online proctor. Check **www.ets.org/gre/at-home** for the most up to date information.

Register Online

You can register online (if you are paying with a credit or debit card) at **www.ets.org/gre**. Once the registration process is complete, you can print out your voucher immediately (and can reprint it if it is lost). If you register online, you can confirm test center availability in real time.

Register by Phone

Call 1-800-GRE-CALL or 1-800-473-2255. Your confirmation number, reporting time, and test center location will be given to you when you call. Payments can be made with an American Express, Discover, JCB, MasterCard, or Visa credit or debit card.

GRE Checklist

Before the Test

- Choose a test date.
- Register online at **www.ets.org/gre** or by phone at 1-800-GRE-CALL.
- Receive your admission voucher in the mail or online.

- If you are taking the GRE at a testing center, visit the location before your official test date.
  - Know the directions to the building and room where you'll be tested.
- Create a test prep calendar to ensure that you're ready by the day of the test.
  - On a calendar, block out the weeks you have to prepare for the test.
  - Based on your strengths and weaknesses, establish a detailed plan of study and select appropriate lessons and practice. (Don't forget to include some days off!)
- Stick to the plan; as with any practice, little is gained if it isn't methodical. Skills can't be "crammed" at the last minute.
- Reevaluate your strengths and weaknesses from time to time and revise your plan accordingly.

The Day of the Test

- Make sure you have your GRE admission voucher and acceptable ID.
- If you are taking the test at a center, leave yourself plenty of time to arrive at the test site stress-free.
  - Arrive at the test site at least 30 minutes early for the check-in procedures.
- Don't worry—you're going to do great!

GRE Subject Tests

Subject Tests are designed to test the fundamental knowledge that is most important for successful graduate study in a particular subject area. To do well on a GRE Subject Test, you must have an extensive background in the particular subject area—the sort of background expected of a student who majored in the subject. Subject Tests enable admissions officers to compare students from different colleges with different standards and curricula. Not every graduate school or program requires Subject Tests, so check admissions requirements at those schools in which you're interested.

Organization, Scoring, and Test Dates

All Subject Tests are administered in paper-based format and consist exclusively of multiple-choice questions that are designed to assess knowledge of the areas of the subject that are included in the typical undergraduate curriculum.

On Subject Tests, you'll earn one point for each multiple-choice question that you answer correctly. Your raw score is then converted into a scaled score, which can range from 200–990. The range varies from test to test.

Some Subject Tests also contain subtests, which provide more specific information about your strengths and weaknesses. The same questions that contribute to your subtest scores also contribute to your overall score. Subtest scores, which range from 20–99, are reported along with the overall score. For further information on scoring, you should consult the relevant Subject Test Descriptive Booklet, available from ETS. Subject Tests are offered three times a year: in April, September, and October. Note that not all of the Subject Tests are offered on every test date; consult **www.ets.org/gre** for upcoming test dates and registration deadlines.

Subjects

Currently, six Subject Tests are offered.

Biology

This test consists of about 188 questions divided among three subscore areas: cellular and molecular biology, organismal biology, and ecology and evolution.

Chemistry

This test consists of about 130 questions. There are no subscores, and the questions cover the following topics: analytical chemistry, inorganic chemistry, organic chemistry, and physical chemistry.

Literature in English

This test consists of about 230 questions on literature in the English language. There are two basic types of questions: factual questions that test your knowledge of writers and literary or critical movements typically covered in the undergraduate curriculum, and analytical questions that test your ability to read various types of literature critically.

Mathematics

This test consists of about 66 questions on the content of various undergraduate courses in mathematics. Most of the test assesses your knowledge of calculus, linear algebra, abstract algebra, and number theory.

Physics

This test consists of approximately 100 questions covering mostly material from the first three years of undergraduate physics. Topics include classical mechanics, electromagnetism, atomic physics, optics and wave phenomena, quantum mechanics, thermodynamics and statistical mechanics, special relativity, and laboratory methods. About 9 percent of the test covers advanced topics, such as nuclear and particle physics, condensed matter physics, and astrophysics.

Psychology

This test consists of approximately 205 questions drawn from courses most commonly included in the undergraduate curriculum. In addition to a total score, there are also six subscores corresponding with these sections: biological, cognitive, social, developmental, clinical, and measurement and methodology.

For more information, consult ETS's Subject Test section at **www.ets.org/gre/subject**.

CHAPTER 2

MULTI-STAGE TEST MECHANICS

How the MST Works

The multi-stage test, or MST, differs in some critical ways from the typical standardized test. An MST is a computer-based test that you take at a special test center at a time you schedule. Below is a chart that highlights some of the key features of the GRE MST:

MST FEATURES
The test adapts one section at a time, altering the difficulty level of your second Quantitative and Verbal sections based on your performance on the first of each.
You may answer questions in any order within a section and change your answers to previously answered questions within a section.
An onscreen calculator is provided for the Quantitative Reasoning sections.
Mark & Review buttons are available to help you keep track of questions you want to revisit.
The MST lasts about 4 hours, including breaks.

Now that you have a sense of the overall format and structure of the GRE MST, let's look more closely at what the term *multi-stage test* means, how the MST adapts to your performance, and how these factors determine your score.

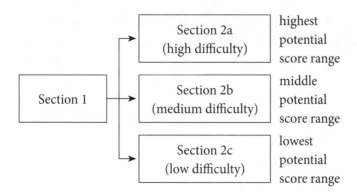

The previous chart depicts a simplified version of how adaptivity works on the MST. Depending on your performance on the first Quantitative or Verbal section, you may get channeled into a harder or an easier second Quantitative or Verbal section. The difficulty of the second section determines your score range—roughly speaking, the "ceiling" and "floor" of your potential Quantitative or Verbal scores. Ultimately, your score will be determined by two factors: (1) the difficulty of the questions you receive and (2) the number of questions you answer correctly.

Therefore, it is important to do as well as possible on the first section, since that will put you in the best position to achieve a great score. That said, your performance on the second section is still a crucial determinant of your ultimate score. (Note that the test only adapts within a given subject. In other words, your performance on the Verbal section will not affect the difficulty of a subsequent Quantitative section.)

Understanding the adaptive nature of the MST is interesting and somewhat useful in your prep, but it is actually counterproductive to think too much about it on Test Day. Many test takers try to gauge how they are doing on the exam by assessing the difficulty of the second section they receive. Doing this on Test Day is, at best, a waste of brainpower. At worst, it can cause you to become distracted by counterproductive thoughts ("These questions are too easy! What am I doing wrong?"). Just focus on solving the questions in front of you and do your best.

Simply put, the more questions you get right on the first section, the better off you'll be. The same goes for the second section. Therefore, your goal will be to get as many questions right as possible—not terribly mind-blowing! But how do you do that? Specifically, how can you use the structure of the MST to your advantage as you try to achieve this goal?

Let's now discuss the best ways to navigate the MST and how you can use these functionalities on Test Day to get as many correct answers as possible.

Navigating the GRE MST Interface

Let's preview the primary computer functions that you will use to move around on the MST. ETS calls them "testing tools." They're basically tabs that you can click with your mouse to navigate through the section. The following screen is typical for a multi-stage test.

Directions: Choose the word or set of words for each blank that best fits the meaning of the sentence as a whole.

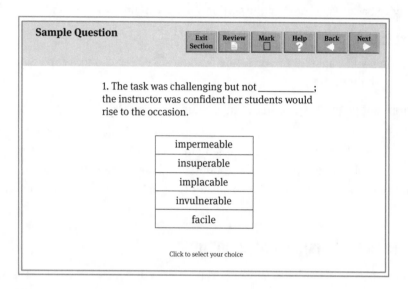

Here's what the various buttons do:

The Time Button (not pictured)

Clicking on this button turns the time display at the top of the screen on or off. When you have five minutes left in a section, the clock will automatically turn on, and the display will change from hours and minutes to hours, minutes, and seconds.

The Quit Test Button (not pictured)

Hitting this button ends the test prematurely. *Do not* use this button unless you want all of your scores canceled and your test invalidated.

The Exit Section Button

This allows you to exit the section before the time is up. Try not to end the section early—use any extra time to review any problems you flagged or felt concerned about.

The Review Button

This button will allow you to view your progress on all the questions you have looked at so far within the section you're working on. The items you have marked for review will have a check mark next to them. The chart on the screen will also have a column indicating whether or not you have answered a question.

The Mark Button

This button allows you to mark a question for review later. The question will have a check mark next to it in the review section.

The Help Button

This button leads to directions and assistance on how to use the test interface. But beware: the test clock won't pause just because you click on Help.

The Back Button

This button allows you to return to previous questions within the section. Note that you may only go back to questions in the section you're currently working on.

The Next Button

Hit this when you want to move on to the next question. You cannot proceed until you have hit this button.

Calculator (not pictured; Quantitative Reasoning section only)

This button opens the onscreen calculator on Quantitative Reasoning sections. It's a pretty basic calculator, and the questions tend to be conceptual in nature, but the calculator still can help you to avoid simple computational errors. Note that you can click on the "Transfer Display" button on the calculator to transfer your answer into a numeric entry box.

MST Section Management Techniques

Section management is an especially important skill to develop for the GRE. The MST allows you to move around within the section you're working on. This can be a great help if you know how to use this functionality to your advantage, but it can also be a source of uncertainty—with the ability to approach each section in whatever order you wish, where should you start? How can you best use the allotted time to rack up as many points as possible? Here are some principles to follow:

Approach the exam as you would a paper-based one. Since it's impossible (and certainly not a good use of your mental effort) to judge the difficulty level of questions while you're working on them, just focus on doing the best you can on each question—as far as you are concerned, they are all of equal importance to your score. Pace yourself so that you can capitalize on all the questions that you are capable of getting correct.

Don't get bogged down on any one question. If you feel that you are getting stuck, mark the question and go to the next one. Use the Mark and Review buttons to tag questions that you wish to return to later in the section. Sometimes when you take a second look at a question, you'll immediately see how to approach those aspects you previously found challenging.

You can also use the Mark button to indicate that you should come back and review the question if you have time at the end of that section. You can do this whether or not you've answered the question. This way, you can better organize your time by keeping track of which questions you are done with and which ones need a second look. Even if you are marking a question to come back to later, you may want to enter an answer the first time through. If you run out of time, you'll be glad that you at least put in a guess.

Use extra time at the end of a section to check your work. This is a major advantage of the MST. Always check the review screen before you finish a section to ensure you haven't forgotten to answer a question.

You may find that it is beneficial to start with some of the question types that take less time to answer. For example, you may find that you score highest on the Verbal section when you answer the Sentence Equivalence questions first. Use the practice sets in this book and your online MSTs to find the approach that works best for you.

There is no penalty for guessing on the GRE. As far as the MST is concerned, leaving an answer blank is the same as selecting an incorrect answer. Therefore, you should guess on every question so you at least have a chance of getting it right. But you should always guess strategically. This book will provide many tools, such as elimination strategies and estimation, that will make you an excellent strategic guesser.

Finally, the onscreen timer can work to your advantage, but if you find yourself looking at it so frequently that it becomes a distraction, you should turn it off for 10 or 15 minutes and try to refocus your attention on the test. You may be concerned about your pacing, but being distracted by the timer can be just as damaging to your score as running out of time. As with a traditional paper-and-pencil test, you don't want to get hung up on clock management.

MST: The Upside

To sum up, there are many good things about the MST, including the following:

- There will be only a few other test takers in the room with you—it won't be like taking a test in one of those massive lecture halls with distractions everywhere.

- You get a 10-minute break after the third section and a 1-minute break between each of the other sections. The breaks are optional, but you should use them to relax, stretch, and clear your head before the next section.

- You can sign up for the GRE just two days before the test (though we recommend signing up much earlier!), and registration is very easy.

- The MST is convenient to schedule. It's offered at more than 175 centers, up to seven days a week (depending on the center), all year long.

- Perhaps the MST's best feature is that it gives you your unofficial Verbal Reasoning and Quantitative Reasoning scores immediately.

MST: The Downside

There are also some less attractive features of the MST:

- The MST is a long test requiring lots of endurance.

- As with any computer-based test, you can't cross off an answer choice to use the process of elimination. Use your scratch paper to avoid reconsidering choices you've already eliminated.

- You have to scroll through Reading Comprehension passages and read them onscreen.

- You'll be given scratch paper to make notes or perform calculations, but if you need more, you'll have to turn in the scratch paper that you've already used before obtaining new paper.

- Many people find that spending considerable time (especially four hours!) in front of a computer screen tires them out and causes eyestrain.
- Having a calculator provided for you on the Quantitative Reasoning sections may seem like a gift, but it comes with a price. The questions on the Quantitative Reasoning section are now more conceptual and less calculation based. Basically, you won't have to worry about doing long division, but the problems will be less straightforward.
- Being able to go back and change your answers may be a plus, but it can lead to pacing issues for some test takers, who will leave questions blank and then either forget to come back to them or run out of time.
- If you wish to take the GRE again, there is a mandatory waiting period: you can only test every 21 calendar days. So if you don't get the scores you need the first time, you'll need to wait three weeks until you can test again. This can be a problem if you're on a tight deadline.

Paper-Based GRE Strategies

If you are located outside of the United States, Canada, Guam, the U.S. Virgin Islands, and Puerto Rico, you may take the paper-based version of the GRE (check—**www.ets.org/gre** for test dates). It consists of six sections: two Analytical Writing sections, two Verbal Reasoning sections, and two Quantitative Reasoning sections. There is no experimental or research section on the paper-based GRE.

Note that registration for the paper-based test fills up much more quickly than for the MST. You will need to plan ahead to register for the test.

You have approximately 3 hours and 30 minutes to complete the entire test. The test-taking strategies for the paper-based test are different from those for the MST. One strategy we recommend is to keep track of answers you've eliminated by crossing out wrong answer choices in your test booklet. Here are some targeted strategies for each section of the paper-based GRE.

Analytical Writing

For the Analytical Writing section, if you are not using a transcriber, you will have to handwrite your essay, so we suggest you write clearly and legibly. For more tips and strategies for conquering the Analytical Writing section, refer to chapter 20.

Verbal Reasoning Section

Before you start a Verbal Reasoning section, glance over it completely but quickly to familiarize yourself with it. With Reading Comprehension, you can preview the question stems to help guide your reading, but don't try to memorize them or answer the questions without reading the passages. We recommend that you answer the questions you're most comfortable with first. Make sure you set aside at least 15 minutes in each Verbal Reasoning section for Reading Comprehension.

Always try to be aware of how long you're spending on each question; this might require more effort than it does on the MST, since you won't have an onscreen timer. If you find yourself getting hung up on a hard question, move on and come back to it later if you have time. You want to give yourself every opportunity to answer as many questions as you are capable of answering correctly.

The Verbal Reasoning sections on the paper-based test have 25 questions—5 more than each section on the MST. The question types and formats on the paper-based Verbal sections are the same as those on the MST, with one exception: the question format that requires you to highlight a sentence, Select-in-Passage, is not available.

Quantitative Reasoning Section

As on the Verbal Reasoning sections, it will behoove you to stay aware of your pacing on the Quantitative Reasoning sections. Calculators are now permitted on the GRE and will be provided at the testing center. Still, don't forget to use your scratch paper for any calculations that are more quickly or accurately performed by hand. Feel free to skip around within this section as well and do all the problems you can do; then come back to the harder ones.

The Quantitative Reasoning sections of the paper-based test have 25 questions—5 more than each section on the MST. The question types and formats on the paper-based Quantitative sections are the same as those on the MST. You will also mark all of your answers directly in the test book, which means you don't have to worry about filling in a separate answer grid!

This chapter has given you an understanding of the GRE MST and paper-based test formats. Let's now turn to the test sections and get you ready for each one.

PART TWO

VERBAL REASONING

CHAPTER 3

INTRODUCTION TO VERBAL REASONING

Overview

The Verbal Reasoning section of the GRE tests complex reasoning skills and your ability to analyze the relationships between words and sentences. Vocabulary will be tested contextually, and the reading passages are both dense and written with a sophisticated level of diction. The goal of the test's content, with its emphasis on analytical skills, is to make the test an accurate indicator of your ability to understand what you're reading and apply reasoning skills to the various question types. These skills will translate directly to study at the graduate level.

In this section of the book, we'll take you through all the types of Verbal Reasoning questions you'll see on the GRE and give you the strategies you'll need to answer them quickly and correctly. Also, the vocabulary words you'll most frequently encounter on the test are included in Appendixes A, B, and C in the "GRE Resources" section at the back of this book. Think of the glossary and word lists there as building blocks for the questions you will see on the test.

Verbal Reasoning Question Types

The GRE contains two Verbal Reasoning sections with approximately 20 questions each. Each section will last 30 minutes and be composed of a consistent, predictable selection of the following question types:

- Text Completion
- Reading Comprehension
- Sentence Equivalence

The Verbal Reasoning portion of the GRE draws heavily upon your vocabulary and assesses your comprehension of written material. Specifically, it evaluates your ability to do the following:

- Analyze sentences and paragraphs
- Derive a word's meaning based on its context
- Detect relationships among words
- Understand the logic of sentences and paragraphs
- Draw inferences
- Recognize major, minor, and irrelevant points
- Summarize ideas
- Understand passage structure
- Recognize an author's tone, purpose, and perspective

Within each section of Verbal Reasoning questions on the GRE, you will see an assortment of question types.

Pacing Strategy

The GRE allows you to move freely backward and forward within each section, which can be a big advantage on Test Day. If you get stuck on a particular question, you can flag it and come back to it later when you have time. You only score points for correct answers, so you don't want to get bogged down on one problem and lose time you could have used to answer several other questions correctly. You also are not penalized for incorrect answers, so never leave a question blank.

You will have 30 minutes to work on each Verbal Reasoning section. The approximately 20 questions in each section will be an assortment of Text Completion, Sentence Equivalence, and Reading Comprehension items. However, these types of questions are not distributed equally. The following chart shows how many questions you can expect of each type, as well as the average amount of time you should spend per question type.

	TEXT COMPLETION	SENTENCE EQUIVALENCE	READING COMPREHENSION
Number of Questions	approx. 6	approx. 4	approx. 10
Time per Question	1–1.5 minutes, depending on the number of blanks	1 minute	1–3 minutes, depending on the length, to read the passage and 1 minute to answer each question

Use these timing estimates as you work on practice questions and exams. With repetition, you will become comfortable keeping to the same amounts of time on Test Day. Additionally, you will be prepared to use the Mark and Review buttons to your advantage while taking the actual test.

Navigating the Verbal Reasoning Section of This Book

The next chapter, Verbal Foundations and Content Review, will review the classic verbal concepts and topics that you will encounter on the GRE. This section of the book also includes individual chapters on Text Completion, Sentence Equivalence, and Reading Comprehension questions. Each of those chapters includes an introduction and definition of the relevant question types, followed by a review and examples of the strategies to follow to answer those questions quickly and correctly. In addition, you'll find a practice set with answers and explanations for each of the question types you'll encounter on the GRE.

Finally, at the end of this section, you'll find the Verbal Reasoning Practice Sets, which include not only practice questions but also answers and explanations. Use the Verbal Reasoning Practice Sets to test your skills and pinpoint areas for more focused study. When you are finished with this section of the book, you will have prepared for every question type you might encounter on the Verbal Reasoning section of the GRE.

CHAPTER 4

VERBAL FOUNDATIONS AND CONTENT REVIEW

Introduction to Verbal Foundations and Content Review

The GRE Verbal section tests critical thinking skills that are essential to handling graduate-level work. To do well on this section, you will need to grasp how ideas relate to one another in sentences and passages. To measure this skill, the GRE evaluates your mastery of college-level vocabulary and your ability to read dense academic text for meaning. There are many strategies you can use to improve your vocabulary and reading comprehension.

- To improve your vocabulary:
  - Learn words in context
  - Tell stories about words
  - Use flashcards
  - Keep a vocabulary journal
  - Think like a thesaurus—word groups and word roots
  - Use all your senses
  - Use other people
  - Use other languages
  - Use online resources
  - Learn very common GRE words

- To improve your reading comprehension:
  - Attack the passage
  - Change your reading habits

This chapter will cover all of these strategies to improve your GRE vocabulary and reading comprehension, boosting your performance on Text Completion, Sentence Equivalence, and Reading Comprehension questions. In addition, you'll find short practice sets that will introduce you to each of these question types.

The Kaplan Guide to Improving Your Vocabulary

According to the Global Language Monitor, there are over 1,000,000 words in the English language. According to the *Oxford English Dictionary*, there are "only" about 170,000 words in current use. Either way, that's a lot of words. Estimates put the vocabulary of most American college graduates at around 20,000 words. If you've taken a practice test and thought, "There are so many words I don't know!" you're not alone.

Fortunately, you can efficiently build your GRE vocabulary and see a significant increase in your Verbal score. You can do this by choosing a few strategies from the following pages that appeal to you and working with them every day over a number of weeks or months.

Be warned: you won't feel as though you're making progress at first. You'll learn a bunch of new words, then do some practice questions and see a plethora of words you still don't know. That's because there are an awful lot of words. You may feel discouraged. But don't give up! By spending at least 10 minutes a day on vocabulary, using the effective strategies given here, you will reach critical mass so that you can eliminate incorrect answers on Text Completion and Sentence Equivalence questions and choose the answers that match your predictions. Here are some facts that should help you feel confident about this task:

- The testmaker prefers certain types of words. On the test, you can expect to see the kind of vocabulary that commonly appears in literature and in academic journal articles. Also, you can expect to see a preponderance of words with Latin and Greek roots and prefixes. Thus, it is virtually unthinkable that you would need to know what *gabelle* means (a gabelle was a tax on salt in France before the French Revolution, and the word was derived from Arabic). However, a word like *incontrovertible* (from Latin, with *in-* meaning "not" and *controvertible* relating to "controversial," so "not controversial" or "undoubtedly true") is a word that the testmaker would expect you to be familiar with or to be able to figure out. After all, in graduate school you may well need to discuss whether an idea is incontrovertible or not.

- You often don't need to know the exact definition of a word to get a question correct. In fact, often just knowing whether a word has a positive or negative connotation is enough. Consider the word *ignominy*. That's not a word most of us use every day. But think about words you know that start with *igno . . .*, like *ignore* and *ignorant*. It's not nice to ignore someone, and no one wants to look ignorant in front of other people. If the sentence is "It took her years to overcome the _____ of giving such an important speech when she was completely unprepared," you can predict "something bad" for the blank and make a good guess that *ignominy* fits. (In fact, *ignominy* means "shame" or "humiliation"—it's very negative, and it fits the sentence perfectly.)

The following strategies will help you learn the general meaning of the words you're most likely to see on the GRE.

Learn Words in Context

When you're not studying for the GRE, where do you see words and need to know what they mean? In things you read. Therefore, a good way to expand your vocabulary is through reading. When you read, you see words in a context that will help you remember them.

Your neighborhood or campus library has hard-copy books, magazines, and newspapers that you can read for free, and increasingly libraries can loan out ebooks as well. Check with a library near you to see what's available. If you don't want to worry about getting the book back on time, classic literature is generally available for purchase in bookstores or online for low prices. Moreover, a lot of excellent, vocabulary-rich material is available online at no charge. You can have reading material with you, whether in your bag or on your mobile device, all the time, so you can improve your GRE Verbal score throughout the day whenever you have a few minutes!

When you're reading, make sure to have handy (a) a notebook or notes app so you can jot down the words you don't know (see "Keep a Vocabulary Journal" below) and (b) a good dictionary or dictionary app so you can look up the words. (In a lot of e-readers, you can highlight or double-click a word to bring up its definition.) When you look up a word's meaning, also see what the dictionary says about its etymology and synonyms/antonyms and check whether the dictionary shows the word used in a sentence. If it does, compare how the word is used in the sentence you just read with how it's used in the dictionary's example sentence. If it doesn't, then make up your own sentence, using the word in a way that's relevant to you. You might also make flashcards (see "Use Flashcards" later in this chapter) with your new words so you can easily keep practicing them.

Oh, and if you come across any words in this chapter that you're unfamiliar with, write them down and look them up! There's no time like the present to start improving your GRE score.

Here are some ideas for reading where you will encounter a plethora of GRE-type words. As you consider these resources, think about what you like to read. If you try to force yourself to read material you find tedious, you're unlikely to keep up the regular routine your GRE vocabulary growth depends on, so read things you find interesting. Ask yourself these questions:

- Are you a more avid reader of fiction or nonfiction?
- Do you prefer to immerse yourself in books, or does short work better fit your available time or attention span?
- Are there particular topics that interest you?

The lists of resources that follow are far from exhaustive; feel free to explore the library, bookstores, your own bookshelves and those of friends and family, and the Internet for more ideas. And, of course, the Internet is a dynamic entity. So while all URLs provided here work as this book goes to press, we can't guarantee they will work forever.

Magazines

All of the publications listed here are available at newsstands and bookstores and by subscription, and they offer extensive content online at no charge.

- *The Atlantic* (**www.theatlantic.com**) publishes a selection of nonfiction articles and short stories written at a high level. A visit to this publication's website quickly turned up words such as *affluent*, *ensue*, and *notorious*.
- *The Economist* (**www.economist.com**) covers current world events with an international focus. On a visit to this website, we soon encountered *putative*, *sectarian*, and *opulently*.
- *National Geographic* (**www.nationalgeographic.com**) is known in part for the amazing photography that illustrates its stories about the natural environment and human societies. Words found there included *riposte*, *harried*, and *mesmerizing*.
- *The New Yorker* (**www.newyorker.com**) publishes in-depth feature articles on a wide variety of topics as well as short fiction. A visit to the magazine's website quickly turned up words including *candid*, *endemic*, and *neophyte*.
- *Scientific American* (**www.scientificamerican.com**) covers science for a lay audience with topics ranging from dinosaurs to DNA to dreams. This is an excellent resource for readers with a background in the humanities or social sciences to get more comfortable with science reading. A few cool words found here: *herbivorous*, *ravaged*, *malady*.

Again, have you seen any words you don't know? Jot them down and start expanding your GRE vocabulary right now!

Newspapers

By reading newspapers, you will improve not only your vocabulary but also your knowledge of current events, which are often excellent examples to draw from when writing your essays for the Analytical Writing Measure. You will find the following publications a rich source of GRE words.

- *The New York Times* (**www.nytimes.com**) is a daily newspaper of national and international scope. On the website, you can access section front pages and read a certain number of articles a month at no charge. The *New York Times* is also available in print and digital subscriptions, and single issues are available at many newsstands and bookstores.
- *The Wall Street Journal* (**www.wsj.com**) is published Monday through Friday and focuses on national and international news with implications for the economy and business.
- *The Washington Post* (**www.washingtonpost.com**) is a daily newspaper with substantial reporting on national politics and international news.

Literature

If you enjoy fiction, try acquainting yourself with GRE words by reading novels and short stories from the canon of English literature. It doesn't matter if your tastes run more toward Jane Austen or Alice Walker, Ray Bradbury or Charlotte Brontë, Willa

Cather or Arthur Conan Doyle, Ralph Ellison or Ernest Hemingway . . . well, you get the idea. Just read whatever interests you!

Alternatively, grab yourself a smorgasbord of authors in the form of a short-story anthology; collections with titles containing phrases such as "Best Short Stories," "Great Short Stories," or "Classic Short Stories" are good bets.

There are over 60,000 titles available online for free through Project Gutenberg via the website at **www.gutenberg.org**. Alternatively, the website at **https://americanliterature. com** features thousands of classic short stories and novels. The website—which is not actually confined to American literature—has a Short Story of the Day feature; bookmark it and read something different every day.

Nonfiction

Literary nonfiction is a great source of GRE vocabulary as well. Look for collections of classic essays on a range of topics by searching for anthologies with phrases like "Great Essays" or "Best Essays" in the title. Enjoy a particular topic? Search for books with phrases like "Best Science Writing" or "Best Political Writing."

Another good choice for high-level vocabulary is long-form journalism. You'll find these in-depth pieces in the magazines and newspapers listed above. Online, check out **https:// longform.org** for current and historical articles covering just about any topic you can think of and easily searched by subject. (**Longform.org** also features a selection of literary short stories.)

Tell Stories About Words

The previous section explained how seeing words in context can help you remember their meaning. Appendix C: Common GRE-Level Words in Context actually provides context for you. In addition, when you study words using flashcards or lists of words, such as Appendix A: Kaplan's Word Groups and Appendix B: Kaplan's Root List at the back of this book (see below for more on flashcards, word groups, and word roots), you can make up a meaningful context that will help you remember each word.

Take the word *gregarious* as an example. Do you know someone named Greg who is gregarious? (It means "sociable.") Or maybe your friend Greg isn't gregarious at all. Either way, you've got a little story to tell about that word.

Sometimes words look like they mean one thing but actually mean something completely different, and while this may be confusing at first, it can actually be an opportunity to learn the word. Here's how this works. Take the word *noisome* as an example. You might reasonably deduce it means something like "noisy"—but it doesn't. It actually means "offensive" in some way and is especially used to mean "really bad smelling." Now, if you were given a choice of roommates, whom would you prefer: the noisy one or the noisome one? Have you ever had a noisome roommate? When you make up a sentence that contrasts the word with its non-meaning, you won't forget what the word really means.

Here's another example. Most people instinctively think the word *pulchritudinous* must have a negative connotation; it just looks and sounds unpleasant. However, it actually means "very beautiful." Are you surprised when a pulchritudinous movie star dates someone who isn't very attractive?

The etymology of a word, or how the word has come to mean what it means, can be a great starting point for storytelling about the word. Take the word *de<u>cad</u>ence*. It turns out that the root *cadere* is from the Latin for "to fall." Thus, you might fall hard for that *decadent* chocolate cake and fall right off your diet. Someone with a <u>cad</u>averous appearance looks very ill, as though she might fall right over dead any minute and become a corpse (a <u>cad</u>aver). The past participle of *cadere* in Latin is *cas*, so a <u>cas</u>cade is a waterfall. You might have heard the expression "a cascade effect," meaning a series of events that come one after another in a manner similar to a waterfall. Can you imagine going over a *cascade* with your *decadent* chocolate cake in hand and becoming a *cadaver*? Or, less dramatically, eating *decadent* chocolate cake during a picnic by a beautiful *cascade* and not becoming a *cadaver*? Again, by telling these little stories and forming vivid mental images, you'll lock in the meanings of words and won't forget them.

Stories don't have to be based on personal experience or made up. They can come from current events, popular culture, or history. Here's a history lesson with a GRE vocabulary lesson inside it: During World War II, the Germans used the *Enigma* machine to *encrypt* messages. However, the Allies figured out how to *decrypt* these messages, and knowing what the Germans were planning was a great benefit to the Allied side. *Enigma* means "mystery," so it was a good name for an *encryption* machine since *encrypt* means "to put a message into code." As you might imagine, *decrypt* means the opposite—"to decode." The adjectives *enigmatic* and *cryptic* mean "mysterious" and "secret," respectively. You can see that by connecting the words you learn in a story, you can commit their meanings to memory.

Bottom line: Memorizing lists of hundreds of words and their definitions would be very boring. Plus, it can be a futile strategy since you may forget the words soon after you learn them, well before Test Day. Instead, think up a sentence or story that uses the word. If it's funny or weird, or has special personal significance, it will be extra memorable— and the word will stick with you, too.

Use Flashcards

Flashcards are one of the most popular ways of preparing for the GRE Verbal section. You have several options, depending on whether you prefer cards you can hold in your hand or the convenience of a phone app. The purchase of a boxed set of flashcards may include access to a phone app as well, so you may be able to kill two birds with one stone.

If you choose to work with printed cards, you can buy a set of flashcards, such as *Kaplan GRE Vocabulary Flashcards*. Look for cards that include each word's part of speech. A lot of words mean different things depending on whether they're being used as, for example, a noun or a verb. For instance, a malevolent person seeking vengeance might *desert* ("abandon") his foe in the *desert* ("arid area") without leaving her any water. Also, look for cards that include not only the definition of the word but also a sentence using the word. As we said before, learning the word in context is the best way to remember it.

Finally, cards that include synonyms for the word are extra helpful because the associations with other words will help you learn this word and you'll learn groups of words at a time (see "Think Like a Thesaurus" later in the chapter).

Another option is to make your own cards. This is certainly more work, but by the time you look up the word and then write out its part of speech, its definition, any synonyms, and a sentence using it, you may know the word pretty well.

Consider color coding your flashcards. Here's one way to do this: If a word has a positive connotation, write it in green or put a green dot next to it; if it has a neutral connotation, write it in black or use a black dot; if it has a negative connotation, write it in red or use a red dot. Then on the test, if you see the word *penury* and can't quite remember the definition, you might still remember seeing it on the flashcard with a big red dot next to it and know it's negative (*penury* means "extreme poverty"). As we said at the beginning of this chapter, often just knowing the charge of a word is enough to choose it as a correct answer or eliminate it as incorrect on the GRE.

It's hard to beat the convenience of flashcards on your phone. Waiting in line at the store? Waiting for someone to text you back? Waiting for the bus? Hey, how much of our lives do we spend waiting anyway? Well, wait no more. Instead, whip out your phone and add a few more words to your GRE vocabulary. Look for the same things in a phone app as in hard-copy cards: part of speech, definition, synonyms, and an example sentence.

Keep a Vocabulary Journal

Keeping a vocabulary journal may sound like a lot of work, but it's actually an efficient way to capture words so their meanings stick with you. A number of studies have shown that writing out words by hand helps some people learn better. So get a notebook and start keeping that vocabulary journal.

What do you write in a word journal? Pretty much the same things you would put on homemade flashcards: unfamiliar words, their definitions, synonyms and antonyms, and sentences using the words. However, you have more room in a notebook, so you can write more. For example, you could make notes about the etymology of a word, or you could write a couple of different sentences using the word. Use different colors of ink or highlighters to help remember the positive, negative, or neutral tone of words or to make the word stand out in the example sentences you write. Some students like to illustrate the word by drawing a picture or affixing a picture from a magazine or that they print out from a website. Every couple of pages, you could write a brief story (a few sentences) that uses all the words on those pages and maybe some of their synonyms and antonyms as well.

Fill Up a Notebook? Start Another One!

When you encounter a word you don't know, you may not have time to look it up just then. No problem. Write it down anyway and give it half a page. Later when you're studying, you can fill in some of the information about the word. Then when you review it again in a few days, you can add more information. By Test Day, you will be completely sanguine about your recall of every word in your journal. (Don't know the word *sanguine*? Make it the first word in your notebook!)

Think Like a Thesaurus—Word Groups and Word Roots

Learning words one at a time is all well and good, but wouldn't it be better to learn them in bunches? That's where word groups and word roots really help. We've already alluded to these in previous sections of this chapter. For example, if you're using flashcards or a vocabulary journal to study, use them to associate a word with its synonyms—a group of words with similar meanings. That's what we mean by a "word group." And in "Tell Stories About Words," we discussed using a word's root (like *cadere* in *decadent* and *cadaver*) to associate that word with related words.

Word Groups

Remember that to get a Text Completion or Sentence Equivalence question correct, you often only need to know a word's approximate meaning. Here's how you can use word groups to know exactly that. In Kaplan's word groups (the complete list is in Appendix A), you'll find this list:

Investigate

appraise

ascertain

assay

descry

peruse

A good point of entry to this list is the relatively common word *appraise*, which means "to determine the value of something." You may have performance *appraisals* at work (and if your boss thinks you're doing a good job, then he will *praise* you). You may also have had or heard of having a home or a piece of art *appraised* in order to *ascertain* its worth. *Ascertain* is another word in this list that, if you don't already know it, is easy to learn because it means "to make *certain* of."

The other words in this group are less commonly used, but you can quickly master them by associating them with the words you do know. *Assay* can mean "to evaluate, analyze, or test." For example, by *assaying* your strengths and weaknesses on the GRE, you can ascertain what topics you most need to study. Or perhaps you will *assay* your vocabulary knowledge by asking a friend to test you on the words in this book, because such an *appraisal* will help you determine which words to study. Then after *assaying* your current GRE skill by taking a practice test, you will raise your score by *perusing* ("reading thoroughly") this book. These words are by no means synonyms, but they all relate to a careful study or evaluation of something. By making up a story that associates these words in a personally meaningful way, you can efficiently pick up their general sense.

Now let's say that in the middle of the GRE, you see the word *descry* and you can't remember that it means "to detect by looking carefully." Uh-oh. But you do remember seeing it in that list with *appraise* and *ascertain*, so you know it must relate to a thorough examination. Is it a good fit for the blank in this sentence?

Although the sailor climbed the mast every morning to carefully scan the misty horizon with the ship's telescope, he was unable to _____ even a hint of land.

The word "Although" sets up a contrast between the great effort the sailor is putting forth to search for land and his inability to find it. *Descry* it is!

Word Roots

Word roots work much the same way. By studying words grouped by their roots, you can learn the meanings of handfuls of words at a time. This is an efficient way to study. As we saw above, you can also use word roots as the basis for making up sentences about words that help you remember them.

Remember the words *desert* (verb) and *desert* (noun) from the section on flashcards? These words are what are known as *homographs*, because they are spelled or written (the root *graph*) the same (*hom*) way. *Homophones* are words that are pronounced (*phon*) the same way, like *air* and *heir* or *bore* and *boar*. In Appendix B, you'll find Kaplan's list of word roots. Here's what it says about these three roots:

(H)OM: same	GRAM/GRAPH: to write, to draw	PHON: sound
anomaly: deviation from the common rule	**diagram:** a figure made by drawing lines; an illustration	**euphony:** the quality of sounding good
homeostasis: a relatively stable state of equilibrium	**epigram:** a short poem; a pointed statement	**megaphone:** a device for magnifying the sound of one's voice
homogeneous: of the same or a similar kind of nature; of uniform structure of composition throughout	**grammar:** a system of language and its rules	**phonetics:** the study of the sounds used in speech
homonym: one of two or more words spelled and pronounced alike but different in meaning	**graph:** a diagram used to convey mathematical information	**polyphony:** the use of simultaneous melodic lines to produce harmonies in musical compositions
homosexual: of, relating to, or exhibiting sexual desire toward a member of one's own sex	**graphite:** mineral used for writing, as the "lead" in pencils	**telephone:** a device for transmitting sound at a distance
	photograph: a picture, originally made by exposing chemically treated film to light	

Just as with word groups, you can find a point of entry to a word root by starting with a word you know. You certainly know what *grammar* is because you've studied it in school, and you know what a *photograph* and a *diagram* are, but the word *epigram* is less common. If you don't know what *epigram* means, you can learn it now: Was her terse *epigram* written with good *grammar*? In his presentation, what worked best to get his point across: his *diagram*, his *photograph*, or his *epigram*? An *epigram* is something short written to make a point.

The history of words' meanings provides stories that help with learning them, too. For example, starting with the Ancient Greeks and continuing into early modern times, physicians believed that four humors based on bodily fluids determined health. Today we still have the words *sanguine* ("optimistic, confident," from old words for "blood"), *choleric* and *bilious* ("irritable," from words for "yellow bile"), *phlegmatic* ("calm, lacking energy," from "phlegm"), and *melancholic* ("sad, gloomy" from words for "black bile"). So the same medical beliefs that led to draining blood from sick people to make them "better" live on in our language.

Do be careful when studying word roots. Watch out for these potential pitfalls:

- **Just because two words look similar does not mean they share the same root.** Here's an example. The words *aver* and *avert* differ by only one letter. However, *aver* ("to state or prove as true") comes from the Latin *verus* ("truth") and shares a root with *verity, verify, verdict, veracity,* and *verisimilitude,* while *avert* ("to turn away, prevent") comes from the Latin *vertere* ("to turn") and is related to *convert, subvert, introvert, extrovert, incontrovertible* (from the top of the chapter), and *vertigo.* The two words have no relationship.

- **The same root or prefix can have different meanings.** Take for example *embellish* and *belligerent.* Both have *bell* as a root, but *embellish* means "to make prettier" and comes from the Latin *bellus* for "pretty," while *belligerent* means "at war or eager to fight" and comes from the Latin *bellum* for "war." Confusing? Yes. However, this is yet another opportunity to learn these similar-looking words, because you can tell a story that associates them but makes their different meanings clear. For example, if you accused someone of *embellishing* his war stories, he might become angry and *belligerent.* Have you ever pointed out that someone was stretching the truth and seen them get angry? If so, then you've got *embellish* and *belligerent.* Next!

- **Smaller words inside larger words aren't necessarily a Greek or Latin root.** Consider the word *adumbrate.* It would be easy to see the word *dumb* ("not intelligent" or "not able to speak") in the middle and think that was the root. In fact, the root is *umbr* ("shadow"), the same root as in *umbrella,* which shades you from the sun or rain. The prefix *ad-* means "toward," and *adumbrate* means "to foreshadow," or to give a hint of what's coming, as in "The ticking clock in the first paragraph *adumbrates* the fact that the protagonist runs out of time at the end of the story."

In addition to Appendix B in the back of this book, there are many print and online resources you can use to learn more about word roots. Most dictionaries provide a short summary of words' origins. In addition, some students have found *Word Power Made Easy,* by Norman Lewis, entertaining as well as chock-full of engaging descriptions of what words mean. A popular website for finding out about the history of words is **www.etymonline.com.** The site has search functionality and a bibliography.

Use All Your Senses

We've emphasized the importance of reading words in the context of other words, but reading isn't the only way to learn words.

Plus, learning words in other ways can be fun—it can feel like playing charades or Pictionary. Here are some ideas that engage different parts of your brain in learning:

- Say the word aloud. Speaking engages Broca's area of the brain, just above the left ear in most people. Plus, you hear yourself say the word, engaging still more of the brain. While you're at it, say the word's definition and a sentence using the word out loud, too. Want to make the word even more memorable? If you're comfortable doing so, say the word in a funny voice that matches the meaning or "charge" of the word. You'd say *insouciant* ("carefree") in a very different voice than you'd say *moribund* ("near death").

- Make up a song with the words you are learning in it. Singing engages even more of the brain than speaking. If you learned the English alphabet song as a kid, you could probably still sing it, along with a lot of other children's songs. This can be a great way to learn a group of related words.

- Not going to sing, not even in the shower? Write a poem with the word in it. No pressure—you're not trying to win the Nobel Prize in Literature, just learn vocabulary words. Everyone can write haiku (traditionally, a three-line poem with five syllables on the first line, seven on the second, and five on the third). Or maybe you could write silly rhymes like Dr. Seuss.

- Draw a picture representing the word. For instance, you might draw someone wagging her finger and looking disapproving to illustrate *discountenance* ("to disapprove"). Work the word into the picture if you can. Or you can write words in your journal or on flashcards in a font that you design to match their meaning or charge.

- If you're having someone quiz you on GRE words and you find yourself answering with a hand gesture—"Oh, *attenuate* . . . that means, you know [move your hand while bringing your thumb and fingers together]"—go with it! *Attenuate* means "to become thinner or weaker," and if you can associate a hand gesture with that definition, then you know the word.

- You don't need to stop with hand gestures. Feel free to move your whole body to act out the meaning or charge of a word. For *exalt* ("to praise"), maybe you jump up and give an invisible friend a high-five; for *commiserate* ("to sympathize"), maybe you give your invisible friend a hug.

Use Other People

You don't need to learn GRE vocabulary on your own. Your friends, family members, and coworkers may be excited to get in on the action. If you carry flashcards around with you, whip out a few and ask someone to quiz you. As they learn the words too, they may think of sentences or little stories that will help you remember them. This can definitely be a group project.

You can also incorporate the words you are learning into your everyday conversation. Did you make a mistake at work? You can tell your coworkers, "I hope our boss merely *reproves* ("gently criticizes") me instead of *castigating* ("harshly scolding") me." They may be impressed. More likely they'll be amused, or possibly *bemused* ("confused"). Maybe they'll even want to get in on the fun. Feel tired after a long day? Tell your friends you are *flagging* and *enervated*. They'll say that if you've been using words like that all day, it's no wonder. Then you could say that a promise of ice cream afterward would *indubitably galvanize* you into wanting to go out to a movie.

Use Other Languages

If you've ever studied (or grew up speaking) a Romance language such as Spanish, French, or Italian, it will help you on the GRE. If you've ever studied Latin, even just for a year a long time ago, it will help a lot. The only language tested on the GRE is English. However, if you've learned a Romance language, you've probably noticed that quite a few words were spelled similarly and had similar meanings in that language and in English. Here are just a few examples:

English	French	Spanish
affable (friendly)	affable	afable
apprehend (to learn)	apprendre	aprender
extraordinary (exceptional)	extraordinaire	extraordinario
indubitable (undoubted)	indubitable	indudable
liberty (freedom)	liberté	libertad
salutary (healthful)	salutaire	saludable

Overlaps between words in these languages usually indicate a common Latin root, so when you noticed the similarities, you were learning the roots of words. This knowledge will help you recognize other related words in English.

Use Online Resources

Several publishers of dictionaries host websites with not only the ability to search for words' meanings but also a thesaurus feature, quizzes and games, and a word-of-the-day feature. Sign up to get the word of the day and wake up every morning to a new word on your phone. Then make sure to use the word at least three times during the day! Most online dictionaries are also available via mobile apps. Here are some sites to check out:

- **www.dictionary.com** (largely based on the *Random House Dictionary*)
- **www.macmillandictionary.com** (based on the *Macmillan English Dictionary*)
- **www.merriam-webster.com** (based on *Merriam-Webster's Collegiate Dictionary*)
- **www.oxforddictionaries.com** (produced by the publishers of the *Oxford English Dictionary*)

Another site that many GRE students enjoy is **www.freerice.com**, which will quiz you on one word after another. The words start out very easy, but as you answer correctly, your level goes up and the words get tougher. For every question you get right, this nonprofit website donates rice to the United Nations' World Food Programme. You'll see bowls filling up with rice as you answer questions correctly. So build your vocabulary and feed hungry people—truly a win-win.

These resources aren't targeted at the kinds of words that show up frequently on the GRE, the way the words in Appendixes A, B, and C of this book are. Nonetheless, these are fun, convenient ways to help you sharpen your vocabulary consciousness every day. By looking at a "word of the day" every morning as you wait for your bread to toast, you're preparing your brain to learn words all day. The same thing happens when you take a break from whatever else you're doing and play a few rounds of a vocabulary game. And did we mention these are *fun*? There's no rule against having fun while you expand your word knowledge. In fact, approaching your prep in a spirit of play will make it even more effective!

Learn Very Common GRE-Level Words

Maybe you're ready to use some of these strategies to improve your vocabulary and your GRE score, but you're not sure where to start. After all, there are a lot of words. Rest assured, no one knows all the words in the English language, nor will the GRE test them all. Your best bet is to memorize common college-level vocabulary words, such as the ones on this list, because words like these are the most likely to appear on the GRE.

ABSTAIN	ADULTERATE	ANOMALY
APATHY	ASSUAGE	AUDACIOUS
CAPRICIOUS	CORROBORATE	DESICCATE
ENGENDER	ENIGMA	EPHEMERAL
EQUIVOCAL	ERUDITE	FERVID
GULLIBLE	HOMOGENEOUS	LACONIC
LAUDABLE	LOQUACIOUS	LUCID
MITIGATE	OPAQUE	PEDANT
PLACATE	PRAGMATIC	PRECIPITATE
PRODIGAL	PROPRIETY	VACILLATE
VOLATILE	ZEAL	

Start with these, which are listed in Appendix C: Common GRE-Level Words in Context at the end of this book. Then move on to the 150 other very common GRE words in that section. It is very likely that at least a few of these words will appear on your GRE test, and they're an excellent starting point for learning even more words.

Some Final Thoughts

You've been in school a long time, and you've read a lot of words. You may feel as though a lot of GRE vocabulary is new to you, but it almost certainly isn't. At some point, you've seen almost every word you'll see on Test Day, and you understood it well enough in context to understand what you were reading. Those words have left some trace in your brain's neural pathways. Your job in studying words is to activate those connections and strengthen them so the words' meanings are readily available to you during the test.

Not only have you seen most of these words before (even if you don't remember them), but once you start to learn them, you'll begin to see and hear them everywhere—on your favorite television shows, in news stories, even in social media memes. This will be more reinforcement of your learning!

Choose a couple of strategies from this chapter to use every day. When you take the practice test toward the end of this book, make sure to review the explanations for each question thoroughly and use your vocabulary-learning strategies to study every word you weren't sure of. This definitely applies to words in the Text Completion and Sentence Equivalence questions, but if you encounter words in Reading Comprehension passages that are unfamiliar, make sure to learn those words, too.

To acquaint you with the types of GRE questions that test critical thinking skills along with vocabulary knowledge, here is a short practice set of Text Completion and Sentence Equivalence questions. See how many words you know and don't know and then, as you read the explanations, think about how you are going to learn the obscure words so they'll be familiar the next time you see them.

Text Completion and Sentence Equivalence Practice Set

Directions: For each blank, select one entry from the corresponding column of choices. Fill all blanks in the way that best completes the text.

1. All Jon cared about was getting an A, so because the team project did not count toward his grade in the course, he felt _____ the work and did not do his share.

   Ⓐ apathy toward

   Ⓑ zeal for

   Ⓒ loathing for

   Ⓓ cheerful about

   Ⓔ antagonism toward

2. To her friends' (i) _____, because she had never expressed an interest in travel, Lovia decided to teach English in Thailand, (ii) _____ in that country for a year.

Blank (i)		Blank (ii)	
A	delight	**D**	sojourning
B	astonishment	**E**	retiring
C	dismay	**F**	persevering

3. The citizens met with their senator to express (i) _____, arguing that if tax rates (ii) _____ any further, taxes would become (iii) _____, allowing hard-working individuals to keep little of their well-earned income.

Blank (i)		Blank (ii)		Blank (iii)	
A	euphoria	**D**	economized	**G**	congruent
B	composure	**E**	escalated	**H**	confiscatory
C	apprehension	**F**	elaborated	**I**	consummate

Directions: Select the <u>two</u> answer choices that, when used to complete the sentence, fit the meaning of the sentence as a whole <u>and</u> produce completed sentences that are alike in meaning.

4.   Our manager holds as a _____ that an employee with a messy desk is irredeemably lazy, and she therefore demands that all members of her staff keep their work areas meticulously organized.

   A   whim
   B   dogma
   C   hypothesis
   D   fancy
   E   tenet
   F   polity

5.   Elena liked Joe a great deal, but she soon tired of his friends, pseudointellectuals who propounded inane theories based on _____ interpretations of neo-Marxism and existentialism.

   A   spurious
   B   terse
   C   fallacious
   D   succinct
   E   bellicose
   F   blithe

6.   Despite the many pleasures of staying in a hotel, such as a hot shower and clean sheets, many people _____ such comforts in favor of cold water from a nearby stream and a sleeping bag in order to savor a revitalizing proximity to nature.

   A   extol
   B   deprecate
   C   renounce
   D   spurn
   E   discountenance
   F   eulogize

Answers and explanations follow on the next page. ▶ ▶ ▶

Text Completion and Sentence Equivalence Practice Set Answer Key

1. A	4. B, E
2. B, D	5. A, C
3. C, E, H	6. C, D

Text Completion and Sentence Equivalence Practice Set Answers and Explanations

1. A

The sentence begins by telling you that Jon only cares about getting an A, and then it says that the team project did not affect his grade. The blank needs a term for how Jon "felt" about the project, and the key words "so because" indicate that the blank will be consistent with the information given. Furthermore, the key word "and" in the last part of the sentence means the blank will be consistent with Jon not doing his share of the work. Predict that Jon will not care about the team project or will feel "indifference" toward it. Answer choice (**A**) *apathy toward* is a match for your prediction and the correct answer. *Apathy* is composed of *a–* ("not") and *path* ("emotion") and is related to words like *empathy*, *sympathy*, and *antipathy*. Learn these words as a group with the same root.

The word *zeal* ("strong interest"), in choice (B), is the opposite of what is needed. Note that *zealous* means "very enthusiastic" and a *zealot* is "a fanatic" for some cause. Another word beginning with *z*, *zest*, also means "great enthusiasm." Learn these words as a group with related meanings. Choice (D) *cheerful about* is incorrect for the same reason; it is positive, but you need a neutral or mildly negative word. Choice (C) *loathing* means "extreme dislike," and choice (E) *antagonism toward* means "dislike" or "conflict"; both words are too negative. While Jon does not care about the project, he has no reason to hate it. When you studied literature, you may have learned that the *protagonist* is the main character of the story and the *antagonist* is the person with whom the main character experiences conflict.

2. B, D

The sentence says that Lovia had never been interested in travel, but she is going to Thailand. Her decision would come as a "surprise" to her friends, and choice (**B**) *astonishment* is correct for blank (i). There is no evidence to support the idea that her friends are feeling either *delight* (A) or *dismay* (C) about her decision. You need a neutral word for this blank.

Lovia will be abroad for a year, so the choice that fits blank (ii) is (**D**) *sojourning* ("staying temporarily"). This word is related to *journey*, which also relates to travel, and to *journal*. You might think of a personal journal as a record of one's "trip" through life. She is not (E) *retiring* because she will be working as a teacher. (F) *persevering* means "being persistent" or "overcoming obstacles," and nothing in the sentence indicates that she will encounter adversity.

3. C, E, H

People can "express" a wide range of thoughts and feelings (blank (i)), and tax rates can go up, go down, or stay the same (blank (ii)). Start with the third blank, which has the most context clues.

The word for blank (iii) must be consistent with the last part of the sentence, which is about not letting people keep their money—or taking their money away from them. The match is choice (**H**) *confiscatory* ("seizing property"). This word's root is the same as in the word *fiscal*, meaning "financial": your *fiscal* condition is reduced if the authorities *confiscate* your property. Choice (G) *congruent* means "in agreement"; when you study geometry for the Quantitative section, you will study *congruent* shapes, which are identical to or in complete agreement with each other. Choice (I) *consummate*, when used as an adjective, means "perfect." This word has the same root as *summit*, or "highest point," and if someone describes you as the *consummate* professional, she is saying that you bring together (*con–*) the highest or best qualities of a professional.

Given that the tax rates might become *confiscatory*, the citizens must be concerned that taxes will "rise," so this is your prediction for blank (ii). Choice (**E**) *escalated* is correct. Think of riding up an *escalator* in a building. Or think of *scaling*, or climbing, a wall—*escalate* and *scale* share the same root. Choice (D) *economized* would relate to "spending less money," and choice (F) *elaborated* would mean "to develop." Neither of these choices describes rising taxes.

Now for blank (i): Because the citizens believe taxes will go up and take most of their money, and they are meeting with their senator about this prospect, they are undoubtedly worried. Choice (**C**) *apprehension* conveys worry or fear and is correct. *Apprehension* is an interesting word because it can mean "capture," "understanding," or "fear." Here's a sentence to think about: If the criminal had *apprehended* that the police would soon *apprehend* him, he would have felt *apprehension*. Choice (A) *euphoria* means "bliss" and is the opposite of what these folks are feeling. Choice (B) *composure* means "calm" and also does not reflect what the citizens feel.

4. B, E

When this manager sees a messy desk, she forms a harshly negative opinion of the employee, and as a result ("therefore"), she "demands" that her staff keep their desks clean. Based on the sentence, you can conclude that the manager holds a "strong belief" on this subject. Answer choices (**B**) *dogma* and (**E**) *tenet* both mean an "idea held to be true" and are the correct answers. If someone is *dogmatic*, that person is very opinionated. Imagine someone refusing to let go of an idea like a dog refusing to let go of a bone! *Tenet* comes from the Latin word meaning "to hold" and shares its root with *tenable* ("can be held, defensible") and *tenacity* ("holding on persistently").

Choices (A) *whim* and (D) *fancy* both relate to a "passing thought." While these words can have similar meanings, they do not fit the context of this sentence. Choice (C) *hypothesis* is a "guess" or a starting point for exploring a problem, not a strongly held belief. Choice (F) *polity* means a "government" (think "politics") and does not fit the sentence.

5. A, C

Elena liked Joe, but the key word "but" indicates she has a negative view of his friends. Why? They are "pseudo-intellectuals" and their theories are "inane." The prefix *pseudo–* means "fake," and *inane* means "silly." Either one of these clues tells you that they don't understand the complex philosophies mentioned in the sentence. Predict that the word in the blank means their "interpretations" are actually misinterpretations; that is, they are "false." Choices (**A**) *spurious* and (**C**) *fallacious* both relate to "falseness" and fit the sentence. The word *spurious* is derived from the Latin word for "illegitimate child." It is not etymologically related to the word *spur*, but you can think of a railroad spur, which looks like any other track but is not the main line and doesn't go very far. *Fallacious*, like *fallacy* and *false*, comes from a Latin word for "deceive."

Choices (B) *terse* and (D) *succinct* both relate to "not using many words," and the sentence gives no reason to believe Joe's friends do not talk much (one rather imagines the opposite). Choice (E) *bellicose* means "looking for a fight" (the root is *bell* meaning "war"), and while this is a negatively charged word, it does not fit the clues in the sentence; his friends are wrong but not necessarily argumentative. Choice (F) *blithe* means "cheerful" or "without worries" (it shares a root in Old English with *bliss*, which is "extreme happiness"); this is a positively charged word.

6. C, D

The key word "Despite" signals a contrast, so people who camp instead of staying indoors "reject" the comforts of a hotel. Choice (**C**) *renounce* means "to put aside," and choice (**D**) *spurn* means "to reject scornfully." You may have heard or read the expression "to *spurn* someone's advances," meaning to let someone know that you are absolutely not interested in a romantic relationship. These words both give the sentence the same sense and are correct.

Choices (A) *extol* and (F) *eulogize* both mean "to praise highly." People who opt for camping would praise being close to nature highly, according to the sentence, but this blank relates to the hotel experience. Thus, these are the opposite of what is needed. By the way, don't confuse a *eulogy* with an *elegy*: Both are often written about someone who has died, but a eulogy is prose while an elegy is a poem and the focus of a eulogy is on praising the subject while an elegy's focus is on expressing grief. Choices (B) *deprecate* and (E) *discountenance* are negatively charged, which might have made them tempting. However, both mean "to express disapproval," and while the sentence indicates that nature lovers reject staying in a hotel for themselves, there is no evidence that they disapprove of other people staying in hotels.

The Kaplan Guide to Improving Your Reading Comprehension Skills

Many people preparing to take the GRE give Reading Comprehension little attention. There are a few reasons for this. One is that they've been reading since they started school as children, so the idea that they need to practice reading now seems ridiculous. "I know how to read!" they think. "So why put limited study time into reading?"

Another reason is that the correct answers to Reading Comprehension questions can seem subjective. A test prepper might take a practice test or try some practice questions and think, "I'm never going to understand why this answer is better than that one. I'm just never going to grasp how the testmaker thinks. Better to invest my study time elsewhere."

Yet another rationale is that learning all the words that might appear on the Verbal section seems like such a daunting task (see the previous section of this chapter for tips to make it less intimidating) that test takers allocate all their Verbal study time to vocabulary, with none left over for reading.

Let's rebut these one at a time:

- GRE Reading Comp requires a particular kind of reading. You are probably skilled at reading for school and work, and you may enjoy reading for fun. But to do well on the GRE Verbal section, you need to read to answer very specific kinds of questions, and this is a skill that takes practice.
- The answers to Reading Comp questions are *not* subjective. The test will not make you guess among correct answers, one of which is "better" than the others. Instead, there are *right* answers and *wrong* answers, and every wrong answer is incorrect for a reason. You can objectively evaluate answer choices based on information in the passage.
- Only half the Verbal section consists of Text Completion and Sentence Equivalence questions. The other half is Reading Comp. Thus, it is important to your Verbal score that you master the reading passages and questions.

If you have taken a practice test and answered almost all the Reading Comprehension questions correctly, then by all means, invest your preparation efforts elsewhere. If that is not the case, read on.

Attack the Passage

The GRE will present you with academic passages, most of one paragraph but some of several paragraphs, and it will ask you predictable types of questions about certain features of the text. The GRE is primarily concerned with your ability to grasp the main idea of what you read, differentiate fact from opinion and one person's opinion from another's, make supported inferences based on the text, and understand how the author has developed her ideas or the structure of the passage. The GRE will also ask you to analyze the logic of arguments. While some questions will test your ability to accurately identify a fact or idea in the passage, the test is always open book. That is, as questions come up on the right side of the screen, the passage will always be available on the left side of the screen for you to research.

Note that the GRE is *not* interested in testing your ability to learn facts about philosophy or physics or physiology. Thus, you are *not* studying to learn something about a topic, as you are accustomed to doing in school. Passages are often full of details that you will not see a question about, so time spent learning them is time wasted.

In fact, if the word *reading* triggers you to begin *studying*, as you would if you needed to take a test or write a paper for class, then don't think of this task as "reading." Instead, think of it as *attacking the passage.*

Attacking the passage means interrogating the passage, actively asking the same questions the test is likely to ask you. What's the author's point? Why is the author comparing X to Y? What is the author's attitude toward Z? By asking these questions as you read, you will be ready for the questions the test asks you. Watch a GRE expert take apart a science passage:

> There is no doubt that dogs have been domesticated for thousands of years, since the last Ice Age. What is less certain is the process of domestication that brought wolves, a predator of livestock and a danger to humans themselves, into the family as helper and companion.

> GRE expert's mental paraphrase: *What is the author's topic? Domestication of dogs. What is the author's position? Apparently, that we don't know exactly how Spot got to sleep on the bed.*

Attacking the passage means focusing on key words that signal important ideas and changes in a passage's direction, which are often the targets of questions. Focus on these sentences, making sure you understand what the author is saying. Key words also indicate when the author is using an example to illustrate a main point or breaking an overall process into a sequence of events or steps. You can read these sentences more lightly, simply noting where the information is if you need it.

> There is no doubt that dogs have been domesticated for thousands of years, beginning during the last Ice Age. What is less certain is the process of domestication that brought wolves, a predator of livestock and a danger to humans themselves, into the family as helper and companion. One widely accepted theory is that Paleolithic humans captured wolf cubs and raised them to serve as alarms when other large predators, such as cats in the *Smilodon* genus, approached. However, . . .

> GRE expert's mental paraphrase: *Sure enough, "One . . . theory" indicates that there is more than one idea about this. Then "However" signals a contrasting theory. It will be interesting to see whether the author takes a side.*

Attacking the passage means mentally paraphrasing as you read. GRE passages are often written in dense academic language, which makes answering questions about them harder. You can make answering questions easier by recasting the concepts in the same language you would use to explain them to a friend.

There is no doubt that dogs have been domesticated for thousands of years, beginning during the last Ice Age. What is less certain is the process of domestication that brought wolves, a predator of livestock and a danger to humans themselves, into the family as helper and companion. One widely accepted theory is that Paleolithic humans captured wolf cubs and raised them to serve as alarms when other large predators, such as cats in the *Smilodon* genus, approached. However, some paleoanthropologists are skeptical that humans would have befriended members of a species they viewed as inimical and sought to decimate. These scientists posit that some wolves—those best at reading human body language indicating hostile or tolerant intent and at adopting submissive, ingratiating behaviors such as tail wagging—approached early human settlements, first to scavenge and then to solicit handouts.

GRE expert's mental paraphrase: *So some scientists think taming wolves was our idea. But others think buddying up to us was actually their idea.*

Attacking the passage means taking notes, or making a Passage Map. Writing down the passage's broad Topic, its narrower Scope (the aspect of the Topic the author's interested in), and the author's Purpose, as well as the key ideas from each paragraph, will accomplish three goals. First, by digesting these important elements of the passage so you can briefly jot them down in a few words, you will ensure you really understand them. Second, if you capture the essential elements of the passage in your map, you can answer many questions just from your notes, saving time. Third, just as a road map tells you how to get to your friend's house, your Passage Map will tell you where to find that detail the GRE is asking about, again saving time.

There is no doubt that dogs have been domesticated for thousands of years, beginning during the last Ice Age. What is less certain is the process of domestication that brought wolves, a predator of livestock and a danger to humans themselves, into the family as helper and companion. One widely accepted theory is that Paleolithic humans captured wolf cubs and raised them to serve as alarms when other large predators, such as cats in the *Smilodon* genus, approached. However, some paleoanthropologists are skeptical that humans would have befriended members of a species they viewed as inimical and indeed sought to decimate. These scientists posit that some wolves—those best at reading human body language indicating hostile or tolerant intent and at adopting submissive, ingratiating behaviors such as tail wagging—approached early human settlements, first to scavenge and then to solicit handouts. Natural selection then favored those wolves most pleasing to humans, specifically those most friendly and trainable, as these animals would elicit the most food and shelter; their descendants are today's dogs, from Chihuahuas to Great Danes. Thus, if we accept that wolves took the initiative to join their lives with ours, it is not a much greater leap to believe that our species have coevolved such that those humans with traits that best satisfied wolves benefited most from wolves' protection and passed on those canid-friendly characteristics to their offspring. It is no wonder that so many people love dogs.

GRE expert's Passage Map:

Topic: Domestication of wolves/dogs

Scope: Theories of how it happened

Purpose: To argue for idea that wolves approached humans

Theory #1: Humans caught wolf cubs, used them for protection

Theory #2: Wolves chose to hang out near human settlements, get fed. If true, then we "coevolved"—people selected for wolf-pleasing traits. People ♥ dogs → theory #2.

Attacking the passage does not mean reading faster. It means reading at a speed that allows you to do all of the above: interrogate the text, spot key words and focus on the important ideas they highlight, mentally paraphrase, and map the passage. At first, this may mean reading more slowly than you will read on Test Day, given the Verbal section's timing. However, as you practice, you will get faster. Even better, when you are thoroughly prepared to answer the questions, they will take much less time, thereby saving you time overall.

Bottom line: If you read the passage but then can't answer the GRE's questions about it, then reading it didn't do you much good. Instead, *attack the passage* using the strategies briefly introduced here and discussed in much greater depth in chapter 7. Then also use the approaches in chapter 7 for analyzing the questions, researching and predicting the answers, and avoiding common types of wrong answers to master Reading Comprehension.

Change Your Reading Habits

It can be hard to put away old reading habits in favor of *attacking the passage*. Fortunately, you don't need to practice this skill only when you're studying for the GRE.

In fact, you can practice anytime you are reading for school, for work, to keep up with current events, or any other reason. Approach the textbook chapter, memo, article, or whatever it may be as though you were taking the GRE. By practicing this type of reading whenever you have a chance, you will soon work past the initial awkwardness, and reading this way will become second nature. Plus, you are adding to the total time you are investing in your GRE score.

Then when you practice with GRE-type passages and questions, like the ones you'll find next in this chapter and throughout this book (Chapter 7: Reading Comprehension, Chapter 8: Verbal Reasoning Practice Sets, Chapter 25: Practice Test), as well as in your online practice tests (MSTs), you will see significant improvement!

Reading Comprehension Practice Set

Questions 1–3 are based on the passage below.

In modern literary history, both budding and well-established authors have used secondary careers as book reviewers to hone their craft. George Orwell stands out as perhaps the most notable example with his prolific career as both a book reviewer and author. Analysis of his critiques of contemporaneous works offers insight into his belief that his personal world view should be reflected in the writings of his peers. Unrivaled in his keen insight into the core arguments of the seminal works of his time, Orwell was adept at pointing out fatal flaws in logic and never hesitated to enumerate what was wanting, even at the cost of infuriating other authors, both foes and friends. Indeed, Orwell's review of H. G. Wells' *Mind at the End of Its Tether* led to the end of their friendship, a fact in which there is a tinge of irony. While Orwell casts Wells' work as a disjointed and pessimistic diatribe about a bleak future, the description rings eerily similar to some reviews of Orwell's own masterpiece, *1984*.

1. The author of the passage would likely agree with each of the following statements about George Orwell EXCEPT:

    Ⓐ Orwell critiqued the works of many of his contemporaries.

    Ⓑ Orwell valued journalistic integrity over personal relationships.

    Ⓒ In *1984*, Orwell delved into some of the same bleak themes that Wells did in *Mind at the End of Its Tether*.

    Ⓓ Orwell's reviews had greater literary value than his novels.

    Ⓔ Orwell was skilled at dissecting the key ideas presented in other authors' works.

Consider each of the choices separately and select all that apply.

2. Which of the following statements accurately describes Orwell's approach to reviewing books?

    A Objective criticism tempered by mutual admiration

    B Invective-laden diatribe prompted by a competitive nature

    C Insightful analysis unswayed by personal attachment

3. According to the passage, Orwell's review of *Mind at the End of Its Tether*

   (A) ironically led to record sales of *Mind at the End of Its Tether*

   (B) cast in a negative light themes that he addressed in his novel *1984*

   (C) was irrelevant because it lacked a clear understanding of Wells' core argument

   (D) is a testament to his singular focus on pointing out flaws in the works of his contemporaries

   (E) marked the pinnacle of his prolific career as a book reviewer

Questions 4–6 are based on the passage below.

The problematic relationship between Heidegger's political views and his seminal status as a philosopher is a continuing point of contention in the historical assessment of his achievements. His contributions to Continental philosophy in works such as *Sein und Zeit* have been read, in some circles, through the critical lens of his affiliation with National Socialism in Nazi Germany during the Second World War. His writing during that time covered a broad range of subjects, including philosophy, politics, and aesthetics. His work on ontology directly influenced his contemporary philosophical thinkers, such as Jean-Paul Sartre. Though he is widely regarded within philosophical circles as one of the preeminent luminaries, along with Husserl, in the modern development of ontology, certain scholars and thinkers militate against the value of his thought in its entirety. To regard Heidegger's work highly would be, in their eyes, to absolve him of his support of the politics of Nazism, even though he is being evaluated solely on the basis of his contributions to the study of philosophy and not in any political context.

4. Select the sentence in the passage in which the author summarizes the competing attitudes toward Heidegger within the academic community.

Consider each of the choices separately and select all that apply.

5. The author asserts which of the following about Heidegger?

   A Some academics view him positively for both his political and philosophical work.

   B His legacy has been affected by opinions he expressed during World War II.

   C Some academics view him positively, while others cannot countenance him at all.

6. Which conclusion is implied by the author in his description of the status of Heidegger's legacy?

    (A) Heidegger's work should not be given serious recognition due to his political views.

    (B) The Second World War fostered a climate of intellectual innovation in Europe.

    (C) It is possible to critically evaluate Heidegger's contributions to philosophy while not absolving him of responsibility for his political views.

    (D) Scholars should consider the entire body of work of a thinker, in every field to which he or she contributed, when assessing that thinker's legacy in any one field.

    (E) It is impossible to divorce the study of politics from the study of philosophy.

Questions 7–10 are based on the passage below.

A common misconception is that color refers only to a wavelength of light in the visual spectrum, from about 400 nanometers (violet) to about 700 nanometers (red). When an object reflects light of a given wavelength, we see that object as the corresponding color. So, for example, we might see a Braeburn apple as red and a Granny Smith apple as green because they reflect light of different wavelengths. However, color is not merely a property of an external physical object but rather the result of an interaction among that object, the light that shines on it, and, finally but most significantly, the manner in which the human eye and brain make sense of the reflected light stimulus. Thus, the study of color can properly fall as much within the realm of psychology as that of physics.

Experience is one psychological factor that informs our perception of color. For example, a child eating by a campfire that emits a great deal of yellow light may believe that the melted Cheddar cheese served on white bread on a white paper plate is actually a white cheese like Swiss or Monterey Jack. This occurs because the yellow light reflects off both the plate and the bread, which the child knows are white, and off the cheese, which the child isn't sure about. All the objects therefore appear to be the same color, and the child assumes that color is white. On the other hand, an adult with experience viewing things in firelight would intuitively adjust her perception to account for the yellow light and would not make the same mistake.

Color is also perceived differently depending on its context. The noted abstract painter Josef Albers produced an influential body of work based on this phenomenon, including his series *Homage to the Square* featuring nested squares of different colors. In one psychological experiment testing perception, the letter *X* is presented against two colored backgrounds. Although the letter is identical each time it is presented, it appears olive green in one context and lavender in the other context. This effect is achieved when the *X* is given a low-saturation blue color, or gray-blue, and the backgrounds are also low-saturation colors with hues on either side of blue on the color wheel. Because blue falls between purple and green on the color wheel, a gray-blue *X* against a gray-purple background will look gray-green, or olive, and the same *X* against an olive background will look gray-purple, or lavender. In a similar manner, an intermediate color will look different against different primary color backdrops; teal, for instance, will look green against a blue background and blue against a green background.

Other subjective factors also influence the experience of color. These include cultural norms (Westerners most often name blue as their favorite color, whereas in China red is preferred) and simply what we learn about color. Consider that if a child learns that stop signs are "red," the child will call them "red." Another person in that society will also have learned to call stop signs "red." However, whether the two people are experiencing the same color is unknown since that experience exists only in the mind. Therefore, if one were to tell an interior designer that color is an immutable physical property of objects, one would meet with skepticism. Before placing the electric blue sofa in a client's living room, the designer considers the color of light the various light fixtures will emanate, the colors of the carpet and walls, and her client's feelings about electric blue, which after all may not even be the same color in the client's mind as it is in the designer's.

7. Which of the following statements best expresses the main idea of the passage?

(A) Color is primarily a psychological construct, and therefore the study of physics is not relevant to an understanding of how color is perceived.

(B) The phenomenon of color is a combined effect of the wavelength of light that shines on an object, the wavelength of light reflected by the object, and the human mind's perception of the light stimulus that comes to the eye.

(C) Scientists have determined that although people may perceive color differently in different situations, color is an immutable characteristic of objects.

(D) Creative professionals, such as artists and interior designers, view color significantly differently than do scientists.

(E) To say that an object is a particular color is meaningless because color is a subjective perception influenced by experience, culture, and context and cannot therefore be ascertained to be a specific physical characteristic.

8. The author would be most likely to agree with which of the following ideas?

  (A) When attempting to achieve a particular aesthetic effect, a graphic designer should consider how the color used for the border of an advertisement will appear next to the color of the text.

  (B) A decorator working for a client in China would not purchase an electric blue sofa for that individual's living room, because blue is not a preferred color in China.

  (C) Companies designing packaging for their products should avoid using gray tones because these would cause different customers to see the colors differently, thereby rendering the brand message inconsistent.

  (D) Because red is a primary color, a wall should not be painted red if a sofa of an intermediate color will be placed against it, as the sofa's color may be distorted by its proximity to the wall.

  (E) Artists often explore the interaction of adjacent colors when juxtaposing different forms in the composition of their paintings.

Consider each of the choices separately and select all that apply.

9. According to the passage, which of the following accurately describes human perception of color?

  [A] A low-saturation color against a low-saturation background of an adjacent hue on the color wheel will appear a similar shade as the other adjacent hue.

  [B] An intermediate color against a background that is one of the intermediate color's component primary colors will be difficult to distinguish from that background.

  [C] Letters written in an intermediate color or in a low-saturation color are more likely to be misread by children than by adults.

10. The author mentions Josef Albers in paragraph 3 in order to

  (A) argue that artists are aware of how humans perceive color and use this phenomenon to enhance the impact of their work

  (B) illustrate the idea that color is fundamentally a subjective, aesthetic phenomenon rather than a scientific one

  (C) demonstrate that a child would probably see a painting in the *Homage to the Square* series differently than would an adult

  (D) explain that humans perceive the color of regular shapes, such as squares, differently than they perceive the color of less regular shapes, such as food on a plate or a letter of the alphabet

  (E) provide an example that reinforces the importance of the concept that color is a subjective experience manufactured in part within the human mind

Reading Comprehension Practice Set Answer Key

1. **D**
2. **C**
3. **B**
4. **Though he is widely regarded within philosophical circles as one of the preeminent luminaries, along with Husserl, in the modern development of ontology, certain scholars and thinkers militate against the value of his thought in its entirety.**
5. **B, C**
6. **C**
7. **B**
8. **A**
9. **A**
10. **E**

Reading Comprehension Practice Set Answers and Explanations

1. D

For this Inference EXCEPT question, examine each answer choice in light of the passage. The fourth sentence points out that Orwell reviewed "the seminal works of his time," which would be the books written by his contemporaries. The author would thus agree with the statement in (A), so it can be eliminated. The last two sentences show that Orwell's negative review of Wells' final work led to the end of their friendship, so (B) is out. The final sentence shows that the pessimistic view of the future in Wells' work is similar to that presented in Orwell's *1984*. The author would also agree with the statement in (C), so eliminate it as well. While the passage highlights Orwell's work as a reviewer, it states that he had a "prolific career as *both* a book reviewer and author." There is no evidence in the passage to support the idea that Orwell's work as a reviewer outweighed his work as an author. The author of the passage would not agree with this statement, so **(D)** is correct. The fourth sentence eliminates (E). The phrase "unrivaled in his keen insight into the core arguments of the seminal works of his time" is another way to say that Orwell was skilled at dissecting the key ideas presented in the work of other authors.

2. C

All-that-apply questions require consideration of each of the answer choices separately. In (A), objective criticism does describe Orwell's approach, but the second part of the statement—that the criticism was tempered by mutual admiration—is proved false by Orwell's negative review of his friend Wells' work and the subsequent end of their friendship. Eliminate (A). The "invective-laden diatribe" in (B) is an unnecessarily extreme reference to Orwell's review of Wells' book. While it may be true that Orwell felt some competitive rivalry with his contemporaries, there is no evidence for this idea in the passage. Eliminate (B). The passage mentions both Orwell's "unrivaled keen insight" and the fact that he did not allow his friendship with Wells to affect the review that he wrote. Therefore, there is support in the passage for both parts of statement **(C)**, making this choice the only correct answer.

3. B

This question asks for an accurate description of the effects of Orwell's review of *Mind at the End of Its Tether*. The last two sentences of the passage talk about how the review ended Orwell and Wells' friendship and the irony of Orwell's negative review of the book given its similarities to his own novel, *1984*. **(B)** is correct because it picks up on the fact that Orwell's negative review of *Mind at the End of Its Tether* addressed themes also found in *1984*. (A) is incorrect because sales of *Mind at the End of Its Tether* are not mentioned in the passage. (C), (D), and (E) all use extreme language—"irrelevant," "singular," and "pinnacle"—that is not supported in the passage.

4. Though he is widely regarded within philosophical circles as one of the preeminent luminaries, along with Husserl, in the modern development of ontology, certain scholars and thinkers militate against the value of his thought in its entirety.

The sentence you're looking for is one that sums up how the intellectual community, as a whole, views Heidegger. This means the sentence should encompass all parties, both those that are receptive to him and those that view him negatively. The second sentence, "His contributions to Continental philosophy in works such as *Sein und Zeit* have been read, in some circles, through the critical lens of his affiliation with National Socialism in Nazi Germany during the Second World War," may be tempting, but this is telling you the way in which his work has been interpreted, not the reactions or attitudes of the academic community. It also doesn't mention any "competing" feelings toward his work. The last sentence provides justification for *why* certain scholars view him as they do, but it does not account for the other schools of thought. The next-to-last sentence, "Though he is widely regarded within philosophical circles as one of the preeminent luminaries, along with Husserl, in the modern development of ontology, certain scholars and thinkers militate against the value of his thought in its entirety," sums up the complete range of reaction to Heidegger across the academic community.

5. B, C

Choice (A) is incorrect. The author nowhere explicitly states or implies that anyone has a positive reaction to Heidegger's political views. She only intimates that scholars working in the study of philosophy have been influenced by his work in that field. Choice **(B)** is correct because the author states that Heidegger's work, even in philosophy, has been viewed through this "critical lens." Answer choice **(C)** is also correct. The author cites philosophers, such as Sartre, who have reacted positively to Heidegger's philosophy and asserts that those who view him negatively do so because they cannot abide by absolving him of guilt for his support of the Nazis.

6. C

This question asks you to engage the text at a deep level and to infer what the author is suggesting. It is important to pay close attention to the author's tone. The passage's Main Idea is the evaluation of a thinker's body of work by academic scholars in different fields. The author points out both Heidegger's tremendous accomplishments in the field of philosophy and his less-than-admirable involvement with the Nazi party. Choice (B) is dealt with nowhere in the passage. Choice (E) goes beyond the scope of the passage. Choice (A) is incorrect, because the author emphasizes Heidegger's influence on philosophers like Sartre and makes certain to point out that it is in "their eyes" that Heidegger is so viewed, not the author's own. Choice (D) is incorrect because it is the opposite of what the author implies. Choice **(C)** is the correct answer because, in the last sentence of the passage, the author stresses that it is only Heidegger's contributions to philosophy that are being considered, not his political views. The author seems to be suggesting that the two can be judged apart from one another.

7. B

In the first paragraph, the author states that color is not only a function of wavelength, and then the key word "However" signals what color actually is: "not merely" a physical property, "but rather" the product of an interaction among the object's properties (specifically, how it reflects light), the light itself, and the human observer. The rest of the passage elaborates on this interaction of the physical properties of light and the perception of light. Answer choice **(B)** states this idea and is correct.

Choice (A) is extreme because of the words "primarily" in the first part and "not relevant" in the second part; in the last sentence of paragraph 1, the author says the study of color is appropriate for both psychology and physics. The word "immutable" in choice (C) means "unchanging" and thus directly contradicts the Main Idea of the passage, which is that color is a construct of multiple factors and these factors can vary for any given object. Choice (D) might be inferred from the passage, but this is not the main point of the passage, which is about the nature of color and not about people's reactions to color. Choice (E) is extreme due to the word "meaningless." Although objects may appear different colors to different people under different conditions, and one can never be sure what another person means by the word *red*, the author never says it is without meaning to, for example, describe an apple as red.

8. A

To prepare to answer this Inference question, review the points the author has made in the passage. The correct answer must be true given what the author has said. In paragraph 3, the author states that the color of an object changes depending on nearby colors. Therefore, answer choice (**A**) is supported.

Choice (B) misuses the detail that blue is not the favorite color of most Chinese. This does not mean that no Chinese person would like an electric blue sofa—after all, most people own objects of many colors, including colors that are not their favorite—and some Chinese people may prefer blue. Choice (C) is not supported. Using low-saturation or grayish tones next to each other can result in colors looking different than they would in isolation or next to other colors, but it does not result in different people perceiving the colors differently. Choice (D) is a distortion. The passage states that an item of an intermediate color that is placed near a color-wheel-adjacent primary color, such as orange placed near red, will look more like the primary color on the other side of it (orange next to red will look more yellow). Nothing suggests this effect is undesirable, so choice (D)'s "should not" is unsupported. Also, the passage only discusses the interaction of intermediate and primary colors that are next to each other on the color wheel, but this answer choice refers to any intermediate color being placed next

to red. Finally, although one artist, Josef Albers, worked with color in this way, the passage does not suggest that artists in general "often" do this, and choice (E) is incorrect.

9. A

"According to the passage" signals a Detail question. Research each answer choice to determine whether it matches an idea stated in the passage. Choice (**A**) is stated in paragraph 3, as shown by the example of gray-blue looking either gray-purple or gray-green when placed against a background of the other color. Answer choice (B) is a 180, or the opposite of what is true. An intermediate color placed next to a component primary color will look more like the other component primary color, thus contrasting more sharply. Choice (C) is incorrect. According to paragraph 2, children may interpret colors differently than do adults because children lack experience interpreting color under different lighting conditions, but this has nothing to do with intermediate or low-saturation colors.

10. E

"In order to" signals a Logic question. It is asking why the author included Albers in the passage. Review your Passage Map. It should note that the author's overall purpose is to explain why color is as much psychological construct as physical property. Then the Main Idea of paragraph 3, where Albers is mentioned, is that people see color differently depending on context. Thus, paragraph 3 is about a particular aspect of how color is a psychological construct. The author must mention Albers to support this idea, and answer choice (**E**) correctly states this.

The author is not making an argument about artists, so (A) is out. Choice (B) is incorrect because the author says in paragraph 1 that color does result in part from the physical properties of light and can properly be studied by physicists; the author does not mention Albers to say that color is solely a nonscientific phenomenon. (C) uses an idea from paragraph 2; this is not the point being made in paragraph 3. (D) states a comparison between different types of shapes that the passage never makes.

CHAPTER 5

TEXT COMPLETION

Introduction to Text Completion

In the Text Completion question type, you will be asked to select one entry for each blank from the corresponding column of choices. Each question may include as many as three blanks.

You will find about six Text Completion questions in each Verbal Reasoning section. In each of these questions, one or more words from a sentence or paragraph will be missing. This question type tests your ability to read critically—to recognize the meaning of the sentence or paragraph as a whole and to select words that logically fit the blanks.

The directions for Text Completion will look like this:

Each sentence below has one or more blanks, each blank indicating that something has been omitted. Beneath the sentence are five words for one-blank questions and sets of three words for each blank for two- and three-blank questions. Choose the word or set of words for each blank that best fits the meaning of the sentence as a whole.

A Text Completion question with one blank will look like this:

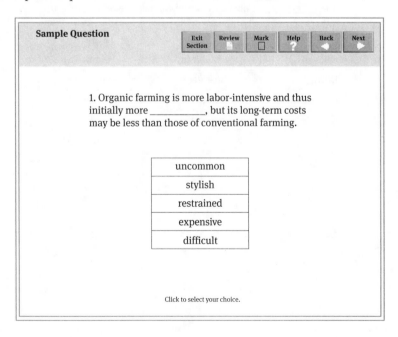

A Text Completion question with two blanks will look like this:

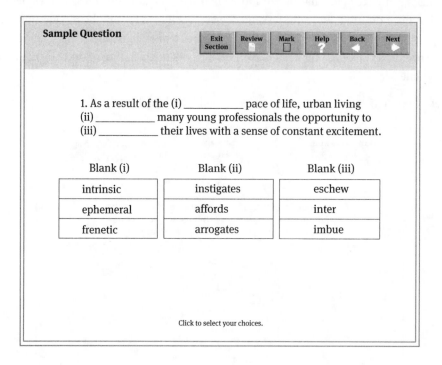

A Text Completion question with three blanks will look like this:

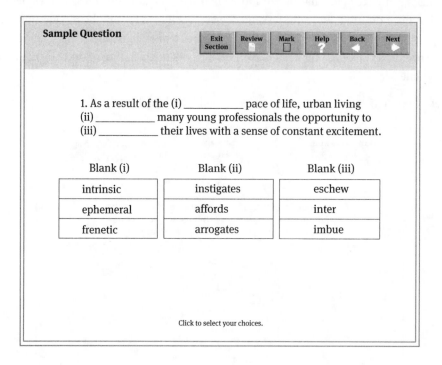

THE KAPLAN METHOD FOR TEXT COMPLETION

STEP 1 Read the sentence or sentences, looking for clues.

STEP 2 Predict an answer for each blank.

STEP 3 Select the best match(es) from among the choices.

STEP 4 Confirm your answer by reading your selected choice(s) into the sentence(s).

How the Kaplan Method for Text Completion Works in Questions with Only One Blank

Now let's discuss how the Kaplan Method will help you answer these questions correctly.

[**STEP 1**]

Read the sentence, looking for clues.

There are always clues in the sentence that will point you to the right answer. The missing words in Text Completion questions will usually have a relationship with key words in the sentence. Key words and key phrases are descriptors that lead to the meaning of the missing words.

A road sign is a structural key word that signals a connection between ideas; it also determines the direction of the relationship. There are road signs in the GRE that tell you to go straight ahead and those that tell you to take a detour. A semicolon also functions as a road sign, indicating a close connection between two clauses.

"Straight-ahead" road signs are used to make one part of the sentence support or elaborate upon another part. They continue the sentence in the same direction. The positive or negative connotation of what follows is not changed by these clues.

"Detour" road signs change the direction of the sentence. They make one part of the sentence contradict or qualify another part. The positive or negative connotation of an answer is changed by these clues.

Review the following examples of road signs. Interpreting the road sign will help you to determine which way the sentence is going and predict what words will best complete the blanks.

Straight-ahead road signs:	Detour road signs:
And	*But*
Since	*Despite*
Also	*Yet*
Thus	*However*
Because	*Unless*
; (semicolon)	*Rather*
Likewise	*Although*
Moreover	*While*
Similarly	*On the other hand*
In addition	*Unfortunately*
Consequently	*Nonetheless*
	Conversely

[STEP 2]

Predict an answer.

Once you've found the road sign and the key word(s) relevant to the blank, predict an answer for the blank. Your prediction does not have to be a sophisticated or complex word or phrase; it just needs to be a paraphrase that logically fits into the sentence. By predicting, you avoid the temptation of trying every answer choice on its own, which can take up valuable time on Test Day.

[STEP 3]

Select the best match from among the choices.

Quickly go through the choices, see which one most closely matches, and eliminate whichever choices do not fit your prediction. If none of the choices match your prediction, reread the question and revisit Steps 1 and 2.

[STEP 4]

Confirm your answer by reading your selected choice into the sentence.

This step is simply double-checking that you did your work correctly and that your answer choice is correct in context. If your answer makes sense when you read your choice back into the sentence, you can confirm and move on. If your choice does not make sense when you read it back into the sentence, you should reread the question and revisit Steps 1–3.

How to Apply the Kaplan Method for Text Completion in Questions with One Blank

Now let's apply the Kaplan Method to a Text Completion question that only has one blank:

> The yearly financial statement of a large corporation may seem _____ at first, but the persistent reader soon finds its pages of facts and figures easy to decipher.
>
> (A) bewildering
> (B) surprising
> (C) inviting
> (D) misguided
> (E) uncoordinated

[STEP 1]

Read the sentence, looking for clues.

The sentence contains the detour road sign "but," which indicates that the correct answer will mean the opposite of another key word or key phrase in the sentence. The key phrase to note in this example is "easy to decipher."

[STEP 2]

Predict an answer.

By knowing that the blank must contrast with the phrase "easy to decipher," you can predict that the missing word will be similar to "difficult to understand."

[STEP 3]

Select the best match from among the choices.

Quickly go through the choices and see which one most closely matches "difficult to understand," which in this case is choice (**A**) *bewildering*.

[STEP 4]

Confirm your answer by reading your selected choice into the sentence.

Plugging the word *bewildering* into the sentence fits the context: "The yearly financial statement of a large corporation may seem *bewildering* at first, but the persistent reader soon finds its pages of facts and figures easy to decipher."

Now let's apply the Kaplan Method to a second Text Completion question that only has one blank:

> Although the initial cost of installing solar panels to produce electricity can be _____, the financial benefits are realized for years to come in the form of reduced electric bills.
>
> (A) encouraging
>
> (B) minimal
>
> (C) exciting
>
> (D) misleading
>
> (E) exorbitant

[STEP 1]

Read the sentence, looking for clues.

The sentence contains the detour road sign "although," which indicates that the correct answer will mean the opposite of a key word or key phrase in the sentence. The key phrase to note in this example is "reduced electric bills."

[STEP 2]

Predict an answer.

By knowing that the blank must contrast with the phrase "reduced electric bills," you can predict that the correct answer will be similar to "increased or high payments or costs."

[STEP 3]

Select the best match from among the choices.

Quickly go through the five choices and see which one most closely matches "increased or high payments or costs," which in this case is choice (**E**) *exorbitant*.

[STEP 4]

Confirm your answer by reading your selected choice into the sentence.

Plugging the word *exorbitant* into the sentence fits the context: "Although the initial cost of installing solar panels to produce electricity can be *exorbitant*, the financial benefits are realized for years to come in the form of reduced electric bills."

How the Kaplan Method for Text Completion Works for Questions with Two or Three Blanks

For Text Completion questions with multiple blanks, use the same general approach that you would use when there is only one blank. Because there are multiple blanks, you might feel like you have to predict an answer for each blank as you encounter it. Sometimes, though, it is difficult to make a prediction for the first blank because there is just not enough context to do so. In such a situation, simply read the entire sentence or sentences before making your predictions. Then predict an answer for the easiest blank first, then the next easiest, and so on. As you make predictions for the easier blanks, your understanding of the sentence or sentences becomes more concrete, and your predictions for the harder blanks will be that much stronger.

[**STEP 1**]

Read the sentence or sentences, looking for clues.

Your approach in Step 1 is essentially the same as it is for one-blank questions. Just be sure that you are not in a rush to start making predictions. Take your time to understand how the entire stimulus fits together.

[**STEP 2**]

Predict an answer for each of the blanks.

Once you have a clear understanding of the context of the sentence or sentences, take a moment to identify the easiest blank to work with. Look for road signs and key words relevant to that blank and predict an answer. With more context in which to interpret the remaining blanks, you are ready to make a prediction for the remaining blanks.

[**STEP 3**]

Select the best matches from among the choices.

This step is the same as it is with one-blank questions. The only difference is that you will select an answer choice for each of the blanks.

[**STEP 4**]

Confirm your answer by reading your selected choices into the sentence or sentences.

This step is the same as it is for one-blank questions.

How to Apply the Kaplan Method for Text Completion in Questions with Two or Three Blanks

Now let's apply the Kaplan Method to a Text Completion question with two blanks:

> Everyone believed the team was favored with athletic talent and a seasoned, successful coaching staff; consequently, it was difficult to (i) _____ why the team was (ii) _____ so badly against one of the worst teams in the division.

	Blank (i)		Blank (ii)
A	fathom	**D**	elevating
B	interpolate	**E**	dominating
C	explore	**F**	floundering

[STEP 1]

Read the sentence or sentences, looking for clues.

In this sentence, the straight-ahead road sign "consequently" indicates that the correct answer will support or elaborate on another word or phrase in the text. The key word to note in this example is "badly."

[STEP 2]

Predict an answer for each of the blanks.

The first clause in the sentence indicates that the team should have been good. However, the team was doing poorly, and this is "difficult" for everyone because it did not make sense. In other words, it was difficult to "understand" why the team was not doing well. The second blank must support or elaborate on the phrase "so badly," so you can predict that the correct answer will be similar to "playing so poorly."

[STEP 3]

Select the best matches from among the choices.

For the first blank, the answer choice most like "understand" is (**A**) *fathom*. For the second blank, the choice that most closely matches "playing poorly" is choice (**F**) *floundering*.

[STEP 4]

Confirm your answer by reading your selected choices into the sentence.

Plugging the selected words into the sentence fits the context: "Everyone believed the team was favored with athletic talent and a seasoned, successful coaching staff; consequently, it was difficult to *fathom* why the team was *floundering* so badly against one of the worst teams in the division."

Now let's apply the Kaplan Method to a Text Completion question with three blanks:

It seemed there would be no resolving the matter since both sides felt they had reached an (i) _____; neither side would (ii) _____, and the resulting (iii) _____ would keep their relationship strained and fragile for years to come.

Blank (i)	
A	apogee
B	epiphany
C	impasse

Blank (ii)	
D	capitulate
E	regress
F	impugn

Blank (iii)	
G	acrimony
H	cacophony
I	sinecure

[STEP 1]

Read the sentence or sentences, looking for clues.

In this sentence, there are clues in the phrases "no resolving the matter" and "strained and fragile," which, along with the straight-ahead road signs "since" and "and," suggest that the correct answers are going to describe or support a conflict between disagreeing parties. In this example, you may already sense the words that complete at least one of the blanks just from the construction of the sentence.

[STEP 2]

Predict an answer for each of the blanks.

The first blank must support or elaborate on the phrase "no resolving the matter," so predict something that suggests the sides reached a point of no more negotiating. Now that you've predicted that blank, the others are easier. Neither side would "back down," and the resulting "bitterness" kept the relationship strained.

[STEP 3]

Select the best matches from among the choices.

Quickly go through the choices and select the ones that most closely match your predictions. For the first blank, **(C)** *impasse* matches the idea that they've reached a point of no more negotiating. As a result, they are not willing to "back down" or **(D)** *capitulate*, and the result is "bitterness" or **(G)** *acrimony*.

[STEP 4]

Confirm your answer by reading your selected choices into the sentence.

Plugging the words *impasse*, *capitulate*, and *acrimony* into the sentence fits the context: "It seemed there would be no resolving the matter since both sides felt they had reached an *impasse*; neither side would *capitulate*, and the resulting *acrimony* would keep their relationship strained and fragile for years to come."

Kaplan's Additional Tips for Text Completion Questions

Look for what's directly implied and not an ambiguous interpretation

The questions you'll encounter are written in sophisticated but still logical and straight-forward prose. Therefore, the correct answer is the one most directly implied by the meanings of the words in the sentence. These sentences are constructed to allow you to identify the answer using the inferential strategies you just practiced.

Don't be too creative

Read the sentence literally, not imaginatively. Pay attention to the meaning of the words instead of to any associations or feelings that might come up for you.

Paraphrase long or complex sentences

You may encounter a sentence that, because of its length or structure, is hard to get a handle on. When faced with a complex sentence, slow down and put it in your own words. You could break it into pieces as well and tackle one phrase at a time.

Use word roots

In the GRE Resources section at the back of this book, you can learn the Latin and Greek roots of many common GRE words. If you can't figure out the meaning of a word, take a look at its root to try to get close to its meaning. Etymology can often provide clues to meaning, especially when you couple a root definition with the word in context.

TEXT COMPLETION CONCEPT CHECK

Before you move on, check your understanding by considering these questions:

· What role do road signs and context clues play in Text Completion sentences?

· Why is it important to make a prediction before evaluating answer choices in Text Completion questions?

· After you find an answer choice or choices that match your prediction, what should you do next?

If you feel like you've got the hang of it, great! Proceed to the practice set that starts on the next page.

If you'd like a quick video review of this chapter, or if you would like some additional guided practice, head to your online resources. Under **Text Completion**, click **Strategy for Text Completion** to watch a quick video review of this chapter. Or click **Text Completion Guided Practice** to apply what you've learned.

Text Completion Practice Set

Try the following Text Completion questions using the Kaplan Method for Text Completion. If you're up to the challenge, time yourself; on Test Day, you'll want to spend between one and one and a half minutes on each question, depending on the number of blanks.

1. Many know him for his great scientific achievements, but Benjamin Franklin always believed that public service should (i) _____ science. Accordingly, his political contributions to the formation of the United States were (ii) _____.

Blank (i)		Blank (ii)	
A	impede	D	substantial
B	replicate	E	paltry
C	outweigh	F	abhorrent

2. The giant squid's massive body, adapted for deep-sea life, breaks apart in the reduced pressures of shallower ocean depths, making the search for an intact specimen one of the most _____ quests in all of marine biology.

   Ⓐ meaningful
   Ⓑ elusive
   Ⓒ popular
   Ⓓ expensive
   Ⓔ profitable

3. Despite the threat of sanctions from numerous other countries, the (i) _____ nation has repeatedly ordered its armies to (ii) _____ the borders of the disputed territory.

Blank (i)		Blank (ii)	
A	desultory	D	breach
B	parsimonious	E	circumnavigate
C	truculent	F	circumvent

4. For the people of ancient cultures who resided in desert climates, laws of hospitality dictated that (i) _____ must be welcomed as friends in the homes of their hosts; this code of conduct, typically grounded in religious belief, was considered (ii) _____ as it ensured basic survival for those who were traveling through the harsh, arid environment.

Blank (i)		Blank (ii)	
A	adversaries	D	discretionary
B	sojourners	E	sacrosanct
C	occupants	F	injudicious

5. Scientists have long (i) _____ that there are oceans of liquid water beneath the surface of Europa, one of Jupiter's largest moons; if such (ii) _____ seas do in fact exist, then this satellite may prove to be the most likely location for extraterrestrial life in our solar system.

Blank (i)		Blank (ii)	
A	postulated	**D**	embryonic
B	refuted	**E**	pestilential
C	overlooked	**F**	subterranean

6. Franklin Pierce was an expansionist American president who signed the treaty authorizing the Gadsden Purchase of land from Mexico, but his similar attempt to (i) _____ Cuba was unpopular, even within his own party. He further cemented the (ii) _____ of his political opponents with his pro-slavery policies, which ultimately led his party to (iii) _____ him and reject his bid for a second term.

Blank (i)		Blank (ii)		Blank (iii)	
A	boycott	**D**	enmity	**G**	galvanize
B	bolster	**E**	approbation	**H**	abide
C	annex	**F**	largess	**I**	repudiate

7. The (i) _____ gave such an impassioned speech that even the most forlorn members of the crowd were briefly moved to (ii) _____.

Blank (i)		Blank (ii)	
A	orator	**D**	despair
B	miscreant	**E**	duress
C	interloper	**F**	ebullience

8. The (i) _____ nature of the monarch's reign, which was characterized by frequent shows of force and what were thought by many to be egregious violations of individual rights, was not negated by the ruler's (ii) _____ acts of generosity. In time, he might well be remembered as a (iii) _____ rather than a benevolent king.

Blank (i)		Blank (ii)		Blank (iii)	
A	inscrutable	**D**	intermittent	**G**	prolocutor
B	mercenary	**E**	insipid	**H**	despot
C	draconian	**F**	legitimate	**I**	figurehead

9. Although the young woman initially refused to enter the heated debate, claiming to be (i) _____ its outcome, her calm demeanor quickly turned (ii) _____ as she listened to one participant's argument, revealing herself to be actually rather opinionated about the (iii) _____ issue.

Blank (i)		Blank (ii)		Blank (iii)	
A	indifferent to	D	phlegmatic	G	inscrutable
B	cognizant of	E	conciliatory	H	trivial
C	partial to	F	cantankerous	I	contentious

10. The lawyer's explosive, rude remarks convinced many that he was (i) _____ and of (ii) _____ character, suddenly making his future as a politician seem (iii) _____.

Blank (i)		Blank (ii)		Blank (iii)	
A	indifferent	D	courageous	G	guaranteed
B	charming	E	virtuous	H	precarious
C	volatile	F	ignoble	I	facetious

Text Completion Practice Set Answer Key

1. C, D
2. B
3. C, D
4. B, E
5. A, F

6. C, D, I
7. A, F
8. C, D, H
9. A, F, I
10. C, F, H

Text Completion Practice Set Answers and Explanations

1. C, D

The detour road sign "but" is the key to the first sentence. It indicates that the next idea will contrast with the fact that Franklin is known for his scientific achievements. Since the next idea is Franklin's belief about public service and science, predict that Franklin believed his work in public service to be more important than his work in science. This leads to **(C)** *outweigh* as the correct answer for the first blank. (A) *impede* means "slow the progress of," which is extreme. Franklin may have valued public service more than science, but there is no context to support the idea that he believed that public service should actually slow the progress of science. (B) *replicated*, which means "duplicated" or "repeated," expresses a relationship between public service and science that is not indicated by the sentence.

The second sentence begins with the straight-ahead road sign "Accordingly," and therefore follows the train of logic from the first sentence. Franklin believed that public service was even more important than work in science, yet he achieved greatness in science. Thus, you can predict that his political contributions were also "significant." **(D)** *substantial*, or "having great meaning or lasting effect," is a perfect match for this prediction and is the correct answer for the second blank. (E) *paltry* means "inferior," "trivial," or even "despicable" and is the opposite of what is required here. (F) *abhorrent*, or "causing or deserving strong dislike or hatred," does not fit in with the logic of the sentence.

2. B

The key word here is "intact," which means that although specimens have been collected, they have rarely (if ever) been in one piece when recovered. You can fairly assume that recovering an intact specimen is difficult. When you look for a synonym for "difficult" in the answer choices, you recognize **(B)** *elusive* as your answer.

3. C, D

The first part of the sentence describes measures—namely, sanctions—that have been taken to stop a nation's actions in a disputed territory. The word "despite" at the beginning of the sentence acts as a detour road sign, indicating that the first half of the sentence contrasts with the second half. You can infer that the sanctions did not have the desired effect on the country and that it continued its undesirable activities.

The first blank describes the type of country that would continue to use force in a disputed territory despite the threat of sanctions. You can predict the adjective "aggressive," which matches **(C)** *truculent*. (A) *desultory*, which means "lacking a plan," and (B) *parsimonious*, which means "frugal," do not make sense in this context.

The second blank indicates what the nation has done to incur the threat of sanctions. Since the issue involves the disputed territory's borders, you can predict that the nation's armies entered the disputed territory unlawfully, which matches **(D)** *breach*. (E) *circumnavigate* means to "go around rather than through" an area, while (F) *circumvent* means "to avoid altogether."

4. B, E

The context clues that point to the meaning of the first blank can be found both before and after the semicolon. In the first half of the sentence, the references to "hospitality" and being "welcomed as friends" indicate that the missing word refers to a group of people. In the second half of the sentence, this same group is described as "those who were traveling." You can, therefore, predict "travelers" for the missing word. This prediction matches **(B)** *sojourners*, which refers to people staying in a place for a short time. Choice (A) *adversaries* means "enemies," but no context clues indicate that the travelers are hostile. Choice (C) *occupants* refers to people who live in a particular place, so it would be the opposite of "travelers."

The second blank describes how ancient people viewed the law of hospitality. As the sentence states, this law was usually "grounded in religious belief" and "ensured basic survival" for travelers, so you can predict that this law was regarded as very important and even sacred. Eliminate (D) *discretionary*, which means "optional," and (F) *injudicious*, which means "foolish." Choice **(E)** *sacrosanct*, which means "sacred" or "inviolable," is a strong match for the prediction and the correct answer.

5. A, F

The semicolon is a straight-ahead road sign that indicates that the second clause builds on the first. The first blank describes the scientists' attitude in regard to oceans on Europa. The "if" in the second clause of the sentence indicates that their existence is not certain, so predict that the scientists "hypothesized" that such lakes exist. **(A)** *postulated* is a perfect match for this prediction and is correct. (B) *refuted*, or "declared untrue," is too negative; the sentence does not imply that there is evidence that proves the lakes are not there. Similarly, there's no reason to believe that the scientists have (C) *overlooked* these oceans.

The second blank describes the oceans themselves. All that is known about them from the clues in the sentence is that they are under the surface of one of Jupiter's moons, so the right answer will relate to that idea. **(F)** *subterranean* means "underground" and fits perfectly. (D) *embryonic* may seem tempting because the oceans are said to be potential sources of life; however, the missing word refers to the oceans themselves, not whatever life may exist within them. When used in such a context, embryonic means "new" or "not yet fully developed," which doesn't fit the context. (E) *pestilential*, which means "harmful" or "virulent," is too negative to fit the sentence.

6. C, D, I

The first sentence mentions that Pierce was known for purchasing land, and the key word "similar" signals that the first blank should also mean something like "purchase" or "obtain." **(C)** *annex* is a match for this idea and is the correct answer. (A) *boycotting* Cuba would mean cutting off relations with the country, which is not equivalent to the purchase of land from Mexico described in the first portion of the sentence, and (B) *bolster* would imply that Pierce was strengthening Cuba in some way, rather than acquiring it.

"Further" is the clue for the second blank, a continuation from the first sentence. The fact that Pierce's attempt to grab land in Cuba was unpopular "even within his own party" suggests that his actions were even more unpopular among his political opponents. **(D)** *enmity* is a match. He certainly wouldn't garner (E) *approbation* (meaning "praise") or (F) *largess* (meaning "generosity") from them.

The final blank is part of a very helpful construction on the GRE: when the sentence contains the blank, followed by "and" and another word, the other word is typically a great prediction for the blank. Here, it makes perfect sense to say that his party rejected Pierce *and* his bid for renomination. **(I)** *repudiate* is a synonym for reject and is correct. (G) *galvanize* would mean that he was energized by his unpopularity, which is not supported by the sentence. (H) *abide* would imply that his party was overlooking his problems and putting up with him, which is certainly different from their rejection of him.

7. A, F

The key phrase for the first blank is "impassioned speech." You can tell the correct answer for the first blank is someone who can speak expressively. (B) *miscreants* and (C) *interlopers* are not necessarily excellent speakers, but *orators* are. The correct choice is **(A)**.

For the second blank, the key phrase is "even the most forlorn"; "even" works as a detour road sign, and "forlorn" is negative, so you want a positive term. Since (D) *despair* and (E) *duress* are not positive, the answer is **(F)** *ebullience*.

8. C, D, H

The first blank describes the nature of the monarch's reign, which included "frequent shows of force" and "egregious violations of individual rights." These negative phrases indicate the first blank should mean something like "severe or harsh use of power." This prediction matches **(C)** *draconian*. Choice (A) *inscrutable* means "incomprehensible," but no context clues indicate that the king's actions were difficult to understand. (B) *mercenary*, which means "greedy," is a negative quality but not one supported by the clues.

The second blank describes the king's acts of generosity. Since the king's reign was "characterized" by abuses of power, you can predict that it was unusual for the king to act in a generous manner. This prediction matches **(D)** *intermittent*, which means "sporadic" or "irregular." (E) *insipid* is the opposite and means "commonplace" and "boring," while (F) *legitimate* means "lawful."

To complete the third blank, note the detour road sign "rather than." The third missing word is thus set up to contrast with the phrase "benevolent king." These clues indicate that the king's legacy will reflect his reign, which was oppressive. You can predict that the king would be remembered as a tyrant, which matches **(H)** *despot*. (G) *prolocutor*, which means "spokesperson," lacks the negative charge needed here. (I) *figurehead* is a term that describes a leader with no real power.

9. A, F, I

The detour road sign "Although" indicates that there are two parts of the sentence that contrast with one another. The first blank refers to what the young woman claimed about her attitude toward the debate's outcome. This claim contrasts with the fact that she quickly reveals herself to be "opinionated." A good prediction for the first blank would be the phrase "impartial to," which matches **(A)** *indifferent to*. Choice (B) *cognizant of* means "aware of," which does not match the prediction, and (C) *partial to* is the opposite of the prediction.

The second blank describes how the young woman's demeanor changed from "calm" to something else as she listened to one of the debaters. The change indicated that the young woman was not impartial but actually "opinionated," so you can predict that her demeanor became either noticeably positive or negative. Eliminate (D) *phlegmatic*, which means "calm," and (E) *conciliatory*, which describes something that is meant to calm. Choice **(F)** *cantankerous* means "argumentative," which fits the predicted meaning.

The third blank describes the type of issue that is being debated. Earlier in the sentence, the debate is described as "heated," so you can predict that the issue or topic is "controversial." This prediction matches **(I)** *contentious*. Eliminate (G) *inscrutable*, which means "mysterious," and (H) *trivial*, which means "unimportant."

10. C, F, H

For the first blank, the key phrase is "explosive, rude remarks." Choice (A) *indifferent* suggests neutrality, but being explosive and rude is far from being neutral. The second choice, *charming* (B), does not make sense because someone who is "explosive" and "rude" is not seen as being charming. Choice **(C)** *volatile* means "unstable," the same as "explosive."

Since we know the lawyer is explosive, rude, and volatile, we can predict his character will be seen in negative ways. Because (D) *courageous* and (E) *virtuous* have positive connotations, choice **(F)** *ignoble* is the correct choice.

With the information that he is explosive, rude, volatile, and ignoble, predict what kind of "future as a politician" the lawyer will have. This is the key phrase for identifying the third blank. His character suggests he is not popular, so we can conclude his future is not (G) *guaranteed*. Choice (I) *facetious* means "flippant," which does not make sense as a description of the politician's future. Choice **(H)** *precarious* means "uncertain," which fits the context of the sentence and is the correct choice.

[CHAPTER 6]

SENTENCE EQUIVALENCE

Introduction to Sentence Equivalence

Each Verbal Reasoning section features approximately four Sentence Equivalence questions. In each sentence, one word will be missing, and you must identify two correct words to complete the sentence. The correct answer choices, when used in the sentence, will result in the same meaning for *both* sentences. This question type tests your ability to figure out how a sentence should be completed by using the meaning of the entire sentence.

The directions for Sentence Equivalence will look like this:

> Select the **two** answer choices that, when inserted into the sentence, fit the meaning of the sentence as a whole **and** yield complete sentences that are similar in meaning.

A Sentence Equivalence question will look like this:

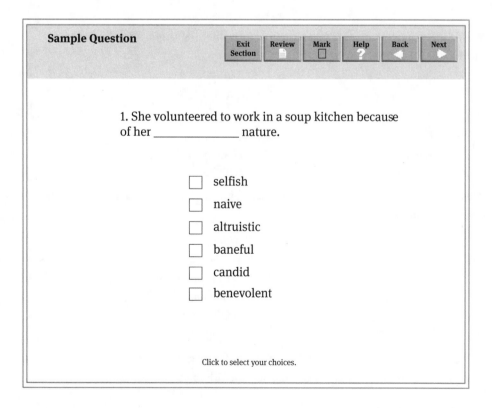

> **THE KAPLAN METHOD FOR SENTENCE EQUIVALENCE**
>
> **STEP 1** Read the sentence, looking for clues.
>
> **STEP 2** Predict an answer.
>
> **STEP 3** Select the two choices that most closely match your prediction.
>
> **STEP 4** Confirm your answer by reading your selected choices into the sentence.

How the Kaplan Method for Sentence Equivalence Works

Now let's discuss how the Kaplan Method will help you answer these questions correctly.

[STEP 1]

Read the sentence, looking for clues.

As you read the sentence, pay attention to the part of speech that the answer choice will be and compare it with the answer choices. Also look for specific words in the sentence that will help you to understand its meaning. These are called "key words" or "road signs"—descriptive phrases or contextual clues that suggest the meaning of the missing word.

Words that connect one part of a sentence to another ("straight-ahead" road signs) include the following:

And	*Likewise*
Since	*Moreover*
Also	*Similarly*
Thus	*In addition*
Because	*Consequently*
; (semicolon)	

Words that indicate one part of the sentence contradicts another part of the sentence ("detour" road signs) include these:

But	*Although*
Despite	*While*
Yet	*On the other hand*
However	*Unfortunately*
Unless	*Nonetheless*
Rather	*Conversely*

Being aware of these road signs will help you to figure out the meaning of the sentence and the relationship of the missing word to other ideas in the sentence.

[STEP 2]

Predict an answer.

Once you have read the sentence and identified clues to words that will complete the sentence, predict an answer. Your prediction should be a word that you choose on your own *before* you look at the answer choices. The prediction word should also be a simple word that logically completes the sentence.

[STEP 3]

Select the two choices that most closely match your prediction.

Quickly review the six answer choices and choose the two words that, when plugged into the sentence, most closely make the intended meaning of the sentence match your prediction. Eliminate the answer choices that do not fit your prediction.
Sometimes you will need to adjust your prediction in order to find two answer choices that match each other.

[STEP 4]

Confirm your answer by reading your selected choices into the sentence.

Read the sentence with each answer choice plugged in to check that you have selected the correct answers. Make sure that both answer choices make sense in the context of the sentence. Pay close attention to the charge of a word's meaning. For example, "dislike" and "despise" both mean the same thing, but "despise" has a much *stronger* degree of charge to that meaning. Each sentence should have the same meaning. If one or both of your answers do not make sense when you reread the sentence, revisit the question and repeat Steps 1, 2, and 3.

How to Apply the Kaplan Method for Sentence Equivalence

Now let's apply the Kaplan Method to a Sentence Equivalence question.

1. She volunteered to work in a soup kitchen because of her _____ nature.

- [A] selfish
- [B] naive
- [C] altruistic
- [D] baneful
- [E] candid
- [F] benevolent

[STEP 1]

Read the sentence, looking for clues.

One way to determine the correct answer in this sentence is to figure out the part of speech of the missing word. The missing word in this sentence is an adjective because it modifies the noun "nature." Another clue in this sentence is the key word "volunteer." A volunteer is someone who offers her time or skills without pay. The blank will be an adjective with a positive connotation that describes the type of person who volunteers.

[STEP 2]

Predict an answer.

By knowing that the blank must describe someone who offers her time or skills without pay, you can predict that the correct answer will be similar to "helpful."

[STEP 3]

Select the two choices that most closely match your prediction.

Quickly review the six answer choices to see which two words most closely match "helpful," which in this case are choice (**C**) *altruistic* and choice (**F**) *benevolent*.

[STEP 4]

Confirm your answer by reading your selected choices into the sentence.

Plug each answer choice into the sentence to see if it matches the context. Make sure that each sentence has the same meaning:

"She volunteered to work in a soup kitchen because of her <u>altruistic</u> nature."

"She volunteered to work in a soup kitchen because of her <u>benevolent</u> nature."

Now let's apply the Kaplan Method to a second Sentence Equivalence question.

2. While the first speaker at the conference was confusing and unclear, the second speaker was _____.

     A   articulate

     B   experienced

     C   melancholy

     D   ambiguous

     E   eloquent

     F   vociferous

[STEP 1]

Read the sentence, looking for clues.

In this sentence, the clue word "while" is a detour road sign. "While" indicates that the second part of the sentence will mean the opposite of the first part of the sentence. The first speaker was described as "confusing" and "unclear," which are the key words in this question. The correct answer means the opposite.

[STEP 2]

Predict an answer.

By knowing that the blank will mean the opposite of "confusing" and "unclear," you can predict that correct answers will be similar to "clear."

[STEP 3]

Select the two choices that most closely match your prediction.

Quickly go through the six answer choices and see which two words most closely match "clear" in the context of speaking. In this case, these are choice (**A**) *articulate* and choice (**E**) *eloquent*.

[STEP 4]

Confirm your answer by reading your selected choices into the sentence.

Plug each answer choice into the sentence to see if it matches the context. Make sure that each sentence has the same meaning:

"While the first speaker at the conference was confusing and unclear, the second speaker was <u>articulate</u>."

"While the first speaker at the conference was confusing and unclear, the second speaker was <u>eloquent</u>."

Kaplan's Additional Tips for Sentence Equivalence

Consider all answer choices

Make sure to read and check all answer choices in the sentence before making your final choice. An answer may fit well in the sentence and closely match your prediction, but if there is no other answer choice that also completes the sentence with the same meaning, it isn't correct.

Paraphrase the question

If you rephrase a difficult or longer sentence into your own words, it will be easier to make a prediction for the answer. Paraphrasing will also make sure that you understand the meaning of the sentence.

Look beyond synonyms

Simply finding a synonym pair in the answer choices will not always lead you to the correct answer. Answer choices may include a pair of words that are synonyms but do not fit in the context of the sentence. Both of those two choices will be incorrect. The meaning of each sentence must be the same *and* correct. Be sure to try both words in the sentence, checking that each sentence has the same meaning, before making your final choice.

Use prefixes, suffixes, and roots

Think about the meaning of the prefixes, suffixes, and roots in words that you know if you are struggling to figure out the definition of a word.

SENTENCE EQUIVALENCE CONCEPT CHECK

Before you move on, check your understanding by considering these questions:

- Why is it important to make a prediction before evaluating answer choices in Sentence Equivalence questions?

- How many answers will you select for Sentence Equivalence questions?

- If you see an answer choice that you believe is a correct answer but there is no conceptual match in the other choices, what should you do?

If you feel like you've got the hang of it, great! Proceed to the practice set that starts on the next page.

If you'd like a quick video review of this chapter, or if you would like some additional guided practice, head to your online resources. Under **Sentence Equivalence**, click **Strategy for Sentence Equivalence** to watch a quick video review of this chapter. Or click **Sentence Equivalence Guided Practice** to apply what you've learned.

Sentence Equivalence Practice Set

Try the following Sentence Equivalence questions using the Kaplan Method for Sentence Equivalence. For each question, select two choices. If you're up to the challenge, time yourself; on Test Day, you'll want to spend only about one minute on each question.

1. While the abstract impressionist painter Lee Krasner may not be as well-known to the general public as her husband Jackson Pollock, her work is held in esteem by _____; indeed, she is one of the only female artists to have been featured in a retrospective at the Museum of Modern Art.

    [A] detractors

    [B] neophytes

    [C] the cognoscenti

    [D] connoisseurs

    [E] malcontents

    [F] the uninitiated

2. Although *Don Quixote*, published in 1605, is a _____ work of Western literature and an early example of the modern novel, it is not, as is sometimes claimed, the first novel; an even earlier contender for that designation is *The Tale of Genji*, an 11th-century work of Japanese literature.

    [A] seminal

    [B] derivative

    [C] uninspired

    [D] canonical

    [E] serial

    [F] antithetical

3. Although the lab assistant openly apologized for allowing the samples to spoil, her _____ did not appease the research head, and she was let go.

    [A] insincerity

    [B] frankness

    [C] falsehoods

    [D] candor

    [E] inexperience

    [F] hesitation

4. Human infants are born with motor capabilities that are barely _____ compared to those of other animal species that can survive on their own hours after birth; this is thought in part to be the result of a biological prioritization in humans of complex reasoning and language skills over motor development early in life.

    A impetuous

    B consummate

    C inchoate

    D sedentary

    E incipient

    F volatile

5. The firefighter, desperate to save the children on the second floor of the fiery house, rushed into their bedroom; his colleagues, more wary of the _____ structure, remained outside.

    A stalwart

    B precarious

    C stout

    D irrefragable

    E tottering

    F fecund

6. While the subject of numerous studies and self-help books, attaining happiness is often made more challenging by the fact that the concept of happiness itself is open to broad interpretation; psychologists are undecided whether happiness is merely _____ emotion that one can experience only momentarily, a fixed state of being that one achieves, or something in between.

    A a coincidental

    B an inherited

    C a transient

    D an incessant

    E an intrinsic

    F an ephemeral

7. In honor of his lost homeland, the exiled poet wrote a moving _____ that described the beauty of his native country's people, culture, and landscapes.

   A elocution

   B paean

   C oratory

   D panegyric

   E diatribe

   F harangue

8. While the ethics committee ultimately _____ the executive, the taint of scandal followed her long after the investigation into her private business dealings had concluded.

   A discharged

   B repudiated

   C dismissed

   D exculpated

   E lionized

   F exonerated

9. No matter how hard Benjamin tried to coax the kitten off of the tree branch, the tiny creature remained _____, clinging to the bark with all its strength.

   A intractable

   B enervated

   C obstinate

   D diffident

   E lackadaisical

   F incapacitated

10. Despite the legend that portrays him as unable to lie about cutting down a cherry tree, George Washington was hardly as _____ as the apocryphal story would make him seem. In fact, he was a shrewd general who used deception and misdirection efficaciously during the American Revolutionary War.

   A hapless

   B guileless

   C duplicitous

   D listless

   E artless

   F mendacious

Sentence Equivalence Practice Set Answer Key

1. **C, D**	6. **C, F**
2. **A, D**	7. **B, D**
3. **B, D**	8. **D, F**
4. **C, E**	9. **A, C**
5. **B, E**	10. **B, E**

Sentence Equivalence Practice Set Answers and Explanations

1. C, D

"While" sets up a contrast; Lee Krasner is not well known to the public, but one group of people, described by the missing word, respected her work. There's a further clue after the semicolon: her work has been featured in a prominent museum. Thus, you can predict that the blank must mean something like "art experts."

(C) *the cognoscenti* and **(D)** *connoisseurs* both mean "experts," especially in connection to the arts, so they are the two correct answers. (B) *neophytes* and (F) *the uninitiated* are the opposite of what's needed; both refer to novices or those who are untrained. (A) *detractors* ("those who disparage or criticize") and (E) *malcontents* ("rebels" or "troublemakers") are both too negative to fit the context of the sentence.

2. A, D

The missing word describes *Don Quixote*'s relation to Western literature. The fact that it is sometimes called the first novel implies that it holds a special place in Western literature, so you can predict that the blank will mean something like "important."

(A) *seminal*, meaning "influential," and **(D)** *canonical*, meaning "recognized" or "time-honored," both match this prediction and are correct. (B) *derivative* would imply that *Don Quixote* is based on modern novels; this is the opposite of their actual relationship. (C) *uninspired* means "dull" or "uninteresting" and is again the opposite of what you need. (E) *serial*, or "arranged in a series," doesn't fit the context as there is no indication that *Don Quixote* was published as a series of chapters. Finally, (F) *antithetical* means "opposite." Since the sentence indicates that *Don Quixote* is an early modern novel, this choice can be eliminated.

3. B, D

The clue in this sentence is the detour road sign "although," which indicates contrast. Her "open" apology would be expected to "appease" her boss, but she was fired anyway; paraphrasing further, she did something good but suffered bad consequences. The word in the blank will express the good thing she did, so you can predict that the correct answers will be similar to "honesty." Choices (A), (C), (E), and (F) are not synonyms for "honesty," leaving choices **(B)** and **(D)**. **(B)** *frankness* and **(D)** *candor* both carry the meaning of "forthright." They're your answers.

4. C, E

When taken as a whole, the sentence provides a reason why human infants might be born in a state that is less developed than that of other animal species. Indeed, "barely developed" would be a good prediction to complete the sentence. Both **(C)** *inchoate* and **(E)** *incipient* mean "just beginning to develop" and are the correct answers.

(A) *impetuous* means "impulsive," which does not fit the context of the sentence at all. (B) *consummate* means "complete" or "perfect" and is the opposite of the meaning of the missing word. (D) *sedentary* means "not moving around" and would imply that human infants avoid moving because they are lazy. Finally, (F) *volatile* means "changeable" or "explosive" and can be eliminated because, while the infants are still developing, there is no indication that they are changing unpredictably.

5. B, E

There's a somewhat subtle contrast clue here. One of the firefighters is rushing into a burning building to rescue children, while others are "more wary" of the structure. The blank must describe why the firefighters are concerned the building is dangerous; a good prediction would be "unsafe." Evaluate the choices to find two matches for the prediction. **(B)** *precarious* and **(E)** *tottering* both mean "unstable," so they're the correct answers.

(A) *stalwart* and (C) *stout* are the opposite of the prediction; they both mean "sturdy." (D) *irrefragable* means "impossible to refute," while (F) *fecund* means "fertile."

6. C, F

The first part of the sentence explains that there are multiple definitions of "happiness," while the second part highlights two of those definitions. The first definition, which contains the blank, describes a type of "emotion" that can only be experienced "momentarily." You can predict that the blank means something like "temporary."

Choices **(C)** *a transient* and **(F)** *an ephemeral* both mean "short-lived" and are therefore the correct answers. (A) *a coincidental* would refer to something that happens to occur at the same time as something else, so it is incorrect. (B) *an inherited* refers to a trait passed down from one's parents, and (D) *an incessant* describes something that is unceasing, so both are closer in meaning to "fixed" than to "fleeting." Similarly, (E) *an intrinsic* describes a trait that is part of one's very nature, rather than a state that is temporary.

7. B, D

Analyze the word charge of the context clues that relate to or describe the blank. In this sentence, the words "honor," "moving," and "beauty" have a positive word charge, indicating that the poet wrote a poem that praised his native country. Predict that the missing word will be similar in meaning to the word "tribute." This prediction matches both **(B)** *paean* and **(D)** *panegyric*, each of which means "an expression of praise."

The other answer choices may have been tempting as each is related to speech or the use of words. Choice (A) *elocution* is the manner in which one pronounces words, but it does not refer to the content of a text. Similarly, (C) *oratory* means "the art of public speaking," but it does not refer to the text of a speech. Choices (E) *diatribe* and (F) *harangue* both mean "a critical and aggressive speech," which is the opposite of the prediction.

8. D, F

The detour road sign "While" indicates that the "taint of scandal" followed the executive in spite of the ethics committee's actions. Since the second half of the sentence is set up to contrast with the first half, you can infer that the ethics committee did something positive for the executive. A strong prediction for the missing word would be "acquitted" or "cleared of wrongdoing." This prediction matches **(D)** *exculpated*, which means "to have blame removed," and **(F)** *exonerated*, which means "to have one's innocence proven."

Choices (A) *discharged* and (C) *dismissed* may have been tempting answer choices since they are synonyms. However, both words mean "to be relieved of duty," which would be a negative act against the executive rather than the positive act indicated. Choice (B) *repudiated* means "rejected," which also has a negative charge. (E) *lionized* is a positive word that means "celebrated," but no clues in the sentence indicate that the executive deserved praise, and no other answer choice has a synonymous meaning.

9. A, C

The phrase "no matter how hard" at the beginning of the sentence acts as a detour road sign, indicating that Benjamin's efforts to get the kitten off the branch were unsuccessful. The word "remained" is a straight-ahead road sign that implies the kitten had been clinging to the branch for a while. You can predict that the missing word, which describes the kitten, means something like "stubborn." This prediction matches **(A)** *intractable* and **(C)** *obstinate*, both of which mean "stubborn" or "immovable."

Choices (B) *enervated* and (F) *incapacitated* might have been tempting since they are synonyms, but both mean "weakened" and, therefore, do not match the prediction. Choice (D) *diffident*, which means "shy," might be a tempting word to use when describing a kitten, but the context clues do not support this meaning. Similarly, (E) *lackadaisical*, which means "lazy," would contrast with the description of the kitten, which was hanging on "with all of its strength."

10. B, E

Several clues point to the meaning of the blank. "Despite" and "hardly" indicate that the missing word contrasts with the expectation of George Washington's character. The story about his being "unable to lie" is "apocryphal" or unlikely to be true, and the second sentence states that Washington was actually "shrewd," using "deception and misdirection." A great prediction for the blank would be "honest." This would contrast with what the sentence claims to be Washington's true "shrewd" nature.

(B) *guileless* and **(E)** *artless* both mean "honest and innocent" and are thus correct. Be careful with (C) *duplicitous* and (F) *mendacious*, which are synonyms but mean "deceptive," which is the opposite of the meaning of the blank. (A) *hapless*, or "unlucky," and (D) *listless*, or "lacking energy," do not fit the meaning of the sentence.

CHAPTER 7

READING COMPREHENSION

Introduction to Reading Comprehension

Reading Comprehension is the only question type that appears on all major standardized tests, and with good reason. No matter what academic discipline you pursue, making sense of densely written material is a core skill necessary for success in graduate school. That's why Reading Comprehension passages are on the GRE—to test this skill. Fittingly, ETS adapts its content from actual, graduate-level documents. The GRE traditionally takes its topics from four disciplines: social sciences, biological sciences, physical sciences, and the arts and humanities.

There are roughly 10 reading passages and 20 questions spread between the two Verbal Reasoning sections of the GRE. Some passages are only one paragraph in length, while others are longer. Each passage is then followed by one to six questions that will require you to perform one or more of the following skills: ascertain a passage's scope and purpose, consider what inferences can properly be drawn from the statements in a passage, research details in the text, understand the meaning of words and the function of sentences in context, and analyze the assumptions inherent in an argument.

Because the number of questions for each passage varies, there will always be a sentence introducing the passage that tells you exactly how many questions are associated with the passage. Here is an example of an introductory sentence and the passage that follows; these appear on the left of your screen. The first question about the passage also appears, on the right.

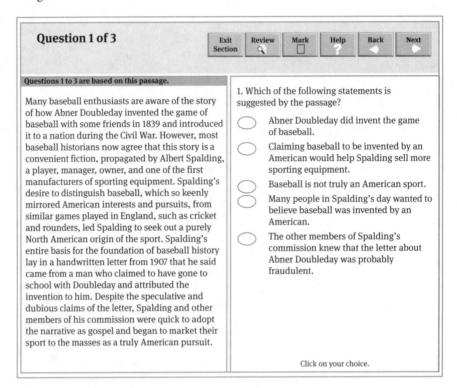

Reading Comprehension questions take one of three forms. The first, and most familiar, is the standard multiple-choice question. A question of this type will ask you to select the best answer from a set of five possible answers. The question shown above is a multiple-choice question.

The second type of question will present you with three answer choices, of which one or more are correct. Note the language in the box above the question stem: "Consider each of the choices separately and select all that apply." In these **all-that-apply** questions, you will not receive partial credit for selecting only *some* of the right answers—you must select *all* of the correct choices, and no incorrect ones, to receive full credit for the question.

Here's an example of an all-that-apply question:

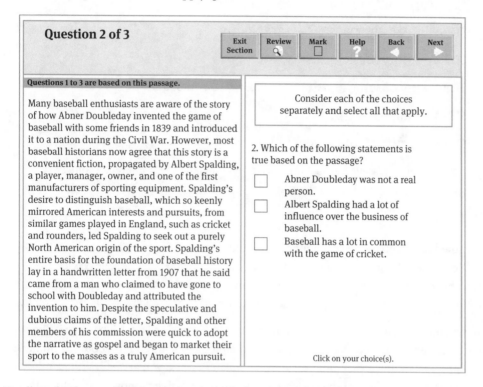

Finally, a third type of question asks you to find and then select within the passage a sentence that includes an important detail or that performs a certain function. In these **select-in-passage** questions, you will use your mouse to click on the sentence that specifically fulfills the task set out in the question stem. Here is an example of a select-in-passage question:

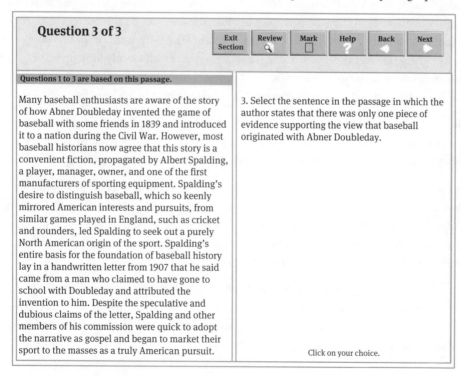

> **THE KAPLAN METHOD FOR READING COMPREHENSION**
>
> **STEP 1**   Read the passage strategically.
>
> **STEP 2**   Analyze the question stem.
>
> **STEP 3**   Research the relevant text in the passage.
>
> **STEP 4**   Make a prediction.
>
> **STEP 5**   Evaluate the answer choices.
>
> *Note:* When a passage has just one question associated with it, Steps 1 and 2 are switched; read the question stem first, then read the passage.

As noted in Chapter 4: Verbal Foundations and Content Review, many students think that because they have read a large number of academic texts for college classes, they can apply the same skills to achieve success on the GRE. However, answering Reading Comprehension questions correctly requires a different approach.

In school, you read to learn things about a subject. However, if a GRE passage is about the behavior of enzymes, you are not taking a biology test, and if it is about the influence of Appalachian music on composer Aaron Copland's work, you are not taking a music theory test. The makers of the GRE are not testing your subject knowledge; rather, they are interested in your critical thinking skills. Moreover, GRE Reading Comprehension questions are open book—the passage stays on the screen throughout the question set, meaning that if a question asks about a detail, you can research it in the passage. Thus, memorizing details as you read is wasted effort. In fact, answering Detail questions from memory often leads to the wrong answer because the GRE supplies incorrect answer choices that are subtle distortions of passage content. The GRE wants to know whether you can grasp the overall structure of a passage so you can efficiently look up information you need to answer a question—a skill you'll use when completing papers and projects in graduate school—and *it rewards test takers who use this approach*.

Instead of reading to learn the material, focus on the big picture: *Why* did the author write the passage, and what are the passage's topic and scope? Sifting out these big-picture concepts from the surrounding details—reading *strategically*—is the key to success.

But reading strategically is only part of the battle. After all, you don't get any points for reading well. Instead, your goal is to answer questions correctly. And to answer Reading Comprehension questions correctly, you need to know the specific task a question asks you to perform, how to accomplish that task effectively, and how to avoid the GRE's common and predictable wrong-answer traps.

If learning a new way to read passages and answer questions seems daunting, don't worry. The GRE is a standardized test, and that means that the passages and questions in every Reading Comprehension section follow the same predictable patterns, over and over again. Success in the Reading Comprehension section, then, is simply a result of mastering a small handful of skills, including the ability to read the passage strategically, research the passage or your notes on the passage to answer specific questions, make clear predictions, and know what differentiates right answers from wrong answers. Those skills are intimately tied to the Kaplan Method for Reading Comprehension, a step-by-step approach that will help you maximize your performance in this section.

How the Kaplan Method for Reading Comprehension Works

[**STEP 1**]

Read the passage strategically.

Note that this step is not simply "Read the passage." Step 1 is to read *strategically*. Reading strategically means giving more weight to some parts of the passage than to others.

That means that as you read, you will make sure to fully understand certain parts of the passage (things like the author's opinion, each paragraph's main idea, new theories, interesting discoveries) and read lightly through parts of the passage that are not as important (background information, supporting examples, rhetorical asides). Doing this will help you read efficiently while still capturing the important big-picture information that you'll need to answer questions. Noting the big-picture information means identifying the Topic, Scope, and Purpose of a passage. The Topic is what the passage is about, very broadly stated. The Scope is that specific aspect of the topic that interests the author. The Purpose is the author's reason for writing the passage.

On the GRE, authors write passages for the following reasons:

- To **explain** an aspect of a topic
- To **describe** the features of a thing or event
- To **analyze** how something works
- To **compare and contrast** two or more things—the author may simply describe how they are similar and/or different, or the author may also express an opinion about which is better
- To critique or **evaluate** how well or poorly something achieves a purpose—the author may only present other people's critiques or may offer her own opinion
- To **argue** for a position—the author has an opinion
- To **rebut** someone's position—the author disagrees with someone else's opinion

Here are some examples of big-picture summaries. Try to imagine the passage that each of these reflects.

Topic: World War II	**Topic:** Genetic diversity	**Topic:** Ethical systems
Scope: Impact of London blitz on children	**Scope:** Hypothesis about role viruses may play in causing genetic mutations	**Scope:** Use of utilitarianism and Kantian ethics in business
Purpose: To describe negative effects	**Purpose:** To evaluate evidence for/against	**Purpose:** To compare/ contrast effects on profits

Just from knowing the Topic, Scope, and Purpose, you probably find that you have a pretty good grasp of the gist of these passages, without even having read them. When you capture this information from a passage you read, you will have a solid foundation to answer GRE Reading Comprehension questions.

In addition, part of strategic reading is taking notes on the passage, or making a Passage Map. This means writing down the Topic, Scope, and Purpose, as in the examples above, as well as the following information:

- Main Idea of each paragraph
- Any opinion(s) offered—whose opinion and what it is
- Definition of any specialized term(s) central to the Main Idea
- Key examples—a few words identifying the example and what idea it illustrates

Your goal is not to rewrite the passage. After all, the passage is always going to be there on the screen, and writing down too much information would take too much time. Instead, in addition to mentally paraphrasing as you read, summarize important concepts and opinions, as well as terms and examples that are central to the author's Main Idea, by jotting down a few words on your scratch paper. You can and should use abbreviations and symbols, and sometimes a quick sketch will capture a concept more quickly and succinctly than words. Finally, no one will ever read this except you, so it doesn't need to be neat; as long as you understand what you've written, your Passage Map is doing its job.

One question that many students have initially is: How do I know what's important in a passage? Fortunately, GRE passages will tell you what's important with *key words*—including the same kind of key words you are already familiar with from Text Completion and Sentence Equivalence questions. Particularly important are key words of *emphasis* and of *contrast.* Emphasis key words (such as *very, important,* and *clearly*) are strong adjectives or adverbs that highlight the author's opinion or an idea the author views as significant or noteworthy. Contrast key words (such as *but, yet,* and *however*) often indicate a significant conflict, disagreement, or change in thinking.

Strategic Reading: How to Use Key Words

When you strategically read a Reading Comprehension passage, you determine the passage's big picture: the passage's Topic, Scope, and Purpose. The GRE provides savvy readers with key words as clues to when to slow down and digest important parts of a passage and when to move quickly past unimportant details. Take a look at the following sentences:

> The students attended Dr. Robinson's lecture on international financial markets.

> The students have a solid understanding of global currency exchange rates.

Based on these two sentences, can you infer the contents of Dr. Robinson's lecture or its value to the students? Without key words indicating the relationship between the sentences, you simply cannot determine what Dr. Robinson spoke about or whether the students learned anything. But add just one little phrase to the beginning of the second sentence, and a deduction can be made:

> The students attended Dr. Robinson's lecture on international financial markets.

> **As a result,** the students have a solid understanding of global currency exchange rates.

Now it's clear: the students gained their understanding of global currency exchange rates *because* they attended Dr. Robinson's lecture. But what if you saw this phrasing instead?

> The students attended Dr. Robinson's lecture on international financial markets.

> **Nevertheless,** the students have a solid understanding of global currency exchange rates.

In this instance, either Dr. Robinson didn't cover the topic of global currency exchange rates, or he did so inadequately. Either way, it's apparent that the students gained their knowledge of global currency exchange rates from some other source.

Here are the different types of key words that will help you locate central ideas and opinions and grasp the structure of the passage:

- **Emphasis** and **opinion** key words are used when the author wants to call attention to a specific point. These come in two varieties. Emphasis key words, such as *very* and *critical*, point to ideas that are important to the author. Opinion key words, such as *beneficial* or *dead end*, emphasize a positive or negative charge and point to attitudes toward or judgments about ideas. These opinions are frequently the focus of GRE questions. Be sure to distinguish between the author's opinions and those of others.

- **Contrast** key words such as *but, however, nevertheless,* and *on the other hand* tell you that a change or disagreement is coming.

- **Continuation** key words such as *moreover, furthermore, also*, and *in addition* tell you to expect more of the same line of reasoning.
- **Logic** key words, which play an important role in answering Reasoning questions, alert you to an argument. **Conclusion** key words such as *therefore* and *thus* indicate a supported claim or main point. **Evidence** key words like *because, since*, and *for* announce the reasons used to support that conclusion. Again, be careful to distinguish between an argument the author is making and someone else's argument, which the author may be explaining without taking a position, agreeing with, or rebutting.
- **Illustration** key words let you know that what follows is an example of a broader point. One example, of course, is *example. For instance* is another favorite in GRE passages.
- **Sequence/grouping** key words delineate how events or characteristics are related. *First, second*, and *third* are examples, as is a sequence like *17th century, 18th century*, and *today*. Science passages may group complicated phenomena using simpler key words (*at a higher temperature* and *at a lower temperature*, for example). Look for these key words especially in passages explaining steps in a scientific, social, or artistic process.

Of course, you don't get any points on the GRE for classifying a key word or for writing down a note on your scratch paper. Instead, the purpose of focusing on key words is to identify those parts of the passage that help you understand its big picture while at the same time ignoring less important details. Key words also help you take control over your reading by helping you predict the function of the text that follows. Imagine that you saw a passage with the following structure on Test Day. Can you anticipate the kinds of details that would fill each of the blanks?

The northern rabbit is exceptionally suited to cold climates because _____ _____. Moreover, _____. However, one danger to this species' survival is _____. Furthermore, _____.

The emphasis key word "exceptionally" tells you that the author believes the northern rabbit's adaptation to cold climates is significant, and you can expect the following text to focus on this idea. The evidence key word "because" indicates the author will provide a reason the rabbit survives the cold so well. "Moreover," a continuation key word, signals another reason. Then the contrast key word "[h] owever" indicates a change in direction, so the next two blanks will include text describing potential threats to the northern rabbit's survival. While you can't predict the exact features that aid the rabbit (a special type of insulating fur? hibernation strategies?) or the specific dangers it faces (cold-climate predators? lack of food in the winter?), you do understand the overall structure of the passage. The details might change, but as long as the key words remain the same, the overall gist of the passage does not. You actually know a lot about this passage just from the outline above, without any details!

Are key words just as helpful when the passage begins discussing ideas and terms that you're unfamiliar with?

> Many biologists attribute Tasmanian devils' susceptibility to certain types of facial cancers to a lack of genetic diversity in the devils' overall population. These scientists base their conclusions on evidence showing that _____ _____. However, new research _____.
> In fact, _____.

This passage, like the one before it, is a scientific passage with a species of animal as the topic. However, the text is denser, and the terms the author uses—"certain types of facial cancers" and "lack of genetic diversity"—might throw off some untrained test takers who focus too much on details about the topic and not on the passage's overall structure. A well-trained test taker knows that "these scientists" will base their conclusions on data that show a connection between the concepts in the first sentence. As the expert reads, she knows that what follows "[h]owever" will introduce ideas that differ from those of "[m]any biologists." By focusing on key words, the expert knows to expect that the "new research" will present an alternative cause of the facial cancer. Furthermore, by starting a sentence with "In fact," the author may be signaling his own opinion on the matter—stating something he believes to be the truth. Again, simply on the basis of the outline above, you already know the gist of the passage.

With each GRE Reading Comprehension passage, focus on key words to help you separate unimportant background information from the author's Topic, Scope, and Purpose in writing, and to help you grasp the structure of the passage. Again, because the passage remains on screen as you answer the questions, you will be able to research details as necessary. In this way, you will read efficiently and be well prepared to answer questions correctly.

Note: When a passage has just one question associated with it, Steps 1 and 2 are switched; read the question stem first, then read the passage.

[**STEP 2**]

Analyze the question stem.

Once you have strategically read a passage to determine its Topic, Scope, and Purpose and have made a Passage Map, it is time to start answering the questions. Luckily, because the GRE is a standardized test, the questions that accompany a passage almost always fall into one of just a handful of categories:

- **Global.** These ask about the passage as a whole. Look for language in the question stem that asks you to determine a passage's main idea, primary purpose, or overall structure. Here are some examples of Global question stems:

   Which of the following most accurately describes the primary purpose of the passage?

   The author's tone could best be described as

- **Detail.** These ask you to research the text and identify a specific detail mentioned in the passage. Look for language in the question stem such as "according to the author" or "is mentioned in the passage." Here are some examples of Detail question stems:

   According the passage, the primary cause of unemployment in micronations is a lack of

   Which of the following was mentioned in the passage as a result of high employment?

- **Inference.** These questions ask for something that, though not stated explicitly in the text, must be true based on the information that is provided in the passage. Look for language in the question stem like "suggests," "implies," or "most likely agrees." Here are some examples of Inference question stems:

   The passage most strongly suggests that which of the following is true?

   With which of the following characterizations of medieval comedies would the author most likely agree?

- **Logic.** This type of question asks you to describe why the author included a certain word, phrase, or statement. Look for language like "in order to" or "primarily serves to." Here are some examples of Logic question stems:

   The author mentions Tussey's theory of copyright systems primarily in order to

   Which of the following most accurately describes the reason the author included the results of the experiments in lines 9–12?

- **Vocab-in-Context.** These relatively straightforward questions ask you to identify the specific way a word is used in the passage. Here are some examples of Vocab-in-Context questions:

    As it is used in line 16, "brilliant" most nearly means

    Which of the following most closely corresponds to the meaning of the word "effect" as it is used in line 26?

- **Reasoning.** These questions ask you to analyze an author's reasoning in an argument. They may ask you to identify an argument's assumption, point out a flaw in the author's reasoning, or strengthen or weaken the reasoning. Here are some examples of Reasoning questions:

    The ethicist's argument requires the assumption that

    Which of the following would cast the most doubt on the conclusion drawn by the scholar?

Now be honest: Did you just skim through that list of question types without taking the time to catalog and understand how the tasks are different? If you did, you're not alone. But take another look. The fact is, knowing the type of question you're dealing with is incredibly helpful. For one thing, different question types require different research and prediction steps. For another, different question types have different types of flawed answer choices, which you can learn to avoid. Knowing how to research a question effectively and how to avoid wrong answer traps will allow you to choose correct answers confidently and improve your performance.

Analyze the Question Stem: Exercise

In the following exercise, identify each question as one of the following types: Global, Detail, Inference, Logic, Vocab-in-Context, or Reasoning. In addition, for each example question, ask yourself:

- Are there any clues in this stem that will help me research a specific part of the passage?
- Would I be able to formulate a strong prediction for this question?

The pages following this drill will provide answers and explanations to these questions.

1. The passage implies which of the following about [xxxxx]?
   - (A) Global
   - (B) Detail
   - (C) Inference
   - (D) Logic
   - (E) Other

2. According to the passage, each of the following is true about [xxxxx] EXCEPT:
   - (A) Global
   - (B) Detail
   - (C) Inference
   - (D) Logic
   - (E) Other

3. The author mentions [xxxxx] in order to
   - (A) Global
   - (B) Detail
   - (C) Inference
   - (D) Logic
   - (E) Other

4. The main point of the passage is
   - (A) Global
   - (B) Detail
   - (C) Inference
   - (D) Logic
   - (E) Other

5. Which of the following most accurately describes a flaw in the argument above?
   - (A) Global
   - (B) Detail
   - (C) Inference
   - (D) Logic
   - (E) Other

6. As it is used in context, the word "[xxxxx]" in line xx most nearly means
   - (A) Global
   - (B) Detail
   - (C) Inference
   - (D) Logic
   - (E) Other

7. An appropriate title for the passage would be

    (A) Global

    (B) Detail

    (C) Inference

    (D) Logic

    (E) Other

8. The author makes which of the following statements concerning [xxxxx]?

    (A) Global

    (B) Detail

    (C) Inference

    (D) Logic

    (E) Other

9. The passage provides support for which of the following assertions about [xxxxx]?

    (A) Global

    (B) Detail

    (C) Inference

    (D) Logic

    (E) Other

10. Which of the following best supports the author's conclusion that [xxxxx]?

    (A) Global

    (B) Detail

    (C) Inference

    (D) Logic

    (E) Other

11. The function of the example in line xx is to

    (A) Global

    (B) Detail

    (C) Inference

    (D) Logic

    (E) Other

12. The author indicates explicitly that which of the following has been [xxxxx]?

    (A) Global

    (B) Detail

    (C) Inference

    (D) Logic

    (E) Other

Answers and Explanations

1. C

When you see "implies" or "suggests" in a question stem, you're dealing with an Inference question.

2. B

Language that points you to find something directly stated in the passage (here, the phrase "according to the passage") indicates a Detail question.

3. D

The phrase "in order to" means that this is a Logic question. Your task is to determine why the author has included the specific phrase or statement.

4. A

This is a Global question that asks for the entire passage's main point.

5. E

To answer this Reasoning question, separate the argument's conclusion from its evidence and then describe the way in which the evidence fails to fully support the conclusion.

6. E

This is clearly a Vocab-in-Context question.

7. A

Since the title of a passage reflects the content of the passage as a whole, this is a Global question.

8. B

Since the question asks for a specific statement made by the author, this is a Detail question.

9. C

The correct answer will be something that can be directly inferred from information in the passage.

10. E

This is a Reasoning question because the answer will support the conclusion. Notice that the word "support" is used differently than in the previous question. In this question, the answer strengthens (supports) the conclusion in the passage; in the prior question, the passage supported the answer.

11. D

This is a Logic question. It is asking what role the example plays in the passage, not for information or an inference about the example.

12. B

The word "explicitly" means that the question deals with something that is contained in the passage, not something that needs to be inferred.

How did you do? Were you able to correctly identify each question's type? How would you have proceeded differently to answer each of the different types of questions? It is easy to overlook the value of identifying question types in the Reading Comprehension section. However, knowing the type of question you're dealing with will help you research the passage more effectively. That, in turn, will help you more quickly formulate a prediction and more quickly find the correct answer.

[**STEP 3**]

Research the relevant text in the passage.

Once you have analyzed and fully understood the question stem, use your Passage Map for guidance. Global questions and some Inference and Logic questions are so general that you can simply use your understanding of the passage's Topic, Scope, and Purpose as well as the structure of the passage to answer them. You can answer questions such as "What is the purpose of this passage?" or "Which of these statements expresses the author's conclusion?" directly from your notes.

Sometimes, however, the question stem will ask you to find a specific detail in the passage, draw an inference about a specific situation mentioned by the author, or identify the function of a specific phrase or sentence. Pay close attention to the research clues in the question stem, noting which part of the passage will help you answer the question. Then consult your Passage Map to refresh your memory of the Main Idea in that part of the passage. Finally, return to the passage and research the text of interest.

Take a look at the following two question stems. What would you say is the biggest difference between them?

1.   The author of the passage would be most likely to agree with which of the following?

2.   The author of the passage would be most likely to agree with which of the following statements regarding the nocturnal habits of newly discovered species in the Himalayan range?

Both are Inference questions. Both ask you to determine what the author of the passage would be likely to agree with. But where the questions differ is in your ability to research a specific part of the passage. In the first question stem, there are no clues pointing you to a specific portion of the passage. Instead, you'll have to consult your big-picture summary (topic, scope, purpose) and evaluate *each answer choice,* checking it against the passage.

For the second question stem, though, notice the numerous clues it provides. It asks you to determine the author's opinion of something explicitly stated in the passage—the nocturnal habits of newly discovered species in the Himalayan range. Untrained test takers might look at such a question stem and assume that their task is to answer the question based on their memory of the passage. But that's often a losing strategy. Your memory of the details of the passage will likely be fuzzy, plus wrong answers will often present subtle distortions of ideas in the text, even using words and phrases from the passage. Instead, check your Passage Map for key information you may have noted about these animals and to confirm where in the text the author discusses them. Then go to the passage itself and reread just the section with the author's comments on the nocturnal habits of these animals.

Researching the passage to determine the correct answer to a question is a skill that you can develop, just like every other step of the Kaplan Method. Each question type requires a slightly different research strategy.

- **Global.** Attack Global questions by using the Topic, Scope, and Purpose you noted as you read the passage. *Eliminate* answers that reflect only a part of the passage or supporting ideas rather than the Main Idea.

- **Detail.** Because Detail questions ask you to find a specific detail in the passage, these questions will almost never include line references. Instead, you will have to use your knowledge of the passage or your Passage Map to research the relevant part of the passage. Correct answers to Detail questions will always be close paraphrases of the text, so make it a habit to research the passage and find direct support for your answer. *Eliminate* answer choices that distort what the author actually said about the matter at issue or that provide a correct detail about something else.

- **Inference.** Attack open-ended Inference questions that do not point you back to a specific part of the passage (like question number 1 above) as you would a Global question. Consult your big-picture summary and consider the author's Main Idea and Purpose. Because your predictions for these questions will of necessity be very general, you may need to check each answer choice against the information in the passage.

  For Inference questions that give specific research clues, consult the specific part of the passage referenced in the question. Take note of the particular language in the question stem: Are you being asked to infer something that the author believes, or are you inferring someone else's opinion? Focus on key words that surround the relevant text in the passage.

  When evaluating answer choices for Inference questions, *eliminate* choices that reflect the author's (or someone else's) opinion but are worded too strongly (are Extreme) and those that are reasonable statements but wander beyond the scope of the passage (Outside the Scope).

- **Logic.** Logic questions often contain line references or quote specific text from the passage. Consult your Passage Map for the author's overall purpose and for notes you've made about the specific part of the passage the referenced quote or phrase is from. Then go to the passage and read before and after the referenced text. Your task for these questions is to understand why the author included something in the passage, so consider how the passage would be affected if the reference text were not there. What function does it serve in the larger context of the passage? *Eliminate* choices that do not align with the author's purpose in writing.

- **Vocab-in-Context.** These questions are relatively straightforward, and researching is often simply a matter of finding the word in question in the passage, then considering how that word is used in context. The words asked about will have more than one meaning, usually a common one and one or more uncommon ones, and often the author has used the word with a less common meaning. Ask: What word could one use to replace the word referenced in the question? Use that prediction as you evaluate the answer choices.

- **Reasoning.** In Reasoning questions, you will most often be asked to analyze an argument, so your first task should be to identify the argument's conclusion and its evidence. The conclusion of an argument is simply the claim that the author is trying to convince you of; the evidence, then, is the information used to support that conclusion. Once you've separated an author's claim from her evidence for that claim, your task is to identify the author's assumption. The assumption in an argument is any unstated fact that must be true in order for the argument to make sense.

Reasoning questions come in a variety of forms. A question might ask you to simply find an assumption of an argument, while another might ask you to identify a reasoning flaw. Some Reasoning questions will have you strengthen or weaken an argument, while others test your ability to resolve a paradox. See the section "How to Approach Reasoning Questions" toward the end of this chapter for examples of different types of Reasoning questions and predictable patterns to look for.

[STEP 4]

Make a prediction.

Making predictions is one of the hallmarks of expert GRE readers. Unprepared test takers fall into the testmaker's trap of using the *answer choices* to guide their thinking, but the testmaker does not write answers to help you clarify your thinking. If you approach the answer choices in this way, you may find yourself attempting to justify each choice as correct, and more than one answer choice will often appear reasonable.

Instead, use the information in the *passage* to arrive at a correct answer. After you have read the passage, identified the type of question you're dealing with, and researched as appropriate, take a few seconds to imagine what the correct answer should look like. This is your prediction. Then, when you begin to read the answers, you will be able to rule out those that do not match your prediction—that do not match information in the passage—even if they seem like reasonable or relevant statements. It is, after all, much easier to find the answer choice you are looking for if you already have an idea what it looks like.

Of course, it is unusual that an answer choice will exactly match your prediction, word for word. Often, for example, your prediction will be general and the correct answer will be a specific instantiation of your general idea. However, the *concept* in the correct answer will match, and this is what's important, not the exact language that is used. Note that if you mentally paraphrase the passage as you read, casting it into your own words, you will be prepared to recognize ideas in and inferences based on the passage when they are expressed in different terms.

Some question types, like open-ended Inference questions, might not lend themselves to a precise prediction. Other question types, like Detail questions, will nearly always lend themselves to a strong prediction. In your practice, you'll start to figure out which question types take general and more specific predictions.

It might help to think of GRE Reading Comprehension questions as short-answer instead of multiple-choice. If you imagine that the questions require you to write a short-answer response, you will formulate a short sentence as an answer—and this is your prediction! You will then use that prediction as you evaluate the choices, eliminating those that don't match and homing in on the choice or choices (for all-that-apply questions) that do.

If this step seems daunting, or if you find that no matter how hard you try to pause and predict an answer before evaluating the choices, you always rush through to the answers, try this exercise. Get some sticky notes and, during your next practice set of Reading Comprehension questions, cover up the answer choices with a sticky note. In your notebook, jot down what you think would be an appropriate response to the question.

With a strong prediction, you'll be much less likely to be tempted by wrong answer choices. Indeed, if you see an answer choice that matches your prediction, confidently select it and move on to the next question.

[STEP 5]
Evaluate the answer choices.

The first four steps of the Kaplan Method are all preparation for the final step: correctly answering the question. This step can be frustrating. How often have you found yourself in this position: you've read the passage and understand it; you've read the question stem and know your task; you've researched the passage and have an idea what the right answer choice looks like; but when you get to the answers, you find that two choices appear acceptable?

The testmaker is adept at writing deceptively appealing incorrect answer choices: that is, wrong answers that appear at first glance to be just as good as the correct answer. To recognize wrong answer choices on the GRE, it is valuable to know the ways in which the testmaker consistently creates wrong answers. In fact, just as there are predictable types of questions that the GRE recycles over and over again, there are also predictable and repeatable types of wrong answers.

- **Outside the Scope.** These answer choices misrepresent the scope of a particular part of the passage, often by drawing an irrelevant comparison to something not mentioned in the passage.
- **Extreme.** Be careful when you see answer choices that include extreme language like *always, never, mostly, rarely,* and so on. The passage must support such strong/extreme language for the choice to be correct.
- **Distortion.** These incorrect answer choices use specific language from the passage but then distort the context or meaning of the details in the passage.
- **180.** These answer choices contradict (either subtly or explicitly) the statements made in the passage.
- **Half-Right/Half-Wrong.** These are especially common in longer answer choices, where the first clause of a long sentence is correct but then the second half goes awry.

Certain types of wrong answers will appear more frequently in certain types of questions and less frequently in others. For example, Outside the Scope and Extreme answer choices tend to show up in Inference questions, while Distortion answer choices are common in Detail and Function questions.

As you practice, pause and reflect not only on why *right* answers are *right* but also on what makes *wrong* answers *wrong*. Having a strong grasp what kinds of flawed answer choices to expect is nearly as powerful as researching accurately and making strong predictions. In time, you'll be able to quickly and effectively eliminate incorrect choices and zero in on the correct one.

By practicing the five steps of the Kaplan Method, you'll build your ability to attack Reading Comprehension passages with a consistent, methodical approach and reliably answer questions correctly. Now that you know what each step of the method entails, and why each step is so beneficial to your GRE score, let's take an even deeper look at each step using examples.

How to Apply the Kaplan Method for Reading Comprehension

[**STEP 1**]

Read the passage strategically.

Apply your strategic reading skills to the passage below. Focus on how the author's use of emphasis and contrast key words telegraphs not just the author's intent but also the passage's overall structure. For each sentence, focus less on what is being said and more on why the author has included it. Is it simply background information? Is it the author's Main Idea? Is it someone else's opinion or belief? *By asking and answering these questions as you read, you will be well prepared for the questions the test asks.* Also, instead of trying to hold key ideas in your head, jot them down on scratch paper—make a Passage Map.

Questions 1 to 3 are based on this passage.

> Many baseball enthusiasts are aware of the story of how Abner Doubleday invented the game of baseball with some friends in 1839 and introduced it to a nation during the Civil War. However, most baseball historians now agree that this story is a convenient fiction, propagated by Albert Spalding, a player, manager, owner, and one of the first manufacturers of sporting equipment. Spalding's desire to distinguish baseball, which so keenly mirrored American interests and pursuits, from similar games played in England, such as cricket and rounders, led Spalding to seek out a purely North American origin of the sport. Spalding's entire basis for the foundation of baseball history lay in a handwritten letter from 1907 that he said came from a man who claimed to have gone to school with Doubleday and attributed the invention to him. Despite the speculative and dubious claims of the letter, Spalding and other members of his commission were quick to adopt the narrative as gospel and began to market their sport to the masses as a truly American pursuit.

Below, check out how a GRE expert thinks as she reads the passage strategically, differentiating important information from background information.

> Many baseball enthusiasts are aware of the story of how Abner Doubleday invented the game of baseball with some friends in 1839 and introduced it to a nation during the Civil War.

This is background information describing what "[m]any baseball enthusiasts" (not the author) believe. What follows might be new information that shows this understanding to be incorrect.

However, most baseball historians now agree that this story is a convenient fiction, propagated by Albert Spalding, a player, manager, owner, and one of the first manufacturers of sporting equipment.

The contrast key word "[h]owever" indicates that what is commonly known is incorrect. Instead, the story of Doubleday was probably made up by a person named Spalding.

Spalding's desire to distinguish baseball, which so keenly mirrored American interests and pursuits, from similar games played in England, such as cricket and rounders, led Spalding to seek out a purely North American origin of the sport.

Here, the author tells us why Spalding created this fictional story: Spalding wanted to create an "American" backstory, not an English one.

Spalding's entire basis for the foundation of baseball history lay in a handwritten letter from 1907 that he said came from a man who claimed to have gone to school with Doubleday and attributed the invention to him.

This is a detail that explains why Spalding credited baseball's invention to Doubleday—it concerns a letter (the details about the letter are not important—I can return later to research them if necessary).

Despite the speculative and dubious claims of the letter, Spalding and other members of his commission were quick to adopt the narrative as gospel and began to market their sport to the masses as a truly American pursuit.

The key word "[d]espite" shows a contrast: while the letter didn't seem authentic, Spalding pushed the theory anyway. Why? To market the sport as uniquely "American."

Notice what a proficient GRE reader does. As she reads strategically, she "sums up" each sentence by mentally putting it into her own words. By paraphrasing, she separates key insights from nonessential background information. By the end, she understands the gist of the passage and has an excellent understanding of the passage's Topic, Scope, and Purpose. Here is this reader's Passage Map:

Topic: Origin of baseball

Scope: Did Abner Doubleday invent baseball?

Purpose: To explain why Albert Spalding spread the story that Doubleday invented baseball

¶1   Wanted to market the sport as American

       Claimed to have found a letter, but very sketchy

Your Passage Map probably doesn't use exactly the same words—everyone will map a passage a little differently—but your map should have captured the same ideas. Now apply Steps 2–5 to answer some questions about this passage.

1. Which of the following statements is suggested by the passage?

    (A) Abner Doubleday did invent the game of baseball.

    (B) Claiming baseball to be invented by an American would help Spalding sell more sporting equipment.

    (C) Baseball is not truly an American sport.

    (D) Many people in Spalding's day wanted to believe baseball was invented by an American.

    (E) The other members of Spalding's commission knew that the letter about Abner Doubleday was probably fraudulent.

[STEP 2]

Analyze the question stem.

The key phrase is "suggested by," which indicates this is an Inference question. The correct answer is not explicitly stated in the text but can be discerned by an accurate reading of the text.

[STEP 3]

Research the relevant section in the text.

This Inference question does not point to a particular statement in the passage, so you cannot research a particular sentence or section of the passage before approaching the answer choices. However, you can review your Passage Map so you have a firm grasp of the big picture of the passage; answer choices that contradict this or lie outside the scope of the passage can be eliminated. If any choices remain, you'll need to check each one against the information provided in the text until you find one that is fully supported.

[STEP 4]

Make a prediction.

Because of the open-ended nature of the question, you cannot formulate a precise prediction. However, your review of the Passage Map shows that because Spalding wanted to market baseball to Americans, he spread the story about an American, Doubleday, inventing it, even though Spalding had little evidence of this. Look for an answer choice that aligns with this main thrust of the passage, and look to eliminate choices that do not align.

[STEP 5]

Evaluate the answer choices.

Eliminate choice (**A**) because it contradicts the main thrust of the passage, which is that "most baseball historians," and the author, agree that Doubleday did not invent baseball. This was just a story that Spalding made up. Choice (B) might require some research. Spalding did make sporting equipment, and he was an avid promoter of baseball. However, he had a number of connections to baseball, and nowhere is it implied that he wanted to expand the fan base for the sport to increase sales of equipment. Choice (C) is Outside the Scope; the passage says that evidence for Doubleday's inventing baseball is very weak, but it never discusses who did invent the sport. Choice (E) can be researched in the last sentence, which mentions that "other members of [Spalding's] commission" promoted the story about Doubleday. However, the passage never says whether they believed the story or were skeptical of it. The correct answer is choice (**D**), which is supported by evidence in the passage. Spalding and his commission were eager to spread a story about an American inventor because they knew it would help market the sport to Americans.

Now try an all-that-apply question on the same passage.

Consider each of the choices separately and select all that apply.

2.   Which of the following statements is true based on the passage?

   A   Abner Doubleday was not a real person.

   B   Albert Spalding had a lot of influence over the business of baseball.

   C   Baseball has a lot in common with the game of cricket.

[STEP 2]

Analyze the question stem.

The phrase "based on the passage" means this is an Inference question. As with all GRE Inference questions, while the correct answer(s) won't be directly stated in the passage, it or they must be true given what is stated in the passage.

[STEP 3]

Research the relevant text in the passage.

This is another open-ended Inference question. Again, use your Passage Map to refresh your memory of the key ideas of the passage—any choice that contradicts these or is a 180, wanders Outside the Scope, or is too Extreme can be eliminated immediately. Be prepared to research any remaining choices in the appropriate place in the text.

[**STEP 4**]

Make a prediction.

While a precise prediction is not possible, having read the passage strategically and already answered one open-ended Inference question about it, you have a strong sense of what kinds of statements would and would not be supported by the text.

[**STEP 5**]

Evaluate the answer choices.

Choice (A) is Outside the Scope of the passage, which only concerns whether Doubleday invented baseball; it does not discuss whether he existed at all. Choice (**B**) can reasonably be inferred. According to the second sentence, Spalding was a baseball player, manager, and owner, and according to the last sentence, he was a member of a commission that promoted the sport. In addition, he is believed responsible for perpetuating a widely believed myth about the origins of baseball. Thus, he was certainly influential in the game, and (**B**) is correct. Choice (**C**) is supported by the third sentence, in the middle of the passage, which describes cricket as a game "similar" to baseball. The similarity of the games was a reason Spalding was so eager to differentiate baseball by inventing an American origin story.

Now try a select-in-passage question. There is no need to approach this type of question any differently. Indeed, you can think of it as a multiple-choice question. There are five sentences in this passage, so they are your five answer choices.

3. Select the sentence in the passage in which the author states that there was only one piece of evidence supporting the view that baseball originated with Abner Doubleday.

[**STEP 2**]

Analyze the question stem.

A key to choosing the correct answer to select-in-passage questions is to read the question very carefully. A rushed reading might focus on words like "Abner Doubleday" and "baseball," and the test taker might think, "The whole passage is about that. How do I figure out which sentence to pick?" The words pointing you to the one and only sentence that fits the bill are "there was only one piece of evidence" for the Doubleday story. Only one sentence discusses the evidence for this origin myth.

[**STEP 3**]

Research the relevant text in the passage.

From your Passage Map, you know that the evidence was a letter.

[**STEP 4**]

Make a prediction.

You will look for the sentence that mentions the letter and says it was the only basis for the story.

[**STEP 5**]

Evaluate the answer choices.

You might recall that the passage begins by presenting background information and introducing the topic, that the story about Doubleday was largely the creation of Spalding. Only later does the passage discuss how Spalding came up with the story. So begin your scan for the correct sentence at the end of the passage. You'll quickly find the fourth sentence: **Spalding's entire basis for the foundation of baseball history lay in a handwritten letter from 1907 that he said came from a man who claimed to have gone to school with Doubleday and attributed the invention to him.** That fits the criteria of the question perfectly.

Some test takers feel less comfortable with passages about certain topics. Readers with a strong background in science may feel nervous about humanities passages, and readers well versed in the social sciences may approach physical science passages with some anxiety. However, the Kaplan Method and your strategic reading skills work equally well for all passages, no matter what your personal familiarity with the subject matter.

The last passage concerned history. Now try a passage with science content.

[**STEP 1**]

Read the passage strategically.

Practice each step of the Kaplan Method with this passage and its associated questions. Read this passage strategically, using key words, mentally paraphrasing, and making a Passage Map. Then use your knowledge of the Reading Comprehension question types to analyze the question stem, research the necessary information, form a prediction, and evaluate the choices.

- For Step 1, map the passage on your scratch paper.
- For Steps 2–4, jot down your thinking to help yourself become conscious of each step. This type of practice will help you analyze what you are doing right and where you go wrong when you miss questions.
- For Step 5, eliminate incorrect answer(s) that do not address the question or are not supported by the passage. Choose the correct answer(s) that matches your prediction.

Questions 4 and 5 are based on this passage.

Many tea drinkers believe that different teas—black, green, oolong, and so forth—come from different plants. In fact, however, all tea leaves come from *Camellia sinensis*, a large evergreen shrub. Native to China, the plant is now cultivated throughout Asia and in Africa, Europe, and North and South America. The character of various teas depends in some measure on the climate and soil where the plant is grown but mostly on how the leaf is processed after it is harvested. An interesting case is black pu-erh tea, a specialty of China's Yunnan province. Unlike green or oolong tea, black pu-erh tea undergoes an oxidation process with the help of naturally occurring enzymes or, in the world of tea, is said to be "fermented." It then undergoes an additional step that differentiates it from other black teas: after oxidation, the leaves are aged in humid conditions, sometimes for several decades. Like all other teas, pu-erh contains antioxidants, which may help protect regular consumers from some cancers. It also contains caffeine, though not as much as most other black teas. What really sets it apart from all other teas is the fact that it naturally contains small quantities of lovastatin, a medication that physicians prescribe to lower cholesterol. It is possible that certain fungi that colonize the tea leaves produce lovastatin as a metabolic by-product. Most pu-erh connoisseurs, while appreciative of the tea's potential health benefits, are more intrigued by its taste, which they describe with words such as *woody*, *earthy*, and *leathery*. Clearly, an adventurous palate is necessary to enjoy this unusual beverage. Fortunately, those seeking a more conventional tea flavor have many options.

How did that go? Did you notice emphasis key words that pointed to the author's opinion or significant details? Did you identify contrast key words indicating a change in direction or an unexpected discovery? Were you able to capture the passage's Topic, Scope, and Purpose and the Main Ideas in your Passage Map?

Here is a visual representation of how a GRE expert reads. This reader has trained himself to focus on key words and phrases, and these seem to leap out of the passage at him as though in bold print. These highlight the structure of the passage and point to the main ideas. He reads the less important details with less attention.

Many tea drinkers believe that different teas—black, green, oolong, and so forth—come from different plants. **In fact, however,** all tea leaves come from *Camellia sinensis*, a large evergreen shrub. Native to China, the plant is now cultivated throughout Asia and in Africa, Europe, and North and South America. The character of various teas depends in some measure on the climate and soil where the plant is grown **but mostly** on how the leaf is processed after it is harvested. An **interesting case** is black pu-erh tea, a specialty of China's Yunnan province. **Unlike** green or oolong tea, black pu-erh tea undergoes an oxidation process with the help of naturally occurring enzymes or, in the world of tea, is said to be "fermented." It then undergoes an **additional step** that **differentiates** it from other black teas: after oxidation, the leaves are aged in humid conditions, sometimes for several decades. **Like all other teas,** pu-erh contains antioxidants, which may help protect regular consumers from some cancers. It **also** contains caffeine, though not as much as most other black teas. **What really sets it apart** from all other teas is the fact that it naturally contains small quantities of lovastatin, a medication that physicians prescribe to lower cholesterol. It is **possible** that certain fungi that colonize the tea leaves produce lovastatin as a metabolic by-product. **Most** pu-erh connoisseurs, while appreciative of the tea's potential health benefits, are more **intrigued** by its taste, which they describe with words such as *woody, earthy,* and *leathery*. **Clearly,** an **adventurous** palate is necessary to enjoy this **unusual** beverage. **Fortunately,** those seeking a more conventional tea flavor have many options.

Take a look at the following Passage Map and see how yours compares. Again, there are many "right" ways to map a passage—just make sure you noted the important ideas.

Topic: Tea

Scope: Pu-erh tea—how it's made, characteristics

Purpose: Compare/contrast with other teas

¶1   Tea—same plant, grown widely, differences come from processing

      All teas—antioxidants

      Black teas—oxidized, caffeine

      Black pu-erh tea—also aged, lovastatin, unusual taste

Now that you have read the passage strategically and made your map, try answering this question.

Consider each of the choices separately and select all that apply.

4. The passage suggests that which of the following would be a correct statement about tea subjected to an aging process?

  A The aging process removes caffeine and antioxidants from tea leaves.

  B The aging process may be responsible for the presence of a medically signifi-cant agent.

  C Aged tea leaves produce a brew with a flavor distinct from that of unaged leaves.

Step 2—What kind of question is this?

Step 3—Where do you research?

Step 4—What is your prediction?

Step 5—What is your answer?

[STEP 2]

Analyze the question stem.

The key word "suggests" means this is an Inference question. This question asks about a specific idea in the passage, "tea subjected to an aging process." The correct answer(s) must be true given the information that is provided in the passage.

[STEP 3]

Research the relevant section in the text.

The "tea subjected to an aging process" discussed in the passage is black pu-erh tea. According to the Passage Map, black pu-erh tea is different from other teas in two ways: it contains lovastatin and it has an unusual flavor. If these details are not captured in your Passage Map, you can find them in the latter half of the passage, where black pu-erh tea is compared and contrasted with other teas.

[STEP 4]

Make a prediction.

You can infer that the ways in which pu-erh tea differs from other teas are due to the aging process it undergoes. The correct answer(s) will concern the cholesterol-lowering agent lovastatin and/or the tea's distinctive taste.

[STEP 5]
Evaluate the answer choices.

Answer choices (**B**) and (**C**) match this prediction. Choice (A) is Half-Right/Half-Wrong: the passage states that pu-erh contains "not as much" caffeine as other black teas, so the aging process can be inferred to remove some caffeine. However, the passage says that pu-erh tea (and all teas) contains antioxidants and does not indicate that the tea has fewer antioxidants than do other teas.

Now try another question about this passage.

5. Based on the passage, which of the following can be inferred about black teas?

   (A) Black teas taste more like green or oolong tea than like pu-erh tea.

   (B) People seeking health benefits from tea can experience exactly the same effects from black teas as from all other teas except pu-erh tea.

   (C) People who enjoy new and unusual foods will prefer pu-erh tea to black teas.

   (D) Black teas are oxidized but not subsequently stored in humid conditions to be aged.

   (E) Although black teas contain caffeine, they do not contain any substances that may protect against cancer.

Step 2—What kind of question is this?

Step 3—Where do you research?

Step 4—What is your prediction?

Step 5—What is your answer?

[STEP 2]
Analyze the question stem.

The word "inferred" leaves little doubt this is an Inference question. Again, this question is directed at specific information in the passage—this time what the passage says about black teas.

[**STEP 3**]

Research the relevant section in the text.

Review what the passage says about black teas. In discussing the processing steps that differentiate types of tea, the passage says that pu-erh tea is oxidized but that what makes it different from black tea is that it is also aged. Therefore, black teas are also oxidized, but they are not aged. The passage also says that most black teas contain more caffeine than black pu-erh. Moreover, the passage says that pu-erh is like "all other teas" in containing antioxidants, so black teas must contain antioxidants.

[**STEP 4**]

Make a prediction.

The correct answer will correspond to one or more of the ideas in Step 3.

[**STEP 5**]

Evaluate the answer choices.

Choice (**D**) says black teas are oxidized but not aged and is correct. Choices (A) and (B) both use comparisons between black teas and other teas that the passage does not support. Although the author says it is necessary to have an "adventurous palate" to enjoy pu-erh tea, this does not mean that people with adventurous tastes will prefer pu-erh tea to others; perhaps they will enjoy all kinds of tea equally. Therefore, choice (C) is incorrect. Because all teas contain antioxidants, which may protect against cancer, (E) is incorrect.

Now apply your Reading Comprehension skills to a longer passage, this one with a topic in the social sciences. Again, remember that neither the length of the passage nor the subject matter changes your approach. Use the Kaplan Method and your strategic reading skills to identify the important information and answer GRE questions.

- For Step 1, map the passage on your scratch paper.
- For Steps 2–4, jot down your thinking to help yourself become conscious of each step. This type of practice will help you analyze what you are doing right and where you go wrong when you miss questions.
- For Step 5, eliminate incorrect answer(s) that do not address the question or are not supported by the passage. Choose the correct answer(s) that matches your prediction.

[**STEP 1**]

Read the passage strategically.
Questions 6 to 9 are based on this passage.

As the business world becomes ever more globalized and dynamic, freelance knowledge workers have come into their own. Technology drives rapid change in products and markets, and to keep up, companies find value in an on-demand workforce, one that they can adjust at will as new skills are needed. At the same time, the Internet means that a worker across the country or on the other side of the world can be as connected to a project's workflow as someone seated in the company's headquarters. Reflecting this reality, the U.S. Census Bureau's count of "nonemployer businesses" rose 39 percent from 2002 to 2017, and according to one study, 57 million Americans—more than one-third of the workforce—engage in freelance work. The growth of so-called contingent labor is forecast to continue unabated. Clearly, not all labor is equally empowered in the new paradigm. The barista placing the artistically styled froth on a customer's latte must be in the coffee shop. However, the systems analyst upgrading the shop's financial system that tracks the sales of lattes can be anywhere. Thus, workers with intellectual capital are in prime position to choose where they work and for whom.

The transition to a labor market of independent professionals has social and cultural implications. In much of the world, work is a major source of identity, so when work changes, identity changes. Instead of identifying as Widgets Incorporated employees who, whether they are an executive or a janitor, will someday earn a gold watch with the Widgets logo engraved on the back, workers identify as designers or social media gurus or software engineers. Rather than forging a common bond with coworkers in a mix of jobs around the proverbial water cooler, freelancers build geographically dispersed networks with other self-employed professionals with similar skill sets. Furthermore, in the twenty-first century the workplace has become a primary site of social connections and thus an important thread in the fabric of social cohesion, but instead of going to an office for a large portion of the day where they assume their workday persona, the new entrepreneurs work at home—even in bed, where they tap out messages to clients on their smartphone while wearing pajamas. And instead of relying on company benefits packages when working or government-administered unemployment payments when not working, these workers attempt to provide for themselves in defiance of the vicissitudes of life. Not partaking in any communal safety net, they argue that in an era when layoffs are commonplace, being self-employed is little more precarious than working for an employer. The cumulative result of these changes may be, on the one hand, an integration of personal and work life not seen since the Industrial Revolution moved people from farms into factories and, on the other hand, the atomization of society as individual contributors of labor rent themselves out impermanently to companies around the globe without meeting their coworkers face-to-face. Contributing further to social disruption is the bifurcation of the labor market into the independent self-employed and those still dependent on traditional jobs. It remains to be seen whether this new generation of professionals will appreciate the degree of vulnerability that accompanies their freedom and reach out to find common cause with employees who still draw a steady paycheck, working together to address issues of security and dignity in the workplace.

[**STEPS 2-5**]

6. The author is primarily concerned with

    (A) how working conditions differ for freelancers and traditionally employed individuals

    (B) the growth of freelance employment and its ramifications for workers and society

    (C) the economic implications of a shift in the labor market toward freelance workers

    (D) why some professional knowledge workers choose to freelance

    (E) recent and forecast statistical trends in freelance employment

Step 2—What kind of question is this?

Step 3—Where do you research?

Step 4—What is your prediction?

Step 5—What is your answer?

7. Select the sentence that best summarizes the author's conclusion about the historic impact of the growth of the independent workforce.

Step 2—What kind of question is this?

Step 3—Where do you research?

Step 4—What is your prediction?

Step 5—What is your answer?

Consider each of the choices separately and select all that apply.

8. Based on the passage, one can infer that the author would likely agree with all of the following statements about self-employed freelancers EXCEPT:

    [A] Unlike traditional employees, who are dependent on the local economy, freelancers can contract with companies anywhere in the world and so do not experience sudden changes in workload and income.

    [B] Freelancers who can use the globalized, technology-enhanced business environment to their advantage generally perform mental rather than physical labor.

    [C] Compared to workers in the traditional workforce, freelancers are likely to use the Internet to build relationships with people of different socioeconomic status from themselves.

Step 2—What kind of question is this?

Step 3—Where do you research?

Step 4—What is your prediction?

Step 5—What is your answer?

9. The author mentions "government-administered unemployment payments" in paragraph 2 in order to

    (A) support the conclusion that freelance knowledge workers are financially insecure

    (B) argue that the increase in the percentage of freelancers in the workforce is of benefit to society

    (C) illustrate a way in which self-employed individuals impose a burden on the social safety net

    (D) reject the notion that freelance professionals should be required to pay unemployment taxes

    (E) provide evidence for the idea that freelancers are less integrated with society at large than are traditional employees

Step 2—What kind of question is this?

Step 3—Where do you research?

Step 4—What is your prediction?

Step 5—What is your answer?

Answers and Explanations

Examine the following Passage Map. How does yours differ from the example? Below the map, you'll see each step of the Kaplan Method fully explained for each question. Did you correctly identify each question type? Did you research the relevant information? Did you craft an appropriate prediction?

Topic: Freelance workers

Scope: Trend and social implications

Purpose: To argue that society is less cohesive due to FWs

¶ 1: Rapid growth of freelance workforce, expected to continue FWs mostly knowledge workers

¶ 2: Social/cultural consequences

    Identity—with skills, not employer

    Work at home alone, not in office   } Loss of social cohesion

    Self-reliant, don't depend on employer, government

    Both FWs & traditional employees face economic uncertainty. Will they work together?

6. The author is primarily concerned with

STEP 2: The phrase "primarily concerned with" indicates this is a Global question.

STEP 3: Consult your Passage Map—the author is interested in the social implications of a growing freelance workforce.

STEP 4: "How the growth of the contingent workforce will impact society"

STEP 5: B

The first paragraph discusses the fact that freelance employment is becoming more common for knowledge workers, and the second paragraph argues that this trend will have "social and cultural implications," resulting in shifts in personal identity and "social disruption." Choice **(B)** is the correct answer to this Global question.

Although paragraph 2 mentions a number of ways in which freelancers' lifestyles differ from those of employees, the author mentions these details to support the larger point that an increase in freelancing is changing society. Therefore, choice **(A)** is incorrect. The author mentions the economic vulnerability of freelancers but only to support the discussion of their different approach to security from traditional employees, so choice (C) is incorrect. One can infer that freelancers enjoy the freedom of this mode of work and this may be why they choose self-employment, but explaining this is not the author's primary goal. Choice (D) is not correct. Choice (E) only reflects the ideas in the first paragraph; the author is concerned with more than statistical trends.

7. Select the sentence that best summarizes the author's conclusion about the historic impact of the growth of the independent workforce.

STEP 2: This is a Detail question.

STEP 3: According to the Passage Map, the impact of freelance workers is discussed in paragraph 2, so you will look there for the answer. A number of sentences describe changes brought about by growing numbers of these workers, but only one—toward the end of the paragraph—sums up the author's conclusion and puts the trend into historical perspective.

STEP 4: The correct answer will be the sentence that mentions a historical fact and includes a key word or phrase suggesting a wrap-up of the author's ideas.

STEP 5: The cumulative result of these changes may be, on the one hand, an integration of personal and work life not seen since the Industrial Revolution moved people from farms into factories and, on the other hand, the atomization of society as individual contributors of labor rent themselves out impermanently to companies around the globe without meeting their coworkers face to face.

The author discusses the effects of the increase in freelancing in paragraph 2, and she sets it in historical context in this sentence, where she compares it to the Industrial Revolution.

8. Based on the passage, one can infer that the author would likely agree with all of the following statements about self-employed freelancers EXCEPT:

STEP 2: The word "infer" signals an Inference question. Additionally, the phrase "the author would likely agree" implies that you are being asked to make an inference rather than find a detail explicitly stated in the passage. And because this is an EXCEPT question as well as an all-that-apply question, your task is to select all the choices that the author would not agree with.

STEP 3: Use your Passage Map to refresh your memory of ideas the author has stated and therefore would agree with. The question hasn't given you any guidance about where in the passage to research, so save that effort until you have answer choices to evaluate.

STEP 4: You can't formulate a specific prediction for a question like this one. After all, there are an infinite number of ideas the author would not agree with. However, in Step 5 you can compare the answer choices to ideas you know the author *would* agree with and eliminate them. On the cross-out list would be ideas like these (from the Passage Map): freelance workforce is growing; knowledge workers are in the best position to freelance; freelance workers identify with their job title, not a company, and they work at home alone and are self-reliant; growth of freelance workforce means society is becoming less cohesive; both freelance and traditional workers face insecurity.

STEP 5: A, C

In the first paragraph, the author says the demand for freelancers is increasing in part because companies want a workforce they can "adjust at will." In the last sentence, the author concludes by saying that freelancers have a "degree of vulnerability" that gives them common ground with other workers. Therefore, freelancers are not always financially secure, and the author would disagree with choice (**A**), making it a correct answer to this EXCEPT question.

In the second paragraph, the author states that freelancers integrate different aspects of their own lives but are less connected to coworkers, resulting in an "atomization of society." They do build networks, but mostly with people similar to themselves. Therefore, the author would disagree with choice (**C**), making it another correct answer. In paragraph 1, the author contrasts knowledge workers with a coffee shop barista and indicates that professionals with "intellectual capital are in prime position" to succeed as freelancers. Therefore, the author would agree with choice (B), and this choice is incorrect.

9. The author mentions "government-administered unemployment payments" in paragraph 2 in order to

STEP 2: The phrase "in order to" tells you this is a Logic question. You are being asked *why* the author mentions this detail, not for further information about it.

STEP 3: According to your Passage Map, paragraph 2 is about the social consequences of the growth in the freelance workforce, specifically how this trend is causing society to become less cohesive. Reading the target sentence, you find the contrast key words "instead of": "company benefits" and "unemployment benefits" are being contrasted with freelance workers' "attempt[s] to provide for themselves." The next sentence continues the contrast, starting with the word "[n]ot" and saying freelance workers reject "communal benefits."

STEP 4: Predict that the author mentions this detail to support the idea that in contrast to traditional employees, freelance workers depend on themselves rather than on society.

STEP 5: E

The purpose of paragraph 2 is to argue that the increase in freelancers has profound social implications, namely that freelancers' work and personal lives are more integrated but these workers are less integrated with society. "Government-administered unemployment payments" are mentioned in a sentence that contrasts programs organized to protect the well-being of a group with the self-reliance of freelancers. Therefore, this detail is mentioned to support the idea that self-employed people are less connected to the social safety net, and answer choice **(E)** is correct.

The detail in this question is mentioned to support the idea that freelancers provide for themselves, not that sometimes they cannot do so; choice (A) is incorrect. If anything, the author seems troubled by the effect of a larger contingent labor force on society, so choice **(B)** does not work. Freelancers are self-reliant, according to the author, so (C) does not make sense. Finally, although it might logically follow that people who do not receive unemployment benefits should not pay unemployment taxes, the passage never discusses taxes of any kind, and choice (D) is out of scope.

How to Approach Reasoning Questions

Reasoning questions ask you to analyze and deconstruct an author's argument. The test might then ask you to do a number of things: identify one of the assumptions in the argument, point out the flawed reasoning in the argument, strengthen the argument by affirming the relationship between the evidence and the conclusion, or weaken the argument by introducing a previously overlooked alternative explanation. Just like every other question on the GRE, these questions follow predictable patterns and are beatable.

Anatomy of an Argument

Before we get into those common patterns, let's briefly discuss how arguments are constructed. You might think of an argument as a disagreement between two parties. On the GRE, however, the word *argument* means that an author is advocating for a position or claim. When one person makes an argument, she does so by providing **evidence** that is used in support of a **conclusion**. A conclusion is often an opinion, a bold claim, a recommendation, a prediction, or the rebuttal of someone else's viewpoint. Evidence is the facts and/or opinions presented in support of the author's claim. To demonstrate, take a look at this argument. Can you tell which piece is the evidence and which is the conclusion?

> Michael refuses to eat things he is allergic to. Therefore, he definitely won't be ordering the salmon.

The second sentence is the conclusion, and the first is the evidence. How do you know? Well, the clearest giveaway is the conclusion key word "[t]herefore." On the GRE, authors will often telegraph their conclusions by using clear key words. Additionally, though, notice that the second sentence is a prediction. It's what the author believes will happen, based on the information provided in the first sentence. Using this kind of logic, you can separate evidence from conclusion, even in arguments without clear conclusion key words.

Now that you've pulled that argument apart, can you spot the assumption—that is, the fact the author believes must be true but hasn't explicitly stated? If you're having trouble, ask yourself this: Is there any new term or idea that appears in the conclusion but was nowhere to be found in the evidence? The conclusion discusses "Michael," and so does the evidence. But aha! Check out that term "salmon" in the conclusion. The evidence never mentions salmon. Instead, the evidence discusses things that Michael "is allergic to." Connect the two: the author assumes that Michael is allergic to salmon.

Common Types of Arguments

To perform well on Reasoning questions, it helps tremendously to be able to identify common argument patterns.

Scope Shift Arguments

Arguments like the one about Michael and salmon—one in which the author moves from discussing one thing in the evidence to a different thing in the conclusion—are called scope shift arguments. Try analyzing another, more complex one. First pull apart the evidence and the conclusion. Then look for different terms that the author assumes must be related.

> Scientists who have devoted their lives to curing cancer work long hours away from their friends and family. Such social isolation can lead to emotional distress, even in researchers with the most stable of personalities. Therefore, scientists who devote their lives to curing cancer are at a greater risk than other people of suffering from symptoms of depression and anxiety.

How did that go? Did you correctly identify the last sentence as being the argument's conclusion? Once you identified the conclusion, did you notice a new term or idea that had not been explicitly mentioned before? Take a look at the argument again. This time, the different terms in the evidence and the conclusion are bolded.

> Scientists who have devoted their lives to curing cancer work long hours away from their friends and family. Such social isolation can lead to emotional distress, even in researchers with the most stable of personalities. Therefore, scientists who devote their lives to curing cancer are at a greater risk than other people of **suffering from symptoms of depression and anxiety**.

The author's assumption must be that emotional distress tends to lead to depression and anxiety. Now, imagine if that weren't true. What if it were established that a higher level of emotional distress does *not* correlate with higher levels of depression and anxiety? If that were true, the author's argument would no longer make sense. Therefore, the author must be assuming that emotional distress impacts whether one develops depression and anxiety.

If you were asked to weaken this argument, you would look for an answer choice that indicates emotional distress and risk for depression and anxiety are unrelated. If asked to strengthen the argument, you would choose an answer that supports such a relationship.

Representativeness Arguments

Another common argument pattern is one in which the conclusion is about a different population than the evidence. Take a look at this argument and see if you can determine the author's assumption. What logical leap does the author make as he moves from evidence to conclusion?

> Recently, Big Tech Corporation conducted a survey that asked workers to rate their direct managers. Of the workers who responded, over 70% rated their direct manager as "good" or "excellent." Clearly, the responses indicate that a majority of workers at Big Tech Corporation have a positive relationship with their direct manager.

This argument makes a number of assumptions. For one thing, the author assumes that people were being truthful in their responses. But if the survey was not anonymous, then respondents might reply in a manner that flatters their direct manager. Additionally, did you notice the scope shift between workers rating the managers as good or excellent and the claim that workers have a positive relationship with those managers? Perhaps a worker finds that a manager is good at his job, but the relationship between the two is chilly.

There is still another assumption in this argument. Note the language "[o]f the workers who responded . . ." What if only 8 workers out of 100 responded? That would be too small a sample to draw a valid conclusion about Big Tech employees in general. Maybe only people who have good relationships with their managers responded to the survey; the others were too afraid or too unmotivated. The problem here, then, is one of representativeness. The author assumes that the respondents (however few) must represent the company as a whole.

On the GRE, be on the lookout for any argument in which information about one group is used to draw a conclusion about a larger group or a different group. If you are asked to weaken the argument, look for an answer that indicates the group in the evidence differs on a key characteristic from the group in the conclusion. If you are asked to strengthen the argument, look for a statement that says the two groups are similar in an important way.

Causal Arguments

There is yet another type of argument that you might encounter on the GRE. See if you can spot the logical jump that the dean of student security makes in this argument.

> Last month, Big University instituted a new security system that allows only those with official identification to enter academic buildings. Since that time, there have been fewer reports of unauthorized access in academic buildings at Big University. The dean of student security has concluded that the new security system is working.

Did you notice that the evidence presents two things that occurred at the same time (or in the same relative time frame) and, from that data, the dean drew the conclusion that one of those things must have caused the other thing to happen? This is a classic argumentative flaw in which correlation is confused with causation.

Causal arguments are easy to spot because their conclusions nearly always fit the pattern of "therefore, one thing is making another thing happen." In the argument above, we see that pattern by paraphrasing the conclusion as "The security system is causing the decrease in unauthorized entries." The dean is jumping too quickly to a claim of causation, without taking into account other factors. Couldn't something else be causing the reduction in unauthorized access? What if summer break began last month—then there would be fewer students on campus, which might explain the reduction in unauthorized entrances.

Note that there is also a scope shift in this argument. The dean assumes that "fewer reports" of improper access indicates fewer actual such incidents ("the new security system is working"). However, maybe unauthorized individuals are gaining entrance to the building just as much as before, but for some reason people are less likely to call security.

Scope shift, representativeness, and causal arguments make up the bulk of argument patterns you'll see on Test Day. Recognizing these patterns will help you spot the implicit assumptions in an argument. And once you recognize an argument's assumption(s)— that logical leap the author makes from the evidence to the conclusion—you'll be able to choose the answer that strengthens or weakens an argument, points out its reasoning flaw, or simply describes the assumption.

READING COMPREHENSION CONCEPT CHECK

Before you move on, check your understanding by considering these questions:

- What is the Kaplan Method for Reading Comprehension?
- How would you describe *strategic reading* in the context of GRE Reading Comprehension passages?
- What are the Reading Comprehension question types?
- What is the value of researching and predicting before evaluating answer choices?

If you feel like you've got the hang of it, great! Proceed to the practice set that starts on the next page.

If you'd like a quick video review of this chapter, or if you would like some additional guided practice, head to your online resources. Under **Reading Comprehension**, click **Strategy for Reading Comprehension** to watch a quick video review of this chapter. Or click **Reading Comprehension Guided Practice** to apply what you've learned.

Reading Comprehension Practice Set

Now it's your turn. In the passage and question set below, apply the Kaplan Method for Reading Comprehension, being cognizant of each step. If you're up to the challenge, time yourself. If you set a timer, give yourself nine minutes. On Test Day, you'll want to invest about one to one and a half minutes in reading each passage paragraph and one minute in answering each question.

Questions 1 and 2 are based on the passage below.

Recent advances in organ transplant methods have included a resurgence in interest in xenotransplantation—any procedure in which the transplant materials are taken from a non-human source—due to its potential to eliminate any issues related to scarcity in the availability of human organs for transplant. Scientific interest in using organic material from non-human sources to improve health, and even stave off death, is certainly not new. Anecdotal evidence of humans' attempts to transplant limbs from animals in order to achieve superhuman feats, both successful and unsuccessful, has existed since ancient times and is deeply woven into Greek mythology. The early 19th century included more forays into the potential for non-human primate organs to be used for human transplantation, though from a scientific perspective, the record of success left much to be desired. Work in this field has not been without its critics, as animal welfare groups have spoken about the concerns of genetically modifying animals for the sole purpose of organ harvesting and the long-term consequences of ignoring the ethical implications for much of the xenotransplantation timeline. Whether society ultimately decides the potential benefits to humans in need of organ transplants outweigh the possible exploitation of thousands of animals remains to be seen.

1. In the passage above, what roles do the highlighted sentences serve?

    (A) The first sentence is the main idea, and the second sentence restates the main idea.

    (B) The first sentence makes the central argument of the passage, and the second sentence provides a supporting example.

    (C) The first sentence is an example, and the second sentence is the author's conclusion.

    (D) The first sentence is an explanation, and the second sentence is an analysis of that explanation.

    (E) The first sentence introduces the topic, and the second sentence presents a criticism.

2. According to the passage, all of the following statements are true EXCEPT:

(A) Xenotransplantation mitigates many of the risks associated with human organ transplant.

(B) The scientific interest in xenotransplantation is not new.

(C) The record of success for primate organs transplanted into humans is not extensive.

(D) Greek mythology contains stories of combining human and animal physical characteristics.

(E) The ethical questions surrounding xenotransplantation are, as of yet, unanswered.

Questions 3–5 are based on the passage below.

Although it is an imperfect model for describing a complex market, the theory of supply and demand is a reasonably accurate method of explaining, describing, and predicting how the quantity and price of goods fluctuate within a market. Economists define supply as the amount of a particular good that producers are willing to sell at a certain price. For example, a manufacturer might be willing to sell 7,000 sprockets if each one sells for $0.45 but would be willing to sell substantially more sprockets, perhaps 12,000, for a higher price of $0.82. Conversely, demand represents the quantity of a given item that consumers will purchase at a set price; in the most efficient market, all buyers pay the lowest price available, and all sellers charge the highest price they are able. The intersection of these occurrences is graphically represented in supply and demand curves that show the prices at which a product becomes too expensive or too readily available.

3. Which of the following best expresses the purpose of the passage?

(A) Explaining why buyers in a given market tend to seek the lowest price on available goods

(B) Offering a dissenting perspective on an obsolete economic model

(C) Persuading readers that the model of supply and demand is the best method for understanding market forces

(D) Providing an explanation of the two primary elements of an economic model and how they intersect

(E) Analyzing the fluctuation of supply and demand within a market

Consider each of the choices separately and select all that apply.

4. If the producer of sprockets nearly doubles its prices as described in the passage, it follows that

    A buyers in the market will be likely to purchase more of the sprockets being sold

    B the price of sprockets will continue to increase

    C buyers in the market will be likely to purchase fewer of the sprockets being sold

5. Select the sentence in the passage that illustrates an abstract concept presented by the author.

Reading Comprehension Practice Set Answer Key

1. **E**
2. **A**
3. **D**
4. **C**
5. **For example, a manufacturer might be willing to sell 7,000 sprockets if each one sells for $0.45 but would be willing to sell substantially more sprockets, perhaps 12,000, for a higher price of $0.82.**

Reading Comprehension Practice Set Answers and Explanations

1. E

This Logic question asks for the role of the two highlighted sentences. The first highlighted sentence introduces the concept of xenotransplantation, explaining what it is and providing historical context. In the second highlighted sentence, the author presents an opposing ethical view of the technology but never takes a definite side on the ethics of using it. Therefore, neither sentence is an argument of the author's. Eliminate (B) and (C) because the first sentence is neither an argument nor an example.

Now determine whether the remaining choices correctly identify the role of the second highlighted sentence. This sentence describes the criticism leveled by the animal welfare groups. **(E)** is the correct answer. To get there by process of elimination, note that the second highlighted sentence does not restate anything, so (A) is incorrect. The second highlighted sentence also does not directly analyze anything stated in the first sentence, so (D) is likewise incorrect.

2. A

"According to the passage" signals a Detail question. The "EXCEPT" means the correct answer is a fact or idea that is *not* stated in the passage; the four incorrect answers present material that *is* in the passage. Forming a precise prediction of the correct answer is not possible, but by consulting the Passage Map and reviewing what the author says about xenotransplantation, it is possible to eliminate choices that reflect that information.

In reading the passage, you should have noted that xenotransplantation is an alternative intended to deal with the scarcity of human organs for transplant but not to reduce any actual risks involved in human organ transplant. **(A)** incorrectly identifies the problem that xenotransplantation is intended to solve, making it the correct answer to this EXCEPT question.

(B) is confirmed by the second sentence. (C) is given in the passage's fourth sentence. (D) is present in the third sentence of the passage where it states "Anecdotal evidence…is deeply woven into Greek mythology." (E) is stated in the final sentence.

3. D

The passage as a whole discusses the basic elements of the model of supply and demand, defining the two terms and describing how they work. That's choice **(D)**. Choice (A) is too narrow, focusing on only one of the two forces described. Choice (B) is out of scope because there's no mention of the model being obsolete; also, the author simply describes the model—she doesn't dissent from its contentions. Although the passage asserts that the supply and demand model is "reasonably accurate," the passage is primarily concerned with explaining the model, not with persuading readers that it is the "best" model. Therefore, you can rule out (C). Although the theory of supply and demand does allow for the analysis of market forces, (E), the passage itself provides only description, not analysis.

4. C

You are told that producers want to charge as much as possible and buyers want to pay as little as possible, so it makes sense that as prices rise, demand falls, choice **(C)**. Choice (A) is the opposite of what the passage implies, which is that demand decreases as prices rise. There's no evidence presented that this change in price will lead to further price increases, so you can rule out (B).

5. For example, a manufacturer might be willing to sell 7,000 sprockets if each one sells for $0.45 but would be willing to sell substantially more sprockets, perhaps 12,000, for a higher price of $0.82.

The abstract concepts addressed in the passage are those of supply and demand, and the only example that illustrates supply and demand occurs in sentence 3. Sentence 1 introduces the supply and demand model. Sentence 2 defines the term *supply*. Sentence 4 explains demand, and sentence 5 describes a graphical representation of the two forces.

CHAPTER 8

VERBAL REASONING PRACTICE SETS

In this chapter, you will take three practice sets consisting of 20 questions each. After each practice set is a diagnostic tool to help you learn from your mistakes and continue your practice with more awareness of the traps you may encounter.

Review of the Kaplan Methods for Verbal Reasoning

Review the steps and strategies you have studied for answering each type of question quickly, efficiently, and correctly before starting your practice sets.

THE KAPLAN METHOD FOR SHORT VERBAL

STEP 1 Read the sentence or sentences, looking for clues.

STEP 2 Predict an answer for each blank.

STEP 3 Select the best match or matches from among the choices.

STEP 4 Confirm your answer by reading your selected choice or choices into the sentence or sentences.

THE KAPLAN METHOD FOR READING COMPREHENSION

STEP 1 Read the passage strategically.

STEP 2 Analyze the question stem.

STEP 3 Research the relevant text in the passage.

STEP 4 Make a prediction.

STEP 5 Evaluate the answer choices.

Verbal Reasoning Practice Set 1

Directions: Each sentence below has one or more blanks, each blank indicating that something has been omitted. Beneath the sentence are five words for one-blank questions and sets of three words for each blank for two- and three-blank questions. Choose the word or set of words for each blank that best fits the meaning of the sentence as a whole.

1. The cockpit recording from the downed airliner was initially _____, but after careful analysis, experts were able to determine much of what the pilots had been shouting.

   (A) disturbing

   (B) streamlined

   (C) coherent

   (D) unintelligible

   (E) esoteric

2. In spite of its popularity, *The Merchant of Venice* remains a (i) _____ play, with many critics (ii) _____ the extent of Shakespeare's anti-Semitism.

Blank (i)		Blank (ii)	
A	controversial	D	assuaging
B	celebrated	E	augmenting
C	histrionic	F	debating

3. Considered one of his most (i) _____ works, Mozart's *Requiem in D Minor* has a certain (ii) _____ in Western culture because of its incomplete status at the time of his death, and many (iii) _____ stories have arisen surrounding it; unfortunately, the truth is lost to us.

Blank (i)		Blank (ii)		Blank (iii)	
A	ignominious	D	obscurity	G	fraudulent
B	inconspicuous	E	indifference	H	apocryphal
C	famous	F	mystique	I	verified

4. Although Thomas Paine was most (i) _____ his political pamphlets, he was in fact (ii) _____ writer on many different subjects.

Blank (i)		Blank (ii)	
A	inimical to	D	an abstruse
B	condemned for	E	a prolific
C	famous for	F	a terrible

5. Because Rachel's success had convinced her of her own (i) _____, she never (ii) _____ her errors.

	Blank (i)
A	ineptitude
B	impeccability
C	resilience

	Blank (ii)
D	publicized
E	overlooked
F	discerned

6. St. Elmo's fire is a weather phenomenon that, (i) _____ it has been documented since ancient times, was not (ii) _____ until recently.

	Blank (i)
A	because
B	since
C	although

	Blank (ii)
D	incinerated
E	reported
F	understood

Questions 7–10 are based on the passage below.

It has been commonly accepted for some time now that certain scenes in Shakespeare's *Macbeth* are interpolations from the writing of another author; act III, scene 5, and parts of act IV, scene 1, have been determined to be the writing of one of his contemporaries, Thomas Middleton. This can be regarded as both illuminating and problematic, depending upon how the play is being studied. It allows us to infer a great deal about the conventions and practices of writing for the stage at the time. For example, playwriting may have been more collaborative than previously thought, or perhaps Elizabethan notions of plagiarism were different from ours. While historically significant, this does complicate our interpretation of the characters in the play. It is more difficult to assess authorial intention with regard to a character's motives if the text has been redacted by multiple authors.

Consider each of the choices separately and select all that apply.

7. According to the passage, it is correct to say that:

[A] The author feels that Shakespeare is guilty of plagiarism.

[B] The interpolations found in plays such as *Macbeth* make the assessment of authorial intention more straightforward.

[C] Our current understanding of plagiarism may have arisen after Shakespeare's time.

Consider each of the choices separately and select all that apply.

8.   Which of the following could aid in the further study of the interpolations discussed in the above passage?

   [A]   an investigation into the existence and prevalence of collaborative writing partnerships during Shakespeare's time

   [B]   an examination of the themes and techniques of other writers contemporary with Shakespeare

   [C]   a search through legal documents of Shakespeare's time for references to plagiarism or intellectual property rights

Consider each of the choices separately and select all that apply.

9.   Which CANNOT be inferred from the passage?

   [A]   The example of interpolation discussed in the passage would be illegal today.

   [B]   Authors and playwrights in Shakespeare's time might have recruited assistance when composing their works.

   [C]   Shakespeare used Middleton's writing without his consent.

10.   In the passage, the two highlighted statements play which of the following roles?

   (A)   The first explains a concept, and the second presents an example of that concept.

   (B)   The first presents an example of the main subject of the passage, and the second is a conclusion based on that example.

   (C)   The first states the conclusion of the argument as a whole, and the second provides support for that conclusion.

   (D)   The first provides evidence for a conclusion that the passage as a whole opposes, and the second presents the objection to that conclusion.

   (E)   The first states the primary conclusion of the passage, and the second states the secondary conclusion.

Directions: For the following questions, select the **two** answer choices that, when inserted into the sentence, fit the meaning of the sentence as a whole **and** yield complete sentences that are similar in meaning.

11.   Known to all as having a silver tongue, the orator easily distracts audiences from the meaning of his words with his _____ speech.

   [A]   mellifluous

   [B]   concise

   [C]   stumbling

   [D]   laconic

   [E]   euphonic

   [F]   strident

12. While medical experts have long touted the importance of sleep to optimal health, many adults will forgo the _____ effects of taking a nap for fear of seeming idle.

   A   soporific

   B   detrimental

   C   beneficial

   D   perceptible

   E   deleterious

   F   salubrious

13. The celebrated playwright's most recent work, intended to be a serious exploration of the meaning of existence, was roundly _____ by theatergoers, who found the lofty themes and abstruse language to be overwrought and almost comical.

   A   lampooned

   B   extolled

   C   lionized

   D   disregarded

   E   contemplated

   F   ridiculed

14. Word painting is a musical technique in which the progression of the notes _____ the meaning of the lyrics; a famous example of this can be found in Handel's *Messiah*, in which the notes rise with the mention of "mountains" and fall with the mention of "low."

   A   affects

   B   mimics

   C   contrasts

   D   reflects

   E   opposes

   F   renounces

Directions: Each passage in this group is followed by questions based on its content. After reading a passage, choose the best answer to each question. Answer all questions following a passage on the basis of what is stated or implied in that passage.

Questions 15 and 16 are based on the passage below.

In the decades leading up to the 1970s, the primarily French-speaking Canadian province of Québec saw its proportion of native French speakers diminish from year to year. The attrition of French was attributed to the preeminence of English in the workplace, particularly in affluent, "white-collar" jobs. The French-speaking majority was economically marginalized within its own province, as it was left with the choice of either working in lower-paying jobs or teaching its children English as a first language. The latter option would further erase Québec's cultural autonomy and singularity within a country that primarily spoke English. Facing the risk of linguistic extinction, the province passed *Loi 101* (Law 101): The Charter of the French Language. It established French as the only official language of the province, established the primacy of French in the workplace, and led to more economic equity. Since its passage in 1977, the percentage of people in Québec who speak French as a first language has begun to rise.

15. Which of the following is suggested in the passage as a reason for the decline of French in Québec?

   (A) the disparity of economic opportunities available to French and English speakers

   (B) an influx of English-speaking immigrants

   (C) efforts of French Canadians to further integrate themselves with Canadian culture

   (D) the emigration of French Canadians

   (E) the outlawing of French in the other provinces

16. According to the passage, *Loi 101* was significant in that it

   (A) was a final, unsuccessful attempt at enforcing the usage of French in Québec

   (B) curtailed the economic supremacy of English

   (C) restricted the teaching of English in schools

   (D) highlighted the distinctiveness of the cultural identity of Québec from that of the rest of Canada

   (E) provided for bilingual education

Questions 17–19 are based on the paragraph below.

The advent of online education in the first decade of the 21st century was the result of and a response to a number of factors that were both internal and external to the field of higher education. Traditional tertiary institutions, especially those that were privately endowed, raised tuition rates far in excess of the rate of inflation. This, in concert with a larger demand for postsecondary education for working adults, helped facilitate the introduction of online learning. However, it should be acknowledged that the relative simplicity of using the Internet as a platform, as well as its cost-effectiveness, was seized upon by entrepreneurs in the private sector. Online education is largely in the hands of for-profit companies. The question now becomes whether the democratization of higher education is worth the price of removing it from nonprofit, research-based universities.

17. The passage is concerned primarily with

    (A) the advent of online education

    (B) adult-oriented educational systems

    (C) the usefulness of the Internet in postsecondary education

    (D) economic and technological factors that influenced the development and current state of online education

    (E) the advantages and disadvantages of online education

18. The author's use of the term "seized upon" evokes an image of _____ on the part of the entrepreneurs.

    (A) accidental realization

    (B) opportunistic tactics

    (C) violent appropriation

    (D) collusive behavior

    (E) market manipulation

19. The highlighted section refers to

    (A) the cost of online education

    (B) the popularity of online courses

    (C) making education available to a wider range of students

    (D) the role of voting in class selection

    (E) whether or not a democratic society should have online education

Question 20 is based on the passage below.

Thermodynamics is concerned with changes in the properties of matter when we alter the external conditions. An example of this is a gas being compressed by the motion of a piston. The final outcome depends on how the change is made—if the piston is moved in slowly, we say that the compression is "reversible." This means that if we pull the piston back out, we retrace the same sequence of properties but in the reverse order; hence, the temperature of the gas will be the same when the piston has been pulled out as it was before the piston was pushed in. However, if the piston is moved in and out quickly, then the initial state (and temperature) will not be recovered—the gas will always be hotter than it was at the beginning. This is a manifestation, although not a statement, of the second law of thermodynamics. It also makes a difference whether there is a transfer of heat between the cylinder of gas and the external surroundings. If the cylinder is insulated, then the gas will heat on compression and cool on expansion (refrigeration uses this principle). On the other hand, if the cylinder can exchange heat with the surroundings, it will remain at the same temperature if the compression is slow enough.

20. This passage is primarily concerned with

   (A) describing the motion of a piston to demonstrate the laws of thermodynamics

   (B) explaining the conservation of heat during the motion of a piston

   (C) demonstrating how the second law of thermodynamics applies to pistons

   (D) explaining how thermodynamics function

   (E) discussing reversible compression

Answers and explanations follow on the next page. ▶ ▶ ▶

Verbal Reasoning Practice Set 1 Answer Key

1. **D**
2. **A, F**
3. **C, F, H**
4. **C, E**
5. **B, F**
6. **C, F**
7. **C**
8. **A, B, C**
9. **A, C**
10. **B**
11. **A, E**
12. **C, F**
13. **A, F**
14. **B, D**
15. **A**
16. **B**
17. **D**
18. **B**
19. **C**
20. **A**

Diagnose Your Results

Diagnostic Tool

Tally up your score and write your results below.

Total

Total Correct: _____ out of 20 correct

By Question Type

Text Completions (questions 1–6) _____ out of 6 correct
Sentence Equivalence (questions 11–14) _____ out of 4 correct
Reading Comprehension (questions 7–10, 15–20) _____ out of 10 correct

Look back at the questions you got wrong and think about your experience answering them.

[STEP 1]
Find the roadblocks.

If you struggled to answer some questions, then to improve your score, you need to pinpoint exactly what "roadblocks" tripped you up. To do that, ask yourself the following two questions:

Am I weak in the skills being tested?

The easiest way to determine this is to think in terms of what skills are required for each question type. If you're having trouble with Sentence Equivalence or Text Completion, you probably need to review your vocabulary word lists. Maybe you need to brush up on using word etymology to your advantage. If Reading Comprehension questions are bothersome, you need to work on your critical reading skills.

Did the question types throw me off?

Then you need to become more comfortable with them! Sentence Equivalence questions have a unique format, and Reading Comprehension can be daunting with its dense, complex passages. If you struggled, go back to the beginning of this chapter and review the Kaplan principles and methods for the question types you found challenging. Make sure you understand the principles and how to apply the methods. These strategies will help you improve your speed and efficiency on Test Day. Remember, it's not a reading or vocabulary test; it's a critical-reasoning test (even though your reading habits and command of vocabulary are indispensable tools that will help you earn a high score). Once you've done this review, go on to the next practice set in this chapter.

[STEP 2]
Find the blind spots.

Did you answer some questions quickly and confidently but get them wrong anyway?

When you come across wrong answers like these, you need to figure out what you thought you were doing right, what it turns out you were doing wrong, and why that happened. The best way to do that is to **read the answer explanations!**

The explanations give you a detailed breakdown of why the correct answer is correct and why all the other answer choices are incorrect. This helps to reinforce the Kaplan principles and methods for each question type and helps you figure out what blindsided you so it doesn't happen again.

[STEP 3]
Reinforce your strengths.

Now read through all the answer explanations for the ones you got right. You should check every answer because if you guessed correctly without actually knowing how to get the right answer, reading the explanations will make sure that whatever needs fixing gets fixed. Work through them one more time. Again, this helps to reinforce the Kaplan principles and methods for each question type, which in turn helps you work more efficiently so you can get the score you want. Keep your skills sharp with more practice.

Verbal Reasoning Practice Set 1 Answers and Explanations

1. D

The word "but" signals a contrast from what came before it. The experts had to analyze the recording carefully to know what was being said, so at first the recording must have been "unclear" or "hard to make out." **(D)** *unintelligible* perfectly describes a recorded conversation that is hard to make out, and is therefore the correct answer. Neither (A) *disturbing* nor (E) *esoteric*, which means "understood only by the specially initiated," is a fitting answer. Although the recording may indeed have been disturbing or may have used specialized terminology only understood by a small number of listeners, neither of these words describe a situation in which experts would have trouble determining what was said in the recording. (B) *streamlined* means "aerodynamic," and while the plane itself certainly would be streamlined, here the word does not apply to the cockpit recording. Finally, (C) *coherent*, or "understandable," is the opposite of what is needed.

2. A, F

Begin by taking note of the phrase "in spite of," which suggests that there will be an opposing idea in the sentence. The sentence describes the play as popular, so you can rule out choices (B) *celebrated* and (C) *histrionic* for the first blank because you are looking for a word contrasting with popularity. Based on the remaining option, **(A)** *controversial*, you are looking for a solution to the second blank that connotes uncertainty. Choices (D) *assuaging* and (E) *augmenting* are not possible, since neither means uncertainty. It is therefore answer choice **(F)** *debating* for the second blank. Read the sentence with the blanks filled in: if the play is controversial, it is not universally popular, and it makes sense that critics would debate some aspect of it.

3. C, F, H

When there are so many missing parts, it is often best to begin with whatever complete clause you can find; in this case, the final one. This will allow you to fill in the third blank. You are told that we do not know the truth, which allows you to eliminate both choices (G) *fraudulent* and (I) *verified*, because both indicate that concrete

knowledge exists on the matter. Answer choice **(H)** *apocryphal* is the only possible answer. If you know that many apocryphal stories arose surrounding the work, you can make headway into both of the other blanks.

For the first blank, assume that if many stories are made up about something, it is widely talked about—this eliminates choice (B) *inconspicuous* without a doubt, and between choices (A) *ignominious* and **(C)** *famous*, the choice is fairly straightforward. When you know something is much talked about because it is "incomplete," you can suppose that a neutral synonym of "well known" is going to be much more likely than a negative synonym of "shameful."

Finally, for the second blank, you can reject choices (D) *obscurity* and (E) *indifference* because you know the composition is well known, so answer choice **(F)** *mystique* is the only logical choice (and is supported by the mention of *apocryphal* stories). Let's check our answer: "Considered one of his most *famous* works, Mozart's *Requiem in D Minor* has a certain *mystique* in Western culture, and many *apocryphal* stories have arisen surrounding it; unfortunately, the truth is lost to us." Everything fits in perfectly when you read back the sentence with the correct words filled in.

4. C, E

"Although," a detour road sign, starts off the sentence, indicating that the ideas of the first and second clause will be opposites. While external knowledge might tell you that Paine was, in fact, a famous writer, it is important to remember that the correct answer will be derived from clues in the sentence alone. Also, the key words "political pamphlets" and "many different subjects" tell us what is being contrasted here: one subject (politics) versus many subjects. You might predict that Paine was well known for his political writing but was actually a good writer on many subjects.

For the first blank, **(C)** *famous for* is a perfect match for your prediction. Choices (A) *inimical to* and (B) *condemned for* are both negative and, therefore, incorrect. Then for the second blank, neither (D) *abstruse* nor (F) *terrible* indicates that Paine wrote well. However, a **(E)** *prolific* author writes a lot, and it can be presumed that writing comes easily to him. Therefore, (**E**) is the correct answer for the second blank.

Choices (D) *abstruse* and (F) *terrible* could work in a different sentence, but there is no choice for the first blank that will allow the resulting sentence to make sense. The answer will always be clear and definite—choices (C) *famous for* and (E) *prolific* create a sentence that makes sense without requiring any other knowledge or qualifications.

5. B, F

Rachel was convinced that whatever is in the first blank described her. Furthermore, it was Rachel's success that led her to this belief. A good prediction for the first blank would therefore be "superiority" or "dominance." (**B**) *impeccability*, or "flawlessness," is a good match for the prediction and is the correct answer. (A) *ineptitude*, or "incompetence," can be eliminated quickly because it is the opposite of what Rachel's success would convince her of. (C) *resilience*, or "an ability to recover from or adjust easily to misfortune or change," might have been tempting because one can imagine Rachel having to recover from misfortunes along the way to success. However, the sentence doesn't indicate that Rachel actually dealt with misfortunes, and "resilience" doesn't fit in with the rest of the sentence.

"Because" shows a relationship of cause and effect and indicates that the second blank will be something Rachel never did due to her belief in her own impeccability. A good prediction would be that she never "realized," "admitted," or "acknowledged" her errors. (**F**) *discerned*, which means "detected" or "recognized," is a good match and is correct. (D) *publicized*, which means "brought to the attention of the public," can be eliminated because there is no reason to think that Rachel's desire to avoid making her errors public would be different from anyone else's. (E) *overlooked* is the opposite of what is needed here.

6. C, F

Based on the choices, you know that there will be a conjunction between the clauses of the first and second blanks. The contrast of "ancient times" and "recently" tells you to predict a word for the first blank that

suggests contrast, which eliminates choices (A) *because* and (B) *since*, leaving you with answer choice (**C**) *although*.

You know St. Elmo's fire has been documented for a long time, so discount choice (E) *reported* for the second blank. Choice (D) may be tempting, because *incinerated* is related to fire, but it does not make sense in this sentence. That leaves (**F**) *understood*, which does make sense as a contrast with the phenomenon's having been documented.

7. C

This type of question gives you three statements and asks you to select which ones are true. Break it down statement by statement. Statement (A) is untrue because the term "plagiarism" is used in the passage in the phrase "perhaps Elizabethan notions of plagiarism were different from ours"—which indicates that one cannot be certain of what might have constituted plagiarism at the time. Statement (B) is a 180: the passage does refer to the assessment of authorial intention if the text has been redacted by several authors, but the passage states the exact opposite of statement (B). Statement (**C**) is correct because you are told that our current notion of plagiarism might be different from the notion of plagiarism in Shakespeare's time.

8. A, B, C

This Inference question asks you to consider possibilities *based* on what is in the text but not necessarily stated *within* it. (**A**) The passage raises the question of how collaborative writing for the stage may have been during Shakespeare's time. Conducting an investigation into the existence of collaborative writing partnerships would be a good way to determine an answer for this question. (**B**) Familiarizing yourself with the style of other writers who might have helped write or had their work used in the writing of Shakespeare's plays would help in the determination of the actual authorship of passages in *Macbeth* (and other plays), as well as provide insight into authorial intention. Finally, (**C**) is an interesting alternative to a strictly literary study and would help to solve the question posed in the text of what constituted plagiarism in the Elizabethan era. All three are good choices for further study.

9. A, C

This is an Inference EXCEPT question: you must select the answers you *cannot* infer from the passage. **(A)**, that this example of interpolation would be illegal today, is impossible to tell as the passage does not address issues of legality and we do not even know whether Middleton was a willing collaborator. (B) is suggested within the passage in the supposition that writing such as *Macbeth* might have, in fact, been collaborative—this allows you to eliminate choice (B). **(C)** you know to be also a correct response for the same reason you specified for **(A)**—you do not know precisely Middleton's role in the composition. Answer choices **(A)** and **(C)** are both correct.

10. B

In this question, you are asked to determine the rhetorical roles of the two highlighted statements. The first highlighted statement is used as an example of the interpolations that the first clause in the sentence mentions. The highlighted portion states that parts of Shakespeare's work were in fact written by his peer Middleton. So the first highlighted portion appears to be an example.

The second highlighted statement presents an opinion regarding the impact of interpolations on literary analysis. According to this statement, because others wrote certain parts of Shakespeare's work, it is more difficult to determine a character's motives. Your prediction should be that the first statement is an example and the second is an opinion or conclusion (remember that in arguments, the words "opinion" and "conclusion" will often be used interchangeably). Answer choice **(B)** matches this prediction perfectly.

The other choices miss the mark completely. For instance, choice (A) incorrectly states that the second highlighted portion is the example. Similarly, choice (C) indicates that the first statement is the opinion and the second is the evidence, the exact opposite of our prediction. (D) states that the passage opposes an argument, but there is no conflict addressed in the passage. Finally, choice (E) identifies both statements as conclusions, which is not correct.

11. A, E

The key here is that the sentence tells us that his "silver tongue" makes it hard to concentrate on the meaning of his words. To have a silver tongue is to be noted for the pleasantness of one's speech, so you are looking for a pair of answers that mean "pleasing." (C) *stumbling*, (D) *laconic*, and (F) *strident* all are unrelated to the pleasantness of his tone, and while (B) *concise* language may be an attribute of a skilled orator, it will not create a similar sentence to one created by either of the other two possible answers. **(A)** *mellifluous* and **(E)** *euphonic* both mean "to be sweet or pleasing," and both are often used in reference to speech.

12. C, F

The beginning of this sentence focuses on how important sleep is to good health. You can therefore predict that taking a nap produces positive effects on health. (A) *soporific* means "to make sleepy," which is not a logical effect of napping. (B) *detrimental* and (E) *deleterious* both mean "harmful," which is the opposite of the predicted meaning "positive." (D) *perceptible*, meaning "noticeable," might make sense in the context, but the word charge is not positive enough to match the prediction, and there is no second choice that would give the sentence a similar meaning. **(C)** *beneficial*, meaning "favorable," and **(F)** *salubrious*, meaning "health-giving," both correctly convey the idea that the effects of napping are positive and healthy and are the right answers.

13. A, F

The playwright in this sentence is described as "celebrated," which may initially imply a generally favorable response to his most recent play. Although there is no contrast word in the sentence, the language used to describe the audiences' opinion gives the opposite impression. The words "lofty," "abstruse," and "overwrought" indicate that the play was too self-important and complicated, to the point of being "almost comical." You can predict that theatergoers responded negatively to the performance. **(A)** *lampooned* and **(F)** *ridiculed* both mean "mocked" or "made fun of" and are correct. (B) *extolled* and (C) *lionized* both mean "praised" and are the opposite of what you need. (D) *disregarded* means "ignored" and is not supported by the context; the theatergoers clearly saw the play and shared their opinions about it. (E) *contemplated* means "considered," which may be true but does not have a negative enough connotation to fit the context clues.

14. B, D

While you might have no background in musical techniques, you never need information from outside the sentence to deduce the correct answer. The example given tells you that the progression of notes in the music seems to imitate the words of the lyrics. So, you need a word that gives the meaning "the progression of the notes mirrors the meaning of the lyrics." Choices (C) *contrasts*, (E) *opposes*, and (F) *renounces* are antonyms of the desired answer. While (A) *affects* could work in the sentence, it lacks a synonym and does not properly refer to the desired meaning of "mirrors." Answer choices (B) *mimics* and (D) *reflects* do, however, and thus you know that they are your desired choices.

15. A

You are asked why the use of the French language declined in Québec. Researching the passage, you see this mentioned in the first few lines. Specifically, you are told that the "preeminence" of the English language in the best jobs forced people to switch. This indicates that in order to take advantage of the best economic opportunities, one had to speak English. The passage suggests that French became an economically unviable language, stating that "the French-speaking majority was economically marginalized." Thus, the two groups had access to significantly different economic and professional opportunities. This is reflected in answer choice (A).

Choices (B) and (D) are out of scope, as immigrant and emigrant populations are not mentioned. Furthermore, choice (E) is also beyond the scope of the passage, which does not mention the outlawing of French in other provinces. Finally, choice (C) is a 180, as the passage states the French sought to maintain their autonomy, not integrate themselves into other cultures.

16. B

This question asks you to summarize the significance of the law mentioned in the latter part of the passage. Based on the final sentence of the passage (which mentions the rise in French as the primary language), (A) is untrue—it was not an unsuccessful attempt. (B) is true because the passage specifies that the law "established the primacy of French in the workplace." No mention is made of language in schools, so you can dismiss options (C) and (E). Finally, while the cultural identity of Québec is mentioned in the passage, the only results of *Loi 101* specified are the economic equity of the languages and the rise in the usage of French, so you can also reject (D) as a possible answer. Answer choice (B) is the only option that is based on the information in the passage.

17. D

You must be careful here. Just because (A) is a direct quotation of the opening of the passage does not make it the correct answer, and, indeed, the passage moves away from the origins of online education and into other facets of its expansion. (B) is not discussed in the passage, even though the author makes note that the demand for adult-oriented education was one of the contributing factors to the rise of online learning. Neither (C) nor (E) properly describes the entire scope of the passage. Only answer choice (D) can be said to encompass the entirety of the passage.

18. B

Here you are called to define a phrase based on its context. What you are looking for is an answer that accurately reflects what is described in the passage: the entrepreneurs saw an untapped potential for profit in the unanswered demand for online learning and "seized upon" it. (A) is a poor choice because it implies that their success in capitalizing on the demand was unintentional. (B) is a much better solution because it evokes the image of the entrepreneurs taking the opportunity available. (C) is highly unlikely because no mention of violence is made in the passage (and, indeed, in reference to online education this would be an unlikely choice to begin with). (D) can be eliminated as there is no mention of collusion on the part of for-profit education companies; similarly, (E) can be eliminated because those companies are never said to have manipulated the market in order to gain control of the online education market. Answer choice (B) is the only possible answer.

19. C

This type of question asks you to define the highlighted phrase based on the context. The key word here is "democratization." While the cost-effectiveness of online education is mentioned earlier in the passage, it is unlikely that (A) *the cost of online education* is the correct answer because the sense of the final sentence is that it remains to be seen whether making higher education more widely available through online institutions "is worth the price of removing it from nonprofit, research-based universities." Based on this, you can also discount (B) *the popularity of online courses* and (D) *the role of voting in class selection* because while they may be linked conceptually to the term "democracy," the context tells us this is not what the phrase here concerns. Answer choice (**C**) *making education available to a wider range of students* matches our prediction and properly clarifies the usage of the highlighted phrase in the passage. You can discount (E) because it goes well beyond the scope of the passage.

20. A

In a Global question such as this one, the correct answer will reflect the scope and purpose you noted while reading the passage. While the broad topic of the passage is thermodynamics, the bulk of the passage describes the motion of a piston and how the effects of that motion demonstrate the laws of thermodynamics. (**A**) expresses this idea exactly. (D) may be tempting since "thermodynamics" is the first word of the passage, but (D) is too broad and leaves out any mention of the piston, which plays a key role in the passage as a whole. Choices (B), (C), and (E) refer to specific subjects mentioned in the passage but do not refer to the passage as a whole.

Verbal Reasoning Practice Set 2

Directions: Each sentence below has one or more blanks, each blank indicating that something has been omitted. Beneath the sentence are five words for one-blank questions and sets of three words for each blank for two- and three-blank questions. Choose the word or set of words for each blank that best fits the meaning of the sentence as a whole.

1. Mary's former classmates were taken aback by her _____ behavior at the reunion for, during her school years, she was frequently reprimanded for creating disturbances with her exuberant outbursts and playful antics.

   (A) gregarious

   (B) discourteous

   (C) obsequious

   (D) reticent

   (E) scurrilous

2. Hindsight often has the effect of changing the collective perception of certain historical events. Some incidents seem to be of exceptional importance when they first occur, but they ultimately prove to have few (i) _____ for future generations. Others appear to be rather (ii) _____ to contemporaries, and it is only later that their true significance is understood.

	Blank (i)		Blank (ii)
A	vagaries	D	monumental
B	misapprehensions	E	picayune
C	repercussions	F	outlandish

3. Who among us isn't guilty of mistaking a polite rhetorical question such as a (i) _____ "How are you?" for a genuine inquiry and responding with (ii) _____ description of the minutiae of our day?

	Blank (i)		Blank (ii)
A	supercilious	D	a prolix
B	perfunctory	E	a pithy
C	gregarious	F	an abstruse

4. Though she was typically able to (i) _____ the energy required to deal with such an unruly group of students, the exhausted vice principal found herself unable to (ii) _____ the (iii) _____ kindergartners.

	Blank (i)		Blank (ii)		Blank (iii)
A	incite	D	pacify	G	intransigent
B	parry	E	abrogate	H	noisome
C	marshal	F	rouse	I	restive

5. (i) ＿＿＿＿＿ mushrooms are popular in many cuisines, it is
(ii) ＿＿＿＿＿ to eat those found in the wild, as many frequently found
mushrooms resemble edible mushrooms but are, in fact, (iii) ＿＿＿＿＿.

Blank (i)		Blank (ii)		Blank (iii)	
A	Considering	D	imprudent	G	poisonous
B	While	E	cheaper	H	bland
C	Because	F	ingenuous	I	toothsome

6. Though the poet's work was praised highly by critics, sales of his anthologies
were (i) ＿＿＿＿＿; it is possible the poor sales were due to his language
being too (ii) ＿＿＿＿＿ to be readily understood.

Blank (i)		Blank (ii)	
A	scanty	D	lucid
B	robust	E	prosaic
C	singular	F	abstruse

Question 7 is based on the passage below.

Computer programs exist that attempt to generate random numbers, but no such
program can fully replicate a truly random selection. Computer programs are, by
definition, a set of instructions that use an input to generate an output. If both
the input and the algorithm are known, the result is fully predictable. Even the
best random number generation programs can only be called pseudo-random
because the input itself is generated by the program. As a result, a pattern will
emerge within the results, even if the program is sophisticated enough to make
the pattern very complicated, and that pattern can be used to predict future
results. True random number generation often depends on measurement of an
unpredictable physical phenomenon, such as weather patterns or atmospheric
radiation, and using that measurement as an input to generate a result.

7. The passage provides information sufficient to infer each of the following
statements EXCEPT:

Ⓐ The outputs of random number generators that provide their own input could,
with enough information about past results, eventually be predicted.

Ⓑ If a person knew both the algorithm that a corporation used to generate a truly
random number and the atmospheric measurements that served as the input, the
person would be able to generate the same output obtained by the corporation.

Ⓒ With a sufficiently large table of the results of a pseudo-random number generator over time, it would be possible to derive the input and algorithm used
to generate those results.

Ⓓ The integrity of applications for which the unpredictability of the result is vital,
such as lotteries or data encryption, can be best preserved by using a method
of random number generation that is truly random.

Ⓔ It is impossible to know the exact amount of atmospheric radiation emitted at
a particular location and time until after a measurement is taken.

Questions 8–10 are based on the passage below.

Toward the end of the 19th century, many scientists thought that all the great scientific discoveries had already been made and that there was not much left to do beyond some "tidying up." Max Planck, born in 1858, turned this notion upside down with his study of black-body radiation. Even in a vacuum, a hot body will tend to come to thermal equilibrium with a colder body by radiative heat transfer. This is the principle by which we derive energy from the sun. However, measurement of black-body radiation frequencies across a range of temperatures resulted in a parabolic curve, which theory in Planck's time could not explain. After many years of work devoted to this problem, Planck succeeded in quantitatively explaining the experimental data; his key insight was that energy comes in small, discrete packets, called quanta. His theory was the birth of what is called quantum mechanics, the revolutionary theory of matter that is fundamental to the modern understanding of physics, chemistry, and molecular biology.

8. Select the sentence that best describes the importance of Max Planck's work to modern science, as described in the passage.

9. Which of the following would best paraphrase the opening sentence?

   Ⓐ By the late 1800s, much of the scientific community felt it had completed the majority of its work and minor revisions were its only remaining task.

   Ⓑ By 1900, few scientists were still making significant discoveries, and most projects were revising current theories.

   Ⓒ At the end of the 19th century, scientists were concerned that they had run out of discoveries to make and could only perfect already proven theories.

   Ⓓ By 1900, the scientific community had declared that it had come to understand the natural laws of the universe.

   Ⓔ At the end of the 19th century, scientists ceased trying to formulate new theories.

10. Which of the following best describes the relationship between the highlighted portions of the passage?

    Ⓐ Topic and scope

    Ⓑ Theory and debunking

    Ⓒ Problem and solution

    Ⓓ Hypothesis and analysis

    Ⓔ Thesis and synthesis

Directions: For the following questions, select the **two** answer choices that, when inserted into the sentence, fit the meaning of the sentence as a whole **and** yield complete sentences that are similar in meaning.

11. After naturally occurring smallpox was eradicated, the World Health Organization chose to _____ the remaining samples of the virus in hopes that they might be later used in developing the means to combat other viruses.

    A eliminate

    B duplicate

    C preserve

    D retain

    E extirpate

    F cultivate

12. The *Magna Carta* was one of the most _____ political declarations of the Middle Ages because it declared the monarch's powers to be limited by the law; although its practical effects were not immediate, it is commonly seen as the genesis of constitutional law in England.

    A remarkable

    B immense

    C pivotal

    D recondite

    E ancient

    F momentous

13. Though _____ filled the streets, people seemed unconcerned with the appearance of their city.

    A detritus

    B refuge

    C gaudiness

    D bedlam

    E refuse

    F barrenness

14. G. K. Chesterton's sense of humor is exemplified in his often _____ responses to his friend and rival George Bernard Shaw.

    A punctilious

    B vociferous

    C waggish

    D vicious

    E scathing

    F witty

Directions: Each passage in this group is followed by questions based on its content. After reading a passage, choose the best answer(s) to each question. Answer all questions following a passage on the basis of what is stated or implied in that passage.

Questions 15–18 are based on the passage below.

There is an anthropological theory that states that societies may be divided into one of two broad categories by their cultural motivators: shame or guilt. In a shame-based society, the ethical motivations are primarily external; one's behavior is governed based on potential effects on the social group (such as dishonoring one's family). By contrast, guilt-based societies rely more heavily on internal motivations; one's behavior is governed based on a set of internal guidelines. There is no society where one or the other is entirely absent, but the distinction lies in that, based on the accepted values of the society, one will come to be dominant over the other. It would seem that early Medieval Europe was primarily a shame-based society; indeed, the forms of shame-based motivators in courtly society were extremely highly developed, with express social laws governing various behaviors. This sort of shame may be seen to be divided into many forms, such as positive and negative shame; that is, prospective and retrospective (knowledge of the honor one will accrue or the shame one will avoid through future actions, and humiliation or other punishment after something harmful has been done, respectively), ethical and nonethical (dealing with higher, such as theological and abstract, concepts, and quotidian matters, respectively), and so on. These social structures may also be found in the contemporary tales of the chivalric world. An example of such may be seen in the frequent plot device of the knight committing adultery with the wife of his lord. Adultery with the wife of one's lord is a matter of treason and an explicit moral wrong, and yet the condemnation in these stories seems to focus on the perpetrator's violation of social norms (treason) rather than moral standards (adultery).

Consider each of the choices separately and select all that apply.

15. Which of the following CANNOT be inferred from the passage?

    A Early Medieval Europe was unconcerned with moral codes.

    B Some cultures are neither shame-based nor guilt-based.

    C Guilt-based societies have few laws.

16. Select the sentence that describes the scope of the passage.

Consider each of the choices separately and select all that apply.

17. What can we infer about a society that focuses primarily upon a moral code of right and wrong?

    A It would be guilt-based.

    B It would tolerate adultery.

    C It would not have laws governing behavior.

18. Based on the passage, a society that prizes the harmony of the social group would most likely be

    (A) guilt-based

    (B) shame-based

    (C) extremely permissive

    (D) governed by a chivalric order

    (E) bereft of citizens with an internal code of moral right and wrong

Questions 19 and 20 are based on the passage below.

At the atomic scale, all matter exhibits properties commonly associated with both waves and particles. The classic experiment that demonstrates wavelike properties is the double-slit experiment, first performed by Thomas Young at the beginning of the 19th century. If a beam of light passes through two narrow slits and is projected onto a screen behind the slits, a pattern of light and dark fringes can be observed. The explanation for this is based on an analogy with ripples in water. If we drop two stones some distance apart, the ripples start to interfere with each other, sometimes amplifying when two crests or troughs meet, sometimes canceling when a crest meets a trough. A similar explanation holds for interference effects with visible light; the two slits act as independent sources in the same way as do the stones in water. This experiment provided convincing evidence in support of Christiaan Huygens's wave theory of light, which eventually supplanted the older particle theory of Isaac Newton. However, in the 20th century, Einstein showed that Newton was not entirely wrong. His analysis of the photoelectric effect showed that light could behave as a particle as well as a wave. Surprisingly, electrons, which we tend to think of as particles, also demonstrate interference effects, showing that they too are waves as well as particles.

19. Which of the following best summarizes the findings of Young's experiment, as described in the passage?

    (A) The waves from independent light sources interact with one another in predictable patterns.

    (B) Two light sources can cancel each other out, creating the observed dark fringes.

    (C) Light exhibits properties of both particles and waves.

    (D) Newton's theory was permanently debunked.

    (E) Newton's theory was correct all along.

20. Based on the passage, what would we expect the light fringes in Young's experiment to represent?

    (A) the light particles from both slits landing on the screen

    (B) the amplification created by the combination of both sets of waves of light

    (C) the projection onto the screen where the light is not blocked out by the object with the slits

    (D) the amplification created by light particles

    (E) the projection onto the screen where the light is blocked by the object with the slits

Answers and explanations follow on the next page. ▶ ▶ ▶

Verbal Reasoning Practice Set 2 Answer Key

1. D
2. C, E
3. B, D
4. C, D, I
5. B, D, G
6. A, F
7. C
8. His theory was the birth of what is called . . .
9. A
10. C
11. C, D
12. C, F
13. A, E
14. C, F
15. A, B, C
16. It would seem that early Medieval Europe was primarily a shame-based society . . .
17. A
18. B
19. A
20. B

Diagnose Your Results

Diagnostic Tool

Tally up your score and write your results below.

Total

Total Correct: _____ out of 20 correct

By Question Type

Text Completions (questions 1–6) _____ out of 6 correct

Sentence Equivalence (questions 11–14) _____ out of 4 correct

Reading Comprehension (questions 7–10, 15–20) _____ out of 10 correct

Repeat the steps outlined on the Diagnose Your Results page that follows the Verbal Reasoning Practice Set 1 answer key.

Verbal Reasoning Practice Set 2 Answers and Explanations

1. D

The phrase "taken aback" indicates that Mary's former classmates were surprised by how much her behavior had changed since her school years. Since Mary was "exuberant" and prone to "playful antics," you can determine that she was outgoing as a child. The missing word describes how Mary behaves now, which you can expect to be the opposite of outgoing. A strong prediction would be "shy" or "quiet." You can thus quickly rule out (A) *gregarious*, which means "sociable." (B) *discourteous*, which means "impolite," and (E) *scurrilous*, which means "offensive" or "insulting," can both be eliminated as no clues indicate that Mary is now rude. (C) *obsequious* means "fawning" or "servile," which is unsupported by the context. (D) *reticent*, meaning "shy" or "introverted," provides the correct meaning to complete the sentence.

2. C, E

The first sentence describes how the perception of certain events' historical importance may change over time. The second sentence discusses how some events first seem very important, while the word "but" indicates that these events may ultimately prove to be unimportant. You can predict that an unimportant event will have few consequences for future generations. (C) *repercussions* matches this prediction and is correct. (A) *vagaries*, which refers to "sudden or unexpected changes," is not supported by the meaning of the sentence. (B) *misapprehensions* means "misunderstandings" and is also unsuitable for the context.

The word "others" at the beginning of the third sentence indicates that an opposite situation will be described in this sentence. Since the previous sentence discussed how some events seem important when they occur, you can predict that this sentence will describe how other events at first seem unimportant. (E) *picayune*, which means "trivial," is a perfect match for this prediction and is correct. (D) *monumental*, which means "of great importance," is the opposite of the prediction. (F) *outlandish*, meaning "bizarre," is incorrect because it is not supported by the context.

3. B, D

The first half of the sentence provides a number of clues for the first blank, stating that "How are you?" in this context is a "polite rhetorical question" and that it would be a mistake to think of it as a "genuine inquiry." (B) *perfunctory*, meaning "casual" or "offhand," is an appropriate description of a question that is superficial or simply going through the motions. This is the correct answer for the first blank. (A) can be ruled out since there is no indication in the sentence that the person asking the question is *supercilious* or "arrogant." (C) describes the opposite of the situation described in the sentence as a *gregarious* or "outgoing" person might actually care about the answer to her question.

Given the casual nature of the question, a response that describes the "minutiae of our day" would be unnecessarily lengthy. (D) *prolix* is a perfect match and is correct. (E) *pithy* is incorrect because it means "short," and a short response would actually be appropriate for the polite rhetorical question. (F) *abstruse*, or "difficult to understand," misses the clues in the sentence.

4. C, D, I

There is enough context to make a strong prediction for the first blank; it would seem that the vice principal would want to "gather" the necessary energy to deal with the "unruly" students. (C) *marshal* in this context means "summon," so it is a good fit for the prediction and is correct. (A) *incite* means to "provoke" or "urge someone on," which does not fit the context. (B) *parry*, meaning "ward off" or "avoid," is the opposite of the intention of the sentence.

Because they are close together and are directly related to one another, the remaining two blanks can be considered at the same time. Consider the clue from the first half of the sentence, that this is an "unruly group of students." The vice principal's task, then, is to calm this uncontrollable, rowdy group. (D) *pacify* is a good synonym for calm, and (I) *restive* means hyperactive or difficult to control, even though it looks like it means "resting." Likewise, (H) *noisome* might look tempting at a glance, but noisome means "foul or smelly," not noisy.

If the students were just waking up from a nap and were slow to get moving, (F) *rouse* might be appropriate; however, here, this choice is the opposite of the described scenario. (G) *intransigent* would imply that the students were inflexible or stubborn in sticking to an idea, which does not convey the idea that the students are "unruly."

5. B, D, G

Three-blank sentences take a little longer to work out. When looking at the choices for the first blank, you can see that it is a conjunction, but you cannot be sure of which until you solve the rest of the sentence. The best place to begin in this sentence is actually at the end—you are given a very useful hint with the detour road sign "but," telling you that blank (iii) will be an antonym to "edible." While looking through the choices, you can see that the correct answer is answer choice **(G)** *poisonous*. While you might not want to eat something (H) *bland*, this is not a direct antonym to "edible." Choice (I) *toothsome* means "palatable" or "desirable" and is the opposite of what the blank needs.

From here, work backward to the second blank. Since you now know that you are talking about eating possibly poisonous mushrooms, you can predict that blank (ii) will say that it is "unwise" to do so. Choice (E) *cheaper* is irrelevant to the context (and no mention of money is made elsewhere), and choice (F) *ingenuous*, meaning "innocent" or "sincere," is unrelated to the sentence. Answer choice **(D)** *imprudent* is a synonym of "unwise" and is therefore the answer you need.

Return to the first blank in the sentence. You are told that mushrooms are popular in many cuisines, and you are looking for an answer that connects the two ideas. Predict roughly "*although* mushrooms are popular in many cuisines, it is imprudent . . ."; what you are looking for is a conjunction marking this contradicting idea. Answer choice **(B)** *While* is the correct choice. For sentences with three blanks, especially, it is important to reread the sentence with all the blanks filled in: "*While* mushrooms are popular in many cuisines, it is *imprudent* to eat those found in the wild, as many frequently found mushrooms resemble edible mushrooms but are, in fact, *poisonous*." The sentence makes perfect sense.

6. A, F

Within the first half of the sentence, you are given the detour road sign "though" to contrast the high praise with the sales. Thus, choices (B) *robust* and (C) *singular* cannot be correct because they are too positive. Answer choice **(A)** *scanty*, on the other hand, contrasts appropriately with high praise, and it fits perfectly with "poor sales" later in the sentence.

The second half of the sentence offers a possible explanation for why the sales were poor, suggesting that it was too hard to understand the poet's language, which immediately removes choice (D) *lucid*. Choice (E) *prosaic* might trip you up; however, answer choice **(F)** *abstruse* is clearly the better choice for the second blank—it is an adjective indicating that the prose is difficult to understand.

7. C

The four wrong answers to this Inference EXCEPT question are statements that must be true according to the information provided by the passage. The correct answer, therefore, is something that cannot be deduced using the information provided. This is **(C)**. While the passage does say that knowing the input and algorithm allows one to fully determine the results of a random number generator, and that pseudo-random programs produce results that have patterns that are ultimately predictable, this only means that it is possible to determine future results. It does not necessarily mean that it is possible to reverse-engineer the initial input and algorithm from the results.

(A) is supported by combining the given definition of pseudo-randomness ("the input itself is generated by the program") and the idea that pseudo-randomness produces patterns that are predictable. Likewise, (D) must be true, since a pseudo-random number generator is predictable, whereas a truly random program is not.

The passage describes atmospheric radiation as "unpredictable," making it a good source for true randomness, so (E) is true and can be eliminated. On the other hand, if someone obtained the measurements after they were taken and knew the algorithm being used to generate the random number, they would be able to generate the same result obtained by the original program since true-random number generation depends on the input being unpredictable, not the algorithm. As a result, (B) is also true.

8. His theory was the birth of what is called . . .

This sentence provides a summary of the importance of his work.

9. A

While reading the paragraph, paraphrase the text in your head to make sure you understand it. The key aspect of this sentence is that, at the time, there were a number of scientists who believed that the major discoveries had been made and the remaining scientific work was to tweak and perfect current theories. With that in mind, you can look through the options to see which best fits this idea. Answer choice (A) is an excellent paraphrase of the sentence. (B) is problematic because there is a fundamental difference between scientists believing all the great discoveries to have been made and scientists making few new significant discoveries. You can also reject choices (C), (D), and (E) because their description of "scientists" and the "scientific community" as a whole is too broad. The original sentence only states "many scientists," suggesting that there were dissenters, such as Planck.

10. C

What you must keep in mind here is that you are asked for the relationship between the two highlighted phrases, not their relationship to the passage as a whole. A good way to attack this sort of question is to paraphrase each of the phrases and identify what it is saying on its own. The first phrase states an issue: that the current theory could not explain the parabolic curve scientists observed. The second phrase tells us of Planck's break-through discovery of quanta. Thus, you can predict that the answer will tell us the relationship is between the limitations of the current theory and Planck's solution. (A) is a trap because it uses words you frequently see elsewhere and are admonished to remember when considering any Reading Comprehension passage. However, *topic and scope* are irrelevant to this question, and choice (A) can be dismissed. (B) may be tempting because the first highlighted portion does contain the word "theory." However, based on the wording of the first phrase, it is

clear that the issue with the current theory was recognized by the scientific community; thus, Planck's solution was not a challenge to a widely accepted belief, and "debunking" is not appropriate. In answer choice (C), you are given *problem and solution,* which matches your prediction and is the correct answer. (D) is out of scope; a *hypothesis* is not brought up here, nor is that hypothesis being explained further. (E) is incorrect since the first highlighted sentence is not a *thesis*, or summary, of the paragraph, but rather an issue that needs to be addressed.

11. C, D

While you might be tempted to stray toward the answers meaning "destroy" due to the previous mention of eradication and due to the danger of the material (smallpox), you must carefully read through the sentence. It informs us that there is hope that the samples may have further uses, so you know they must be preserved. You can thus reject (A) *eliminate* and (E) *extirpate*. You are left with two pairs of synonyms, choices (B) *duplicate* and (F) *cultivate* as well as (C) *preserve* and (D) *retain*, so you must choose one of the sets. You are able to do this by focusing on what is in the sentence alone—the word "later" suggests saving the samples, not working with them immediately, so answer choices (C) and (D) are correct.

12. C, F

With strong words like "most," "declarations," and "genesis," the answer will be likewise a word of emphatic meaning. Furthermore, the sentence tells us of the importance of the *Magna Carta*, so you can predict synonyms of "significant" or "revolutionary." Choices (D) *recondite* and (E) *ancient* are both meaningless in the sentence, and you can eliminate them. Choice (B) *immense* can likewise be dismissed because nowhere is the size of the *Magna Carta* described, nor are there any synonyms among the other options. While choice (A) *remarkable* may be tempting, both answer choices (C) *pivotal* and (F) *momentous* connote a significant turning point, which (A) does not.

13. A, E

The key here is that the appearance of the city seems to be lacking, so you are looking for words that imply a deficiency in charm or physical beauty. Choice (D) *bedlam* could only make sense without the second clause, and choice (F) *barrenness* is a lack of something, so it could not fill the streets; furthermore, both are lacking synonyms in the other options. Choice (C) *gaudiness* does imply a lack of taste, but it is without a synonym as well. (**A**) *detritus* means "waste" or "debris," which is an excellent option for the blank, and with further investigation you can see it has a synonym in (**E**) *refuse*. (B) *refuge* is a trap for the careless, resembling *refuse* and being right below a synonym of *refuse*—be careful when you read the answers!

14. C, F

The words in the blank will describe Chesterton's particular style of humor. You are given a further clue to the answer in the description of Shaw as his "friend and rival." With this description in mind, you can dismiss choices (B) *vociferous*, (D) *vicious*, and (E) *scathing* as behavior unlikely to be shown toward a friend—remember, if the solution would demand further qualification such as "Chesterton was known to be as harsh to his friends as to his critics," then it is highly unlikely to be the correct answer. (A) *punctilious* is not a synonym of the remaining two answer choices, (**C**) *waggish* and (**F**) *witty*.

15. A, B, C

You are looking for statements that go beyond what can reasonably be inferred in the passage. (**A**) is a good choice, because while the passage mentions that it was "primarily a shame-based society," there is no mention of a lack of concern with moral codes; further, the passage notes that neither classification of societies is without some influence of the other. (**B**) also cannot be inferred; in fact, it is contradicted in the fourth sentence. As for (**C**), while the passage mentions the complexity of the social guidelines of shame-based societies, there is no way you can infer that guilt-based societies have few laws. All three of the answers are correct.

16. It would seem that early Medieval Europe was primarily a shame-based society...

This sentence provides us with the particular focus of the passage on Medieval Europe, narrowed down from the topic of shame- and guilt-based societies in general.

17. A

The difference between the two kinds of societies, according to the author, is a matter of internal (guilt) and external (shame) motivators. What you must consider, then, is where a moral code might be placed. You are given one particularly useful clue in the phrase "internal guidelines" in sentence 3, which, even if it lacks the strength of a sense of moral right and wrong, still allows us to classify the society in the question as guilt based. Furthermore, in the example at the end of the passage, it is suggested that "moral standards" are an example of a trait of a guilt-based society. The answer is (**A**). Choice (B) is incorrect; don't be distracted by the description at the end of the passage that describes how medieval Europe, a shame-based society, dealt with adultery. Choice (C) is beyond the scope of the passage.

18. B

For this question, you must consider the description of the society in the question compared to what you are given in the passage. Early in the passage, you see mention of dishonoring one's family as an example of a damaging effect on the social group. Societies motivated by effects on the social group are shame-based, not guilt-based, so eliminate choice (A). Choice (**B**), the correct choice, matches the prediction. Choice (C) is incorrect because there are certainly rules in a shame-based society. Similarly, you can reject (E); it goes beyond the scope of the passage, which does not offer any evidence to suggest that individuals within a society that emphasizes social cohesion do not have an internally regulated morality. (D) is incorrect because there is insufficient information to support such an assertion.

19. A

The key to this question lies in the analogy of the ripples in the water, where two troughs or crests amplify each other but one trough and one crest negate each other. Likewise, with the light waves, the two separate light sources produce waves that interact with one another and, like the crests and troughs of the water, have predictable results: the light and dark fringes. Choice (B) describes a part of Young's findings, but you must reject it because it does not adequately describe the whole of his findings. Choice (C) cannot be the correct answer either, because the passage notes that it was not until Einstein that particle theory was returned to the theory of light. And likewise for choice (D); you are told Einstein proved that Newton's theory was not entirely accurate and so it was not permanently debunked. Similarly, you cannot claim he was entirely correct, so (E) is out as well. This leaves choice (**A**), which matches your prediction.

20. B

The answer, again, comes from the ripple analogy, where two meeting crests are amplified. Thus, choice (**B**) is likely to be the correct answer. You can dismiss (A) since

Young's experiment is concerned solely with light as a wave, not as a particle, and answer choice (C) fails to take into account the purpose of his experiment: separating a single light source into two streams and recombining them on the screen. As for choice (D), amplification of light particles is mentioned as a possibility, but this is out of the scope of the question. Choice (E) refers to Huygens's wave theory of light but not Young's experiment. You have a clear answer in choice (**B**).

Verbal Reasoning Practice Set 3

Directions: Each sentence below has one or more blanks, each blank indicating that something has been omitted. Beneath the sentence are five words for one-blank questions and sets of three words for each blank for two- and three-blank questions. Choose the word or set of words for each blank that best fits the meaning of the sentence as a whole.

1. Veteran technical support staff members feel that their services are _____ by the use of computer programs to do the same work; they claim that technical support can't be provided procedurally but rather is a case-by-case effort that requires a skill set built upon training and experience.

   (A) devalued

   (B) tarnished

   (C) ridiculed

   (D) vituperated

   (E) impaired

2. The spice saffron is made from the stigma of the *Crocus sativus* plant; the (i) _____ number of blossoms required to produce saffron and the (ii) _____ of the flower makes the spice the most expensive in the world.

Blank (i)		Blank (ii)	
A	vast	D	color
B	meager	E	hardiness
C	unique	F	delicacy

3. The field of cryptozoology is the search for animals unknown to science and those for which we have no scientific attestation; (i) _____ physical evidence, it relies upon (ii) _____ sightings for proof of creatures such as the Loch Ness Monster.

Blank (i)		Blank (ii)	
A	ignoring	D	anecdotal
B	lacking	E	imagined
C	needing	F	nominal

4. Companies that give employees the flexibility to (i) _____ their more (ii) _____ responsibilities in favor of more exciting projects see dramatically increased productivity compared to businesses that are more (iii) _____ in their minute-to-minute structuring of daily routine.

Blank (i)		Blank (ii)		Blank (iii)	
A	undertake	D	quotidian	G	disingenuous
B	eschew	E	latent	H	lax
C	supplement	F	arresting	I	authoritarian

5. The neglect of the old theater was (i) _____ in the extreme (ii) _____ of the building, which was no longer safe to enter.

	Blank (i)
A	hinted at
B	suggested
C	manifest

	Blank (ii)
D	dilapidation
E	depilation
F	radiance

6. The countless (i) _____ days left everyone (ii) _____ for the sudden downpour; the deluge brought traffic to a halt as it (iii) _____ the roads.

	Blank (i)
A	arid
B	calm
C	humid

	Blank (ii)
D	waiting
E	unprepared
F	anxious

	Blank (iii)
G	inundated
H	soaked
I	sprayed

Questions 7–10 are based on the passage below.

The origins of the English language can be traced back to the Saxon and other Germanic settlers in Britain beginning in the 5th century CE. The English language's unusual nature can be attributed to the diverse linguistic origins of the groups that contributed to its development and their role in English society. Although English belongs to the Germanic language family and its grammatical and syntactical rules reflect this, English vocabulary can be seen to be from multiple origins. In fact, a large part of the vocabulary was not derived from the Germanic languages at all but is rather of Latin origin. This can be explained by the influence on Old English of Old French and Latin during the Norman Invasion in the 11th century. By the time of the Norman Invasion, Old English was already a language, with both its grammar and vocabulary based in the Germanic language family. However, the establishment of a ruling class who spoke a Romance language caused significant changes in the indigenous tongue. It is also interesting to note that there is a distinct correlation between the length of a word and its origin—most of the shorter words in the English language are derived from the Germanic languages, whereas the longer words are from a Latin background. One theory to explain this is that these more elaborate and complex words were primarily used by the elite after the Norman Invasion—who would have favored a Latin-based (or Romance) vocabulary—whereas words with the same meaning in the Old English were used primarily by the lower classes and thus fell into disuse. Modern English words, then, concerning more complex and theoretical rather than utilitarian ideas (astronomy, poetry, and epistemology), can generally be found to be of Romance origin, whereas more mundane words, such as pronouns and auxiliary verbs, can be traced back to a Germanic origin.

7.   Which of the following is implied by the passage?

   Ⓐ English was more heavily influenced by Germanic languages than by Romance languages.

   Ⓑ In the 11th century, English speakers of the lower classes did not discuss abstract, theoretical topics.

   Ⓒ No auxiliary verbs in English can be traced back to a Latin-based origin.

   Ⓓ English owes some of its abnormality to the Norman Invasion.

   Ⓔ Fewer words in English are derived from Latin than from the Germanic languages.

Consider each of the choices separately and select all that apply.

8.   The passage suggests that the word "they," a pronoun, would most likely have which of the following origins?

   ☐A Germanic

   ☐B Romance

   ☐C Norse

9.   Based on the passage, what is a likely reason why English has not been reclassified as a Romance language?

   Ⓐ It developed as a Germanic language in its first incarnation, Old English.

   Ⓑ The core of the language, its grammar and syntax, is still Germanic.

   Ⓒ A larger portion of the English vocabulary is Germanic rather than Romance.

   Ⓓ The Normans felt an affinity for the local tongue, which was Germanic.

   Ⓔ Neither linguistic heritage has a claim to preeminence.

Consider each of the choices separately and select all that apply.

10.   Which of the following can be inferred from the passage?

   ☐A Searching for meaning based on the Latin root of a word is less likely to be useful in shorter words.

   ☐B The language spoken by the Saxon and Germanic settlers entirely supplanted the indigenous tongue of 5th-century Britain.

   ☐C The discussion of complex ideas during the Norman era in England was primarily the domain of the ruling class.

Directions: For the following questions, select the **two** answer choices that, when inserted into the sentence, fit the meaning of the sentence as a whole **and** yield complete sentences that are similar in meaning.

11. As modern scholarship continues to dim the possibility that Homer was a single historic figure, the question of authorship of his works has been raised; although we might never know who wrote them, scholars still need some way to refer to the author or authors of the *Iliad* and *Odyssey*, so the term "Homeric tradition" has been _____ as a possible new terminology.

    A selected
    B established
    C appropriated
    D bestowed
    E suggested
    F proposed

12. _____ commercial arsenic usage has diminished, its ongoing presence in water and soil continues to be a major public health concern, given the extremely high toxicity of the substance.

    A After
    B Although
    C Inasmuch as
    D Considering
    E While
    F Because

13. Early sewing machines were poorly received by textile workers, who feared the technology would _____ the demand for their skills; despite their protests, the sewing machine became popular both in the factory and in the home.

    A overwhelm
    B diminish
    C obviate
    D mitigate
    E eliminate
    F belittle

14. The protest march quickly turned into a riot, and in the response by police, several people on either side were killed and dozens more wounded; it would later be _____ remembered by both sides as a tragic accident, and no blame would be assigned.

A indignantly

B mournfully

C spitefully

D bitterly

E soberly

F melancholically

Questions 15–17 are based on the passage below.

Kleptoplasty (from the Greek *kleptes,* meaning "thief") is a phenomenon whereby host organisms ingest a chlorophyll-utilizing species, typically algae, and use the energy-producing organelles called chloroplasts contained within the consumed species to help meet their own metabolic needs. In this way, kleptoplasty is an example of symbiosis, a close relationship between two different species. Further, it is an *endo*symbiosis, such that one of the species resides completely within another. Unlike the example of mitochondria, thought to have once been fully separate bacteria that came to live within animal cells and perform a mutualistic metabolic function, the algae are only partially utilized; most of the organism is digested and discarded, leaving only the chloroplasts to be retained by the host. Most kleptoplastic species are unicellular ciliates or dinoflagellates. The only known members of the animal kingdom that practice kleptoplasty are several species of sarcoglossan sea slugs. These "solar-powered" sea slugs incorporate whole chloroplasts into their body cells, where the stolen plastids can convert sunlight into useful energy for as long as ten months in some species.

Chloroplasts produce energy by using sunlight to power a series of reactions that result in sugars that can be used as a food source for the host organism. Algae have genes that encode proteins that act as enzymes that support this process. PRK, for example, is an enzyme that is responsible for the regeneration of ribulose-1,5-bisphosphate, an organic molecule used in the reductive pentose phosphate pathway (RPPP) of photosynthesis. Sea slugs lack the PRK gene, so for many kleptoplastic species, once the raw materials within the chloroplasts are exhausted, photosynthesis ceases and new chloroplasts must be obtained. As a result, until recently it remained a mystery how some sarcoglossan sea slug species were able to sustain chloroplast function for many months.

Genome sequencing revealed the answer. Polymerase chain reaction (PCR) analysis of the genome of individual sarcoglossan sea slugs of species *Elysia chlorotica* that had been exposed to chlorophyll-utilizing algae revealed that these individuals did in fact have the PRK gene, whereas individuals that had not been exposed to algae lacked the gene. Radioactive labeling confirmed the surprising result: *E. chlorotica* incorporates genes from the algae into its own genome. This process, known as horizontal gene transfer, is common in bacteria and unicellular eukaryotes but is rare to find in more complex species.

15. According to the passage, the main difference between the sarcoglossan sea slug species discussed in paragraph 1 and other sea slug species is that

   (A) they can incorporate the PRK gene into their genome, whereas other sea slugs cannot

   (B) they obtain energy primarily by digesting only certain components of algae, whereas other sea slugs obtain their energy from digesting the entire organism

   (C) they obtain at least some of their metabolic energy from chloroplasts, whereas other sea slugs do not

   (D) they lack the enzyme to regenerate compounds necessary for photosynthesis, whereas other sea slugs produce this enzyme

   (E) they lack mitochondria to perform metabolic functions, whereas other sea slugs utilize mitochondria as their primary source of energy

16. Which of the following best expresses the main point of the passage?

   (A) Until recently, scientists found it difficult to understand the exact mechanisms of kleptoplasty due to misconceptions about the relationship between sea slugs and algae.

   (B) *Elysia chlorotica* incorporates algal genes into its own genome, solving a problem that would leave it unable to survive in the wild.

   (C) Ribulose-1,5-bisphosphate is an organic compound used in photosynthesis that kleptoplastic species lack the ability to produce on their own.

   (D) Kleptoplasty is unusual compared to other forms of symbiotic relationships in that the species that practice it derive some benefit from horizontal gene transfer.

   (E) Kleptoplastic species not only use the biochemical machinery of another species to meet their own metabolic needs but can also incorporate genetic material to facilitate this process.

Consider each of the choices separately and select all that apply.

17. The passage provides support for which of the following statements about *E. chlorotica*?

   A   In the absence of algae, *E. chlorotica* typically lacks the ability to synthesize ribulose-1,5-bisphosphate.

   B   Some of the characteristics of *E. chlorotica* are not commonly found within the animal kingdom.

   C   *E. chlorotica* is the only sarcoglossan sea-slug species that incorporates the PRK gene into its genome.

Questions 18–20 are based on the passage below.

John Finnis developed his theory of natural law based on the structure that Thomas Aquinas provided, filling in areas where he felt that Aquinas's theory was lacking; he also amended other aspects of the theory to respond to a world much more culturally diverse than the one in which Aquinas lived. Unlike Aquinas, who gives only a vague account of the first precepts of the natural law, Finnis locates a specific number of basic human goods. Finnis avoids the charge that his theory falls into the "naturalistic fallacy" by asserting that these goods are not moral in themselves but become moral through human participation in them. In addition, these goods are not hierarchical, which allows a much greater range of freedom in choosing actions. Finally, Finnis's theory does not require the presence of God. Though curiosity about the nature of the universe is one of his basic human goods, the actual existence of God is not required by his theory.

Finnis's theory raises as many questions as it answers. While formulating an interesting answer to the "is/ought" problem and giving a much more robust definition of human volition than Aquinas, his solutions create their own problems. His account of the goods is stripped of any method for evaluation. The boundaries of each good are difficult to discern. Further, by asserting that each good is self-evident and equal to all the others, Finnis makes any action taken in furtherance of any of them equivalent morally. Finally, by removing the precepts of natural law from our natural habits and inclinations, placing them instead in self-evident goods, Finnis seems not to be describing our nature at all.

18. Based on the passage, what is the most likely meaning of "good" according to Finnis?

    Ⓐ A physical object, such as foodstuffs or textiles

    Ⓑ A morally correct action as determined by God

    Ⓒ An action that helps us achieve a desirable, material end

    Ⓓ Something self-evident that we ought to strive to embrace

    Ⓔ Something that is naturally occurring

19. Based on the passage, the existence of which of the following would most likely undermine Finnis's definition of "goods"?

    Ⓐ Proof of the existence of God

    Ⓑ Goods that demand opposing actions

    Ⓒ The demands of our natural desires

    Ⓓ The definition of additional goods

    Ⓔ A method for evaluating goods

Consider each of the choices separately and select all that apply.

20. According to the passage, which of the following is NOT an improvement of Finnis's theory of natural law over Aquinas's?

    [A] Avoiding the "naturalistic fallacy"

    [B] Removing the necessity of God in his definition of "good"

    [C] Curtailing freedom in human actions

Verbal Reasoning Practice Set 3 Answer Key

1.	A	11.	E, F
2.	A, F	12.	B, E
3.	B, D	13.	C, E
4.	B, D, I	14.	B, F
5.	C, D	15.	C
6.	A, E, G	16.	E
7.	D	17.	A, B
8.	A	18.	D
9.	B	19.	B
10.	A	20.	C

Diagnose Your Results

Diagnostic Tool

Tally up your score and write your results below.

Total

Total Correct: _____ out of 20 correct

By Question Type

Text Completions (questions 1–6) _____ out of 6 correct

Sentence Equivalence (questions 11–14) _____ out of 4 correct

Reading Comprehension (questions 7–10, 15–20) _____ out of 10 correct

Repeat the steps outlined on the Diagnose Your Results page that follows the Verbal Reasoning Practice Set 1 answer key.

Verbal Reasoning Practice Set 3 Answers and Explanations

1. A

The increase in automated support suggests a decline in demand for technical support workers, and the second half of the sentence tells you that you are looking for an answer that indicates that their services are being undervalued. (B) *tarnished*, (C) *ridiculed*, and (D) *vituperated* all suggest, beyond a negative image, a directly hostile one, which is not indicated by the sentence. (E) *impaired* might be acceptable from the first part of the sentence alone, but the value of their services implied by the second half can only support (**A**) *devalued*.

2. A, F

The first half of the sentence is just background, so it is from the second half that you must take your clues. It tells us that producing saffron is very costly, so you can anticipate that the number of blossoms required is a large rather than small number. Based on this, you can reject (C) *unique* and (B) *meager* for the first blank, leaving (**A**) *vast*.

The second blank implies a quality of the flower that makes it rare. The correct choice for the second blank is (**F**) *delicacy*. (D) *color* is irrelevant, and (E) *hardiness* is the opposite of your prediction.

3. B, D

The hint you are given is that cryptozoology lacks "scientific attestation"; that is, it has no scientific reason to be supported. So for the first blank, you are looking for a word that means "without." (A) *ignoring* would mean an intentional rejection of scientific evidence, rather than an absence thereof. (C) *needing* would work, but there is no choice for blank (ii) that has to do with physical evidence. Furthermore, "relies upon" points us to a limitation of their evidence. Therefore, (**B**) *lacking* makes the most sense for the first blank.

With regard, again, to scientific attestation, you can infer that the second blank implies that the sightings are not backed by scientific data, so you are looking for a solution that means "unscientific" or "unreliable." (E) *imagined* makes little sense, because it implies the sightings are not just inadequate but fictitious. (**D**) *anecdotal* provides us with the sense of unverifiable sightings and completes the first blank with "lacking" for the sense of being without. (F) *nominal* does not fit at all, as it means negligible, or in name only.

4. B, D, I

Because the first two blanks are so close to one another and are directly related, it is helpful to make a prediction for both of them together. Since the employees are being allowed to approach "more exciting projects," it must be true that they are allowed to avoid the boring ones, so a prediction of "avoid" for blank (i) and "boring" for blank (ii) works well. (**B**) *eschew* and (**D**) *quotidian* are great synonyms for these predictions and are correct. (A) *undertake* and (F) *arresting*, meaning "exciting," are the opposite of the meaning of this portion of the sentence. (C) *supplement* misses the mark as well; "in favor of" indicates replacement of one set of tasks for another, while *supplement* would imply simply adding the exciting tasks while still doing the boring ones. Finally, (E) *latent* means "hidden" or "undeveloped," which does not fit the clues provided by the sentence.

The clues for blank (iii) span the entire sentence. The author is comparing companies that allow "flexibility" to companies that do not, so blank (iii) should mean something along the lines of "strict." Of the answer choices, only (**I**) *authoritarian* is a match. (H) *lax* would describe the more flexible companies mentioned earlier, and there is no indication that the companies are being (G) *disingenuous*, or "insincere."

5. C, D

The key word here is "extreme," which indicates that you are looking for a word with very strong meaning for the first blank. Furthermore, you know that the building is "no longer safe to enter," so the second blank must refer to some sense of structural decay. Thus, you can expect the full sentence to be something like "The neglect of the old theater was apparent in the extreme deterioration of the building." For the first blank, (A) *hinted at* and (B) *suggested* can both be eliminated because they are too weak in meaning for "extreme." Furthermore, both words mean the same thing, so neither could be the single correct answer for the first blank. (**C**) *manifest* makes the most sense.

Out of the options for the second blank, (**D**) and (E) are very similar-looking words, but only (**D**) *dilapidation* refers to buildings—(E) *depilation* refers to hair removal. Always study the words carefully! (F) *radiance* is the opposite of what you need.

6. A, E, G

While you expect the final clause, which is preceded by a semicolon, to be related thematically to the rest of the sentence, grammatically it stands on its own. You can therefore figure out the third blank first without needing the other two. The key here is the word "deluge"—you know this is a major rainstorm. Hence, for the third blank, you can reject both (H) *soaked* and (I) *sprayed* because both are much weaker words than (**G**) *inundated*.

For the second blank, the key clue is "sudden." If it was sudden, then you can assume people were not expecting it—you can thus predict a word synonymous with "not expecting." (D) *waiting* and (F) *anxious* would both imply people were expecting the downpour; thus, (**E**) *unprepared* is the correct choice.

Finally, for the first blank, this word will be the reason that people were not expecting a sudden storm. (C) *humid* doesn't work here, but between (**A**) *arid* and (B) *calm*, you may need to pause for a moment. (B) *calm* might work—it certainly contrasts with the eventfulness of the weather that followed—but (**A**) *arid* is a better answer because it implies that the weather was specifically very dry—the antithesis of the wetness of the storm. Plugging it all in, "The countless *arid* days left everyone *unprepared* for the sudden downpour; the deluge brought traffic to a halt as it *inundated* the roads." You can see that everything agrees.

7. D

This question is an Inference question. Therefore, we must eliminate the answer choices that don't necessarily follow from the passage. (A) is incorrect because we can't say with certainty that Germanic languages had a greater influence than Romance languages did. Yes, the Germanic influence came first and had a greater influence on grammar, but that does not mean its influence

on English as a whole is greater. (B) is out of scope and extreme. Nothing suggests that the lower classes could *never* discuss abstract theoretical topics. For (C), although we are told most mundane words, like auxiliary verbs, are of Germanic origin, that doesn't mean that *all* auxiliary words must be of Germanic origin. (E) is also incorrect because we aren't given any clues as to how many words are derived from each language family. (**D**) is correct because it's directly implied in the passage. The second sentence says that English has an "unusual nature," and the passage goes on to state that this is due to its vocabulary stemming from multiple origins, such as what was brought over by the Norman Invasion.

8. A

The question states that "they" is a pronoun, so look in the passage for clues as to where pronouns are likely to be derived. The final sentence explicitly states that English pronouns are of Germanic origin, so you can safely select (**A**) as your answer. Although Old English and Norse are related, this is not mentioned in the passage, and choice (C) is meant as a distractor.

9. B

To answer this question, you are required to make a small inference from the text. The third sentence begins with a detour road sign, "Although," which indicates that the immediately following clause is a fact—in this case that English is a part of the Germanic language family and that the rules governing its structure reflect this. From this you can infer that the structural rules of a language are significant in its classification, which tells you that answer choice (**B**) is correct. (A) is factually correct, but there is no indication that the language's first incarnation is related to its current classification, so you cannot accept that as an explanation based on the passage. (C) concerns the balance of vocabulary origins between Germanic and Romance, but while the passage does speak of this at length, no mention of number of words as related to the classification of the language is made. (D) is not an option, as the Normans regarded English as lower class. (E) is incorrect, as the core of the language is noted to be Germanic. (**B**) is the correct choice.

10. A

As always, you must be careful about what you infer from a passage. For answer choice (**A**), you would need to find something in the text that would suggest that the shorter the word, the less likely it may be derived from Latin—which you can find in the third-to-last sentence. There is no mention of the indigenous language before the arrival of the Germanic peoples, so you can dismiss (B). (C) might seem tempting because the author notes that the words used for complex ideas today are primarily those that were used by the ruling class. However, while discussing complex ideas might seem more likely to be the habit of those with leisure time and education, the passage does not specify anything that would allow us to draw this conclusion, and (C) must be rejected.

11. E, F

From the sentence, you learn that scholars are in need of a new "way to refer to the author or authors"; furthermore, judging by the tone and topic of the sentence, you can safely assume that the answers you need will have a neutral tone. While it may seem possible for the solutions to render the phrase "the term *Homeric tradition* has been *rejected*," the straight-ahead road sign "so" renders this unlikely. You can predict that the answers will mean "the term has been put forward." The key to this question is the word "possible" near the end of the sentence. (A) *selected* and (B) *established* cannot be correct because that would mean the term has been decided upon. (C) *appropriated* and (D) *bestowed* likewise fail to match our prediction, leaving (**E**) *suggested* and (**F**) *proposed* as the choices that suggest that the term has been offered as an option but no decision has been made. That fits nicely with "possible."

12. B, E

From the meaning of the sentence, you can see that the correct answer choices will render the meaning "commercial arsenic usage has diminished, *but* its ongoing presence is a major health concern." Because the blank is placed at the start of the first clause, you need a sense of contradiction that gives the meaning "even though." (A) *After*, (C) *Inasmuch as*, (D) *Considering*, and (F) *Because* all lack the contradiction you need, leaving only (**B**) *Although* and (**E**) *While*, which are synonyms of each other and match the prediction.

13. C, E

The key to this sentence is to note that the textile workers feared a negative effect on the demand for their skills as a result of the sewing machine. The answer, then, must be indicative of their displeasure with the technology; furthermore, words like "poorly" and "protests" suggest that they felt very strongly about their fear of a decline in their trade, so you must also find words that reflect the strength of their views. (A) *overwhelm* is the opposite of what you need and can be rejected. (B) *diminish*, (D) *mitigate*, and (F) *belittle* are all possible choices, but none of these words are strong enough to convey the meaning you are looking for. (**C**) *obviate* and (**E**) *eliminate* suggest an absolute removal of demand for the worker's skills and match both the meaning and the strength of the prediction.

14. B, F

You are told in the final clause that it would be remembered as a "tragic accident" and that no blame was assigned. You are looking for adverbs that reflect this and can expect to find synonyms of "sadly," but you must be careful not to choose answers that suggest vitriol or blame. Based on this, you can see that (A) *indignantly*, (C) *spitefully*, and (D) *bitterly* can all be eliminated. (**B**) *mournfully* is an excellent choice because you often hear about mourning of a tragic accident. (E) *soberly*, meaning in this context "clearly," does not have any synonyms among the remaining answers. (**F**) *melancholically* is a direct synonym of (**B**) and matches your predicted answer.

15. C

The necessary reference occurs at the end of paragraph 1: the sarcoglossan sea slugs are "[t]he only known animals that practice kleptoplasty." The correct answer must match this idea by saying, in some way, that the sarcoglossan sea slugs obtain and get energy from chloroplasts, while other sea slugs do not. (**C**) is a match.

(A) may be tempting, but the passage does not state that other slugs are incapable of incorporating the PRK gene into their genome, nor is it ever stated that all of the kleptoplastic species can. (In fact, it can be inferred that many do not since the passage says that many kleptoplastic species quickly run out of the enzymes needed to maintain photosynthesis.) (B) is also very close, since the passage mentions that the kleptoplastic slugs do digest most of the algae rather than incorporating them, but they do not use this digestion as their primary food source; it is instead the incorporation of whole chloroplasts that is their primary source of energy from the algae. It is not stated that other sea slugs produce the PRK enzyme, so (D) can be eliminated. Similarly, while the passage mentions that the symbiosis that led to incorporation of mitochondria as being different from the partial symbiosis of algae, the passage does not state that kleptoplastic sea slugs lack mitochondria, ruling out (E).

16. E

The passage as a whole defines what kleptoplasty is and describes a surprising experimental result. Choice **(E)** summarizes both the definition and the result and is therefore correct.

(A) is a distortion of the author's point. The mechanisms of kleptoplasty itself were well understood, even though the nature of its longevity in certain species were not. Both (B) and (C) are too specific. (B) focuses on paragraph 3 and includes information that the author never mentions; it is never stated that *E. chlorotica* cannot survive without incorporating the PRK gene. (C) focuses on a mere detail from paragraph 2.

Finally, choice (D) is not actually mentioned in the passage at all. It is not stated that horizontal gene transfer is unique to kleptoplastic species when compared to "other forms of symbiotic relationships," nor is it stated that all kleptoplastic species use horizontal gene transfer.

17. A, B

E. chlorotica is mentioned in paragraph 3 as being an example of a kleptoplastic species that incorporates the PRK gene into its genome when exposed to another organism that has this gene. **(A)** is supported with information from paragraph 2; in the absence of algae, *E. chlorotica* lacks the PRK gene, which is responsible for producing the PRK enzyme that synthesizes ribulose-1,5-bisphosphate. **(B)** is likewise supported, since both kleptoplasty and horizontal gene transfer

are described as being rare among animals. Regarding choice (C), the passage describes *E. chlorotica* as an example of a species that can incorporate the PRK gene. Indeed, the scientists were surprised to find that gene transfer was the cause of the longevity of the chloroplasts used by *E. chlorotica*, but to say that it is the *only* such species is extreme; it is mentioned in paragraph 2 that other species can maintain the reaction for prolonged periods of time, so it is plausible that they use the same mechanism.

18. D

Remember, even in weighty passages like these, all the information that you need is in the text. (A) *a physical object* is not the right answer because the passage is talking about natural law and human behavior. You can also eliminate (B) *a morally correct action as determined by God* because the passage specifies that "Finnis's theory does not require the presence of God." (C) *action that helps us achieve a desirable, material end* can be rejected for the same reason as (A). Furthermore, you are given an example of one basic human good, according to Finnis: curiosity about the nature of the universe. **(D)** *something self-evident that we ought to strive to embrace* is supported by the text both in the phrase "each good is self-evident" and Finnis's example of how something is made good by human participation. (E) *what is naturally occurring* could only be a reasonable possibility based on the repeated usage of the term "natural"; however, "natural law" is a metaphysical concept, and (E) is also incorrect.

19. B

The key to answering this question is to bear in mind Finnis's definition of "goods" that you considered in the previous question. You can learn from the passage that they are self-evident and all equal, which points us toward **(B)** *goods that demand opposing actions*—if they are all equally important, then how can we choose between actions that would each further one good while distancing ourselves from the other? (A) *proof of the existence of God* is a poor choice, because while his argument does not rely on the existence of God as Aquinas's did, nowhere does the author imply that Finnis's theory hinged on the nonexistence of God. (C) *the demands of our natural desires* is likewise incorrect because of the emphasis on human volition and the notion that some actions are inherently "good" and others are not—to give in to your desires would not undermine his definition but simply fail to follow his admonition. (D) *the definition of additional goods* would not necessarily weaken his definition so long as the new goods were not in opposition to his already established goods. Similarly, (E) *a method for evaluating goods* could help fix a weakness in Finnis's theory rather than undermine it.

20. C

This is a fairly straightforward Reading Comprehension question. It does not require us to make any inferences from the text, just give the text a careful reading to determine whether each answer choice is referred to (and they all are). (A) and (B) are both listed explicitly under the adaptations Finnis made to strengthen Aquinas's argument, so you can dismiss them. **(C)**, our only remaining option, is correct, as its opposite is one of the adaptations.

PART THREE

QUANTITATIVE REASONING

CHAPTER 9

INTRODUCTION TO QUANTITATIVE REASONING

Overview

The Quantitative Reasoning section of the GRE is designed to test your ability to reason quantitatively—to read a math problem, understand what it's asking, and solve it. The mathematical concepts tested on the GRE are similar to those tested on the SAT. You will see questions related to arithmetic, algebra, geometry, and data interpretation. There is no trigonometry or calculus on the GRE. The emphasis in the Quantitative Reasoning section is on your ability to reason, using your knowledge of the various topics. The goal is to make the test an accurate indicator of your ability to apply given information, think logically, and draw conclusions. These are skills you will need at the graduate level of study.

In the next few chapters of this book, we'll help you review the foundational math concepts that the GRE uses to test your reasoning skills. Think of the examples and drills that you see in these chapters as the building blocks for the questions you will see on the test. Once you're on a more solid math footing, we'll then describe the different types of Quantitative Reasoning questions you'll see on the GRE and give you the strategies to answer them quickly and correctly. At the end of this section, we've included a handful of practice sets for you to apply the knowledge that you've learned.

Quantitative Reasoning Question Types

The GRE contains two scored Quantitative Reasoning sections with 20 questions each. You may see a third experimental section, depending on your Test Day experience. Each section—whether scored or experimental—lasts 35 minutes and is composed of a selection of the following question types:

- Quantitative Comparison
- Problem Solving
- Data Interpretation

The Quantitative Reasoning portion of the GRE draws heavily upon your ability to combine your knowledge of mathematical concepts with your reasoning powers. Specifically, it evaluates your ability to do the following:

- Compare quantities using reasoning
- Solve word problems
- Interpret data presented in charts and graphs

What the GRE Quantitative Section is Testing

A common misconception among students preparing for the GRE is that the quantitative section is little more than a test of math skills and aptitude. While it's true that an understanding of math is helpful to perform well in this section, it's more accurate to say that the GRE *uses* basic math concepts as a *way* to test something far more important to your success in graduate school: critical thinking and reasoning skills. The distinction here is important. You don't have to be a math expert to perform at a high level on the GRE. With a solid understanding of foundational math concepts and an ability to think strategically, nearly every question on the GRE can be solved quickly and with little calculation.

The erroneous belief that the GRE tests hard math skills leads many students to make the mistake of jumping into every question with an automatic math-first approach. This can lead to frustration, confusion, and second guessing. "Did I write the algebra correctly? Is this the correct way to express that unknown value?" In contrast, strategic test-takers are in no such rush. They take their time, read through the question stem, and then ask themselves a few questions: "What, exactly, am I being asked to solve here? What concrete information is presented in the question stem?" And perhaps the most important question: "Do I have to do the math—or is there another, more simple or straightforward way to find the answer?"

For example, a strategic test-taker knows that in a multiple-choice question with answer choices containing numerical values, one of those values *must* be the correct answer. Perhaps, then, it easier to just test those choices and see which one "fits" the logic of the question. This is a technique called Backsolving.

Or, in a problem where the question stem and answer choices include variables, a strategic test-taker may find it easier to simply select values for the variables at hand, plug them into the math, and see what results. By doing so, the student has turned complicated and potentially confusing algebra into concrete, simple numbers. This is a strategy called Picking Numbers.

In later sections of this book, we'll describe those strategies in more depth. For now, the important thing to remember is that the GRE is a test of reasoning and critical thinking. In the next few chapters we will help you build your foundational knowledge of basic math skills, but we want you to remember that it's your *strategic* application of those concepts that will lead to your success on Test Day.

Pacing Strategy

As a multi-stage test, the GRE allows you to move freely backward and forward within each section, which can be a big advantage on Test Day. If you get stuck on a particular question, you can mark it and come back to it later when you have time. You only score points for correct answers, so don't get bogged down on one problem and lose time you could have used to answer several other questions correctly.

Each section contains an assortment of Quantitative Comparison, Problem Solving, and Data Interpretation items. However, these types are not distributed equally. The chart that follows shows how many questions you can expect of each question type, as well as the average amount of time you should spend per question type.

	QUANTITATIVE COMPARISON	PROBLEM SOLVING	DATA INTERPRETATION
Number of Questions per Section	approx. 7–8	approx. 9–10	approx. 3
Time per Question per Section	1.5 minutes	1.5–2 minutes	2 minutes

To Calculate or Not

An onscreen calculator will be available during the GRE. Numbers can be entered either by clicking on the numbers on the calculator with your mouse or by entering numbers from the keyboard. There are several points to consider about using the calculator on Test Day. A calculator can be a time-saver, and time is immensely important on a standardized test. But while calculators can speed up computations, they can also foster dependence, making it hard for you to spot the shortcuts in GRE questions. Using the calculator for a long, involved computation to answer a question will gobble up your allotted time for that question—and perhaps for several more. You may even make a mistake in your computation, leading to an incorrect answer. Remember, this is a *reasoning* test. The quantitative questions on the GRE are not designed to require lengthy computations.

If that is the case, why is a calculator provided? A calculator can be an asset for the occasional computation that a few questions require. And it may be a useful tool to confirm that you haven't made an error in freehand calculation. But beyond that, the calculator's use is limited. As you can see in the image to the right, the onscreen calculator provided is a simple four-function calculator. One unique feature on the GRE calculator is that hitting the "Transfer Display" button will enter the calculator's display into the answer box.

Navigating the Quantitative Reasoning Section of This Book

The chapters immediately following this one concern Math Foundations and Content Review. In them, you will review the classic math concepts and topics that you may encounter on the GRE. Use these chapters, and the drills and exercises contained in them, to shore up your understanding of GRE math.

The chapters that follow the Math Foundations and Content Review describe specific strategies for tackling the different GRE question types: Quantitative Comparison, Problem Solving, and Data Interpretation. Each one of those chapters includes an introduction to the relevant question types and then a review with strategies you can follow to answer those questions quickly and correctly. In addition, you'll find a practice set of questions with answers and explanations for each of the question types you'll encounter on the GRE.

Finally, after those chapters, you'll find the Quantitative Reasoning Practice Sets. In those three sets of 20 questions, you'll be able to test your skills and pinpoint areas for more focused study. Once you've worked through all of the chapters in this section of the book, you should be prepared for any question you might encounter on the Quantitative Reasoning section of the GRE.

CHAPTER 10

MATH FOUNDATIONS—ARITHMETIC AND NUMBER PROPERTIES REVIEW

Introduction to Arithmetic and Number Properties Review

The GRE tests your ability to perform operations with numbers (arithmetic) and your understanding of how different kinds of numbers behave (number properties). The following are the arithmetic and number properties topics you will see on the test:

- Arithmetic:
  - Terms
  - Symbols
  - Rules of operation

- Number properties:
  - Adding and subtracting
  - Multiplication and division of positive and negative numbers
  - Absolute value
  - Properties of zero
  - Properties of 1 and −1
  - Factors, multiples, and remainders
  - Exponents and roots

This chapter will cover these concepts with explanations and examples. At the end of the chapter is a practice set to help you improve your mastery.

Arithmetic

Terms

Consecutive numbers: Numbers of a certain type, following one another without interruption. Numbers may be consecutive in ascending or descending order. The GRE prefers to test consecutive integers (e.g., $-2, -1, 0, 1, 2, 3, \ldots$), but you may encounter other types of consecutive numbers. For example:

$-4, -2, 0, 2, 4, 6, \ldots$ is a series of consecutive even numbers.

$-3, 0, 3, 6, 9, \ldots$ is a series of consecutive multiples of 3.

$2, 3, 5, 7, 11, \ldots$ is a series of consecutive prime numbers.

Cube: A number raised to the 3rd power. For example $4^3 = (4)(4)(4) = 64$, showing that 64 is the cube of 4.

Decimal: A fraction written in decimal system format. For example, 0.6 is a decimal. To convert a fraction to a decimal, divide the numerator by the denominator. For instance, $\frac{5}{8} = 5 \div 8 = 0.625$.

Decimal system: A numbering system based on the powers of 10. The decimal system is the only numbering system used on the GRE. Each figure, or digit, in a decimal number occupies a particular position, from which it derives its place value.

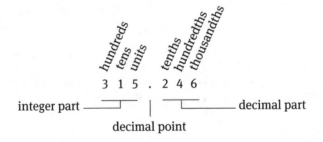

Denominator: The quantity in the bottom of a fraction.

Difference: The result of subtraction.

Digit: One of the numerals 0, 1, 2, 3, 4, 5, 6, 7, 8, or 9. A number can have several digits. For example, the number 542 has three digits: a 5, a 4, and a 2. The number 321,321,000 has nine digits but only four distinct (different) digits: 3, 2, 1, and 0.

Distinct: Different from each other. For example, 12 has three prime factors (2, 2, and 3) but only two distinct prime factors (2 and 3).

Element: One of the members of a set.

Exponent: The number that denotes the power to which another number or variable is raised. The exponent is typically written as a superscript to a number. For example, 5^3 equals $(5)(5)(5)$. The exponent is also occasionally referred to as a "power." For example,

5^3 can be described as "5 to the 3rd power." The product, 125, is "the 3rd power of 5." Exponents may be positive or negative integers or fractions, and they may include variables.

Fraction: The division of a part by a whole. $\frac{\text{Part}}{\text{Whole}} = \text{Fraction}$. For example, $\frac{3}{5}$ is a fraction.

Integer: A number without fractional or decimal parts, including positive and negative whole numbers and zero. All integers are multiples of 1. The following are examples of integers: $-5, -4, -3, -2, -1, 0, 1, 2, 3, 4, 5$.

Number line: A straight line, extending infinitely in either direction, on which numbers are represented as points. The number line below shows the integers from -3 to 4. Decimals and fractions can also be depicted on a number line, as can irrational numbers, such as $\sqrt{2}$.

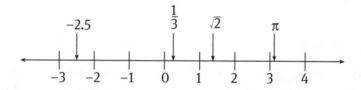

The values of numbers get larger as you move to the right along the number line. Numbers to the right of zero are *positive*; numbers to the left of zero are *negative*. **Zero is neither positive nor negative.** Any positive number is larger than any negative number. For example, $-300 < 4$.

Numerator: The quantity in the top of a fraction.

Operation: A function or process performed on one or more numbers. The four basic arithmetic operations are addition, subtraction, multiplication, and division.

Part: A specified number of the equal sections that compose a whole.

Product: The result of multiplication.

Sequence: An ordered list of terms. The terms of a sequence are often indicated by a letter with a subscript indicating the position of the number in the sequence. For instance, a_3 denotes the third number in a sequence, while a_n indicates the nth term in a sequence.

Set: A well-defined collection of items, typically numbers, objects, or events. The bracket symbols { } are normally used to define sets of numbers. For example, {2, 4, 6, 8} is a set of numbers.

Square: The product of a number multiplied by itself. A squared number has been raised to the 2nd power. For example, $4^2 = (4)(4) = 16$, so 16 is the square of 4.

Sum: The result of addition.

Whole: A quantity that is regarded as a complete unit.

Symbols

$=$ is equal to

$\neq$ is not equal to

$<$ is less than

$>$ is greater than

$\leq$ is less than or equal to

$\geq$ is greater than or equal to

$\div$ divided by

π pi (the ratio of the circumference of a circle to the diameter)

$\pm$ plus or minus

$\sqrt{}$ square root

$\angle$ angle

Rules of Operation

There are certain mathematical laws governing the results of the four basic operations: addition, subtraction, multiplication, and division. Although you won't need to know the names of these laws for the GRE, you'll benefit from understanding them.

PEMDAS

A string of operations must be performed in the proper order. The acronym PEMDAS stands for the correct order of operations:

Parentheses

Exponents

Multiplication
              } simultaneously from left to right
Division

Addition
              } simultaneously from left to right
Subtraction

If you have trouble remembering PEMDAS, you can think of the mnemonic "Please Excuse My Dear Aunt Sally."

Example:

$66(3-2) \div 11$

If you were to perform all the operations sequentially from left to right, without using PEMDAS, you would arrive at an answer of $\frac{196}{11}$. But if you perform the operation within the parentheses first, you get $66(1) \div 11 = 66 \div 11 = 6$, which is the correct answer.

Example:

$$30 - 5(4) + \frac{(7-3)^2}{8}$$
$$= 30 - 5(4) + \frac{4^2}{8}$$
$$= 30 - 5(4) + \frac{16}{8}$$
$$= 30 - 20 + 2$$
$$= 10 + 2$$
$$= 12$$

Commutative Laws of Addition and Multiplication

Addition and multiplication are both commutative, which means that switching the order of any two numbers being added or multiplied together does not affect the result.

Example:

$$5 + 8 = 8 + 5$$
$$(2)(3)(6) = (6)(3)(2)$$

$$a + b = b + a$$
$$xyz = zyx$$

Division and subtraction are not commutative; switching the order of the numbers changes the result. For instance, $3 - 2 \neq 2 - 3$; the left side yields a difference of 1, while the right side yields a difference of -1. Similarly, $\frac{6}{2} \neq \frac{2}{6}$; the left side equals 3, while the right side equals $\frac{1}{3}$.

Associative Laws of Addition and Multiplication

Addition and multiplication are also associative; regrouping the numbers does not affect the result.

Example:

$$(3 + 5) + 8 = 3 + (5 + 8) \quad (a + b) + c = a + (b + c)$$
$$8 + 8 = 3 + 13 \qquad\qquad (ab)c = a(bc)$$
$$16 = 16$$

The Distributive Law

The distributive law of multiplication allows you to "distribute" a factor over numbers that are added or subtracted. You do this by multiplying that factor by each number in the group.

Example:

$$4(3 + 7) = (4)(3) + (4)(7) \quad a(b + c) = ab + ac$$
$$4(10) = 12 + 28$$
$$40 = 40$$

The law works for the numerator in division as well.

$$\frac{a + b}{c} = \frac{a}{c} + \frac{b}{c}$$

However, when the sum or difference is in the denominator—that is, when you're dividing by a sum or difference—no distribution is possible.

$\frac{9}{4 + 5}$ is *not* equal to $\frac{9}{4} + \frac{9}{5}$.

Number Properties

Adding and Subtracting

Numbers can be treated as though they have two parts: a positive or negative sign and a number. Numbers without any sign are understood to be positive.

To add two numbers that have the same sign, add the number parts and keep the sign. For example, to add $(-6) + (-3)$, add 6 and 3 and then attach the negative sign from the original numbers to the sum: $(-6) + (-3) = -9$.

To add two numbers that have different signs, find the difference between the number parts and keep the sign of the number whose number part is larger. For example, to add $(-7) + (+4)$, subtract 4 from 7 to get 3. Because $7 > 4$ (the number part of -7 is greater than the number part of 4), the final sum is negative: $(-7) + (+4) = -3$.

Subtraction is the opposite of addition. You can rephrase any subtraction problem as an addition problem by changing the operation sign from a minus to a plus and switching the sign on the second number. For instance, $8 - 5 = 8 + (-5)$. There's no real advantage to rephrasing if you are subtracting a smaller positive number from a larger positive number. But the concept comes in very handy when you are subtracting a negative number from any other number, a positive number from a negative number or a larger positive number from a smaller positive number.

To subtract a negative number, rephrase as an addition problem and follow the rules for addition of signed numbers. For instance, $9 - (-10) = 9 + 10 = 19$.

To subtract a positive number from a negative number or from a smaller positive number, change the sign of the number that you are subtracting from positive to negative and follow the rules for addition of signed numbers. For example, $(-4) - 1 = (-4) + (-1) = -5$.

Multiplication and Division of Positive and Negative Numbers

Multiplying or dividing two numbers with the same sign gives a positive result.

Examples:

$$(-4)(-7) = +28$$
$$(-50) \div (-5) = +10$$

Multiplying or dividing two numbers with different signs gives a negative result.

Examples:

$$(-2)(+3) = -6$$
$$8 \div (-4) = -2$$

Absolute Value

The absolute value of a number is the value of a number without its sign. It is written as two vertical lines, one on either side of the number and its sign.

Example:

$$|-3| = |+3| = 3$$

The absolute value of a number can be thought of as the number's distance from zero on the number line. Since both 3 and -3 are 3 units from 0, each has an absolute value of 3. If you are told that $|x| = 5$, x could equal 5 or -5.

Properties of Zero

Adding zero to or subtracting zero from a number does not change the number.

$$x + 0 = x$$
$$0 + x = x$$
$$x - 0 = x$$

Examples:

$$5 + 0 = 5$$
$$0 + (-3) = -3$$
$$4 - 0 = 4$$

Notice, however, that subtracting a number from zero changes the number's sign. It's easy to see why if you rephrase the problem as an addition problem.

Example:

Subtract 5 from 0.

$0 - 5 = -5$. That's because $0 - 5 = 0 + (-5)$, and according to the rules for addition with signed numbers, $0 + (-5) = -5$.

The product of zero and any number is zero.

Examples:

$$(0)(z) = 0$$
$$(z)(0) = 0$$
$$(0)(12) = 0$$

Division by zero is undefined. For GRE purposes, that translates to "It can't be done." Since fractions are essentially division (that is, $\frac{1}{4}$ means $1 \div 4$), any fraction with zero in the denominator is also undefined. So when you are given a fraction that has an algebraic expression in the denominator, be sure that the expression cannot equal zero.

Properties of 1 and −1

Multiplying or dividing a number by 1 does not change the number.

$$(a)(1) = a$$
$$(1)(a) = a$$
$$a \div 1 = a$$

Examples:

$$(4)(1) = 4$$
$$(1)(-5) = -5$$
$$(-7) \div 1 = -7$$

Multiplying or dividing a nonzero number by −1 changes the sign of the number.

$$(a)(-1) = -a$$
$$(-1)(a) = -a$$
$$a \div (-1) = -a$$

Examples:

$$(6)(-1) = -6$$
$$(-3)(-1) = 3$$
$$(-8) \div (-1) = 8$$

Factors, Multiples, and Remainders

Multiples and Divisibility

A *multiple* is the product of a specified number and an integer. For example, 3, 12, and 90 are all multiples of 3: $3 = (3)(1)$; $12 = (3)(4)$; and $90 = (3)(30)$. The number 4 is not a multiple of 3, because there is no integer that can be multiplied by 3 to yield 4.

Multiples do not have to be of integers, but all multiples must be the product of a specific number and an integer. For instance, 2.4, 12, and 132 are all multiples of 1.2: $2.4 = (1.2)(2)$; $12 = (1.2)(10)$; and $132 = (1.2)(110)$.

The concepts of multiples and factors are tied together by the idea of *divisibility*. A number is said to be evenly divisible by another number if the result of the division is an integer with no remainder. A number that is evenly divisible by a second number is also a multiple of the second number.

For example, $52 \div 4 = 13$, which is an integer. So 52 is evenly divisible by 4, and it's also a multiple of 4.

On some GRE math problems, you will find yourself trying to assess whether one number is evenly divisible by another. You can use several simple rules to save time.

- An integer is divisible by 2 if its last digit is divisible by 2.
- An integer is divisible by 3 if its digits add up to a multiple of 3.
- An integer is divisible by 4 if its last two digits are a multiple of 4.
- An integer is divisible by 5 if its last digit is 0 or 5.
- An integer is divisible by 6 if it is divisible by both 2 and 3.
- An integer is divisible by 9 if its digits add up to a multiple of 9.

Example:

6,930 is a multiple of 2, since 0 is divisible by 2.

... a multiple of 3, since $6 + 9 + 3 + 0 = 18$, which is a multiple of 3.

... not a multiple of 4, since 30 is not a multiple of 4.

... a multiple of 5, since it ends in zero.

... a multiple of 6, since it is a multiple of both 2 and 3.

... a multiple of 9, since $6 + 9 + 3 + 0 = 18$, which is a multiple of 9.

Properties of Odd/Even Numbers

Even numbers are integers that are evenly divisible by 2; *odd* numbers are integers that are not evenly divisible by 2. Integers whose last digit is 0, 2, 4, 6, or 8 are even; integers whose last digit is 1, 3, 5, 7, or 9 are odd. The terms *odd* and *even* apply only to integers, but they may be used for either positive or negative integers. Zero is considered even.

Rules for Odds and Evens

Odd + Odd = Even
Even + Even = Even
Odd + Even = Odd
Odd × Odd = Odd
Even × Even = Even
Odd × Even = Even

Note that multiplying any even number by *any* integer always produces another even number.

It may be easier to use the Picking Numbers strategy in problems that ask you to decide whether some unknown will be odd or even.

Example:

Is the sum of two odd numbers odd or even?

Pick any two odd numbers, for example, 3 and 5: $3 + 5 = 8$. Since the sum of the two odd numbers that you picked is an even number, 8, it's safe to say that the sum of any two odd numbers is even.

Picking Numbers will work in any odds/evens problem, no matter how complicated. The only time you have to be careful is when division is involved, especially if the problem is in Quantitative Comparison format; different numbers may yield different results.

Example:

Integer x is evenly divisible by 2. Is $\frac{x}{2}$ even?

By definition, any multiple of 2 is even, so integer x is even. And $\frac{x}{2}$ must be an integer. But is $\frac{x}{2}$ even or odd? In this case, picking two different even numbers for x can yield two different results. If you let $x = 4$, then $\frac{x}{2} = \frac{4}{2} = 2$, which is even. But if you let $x = 6$, then $\frac{x}{2} = \frac{6}{2} = 3$, which is odd. So $\frac{x}{2}$ could be even or odd—and you wouldn't know that if you picked only one number.

Factors and Primes

The *factors*, or *divisors*, of an integer are the positive and negative integers by which it is evenly divisible (leaving no remainder).

Example:

What are the positive factors of 36?

36 has nine positive factors: 1, 2, 3, 4, 6, 9, 12, 18, and 36. We can group these factors in pairs: $(1)(36) = (2)(18) = (3)(12) = (4)(9) = (6)(6)$.

The *greatest common factor*, or greatest common divisor, of a group of integers is the largest factor that they share.

Example:

What is the greatest common factor of 36 and 48?

To find the greatest common factor (GCF), break down both integers into their prime factorizations and multiply all the prime factors they have in common: $36 = (2)(2)(3)(3)$, and $48 = (2)(2)(2)(2)(3)$. What they have in common is two 2s and one 3, so the GCF is $(2)(2)(3) = 12$.

A *prime number* is an integer greater than 1 that has only two factors: itself and 1. The number 1 is not considered a prime, because it is divisible only by itself. The number 2 is the smallest prime number and the only even prime. (Any other even number must have 2 as a factor and therefore cannot be prime.)

Prime Factors

The *prime factorization* of a number is the expression of the number as the product of its prime factors (the factors that are prime numbers).

There are two common ways to determine a number's prime factorization. The rules given above for determining divisibility by certain numbers come in handy in both methods.

Method #1: Work your way up through the prime numbers, starting with 2. (You'll save time in this process, especially when you're starting with a large number, by knowing the first ten prime numbers by heart: 2, 3, 5, 7, 11, 13, 17, 19, 23, and 29.)

Example:

What is the prime factorization of 210?

$$210 = (2)(105)$$

Since 105 is odd, it can't contain another factor of 2. The next smallest prime number is 3. The digits of 105 add up to 6, which is a multiple of 3, so 3 is a factor of 105.

$$210 = (2)(3)(35)$$

The digits of 35 add up to 8, which is not a multiple of 3. But 35 ends in 5, so it is a multiple of the next largest prime number, 5.

$$210 = (2)(3)(5)(7)$$

Since 7 is a prime number, this equation expresses the complete prime factorization of 210.

Method #2: Figure out one pair of factors and then determine their factors, continuing the process until you're left with only prime numbers. Those primes will be the prime factorization.

Example:

What is the prime factorization of 1,050?

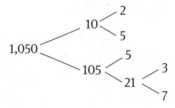

The distinct prime factors of 1,050 are therefore 2, 5, 3, and 7, with the prime number 5 occurring twice in the prime factorization. We usually write out the prime factorization by putting the prime numbers in increasing order. Here, that would be $(2)(3)(5)(5)(7)$. The prime factorization can also be expressed in exponential form: $(2)(3)(5^2)(7)$.

The Least Common Multiple

The *least common multiple* of two or more integers is the smallest number that is a multiple of each of the integers. Here's one quick way to find it:

(1) Determine the prime factorization of each integer.

(2) Write out each prime number the maximum number of times that it appears in any one of the prime factorizations.

(3) Multiply those prime numbers together to get the least common multiple of the original integers.

Example:

What is the least common multiple of 6 and 8?

Start by finding the prime factors of 6 and 8.

$$6 = (2)(3)$$
$$8 = (2)(2)(2)$$

The factor 2 appears three times in the prime factorization of 8, while 3 appears as only a single factor of 6. So the least common multiple of 6 and 8 is $(2)(2)(2)(3)$, or 24.

Note that the least common multiple of two integers is smaller than their product if they have any factors in common. For instance, the product of 6 and 8 is 48, but their least common multiple is only 24.

In addition to answering questions using the term *least common multiple*, you'll find the concept useful whenever you're adding or subtracting fractions with different denominators.

Remainders

The *remainder* is what is "left over" in a division problem. A remainder is always smaller than the number you are dividing by. For instance, 17 divided by 3 is 5, with a remainder of 2. Likewise, 12 divided by 6 is 2, with a remainder of 0 (since 12 is evenly divisible by 6).

GRE writers often disguise remainder problems. For instance, a problem might state that the slats of a fence are painted in three colors, which appear in a fixed order, such as red, yellow, blue, red, yellow, blue . . . You would then be asked something like, "If the first slat is red, what color is the 301st slat?" Since 3 goes into 300 evenly, the whole pattern must finish on the 300th slat and start all over again on the 301st. Therefore, the 301st would be red.

Exponents and Roots

Rules of Operations with Exponents

To multiply two powers with the same base, keep the base and add the exponents together.

Example:

$$2^2 \times 2^3 = (2 \times 2)(2 \times 2 \times 2) = 2^5$$

or

$$2^2 \times 2^3 = 2^{2+3} = 2^5$$

To divide two powers with the same base, keep the base and subtract the exponent of the denominator from the exponent of the numerator.

Example:

$$4^5 \div 4^2 = \frac{(4)(4)(4)(4)(4)}{(4)(4)} = 4^3$$

or

$$4^5 \div 4^2 = 4^{5-2} = 4^3$$

To raise a power to another power, multiply the exponents.

Example:

$(3^2)^4 = (3 \times 3)^4$

or

$(3^2)^4 = (3 \times 3)(3 \times 3)(3 \times 3)(3 \times 3)$

or

$(3^2)^4 = 3^{2 \times 4} = 3^8$

To multiply two powers with different bases but the same power, multiply the bases together and raise to the power.

Example:

$(3^2)(5^2) = (3 \times 3)(5 \times 5) = (3 \times 5)(3 \times 5) = (3 \times 5)^2 = 15^2$

A base with a negative exponent indicates the reciprocal of that base to the positive value of the exponent.

Example:

$5^{-3} = \frac{1}{5^3} = \frac{1}{125}$

Raising any nonzero number to an exponent of zero equals 1.

Examples:

$5^0 = 1$

$161^0 = 1$

$(-6)^0 = 1$

Commonly Tested Properties of Powers

Many Quantitative Comparison problems test your understanding of what happens when fractions and negative numbers are raised to a power.

Raising a fraction between zero and one to a power produces a smaller result.

Example:

$\left(\frac{1}{2}\right)^2 = \left(\frac{1}{2}\right)\left(\frac{1}{2}\right) = \frac{1}{4}$

Raising a negative number to an even power produces a positive result.

Example:

$(-2)^2 = 4$

Raising a negative number to an odd power gives a negative result.

Example:

$(-2)^3 = -8$

Raising an even number to any positive integer exponent gives an even number. Raising an odd number to any integer exponent greater than or equal to 0 gives an odd number.

Examples:

$8^5 = 32{,}768$, an even number

$5^8 = 390{,}625$, an odd number

Powers of 10

When 10 is raised to an exponent that is a positive integer, that exponent tells how many zeros the number would contain if it were written out.

Example:

Write 10^6 in ordinary notation.

The exponent 6 indicates that you will need six zeros after the 1: 1,000,000. That's because 10^6 means six factors of 10, that is, $(10)(10)(10)(10)(10)(10)$.

To multiply a number by a power of 10, move the decimal point the same number of places to the right as the value of the exponent (or as the number of zeros in that power of 10).

Example:

Multiply 0.029 by 10^3

The exponent is 3, so move the decimal point three places to the right.

$$(0.029)10^3 = 0029. = 29$$

If you had been told to multiply 0.029 by 1,000, you could have counted the number of zeros in 1,000 and done exactly the same thing.

Sometimes you'll have to add zeros as placeholders.

> **Example:**
>
> Multiply 0.029 by 10^6.
>
> Add zeros until you can move the decimal point six places to the right:
>
> $$0.029 \times 10^6 = 0029000. = 29,000$$

To divide by a power of 10, move the decimal point the corresponding number of places to the left, inserting zeros as placeholders if necessary.

> **Example:**
>
> Divide 416.03 by 10,000
>
> There are four zeros in 10,000, but only three places to the left of the decimal point. You'll have to insert another zero:
>
> $$416.03 \div 10,000 = .041603 = 0.041603$$

By convention, one zero is usually written to the left of the decimal point on the GRE. It's a placeholder and doesn't change the value of the number.

Scientific Notation

Very large numbers (and very small decimals) take up a lot of space and are difficult to work with. So, in some scientific texts, they are expressed in a shorter, more convenient form called *scientific notation*.

For example, 123,000,000,000 would be written in scientific notation as 1.23×10^{11}, and 0.000000003 would be written as 3×10^{-9}. (If you're already familiar with the concept of negative exponents, you'll know that multiplying by 10^{-9} is equivalent to dividing by 10^9.)

To express a number in scientific notation, rewrite it as a product of two factors. The first factor must be greater than or equal to 1 but less than 10. The second factor must be a power of 10.

To translate a number from scientific notation to ordinary notation, use the rules for multiplying and dividing by powers of 10.

> **Example:**
>
> $5.6 \times 10^6 = 5,600,000$, or 5.6 million

Rules of Operations with Roots and Radicals

A *square root* of any non-negative number x is a number that, when multiplied by itself, yields x. Every positive number has two square roots, one positive and one negative. For instance, the positive square root of 25 is 5, because $5^2 = 25$. The negative square root of 25 is -5, because $(-5)^2$ also equals 25.

By convention, the radical symbol $\sqrt{}$ stands for the positive square root only. Therefore, $\sqrt{9} = 3$ only, even though both 3^2 and $(-3)^2$ equal 9.

When applying the four basic arithmetic operations, radicals (roots written with the radical symbol) are treated in much the same way as variables.

Addition and Subtraction of Radicals

Only like radicals can be added to or subtracted from one another.

Example:

$$2\sqrt{3} + 4\sqrt{2} - \sqrt{2} - 3\sqrt{3} =$$
$$\left(4\sqrt{2} - \sqrt{2}\right) + \left(2\sqrt{3} - 3\sqrt{3}\right) =$$
$$3\sqrt{2} + \left(-\sqrt{3}\right) =$$
$$3\sqrt{2} - \sqrt{3}$$

This expression cannot be simplified any further.

Multiplication and Division of Radicals

To multiply or divide one radical by another, multiply or divide the numbers outside the radical signs, then the numbers inside the radical signs.

Example:

$$\left(6\sqrt{3}\right)2\sqrt{5} = (6)(2)\left(\sqrt{3}\right)\left(\sqrt{5}\right) = 12\sqrt{15}$$

Example:

$$12\sqrt{15} \div 2\sqrt{5} = \left(\frac{12}{2}\right)\left(\frac{\sqrt{15}}{\sqrt{5}}\right) = 6\sqrt{\frac{15}{5}} = 6\sqrt{3}$$

Simplifying Radicals

If the number inside the radical is a multiple of a perfect square, the expression can be simplified by factoring out the perfect square.

Example:

$$\sqrt{72} = \left(\sqrt{36}\right)\sqrt{2} = 6\sqrt{2}$$

Before you move on, check your understanding of arithmetic and number properties on the GRE by considering a few questions:

· What type of number results when two odd numbers are multiplied together?

· What is the value of x if $|x| = 6$?

· What is the difference between a factor and a multiple?

· What is $7^3 \times 7^4$? What is $2\sqrt{y} \times 5\sqrt{y}$?

If you feel confident in your ability to tackle questions that deal with these concepts, proceed to the practice set that follows.

If you feel like you would like some additional guided practice, head to your online resources. Under **Math Foundations**, click **Arithmetic and Number Properties Guided Practice**. Try each question on your own first. Then watch a video explanation in which a Kaplan GRE instructor describes a strategic approach.

Arithmetic and Number Properties Practice Set

Directions: Try answering these questions to practice what you have learned about arithmetic and number properties. Answers and explanations follow at the end of the chapter.

Basic

1. What is the value of $6(-3 + 1) - 6(3 - 1)$?

2. What is the value of $\left| 6 - 4 \times 2 \right|$?

3. What is the value of $\dfrac{\frac{2}{3}}{\frac{1}{6}}$?

4. How many two-digit multiples of 6 are multiples of 15?

5. If a, b, and c are positive integers and a and c are odd, what is the smallest possible value of b given $a \times b \times c$ is even?

Intermediate

6. How many positive factors of 54 are odd?

7. What is the largest prime factor of 46,000?

8. What is the value of $\dfrac{4^3 \times 9^3}{6^5}$?

9. When integer a is divided by 5, the remainder is 2. When integer b is divided by 5, the remainder is 3. What is the remainder when $a \times b$ is divided by 5?

10. If x is an integer, how many values of x are there such that $|x| < 6$ and $|x| > 3$?

Advanced

11. What is the largest 4-digit multiple of 71?

12. What is the value of $\left(\sqrt{3} + 3\sqrt{27}\right)\left(2\sqrt{3} - \sqrt{27}\right)$?

13. What is the value of $\sqrt{63} \times \sqrt[3]{56} \times 7^{\frac{1}{6}}$?

14. If the digits of integer x are reversed and the resulting number is added to the original x, the sum is 7,777. What is the smallest possible value of x?

15. What is the value of $\left(\sqrt[3]{.125}\right)^{-4}$?

Arithmetic and Number Properties Practice Set Answer Key

1. −6
2. 2
3. 4
4. 3
5. 2
6. 4
7. 23
8. 6

9. 1
10. 4
11. 9,940
12. −30
13. 42
14. 1,076
15. 16

Arithmetic and Number Properties Practice Set Answers and Explanations

Basic

1. −6

Follow PEMDAS, and be careful when dealing with negative numbers.

$$6(-3+1) - 6(3-4) = 6(-2) - 6(-1) =$$
$$-12 - (-6) = -12 + 6 = -6$$

2. 2

Using PEMDAS, first multiply 4 by 2. The expression is now $|6 - 8|$. Then subtract 8 from 6 to get −2. Finally, take the absolute value of −2 to get 2.

3. 4

Dividing by a fraction is equal to multiplying by the reciprocal of that fraction. So, dividing by $\frac{1}{6}$ is equal to multiplying by $\frac{6}{1}$. $\frac{2}{3} \times \frac{6}{1} = \frac{12}{3} = 4$.

4. 3

The least common multiple of 6 and 15 is 30. Every multiple of 30 will also be a multiple of both 6 and 15. That means there are only three two-digit multiples of both 6 and 15: 30, 60, and 90.

5. 2

When multiplying integers, at least one integer must be even to get an even result. If a and c are odd, then b must be even for $a \times b \times c$ to be even. That means the smallest value of b, which must be positive, is 2.

Intermediate

6. 4

The positive factors of 54 are 1, 2, 3, 6, 9, 18, 27, and 54. Of those, four (1, 3, 9, and 27) are odd.

7. 23

Any multiple of 10 will have prime factors of 5×2. In this case, $46,000 = 46 \times 10 \times 10 \times 10 = 23 \times 2 \times 5 \times 2 \times 5 \times 2 \times 5 \times 2$. The number 23 is prime and cannot be broken down further.

8. 6

Whenever there are exponents in a fraction, see if it is possible to get a common base in both the numerator and the denominator. Here, the denominator has a base of 6. There are two ways to simplify the numerator to get a base of 6:

$$\frac{4^3 \times 9^3}{6^5} = \frac{(4 \times 9)^3}{6^5} = \frac{36^3}{6^5} = \frac{(6^2)^3}{6^5} = \frac{6^6}{6^5} \text{ or}$$

$$\frac{4^3 \times 9^3}{6^5} = \frac{(2^2)^3 \times (3^2)^3}{6^5} = \frac{2^6 \times 3^6}{6^5} = \frac{(2 \times 3)^6}{6^5} = \frac{6^6}{6^5}$$

Either way, the final result is $\frac{6^6}{6^5} = 6^{6-5} = 6^1 = 6$.

9. 1

Numbers that leave a remainder of 2 when divided by 5 are numbers that are 2 greater than a multiple of 5, e.g., $7\,(5+2)$, $12\,(10+2)$, $17\,(15+2)\ldots$ Similarly, numbers that leave a remainder of 3 are 3 greater than a multiple of 5, e.g., 8, 13, 18 ...

Pick any two valid numbers to test $a \times b$. If $a = 7$ and $b = 8$, then $a \times b = 56$. When 56 is divided by 5, the result is 11 with a remainder of 1 (as 56 is 1 greater than 55, a multiple of 5).

This will work out for any values of a and b. On Test Day, it may be tempting to try a second set of values. However, when the correct answer is a single number, there is no need to do so. The GRE will not play tricks, and every valid set of numbers will lead to the same result. Have confidence with the numbers you selected and move on.

10. 4

$|x|$ is the distance between 0 and x on a number line. If $|x| < 6$, then x must be less than 6 units away from 0. If x is an integer, that means it is any integer from -5 to 5. If $|x| > 3$, then x must be more than 3 units away from 0. That means x can be 4 or greater, or it can be -4 or less. To satisfy both conditions, x can be -5, -4, 4, or 5.

Advanced

11. 9,940

The largest 4-digit number is 9,999. When 9,999 is divided by 71, the result is 140 with a remainder of 59. That means 9,999 is 59 greater than the nearest multiple of 71. Subtracting 59 from 9,999 will produce the greatest 4-digit multiple of 71. Another way to approach this, after doing the division, is to recognize that 71×141 would produce a number larger than 9,999, so the largest 4-digit multiple of 71 would be 71×140.

12. −30

Use FOIL to multiply:

$$\left(\sqrt{3} + 3\sqrt{27}\right)\left(2\sqrt{3} - \sqrt{27}\right) =$$

$$\sqrt{3}\left(2\sqrt{3}\right) + \sqrt{3}\left(-\sqrt{27}\right) + 3\sqrt{27}\left(2\sqrt{3}\right) + 3\sqrt{27}\left(-\sqrt{27}\right) =$$

$$2(3) - \sqrt{81} + 6\sqrt{81} - 3(27) = 6 - 9 + 6(9) - 81 =$$

$$-3 + 54 - 81 = -30$$

13. 42

The mixture of radicals and exponents can be confusing. Exponents are usually easier to deal with, so start by converting each radical into an exponential term:

$$\sqrt{63} \times \sqrt[3]{56} \times 7^{\frac{1}{6}} = 63^{\frac{1}{2}} \times 56^{\frac{1}{3}} \times 7^{\frac{1}{6}}$$

63, 56, and 7 are all multiples of 7, so factor out 7 from each term:

$$63^{\frac{1}{2}} \times 56^{\frac{1}{3}} \times 7^{\frac{1}{6}} = \left(9^{\frac{1}{2}}\right)\left(7^{\frac{1}{2}}\right) \times \left(8^{\frac{1}{3}}\right)\left(7^{\frac{1}{3}}\right) \times 7^{\frac{1}{6}}$$

$9^{\frac{1}{2}} = \sqrt{9} = 3$ and $8^{\frac{1}{3}} = \sqrt[3]{8} = 2$. Use the rules of exponents to finish:

$$3\left(7^{\frac{1}{2}}\right) \times 2\left(7^{\frac{1}{3}}\right) \times 7^{\frac{1}{6}} = (3 \times 2) \times \left(7^{\frac{1}{2}} \times 7^{\frac{1}{3}} \times 7^{\frac{1}{6}}\right) =$$

$$6 \times 7^{\left(\frac{1}{2} + \frac{1}{3} + \frac{1}{6}\right)} = 6 \times 7^{\left(\frac{3}{6} + \frac{2}{6} + \frac{1}{6}\right)} = 6 \times 7^{\left(\frac{6}{6}\right)} = 6 \times 7^1 = 42$$

14. 1,076

When the digits are reversed, the new number will have the same number of digits. No two 3-digit numbers add up to 7,777 (as the largest 3-digit number is 999, and 999 plus 999 is only 1,998), so x must be a 4-digit number. Let A, B, C, and D represent the digits of x. Adding x to its reverse would look like this.

$ABCD + DCBA = 7777$

The smallest 4-digit numbers would begin with 1, so A should be 1.

$1BCD + DCB1 = 7777$

For the sum to end in 7, D would have to be 6.

$1BC6 + 6CB1 = 7777$

After that, the smallest possible value of B would be 0. In that case, C would have to be 7.

$1076 + 6701 = 7777$

Thus, 1,076 is the smallest possible value of x.

15. 16

Start by converting .125 to a fraction. Once that's done, use the rules of radicals and exponents to simplify:

$$\left(\sqrt[3]{.125}\right)^{-4} = \left(\sqrt[3]{\frac{1}{8}}\right)^{-4} = \left(\frac{\sqrt[3]{1}}{\sqrt[3]{8}}\right)^{-4} = \left(\frac{1}{2}\right)^{-4} =$$

$$\frac{1}{\left(\frac{1}{2}\right)^4} = \frac{1}{\frac{1^4}{2^4}} = \frac{1}{\frac{1}{16}} = 1 \times \frac{16}{1} = 16$$

CHAPTER 11

MATH FOUNDATIONS—RATIOS AND MATH FORMULAS REVIEW

Introduction to Ratios and Math Formulas Review

To solve many GRE Quantitative questions, you will need to be able to work fluently with ratios. You will also need to apply certain math formulas. The following topics will show up on Test Day:

- Ratios:
  - Fractions
  - Decimals
  - Percents
  - Ratios
- Math formulas:
  - Rates
  - Work formula
  - Averages

After studying this chapter, which explains each of these concepts, try the questions in the practice set to improve your understanding.

Ratios

Fractions

The simplest way to understand the meaning of a fraction is to picture the denominator as the number of equal parts into which a whole unit is divided. The numerator represents a certain number of those equal parts.

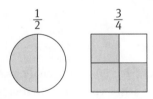

On the left, the shaded portion is one of two equal parts that make up the whole. On the right, the shaded portion is three of four equal parts that make up the whole.

The fraction bar is interchangeable with a division sign. You can divide the numerator of a fraction by the denominator to get an equivalent decimal. However, the numerator and denominator must each be treated as a single quantity.

Example:

Evaluate $\dfrac{5+2}{7-3}$

You can't just rewrite the fraction as $5 + 2 \div 7 - 3$, because the numerator and the denominator are each considered distinct quantities. Instead, you would rewrite the fraction as $(5 + 2) \div (7 - 3)$. The order of operations (remember PEMDAS?) tells us that operations in parentheses must be performed first.

That gives you $7 \div 4$. Your final answer would be $\dfrac{7}{4}$, $1\dfrac{3}{4}$, or 1.75, depending on the form of the answer choices.

Equivalent Fractions

Since multiplying or dividing a number by 1 does not change the number, multiplying the numerator and denominator of a fraction by the same nonzero number doesn't change the value of the fraction—it's the same as multiplying the entire fraction by 1.

Example:

Change $\dfrac{1}{2}$ into an equivalent fraction with a denominator of 4.

To change the denominator from 2 to 4, you'll have to multiply it by 2. But to keep the value of the fraction the same, you'll also have to multiply the numerator by 2.

$$\frac{1}{2} = \frac{1}{2}\left(\frac{2}{2}\right) = \frac{2}{4}$$

Similarly, dividing the numerator and denominator by the same nonzero number leaves the value of the fraction unchanged.

Example:

Change $\dfrac{16}{20}$ into an equivalent fraction with a denominator of 10.

To change the denominator from 20 to 10, you'll have to divide it by 2. But to keep the value of the fraction the same, you'll have to divide the numerator by the same number.

$$\frac{16}{20} = \frac{16 \div 2}{20 \div 2} = \frac{8}{10}$$

Reducing (Canceling)

Most fractions on the GRE are in lowest terms. That means that the numerator and denominator have no common factor greater than 1.

For example, the final answer of $\frac{8}{10}$ that we obtained in the previous example was not in lowest terms, because both 8 and 10 are divisible by 2. In contrast, the fraction $\frac{7}{10}$ is in lowest terms, because there is no factor greater than 1 that 7 and 10 have in common. To convert a fraction to its lowest terms, we use a method called *reducing*, or *canceling*. To reduce, simply divide any common factors out of both the numerator and the denominator.

Example:

Reduce $\frac{15}{35}$ to lowest terms.

$\frac{15}{35} = \frac{15 \div 5}{35 \div 5} = \frac{3}{7}$ (because a 5 cancels out, top and bottom)

Sometimes it may be necessary to repeat the process and keep dividing out common factors until no common factor greater than 1 remains for the numerator and denominator.

Example:

Reduce $\frac{1,040}{1,080}$ to lowest terms.

$$\frac{1,040}{1,080} = \frac{104}{108} = \frac{52}{54} = \frac{26}{27}$$

Adding and Subtracting Fractions

You cannot add or subtract fractions unless they have the same denominator. If they don't, you'll have to convert each fraction to an equivalent fraction with the least common denominator. Then add or subtract the numerators (not the denominators!) and, if necessary, reduce the resulting fraction to its lowest terms.

Given two fractions with different denominators, the least common denominator is the least common multiple of the two denominators, that is, the smallest number that is evenly divisible by both denominators.

Example:

What is the least common denominator of $\frac{2}{15}$ and $\frac{3}{10}$?

The least common denominator of the two fractions will be the least common multiple of 15 and 10.

Because $15 = (5)(3)$ and $10 = (5)(2)$, the least common multiple of the two numbers is $(5)(3)(2)$, or 30. That makes 30 the least common denominator of $\frac{2}{15}$ and $\frac{3}{10}$.

Example:

$$\frac{2}{15} + \frac{3}{10} = ?$$

As we saw in the previous example, the least common denominator of the two fractions is 30. Change each fraction to an equivalent fraction with a denominator of 30.

$$\frac{2}{15}\left(\frac{2}{2}\right) = \frac{4}{30}$$

$$\frac{3}{10}\left(\frac{3}{3}\right) = \frac{9}{30}$$

Then add:

$$\frac{4}{30} + \frac{9}{30} = \frac{13}{30}$$

Since 13 and 30 have no common factor greater than 1, $\frac{13}{30}$ is in lowest terms. You can't reduce it further.

Multiplying Fractions

To multiply fractions, multiply the numerators and multiply the denominators.

$$\frac{5}{7}\left(\frac{3}{4}\right) = \frac{15}{28}$$

Multiplying numerator by numerator and denominator by denominator is simple. But it's easy to make careless errors if you have to multiply a string of fractions or work with large numbers. You can minimize those errors by reducing before you multiply.

Example:

Multiply $\left(\frac{10}{9}\right)\left(\frac{3}{4}\right)\left(\frac{8}{15}\right)$.

First, cancel a 5 out of the 10 and the 15, a 3 out of the 3 and the 9, and a 4 out of the 8 and the 4:

$$\left(\frac{\cancel{10}^{2}}{\cancel{9}_{3}}\right)\left(\frac{\cancel{3}^{1}}{\cancel{4}_{1}}\right)\left(\frac{\cancel{8}^{2}}{\cancel{15}_{3}}\right)$$

Then multiply numerators together and denominators together:

$$\left(\frac{2}{3}\right)\left(\frac{1}{1}\right)\left(\frac{2}{3}\right) = \frac{4}{9}$$

Reciprocals

To get the reciprocal of a common fraction, turn the fraction upside down so that the numerator becomes the denominator and vice versa. If a fraction has a numerator of 1, the fraction's reciprocal will be equivalent to an integer.

Example:

What is the reciprocal of $\frac{1}{25}$?

Inverting the fraction gives you the reciprocal, $\frac{25}{1}$. But dividing a number by 1 doesn't change the value of the number.

Since $\frac{25}{1}$ equals 25, the reciprocal of $\frac{1}{25}$ equals 25.

Dividing Common Fractions

To divide fractions, multiply by the reciprocal of the number or fraction that follows the division sign.

$$\frac{1}{2} \div \frac{3}{5} = \frac{1}{2}\left(\frac{5}{3}\right) = \frac{5}{6}$$

The operation of division produces the same result as multiplication by the inverse.

Example:

$$\frac{4}{3} \div \frac{4}{9} = \frac{4}{3}\left(\frac{9}{4}\right) = \frac{36}{12} = 3$$

Comparing Positive Fractions

Given two positive fractions with the same denominator, the fraction with the larger numerator will have the larger value.

Example:

Which is greater, $\frac{3}{8}$ or $\frac{5}{8}$?

$$\frac{3}{8} < \frac{5}{8}$$

But if you're given two positive fractions with the same numerator but different denominators, the fraction with the smaller denominator will have the larger value.

Example:

Which is greater, $\frac{3}{4}$ or $\frac{3}{8}$?

The diagrams below show two wholes of equal size. The one on the left is divided into 4 equal parts, 3 of which are shaded. The one on the right is divided into 8 equal parts, 3 of which are shaded.

$\frac{3}{4}$ is clearly greater than $\frac{3}{8}$

If neither the numerators nor the denominators are the same, you have three options. You can turn both fractions into their decimal equivalents. You can express both fractions in terms of some common denominator and then see which new equivalent fraction has the largest numerator. Or you can cross multiply the numerator of each fraction by the denominator of the other. The greater result will wind up next to the greater fraction.

Example:

Which is greater, $\frac{5}{6}$ or $\frac{7}{9}$?

$$\overset{45}{\underset{6}{5}}\diagdown\hspace{-0.5em}\diagup\overset{42}{\underset{9}{7}}$$

Since $45 > 42$, $\frac{5}{6} > \frac{7}{9}$.

Mixed Numbers and Improper Fractions

A *mixed number* consists of an integer and a fraction.

An *improper fraction* is a fraction whose numerator is greater than its denominator. To convert an improper fraction to a mixed number, divide the numerator by the denominator. The number of "whole" times that the denominator goes into the numerator will be the integer portion of the mixed fraction; the remainder will be the numerator of the fractional portion.

Example:

Convert $\frac{23}{4}$ to a mixed number.

Dividing 23 by 4 gives you 5 with a remainder of 3, so $\frac{23}{4} = 5\frac{3}{4}$.

To change a mixed number to a fraction, multiply the integer portion of the mixed number by the denominator and add the numerator. This new number is your numerator. The denominator will not change.

Example:

Convert $2\frac{3}{7}$ to a fraction.

$$2\frac{3}{7} = \frac{7(2) + 3}{7} = \frac{17}{7}$$

Properties of Fractions Between −1 and +1

The reciprocal of a fraction between 0 and 1 is greater than both the original fraction and 1.

Example:

The reciprocal of $\frac{2}{3}$ is $\frac{3}{2}$, which is greater than both 1 and $\frac{2}{3}$.

The reciprocal of a fraction between −1 and 0 is less than both the original fraction and −1.

Example:

The reciprocal of $-\frac{2}{3}$ is $-\frac{3}{2}$, or $-1\frac{1}{2}$, which is less than both −1 and $-\frac{2}{3}$.

The square of a fraction between 0 and 1 is less than the original fraction.

Example:

$$\left(\frac{1}{2}\right)^2 = \left(\frac{1}{2}\right)\left(\frac{1}{2}\right) = \frac{1}{4}$$

But the square of any fraction between 0 and −1 is greater than the original fraction, because multiplying two negative numbers gives you a positive product and any positive number is greater than any negative number.

Example:

$$\left(-\frac{1}{2}\right)^2 = \left(-\frac{1}{2}\right)\left(-\frac{1}{2}\right) = \frac{1}{4}$$

Multiplying any positive number by a fraction between 0 and 1 gives a product smaller than the original number.

Example:

$$6\left(\frac{1}{4}\right) = \frac{6}{4} = \frac{3}{2}$$

Multiplying any negative number by a fraction between 0 and 1 gives a product greater than the original number.

Example:

$$(-3)\left(\frac{1}{2}\right) = -\frac{3}{2}$$

Decimals

Converting Decimals

It's easy to convert decimals to common fractions, and vice versa. Any decimal fraction is equivalent to some common fraction with a power of 10 in the denominator.

To convert a decimal between 0 and 1 to a fraction, determine the place value of the last nonzero digit and set that value as the denominator. Then use all the digits of the decimal number as the numerator, ignoring the decimal point. Finally, if necessary, reduce the fraction to its lowest terms.

Example:

Convert 0.875 to a fraction in lowest terms.

The last nonzero digit is the 5, which is in the thousandths place. So the denominator of the common fraction will be 1,000. The numerator will be 875: $\frac{875}{1,000}$.

(You can ignore the zero to the left of the decimal point, since there are no nonzero digits to its left; it's just a "placeholder.")

Both 875 and 1,000 contain a factor of 25. Canceling it out leaves you with $\frac{35}{40}$.

Reducing that further by a factor of 5 gives you $\frac{7}{8}$, which is in lowest terms.

To convert a fraction to a decimal, simply divide the numerator by the denominator.

Example:

What is the decimal equivalent of $\frac{4}{5}$?

$$4 \div 5 = 0.8$$

Comparing Decimals

Knowing place values allows you to assess the relative values of decimals.

Example:

Which is greater, 0.254 or 0.3?

Of course, 254 is greater than 3. But $0.3 = \frac{3}{10}$, which is equivalent to $\frac{300}{1,000}$, while

0.254 is equivalent to only $\frac{254}{1,000}$. Since $\frac{300}{1,000} > \frac{254}{1,000}$, 0.3 is greater than 0.254.

Here's the simplest way to compare decimals: add zeros after the last digit to the right of the decimal point in each decimal fraction until all the decimals you're comparing have the same number of digits. Essentially, what you're doing is giving all the fractions the same denominator so that you can just compare their numerators.

Example:

Arrange in order from smallest to largest: 0.7, 0.77, 0.07, 0.707, and 0.077.

The numbers 0.707 and 0.077 end at the third place to the right of the decimal point—the thousandths place. Add zeros after the last digit to the right of the decimal point in each of the other fractions until you reach the thousandths place:

$$0.7 = 0.700 = \frac{700}{1,000}$$

$$0.77 = 0.770 = \frac{770}{1,000}$$

$$0.07 = 0.070 = \frac{70}{1,000}.$$

$$0.707 = \frac{707}{1,000}$$

$$0.077 = \frac{77}{1,000}$$

$$\frac{70}{1,000} < \frac{77}{1,000} < \frac{700}{1,000} < \frac{707}{1,000} < \frac{770}{1,000}$$

Therefore, $0.07 < 0.077 < 0.7 < 0.707 < 0.77$.

Estimation and Rounding on the GRE

You should be familiar and comfortable with the practice of "rounding off" numbers. To round off a number to a particular place, look at the digit immediately to the right of that place. If the digit is 0, 1, 2, 3, or 4, don't change the digit that is in the place to which you are rounding. If it is 5, 6, 7, 8, or 9, change the digit in the place to which you are rounding to the next higher digit. Replace all digits to the right of the place to which you are rounding with zeros.

For example, to round off 235 to the tens place, look at the units place. Since it is occupied by a 5, you'll round the 3 in the tens place up to a 4, giving you 240. If you had been rounding off 234, you would have rounded down to the existing 3 in the tens place; that would have given you 230.

Example:

Round off 675,978 to the hundreds place.

The 7 in the tens place means that you will have to round the hundreds place up. Since there is a 9 in the hundreds place, you'll have to change the thousands place as well. Rounding 675,978 to the hundreds place gives you 676,000.

Rounding off large numbers before performing a calculation will allow you to quickly estimate the correct answer.

Estimating can save you valuable time on many GRE problems. But before you estimate, check the answer choices to see how close they are. If they are relatively close together, you'll have to be more accurate than if they are further apart.

Percents

The word *percent* means "hundredths," and the percent sign, %, means $\frac{1}{100}$. For example, 25% means $25\left(\frac{1}{100}\right) = \frac{25}{100}$. (Like the division sign, the percent sign evolved from the fractional relationship; the slanted bar in a percent sign represents a fraction bar.)

Percents measure a part-to-whole relationship with an assumed whole equal to 100. The percent relationship can be expressed as $\frac{Part}{Whole}(100\%)$. For example, if $\frac{1}{4}$ of a rectangle is shaded, the percent of the rectangle that is shaded is $\frac{1}{4}(100\%) = 25\%$.

Like fractions, percents express the relationship between a specified part and a whole; more specifically, percents express a relationship of a part out of 100. Thus, 25%, $\frac{25}{100}$, and 0.25 are simply different names for the same part-to-whole relationship.

Translating English to Math in Part-to-Whole Problems

On the GRE, many fractions and percents appear in word problems. You'll solve the problems by plugging the numbers you're given into some variation of one of the three basic formulas:

$$\frac{Part}{Whole} = Fraction$$

$$\frac{Part}{Whole} = Decimal$$

$$\frac{Part}{Whole}(100) = Percent$$

To avoid careless errors, look for the key words *is* and *of. Is* (or *are*) often introduces the part, while *of* almost invariably introduces the whole.

Properties of 100%

Since the percent sign means $\frac{1}{100}$, 100% means $\frac{100}{100}$, or one whole. The key to solving some GRE percent problems is to recognize that all the parts add up to one whole: 100%.

Example:

All 1,000 registered voters in Smithtown are Democrats, Republicans, or independents. If 75% of the registered voters are Democrats and 5% are independents, how many are Republicans?

We calculate that 75% + 5%, or 80%, of the 1,000 registered voters are either Democrats or independents. The three political affiliations together must account for 100% of the voters; thus, the percentage of Republicans must be 100% − 80%, or 20%. Therefore, the number of Republicans must be 20% of 1,000, which is 20%(1,000), or 200.

Multiplying or dividing a number by 100% is just like multiplying or dividing by 1; it doesn't change the value of the original number.

Converting Percents

To change a fraction to its percent equivalent, multiply by 100%.

Example:

What is the percent equivalent of $\frac{5}{8}$?

$$\frac{5}{8}(100\%) = \frac{500}{8}\% = 62\frac{1}{2}\%$$

To change a decimal fraction to a percent, you can use the rules for multiplying by powers of 10. Move the decimal point two places to the right and insert a percent sign.

Example:

What is the percent equivalent of 0.17?

$$0.17 = 0.17(100\%) = 17\%$$

To change a percent to its fractional equivalent, divide by 100%.

Example:

What is the common fraction equivalent of 32%?

$$32\% = \frac{32\%}{100\%} = \frac{8}{25}$$

To convert a percent to its decimal equivalent, use the rules for dividing by powers of 10—just move the decimal point two places to the left.

Example:

What is the decimal equivalent of 32%?

$$32\% = \frac{32\%}{100\%} = \frac{32}{100} = 0.32$$

When you divide a percent by another percent, the percent sign "drops out," just as you would cancel out a common factor.

Example:

$$\frac{100\%}{5\%} = \frac{100}{5} = 20$$

Translation: There are 20 groups of 5% in 100%.

But when you divide a percent by a regular number (not by another percent), the percent sign remains.

Example:

$$\frac{100\%}{5} = 20\%$$

Translation: One-fifth of 100% is 20%.

Common Percent Equivalents

As you can see, changing percents to fractions, or vice versa, is pretty straightforward. But it does take a second or two that you might spend more profitably doing other computations or setting up another GRE math problem. Familiarity with the following common equivalents will save you time.

$\frac{1}{20} = 5\%$ $\frac{1}{2} = 50\%$

$\frac{1}{12} = 8\frac{1}{3}\%$ $\frac{3}{5} = 60\%$

$\frac{1}{10} = 10\%$ $\frac{5}{8} = 62\frac{1}{2}\%$

$\frac{1}{8} = 12\frac{1}{2}\%$ $\frac{2}{3} = 66\frac{2}{3}\%$

$\frac{1}{6} = 16\frac{2}{3}\%$ $\frac{7}{10} = 70\%$

$\frac{1}{5} = 20\%$ $\frac{3}{4} = 75\%$

$\frac{1}{4} = 25\%$ $\frac{4}{5} = 80\%$

$\frac{3}{10} = 30\%$ $\frac{5}{6} = 83\frac{1}{3}\%$

$\frac{1}{3} = 33\frac{1}{3}\%$ $\frac{7}{8} = 87\frac{1}{2}\%$

$\frac{3}{8} = 37\frac{1}{2}\%$ $\frac{9}{10} = 90\%$

$\frac{2}{5} = 40\%$ $\frac{11}{12} = 91\frac{2}{3}\%$

Using the Percent Formula to Solve Percent Problems

You can solve most percent problems by plugging the given data into the percent formula:

$$\frac{\text{Part}}{\text{Whole}}(100\%) = \text{Percent}$$

Most percent problems give you two of the three variables and ask for the third.

Example:

Ben spends $30 of his annual gardening budget on seed. If his total annual gardening budget is $150, what percentage of his budget does he spend on seed?

This problem specifies the whole ($150) and the part ($30) and asks for the percentage. Plugging those numbers into the percent formula gives you this:

$$\text{Percent} = \frac{30}{150}(100\%) = \frac{1}{5}(100\%) = 20\%$$

Ben spends 20% of his annual gardening budget on seed.

Percent Increase and Decrease

When the GRE tests percent increase or decrease, use the correct formula:

$$\text{Percent increase} = \frac{\text{Increase}(100\%)}{\text{Original}}$$

or

$$\text{Percent decrease} = \frac{\text{Decrease}(100\%)}{\text{Original}}$$

To find the increase or decrease, just take the difference between the original and the new. Note that the "original" is the base from which change occurs. It may or may not be the first number mentioned in the problem.

Example:

Two years ago, 450 seniors graduated from Inman High School. Last year, 600 seniors graduated. By what percent did the number of graduating seniors increase?

The original is the figure from the earlier time (two years ago): 450. The increase is $600 - 450$, or 150. So the percent increase is $\frac{150}{450}(100\%) = 33\frac{1}{3}\%$.

Example:

If the price of a $120 dress is increased by 25%, what is the new selling price?

To find the new whole, you'll first have to find the amount of increase. The original whole is $120, and the percent increase is 25%. By plugging in, we find that:

$$\frac{\text{Increase}}{120}(100\%) = 25\%$$

$$\frac{\text{Increase}}{120} = \frac{25}{100}$$

$$\frac{\text{Increase}}{120} = \frac{1}{4}$$

$$\text{Increase} = \frac{120}{4}$$

$$\text{Increase} = 30$$

The amount of increase is $30, so the new selling price is $120 + $30, or $150.

Multistep Percent Problems

On some difficult problems, you'll be asked to find more than one percent or to find a percent of a percent. Be careful: you can't add percents of different wholes.

Example:

The price of an antique is reduced by 20%, and then this price is reduced by 10%. If the antique originally cost $200, what is its final price?

The most common mistake in this kind of problem is to reduce the original price by a total of 20% + 10%, or 30%. That would make the final price 70% of the original, or 70%($200) = $140. This is not the correct answer. In this example, the second (10%) price reduction is taken off of the first sale price—the new whole, not the original whole.

To get the correct answer, first find the new whole. You can find it by calculating either $200 − (20% of $200) or 80%($200). Either way, you will find that the first sale price is $160. That price then has to be reduced by 10%. Either calculate $160 − (10%($160)) or 90%($160). In either case, the final price of the antique is $144.

Picking Numbers with Percents

Certain types of percent problems lend themselves readily to the alternative technique of Picking Numbers. These include problems in which no actual values are mentioned, just percents. If you assign values to the percents you are working with, you'll find the problem less abstract.

You should almost always pick 100 in percent problems, because it's relatively easy to find percentages of 100.

Example:

The price of a share of company A's stock fell by 20% two weeks ago and by another 25% last week to its current price. By what percent of the current price does the share price need to rise in order to return to its original price?

(A) 45%

(B) 55%

(C) $66\frac{2}{3}$%

(D) 75%

(E) 82%

Pick a value for the original price of the stock. Since this is a percent question, picking $100 will make the math easy. The first change in the price of the stock was by 20% of $100, or $20, making the new price $100 − $20 = $80.

The price then fell by another 25%. You know that 25% is the same as $\frac{1}{4}$, and $\frac{1}{4}$ of $80 is $20. Therefore, the current price is $80 − $20 = $60. To return to its original price, the stock needs to rise from $60 to $100, that is, by $100 − $60 = $40. Then $40 is what percent of the current price, $60?

$$\frac{40}{60}(100\%) = \frac{2}{3}(100\%) = 66\frac{2}{3}\%$$

Percent Word Problems

Percent problems are often presented as word problems. We have already seen how to identify the percent, the part, and the whole in percent word problems. Other terms that you might encounter in more complicated percent word problems include those listed below.

Profit made on an item is the seller's price minus the cost to the seller. If a seller buys an item for $10 and sells it for $12, he has made $2 profit. The percent of the selling price that is profit is as follows:

$$\frac{\text{Profit}}{\text{Original selling price}}(100\%) = \frac{\$2}{\$12}(100\%) = 16\frac{2}{3}\%$$

A *discount* on an item is the original price minus the reduced price. If an item that usually sells for $20 is sold for $15, the discount is $5. A discount is often represented as a percentage of the original price. In this case:

$$\text{Percent discount} = \frac{\text{Discount}}{\text{Original price}}(100\%) = \frac{\$5}{\$20} = 25\%$$

The *sale price* is the final price after discount or decrease.

Occasionally, percent problems will involve *interest*. Interest is given as a percent per unit of time, such as 5% per month. The sum of money invested is the *principal*. The most common type of interest you will see is *simple interest*. In simple interest, the interest payments received are kept separate from the principal.

Example:

If an investor invests $100 at 20% simple annual interest, how much does she have at the end of three years?

The principal of $100 yields 20% interest every year. Because 20% of $100 is $20, after three years the investor will have three years of interest, or $60, plus the principal, for a total of $160.

In *compound interest*, the money earned as interest is reinvested. The principal grows after every interest payment received.

Example:

If an investor invests $100 at 20% compounded annually, how much does he have at the end of 3 years?

The first year the investor earns 20% of $100 = $20. So, after one year, he has $100 + $20 = $120.

The second year the investor earns 20% of $120 = $24. So, after two years, he has $120 + $24 = $144.

The third year the investor earns 20% of $144 = $28.80. So, after three years, he has $144 + $28.80 = $172.80.

Ratios

A *ratio* is the proportional relationship between two quantities. The ratio, or relationship, between two numbers (for example, 2 and 3) may be expressed with a colon between the two numbers (2:3), in words ("the ratio of 2 to 3"), or as a fraction $\frac{2}{3}$.

To translate a ratio in words to numbers separated by a colon, replace *to* with a colon.

To translate a ratio in words to a fractional ratio, use whatever follows the word *of* as the numerator and whatever follows the word *to* as the denominator. For example, if we had to express the ratio *of* glazed doughnuts *to* chocolate doughnuts in a box of doughnuts that contained 5 glazed and 7 chocolate doughnuts, we would do so as $\frac{5}{7}$.

Note that the fraction $\frac{5}{7}$ does not mean that $\frac{5}{7}$ of all the doughnuts are glazed doughnuts. There are 5 + 7, or 12 doughnuts altogether, so of the doughnuts, $\frac{5}{12}$ are glazed. The $\frac{5}{7}$ ratio merely indicates the proportion of glazed to chocolate doughnuts. For every five glazed doughnuts, there are seven chocolate doughnuts.

Treating ratios as fractions can make computation easier. Like fractions, ratios often require division. And, like fractions, ratios ultimately should be reduced to lowest terms.

Example:

Joe is 16 years old and Mary is 12 years old. Express the ratio of Joe's age to Mary's age in lowest terms.

The ratio of Joe's age to Mary's age is $\frac{16}{12} = \frac{4}{3}$, or 4:3.

Part:Whole Ratios

In a part:whole ratio, the "whole" is the entire set (for instance, all the workers in a factory), while the "part" is a certain subset of the whole (for instance, all the female workers in the factory).

In GRE ratio question stems, the word *fraction* generally indicates a part:whole ratio. "What fraction of the workers are female?" means "What is the ratio of the number of female workers to the total number of workers?"

Example:

The sophomore class at Milford Academy consists of 15 boys and 20 girls. What fraction of the sophomore class is female?

The following three statements are equivalent:

1. $\frac{4}{7}$ of the sophomores are female.

2. Four out of every seven sophomores are female.

3. The ratio of female sophomores to total sophomores is 4:7.

Ratio vs. Actual Number

Ratios are usually reduced to their simplest form (that is, to lowest terms). If the ratio of men to women in a room is 5:3, you cannot necessarily infer that there are exactly five men and three women.

If you knew the total number of people in the room, in addition to the male-to-female ratio, you could determine the number of men and the number of women in the room. For example, suppose you are able to determine that there are 32 people in the room. If the male-to-female ratio is 5 to 3, then the ratio of males to the total is 5:(5 + 3), which is 5:8. You can set up an equation as $\frac{5}{8} = \frac{\text{\# of males in room}}{32}$. When solving, you will find that the number of males in the room is 20.

Example:

The ratio of domestic sales revenues to foreign sales revenues of a certain product is 3:5. What fraction of the total sales revenues comes from domestic sales?

At first, this question may look more complicated than the previous example. You have to convert from a part:part ratio to a part:whole ratio (the ratio of domestic sales revenues to total sales revenues). And you're not given actual dollar figures for domestic or foreign sales. But since all sales are either foreign or domestic, "total sales revenues" must be the sum of the revenues from domestic and foreign sales. You can convert the given ratio to a part:whole ratio because the sum of the parts equals the whole.

Although it's impossible to determine dollar amounts for the domestic, foreign, or total sales revenues from the given information, the 3:5 ratio tells you that of every $8 in sales revenues, $3 comes from domestic sales and $5 from foreign sales. Therefore, the ratio of domestic sales revenues to total sales revenues is 3:8, or $\frac{3}{8}$.

You can convert a part:part ratio to a part:whole ratio (or vice versa) only if there are no missing parts and no overlap among the parts—that is, if the whole is equal to the sum of the parts.

Example:

In a certain bag, the ratio of the number of red marbles to the number of blue marbles is 3:5. If there are only red and blue marbles in the bag, what is the ratio of the number of red marbles to the total number of marbles?

In this case, you can convert a part-to-part ratio (red marbles to blue marbles) to a part-to-whole ratio (red marbles to all marbles) because you know there are only red and blue marbles in the bag. The ratio of red marbles to the total number of marbles is 3:8.

Example:

Of the 25 people in Fran's apartment building, there are 9 residents who use the roof for tanning and 8 residents who use the roof for gardening. The roof is used only by tanners and gardeners.

QUANTITY A	QUANTITY B
The ratio of people who use the roof to total residents	17:25

In this question, we do not know if there is any overlap between tanners and gardeners. How many, if any, residents do both activities? Since we don't know, the relationship cannot be determined from the information given.

Ratios of More Than Two Terms

Most of the ratios that you'll see on the GRE have two terms. But it is possible to set up ratios with more than two terms. These ratios express more relationships, and therefore convey more information, than do two-term ratios. However, most of the principles discussed so far with respect to two-term ratios are just as applicable to ratios of more than two terms.

Example:

The ratio of x to y is 5:4. The ratio of y to z is 1:2. What is the ratio of x to z?

We want the y's in the two ratios to equal each other, because then we can combine the $x{:}y$ ratio and the $y{:}z$ ratio to form the $x{:}y{:}z$ ratio that we need to answer this question. To make the y's equal, we can multiply the second ratio by 4. When we do so, we must perform the multiplication on both components of the ratio. Since a ratio is a constant proportion, it can be multiplied or divided by any number without losing its meaning, as long as the multiplication and division are applied to all the components of the ratio. In this case, we find that the new ratio for y to z is 4:8. We can combine this with the first ratio to find a new x to y to z ratio of 5:4:8. Therefore, the ratio of x to z is 5:8.

Math Formulas

Rates

A *rate* is a special type of ratio. Instead of relating a part to the whole or to another part, a rate relates one kind of quantity to a completely different kind. When we talk about rates, we usually use the word *per*, as in "miles per hour," "cost per item," etc. Since *per* means "for one" or "for each," we express the rates as ratios reduced to a denominator of 1.

Speed

The most commonly tested rate on the GRE is speed. This is usually expressed in miles or kilometers per hour. The relationship between speed, distance, and time is given by the formula $\text{Speed} = \dfrac{\text{Distance}}{\text{Time}}$, which can be rewritten two ways: $\text{Time} = \dfrac{\text{Distance}}{\text{Speed}}$ and $\text{Distance} = (\text{Speed})(\text{Time})$.

Anytime you can find two out of the three elements in this equation, you can find the third. For example, if a car travels 300 miles in 5 hours, it has averaged $\dfrac{300\,\text{miles}}{5\,\text{hours}} = 60$ miles per hour. (Note that speeds are usually expressed as averages because they are not necessarily constant. In this example, the car moved at an "average speed" of 60 miles per hour but probably not at a constant speed of 60 miles per hour.)

Likewise, a rearranged version of the formula can be used to solve for missing speed or time.

Example:

How far do you drive if you travel for 5 hours at 60 miles per hour?

$$\text{Distance} = (\text{Speed})(\text{Time})$$
$$\text{Distance} = (60\,\text{mph})(5\,\text{hours})$$
$$\text{Distance} = 300\,\text{miles}$$

Example:

How much time does it take to drive 300 miles at 60 miles per hour?

$$\text{Time} = \frac{\text{Distance}}{\text{Speed}}$$
$$\text{Time} = \frac{300\,\text{miles}}{60\,\text{mph}}$$
$$\text{Time} = 5\,\text{hours}$$

Other Rates

Speed is not the only rate that appears on the GRE. For instance, you might get a word problem involving liters per minute or cost per unit. All rate problems, however, can be solved using the speed formula and its variants by conceiving of "speed" as "rate" and "distance" as "quantity."

Example:

How many hours will it take to fill a 500-liter tank at a rate of 2 liters per minute?

Plug the numbers into our rate formula:

$$\text{Time} = \frac{\text{Quantity}}{\text{Rate}}$$
$$\text{Time} = \frac{500\ \text{liters}}{2\ \text{liters per minute}}$$
$$\text{Time} = 250\ \text{minutes}$$

Now convert 250 minutes to hours: 250 minutes ÷ 60 minutes per hour = $4\frac{1}{6}$ hours to fill the tank. (As you can see from this problem, GRE Problem Solving questions test your ability to convert minutes into hours and vice versa. Pay close attention to what units the answer choice must use.)

In some cases, you should use proportions to answer rate questions.

Example:

If 350 widgets cost $20, how much will 1,400 widgets cost at the same rate?

Set up a proportion:

$$\frac{\text{Number of widgets}}{\text{Cost}} = \frac{350 \text{ widgets}}{\$20} = \frac{1,400 \text{ widgets}}{\$x}$$

Isolate the variable to determine that $x = 80$.

So, 1,400 widgets will cost $80 at that rate.

Combined Rate Problems

Rates can be added.

Example:

Nelson can mow 200 square meters of lawn per hour. John can mow 100 square meters of lawn per hour. If Nelson and John work simultaneously but independently, how many hours will it take them to mow 1,800 square meters of lawn?

Add Nelson's rate to John's rate to find the combined rate.

200 m^2 per hour + 100 m^2 per hour = 300 m^2 per hour.

Divide the total lawn area, 1,800 square meters, by the combined rate, 300 square meters per hour, to find the number of required hours, 6.

Combined Work Formula

Proportions can be used to find out how long it takes a number of people (or machines) working together to complete a task. Let's say we have three people. The first takes a units of time to complete the job. In other words, this person's rate of work is 1 job per a units of time, or $\frac{1}{a}$. The second person takes b units of time to complete the job, and the third c units of time. You can add their rates to find the rate at which they complete the job when they work together. Thus, $\frac{1}{a} + \frac{1}{b} + \frac{1}{c} = \frac{1}{T}$, where T is the time it takes all three people to do the job.

Example:

John can weed the garden in 3 hours. If Mark can weed the garden in 2 hours, how long will it take them to weed the garden at this rate, working independently?

Referring to the formula above, call John's time per unit of work a and Mark's time per unit of work b. (There is no need for the variable c, since there are only two people.) By plugging in, you find that

$$\frac{1}{3} + \frac{1}{2} = \frac{1}{T}$$

$$\frac{2}{6} + \frac{3}{6} = \frac{1}{T}$$

$$\frac{5}{6} = \frac{1}{T}$$

$$T = \frac{6}{5} \text{ hours}$$

Many students prefer to memorize the following combined work formula, derived from the formula above, for situations in which two people are working together. As above, T is the total amount of time it takes the two people working together to do the job, a is the time it would take one working alone to complete the task, and b the time for the other working alone to complete the task.

$$T = \frac{ab}{a + b}$$

This formula is especially handy when the question gives you the times it would take each person to do the job and those times are easy numbers to work with. Let's take another look at the above example.

Example:

John takes 3 hours to weed the garden, and Mark takes 2 hours to weed the same garden. How long will it take them to weed the garden together?

$$T = \frac{ab}{a + b} = \frac{3 \times 2}{3 + 2} = \frac{6}{5} \text{ hours}$$

If there are three entities doing a job together and you are given the times it would take each to do the job alone, you can use an extension of the above formula for this situation.

$$T = \frac{abc}{ab + bc + ac}$$

However, this formula involves so many calculations that adding the rates—using the $\frac{1}{a} + \frac{1}{b} + \frac{1}{c} = \frac{1}{T}$ formula—is often more efficient.

Example:

Our gardeners have decided they are tired of weeding and have purchased three robots that are advertised as being good at gardening. Unfortunately, the robots malfunction a lot. Robot A takes 4 hours, robot B takes 6 hours, and robot C takes 10 hours to weed the garden. How long will it take these robots to weed the garden together?

Solving by adding the rates:

$$\frac{1}{T} = \frac{1}{4} + \frac{1}{6} + \frac{1}{10} = \frac{30}{120} + \frac{20}{120} + \frac{12}{120} = \frac{62}{120} = \frac{31}{60}$$

$$T = \frac{60}{31} \text{ hours}$$

Solving by using the formula:

$$T = \frac{a \times b \times c}{ab + ac + bc} = \frac{4 \times 6 \times 10}{4 \times 6 + 4 \times 10 + 6 \times 10} = \frac{240}{24 + 40 + 60} = \frac{240}{124} = \frac{60}{31} \text{hours}$$

Whichever way you calculate it, the three robots take just under 2 hours to weed the garden. John and Mark could have done the job faster themselves.

Be familiar with both arrangements of the combined work formula so you can efficiently solve any question, whether the rates or the times are easier to work with.

Averages

The *average* of a group of numbers is defined as the sum of the terms divided by the number of terms.

$$\text{Average} = \frac{\text{Sum of terms}}{\text{Number of terms}}$$

This equation can be rewritten two ways:

$$\text{Number of terms} = \frac{\text{Sum of terms}}{\text{Average}}$$

$$\text{Sum of terms} = (\text{Number of terms})(\text{Average})$$

Thus, any time you have two out of the three values (average, sum of terms, number of terms), you can find the third.

Example:

Henry buys three items costing $2.00, $1.75, and $1.05. What is the average price (arithmetic mean) of the three items? (Don't let the phrase *arithmetic mean* throw you; it's just another term for *average*.)

$$\text{Average} = \frac{\text{Sum of terms}}{\text{Number of terms}}$$

$$\text{Average} = \frac{\$2.00 + \$1.75 + \$1.05}{3}$$

$$\text{Average} = \frac{\$4.80}{3}$$

$$\text{Average} = \$1.60$$

Example:

June pays an average price of $14.50 for 6 articles of clothing. What is the total price of all 6 articles?

$$\text{Sum of terms} = (\text{Average})(\text{Number of terms})$$

$$\text{Sum of terms} = (\$14.50)(6)$$

$$\text{Sum of terms} = \$87.00$$

Example:

The total weight of the licorice sticks in a jar is 30 ounces. If the average weight of each licorice stick is 2 ounces, how many licorice sticks are there in the jar?

$$\text{Number of terms} = \frac{\text{Sum of terms}}{\text{Average}}$$

$$\text{Number of terms} = \frac{30 \text{ ounces}}{2 \text{ ounces}}$$

$$\text{Number of terms} = 15$$

Using the Average to Find a Missing Number

If you're given the average, the total number of terms, and all but one of the actual numbers, you can find the missing number.

Example:

The average annual rainfall in Boynton for 1976–1979 was 26 inches per year. Boynton received 24 inches of rain in 1976, 30 inches in 1977, and 19 inches in 1978. How many inches of rainfall did Boynton receive in 1979?

You know that total rainfall equals 24 + 30 + 19 + (number of inches of rain in 1979).

You know that the average rainfall was 26 inches per year.

You know that there were 4 years.

So, plug these numbers into any of the three expressions of the average formula to find that Sum of terms = (Average)(Number of terms):

$$24 + 30 + 19 + \text{inches in } 1979 = (26)(4)$$
$$73 + \text{inches in } 1979 = (26)(4)$$
$$73 + \text{inches in } 1979 = 104$$
$$\text{inches in } 1979 = 31$$

Another Way to Find a Missing Number: The Concept of "Balanced Value"

Another way to find a missing number is to understand that the *sum of the differences between each term and the mean of the set must equal zero*. Plugging in the numbers from the previous problem, for example, we find:

$$(24 - 26) + (30 - 26) + (19 - 26) + (\text{inches in } 1979 - 26) = 0$$
$$(-2) + (4) + (-7) + (\text{inches in } 1979 - 26) = 0$$
$$-5 + (\text{inches in } 1979 - 26) = 0$$
$$\text{inches in } 1979 = 31$$

It may be easier to comprehend why this is true by visualizing a balancing, or weighting, process. The combined distance of the numbers above the average from the mean must be balanced with the combined distance of the numbers below the average from the mean.

Example:

The average of 63, 64, 85, and x is 80. What is the value of x?

Think of each value in terms of its position relative to the average, 80.

63 is 17 less than 80.

64 is 16 less than 80.

85 is 5 greater than 80.

So these three terms are a total of $17 + 16 - 5$, or 28, less than the average. Therefore, x must be 28 greater than the average to restore the balance at 80. So $x = 28 + 80 = 108$.

Average of Consecutive, Evenly Spaced Numbers

When consecutive numbers are evenly spaced, the average is the middle value. For example, the average of consecutive integers 6, 7, and 8 is 7.

If there is an even number of evenly spaced numbers, there is no single middle value. In that case, the average is midway between (that is, the average of) the middle two values. For example, the average of 5, 10, 15, and 20 is 12.5, midway between the middle values 10 and 15.

Note that not all consecutive numbers are evenly spaced. For instance, consecutive prime numbers arranged in increasing order are not evenly spaced. But you can use the handy technique of finding the middle value whenever you have consecutive integers, consecutive odd or even numbers, consecutive multiples of an integer, or any other consecutive numbers that are evenly spaced.

Combining Averages

When there is an equal number of terms in each set, and *only when there is an equal number of terms in each set*, you can average averages.

For example, suppose there are two bowlers and you must find their average score per game. One has an average score per game of 100, and the other has an average score per game of 200. If both bowlers bowled the same number of games, you can average their averages to find their combined average. Suppose they both bowled 4 games. Their combined average will be equally influenced by both bowlers. Hence, their combined average will be the average of 100 and 200. You can find this quickly by remembering that the quantity above the average and the quantity below the average must be equal. Therefore, the average will be halfway between 100 and 200, which is 150. Or, we could solve using our average formula:

$$\text{Average} = \frac{\text{Sum of terms}}{\text{Number of terms}} = \frac{4(100) + 4(200)}{8} = 150$$

However, if the bowler with the average score of 100 had bowled 4 games and the bowler with the 200 average had bowled 16 games, the combined average would be weighted further toward 200 than toward 100 to reflect the greater influence of the 200 bowler than the 100 bowler upon the total. This is known as a *weighted average*.

Again, you can solve this by using the concept of a balanced average or by using the average formula.

Since the bowler bowling an average score of 200 bowled $\frac{4}{5}$ of the games, the combined average will be $\frac{4}{5}$ of the distance along the number line between 100 and 200, which is 180. Or, you can plug numbers into an average formula to find the following:

$$\text{Average} = \frac{\text{Sum of terms}}{\text{Number of terms}}$$
$$\text{Average} = \frac{4(100) + 16(200)}{20}$$
$$\text{Average} = \frac{400 + 3{,}200}{20}$$
$$\text{Average} = 180$$

Example:

A teacher surprised her students with a 5-question pop quiz. 10% of the students answered no questions correctly, 20% had 2 right answers, 30% answered 3 questions correctly, 30% had 4 right answers, and 10% had a perfect score. What was the weighted average of the number of correct answers?

$$\text{Weighted Avg} = \frac{0.1(0) + 0.2(2) + 0.3(3) + 0.3(4) + 0.1(5)}{0.1 + 0.2 + 0.3 + 0.3 + 0.1}$$
$$= \frac{0.0 + 0.4 + 0.9 + 1.2 + 0.5}{1} = 3.0$$

RATIOS AND MATH FORMULAS CONCEPT CHECK

Before you move on, check your understanding of ratios and math formulas on the GRE by considering a few questions:

- What is $\frac{2}{7} \div \frac{8}{9}$?
- Which is larger, $\frac{37}{64}$ or $\frac{37}{65}$?
- Do you know the commonly tested formulas on the GRE, including: the percent change formula, the formula to determine speed, the combined work formula, and the average formula?

- If there are 4 apples and 5 pears in a bowl, what is the ratio of apples to total pieces of fruit?

If you feel confident in your ability to tackle questions that deal with these concepts, proceed to the practice set that starts on the next page.

If you feel like you would like some additional guided practice, head to your online resources. Under **Math Foundations**, click **Ratios and Math Formulas Guided Practice**. Try each question on your own first. Then watch a video explanation in which a Kaplan GRE instructor describes a strategic approach.

Ratios and Math Formulas Practice Set

Directions: Try answering these questions to practice what you have learned about ratios and math formulas. Answers and explanations follow at the end of the chapter.

Basic

1. $\dfrac{1}{3} + \dfrac{3}{5} + \dfrac{1}{2} - \dfrac{13}{15} = ?$

2. If $-1 < x < 1$, but x is not 0, which has the greater value, $|x^4|$ or $|x^5|$?

3. The ratio of red to blue to black pens in a box is 3:5:7. If all 75 pens in the box are one of these colors, how many are red?

4. 17 is what percent of 85?

5. What is the value of $\dfrac{\dfrac{1}{4} \times \dfrac{6}{11}}{\dfrac{3}{7}}$?

Intermediate

6. If the average of 6, 3, −2, 5, 11, and x is 5, what is the value of x?

7. Abdul recently made a 200-mile trip. For the first 30 miles, he traveled at an average speed of 45 miles per hour. His average speed for the next 50 miles was 60 mph. Abdul averaged 50 mph for the final portion of his trip. How long did it take Abdul to complete his journey?

8. A certain brand and style of shoe was priced at $120. The store owner was concerned that this shoe was not selling well enough, so she decided to mark the list price down by 15%. Sales of the shoe only increased slightly, so the owner offered an additional 10% discount from the sale price at checkout. Sales tax of 8% is added to all purchases. What would a customer have to pay for the shoes with tax added?

9. Jennifer and Boris are graduate assistants helping a professor grade student tests. When working together, they are able to complete the task in 1 hour and 12 minutes. If Jennifer could have graded the entire batch of tests by herself in 2 hours, how long would it have taken Boris to complete that task by himself?

10. What is the value of $\dfrac{0.003 \times 2.4 \times 10^4}{0.09 \times 4 \times 10^{-2}}$?

Advanced

11. The ratio of x to y is 1:4. If the value of x were increased by 1 without changing the value of y, the ratio of x to y would become 1:3. If $z = x + 2y$, what is the value of z?

12. When working together, Kendra, Latasha, and Melanie can complete a certain task in 4 hours. If Kendra alone could complete the task in 8 hours and Latasha could complete the task in half the time it would take Melanie, how long would it take Latasha to complete the task by herself?

13. In a bag of coins, $\frac{2}{5}$ are pennies, $\frac{1}{3}$ are nickels, $\frac{1}{4}$ are dimes, and there are 5 quarters. If there are no other coins in the bag, what is the total number of coins?

14. If $A{:}B$ is 3:7, $C{:}D$ is 15:11, and $B{:}C$ is 14:5, what is $A{:}D$?

15. Jack drives a car that was manufactured in Europe, so the fuel economy readout on his dashboard is stated in L/km. If the value shown is 0.095, what is the fuel consumption rate stated in the American convention of miles per gallon? (Note: 5 miles $\approx$ 8 km and 1 gal $\approx$ 3.8 L.)

Ratios and Math Formulas Practice Set Answer Key

1. $\dfrac{17}{30}$

2. $|x^4|$

3. 15

4. 20%

5. $\dfrac{7}{22}$

6. 7

7. 3 hours and 54 minutes

8. $99.14

9. 3 hours

10. 20,000

11. 27

12. 12 hours

13. 300

14. 18:11

15. 25 mpg

Ratios and Math Formulas Practice Set Answers and Explanations

Basic

1. $\dfrac{17}{30}$

In order to add or subtract fractions, first convert them so that they have a common denominator. The denominators in this question (3, 5, 2, and 15) are all factors of 30, so multiply the numerator and denominator of each fraction by the number that will result in a denominator of 30:

$$\frac{10}{10}\left(\frac{1}{3}\right) + \frac{6}{6}\left(\frac{3}{5}\right) + \frac{15}{15}\left(\frac{1}{2}\right) - \frac{2}{2}\left(\frac{13}{15}\right) = \frac{10}{30} + \frac{18}{30} + \frac{15}{30} - \frac{26}{30}.$$

Now add all the numerators: $\dfrac{10 + 18 + 15 - 26}{30} = \dfrac{17}{30}$.

2. $|x^4|$

If x is between -1 and 1, it will be a fraction. As positive proper fractions are raised to greater powers, they become smaller and smaller. Negative fractions raised to an even power are positive and raised to an odd power are negative. However, in either case, their absolute value continues to decrease as the exponent gets greater. Since this question asks about absolute values, it does not matter whether the fraction is negative or positive. Because 4 is less than 5, $|x^4| > |x^5|$.

3. 15

Convert the part-to-part ratio to the part-to-whole ratio for red pens: $\dfrac{3}{3 + 5 + 7} = \dfrac{3}{15} = \dfrac{1}{5}$. Set up the proportion $\dfrac{R}{75} = \dfrac{1}{5}$, and cross multiply to get $5R = 75$ and $R = 15$.

4. 20%

Set up the proportion $\dfrac{17}{85} = \dfrac{x}{100}$. Cross multiply to get $1{,}700 = 85x$. Divide both sides by 85 to find that $x = 20$.

5. $\dfrac{7}{22}$

First, multiply the two fractions in the numerator by multiplying the two numerators and the two denominators to get $\dfrac{\frac{6}{44}}{\frac{3}{7}}$ which reduces to $\dfrac{\frac{3}{22}}{\frac{3}{7}}$. Invert the fraction in the denominator and multiply: $\dfrac{3}{22} \times \dfrac{7}{3} = \dfrac{7}{22}$.

Intermediate

6. 7

The formula for computing averages is $\text{Average} = \dfrac{\text{Sum of values}}{\text{Number of values}}$. Rearrange this to Sum of values = Number of values × Average. Including x, there are 6 values, so $6 + 3 - 2 + 5 + 11 + x = 6 \times 5$. Thus, $23 + x = 30$ and $x = 7$.

Another way to handle this question is with the balance approach. The average is 5, so the known numbers above this are 6 and 11. These are 1 and 6 above the average, respectively. The known values below are 3 and -2, which are 2 and 7 below the average, respectively. Without x, then, the values are $1 + 6 - 2 - 7 = -2$, which means 2 below the average overall. Thus, x must be 2 *above* the average in order to balance, making x equal to $5 + 2 = 7$.

7. 3 hours and 54 minutes

Use the Time-Speed-Distance formula in the format $T = \frac{D}{S}$ to determine the time for each leg of Abdul's trip. For the first part, $T = \frac{30}{45} = \frac{2}{3}$. For the second leg, $T = \frac{50}{60} = \frac{5}{6}$. The distance for the third part of the trip is not given, but it can be calculated by subtracting the two known distances from the total: $D_3 = 200 - 30 - 50 = 120$. Apply the equation for time: $T = \frac{120}{50} = 2\frac{2}{5}$. Rather than trying to work with a common denominator to add the times, convert to minutes: $\frac{2}{3}(60) + \frac{5}{6}(60) + 2\frac{2}{5}(60) = 40 + 50 + 144 = 234$. Divide 234 minutes by 60 minutes in an hour to get 3 hours with 54 minutes remaining.

8. $99.14

The first discount is 15%. Since 15% of $120 is $18, this markdown reduces the price to $102. The second discount is applied to the *reduced* price: 10% of $102 is $10.20, so the price, before tax, would be $102 − $10.20 = $91.80. The 8% tax on that amount is $7.344, so the final price would be $91.80 + $7.34 = $99.14, since a customer would not pay a fraction of a cent. (Note: If you did not want to open the calculator for the final calculation, you could use the distributive property to calculate the tax: 8% of $91.80 is $.08(90 + 1 + 0.8) = 7.2 + .08 +.064$, which rounds to $7.34.)

9. 3 hours

The simplified formula for combined work is $T = \frac{AB}{A + B}$. This question provides values for T and the time to complete the task for one worker. Convert the total time to 72 minutes and Jennifer's solo time to 120 minutes and plug these values into the equation: $72 = \frac{120B}{120 + B}$. Cross multiply: $72(120+B) = 120B$. Distribute the multiplication: $72(120) + 72B = 120B$. Group the terms with the variable: $72(120) = 120B - 72B = 48B$. Divide both sides by 24 to get $3(120) = 2B$, so $B = 3(60)$ minutes, which is 3 hours.

10. 20,000

Multiply the values in the numerator and in the denominator, paying close attention to the decimal placement. To multiply 0.003×10^4, move the decimal point 4 places to the right, which requires adding a zero. The numerator becomes $30 \times 2.4 = 72$. After multiplying the first terms, the denominator is 0.36×10^{-2}. To simplify the division, convert this to 36×10^{-4}. A negative exponent in a denominator is equivalent to the same positive exponent in the numerator, so the expression simplifies to $\frac{72 \times 10^4}{36} = 2 \times 10^4 = 20{,}000$.

Advanced

11. 27

Restate the ratios as fractions: initially $\frac{x}{y} = \frac{1}{4}$, so $y = 4x$. If x were increased by 1, the new ratio would be $\frac{x+1}{y} = \frac{1}{3}$. Cross multiply to get $y = 3x + 3$. Set the two values of y equal to each other: $4x = 3x + 3$, which simplifies to $x = 3$. Since $y = 4x$, $y = 4(3) = 12$. Because the question states the increase of x as a hypothetical statement, use the *initial* value for x to calculate z: $3 + 2(12) = 27$.

12. 12 hours

Since there are 3 workers in this question, use the formula for adding rates of multiple workers: $\frac{1}{T} = \frac{1}{K} + \frac{1}{L} + \frac{1}{M}$. The question states that the three women could compete the task together in 4 hours, and it provides the information that $K = 8$. It then states that Latasha can complete the task in half the time that Melanie can. Set $M = 2L$ and plug the values into the equation to get $\frac{1}{4} = \frac{1}{8} + \frac{1}{L} + \frac{1}{2L}$. Multiply each term by the least common multiple of the denominators, $8L$, to clear the fractions: $8L\left(\frac{1}{4}\right) = 8L\left(\frac{1}{8}\right) + 8L\left(\frac{1}{L}\right) + 8L\left(\frac{1}{2L}\right)$. This simplifies to $2L = L + 8 + 4$, so $L = 12$.

13. 300

Since there will not be any partial coins, the number of coins in the bag must be divisible by 5, 3, and 4. The least common multiple (LCM) of those numbers is $3 \times 4 \times 5 = 60$. If there were 60 coins in the bag, there would be $\frac{2}{5}(60) = 24$ pennies, $\frac{1}{3}(60) = 20$ nickels, and $\frac{1}{4}(60) = 15$ dimes. The total number of coins other than quarters is $24 + 20 + 15 = 59$ coins, so there could only be 1 quarter. The question specifies that there are 5 quarters, so there must be $5 \times 60 = 300$ coins.

The question could also be approached using algebra, by setting up the equation $C = \frac{2}{5}C + \frac{1}{3}C + \frac{1}{4}C + 5$, where C represents the total number of coins. Multiply through by the LCM of 60 to get $60C = 24C + 20C + 15C + 300$. Combine like terms: $60C = 59C + 300$, so $C = 300$.

14. 18:11

To facilitate computations, ratios should be stated in fraction format, so write $\frac{A}{B} = \frac{3}{7}$, $\frac{C}{D} = \frac{15}{11}$, and $\frac{B}{C} = \frac{14}{5}$.

Now solve by manipulating the ratios so that they share a numerator or denominator. Multiply both parts of $A{:}B$ by 2 to get $\frac{A}{B} = \frac{6}{14}$. Flip the ratio $B{:}C$ so that $\frac{C}{B} = \frac{5}{14}$. Since both fractions have the same denominator, A and C can be compared directly, and the ratio of A to C $\left(\frac{A}{C}\right)$ is $\frac{6}{5}$. Next, convert this to $\frac{18}{15}$. Flip the ratio $C{:}D$ to get $\frac{D}{C} = \frac{11}{15}$. Again, since the denominators are equal, $\frac{A}{D} = \frac{18}{11}$.

Alternatively, "chain" the ratios to find the answer. Looking at just the variables rather than the numbers, note that $\frac{A}{B} \times \frac{B}{C} \times \frac{C}{D} = \frac{A}{D}$ because the Bs and Cs cancel out. Plug the values of the variables into this equation:

$$\frac{3}{7} \times \frac{14}{5} \times \frac{15}{11} = \frac{3}{1} \times \frac{2}{1} \times \frac{3}{11} = \frac{18}{11}$$

15. 25 mpg

Make the necessary conversions step-by-step. One way to start is by converting km to miles:

$\frac{0.095 \text{ L}}{1 \text{ km}} \times \frac{8 \text{ km}}{5 \text{ mi}} = \frac{(0.095 \times 8) \text{ L}}{5 \text{ mi}}$. (Don't worry about carrying through all the calculations along the way; wait to see if something cancels out later.) Now convert this rate to gallons/mile:

$\frac{(0.095 \times 8) \text{ L}}{5 \text{ mi}} \times \frac{1 \text{ gal}}{3.8 \text{ L}} = \frac{1 \text{ gal}}{5 \text{ mi}} \times \frac{(0.095 \times 8)}{3.8}$. If you notice that 3.8 is 40×0.095, you could simplify this fraction to $\frac{8 \text{ gal}}{5 \times 40 \text{ mi}} = \frac{8 \text{ gal}}{200 \text{ mi}}$. The question asks for the rate in miles per gallon, so invert this rate to get $\frac{200 \text{ mi}}{8 \text{ gal}} = 25$ mpg. If you use the calculator, the result is 0.04 gal/mi. Invert that by calculating $1 \div 0.04 = 100 \div 4 = 25$ mpg.

CHAPTER 12

MATH FOUNDATIONS—ALGEBRA REVIEW

Introduction to Algebra Review

GRE questions often involve variables, or letters that stand for unknown values. To score well, therefore, you will need to be comfortable performing operations on terms with variables in them. Also, being able to translate information in word problems into math will be an important skill so you can solve for unknown values. The following topics are important to your success:

- Algebra:
  - Algebraic terms
  - Basic operations
  - Advanced operations
  - Polynomials and quadratics
  - Alternative strategies for multiple-choice algebra
- Dealing with word problems
- Dealing with logic problems

These topics are explained in the following pages along with examples. A practice set at the end of the chapter gives you an opportunity to practice using these concepts.

Algebraic Terms

You'll encounter the following terminology in your study of algebra and in questions on the GRE.

Variable: A letter or symbol representing an unknown quantity.

Constant (term): A number not multiplied by any variable(s).

Term: A numerical constant; also, the product of a numerical constant and one or more variables.

Coefficient: The numerical constant by which one or more variables are multiplied. The coefficient of $3x^2$ is 3. A variable (or product of variables) without a numerical coefficient, such as z or xy^3, is understood to have a coefficient of 1.

Algebraic expression: An expression containing one or more variables, one or more constants, and possibly one or more operation symbols. In the case of the expression x, there is an implied coefficient of 1. An expression does not contain an equal or inequality sign. x, $3x^2 + 2x$, and $\dfrac{7x + 1}{3x^2 - 14}$ are all algebraic expressions.

Monomial: An algebraic expression with only one term. To multiply monomials, multiply the coefficients and the variables separately: $2a \times 3a = (2 \times 3)(a \times a) = 6a^2$.

Polynomial: The general name for an algebraic expression with more than one term. An algebraic expression with two terms is called a **binomial**.

Algebraic equation: Two algebraic expressions separated by an equal sign or one algebraic expression separated from a number by an equal sign.

Basic Operations

Combining Like Terms

The process of simplifying an expression by adding together or subtracting terms that have the same variable factors is called *combining like terms*.

> **Example:**
>
> Simplify the expression $2x - 5y - x + 7y$.
>
> $2x - 5y - x + 7y = (2x - x) + (7y - 5y) = x + 2y$

Notice that the commutative, associative, and distributive laws that govern arithmetic operations with ordinary numbers also apply to algebraic terms and polynomials.

Adding and Subtracting Polynomials

To add or subtract polynomials, combine like terms.

$$(3x^2 + 5x + 7) - (x^2 + 12) = (3x^2 - x^2) + 5x + (7 - 12) = 2x^2 + 5x - 5$$

Factoring Algebraic Expressions

Factoring a polynomial means expressing it as a product of two or more simpler expressions. Common factors can be factored out by using the distributive law.

> **Example:**
>
> Factor the expression $2a + 6ac$.
>
> The greatest common factor of $2a + 6ac$ is $2a$. Using the distributive law, you can factor out $2a$ so that the expression becomes $2a(1 + 3c)$.

Example:

All three terms in the polynomial $3x^3 + 12x^2 - 6x$ contain a factor of $3x$. Pulling out the common factor yields $3x(x^2 + 4x - 2)$.

Advanced Operations

Substitution

Substitution, a process of plugging values into equations, is used to evaluate an algebraic expression or to express it in terms of other variables.

Replace every variable in the expression with the number or quantity you are told is its equivalent. Then carry out the designated operations, remembering to follow the order of operations (PEMDAS).

Example:

Express $\dfrac{a - b^2}{b - a}$ in terms of x if $a = 2x$ and $b = 3$.

Replace every a with $2x$ and every b with 3:

$$\frac{a - b^2}{b - a} = \frac{2x - 9}{3 - 2x}$$

Without more information, you can't simplify or evaluate this expression further.

Solving Equations

When you manipulate any equation, *always do the same thing on both sides of the equal sign*. Otherwise, the two sides of the equation will no longer be equal.

To solve an algebraic equation without exponents for a particular variable, you have to manipulate the equation until that variable is on one side of the equal sign with all numbers or other variables on the other side. You can perform addition, subtraction, or multiplication; you can also perform division, as long as the quantity by which you are dividing does not equal zero.

Typically, at each step of the process, you'll try to isolate the variable by using the reverse of whatever operation has been applied to the variable. For example, in solving the equation $n + 6 = 10$ for n, you have to get rid of the 6 that has been added to the n. You do that by subtracting 6 from both sides of the equation: $n + 6 - 6 = 10 - 6$, so $n = 4$.

Example:

If $4x - 7 = 2x + 5$, what is the value of x?

Start by adding 7 to both sides. This gives us $4x = 2x + 12$. Now subtract $2x$ from both sides. This gives us $2x = 12$. Finally, let's divide both sides by 2. This gives us $x = 6$.

Inequalities

There are two differences between solving an *inequality* (such as $2x < 5$) and solving an *equation* (such as $2x - 5 = 0$).

First, the solution to an inequality is almost always a range of possible values, rather than a single value. You can see the range most clearly by expressing it visually on a number line.

The shaded portion of the number line above shows the set of all numbers between -4 and 0, excluding the endpoints -4 and 0; this range would be expressed algebraically by the inequality $-4 < x < 0$.

The shaded portion of the number line above shows the set of all numbers greater than -1, up to and including 3; this range would be expressed algebraically by the inequality $-1 < x \leq 3$.

The other difference when solving an inequality—and the only thing you really have to remember—is that *if you multiply or divide the inequality by a negative number, you have to reverse the direction of the inequality sign*. For example, when you multiply both sides of the inequality $-3x < 2$ by -1, you get $3x > -2$.

Example:

Solve for x: $3 - \frac{x}{4} \geq 2$.

Multiply both sides of the inequality by 4: $12 - x \geq 8$.

Subtract 12 from both sides: $-x \geq -4$.

Multiply (or divide) both sides by -1 and change the direction of the inequality sign: $x \leq 4$.

As you can see from the number line, the range of values that satisfies this inequality includes 4 and all numbers less than 4.

Solving for One Unknown in Terms of Another

In general, in order to solve for the value of an unknown, you need as many distinct equations as you have variables. If there are two variables, for instance, you need two distinct equations.

However, some GRE problems do not require you to solve for the numerical value of an unknown. Instead, you are asked to solve for one variable in terms of the other(s). To do so, isolate the desired variable on one side of the equation and move all the constants and other variables to the other side.

Example:

In the formula $z = \dfrac{xy}{a + yb}$, solve for y in terms of x, z, a, and b.

Clear the denominator by multiplying both sides by $a + yb$: $(a + yb)z = xy$.

Remove the parentheses by distributing z: $az + ybz = xy$.

Put all terms containing y on one side and all other terms on the other side: $az = xy - ybz$.

Factor out the common factor, y: $az = y(x - bz)$.

Divide by the coefficient of y to get y alone: $\dfrac{az}{x - bz} = y$.

Simultaneous Equations

We've already discovered that you need as many different equations as you have variables to solve for the actual value of a variable. When a single equation contains more than one variable, you can only solve for one variable in terms of the others.

This has important implications for Quantitative Comparison questions. To have enough information to compare the two quantities, you usually must have at least as many distinct equations as you have variables.

On the GRE, you will often have to solve two simultaneous equations, that is, equations that give you different information about the same two variables. There are two methods for solving simultaneous equations.

Method 1—Substitution

Step 1: Solve one equation for one variable in terms of the other variable.

Step 2: Substitute the result back into the other equation and solve.

Example:

If $x - 15 = 2y$ and $6y + 2x = -10$, what is the value of y?

Solve the first equation for x by adding 15 to both sides.

$x = 2y + 15$

Substitute $2y + 15$ for x in the second equation:

$$6y + 2(2y + 15) = -10$$
$$6y + 4y + 30 = -10$$
$$10y = -40$$
$$y = -4$$

Method 2—Combination

Combine the equations in such a way that one of the variables cancels out. To eliminate a variable, you can add the equations or subtract one equation from the other.

Example:

To solve for x in the two equations $4x + 3y = 8$ and $x + y = 3$, multiply both sides of the second equation by 3 to get $3x + 3y = 9$. Now subtract the second equation from the first.

$$4x + 3y = 8$$
$$\underline{(3x + 3y = 9)}$$
$$x = -1$$

Before you use either method, make sure you really do have two distinct equations. For example, $2x + 3y = 8$ and $4x + 6y = 16$ are really the same equation in different forms; multiply the first equation by 2, and you'll get the second.

Whichever method you use, you can check the result by plugging both values back into both equations and making sure they fit.

Example:

If $m = 4n - 10$ and $3m + 2n = 26$, find the values of m and n.

Since the first equation already expresses m in terms of n, this problem is best approached by substitution.

Substitute $4n - 10$ for m into $3m + 2n = 26$ and solve for n.

$$3(4n - 10) + 2n = 26$$
$$12n - 30 + 2n = 26$$
$$14n = 56$$
$$n = 4$$

Now solve either equation for m by plugging in 4 for n.

$m = 4n - 10$

$m = 4(4) - 10$

$m = 16 - 10$

$m = 6$

So $m = 6$ and $n = 4$.

Example:

If $3x + 3y = 18$ and $x - y = 10$, find the values of x and y.

You could solve this problem by the substitution method. But look what happens if you multiply the second equation by 3 and add it to the first:

$$3x + 3y = 18$$
$$\underline{+(3x - 3y = 30)}$$
$$6x = 48$$

If $6x = 48$, then $x = 8$. Now you can plug 8 into either equation in place of x and solve for y. Your calculations will be simpler if you use the second equation: $8 - y = 10; -y = 2; y = -2$.

The GRE will sometimes reward you for using a shortcut to find the value of an expression containing multiple variables.

Example:

If $5x + 5y = 20$, what is the value of $x + y$?

You don't need the value of either variable by itself, just their sum. If you divide both sides by 5, you have the value of $x + y$.

$$5x + 5y = 20$$
$$5(x + y) = 20$$
$$x + y = 4$$

Example:

If $3x - 5y = 10$ and $6y - 2x = 20$, what is the value of $x + y$?

By aligning the two equations so the terms with the same variables are in the same order, you can see that simply adding the two equations yields the solution.

$$3x - 5y = 10$$
$$\underline{+(-2x + 6y = 20)}$$
$$x + y = 30$$

While you don't know the individual values for x or y, that's okay—you don't need to know them to answer the question.

Symbolism

Don't panic if you see strange symbols like ★, ✧, and ♦ in a GRE problem.

Problems of this type usually require nothing more than substitution. Read the question stem carefully for a definition of the symbols and for any examples of how to use them. Then, just follow the given model, substituting the numbers that are in the question stem.

Example:

An operation symbolized by ✷ is defined by the equation $x ✷ y = x - \frac{1}{y}$. What is the value of 2 ✷ 7?

The ✷ symbol is defined as a two-stage operation performed on two quantities, which are symbolized in the equation as x and y. The two steps are (1) find the reciprocal of the second quantity and (2) subtract the reciprocal from the first quantity. To find the value of 2 ✷ 7, substitute the numbers 2 and 7 into the equation, replacing the x (the first quantity given in the equation) with the 2 (the first number given) and the y (the second quantity given in the equation) with the 7 (the second number given). The reciprocal of 7 is $\frac{1}{7}$, and subtracting $\frac{1}{7}$ from 2 gives you the following:

$$2 - \frac{1}{7} = \frac{14}{7} - \frac{1}{7} = \frac{13}{7}$$

When a symbolism problem involves only one quantity, the operations are usually a little more complicated. Nonetheless, you can follow the same steps to find the correct answer.

Example:

Let $x^\star$ be defined by the equation: $x^\star = \frac{x^2}{1 - x^2}$. Evaluate $\left(\frac{1}{2}\right)^\star$.

$$\left(\frac{1}{2}\right)^\star = \frac{\left(\frac{1}{2}\right)^2}{1-\left(\frac{1}{2}\right)^2} = \frac{\frac{1}{4}}{1-\frac{1}{4}} = \frac{\frac{1}{4}}{\frac{3}{4}} = \frac{1}{4} \times \frac{4}{3} = \frac{1}{3}$$

Every once in a while, you'll see a symbolism problem that doesn't even include an equation. The definitions in this type of problem usually test your understanding of number properties.

Example:

✿x is defined as the largest even number that is less than the negative square root of x. What is the value of ✿81?

- (A) −82
- (B) −80
- (C) −10
- (D) −8
- (E) 8

Plug in 81 for x, then logically work backward. The negative square root of 81 is −9 because $(-9)(-9) = 81$. The largest even number that is less than −9 is −10. (The number part of −8 is smaller than the number part of −9; however, you're dealing with negative numbers, so you have to look for the even number that would be just to the *left* of −9 along the number line.) Thus, the correct answer choice is **(C)** −10.

Sequences

Sequences are lists of numbers. The value of a number in a sequence is related to its position in the list. Sequences are often represented on the GRE as follows:

$$s_1, s_2, s_3, \ldots s_n, \ldots$$

The subscript part of each number gives you the position of each element in the series. s_1 is the first number in the list, s_2 is the second number in the list, and so on.

You will be given a formula that defines each element. For example, if you are told that $s_n = 2n + 1$, then the sequence would be $(2 \times 1) + 1, (2 \times 2) + 1, (2 \times 3) + 1, \ldots$, or $3, 5, 7, \ldots$

Polynomials and Quadratics

The FOIL Method

When two binomials are multiplied, each term in one binomial is multiplied by each term in the other binomial. This process is often called the *FOIL method*, because it involves adding the products of the First, Outer, Inner, and Last terms. Using the FOIL method to multiply out $(x + 5)(x - 2)$, the product of the first terms is x^2, the product of the outer terms is $-2x$, the product of the inner terms is $5x$, and the product of the last terms is -10. Combine like terms to obtain $x^2 + 3x - 10$.

Factoring the Product of Binomials

Many of the polynomials that you'll see on the GRE can be factored into a product of two binomials by using the FOIL method backward.

> **Example:**
>
> Factor the polynomial $x^2 - 3x + 2$.
>
> You can factor this into two binomials, each containing an x-term. Start by writing down what you know:
>
> $$x^2 - 3x + 2 = (x \quad)(x \quad)$$
>
> You'll need to fill in the missing term in each binomial factor. The product of the two missing terms will be the last term in the original polynomial: 2. The sum of the two missing terms will be the coefficient of the second term of the polynomial: -3. Find the pair of factors of 2 that add up to -3. Since $(-1) + (-2) = -3$, you can fill the empty spaces with -1 and -2.
>
> Thus, $x^2 - 3x + 2 = (x - 1)(x - 2)$.

Note: Whenever you factor a polynomial, you can check your answer by using FOIL to multiply the factors and obtain the original polynomial.

Factoring the Difference of Two Squares

A common factorable expression on the GRE is the difference of two squares (for example, $a^2 - b^2$). Once you recognize a polynomial as the difference of two squares, you'll be able to factor it automatically, since any polynomial of the form $a^2 - b^2$ can be factored into the form $(a + b)(a - b)$.

Example:

Factor the expression $9x^2 - 1$.

$9x^2 = (3x)^2$ and $1 = 1^2$, so $9x^2 - 1$ is the difference of two squares.

Therefore, $9x^2 - 1 = (3x + 1)(3x - 1)$.

Factoring Polynomials of the Form $a^2 + 2ab + b^2$ or $a^2 - 2ab + b^2$

A polynomial of either of these forms is the square of a binomial expression, as you can see by using the FOIL method to multiply $(a + b)(a + b)$ or $(a - b)(a - b)$.

To factor a polynomial of either of these forms, check the sign in front of the $2ab$ term. If it's a *plus* sign, the polynomial is equal to $(a + b)^2$. If it's a *minus* sign, the polynomial is equal to $(a - b)^2$.

Example:

Factor the polynomial $x^2 + 6x + 9$.

x^2 and 9 are both perfect squares, and $6x$ is $2(3x)$, which is twice the product of x and 3, so this polynomial is of the form $a^2 + 2ab + b^2$ with $a = x$ and $b = 3$. Since there is a plus sign in front of the $6x$, $x^2 + 6x + 9 = (x + 3)^2$.

Quadratic Equations

A *quadratic equation* is an equation of the form $ax^2 + bx + c = 0$. Many quadratic equations have two solutions. In other words, the equation will be true for two different values of x.

When you see a quadratic equation on the GRE, you'll generally be able to solve it by factoring the algebraic expression, setting each of the factors equal to zero, and solving the resulting equations.

Example:

$x^2 - 3x + 2 = 0$. Solve for x.

To find the solutions, or roots, start by factoring $x^2 - 3x + 2$ into $(x - 2)(x - 1)$.

The product of two quantities equals zero only if one (or both) of the quantities equals zero. So if you set each of the factors equal to zero, you will be able to solve the resulting equations for the solutions of the original quadratic equation. Setting the two binomials equal to zero gives you this:

$$x - 2 = 0 \text{ or } x - 1 = 0$$

That means that x can equal 2 or 1. As a check, you can plug each of those values in turn into $x^2 - 3x + 2 = 0$, and you'll see that either value makes the equation work.

Alternative Strategies for Multiple-Choice Algebra

Backsolving

On GRE Problem Solving questions, you may find it easier to attack algebra problems by Backsolving. To backsolve, substitute each answer choice into the equation until you find the one that satisfies the equation.

Example:

If $x^2 + 10x + 25 = 0$, what is the value of x?

(A) 25

(B) 10

(C)   5

(D) −5

(E) −10

The textbook approach to solving this problem would be to recognize the polynomial expression as the square of the binomial $(x + 5)$ and set $x + 5 = 0$. That's the fastest way to arrive at the correct answer of −5.

But you could also plug each answer choice into the equation until you found the one that makes the equation true. Backsolving can be pretty quick if the correct answer is the first choice you plug in, but here, you have to get all the way down to choice **(D)** before you find that $(-5)^2 + 10(-5) + 25 = 0$.

Example:

If $\frac{5x}{3} + 9 = \frac{x}{6} + 18$, $x =$

(A) 12

(B) 8

(C) 6

(D) 5

(E) 4

To avoid having to try all five answer choices, look at the equation and decide which choice(s), if plugged in for x, would make your calculations easiest. Since x is in the numerators of the two fractions in this equation and the denominators are 3 and 6, try plugging in a choice that is divisible by both 3 and 6. Choices (A) and (C) are divisible by both numbers, so start with one of them.

Choice (A):

$$20 + 9 = 2 + 18$$
$$29 \neq 20$$

This is not true, so x cannot equal 12.

Choice (C):

$$10 + 9 = 1 + 18$$
$$19 = 19$$

This is correct, so x must equal 6. Therefore, choice (C) is correct.

Backsolving may not be the fastest method for a multiple-choice algebra problem, but it's useful if you don't think you'll be able to solve the problem in the conventional way.

Picking Numbers

On other types of multiple-choice algebra problems, especially where the answer choices consist of variables or algebraic expressions, you may want to pick numbers to make the problem less abstract. Evaluate the answer choices and the information in the question stem by picking a number and substituting it for the variable wherever the variable appears.

Example:

If $a > 1$, the ratio of $2a + 6$ to $a^2 + 2a - 3$ is

(A) $2a$

(B) $a + 3$

(C) $\dfrac{2}{a - 1}$

(D) $\dfrac{2a}{3(3 - a)}$

(E) $\dfrac{a - 1}{2}$

You can simplify the process by replacing the variable a with a number in each algebraic expression. Since a has to be greater than 1, why not pick 2? Then the expression $2a + 6$ becomes $2(2) + 6$, or 10. The expression $a^2 + 2a - 3$ becomes $2^2 + 2(2) - 3 = 4 + 4 - 3 = 5$.

So now the question reads, "The ratio of 10 to 5 is what?" That's easy enough to answer: 10:5 is the same as $\dfrac{10}{5}$, or 2. Now you can just eliminate any answer choice that doesn't give a result of 2 when you substitute 2 for a. Choice (A) gives you $2(2)$, or 4, so discard it. Choice (B) results in 5—also not what you want. Choice **(C)** yields $\dfrac{2}{1}$ or 2. That looks good, but you can't stop here.

If another answer choice gives you a result of 2, you will have to pick another number for a and reevaluate the expressions in the question stem and the choices that worked when you let $a = 2$.

Choice (D) gives you $\dfrac{2(2)}{3(3 - 2)}$ or $\dfrac{4}{3}$, so eliminate choice (D).

Choice (E) gives you $\dfrac{2 - 1}{2}$ or $\dfrac{1}{2}$, so discard choice (E).

Fortunately, in this case, only choice **(C)** works out to equal 2, so it is the correct answer. But remember: when using the Picking Numbers strategy, always check every answer choice to make sure you haven't chosen a number that works for more than one answer choice.

Using Picking Numbers to Solve for One Unknown in Terms of Another

It is also possible to solve for one unknown in terms of another by picking numbers. If the first number you pick doesn't lead to a single correct answer, be prepared to either pick a new number (and spend more time on the problem) or settle for guessing strategically among the answers that you haven't eliminated.

Example:

If $\dfrac{x^2 - 16}{x^2 + 6x + 8} = y$ and $x > -2$, which of the following is an expression for x in terms of y?

(A) $\dfrac{1 + y}{2 - y}$

(B) $\dfrac{2y + 4}{1 - y}$

(C) $\dfrac{4y - 4}{y + 1}$

(D) $\dfrac{2y - 4}{2 + y}$

(E) $\dfrac{y + 4}{y + 1}$

Pick a value for x that will simplify your calculations. 4 would work, since 4 is greater than –2, and plugging in 4 for x in the denominator does not cause the denominator to equal 0. When x equals 4, then $x^2 - 16 = 4^2 - 16 = 0$, and so the entire fraction on the left side of the equation is equal to zero.

Now, substitute 0 for y in each answer choice in turn. Each choice is an expression for x in terms of y, and since $y = 0$ when $x = 4$, the correct answer will have to give a value of 4 when $y = 0$. Just remember to evaluate all the answer choices, because you might find more than one that gives a result of 4.

Substituting 0 for y in choices (A), (C), and (D) yields $\dfrac{1}{2}$, $-\dfrac{4}{1}$, and $-\dfrac{4}{2}$, respectively, so none of those choices can be right. But both **(B)** and **(E)** give results of 4 when you make the substitution; choosing between them will require picking another number.

Again, pick a number that will make calculations easy. If $x = 0$, then $y =$

$$\frac{x^2 - 16}{x^2 + 6x + 8} = \frac{0 - 16}{0 + 0 + 8} = \frac{-16}{8} = -2$$

Therefore, $y = -2$ when $x = 0$. You don't have to try the new value of y in all the answer choices, just in **(B)** and (E). When you substitute –2 for y in choice **(B)**, you get 0. That's what you're looking for, but again, you have to make sure it doesn't work in choice (E). Plugging –2 in for y in (E) yields –2 for x, so **(B)** is correct.

Dealing with Word Problems

The key to solving word problems is translation: turning English into math. Rather than having an equation set up for you, *you* have to decide what arithmetic or algebraic operations to perform on which numbers.

For example, suppose the core of a problem involves working with the equation $3j = s - 4$.

In a word problem, this might be presented as "If John had three times as many macaroons as he has now, he would have four fewer macaroons than Susan would."

Your job is to translate the problem from English into math. A phrase like "three times as many as John has" can be translated as $3j$; the phrase "four fewer than Susan" can be translated as "$s - 4$."

Many people dislike word problems. But on the GRE, the math involved is often easier than in other math problems. Once you've translated the language, most word problems boil down to rather simple mathematical concepts and processes—probably because the testmakers figure that the extra step of translation makes the problem difficult enough.

Here's a general approach to any word problem:

1. Read through the whole question once, without lingering over details, to get a sense of the overall problem.
2. Identify and label the variables or unknowns in a way that makes it easy to remember what they stand for.
3. Translate the problem into one or more equations, sentence by sentence. Be careful of the order in which you translate the terms. For example, consider the phrase "5 less than $4x$ equals 9." The *correct* way to translate it is "$4x - 5 = 9$." But many students make the mistake of writing the terms in the order in which they appear in words: "$5 - 4x = 9$."
4. Solve the equation(s).
5. Check your work, if time permits.

Translation Table

This table contains common phrases used in GRE math problems. The left column lists words and phrases that occur frequently; the right column lists the corresponding algebraic symbols.

equals, is, was, will be, has, costs, adds up to, is the same as	$=$
times, of, multiplied by, product of, twice, double, half, triple	$\times$
divided by, per, out of, each, ratio of _ to _	$\div$
plus, added to, sum, combined, and, total	$+$
minus, subtracted from, less than, decreased by, difference between	$-$
what, how much, how many, a number	variable (x, n, etc.)

Example:

Beatrice has three dollars more than twice the number of dollars Allan has.

Translate into $B = 3 + 2A$.

For Word Problems:

Add ...

- when you are given the amounts of individual quantities and asked to find the total.

Example:

If the sales tax on a $12.00 lunch is $1.20, what is the total amount of the check?

$$\$12.00 + \$1.20 = \$13.20$$

- when you are given an original amount and an increase and are then asked to find the new amount.

Example:

The bus fare used to be 55 cents. If the fare increased by 35 cents, what is the new fare?

$$55 \text{ cents} + 35 \text{ cents} = 90 \text{ cents}$$

Subtract ...

- when you are given the total and one part of the total and you want to find the remaining part or parts.

Example:

If a bowl contains 50 total marbles, each of which is colored either solid blue or solid green, and 32 of the marbles are solid blue, what is the number of solid green marbles?

50 total marbles − 32 solid blue marbles = 18 solid green marbles

- when you are given two numbers and asked *how much more* or *how much less* one number is than the other. The amount is called the *difference*.

Example:

How much larger than 30 is 38?

38 (larger) − 30 (smaller) = 8

Multiply ...

- when you are given an amount for one item and asked for the total amount of *many* of these items.

Example:

If 1 book costs $6.50, what is the cost of 12 copies of the same book?

12($6.50) = $78.00

Divide ...

- when you are given a total amount for *many* items and asked for the amount for *one* item.

Example:

If 5 pounds of apples cost $6.75, what is the price of 1 pound of apples?

$6.75 ÷ 5 = $1.35

- when you are given the size of one group and the total size for many such identical groups and are asked how many of the small groups fit into the larger one.

Example:

How many groups of 30 students can be formed from a total of 240 students?

240 ÷ 30 = 8 groups of 30 students

SPECIAL WORD PROBLEMS TIP #1
Don't try to combine several sentences into one equation; each sentence usually translates into a separate equation.

SPECIAL WORD PROBLEMS TIP #2
Pay attention to what the question asks for and make a note to yourself if it is not one of the unknowns in the equation(s). Otherwise, you may stop working on the problem too early.

Dealing with Logic Problems

You won't always have to set up an equation to solve a word problem. Some of the word problems you'll encounter on the GRE won't fall into recognizable textbook categories. Many of these problems are designed to test your analytical and deductive logic. You can solve them with common sense and a little basic arithmetic. Ask yourself how it would be helpful to arrange the information, such as by drawing a diagram or making a table.

In these problems, the issue is not so much translating English into math as simply using your head. The problem may call for nonmath skills, including the ability to organize and keep track of different possibilities, the ability to visualize something (for instance, the reverse side of a symmetrical shape), the ability to think of the exception that changes the answer to a problem, or the ability to deal with overlapping groups.

> **Example:**
>
> If ! and $\int$ are digits and $(!!)(\int\int) = 60\int$, what is the value of $\int$?
>
> Since each of the symbols represents a digit from 0–9, we know that the product of the multiplication equals a value from 600 to 609. We know that the two quantities multiplied each consist of a two-digit integer in which both digits are the same. So list the relevant two-digit integers (00, 11, 22, 33, 44, 55, 66, 77, 88, and 99) and see which two of them can be multiplied together to obtain a product in the 600 to 609 range. Only (11)(55) satisfies this requirement. The $\int$ symbol equals 5.

ALGEBRA CONCEPT CHECK

Before you move on, check your understanding of algebra on the GRE by considering a few questions:

- What is x in terms of y if $2x - y = \dfrac{5 + x}{4}$?
- If $a - 6 = b$ and $2a + 3b = 17$, what is b?
- What are two alternative strategies for tackling multiple-choice algebra questions?
- What are the solutions of x if $x^2 + 7x + 10 = 0$?

If you feel confident in your ability to tackle questions that deal with these concepts, proceed to the practice set that starts on the next page.

If you feel like you would like some additional guided practice, head to your online resources. Under **Math Foundations**, click **Algebra Guided Practice**. Try each question on your own first. Then watch a video explanation in which a Kaplan GRE instructor describes a strategic approach.

Algebra Practice Set

Directions: Try answering these questions to practice what you have learned about algebra. Answers and explanations follow at the end of the chapter.

Basic

1. If $3(x - 6) + 8 - (2 - 4x) = 7 - 4(x + 2)$, what is the value of x?

2. Factor the expression $ac - 2bc - 2bd + ad$.

3. What is the value of $x^3 - x^2 - 7(x - 1)$ if $x = 3$?

4. If $3x - 7 \geq -1$, what is the minimum value of x?

5. If $y = 2x$, and $3(y + 6x) - 7(2y + 3) = 11$, what is the value of y?

Intermediate

6. If $xy + \dfrac{7 + 3x}{4} - 2y = 1$, what is the value of x in terms of y?

7. What are the possible values of x if $9x^2 - 36 = 0$?

8. If $x + 4y = 19$ and $2x - y = 11$, what is the value of y?

9. If $♪\left(x\right) = \dfrac{x^2 + 3}{x - 1}$ and $3r - 4 = 5$, what is the value of $♪(r)$?

10. In a certain sequence, if $x > 2$, then $s_x = s_{x-1} + s_{x-2} + 3$. If $s_1 = 0$ and $s_2 = 4$, what is the value of s_4?

Advanced

11. If $x - 2z = 2(y - z)$, $2x - 6y + z = 1$, and $3x + y - 2z = 4$, what is the value of z?

12. If $@@\left(x\right) = \dfrac{x + 3}{x - 1}$ and $\#\#(y) = y^2 - 2y + 3$, what is the value of $@@(\#\#(2))$?

13. What are the possible values of x if $6x^2 - 10 = 11x$?

14. The values in a particular series beginning with s_3 are a function of the two prior values in that series. Based on the values for this series in the table below, what is the value of s_9?

SEQUENCE NUMBER	VALUE
s_1	0
s_2	1
s_3	1
s_4	3
s_5	5
s_6	11
s_7	21
s_8	43

15. Rafael has three more bus tokens than Taz. Chan has twice as many as Rafael. If Chan had 1 more token, he would have 3 times as many as Taz. How many total tokens does the group have?

Answers and explanations follow on the next page. ▶ ▶ ▶

Algebra Practice Set Answer Key

1. 1
2. $(a - 2b)(c + d)$
3. 4
4. 2
5. −16
6. $x = \dfrac{8y - 3}{4y + 3}$
7. 2, −2
8. 3
9. 6
10. 14
11. 5
12. 3
13. $2\frac{1}{2}$, $-\frac{2}{3}$
14. 85
15. 37

Algebra Practice Set Answers and Explanations

Basic

1. 1

None of the operations in parentheses can be completed, so the first step is to distribute the factors across the terms in parentheses: $3x - 18 + 8 - 2 + 4x = 7 - 4x - 8$. Combine like terms: $7x - 12 = -1 - 4x$. Add $4x$ and 12 to each side of the equation: $7x + 4x - 12 + 12 = -1 + 12 - 4x + 4x$. So, $11x = 11$ and $x = 1$.

2. $(a - 2b)(c + d)$

Notice that the first 2 terms each contain the variable c, so convert these to $(c)(a - 2b)$ by factoring out c. The last 2 terms each contain the variable d, so convert these to $(d)(a - 2b)$. The expression can be restated as $(c)(a - 2b) + (d)(a - 2b)$. Now $(a - 2b)$ is a common term, so factor it out to get $(a - 2b)(c + d)$.

3. 4

Substitute 3 for x in the expression: $3^3 - 3^2 - 7(3 - 1) = 27 - 9 - 7(2) = 4$.

4. 2

Add 7 to both sides of the inequality to get $3x \geq 6$. Divide both sides by 3 to determine that $x \geq 2$. Since "$\geq$" means "greater than or equal to," the minimum value of x is 2.

5. −16

Substitute $2x$ for y in the equation: $3(2x + 6x) - 7(2(2x) + 3) = 11$. Simplify: $3(8x) - 7(4x + 3) = 11$. Complete the multiplications: $24x - 28x - 21 = 11$. Finally, add 21 to both sides of the equation and combine like terms to get $-4x = 32$. Divide both sides by −4 to get $x = -8$. The question asks for the value of y, which is $2x$, so multiply −8 by 2 to get $y = -16$.

Intermediate

6. $x = \dfrac{8y - 3}{4y + 3}$

First, get rid of the fraction by multiplying everything by 4: $4(xy) + 4\left(\dfrac{7 + 3x}{4}\right) - 4(2y) = 4(1)$. The equation becomes $4xy + 7 + 3x - 8y = 4$. Add $8y$ and subtract 7 from both sides to get $4xy + 3x = 4 + 8y - 7$. Factor out x and combine like terms: $x(4y + 3) = 8y - 3$. Finally, divide both sides by $(4y + 3)$, so $x = \dfrac{8y - 3}{4y + 3}$.

7. 2, −2

This is the difference of two squares, a pattern equation that is likely to appear on the GRE. Remember that $a^2 - b^2 = (a + b)(a - b)$. Since $9x^2 = (3x)^2$ and $36 = (6)^2$, the equation becomes $(3x + 6)(3x - 6) = 0$. If $3x + 6 = 0$, then $3x = -6$ and $x = -2$; if $3x - 6 = 0$, then $3x = 6$ and $x = 2$. A shortcut would be to add 36 to both sides to get $9x^2 = 36$ then dividing both sides by 9 to get $x^2 = 4$. Remember that x can be either $+2$ or -2!

8. 3

This question presents 2 linear equations with 2 variables. Systems of equations such as this can be solved by combination or substitution. To combine the 2 equations, adapt one of the equations to make the absolute value of one of its variable's coefficients the same as the absolute value of that variable's coefficient in the other equation. Here, the terms of the first equation can be multiplied by 2 to get $2x + 8y = 38$. Subtract the second equation from this so that the $2x$ cancels out:

$$2x + 8y = 38$$
$$-(2x - y = 11)$$
$$9y = 27, \text{ so } y = 3$$

To solve using substitution, rearrange the first equation to get $x = 19 - 4y$. Substitute that for x in the second equation: $2(19 - 4y) - y = 11$, so $38 - 8y - y = 11$, $27 = 9y$, and $y = 3$.

9. 6

Symbolism questions such as this are algebra questions that can be solved by substitution. In order to find the value of $♪(r)$, first determine the value of r. Since $3r - 4 = 5$, $3r = 9$ and $r = 3$. Substitute 3 for x to get $♪(3) = \dfrac{3^2 + 3}{3 - 1}$. Simplify to $♪(3) = \dfrac{9 + 3}{2} = 6$.

10. 14

A series of numbers beginning with the third number in the series is composed of the previous number in the series plus the second prior number plus 3. So, in order to calculate the value of any number in the series, the value of the 2 preceding numbers is needed. To find the value of s_4, the values of s_3 and s_2 must first be determined. The question provides values for s_1 and s_2, so $s_3 = s_2 + s_1 + 3$, which is $4 + 0 + 3 = 7$. So $s_4 = 7 + 4 + 3 = 14$.

Advanced

11. 5

The question has three variables and three linear equations, so you can solve for any of the variables as long as the equations are distinct. Start by simplifying the first equation: $x - 2z = 2y - 2z$, so $x = 2y$. Now substitute $2y$ wherever x appears in the other equations to end up with two equations with two variables: $2(2y) - 6y + z = 1$ simplifies to $z - 2y = 1$. Similarly, $3(2y) + y - 2z = 4$ becomes $7y - 2z = 4$. Multiply the first of these two equations by 2 to get $2z - 4y = 2$. Now add the equations:

$$2z - 4y = 2$$
$$+(-2z + 7y) = 4$$
$$3y = 6, \text{ so } y = 2$$

Plug that value into $2z - 4y = 2$: $2z - 8 = 2$, so $2z = 10$ and $z = 5$.

12. 3

When confronted with a function of a function, as in this question, start from the inside and work outward. Substitute 2 for y to get $\#\#(2) = 2^2 - 2(2) + 3 = 4 - 4 + 3 = 3$. Now evaluate $@@(3) = \dfrac{3 + 3}{3 - 1} = \dfrac{6}{2} = 3$.

13. $2\dfrac{1}{2}$, $-\dfrac{2}{3}$

First rearrange the equation into standard quadratic form so that it can be factored: $6x^2 - 11x - 10 = 0$. Identify the factors of the last term and those of the coefficient of the first term. The factors of -10 are (-10 and 1), (10 and -1), (-5 and 2), and (5 and -2). The factors of 6 are (1 and 6), (-1 and -6), (2 and 3), and (-2 and -3). Find the pairs that will result in an algebraic sum of -11, which is the coefficient of the middle term. Note that $3 \times (-5) = -15$ and $2 \times 2 = 4$; $-15 + 4 = -11$. So $(2x - 5)(3x + 2)$ are the correct factors. Set each factor equal to zero to find the possible values of x. If $2x - 5 = 0$, then $x = 2\dfrac{1}{2}$; if $3x + 2 = 0$, then $x = -\dfrac{2}{3}$.

14. 85

To predict a forward value for the sequence, determine the equation that quantifies the relationship between any value and "the two prior values." Looking at the overall trend, the values always increase, and the rate of increase accelerates. Start with s_3, which could be the simple sum of s_1 and s_2. However, moving along to s_4, that value is greater than the sum of s_2 and s_3, so there must be a multiplier or exponent in the formula. Continuing forward, try to identify a pattern relating to how much greater each value is than the sum of the two prior values. One way to do this is to set up a table showing the "missing" quantities.

Seq	Value	$s_{x-1} + s_{x-2}$	Difference
s_5	5	$3 + 1 = 4$	$5 - 4 = 1$
s_6	11	$5 + 3 = 8$	$11 - 8 = 3$
s_7	21	$11 + 5 = 16$	$21 - 16 = 5$
s_8	43	$21 + 11 = 32$	$43 - 32 = 11$

Look at the values on the far right: 1, 3, 5, and 11. Those are the values of s_{x-2}. So the equation for this series is $s_x = s_{x-1} + s_{x-2} + s_{x-2} = s_{x-1} + 2(s_{x-2})$. Apply this formula to calculate the value of s_9: $s_9 = 43 + (2)21 = 43 + 42 = 85$.

15. 37

Represent the three people's number of tokens by the first letters of their names and translate the information given into algebraic equations: $R = T + 3$, $C = 2R$, and $C = 3T - 1$. Since there are three distinct linear equations and three variables, you can solve this system of equations. Substitute $2R$ for C in the third equation: $2R = 3T - 1$. Double the first equation to get $2R = 2T + 6$. This gives two different equations for $2R$, so set them equal to each other: $2T + 6 = 3T - 1$. Subtract $2T$ from both sides and add 1 to both sides to get $T = 7$. This means that R has 10 tokens, 3 more than T, and C has twice as many as R, which is 20. The total number of tokens among the three people is $7 + 10 + 20 = 37$.

MATH FOUNDATIONS— STATISTICS REVIEW

Introduction to Statistics Review

On the test, you will see some questions involving charts, such as graphs and tables. In addition, you may be tested on the statistics used to describe sets of numbers. Becoming familiar with the following topics will help you successfully answer these questions:

- Statistics:
  - Median, mode, and range
  - Quartiles
  - Percentiles
  - Standard deviation
  - Frequency distributions
  - Graphs and tables

This chapter explains these concepts with examples. After studying the chapter, try answering the questions in the practice set at the end to evaluate how well you understand this material.

Median, Mode, and Range

You may see these statistics concepts in the GRE Quantitative section.

Median: The middle term in a group of terms that are arranged in numerical order. To find the median of a group of terms, first arrange the terms in numerical order. If there is an odd number of terms in the group, the median is the middle term.

Example:

Bob's test scores in Spanish are 84, 81, 88, 70, and 87. What is his median score?

In increasing order, his scores are 70, 81, 84, 87, and 88. The median test score is the middle one: 84.

If there is an even number of terms in the group, the median is the average of the two middle terms when arranged in numerical order.

Example:

John's test scores in biology are 92, 98, 82, 94, 85, and 97. What is his median score?

In numerical order, his scores are 82, 85, 92, 94, 97, and 98. The median test score is the average of the two middle terms, or $\dfrac{92 + 94}{2} = 93$.

The median of a group of numbers is often different from its average.

Example:

Caitlin's test scores in math are 92, 96, 90, 85, and 82. Find the difference between Caitlin's median score and the average (arithmetic mean) of her scores.

In ascending order, Caitlin's scores are 82, 85, 90, 92, and 96. The median score is the middle one: 90. Her average score is

$$\frac{82 + 85 + 90 + 92 + 96}{5} = \frac{445}{5} = 89$$

As you can see, Caitlin's median score and her average score are not the same. The difference between them is $90 - 89$, or 1.

Mode: The term that appears most frequently in a set.

Example:

The daily temperatures in city Q for one week were 25°, 33°, 26°, 25°, 27°, 31°, and 22°. What was the mode of the daily temperatures in city Q for that week?

Each of the temperatures occurs once on the list, except for 25°, which occurs twice. Since 25° appears more frequently than any other temperature, it is the mode.

A set may have more than one mode if two or more terms appear an equal number of times within the set and each appears more times than any other term.

Example:

The table below represents the score distribution for a class of 20 students on a recent chemistry test. Which score, or scores, are the mode?

SCORE	# OF STUDENTS RECEIVING THAT SCORE
100	2
91	1
87	5
86	2
85	1
84	5
80	1
78	2
56	1

The largest number in the second column is 5, which occurs twice. Therefore, there were two mode scores on this test: 87 and 84. Equal numbers of students received those scores, and more students received those scores than any other score. Note that the modes are the scores that appeared most often, 84 and 87, not the number of times they appeared (5).

If every element in the set occurs an equal number of times, then the set has no mode.

Range: The distance between the greatest and least values in a group of data points.

Find the range of a set of numbers by subtracting the smallest number in the set from the largest. Note that sets with the same mean or median may have very different ranges. For instance, while the median of both the sets $\{-11, -6, -1, 4, 9\}$ and $\{-3, -2, -1, 0, 1\}$ is the same (that is, -1), the numbers in the first set are much more spread out. The range of the first set is $9 - (-11) = 20$, while the range of the second set is $1 - (-3) = 4$.

Quartiles

Not many GRE questions ask about quartiles or the interquartile range, but if you are striving for a high score, read on. When a set of data is divided into four equal sections, those sections are referred to as "quartiles." To determine quartiles, first arrange the terms in your data set in numerical order from least (represented by L) to greatest (represented by G). Next, subdivide the set into two halves, each containing an equal number of terms. The median of the lower half represents the first quartile, which is often written as Q_1, and the median of the upper half is the third quartile, or Q_3. The median of the entire set is Q_2, or M.

The four equal sections of data, in increasing value, are: L to Q_1, Q_1 to Q_2, Q_2 to Q_3, and Q_3 to G.

Example:

Determine L, Q_1, Q_2, Q_3, and G for the following set of numbers: {0, 0, 0, 1, 1, 3, 3, 7, 11, 12, 15, 15, 17, 17, 20, 21}.

The terms are already in numerical order, so you do not need to rearrange them. The easiest values to find are the least value (L) and the greatest value (G). Here, those values are 0 and 21, respectively. The next easiest value to find is Q_2, since it is just the median of the entire set. Because there are 16 terms in the list, the median is the average of the two numbers in the middle of the set. Here, those two numbers are 7 and 11, so the median, or Q_2, is 9.

To find Q_1 and Q_3, split the list into two halves and find the median of each. The first half of the list consists of 0, 0, 0, 1, 1, 3, 3, and 7. The median of this group is the average of the two middle numbers; since both are 1, the median is also 1. This is Q_1. The second group is 11, 12, 15, 15, 17, 17, 20, and 21. The median here is the average of 15 and 17, or 16. This is Q_3.

To summarize: L is 0, Q_1 is 1, Q_2 is 9, Q_3 is 16, and G is 21.

There are other rules that are sometimes used to calculate the location of the quartiles, but this is the rule used by the GRE. Since you can't split a group of numbers in half if there are an odd number of them, it is not likely that a GRE problem requiring you to determine quartiles will present a set for which the number of terms is not even.

Interquartile Range

The difference between the values of the third and first quartile values, $Q_3 - Q_1$, is called the interquartile range. Because outliers fall into the bottom and top quartiles, they do not affect the interquartile range. For instance, set A: {0, 10, 10, 10, 10, 10, 10, 11, 11, 11, 11, 11} and set B: {0, 1, 2, 3, 4, 5, 6, 7, 8, 9, 10, 11} both have 12 elements and a range of 11, but the data distributions within that range are very different for the two sets. The first value in set A (0) is an outlier that skews the value of the range. The interquartile range of set A is $11 - 10 = 1$, and that of set B is $8.5 - 2.5 = 6$. This comparison shows that, with the exception of the outlier, the data in set A are more closely spaced than the data in set B.

A straightforward way to display data dispersion visually by quartiles is to create a *box plot*, also called a *box-and-whisker plot*. Draw the interquartile range (from Q_1 to Q_3, and including M) as a rectangular box, then draw straight lines extending from the sides of the box to the least and greatest values (L and G). A number line is drawn below the box plot to show the numerical values of these points.

As an example, consider the data set: {4, 8, −3, 2, 0, 4, 8, 6}. First, arrange the data in ascending order: {−3, 0, 2, 4, 4, 6, 8, 8}. Next, identify the values needed for the box-and-whisker plot. $L = -3$ and $G = 8$. The median of the entire set, M, is 4. The median of the first half of the set is the average of 0 and 2, so $Q_1 = 1$. Q_3 is the average of 6 and 8, or 7.

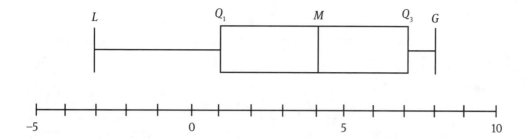

Percentiles

For large groups of numbers, the position of given data points is sometimes stated in percentiles rather than quartiles. The principle is the same as for quartiles, but there are 100 subdivisions instead of 4. Converting quartiles to percentiles is easy: Q_1 is the same value as the 25th percentile, Q_2 is the same value as the 50th percentile, Q_3 is the same value as the 75th percentile, and Q_4 is the same as the 100th percentile.

Standard Deviation

Like the range and the interquartile range, standard deviation is a way to measure the dispersion in a given data set—that is, how spread out the values are. Standard deviation is found by calculating the mean of a group of values, then using a type of averaging to determine how far away the other values in the group are from that mean. If the values in the group are all relatively close to the mean, then the standard deviation is low. Conversely, the more spread out the values are relative to the mean, the higher the standard deviation. For example, consider these two groups of values:

Set A: {0, 25, 50, 75, 100}
Set B: {48, 49, 50, 51, 52}

Both sets have five distinct values, and both have a mean of 50. But because the values in Set A are more widely dispersed (as much as 50 units away from the mean) than the values in Set B (all of which are within 2 units of the mean), Set A has a greater standard deviation than does Set B.

The GRE tests this basic understanding of standard deviation in a variety of ways. For example, the test might ask you to compare the standard deviation of data sets that include variables. While such a question might seem daunting, solve it by focusing on the basic concept of standard deviation—data sets with values that are more spread out have a higher standard deviation.

Example:

If x is a positive integer, which group of values has the greater standard deviation?

Set A: $\{x, 2x, 3x, 4x\}$
Set B: $\{x, 3x, 5x, 7x\}$

Both Set A and Set B contain the positive integer x. In Set A, the second value is twice as large as x, the third value is three times as large as x, and the fourth value is four times as large as x. In Set B, however, the second value is three times as large as x, the third value is five times as large as x, and the fourth value is seven times as large as x. Without even knowing what x is, we know that the values in Set A are more closely grouped together than the values in Set B. Therefore, since the values in Set B are more widely dispersed than those in Set A, Set B has a greater standard deviation.

Another way the GRE could test your understanding of standard deviation is to provide the mean and standard deviation of a group of values, then ask you to determine specific values in that group. For example, imagine a data set that has a mean of 100 and a standard deviation of 20. Even without knowing specific values in the data set, you know that one standard deviation above the mean is 120, and one standard deviation below the mean is 80. Two standard deviations above the mean is 140, and two standard deviations below the mean is 60.

Example:

The mean of Data Set A is 40 and the standard deviation is 10. What value is 1.5 standard deviations below the mean?

The distance from the mean is the number of standard deviations times the value of one standard deviation: $1.5 \times 10 = 15$. And since the question asks for the value that is 1.5 standard deviations *below* the mean, that is $40 - 15 = 25$.

Another variant on the same theme would be to provide the standard deviation of a group of values and one value in that group. If you know how many standard deviations away from the mean that value is, you could calculate the mean itself.

Example:

If 25 is 1.5 standard deviations below the mean of Data Set A and the standard deviation of the data set is 10, what is the mean of Data Set A?

The distance from the mean is the number of standard deviations times the value of one standard deviation: $1.5 \times 10 = 15$.

Since 25 is *below* the mean, the value of the mean is $25 + 15 = 40$.

On Test Day, you probably won't have to calculate the precise standard deviation of a group of values. The types of examples you worked through above were solved with just a basic understanding of standard deviation. That said, knowing how standard deviation is calculated can be useful. For any group of values, follow these steps to calculate standard deviation:

1. Find the group's mean.
2. Determine the difference between the mean and each value in the group.
3. Square each of those differences.
4. Find the mean of the squared differences.
5. Take the non-negative square root of the mean of the squared differences.

Example:

Calculate the standard deviation of 1, 3, 8, 11, and 12.

First, find the mean: $\dfrac{1 + 3 + 8 + 11 + 12}{5} = \dfrac{35}{5} = 7$

Next, determine the difference between each term and 7:
$(1 - 7) = -6$, $(3 - 7) = -4$, $(8 - 7) = 1$, $(11 - 7) = 4$, and $(12 - 7) = 5$.

Square each difference, and find the mean of the squared differences:

$$\frac{(-6)^2 + (-4)^2 + 1^2 + 4^2 + 5^2}{5} = \frac{36 + 16 + 1 + 16 + 25}{5} = \frac{94}{5} = 18.8$$

Finally, find the non-negative square root of that average to determine the standard deviation: $\sqrt{18.8} \approx 4.34$.

When you see a question on the GRE that involves standard deviation, there's no need to panic. Standard deviation is merely a measure of dispersion that essentially represents each value's average deviation from the mean. If you keep this in mind, you can approach the occasional standard deviation question with confidence.

Frequency Distributions

A frequency distribution is a description of how often certain data values occur in a set and is typically shown in a table or histogram. As an example, take a look at the table below, which displays the frequency distribution of singing voices in a choir in two ways. The first delineates the *count* of singers for each vocal range; the second shows the *percentage* of the total choir for the different voices. Counts can be converted to percents by adding all the counts to get the total and then dividing the individual count for each category by that total to obtain the percentages. For instance, in this chart, there are 75 total singers. If 15 of them are tenors, then tenors make up $\dfrac{15}{75} = 0.20 = 20\%$ of the singers.

Soprano	12	16%
Alto	18	24%
Tenor	15	20%
Baritone	12	16%
Bass	18	24%

In a *relative frequency distribution*, also known as a *probability distribution*, the frequency with which given values occur is given in decimal form rather than as percentages. The value of a randomly chosen value from a known distribution of data is called a *random variable X*. The table below is an example of a probability distribution of such a variable. 5% of the values in the distribution are 0, 10% are 1, 20% are 2, and so on. Or, stated differently, the probability that a randomly selected value will be a zero is 0.05, the probability that a randomly selected value will be 1 is 0.10, the probability that a randomly selected value will be 2 is 0.20, etc.

X	P(X)
0	0.05
1	0.10
2	0.20
3	0.30
4	0.25
5	0.10

Note that you can calculate the mean by using a weighted average approach: $0.05(0) + 0.10(1) + 0.20(2) + 0.30(3) + 0.25(4) + 0.10(5) = 0 + 0.10 + 0.40 + 0.90 + 1.00 + 0.50 = 2.90$.

We mentioned before that frequency distributions can be shown as histograms. If the sample set of an experiment is large enough, as in the example below, the histogram begins to closely resemble a continuous curve.

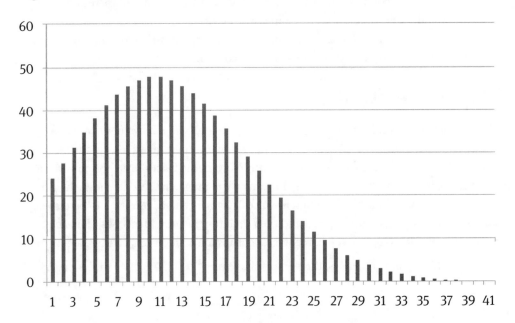

Normal Distribution

There is a special kind of frequency distribution, called the *normal distribution*, that is closely tied to the concept of standard deviation. Many natural data sets, such as the distribution of the heights of adult males in the United States, closely approximate the normal distribution. This distribution is commonly referred to as a *bell curve* because of its shape. Only two parameters are needed to define any normal distribution: the mean and the standard deviation. In a normal distribution, the data are symmetrically distributed around the mean, so the curve to the left of the mean is a mirror image of the curve to the right.

Unlike histograms that display rough and uneven values of raw data, normal distributions are often presented as smoothed curves called continuous probability distributions.

Normal Distributions

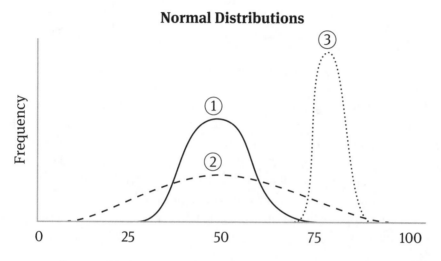

As you can see from the chart, normal distribution curves are not all the same shape, nor do they all have the same mean. The greater the spread of data around the average, the wider the curve; conversely, the more tightly the values are clustered around the mean, the more narrow the curve. In the given graph, Curve 2 is wider and has a greater standard deviation than the narrower Curve 3. And while Curves 1 and 2 have roughly the same mean, Curve 3 has a greater mean.

Some additional key features of normal distributions are as follows:

- The mean, median, and mode of a normal distribution are always equal.

- Normal distributions are more dense in the center and less dense in the tails.

- The probability of a randomly selected value falling somewhere under the curve of a normal distribution is 100%, or 1.

- About 68% of the area of a normal distribution is within one standard deviation of the mean, and about 95% of the area is within two standard deviations of the mean.

The graph below shows some important probability values that hold true for *all* normal distributions. The percentage of the area under any portion of a distribution curve equals the probability that a randomly selected event will fall within that area's range.

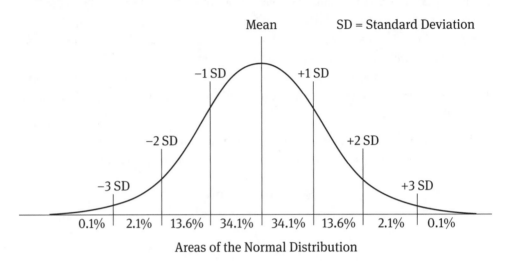

Areas of the Normal Distribution

It's possible you will see a normal distribution represented as a *standard normal distribution*. In such a chart, the mean of the set is centered at 0, and the standard deviation is calibrated to 1. For example, consider a normally distributed population of animals that has a mean weight of 50 kg with a standard deviation of 6 kg. You can imagine such a distribution matching the chart above, where 0 would represent the mean of 50 kg, +1 would be 56 kg (i.e., one standard deviation above the mean), +2 would be 62 kg (two standard deviations above the mean), −1 would be 44 kg (one standard deviation below the mean), and so on.

Following are some examples of how standard deviation and the normal distribution might be tested on the GRE.

Example:

The lengths of adult minnows of a certain species closely approximate a normal distribution, with a mean length of 8.5 centimeters and a standard deviation of 2 centimeters. What is the approximate probability that a randomly selected adult minnow of this species has a length of at least 10.5 centimeters?

10.5 centimeters is 1 standard deviation above the mean. That means the probability that an adult minnow is longer than at least 10.5 centimeters includes the probability that a minnow is between 1 and 2 standard deviations above the mean (13.6%), the probability that a minnow is between 2 and 3 standard deviations above the mean (2.1%), and the probability that a minnow is longer than 3 standard deviations above the mean (0.1%). So, 13.6% + 2.1% + 0.1% = 15.8%.

Apply the same idea to another example.

Example:

The durability of a certain model of light bulb closely approximates a normal distribution with a mean life of 3,400 hours and a standard deviation of 200 hours. Which of the following is closest to the probability that a randomly selected light bulb of this model will last between 3,200 and 3,800 hours?

3,200 hours is 200 hours less than the mean of 3,400, meaning it is 1 standard deviation below the mean. 3,800 hours is 400 hours above the mean, so it is 2 standard deviations above the mean. The area under the curve between 3,200 and 3,800 is the area between the mean and 1 standard deviation *below* the mean (34.1%), the area between the mean and 1 standard deviation *above* the mean (also 34.1%), and the area between 1 standard deviation above the mean and 2 standard deviations above the mean (13.6%). So, there is a 34.1% + 34.1% + 13.6% = 81.8% chance that a randomly selected light bulb of this model will last between 3,200 and 3,800 hours.

At the heart of many of these questions is this simple idea: in a normal distribution, the closer a value is to the mean of the set, the greater its probability of occurring; conversely, the further away a value gets from the mean, the less likely it is to occur.

Example:

Two different standardized tests have scores that approximate the normal distribution. Test A has a mean score of 500 and a standard deviation of 100. Test B has a mean score of 20 and a standard deviation of 6. Which is less likely, a score of 690 on Test A or a score of 29 on test B?

Test A has a mean score of 500, so a score of 690 is 190 points above the mean; since the standard deviation is 100, a score of 690 is $\frac{190}{100} = 1.9$ standard deviations above the mean.

Test B has a mean score of 20, so a score of 29 is 9 points above the mean; since the standard deviation is 6, a score of 29 is $\frac{9}{6} = 1.5$ standard deviations above the mean.

Therefore, a score of 690 on Test A is less likely to occur than is a score of 29 on Test B.

Graphs and Tables

Some questions, especially in Data Interpretation, combine numbers and text with visual formats. Different formats are suitable for organizing different types of information. The formats that appear most frequently on GRE math questions are bar graphs, line graphs, pie charts, and tables.

Questions involving graphs and tables may *look* different from other GRE math questions, but the ideas and principles are the same. The problems are unusual only in the way that they present information, not in what they ask you to do with that information.

Bar Graphs

Here is an example of a bar graph.

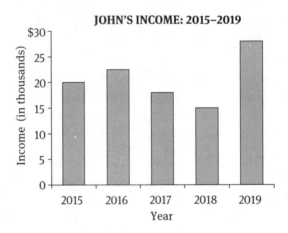

Bar graphs are somewhat less accurate than tables, but that's not necessarily a bad attribute, especially on the GRE, where estimating often saves time on calculations.

What's handy about a bar graph is that you can see which values are larger or smaller without reading actual numbers. Just a glance at this graph shows that John's 2019 income was almost double his 2018 income. Numbers are represented on a bar graph by the heights or lengths of the bars. For example, in the first of the two bar graphs below, the taller bar represents a value of 7.

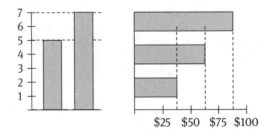

If the height or length of the bar falls between two numbers on the axis, you will have to estimate. For instance, in the second of the two bar graphs given, the shortest bar represents a value about halfway between $25 and $50, or about $37.50.

Histograms

Bar graphs that show relative frequencies or numbers of occurrences are called *histograms*. The *y*-axis on a histogram shows the frequency, while the *x*-axis might show category definitions, values, or ranges, depending on what is being graphed. These graphs can be useful in visualizing patterns and trends in the data.

Inbound Calls per Minute

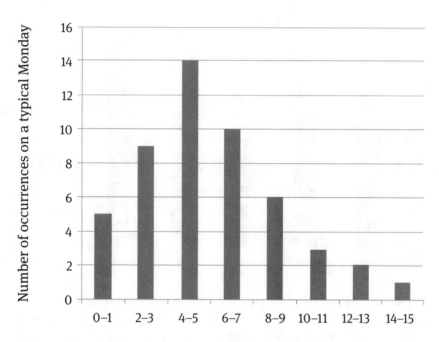

A quick inspection of this graph shows that the mode is 4–5 calls per minute and that the frequency distribution has a long right "tail" of occasional bursts of very high call volume. One drawback of histograms is that estimating the mean of the data can be very difficult.

Segmented Bar Graphs

"Regular" bar graphs only display one value for each bar. Segmented bar graphs, also called *stacked bar graphs*, display multiple quantities on each bar. These quantities represent different subgroups that sum to the amount at the top of each bar.

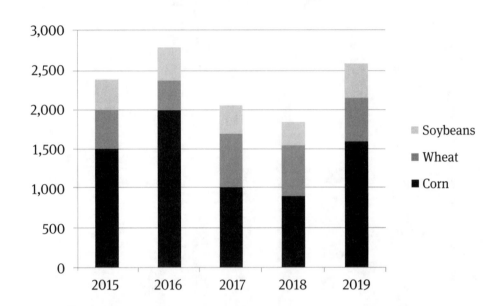

Curtis Farm Crop Production (Bushels)

Values for the first category (in this case, corn) and the total can be read directly on stacked bar charts. For instance, in 2015, the farm produced 1,500 bushels of corn and 2,400 bushels in total. Values for other categories must be calculated by subtracting the value at the bottom of the portion of the bar for that category from the value at the top of that portion of the bar. Here, wheat production is represented by the middle portion, or medium gray area, of each bar. To determine the wheat crop for 2017, find the value at the bottom of the medium gray area of the 2017 bar, 1,000, and subtract that from the value at the top of the medium gray area, 1,700. Since $1,700 - 1,000 = 700$, the wheat production in 2017 was 700 bushels.

Scatterplots

If two measured variables are related to each other, the data are called *bivariate* data. A scatterplot is often the best way to graphically display such data. One variable is plotted on the *x*-axis, and the other is plotted on the *y*-axis. Thus, each ordered pair of measured values represents one data point that is plotted on the graph.

Scatterplots are useful for visualizing the relationships between the two variables. A trend line shows the nature of that relationship and clearly highlights data points that deviate significantly from the general trend. The trend line can either be straight or curved, and it will frequently be drawn on the scatterplot in the question.

Public Elementary and High Schools, by State: 2018–2019

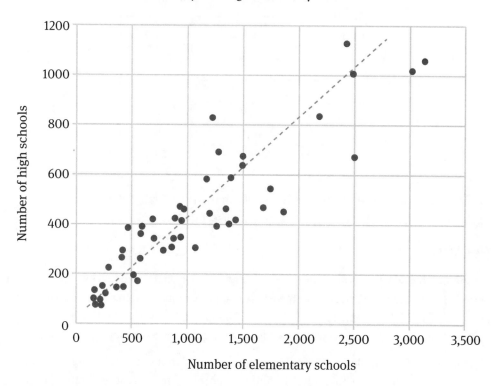

The trend line on this scatterplot slopes upward, meaning that as the number of elementary schools in a state increases, so do the number of high schools. Notice that the scales on the axes are different; even though the apparent slope of the trend line is about 1, the number of high schools increases at a lesser rate than the number of elementary schools. Trend lines can be used to make predictions by interpolating along the trend line or extrapolating beyond the trend line. For instance, to predict the expected number of high schools for a state with 2,000 elementary schools, follow the line for 2,000 up from the *x*-axis until it intersects the trend line at approximately 825 to 850 high schools.

Scatterplots are also useful to spot *outliers*, individual data points that deviate from the trend. For instance, in the scatterplot above, the data point for the state with 2,500 elementary schools and approximately 670 high schools is an outlier.

Line Graphs

Line graphs follow the same general principle as bar graphs, except that instead of using the lengths of bars to represent numbers, they use points connected by lines. The lines further emphasize the relative values of the numbers.

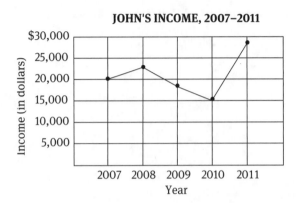

JOHN'S INCOME, 2007–2011

To read John's income for any particular year from this line graph, determine where a line drawn from the appropriate point would intersect the vertical axis.

Pie Charts

Pie charts show how things are distributed. The fraction of a circle occupied by each piece of the "pie" indicates what fraction of the whole that piece represents. In most pie charts, the percentage of the pie occupied by each "slice" will be shown on the slice itself or, for very narrow slices, outside the circle with an arrow or a line pointing to the appropriate slice.

The total size of the whole pie is usually given at the top or bottom of the graph, either as "TOTAL = xxx" or as "100% = xxx." To find the approximate amount represented by a particular piece of the pie, just multiply the whole by the appropriate percent.

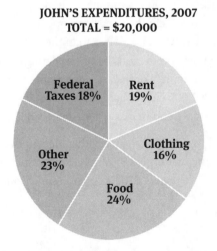

JOHN'S EXPENDITURES, 2007
TOTAL = $20,000

For instance, to find the total tax that John paid to the federal government in 2007, look at the slice of this chart labeled "Federal Taxes." It represents 18% of John's 2007 expenditures. Since his total 2007 expenditures were $20,000, he paid 0.18($20,000) = $3,600 in federal taxes in 2007.

One important note about pie charts: if you're not given the whole and you don't know both the percentage and the actual number that at least one slice represents, you won't be able to find the whole. Pie charts are ideal for presenting the kind of information that ratio problems present in words.

Tables

Tables are in some ways the most accurate graphic presentation format—the only way you can misunderstand a number is to read it from the wrong row or column—but they don't make it easy to spot trends or extremes.

Here's an example of a very simple table.

JOHN'S INCOME: 2007–2011	
YEAR	INCOME
2007	$20,000
2008	$22,000
2009	$18,000
2010	$15,000
2011	$28,000

An easy question might ask for John's income in a particular year or for the difference in his income between two years. To find the difference, you would simply look up the amount for both years and subtract the smaller income from the larger income. A harder question might ask for John's average annual income over the five-year period shown; to determine the average, you would have to find the sum of the five annual incomes and divide it by 5.

STATISTICS CONCEPT CHECK

Before you move on, check your understanding of statistics on the GRE by considering a few questions:

- What are the mean, median, mode, and range of the following set of numbers: $\{3, 9, -8, 2, 0, -4, 9\}$?

- What is the difference between a frequency distribution and a relative frequency distribution?

- Which set has a greater standard deviation: Set A $\{2, 5, 8, 11\}$, or Set B $\{82, 85, 88, 91\}$?

- In a normal distribution, approximately what percent of values are within one standard deviation of the mean?

If you feel confident in your ability to tackle questions that deal with these concepts, proceed to the practice set that starts on the next page.

If you feel like you would like some additional guided practice, head to your online resources. Under **Math Foundations**, click **Statistics Guided Practice**. Try each question on your own first. Then watch a video explanation in which a Kaplan GRE instructor describes a strategic approach.

Statistics Practice Set

Directions: Try answering these questions to practice what you have learned about statistics. Answers and explanations follow at the end of the chapter.

Basic

1. What is the range of the set {3, 8, 2, −6, 0, −2, 7}?

2. If a represents the median of a group of numbers, b is the mode, and c is the range, what is the value of $a + b - c$ for the following group of numbers: 3, 7, −4, 2, −5, 0, −2, 7?

3. A certain teacher gave a grade of A to all students who scored in the 80th percentile or above on a recent test. The distribution of students' scores on that test is shown in the table below. What was the minimum score needed to receive an A on this test?

SCORE RANGE	NUMBER OF STUDENTS
< 70	2
70—74	7
75—79	15
80—84	8
85—89	3
90—94	2
> 94	3
Total Class	40

4. The circle graph below shows the inventory of light bulbs at a local hardware store. If the total number of bulbs in stock was 400, how many were less than 60 watts?

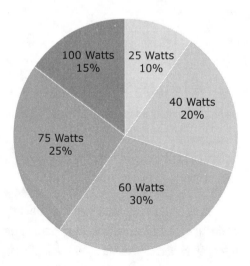

5. Between which two years did sales increase by the greatest amount?

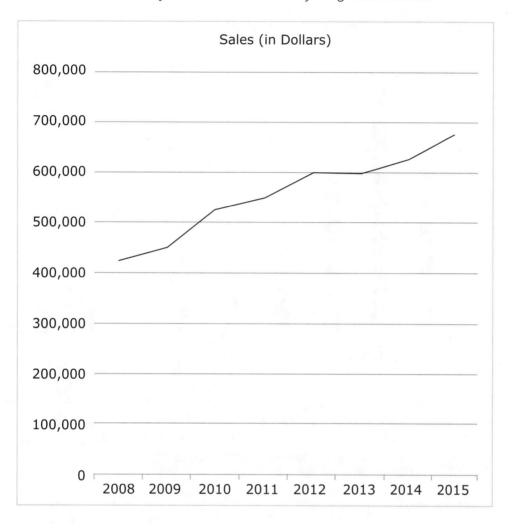

Intermediate

6. The mean of a group of 6 numbers is 15. If the values of one-third of the numbers are increased by 12 each, what is the new mean?

7. In the boxplot shown below, what is the ratio of the range of values in the 75th percentile and above to the range of values in the 25th percentile and below?

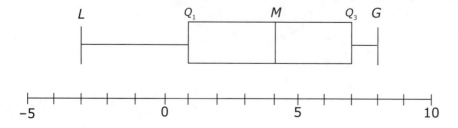

8. The number of inbound calls per minute at a customer service center during a one-hour period is displayed in the column chart below. What was the average number of calls per minute during this period?

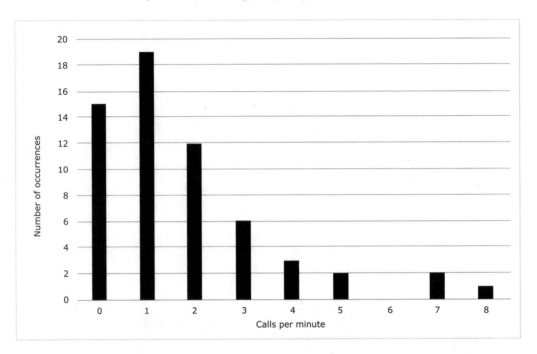

9. A store is open for 10 hours each day. The chart below shows the number of customers each hour for the past week. What was the relative frequency of the number of customers observed between noon and 2:00 pm?

TIME	CUSTOMERS
10 am–11 am	22
11 am–12 pm	38
12 pm–1 pm	60
1 pm–2 pm	44
2 pm–3 pm	33
3 pm–4 pm	27
4 pm–5 pm	31
5 pm–6 pm	38
6 pm–7 pm	49
7 pm–8 pm	58

10. Ebony teaches calligraphy and keeps track of the numbers of her students who are left- and right-handed. Based on the statistics displayed on the graph below, in which year was the ratio of left-handed to right-handed students the highest?

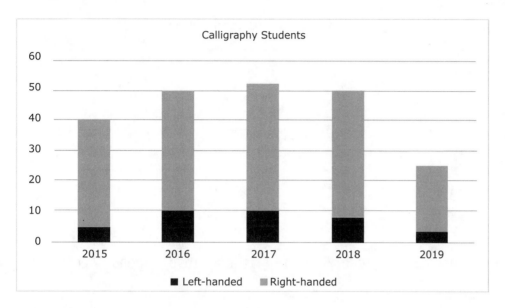

Advanced

11. If list *A* consists of the numbers 1, 3, 3, 3, 3, 3, 3, and 5 and list *B* consists of the numbers 2, 3, 3, 3, 3, 3, 3, and 4, how much greater is the standard deviation of list *A* than that of list *B*?

12. The 7th and 8th grade students in a particular school were given the same mathematics test. A total of 110 7th graders and 100 8th graders completed this test. The overall average score for the two grades was 37.4. If the 7th graders averaged 36.4, what was the average score of the 8th grade students?

13. The average of $\{-1, 3, 0, -2, 4, 2, x, y\}$ is 3 and $x - y = 2$. What is the value of y?

14. The graph below shows the trend in the concentration of a certain pollutant in a river. Based on that trend, to the nearest 0.1 parts per billion, what would have been the concentration in 2015?

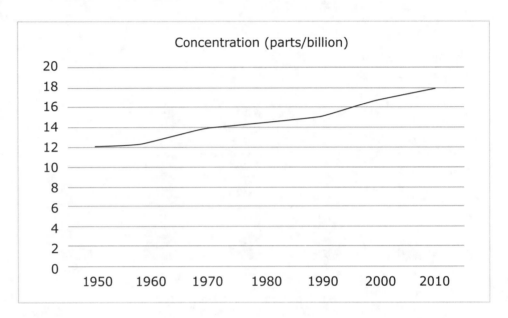

15. What is the range of $\{-3, 0, 2, x, 6, y, 3\}$ if $x^2 + 8x = -16$ and $y^2 - y = 6$?

Answers and explanations follow on the next page. ▶ ▶ ▶

Statistics Practice Set Answer Key

1. 14
2. −4
3. 85
4. 120
5. 2009–2010
6. 19
7. 1:4
8. 1.75

9. 26%
10. 2016
11. 0.5
12. 38.5
13. 8
14. 18.5 parts/billion
15. 10

Statistics Practice Set Answers and Explanations

Basic

1. 14

The range of a group of numbers is the positive difference between the largest and smallest values of the group. For these numbers, that is $8 - (-6) = 8 + 6 = 14$.

2. −4

Arrange the numbers in ascending order: $-5, -4, -2,$ $0, 2, 3, 7, 7$. Because there are 8 numbers, the median will be the average of the 4th and 5th numbers, which is $\frac{0 + 2}{2} = 1$. The mode is 7 since that is the only value that appears more than once. The range is $7 - (-5) = 12$. Plugging these values into the equation given in the question yields $1 + 7 - 12 = -4$.

3. 85

The total number of students in the table is 40. There were $100\% - 80\% = 20\%$ who scored at the 80th percentile or above, so that was $0.2 \times 40 = 8$ students. Count down starting with the highest-scoring category: the total number of students who scored over 94, 90–94, or 85–89 was $3 + 2 + 3 = 8$. So the minimum score to obtain a grade of A was 85.

4. 120

The two types of bulbs that are less than 60 watts are 25 and 40 watts. The percentage of the bulbs in those two power levels is $10\% + 20\% = 30\%$. Since the total number of bulbs is 400, the number of bulbs less than 60 watts is $0.30 \times 400 = 120$.

5. 2009–2010

Examine the chart to find the greatest vertical difference between two adjacent years. This is also the line segment that has the greatest slope. Sales in 2009 were \$450,000, and sales in 2010 were \$525,000. This increase of \$75,000 was greater than for any other equivalent period shown.

Intermediate

6. 19

An average (mean) is the sum of all the values in a group divided by the number of values. In this question, the average is given but the sum is not. Rearrange the formula for averages: sum = (number of values) × (average), which is $6 \times 15 = 90$. Since there are 6 numbers in the group, one-third of that is 2. If those 2 numbers are increased by 12 each, then the sum is increased by 24. Divide the new sum of $90 + 24 = 114$ by 6 to obtain the new average (mean) of 19. (Perhaps you recognized that if one-third of the numbers were increased by 12, the overall average would increase by $12 \div 3 = 4$ to the new value of 19.)

7. 1:4

Box plots are drawn to represent quartiles. Therefore, the range from Q_3 to G represents the 75th percentile and above, and the range from L to Q_1 represents the 25th percentile and below. $G - Q_3$ is $8 - 7 = 1$ and $Q_1 - L$ is $1 - (-3) = 4$, so the ratio is 1:4.

8. 1.75

Calculate the average by multiplying each value by the number of times it occurred, adding those products, and dividing by the total number of minutes, which is 60. First, get the products: $0(15) + 1(19) + 2(12) + 3(6) + 4(3) + 5(2) + 6(0) + 7(2) + 8(1) = 0 + 19 + 24 + 18 + 12 + 10 + 0 + 14 + 8 = 105$. Divide by 60 to obtain the average: $105 \div 60 = 1.75$.

9. 26%

Relative frequency is the number of values with the characteristic of interest expressed as a percent of the total number of values. For this question, that is the number of customers between noon and 2:00 pm expressed as a percent of the total customers. First, find the total number of customers: $22 + 38 + 60 + 44 + 33 + 27 + 31 + 38 + 49 + 58 = 400$. The total number of customers between noon and 2:00 pm is $60 + 44 = 104$, so the percent of the total during that time is $(104 \div 400) \times 100\% = (104 \div 4)\% = 26\%$.

10. 2016

The numbers of left-handed students are shown in the dark-shaded parts of the columns and the right-handed students are in the light-shaded portions. The correct answer will be the year in which the dark-shaded bar is the tallest relative to the light-shaded bar. This would also be the year in which the dark-shaded portion is tallest relative to the total height of the bar, since the former is a part-to-part ratio and the latter is a part-to-whole ratio. This comparison may be faster to visualize than to calculate. A quick glance at the chart shows that the ratios for 2015 and 2019 are much smaller than the others. Compare 2016 and 2017: both had the same number of "lefties," but there were more "righties" in 2017. Similarly, compare 2016 and 2018: both had the same total number of aspiring calligraphers, but there were fewer left-handed students in 2018. Therefore, 2016 had the highest ratio of left-handed students.

Advanced

11. 0.5

Notice that each list consists of 8 numbers, 6 of which are 3, and 2 that have other values. However, in each list those other numbers average 3 (1 and 5 in the first list, 2 and 4 in the second), so the mean of each list is 3. This fact greatly simplifies calculating the differences from the mean for each list. For list A, the differences are 2, 0, 0, 0, 0, 0, 0, and 2; those of list B are 1, 0, 0, 0, 0, 0, 0, and 1. The sum of the squares of these differences is $2^2 + 2^2 = 4 + 4 = 8$ for list A, and $1^2 + 1^2 = 1 + 1 = 2$ for list B. The averages of the squared differences are $8 \div 8 = 1$ and $2 \div 8 = 0.25$. The standard deviations of the two lists are the non-negative square roots of these averages. For list A, the square root of 1 is 1; for list B, the square root of 0.25 is 0.50. Therefore, the difference between the two standard deviations is $1 - 0.5 = 0.5$.

12. 38.5

Because of the numbers involved, this question can be efficiently approached using the balance method for averages. Since the overall average was 37.4, the 7th graders' average of 36.4 was 1.0 below the school average. Those students were cumulatively $1.0 \times 110 = 110$ points below the overall average, so the 8th graders had to be cumulatively 110 points above average. Since there were 100 of them, they had to average $110 \div 100 = 1.1$ above 37.4, which is 38.5.

13. 8

The average of the group is 3 and there are 8 values (including x and y), so the sum of the values is $3 \times 8 = 24$. The sum of the known values is $(-1) + 3 + 0 + (-2) + 4 + 2 = 6$, so $x + y = 24 - 6 = 18$. There are now two equations: $x - y = 2$ and $x + y = 18$. To solve using substitution, rearrange the first equation to $x = y + 2$. Substitute that for x in the second equation: $(y + 2) + y = 18$. So $2y = 16$ and $y = 8$. Alternatively, solve for y by combining the two equations:

$$x + y = 18$$
$$\underline{-(x - y = 2)}$$
$$2y = 16, \text{ so } y = 8$$

14. 18.5 parts/billion

Although there is some variation, the overall trend of the graph is linear and upward. The best estimate of the slope is the overall trend from 1950 to 2010. In 2010 the concentration was 18.0 and in 1950 it was 12.0. Thus, over a period of 60 years, the increase was $18.0 - 12.0 = 6.0$, which equates to 0.1 per year. The increase projected from 2010 to 2015 is $5 \times 0.1 = 0.5$. Add that amount to the 2010 value to get $18.0 + 0.5 = 18.5$ as the estimated value for 2015.

15. 10

In order to determine the range of the group of numbers, the values of x and y are needed. Rearrange the equation for x to: $x^2 + 8x + 16 = 0$. This factors to $(x + 4)^2 = 0$, so the only value for x is -4. At this point, the smallest known value in the group is -4, and the greatest is 6. Set up the equation for y in standard quadratic format: $y^2 - y - 6 = 0$. This factors out to $(y - 3)(y + 2)$, so y can be either 3 or -2. Since both of these values are inside the range of values already known, they have no effect on the overall range of the group, which is $6 - (-4) = 10$.

CHAPTER 14

MATH FOUNDATIONS—COUNTING METHODS AND PROBABILITY REVIEW

Introduction to Counting Methods and Probability Review

You will probably see a few questions on the test that ask you to calculate the probability of an event occurring (or not occurring). You may also see problems dealing with ordering the members of a set and selecting distinct subgroups of items from a set. Understanding and practicing the following concepts will help you handle these questions on Test Day:

- Counting methods:
  - Sets
  - Combination
  - Permutation
- Probability:
  - Probability of multiple events

In this chapter, you will find explanations of each of these topics along with the important formulas to know. At the end of the chapter is a set of practice questions so you can improve your mastery of the concepts.

Counting Methods

Sets

Sets are groups of values that have some common property, such as the negative odd integers greater than -10 or all positive integers that are evenly divisible by 3. The items in sets are called *elements* or *members*. If all the elements in a set can be counted, such as "the number of species of birds in North America," that set is *finite*. If the elements in a set are limitless (e.g., "all positive numbers that are evenly divisible by 3"), that set is *infinite*. The set with no elements is called the *empty set*, which is represented by the symbol Ø. Logically, a set with any members is defined as *nonempty*. If all the elements of set A are among the elements of set B, then A is a *subset* of B. By definition, the empty set is a subset of all sets.

An important characteristic of sets is that elements are unique—that is, they are not repeated. For instance, the set of the numbers 1, 1, 2, 2, and 3 is {1, 2, 3}. Additionally, since order does not matter in sets, {1, 2, 3} is the same set as {3, 2, 1}.

Lists

A list is like a finite set except that the order of the elements matters and that duplicate members can be included. So 1, 2, 3 and 3, 2, 1 are different lists and 1, 2, 3, 2 is a valid list. Because order *does* matter in lists, elements can be uniquely identified by their position, such as "first element" or "fifth element." Notice that sets are usually enclosed within the curly brackets, { }, but lists are not.

Set Operations

The *intersection* of two sets is a set that consists of all the elements that are contained in *both* sets. (You can think of it as the overlap between the sets.) The intersection of sets A and B is written as $A \cap B$. The *union* of two sets is the set of all the elements that are elements of *either* or *both* sets and is written as $A \cup B$. If sets have no common elements, they are referred to as *mutually exclusive*, and their intersection is the empty set.

Drawing *Venn diagrams* is a helpful way to analyze the relationship among sets.

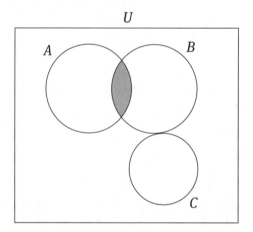

The set of all possible elements that have the characteristics of the sets represented by the circles in a Venn diagram is called a *universal set* and is represented by U. For instance, U could be the set of all species of birds in the world, A the set of species native to Europe, B those native to Asia, and C those native to Australia. In the diagram above, species from other continents are included within U but are not in any specific subset.

The *inclusion-exclusion principle* is a basic counting principle for sets. In the Venn diagram above, the shaded area represents $A \cap B$ (species native to both Europe and Asia), the elements that are within the intersection of A and B. Determining the number of elements in $A \cup B$ is a bit trickier. Merely adding the number of elements in A plus those in B is not correct because that would count the elements that show up in both sets twice. To find the number of elements in the union of two sets, use this formula:

$$|A \cup B| = |A| + |B| - |A \cap B|$$

This formula adjusts for the double-counting of elements that are in both sets. Notice that sets A and C are mutually exclusive, so $|A \cap C| = \emptyset$. For the diagram above, $|A \cup C| = |A| + |C|$.

Multiplication Principle

When choices or events occur one after the other and the choices or events are independent of one another, the total number of possibilities is the *product* of the number of options for each. For example, if a ballot offers 3 candidate choices for Office A, 4 for Office B, and 2 for Office C, the total number of different ways that a voter could fill out the ballot is $3 \times 4 \times 2 = 24$.

Occasionally, a GRE question may require a careful analysis of the number of options for each choice. If a website calls for a 3-letter password but no two letters can be the same, the total possibilities would be $26 \times 25 \times 24 = 15{,}600$ because the stipulation that no two letters be the same reduces the number of choices for the second and third letters.

In situations where choices are "or" rather than "and," as long as the two groups are mutually exclusive, *add* instead of multiplying. A menu has 3 choices for soup and 4 salad options; diners are permitted to select a soup *or* salad with their dinners. In this situation, the total number of choices available is $3 + 4 = 7$.

Combination

A combination question asks you how many unordered subgroups can be formed from a larger group.

Some combination questions on the GRE can be solved without any computation just by counting or listing possible combinations.

> **Example:**
>
> Allen, Betty, and Claire must wash the dishes. They decide to work in shifts of two people. How many shifts will it take before all possible combinations have been used?
>
> It is possible, and not time-consuming, to solve this problem by writing a list. Call Allen "*A*," Betty "*B*," and Claire "*C*." There are three (*AB*, *AC*, *BC*) possible combinations.

The Combination Formula

Some combination questions use numbers that make quick, noncomputational solving difficult. In these cases, use the combination formula $\dfrac{n!}{k!(n-k)!}$, where n is the number of items in the group as a whole and k is the number of items in each subgroup formed. The ! symbol means factorial (for example, $5! = (5)(4)(3)(2)(1) = 120$).

Example:

The 4 finalists in a spelling contest win commemorative plaques. If there are 7 entrants in the spelling contest, how many possible groups of finalists are there?

Plug the numbers into the combination formula, such that n is 7 (the number in the large group) and k is 4 (the number of people in each subgroup formed).

$$\frac{7!}{4!(7-4)!}$$

$$\frac{7!}{4!3!}$$

At this stage, it is helpful to reduce these terms. Since 7 factorial contains all the factors of 4 factorial, we can write 7! as (7)(6)(5)(4!) and then cancel the 4! in the numerator and denominator.

$$\frac{(7)(6)(5)}{(3)(2)(1)}$$

We can reduce further by crossing off the 6 in the numerator and the (3)(2) in the denominator.

$$\frac{(7)(5)}{1} = 35$$

There are 35 potential groups of spelling contest finalists.

When you are asked to find potential combinations from multiple groups, multiply the potential combinations from each group.

Example:

How many groups can be formed consisting of 2 people from room A and 3 people from room B if there are 5 people in room A and 6 people in room B?

Insert the appropriate numbers into the combination formula for each room and then multiply the results. For room A, the number of combinations of 2 in a set of 5 is as follows:

$$\frac{n!}{k!(n-k)!} = \frac{5!}{2!3!} = \frac{(5)(4)(3)(2)(1)}{(2)(1)(3)(2)(1)}$$

Reducing this, you get $\frac{(5)(4)}{(2)} = 10$. For room B, the number of combinations of 3 in a set of 6 is as follows:

$$\frac{n!}{k!(n-k)!} = \frac{6!}{3!3!} = \frac{(6)(5)(4)(3)(2)(1)}{(3)(2)(1)(3)(2)(1)}$$

Reducing this, you get $\frac{(6)(5)(4)}{(3)(2)} = 20$.

Multiply these to find that there are $(10)(20) = 200$ possible groups consisting of 2 people from room A and 3 people from room B.

Sometimes the GRE will ask you to find the number of possible subgroups when choosing one item from a set. In this case, the number of possible subgroups will always equal the number of items in the set.

Example:

Restaurant A has 5 appetizers, 20 main courses, and 4 desserts. If a meal consists of 1 appetizer, 1 main course, and 1 dessert, how many different meals can be ordered at restaurant A?

The number of possible outcomes from each set is the number of items in the set. So there are 5 possible appetizers, 20 possible main courses, and 4 possible desserts. The number of different meals that can be ordered is $(5)(20)(4) = 400$.

Permutation

Within any group of items or people, there are multiple arrangements, or permutations, possible. For instance, within a group of three items (for example: A, B, C), there are six permutations (ABC, ACB, BAC, BCA, CAB, and CBA).

Permutations differ from combinations in that permutations are ordered. By definition, each combination larger than 1 has multiple permutations. On the GRE, a question asking "How many ways/arrangements/orders/schedules are possible?" generally indicates a permutation problem.

To find permutations, think of each place that needs to be filled in a particular arrangement as a blank space. The first place can be filled with any of the items in the larger group. The second place can be filled with any of the items in the larger group except for the one used to fill the first place. The third place can be filled with any of the items in the group except for the two used to fill the first two places, etc.

Example:

In a spelling contest, the winner will receive a gold medal, the second-place finisher will receive a silver medal, the third-place finisher will receive a bronze medal, and the fourth-place finisher will receive a blue ribbon. If there are 7 entrants in the contest, how many different arrangements of award winners are there?

The gold medal can be won by any of 7 people. The silver medal can be won by any of the remaining 6 people. The bronze medal can be won by any of the remaining 5 people. And the blue ribbon can be won by any of the remaining 4 people. Thus, the number of possible arrangements is $(7)(6)(5)(4) = 840$.

Probability

Probability measures the likelihood that an event will occur. Probability can be represented as a fraction, decimal, or percent. For example, if rain today is just as likely as not, then the probability of rain today can be expressed as $\frac{1}{2}$, 0.5, or 50%. You may also see a probability expressed in everyday language: "one chance in a hundred" means the probability is $\frac{1}{100}$. Every probability is expressed as a number between 0 and 1 inclusive, with a probability of 0 meaning "no chance" and a probability of 1 meaning "guaranteed to happen." The higher the probability, the greater the chance that an event will occur.

An *event* may include more than one *outcome*. For example, rolling an even number on a six-sided die is the event that includes only the outcomes 2, 4, and 6. Many GRE probability questions are based on *random experiments* with a defined number of possible outcomes, such as drawing a random card from a full deck. If all the possible outcomes of the experiment are equally likely to occur, you can use this formula to calculate probability:

$$\text{Probability} = \frac{\text{Number of Desired Outcomes}}{\text{Number of Possible Outcomes}}$$

Example:

What is the probability of tossing a fair coin four consecutive times and having the coin land heads up exactly once?

Since a coin is tossed four times and each toss has two possible outcomes, the total number of outcomes, using the multiplication principle, is $2 \times 2 \times 2 \times 2 = 2^4 = 16$. The total number of desired outcomes can be easily counted: HTTT, THTT, TTHT, or TTTH. So there are 4 desired outcomes, and the probability of rolling exactly one head is $\frac{4}{16} = \frac{1}{4} = 0.25$.

The total of the probabilities of all possible outcomes in an experiment must equal 1. For instance, the probability of a tossed coin landing heads up is $\frac{1}{2}$. The probability of the coin landing tails up is also $\frac{1}{2}$. There are no other possible outcomes, and $\frac{1}{2} + \frac{1}{2} = 1$.

By this same logic, if $P(E)$ is the probability that an event *will* occur, then $1 - P(E)$ is the probability that the event *will not* occur. This is a useful fact in many probability questions.

Example:

What is the probability of tossing a fair coin four consecutive times and having the coin land heads up 0, 2, 3, or 4 times?

In the last example, we found that the probability of the coin landing heads up exactly once is 0.25. To find the probability of the coin landing heads up *not* exactly once, subtract that probability from 1: $1 - 0.25 = 0.75$.

In many probability questions involving more than one event, the events are *independent*; one event does not affect the other. If the first toss of a fair coin results in a tail, the probability of the result of the second toss being a tail is still 0.5. In other cases, the results are *not* independent. If there are 4 red disks and 4 green disks in a bag and 2 disks are withdrawn at random without replacement, the probability for the result of the second draw is *dependent* on the result of the first draw. If the first disk drawn is red, then only 3 red disks remain out of a total of 7, and the probability of drawing another red disk on the second draw is $\frac{3}{7}$. If, however, the first draw is green, then 4 of the remaining 7 disks are red, and the probability of drawing red on the second draw is $\frac{4}{7}$.

Probability of Multiple Events

To calculate the probability of two or more independent events occurring, multiply the probabilities of the individual events. For example, the probability of rolling a 3 four consecutive times on a six-sided die would be $\left(\frac{1}{6}\right)\left(\frac{1}{6}\right)\left(\frac{1}{6}\right)\left(\frac{1}{6}\right) = \frac{1}{1,296}$.

You can also calculate the probability of two or more dependent events occurring by multiplying their individual probabilities, but you must calculate the probability of each dependent event as if the preceding event had resulted in the desired outcome or outcomes.

Example:

A bag contains 10 marbles, 4 of which are blue and 6 of which are red. If 2 marbles are removed without replacement, what is the probability that both marbles removed are red?

The probability that the first marble removed will be red is $\frac{6}{10} = \frac{3}{5}$. The probability that the second marble removed will be red will not be the same, however. There will be fewer marbles overall, so the denominator will be one less. There will also be one fewer red marble. (Note that since we are asking about the odds of picking two red marbles, we are only interested in choosing a second marble if the first was red. Don't concern yourself with situations in which a blue marble is chosen first.) If the first marble removed is red, the probability that the second marble removed will also be red is $\frac{5}{9}$. So the probability that both marbles removed will be red is $\left(\frac{3}{\cancel{5}}\right)\left(\frac{\cancel{5}}{9}\right) = \frac{3}{9} = \frac{1}{3}$.

What about the probability of one or another event occurring? On the GRE, you can interpret "the probability of A or B" to mean "the probability of A or B or both," and the formula for calculating this is similar to the inclusion-exclusion principle for sets described earlier in this chapter:

$$P(A \text{ or } B) = P(A) + P(B) - P(A \text{ and } B)$$

Example:

Events A and B are independent. $P(A)$ is 0.60 and $P(A \text{ or } B)$ is 0.94. What is the probability that event B occurs?

Use the formula above: $P(A \text{ or } B) = P(A) + P(B) - P(A \text{ and } B)$. Since the events are independent, $P(A \text{ and } B) = P(A) \times P(B)$. Plug in the values given in the problem: $0.60 + P(B) - (0.60 \times P(B)) = 0.94$, then simplify:

$$0.60 + P(B) - 0.60P(B) = 0.94$$
$$0.60 + 0.40P(B) = 0.94$$
$$0.40P(B) = 0.34$$
$$P(B) = 0.85$$

COUNTING METHODS AND PROBABILITY CONCEPT CHECK

Before you move on, check your understanding of counting methods and probability on the GRE by considering a few questions:

- How many ways can seven books be arranged on a bookshelf?

- How many different groups of three people can be created from a larger pool of ten people?

- From a bag that contains 12 black marbles and 8 blue marbles, what is the probability of selecting 3 black marbles in a row, without replacement?

If you feel confident in your ability to tackle questions that deal with these concepts, proceed to the practice set that starts on the next page.

If you feel like you would like some additional guided practice, head to your online resources. Under **Math Foundations**, click **Counting Methods and Probability Guided Practice**. Try each question on your own first. Then watch a video explanation in which a Kaplan GRE instructor describes a strategic approach.

Counting Methods and Probability Practice Set

Directions: Try answering these questions to practice what you have learned about counting methods and probability. Answers and explanations follow at the end of the chapter.

Basic

1. Paula has 10 books that she'd like to read on vacation, but she only has space for 3 books in her suitcase. How many different groups of 3 books can Paula pack?

2. How many ways are there to fill a candelabra with 4 candle holders from a box of 6 distinctly colored candles?

3. What is the probability of rolling a 6 on two consecutive rolls of a fair six-sided die?

4. What is the probability that one roll of a fair six-sided die will result in an even number?

5. Pablo is allowed to choose 1 of 3 different fruit beverages and 2 of 4 different healthy grain bars for his afternoon snack. How many different combinations does he have from which to choose?

Intermediate

6. A and B are overlapping sets. If $|A|$ has 7 elements, $|B|$ has 5 elements, and $|A \cap B|$ has 3 elements, how many elements are in $|A \cup B|$?

7. What is the probability of the result of 4 independent coin flips being exactly 1 head and 3 tails?

8. A bag contains only 4 orange marbles and 2 blue marbles. Latisha wants to get a blue marble from the bag, but she cannot see what color marble she draws until she takes it out of the bag. Latisha will stop drawing marbles as soon as she gets a blue one. If Latisha does not draw a blue marble in 3 attempts, she stops. What is the probability that she will draw a blue marble?

9. Lee likes both country and pop music. Her playlist has a total of 60 songs that are categorized as pop, country, or rock. If a song is listed as both pop and country, it is considered crossover music. If 24 of Lee's songs are classified as rock music only, 30 are pop, and 18 are country, how many are crossover?

10. A bag contains only red and blue plastic chips. There were 10 chips in the bag and 1 blue chip was removed. The probability of drawing a blue chip was then $\frac{1}{3}$. How many red chips were in the bag?

Advanced

11. In a recent election for two different positions elected by the same voters, Candidates A and B were chosen by a majority of the voters. Two-thirds of the 60% of voters who chose candidate A also voted for Candidate B. The percentage of voters who did not vote for either candidate must have been less than _____?

12. How many different-appearing arrangements can be created using all the letters AAABBC?

13. A certain platoon is made up of 3 squads, each of which has 4 soldiers. When the platoon lines up to enter the mess hall, the squads are allowed to be in any order but the soldiers must line up within their squads according to certain rules. The soldiers in the first squad can line up any way they want as long as they stay with their squad. The squad leader of the second squad insists that the soldiers in that squad be in one particular order. The third squad leader wants the soldiers in that squad to line up in order from either tallest to shortest or shortest to tallest. How many different ways can the platoon line up?

14. Events *A* and *B* are independent but not mutually exclusive. The probability that event *A* occurs is 0.5, and the probability that at least one of the events *A* or *B* occurs is 0.8. What is the probability that event *B* occurs?

15. A six-sided die used for a board game has the letter R on 3 sides, S on 2 sides, and T on the remaining side. What is the probability of rolling an R, an S, and a T on 3 rolls of the die, in any order?

Answers and explanations follow on the next page. ▶ ▶ ▶

Counting Methods and Probability Practice Set Answer Key

1. 120
2. 360
3. $\frac{1}{36}$
4. $\frac{1}{2}$
5. 18
6. 9
7. $\frac{1}{4}$

8. $\frac{4}{5}$
9. 12
10. 6
11. 30%
12. 60
13. 288
14. 0.6
15. $\frac{1}{6}$

Counting Methods and Probability Practice Set Answers and Explanations

Basic

1. 120

Since the books are just being put in a suitcase, order doesn't matter, and the combinations formula can be used.

$$\begin{aligned}
_{10}C_3 &= \frac{10!}{3!(10-3)!} \\
&= \frac{10 \times 9 \times 8 \times 7!}{3!7!} \\
&= \frac{10 \times 9 \times 8}{3 \times 2} \\
&= \frac{720}{6} \\
&= 120
\end{aligned}$$

2. 360

Here, order does matter since the candles are distinctly colored and being placed into slots on the candelabras. There are 6 possible candles for the first slot, 5 for the second, 4 for the third, and 3 for the 4th. To find the total number of possibilities, multiply each of the possibilities for the four slots together ($6 \times 5 \times 4 \times 3$) to get 360.

3. $\frac{1}{36}$

There are 6 equally likely outcomes for one roll of a fair die. One of these outcomes is 6, so the probability of rolling a 6 is $\frac{1}{6}$. The question asks for the probability of rolling a 6 on the first roll *and* the probability of rolling

a 6 on the second roll. These events are independent, so *multiply* the two probabilities: $\frac{1}{6} \times \frac{1}{6} = \frac{1}{36}$.

4. $\frac{1}{2}$

A roll of 2 *or* 4 *or* 6 would meet the criterion in the question. These are mutually exclusive outcomes, so *add* their probabilities: $\frac{1}{6} + \frac{1}{6} + \frac{1}{6} = \frac{3}{6} = \frac{1}{2}$.

5. 18

The number of options Pablo has for the beverage is simply 3, because he can only select one item of the 3 that are available to him. To calculate the number of options for the grain bars, use the combinations formula, because the order in which Pablo selects the 2 grain bars does not matter: $_4C_2 = \frac{4!}{2!(4-2)!} = \frac{4 \times 3 \times 2 \times 1}{2 \times 1 \times 2 \times 1} = 6$. Since Pablo gets to choose a beverage *and* two grain bars, and for each of the 3 beverages he can choose from 6 different options of grain bars, multiply the two numbers of choices: $3 \times 6 = 18$.

Intermediate

6. 9

The formula based on the inclusion-exclusion principle for sets states that $|A \cup B| = |A| + |B| - |A \cap B|$. Substitute the numbers given in the question: $|A \cup B| = 7 + 5 - 3 = 9$.

7. $\frac{1}{4}$

There are two possible outcomes for each flip of the coin: heads or tails. You might be tempted to think that the total number of possible outcomes for 4 consecutive flips would be $4 \times 2 = 8$, but remember that the coin is flipped once *and* then a second time *and* then a third time *and* then a fourth time, so the total number of possible outcomes is actually $2^4 = 16$. If only one head is the result, that could occur on any one of the 4 flips, so there are 4 desired outcomes. The probability is thus $\frac{4}{16} = \frac{1}{4}$.

8. $\frac{4}{5}$

The most efficient way to approach this question is to determine the probability that Latisha will *not* draw a blue marble in 3 attempts and subtract that from 1 to get the probability that she will. There are 6 total marbles, of which 4 are not blue, so the probability that Latisha will not draw a blue marble on the first attempt is $\frac{4}{6} = \frac{2}{3}$. For the second attempt there will only be 5 marbles remaining, 3 of which are not blue, so the probability of not drawing a blue marble on the second attempt is $\frac{3}{5}$.

By the time Latisha tries a third time, there will be 2 blue marbles among the 4 that are left, so the probability of drawing a marble that is not blue is $\frac{2}{4} = \frac{1}{2}$. In order not to draw any blue marbles, Latisha will have to be unsuccessful on the first *and* second *and* third attempts, so the probability of that happening is $\frac{2}{3} \times \frac{3}{5} \times \frac{1}{2} = \frac{6}{30} = \frac{1}{5}$. Therefore, the probability that Latisha will be successful is $1 - \frac{1}{5} = \frac{4}{5}$.

9. 12

The formula for overlapping sets is Total = Group A + Group B − Both + Neither. Since the question defines crossover as country and pop, the rock songs can be considered "neither." Plug the given values into the equation: $60 = 30 + 18 -$ Crossover $+ 24$. Add Crossover to both sides of the equation and subtract 60 from both sides to get: Crossover $= 30 + 18 + 24 - 60 = 12$.

10. 6

After 1 blue chip was removed, there were 9 chips left. If the probability of drawing another blue chip from those remaining 9 was then $\frac{1}{3}$, there must have been $\frac{1}{3} \times 9 = 3$ blue chips, and $9 - 3 = 6$ red chips remaining. Since no red chips were drawn, the original number of red chips must also have been 6.

Advanced

11. 30%

Set up a table to organize the information and derive the values needed to answer this overlapping sets question. The question states that 60% was the total count for A. Put that at the bottom of the "For A" column. The question further states that two-thirds of those voters, which is 40%, also voted for B, so enter that value in the chart as well, at the top of the "For A" column. The total of all the categories must be 100%, as shown in the bottom right cell of the table. Now use these figures to calculate other cells. If 60% of the total voted for A, then 40% of the total did not vote for A. That goes at the bottom of the "Not for A" column. The question does not state what percentage voted for B, but it does mention that B was "chosen by a majority," so enter >50% in the Total column, in the "For B" row. Since 40% of that total is already represented in the "For B/For A" cell, the "For B/Not for A" cell must be greater than 10%, so enter that in the table. Finally, look at the middle cell. If 40% of the total did not vote for A, and at least 10% were "For B," then less than 30% did not vote for either A or B. Put that in the middle cell.

	FOR A	NOT FOR A	TOTAL
For B	40%	>10%	>50%
Not for B		<30%	
Total	60%	40%	100%

12. 60

This question represents a pattern of a counting problem with certain conditions or restrictions added. There are 6! ways to arrange 6 different items. However, in this case, many of those arrangements will appear identical. Consider the configuration in the question, AAABBC. If the A's were not identical there would be 3! = 6 different-appearing ways to arrange them. However, since the A's *are* identical, all 6 of those arrangements have the same appearance. So the number of arrangements must be reduced by a factor of 6. Similarly, there are 2 identical ways to set up any configuration of the B's. The number of different-appearing arrangements is thus $\frac{6!}{3!(2!)}$. This simplifies to $\frac{6 \times 5 \times 4 \times 3 \times 2 \times 1}{3 \times 2 \times 1 \times 2 \times 1} = \frac{5 \times 4 \times 3}{1} = 60$.

13. 288

This question involves the "groups of groups" pattern. First consider how many ways the groups (squads) can be arranged. Since there are 3 distinct squads, that is 3! = 3 × 2 × 1 = 6 different ways. For the squad that is permitted to choose any order they wish, there are 4! = 4 × 3 × 2 × 1 = 24 different ways they can line up. The squad that lines up by height can only have 2 variations and the remaining squad only has one way to line up within the squad. Therefore, the total number of ways that the platoon can line up is 6 × 24 × 2 × 1 = 288.

14. 0.6

Use the formula for two independent events to calculate the probability that event B occurs. Designate the probability that A occurs as P_A, that B occurs as P_B, and the probability that at least one occurs as $P_{A \text{ or } B}$. From the question, $P_A = 0.5$ and $P_{A \text{ or } B} = 0.8$. The formula for $P_{A \text{ or } B}$ is: $P_{A \text{ or } B} = P_A + P_B - P_{A \text{ and } B}$. Since the events are independent, $P_{A \text{ and } B} = P_A \times P_B$. Thus, the formula can be written as $P_{A \text{ or } B} = P_A + P_B - (P_A \times P_B)$. Plug in the known values to get:

$$0.8 = 0.5 + P_B - \left(0.5 \times P_B\right)$$
$$0.8 - 0.5 = P_B - 0.5P_B$$
$$0.3 = 0.5P_B$$
$$0.6 = P_B$$

An alternative approach to this question would be to use the fact that the probability of neither event occurring is $1 - 0.8 = 0.2$. Since this is equivalent to $P_{\text{Not } A} \times P_{\text{Not } B}$, set up the equation: $0.2 = (1.0 - 0.5) \times P_{\text{Not } B}$. So 0.4 is $P_{\text{Not } B}$ and 0.6 is P_B.

15. $\frac{1}{6}$

The desired outcome is R-S-T in any order. The probability of rolling an R (P_R) on any roll is $\frac{3}{6} = \frac{1}{2}$. Similarly, $P_S = \frac{2}{6} = \frac{1}{3}$ and $P_T = \frac{1}{6}$. Thus the probability of rolling one of each is $\frac{1}{2} \times \frac{1}{3} \times \frac{1}{6} = \frac{1}{36}$. There are 3! = 6 different orders in which R-S-T can be rolled, so the total probability of rolling R-S-T in any order is $6 \times \frac{1}{36} = \frac{1}{6}$.

CHAPTER 15

MATH FOUNDATIONS— GEOMETRY REVIEW

Introduction to Geometry Review

Knowing certain two- and three-dimensional geometry formulas is essential to answering many questions, as is knowing the formulas and concepts associated with coordinate geometry. The following concepts are tested on the GRE:

- Geometry:
  - Lines and angles
  - Polygons
  - Triangles
  - Quadrilaterals
  - Circles
  - Coordinate geometry
  - Solids
  - Multiple figures

Use this chapter to gain an understanding of each of these topics. Then use the practice set at the end of the chapter to make sure you can apply the information you've learned to answer questions.

Lines and Angles

A *line* is a one-dimensional geometrical abstraction—infinitely long, with no width. A straight line is the shortest distance between any two points. There is exactly one straight line that passes through any two points.

Example:

In the figure above, $AC = 9$, $BD = 11$, and $AD = 15$. What is the length of BC?

When points are in a line and the order is known, you can add or subtract lengths. Since $AC = 9$ and $AD = 15$, $CD = AD - AC = 15 - 9 = 6$. Now, since $BD = 11$ and $CD = 6$, $BC = BD - CD = 11 - 6 = 5$.

A *line segment* is a section of a straight line of finite length, with two endpoints. A line segment is named for its endpoints, as in segment AB.

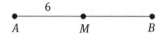

Example:

In the figure above, A and B are the endpoints of the line segment AB, and M is the midpoint ($AM = MB$). What is the length of AB?

Since AM is 6, MB is also 6, and so AB is $6 + 6$, or 12.

Two lines are *parallel* if they lie in the same plane and never intersect regardless of how far they are extended. If line ℓ_1 is parallel to line ℓ_2, we write $\ell_1 \parallel \ell_2$. If two lines are both parallel to a third line, then they are parallel to each other as well.

A *vertex* is the point at which two lines or line segments intersect to form an *angle*. Angles are measured in *degrees* (°).

Angles may be named according to their vertices. Sometimes, especially when two or more angles share a common vertex, an angle is named according to three points: a point along one of the lines or line segments that form the angle, the vertex point, and another point along the other line or line segment. A diagram will sometimes show a letter inside the angle; this letter may also be used to name the angle.

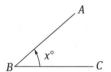

The angle shown in the diagram above could be called $\angle x$, $\angle ABC$, or $\angle B$. (We use a lower-case x because x is not a point.)

Sum of Angles Around a Point

The sum of the measures of the angles around a point is 360°.

$$a + b + c + d + e = 360$$

Sum of Angles Along a Straight Line

The sum of the measures of the angles on one side of a straight line is 180°. Two angles are *supplementary* to each other if their measures sum to 180°.

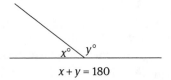

$$x + y = 180$$

Perpendicularity and Right Angles

Two lines are *perpendicular* if they intersect at a 90° angle (a right angle). If line ℓ_1 is perpendicular to line ℓ_2, we write $\ell_1 \perp \ell_2$. If lines ℓ_1, ℓ_2, and ℓ_3 all lie in the same plane, and if $\ell_1 \perp \ell_2$ and $\ell_2 \perp \ell_3$, then $\ell_1 \parallel \ell_3$, as shown in the diagram below.

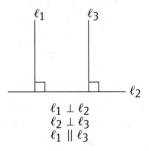

$$\ell_1 \perp \ell_2$$
$$\ell_2 \perp \ell_3$$
$$\ell_1 \parallel \ell_3$$

To find the shortest distance from a point to a line, draw a line segment from the point to the line such that the line segment is perpendicular to the line. Then, measure the length of that segment.

Example:

$\angle A$ of triangle ABC is a right angle. Is side BC longer or shorter than side AB ?

This question seems very abstract, until you draw a diagram of a right triangle, labeling the vertex with the 90° angle as point A.

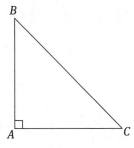

Line segment AB has to be the shortest route between point B and side AC, since side AB is perpendicular to side AC. If AB is the shortest line segment that can join point B to side AC, BC must be longer than AB. Note: The side opposite the 90° angle, called the *hypotenuse*, is always the longest side of a right triangle.

Two angles are *complementary* to each other if their measures sum to 90°. An *acute angle* measures less than 90°, and an *obtuse angle* measures between 90° and 180°. Two angles are *supplementary* if their measures sum to 180°.

Angle Bisectors

A line or line segment *bisects* an angle if it splits the angle into two smaller, equal angles. Line segment *BD* below bisects $\angle ABC$, and $\angle ABD$ has the same measure as $\angle DBC$. The two smaller angles are each half the size of $\angle ABC$.

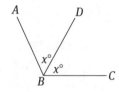

BD bisects $\angle ABC$
$\angle ABD + \angle DBC = \angle ABC$

Adjacent and Vertical Angles

Two intersecting lines form four angles. The angles that are adjacent (next) to each other are *supplementary* because they lie along a straight line. The two angles that are not adjacent to each other are *opposite*, or *vertical*. Opposite angles are equal in measure because each of them is supplementary to the same adjacent angle.

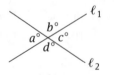

In the diagram above, ℓ_1 intersects ℓ_2 to form angles *a*, *b*, *c*, and *d*. Angles *a* and *c* are opposite, as are angles *b* and *d*. So the measures of angles *a* and *c* are equal to each other, and the measures of angles *b* and *d* are equal to each other. And each angle is supplementary to each of its two adjacent angles.

Angles Around Parallel Lines Intersected by a Transversal

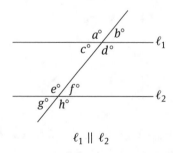

$\ell_1 \parallel \ell_2$

A line that intersects two parallel lines is called a *transversal*. Each of the parallel lines intersects the third line at the same angle. In the figure above, $a = e$. Since *a* and *e* are equal, and since $a = d$ and $e = h$ (because they are opposite angles), $a = d = e = h$. By similar reasoning, $b = c = f = g$.

In short, when two (or more) parallel lines are cut by a transversal, all acute angles formed are equal, all obtuse angles formed are equal, and any acute angle formed is supplementary to any obtuse angle formed.

Example:

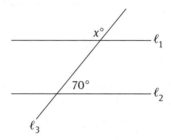

In the diagram above, line ℓ_1 is parallel to line ℓ_2. What is the value of x?

The angle marked $x°$ and the angle adjacent and to the left of the $70°$ angle on line ℓ_2 are corresponding angles. Therefore, the angle marked $x°$ must be supplementary to the $70°$ angle. If $70° + x° = 180°$, x must equal 110.

Polygons

Geometry questions on the GRE will use the following terms to describe polygons.

Polygon: A closed figure whose sides are straight line segments. Families or classes of polygons are named according to their number of sides. A triangle has three sides, a quadrilateral has four sides, a pentagon has five sides, and a hexagon has six sides. Triangles and quadrilaterals are by far the most important polygons on the GRE; other polygons appear only occasionally.

Perimeter: The distance around a polygon; the sum of the lengths of its sides.

Vertex of a polygon: A point where two sides intersect (plural: *vertices*). Polygons are named by assigning each vertex a letter and listing them in order, as in pentagon *ABCDE* below.

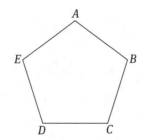

Diagonal of a polygon: A line segment connecting any two nonadjacent vertices.

Regular polygon: A polygon with sides of equal length and interior angles of equal measure.

Small slash marks can provide important information in diagrams of polygons. Sides with the same number of slash marks are equal in length, while angles with the same number of slash marks through circular arcs have the same measure. In the triangle below, for example, $a = b$, and angles X and Z are equal in measure.

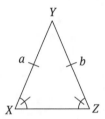

You can figure out the sum of the interior angles of a polygon by dividing the polygon into triangles. Draw diagonals from any vertex to all the nonadjacent vertices. Then, multiply the number of triangles by 180° to get the sum of the interior angles of the polygon. This works because the sum of the interior angles of any triangle is always 180°.

Example:

What is the sum of the interior angles of a pentagon?

Draw a pentagon (a five-sided polygon) and divide it into triangles, as discussed above.

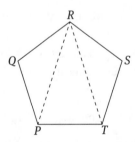

No matter how you've drawn the pentagon, you'll be able to form three triangles. Therefore, the sum of the interior angles of a pentagon is 3 × 180° = 540°.

Triangles

Important Terms

Triangle: A polygon with three straight sides and three interior angles.

Right triangle: A triangle with one interior angle of 90° (a right angle).

Hypotenuse: The longest side of a right triangle. The hypotenuse is always opposite the right angle.

Isosceles triangle: A triangle with two equal sides, which are opposite two equal angles. In the figure below, the sides opposite the two 70° angles are equal, so $x = 7$.

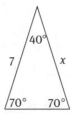

Legs: The two equal sides of an isosceles triangle or the two shorter sides of a right triangle (the ones forming the right angle). Note: The third, unequal side of an isosceles triangle is called the *base*.

Equilateral triangle: A triangle whose three sides are all equal in length and whose three interior angles each measure 60°.

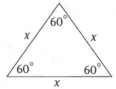

The *altitude,* or *height,* of a triangle is the perpendicular distance from a vertex to the side opposite the vertex. The altitude may fall inside or outside the triangle, or it may coincide with one of the sides.

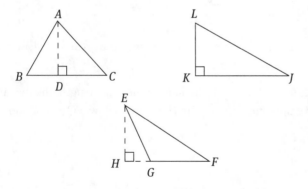

In the diagrams above, AD, EH, *and* LK *are altitudes.*

Interior and Exterior Angles of a Triangle

The sum of the interior angles of any triangle is 180°. Therefore, in the figure below, $a + b + c = 180$.

An *exterior angle of a triangle* is equal to the sum of the remote interior angles. The exterior angle labeled $x°$ is equal to the sum of the remote angles: $x = 50 + 100 = 150$.

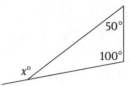

The three exterior angles of any triangle add up to $360°$.

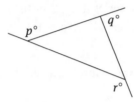

In the figure above, $p + q + r = 360$.

Sides and Angles

The sum of the lengths of any two sides of a triangle is greater than the length of the third side. In the triangle below, $b + c > a$, $a + b > c$, and $a + c > b$.

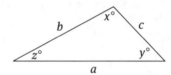

If the lengths of two sides of a triangle are unequal, the greater angle lies opposite the longer side and vice versa. In the figure above, if $x > y > z$, then $a > b > c$.

Since the two legs of an isosceles triangle have the same length, the two angles opposite the legs must have the same measure. In the figure below, $PQ = PR$, and $\angle Q = \angle R$.

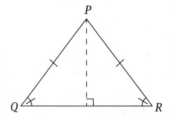

Perimeter and Area of Triangles

There is no special formula for the perimeter of a triangle; it is just the sum of the lengths of the sides.

Example:

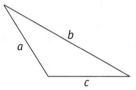

If a, b, and c are integers, and a and b both have a length of 4, what is the largest possible perimeter of the triangle above?

The perimeter is the sum of the lengths of the sides of the triangle. Since a and b are both 4, the perimeter is $4 + 4 + c$.

According to the Triangle Inequality Theorem, the largest possible third side of a triangle must be smaller than the sum of the other two sides. $4 + 4 = 8$, so side c must be smaller than 8. Because all sides are integers and because side c should be as large as possible to create the largest possible perimeter, c must be 7.

$$4 + 4 + 7 = 15$$

The area of a triangle is $\frac{1}{2}(\text{Base})(\text{Height})$.

Example:

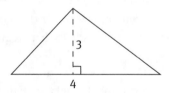

In the diagram above, the base has length 4, and the altitude has length 3. What is the area of the triangle?

$$\text{Area} = \frac{1}{2}bh$$
$$= \frac{bh}{2}$$
$$= \frac{4 \times 3}{2}$$
$$= 6$$

Since the lengths of the base and altitude were not given in specific units, such as centimeters or feet, the area of the triangle is simply said to be 6 square units.

The area of a right triangle is easy to find. Think of one leg as the base and the other as the height. Then the area is one-half the product of the legs, or $\frac{1}{2} \times \text{Leg}_1 \times \text{Leg}_2$.

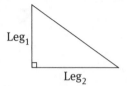

Right Triangles

The right angle is always the largest angle in a right triangle; therefore, the hypotenuse, which lies opposite the right angle, is always the longest side.

Pythagorean Theorem

The *Pythagorean theorem*, which holds for all right triangles and for no other triangles, states that the square of the hypotenuse is equal to the sum of the squares of the legs.

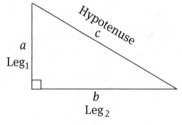

$$(\text{Leg}_1)^2 + (\text{Leg}_2)^2 = (\text{Hypotenuse})^2$$
$$\textbf{or } a^2 + b^2 = c^2$$

The Pythagorean theorem is very useful whenever you're given the lengths of any two sides of a right triangle; as long as you know whether the remaining side is a leg or the hypotenuse, you can find its length by using the Pythagorean theorem.

Example:

What is the length of the hypotenuse of a right triangle with legs of lengths 9 and 10?

$$
\begin{aligned}
(\text{Hypotenuse})^2 &= \left(\text{Leg}_1\right)^2 + \left(\text{Leg}_2\right)^2 \\
&= 9^2 + 10^2 \\
&= 81 + 100 \\
&= 181
\end{aligned}
$$

If the square of the hypotenuse equals 181, then the hypotenuse itself must be the square root of 181, or $\sqrt{181}$.

Pythagorean Triples

Certain ratios of integers always satisfy the Pythagorean theorem. You might like to think of them as "Pythagorean triples." One such ratio is 3, 4, and 5. A right triangle with legs of lengths 3 and 4 and a hypotenuse of length 5 is probably the most common kind of right triangle on the GRE. Whenever you see a right triangle with legs of 3 and 4, with a leg of 3 and a hypotenuse of 5, or with a leg of 4 and a hypotenuse of 5, you immediately know the length of the remaining side. In addition, any multiple of these lengths makes another Pythagorean triple; for instance, $6^2 + 8^2 = 10^2$, so a triangle with sides of lengths of 6 and 8 and a hypotenuse of 10 is also a right triangle.

The other triple that commonly appears on the GRE is 5, 12, and 13.

Special Right Triangles

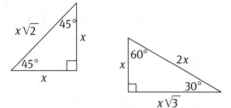

There are two more special kinds of right triangles for which you won't have to use the Pythagorean theorem to find the lengths of the sides. There are special ratios between the lengths of the sides in isosceles right triangles (45°-45°-90° triangles) and 30°-60°-90° triangles (right triangles with acute angles of 30° and 60°). As you can see in the first drawing above, the sides of an isosceles right triangle are in a ratio of $x : x : x\sqrt{2}$ with the $x\sqrt{2}$ in the ratio representing the hypotenuse. The sides of a 30°-60°-90° triangle are in a ratio of $x : x\sqrt{3} : 2x$ where $2x$ represents the hypotenuse and x represents the side opposite the 30° angle. (Remember: the longest side has to be opposite the greatest angle.)

> **Example:**
>
> What is the length of the hypotenuse of an isosceles right triangle with legs of length 4?
>
> You can use the Pythagorean theorem to find the hypotenuse, but it's quicker to use the special right triangle ratios. In an isosceles right triangle, the ratio of a leg to the hypotenuse is $x : x\sqrt{2}$. Since the length of a leg is 4, the length of the hypotenuse must be $4\sqrt{2}$.

Triangles and Quantitative Comparison

All Quantitative Comparison questions require you to judge whether enough information has been given to make a comparison. In geometry, making this judgment is often a matter of knowing the correct definition or formula. For triangles, keep in mind the following:

- If you know two angles, you know the third.
- To find the area, you need the base and the height.
- In a right triangle, if you have two sides, you can find the third. And if you have two sides, you can find the area.
- In isosceles right triangles and 30°-60°-90° triangles, if you know one side, you can find everything.

Be careful, though! Be sure you know as much as you think you do.

Example:

Quantity A	Quantity B
Area of right triangle *ABC*, where $\overline{AB} = 5$ and $\overline{BC} = 4$	6

You may think at first that *ABC* must be a 3:4:5 right triangle. Not so fast! We're given two sides, but we don't know which sides they are. If *AB* is the hypotenuse, then it is a 3:4:5 triangle and the area is $\frac{1}{2}(3 \times 4) = 6$, but it's also possible that *AC*, the missing side, is the hypotenuse. In that case, the area would be $\frac{1}{2}(4 \times 5) = 10$. Because Quantity A can either be equal to Quantity B or can be larger than Quantity B, their relationship cannot be determined from the information given.

Quadrilaterals

A *quadrilateral* is a four-sided polygon. Regardless of a quadrilateral's shape, the four interior angles sum to 360°.

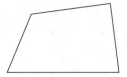

A *trapezoid* is a quadrilateral with at least one pair of parallel sides.

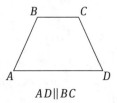

$AD \parallel BC$

A *parallelogram* is a quadrilateral with two pairs of parallel sides. Opposite sides are equal in length; opposite angles are equal in measure; angles that are not opposite are supplementary to each other (measure of $\angle A$ + measure of $\angle D = 180°$ in the figure below).

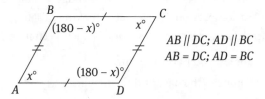

$AB \parallel DC; AD \parallel BC$
$AB = DC; AD = BC$

measure of $\angle A$ = measure of $\angle C$;
measure of $\angle B$ = measure of $\angle D$

A *rectangle* is a parallelogram with four right angles. Opposite sides are equal; diagonals are equal.

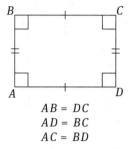

$$AB = DC$$
$$AD = BC$$
$$AC = BD$$

A *rhombus* is a parallelogram with four equal sides. Opposite angles are equal to each other, but they do not have to be right angles.

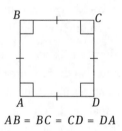

$$AB = BC = CD = DA$$

A *square* is a rectangle with equal sides.

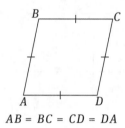

$$AB = BC = CD = DA$$

Perimeters of Quadrilaterals

To find the perimeter of any polygon, you can simply add the lengths of its sides. However, the properties of rectangles and squares lead to simple formulas that may speed up your calculations.

Because the opposite sides are equal, the *perimeter of a rectangle* is twice the sum of the length and the width: Perimeter = 2(Length + Width)

The perimeter of a 5 by 2 rectangle is $2(5 + 2) = 14$.

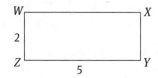

The *perimeter of a square* is equal to the sum of the lengths of the 4 sides. Because all 4 sides are the same length, Perimeter = 4(Side). If the length of one side of a square is 3, the perimeter is $4 \times 3 = 12$.

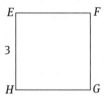

Areas of Quadrilaterals

Area formulas always involve multiplication, and the results are always stated in "square" units. You can see why if you look at the drawing below:

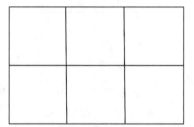

The rectangle is composed of six squares, all equal in size. Let's say that the side of a single small square is 1 unit. Then, we would say that a single square measures "1 by 1." That translates into math as 1×1, or 1^2—in other words, "one square unit."

As you can see from the drawing, there are 6 such square units in the rectangle. That's its area: 6 square units. But you could also find the area by multiplying the number of squares in a row by the number of squares in a column: 3×2, or 6. And since we've defined the length of the side of a square as 1 unit, that's also equivalent to multiplying the length of a horizontal side by the length of a vertical side: again, $3 \times 2 = 6$.

Formulas for Area

To find the area of a rectangle, multiply the *length* by the *width*.

Area of rectangle = ℓw

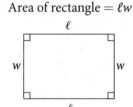

Since the length and width of a square are equal, the area formula for a square just uses the length of a *side*:

$$\text{Area of square} = (\text{Side})^2 = s^2$$

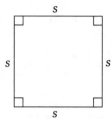

If you're working with a parallelogram, designate one side as the *base*. Then, draw a line segment from one of the vertices opposite the base down to the base so that it intersects the base at a right angle. That line segment will be called the *height*. To find the area of the parallelogram, multiply the length of the base by the length of the height:

$$\text{Area of parallelogram} = (\text{Base})(\text{Height}), \text{ or } A = bh$$

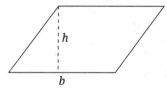

If the figure is a trapezoid with only one pair of parallel sides, average the lengths of the two parallel sides. Then plug that value in for the base in the formula for the area of a parallelogram.

Remember the following:

- In a parallelogram, if you know two adjacent sides, you know all of them; and if you know two adjacent angles, you know all of them.
- In a rectangle, if you know two adjacent sides, you know the area.
- In a square, if you're given virtually any measurement (area, length of a side, length of a diagonal), you can figure out the other measurements.

Circles

Important Terms

Circle: The set of all points in a plane at the same distance from a certain point. This point is called the center of the circle. A circle is labeled by its center point; circle O means the circle with center point O.

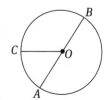

Diameter: A line segment that connects two points on the circle and passes through the center of the circle. *AB* is a diameter of circle *O*, shown previously.

Radius: A line segment that connects the center of the circle with any point on the circle (plural: *radii*). The radius of a circle is one-half the length of the diameter. In circle *O*, *OA*, *OB*, and *OC* are radii.

Central angle: An angle formed by two radii. In circle *O*, *AOC* is a central angle. *COB* and *BOA* are also central angles. (The measure of *BOA* happens to be 180°.) The total degree measure of a circle is 360°.

Chord: A line segment that joins two points on the circle. The longest chord of a circle is its diameter. *AT* is a chord of circle *P* below.

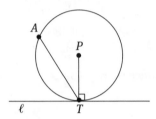

Tangent: A line that touches only one point on the circumference of a circle. A line drawn tangent to a circle is perpendicular to the radius at the point of tangency. In the diagram above, line ℓ is tangent to circle *P* at point *T*.

Circumference and Arc Length

The distance around a polygon is called its *perimeter*; the distance around a circle is called its *circumference*.

The ratio of the circumference of any circle to its diameter is a constant, called *pi* (π). For GRE purposes, the value of π is usually approximated as 3.14.

Since π equals the ratio of the circumference, *C*, to the diameter, *d*, we can say that

$$\pi = \frac{\text{Circumference}}{\text{Diameter}} = \frac{C}{d}.$$

The formula for the circumference of a circle is $C = \pi d$.

The circumference formula can also be stated in terms of the radius, *r*. Since the diameter is twice the length of the radius, that is, $d = 2r$, then $C = 2\pi r$.

An *arc* is a section of the circumference of a circle. Any arc can be thought of as the portion of a circle cut off by a particular central angle. For example, in circle *Q*, arc *ABC* is the portion of the circle that is cut off by central angle *AQC*. Since arcs are associated with central angles, they can be measured in degrees. The degree measure of an arc is equal to that of the central angle that cuts it off. So in circle Q, arc ABC and central angle AQC would have the same degree measure.

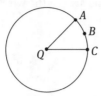

An arc that is exactly half the circumference of its circle is called a *semicircle.*

The length of an arc is the same fraction of a circle's circumference as its degree measure is of $360°$ (the degree measure of a whole circle). For an arc with a central angle measuring $n°$:

$$\text{Arc length} = \frac{n}{360}(\text{Circumference})$$

$$= \frac{n}{360} \times 2\pi r$$

Example:

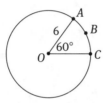

What is the length of arc ABC of circle O above?

$C = 2\pi r$; therefore, if $r = 6$, $C = 2 \times \pi \times 6 = 12\pi$. Since AOC measures $60°$, arc ABC is $\frac{60}{360}$, or $\frac{1}{6}$ of the circumference. Thus, the length of arc ABC is $\frac{1}{6} \times 12\pi$, or 2π.

Area and Sector Area Formulas

The area of a circle is πr^2.

A *sector* is a portion of a circle's area that is bounded by two radii and an arc. The shaded area of circle X is sector AXB.

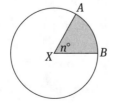

Like arcs, sectors are associated with central angles. And the process and formula used to find the area of a sector are similar to those used to determine arc length. First, find the degree measure of the sector's central angle and figure out what fraction that degree measure is of 360°. Then, multiply the area of the whole circle by that fraction. In a sector whose central angle measures $n°$:

$$\text{Area of sector} = \frac{n}{360}(\text{Area of circle})$$

$$= \frac{n}{360}\pi r^2$$

Example:

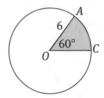

In circle O above, what is the area of sector AOC?

Since $\angle AOC$ measures 60°, a 60° "slice" of the circle is $\frac{60°}{360°}$, or $\frac{1}{6}$ of the total area of the circle. Therefore, the area of the sector is $\frac{1}{6}\pi r^2 = \frac{1}{6}(36\pi) = 6\pi$.

Coordinate Geometry

In coordinate geometry, the locations of points in a plane are indicated by ordered pairs of real numbers.

Important Terms and Concepts

Plane: A flat surface that extends indefinitely in any direction.

x-axis and y-axis: The horizontal (x) and vertical (y) lines that intersect perpendicularly to indicate location on a coordinate plane. Each axis is a number line.

Ordered pair: Two numbers or quantities separated by a comma and enclosed in parentheses. An example would be (8,7). All the ordered pairs that you'll see in GRE coordinate geometry problems will be in the form (x,y), where the first quantity, x, tells you how far the point is to the left or right of the y-axis, and the second quantity, y, tells you how far the point is above or below the x-axis.

Coordinates: The numbers that designate distance from an axis in coordinate geometry. The first number is the x-coordinate; the second is the y-coordinate. In the ordered pair (8,7), 8 is the x-coordinate and 7 is the y-coordinate.

Origin: The point where the x- and y-axes intersect; its coordinates are (0,0).

Plotting Points

Here's what a coordinate plane looks like:

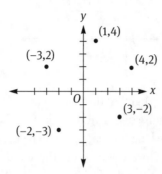

Any point in a coordinate plane can be identified by an ordered pair consisting of its x-coordinate and its y-coordinate. Every point that lies on the x-axis has a y-coordinate of 0, and every point that lies on the y-axis has an x-coordinate of 0.

When you start at the origin and move:

to the right	. . . .	x is positive
to the left	. . . .	x is negative
up	. . . .	y is positive
down	. . . .	y is negative

Therefore, the coordinate plane can be divided into four quadrants, as shown below.

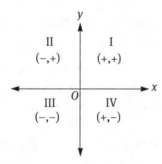

Distances on the Coordinate Plane

The distance between two points is equal to the length of the straight-line segment that has those two points as endpoints.

If a line segment is parallel to the x-axis, the y-coordinate of every point on the line segment will be the same. Similarly, if a line segment is parallel to the y-axis, the x-coordinate of every point on the line segment will be the same.

Therefore, to find the length of a line segment parallel to one of the axes, all you have to do is find the difference between the endpoint coordinates that do change. In the diagram that follows, the length of AB equals $x_2 - x_1$.

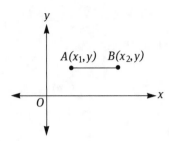

You can find the length of a line segment that is not parallel to one of the axes by treating the line segment as the hypotenuse of a right triangle. Simply draw in the legs of the triangle parallel to the two axes. The length of each leg will be the difference between the x- or y-coordinates of its endpoints. Once you've found the lengths of the legs, you can use the Pythagorean theorem to find the length of the hypotenuse (the original line segment).

In the diagram below, $(DE)^2 = (EF)^2 + (DF)^2$.

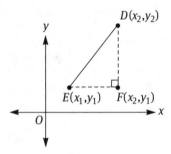

Example:

If the coordinates of point A are (3,4) and the coordinates of point B are (6,8), what is the distance between points A and B?

You don't have to draw a diagram to use the method just described, but drawing one may help you to visualize the problem. Plot points A and B and draw in line segment AB. The length of AB is the distance between the two points. Now draw a right triangle, with AB as its hypotenuse. The missing vertex will be the intersection of a line segment drawn through point A parallel to the x-axis and a line segment drawn through point B parallel to the y-axis. Label the point of intersection C. Since the x- and y-axes are perpendicular to each other, AC and BC will also be perpendicular to each other.

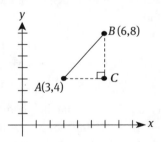

Point C will also have the same x-coordinate as point B and the same y-coordinate as point A. That means that point C has coordinates (6,4).

To use the Pythagorean theorem, you'll need the lengths of AC and BC. The distance between points A and C is simply the difference between their x-coordinates, while the distance between points B and C is the difference between their y-coordinates. So $AC = 6 - 3 = 3$, and $BC = 8 - 4 = 4$. If you recognize these as the legs of a 3:4:5 right triangle, you'll know immediately that the distance between points A and B must be 5. Otherwise, you'll have to use the Pythagorean theorem to come to the same conclusion.

Equations of Lines

Straight lines can be described by linear equations.

Commonly:

$$y = mx + b$$

where m is the slope $\left(\dfrac{\Delta y}{\Delta x}\right)$ and b is the point where the line intercepts the y-axis, that is, the value of y where $x = 0$.

Lines that are parallel to the x-axis have a slope of zero and therefore have the equation $y = b$. Lines that are parallel to the y-axis have the equation $x = a$, where a is the x-intercept of that line.

If you're comfortable with linear equations, you'll sometimes want to use them to find the slope of a line or the coordinates of a point on a line. However, many such questions can be answered without determining or manipulating equations. Check the answer choices to see if you can eliminate any by common sense.

Example:

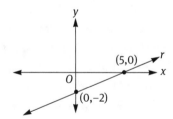

Line r is a straight line as shown above. Which of the following points lies on line r?

(A) (6,6)

(B) (7,3)

(C) (8,2)

(D) (9,3)

(E) (10,2)

Line r intercepts the y-axis at $(0,-2)$, so you can plug -2 in for b in the slope-intercept form of a linear equation. Line r has a rise (Δy) of 2 and a run (Δx) of 5, so its slope is $\dfrac{2}{5}$. That makes the slope-intercept form $y = \dfrac{2}{5}x - 2$.

The easiest way to proceed from here is to substitute the coordinates of each answer choice into the equation in place of x and y; only the coordinates that satisfy the equation can lie on the line. Choice **(E)** is the best answer to start with, because 10 is the only x-coordinate that will not create a fraction on the right side of the equal sign. Plugging in (10,2) for x and y in the slope-intercept equation gives you $2 = \frac{2}{5}(10) - 2$, which simplifies to $2 = 4 - 2$.

That's true, so the correct answer choice is **(E)**.

Graphing Functions and Circles

At the end of the previous section, you saw an example of a line written as an equation: $y = \frac{2}{5}x - 2$. But not all lines need to be written in slope-intercept form; for example, the same line could be written in function notation instead: $f(x) = \frac{2}{5}x - 2$. Just like in an equation written in slope-intercept form, x here represents the x-coordinate, and the function's output is the y-coordinate. Consider what happens when you pick the number 1 for x: $f(1) = \frac{2}{5}(1) - 2 = -\frac{8}{5}$. So when the input is $x = 1$, the output is $y = -\frac{8}{5}$. That means the point $\left(1, -\frac{8}{5}\right)$ is part of $f(x)$'s graph.

Graphing Quadratic Functions

In addition to linear equations, the GRE might also test your ability to plot more complex equations on the coordinate plane. For example, imagine a quadratic equation represented as a function in the form of $f(x) = x^2 + 2x - 2$. While such an expression might seem daunting at first, remember that picking any number for x in the function will produce a y-value. That (x,y) pair can then be plotted on the coordinate plane. Or, you could assign $f(x) = 0$ to determine the x-intercept values when $y = 0$. Even without an extensive understanding of how quadratic equations are graphed on the coordinate plane, your ability to pick numbers and find ordered pairs will help you eliminate wrong answers and potentially find your way to the correct answer.

When a quadratic function is fully plotted on the coordinate plane, it creates a specific shape called a parabola. The most simple parabola, shown on the next page, is that of $y = x^2$. Since 0^2 is equal to 0, the origin is a point on the parabola. What happens when $x = 1$ or -1? Then y also equals 1. But notice what happens when $x = 2$ or -2: the y-value becomes 4. As the parabola moves out along the x-axis in either direction, it grows vertically along the y-axis at a faster rate.

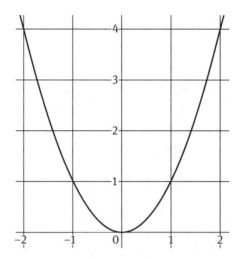

From this basic parabola, the GRE might test how different constants in an equation affect that equation's graph, or how graphs might be shifted, stretched, or shrunk.

In the quadratic function $f(x) = ax^2 + bx + c$, constant a determines which direction the parabola opens. If a is positive, the parabola opens upward. If a is negative, the parabola opens downward. Constant c, on the other hand, represents the vertical shift from the x-axis of the corresponding graph's y-intercept. For example, a c-value of -2 would mean that the parabola is shifted 2 units downward from the x-axis.

Functions' graphs can also be shifted to the left or right. Take, for example, a quadratic function such as $f(x) = x^2 - x - 2$. If 7 were subtracted from every one of that function's possible inputs, the function would become $f(x - 7) = (x - 7)^2 - (x - 7) - 2$, which simplifies to $f(x - 7) = x^2 - 15x + 54$. Notice in these functions' respective graphs below that subtracting 7 from every input of $f(x)$ shifts that function's graph 7 units rightward to create the graph of $f(x - 7)$. Had a constant value been added to every one of the function's inputs, the function's graph would have shifted that number of units leftward.

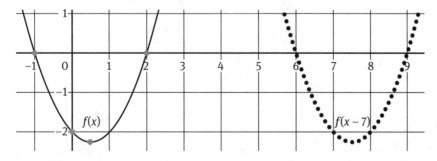

While adding or subtracting constants from a function leads to shifts in that function's graph, multiplying or dividing by constants results in stretching or shrinking that function's graph. For example, if the previous function $f(x)$ is doubled to become $2f(x)$, then for every possible input x, the corresponding output $f(x)$ is doubled. The function thus becomes $2f(x) = 2(x^2 - x - 2)$, which simplifies to $2x^2 - 2x - 4$. By contrast, if $f(x)$ is halved to become $0.5f(x)$, then for every possible input, the corresponding output is halved. The function thus becomes $0.5f(x) = 0.5(x^2 - x - 2) = 0.5x^2 - 0.5x - 1$.

Notice in these functions' respective graphs that follow that $2f(x)$'s graph is $f(x)$'s graph stretched vertically by a factor of 2, while $0.5f(x)$'s graph is $f(x)$'s graph shrunk vertically by a factor of 0.5.

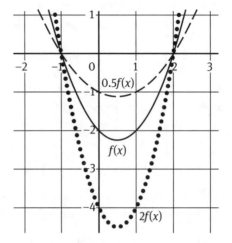

Finally, multiplying a function specifically by -1, or negating that function, results in the reflection of that function across the x-axis. If the previous function $f(x)$ is negated to become $-f(x)$, then $-f(x) = -(x^2 - x - 2)$, which simplifies to $-x^2 + x + 2$. Note from $-f(x)$'s graph below how it is just the upside-down version of $f(x)$'s graph.

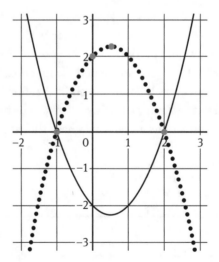

Graphing Circles

It is very rare that the GRE would test the plotting of a circle on the coordinate plane. However, for high scorers, it is good to know that graphing an equation in the form $(x - a)^2 + (y - b)^2 = r^2$ produces a circle, where x and y are points on the coordinate plane and a, b, and r are constants.

The circle's radius is represented by r, the number of units that the circle's center is shifted horizontally from the origin of the xy-plane is represented by a, and the number of units that the circle's center is shifted vertically from the origin is represented by b. Thus, the circle's center is located at the point (a,b).

In the *xy*-plane shown below, the equation of the smaller graphed circle is $x^2 + y^2 = 1$. Thus, $a = b = 0$, meaning that the circle's center is at the origin $(0,0)$; and since $r^2 = 1$, the circle's radius is 1. The equation of the larger graphed circle is $(x - 5)^2 + (y + 3)^2 = 4$. Thus, $a = 5$, $b = -3$, and $r^2 = 4$, so the circle's radius is 2 and the circle's center is at $(5, -3)$.

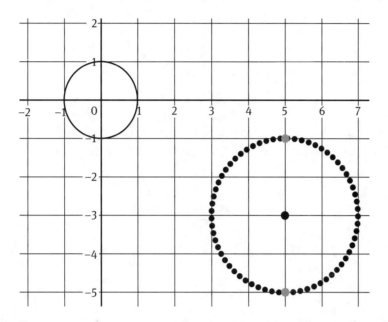

Solids

Important Terms

Solid: A three-dimensional figure. The dimensions are usually called length, width, and height (ℓ, *w*, and *h*) or height, width, and depth (*h*, *w*, and *d*). There are only two types of solids that appear with any frequency on the GRE: rectangular solids (including cubes) and cylinders.

Uniform solid: A solid that could be cut into congruent cross sections (parallel "slices" of equal size and shape) along a given axis. Solids you see on the GRE will almost certainly be uniform solids.

Face: The surface of a solid that lies in a particular plane. Hexagon *ABCDEF* is one face of the solid pictured below.

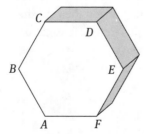

Edge: A line segment that connects adjacent faces of a solid. The sides of hexagon *ABCDEF* are also edges of the solid pictured above.

Base: The "bottom" face of a solid as oriented in any given diagram.

Rectangular solid: A solid with six rectangular faces. All edges meet at right angles. Examples of rectangular solids are cereal boxes, bricks, etc.

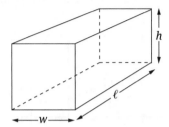

Cube: A special rectangular solid in which all edges are of equal length, e, and therefore all faces are squares. Sugar cubes and dice without rounded corners are examples of cubes.

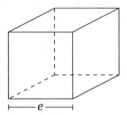

Cylinder: A uniform solid whose horizontal cross section is a circle—for example, a soup can or a pipe that is closed at both ends. A cylinder's measurements are generally given in terms of its radius, r, and its height, h.

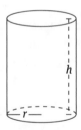

Lateral surface of a cylinder: The "pipe" surface, as opposed to the circular "ends." The lateral surface of a cylinder is unlike most other surfaces of solids that you'll see on the GRE, first because it does not lie in a plane and second because it forms a closed loop. Think of it as the label around a soup can. If you could remove it from the can in one piece, you would have an open tube. If you then cut the label and unrolled it, it would form a rectangle with a length equal to the circumference of the circular base of the can and a height equal to that of the can.

Formulas for Volume and Surface Area

Volume of a rectangular solid = (Area of base)(Height) = (Length × Width)(Height) = lwh

Surface area of a rectangular solid = Sum of areas of faces = $2\ell w + 2\ell h + 2hw$

Since a cube is a rectangular solid for which $\ell = w = h$, the formula for its volume can be stated in terms of any edge:

- Volume of a cube = ℓwh = (Edge)(Edge)(Edge) = e^3
- Surface area of a cube = Sum of areas of faces = $6e^2$

To find the volume or surface area of a cylinder, you'll need two pieces of information: the height of the cylinder and the radius of the base.

- Volume of a cylinder = (Area of base)(Height) = $\pi r^2 h$
- Lateral surface area of a cylinder = (Circumference of base)(Height) = $2\pi rh$
- Total surface area of a cylinder = Areas of circular ends + Lateral surface area = $2\pi r^2 + 2\pi rh$

Multiple Figures

Some GRE geometry problems involve combinations of different types of figures. Besides the basic rules and formulas that you would use on normal geometry problems, you'll need an intuitive understanding of how various geometrical concepts relate to each other to answer these "multiple figures" questions correctly. For example, you may have to revisualize the side of a rectangle as the hypotenuse of a neighboring right triangle or as the diameter of a circumscribed circle. Keep looking for the relationships between the different figures until you find one that leads you to the answer.

Area of Shaded Regions

A common multiple-figures question involves a diagram of a geometrical figure that has been broken up into different, irregularly shaped areas, often with one region shaded. You'll usually be asked to find the area of the shaded (or unshaded) portion of the diagram. Your best bet will be to take one of the following two approaches:

- Break the area into smaller pieces whose separate areas you can find; add those areas together.
- Find the area of the whole figure; find the area of the region(s) that you're *not* looking for; subtract the latter from the former.

Example:

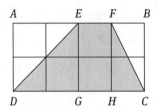

Rectangle *ABCD* above has an area of 72 and is composed of 8 equal squares. What is the area of the shaded region?

The first thing you have to realize is that, for the 8 equal squares to form a total area of 72, each square must have an area of 72 ÷ 8, or 9. Since the area of a square equals the square of the length of a side, each side of a square in the diagram must have a length of $\sqrt{9}$, or 3.

At this point, you choose your approach. Either one will work:

Approach 1:

Break up the shaded area into right triangle *DEG*, rectangle *EFHG*, and right triangle *FHC*. The area of triangle *DEG* is $\frac{1}{2}(6)(6) = 18$. The area of rectangle *EFHG* is $(3)(6)$, or 18. The area of triangle *FHC* is $\frac{1}{2}(3)(6)$, or 9. The total shaded area is $18 + 18 + 9$, or 45.

Approach 2:

The area of unshaded right triangle *AED* is $\frac{1}{2}(6)(6)$, or 18. The area of unshaded right triangle *FBC* is $\frac{1}{2}(3)(6)$, or 9. Therefore, the total unshaded area is $18 + 9 = 27$. Subtract the total unshaded area from the total area of rectangle *ABCD*: $72 - 27 = 45$.

Inscribed/Circumscribed Figures

A polygon is inscribed in a circle if all the vertices of the polygon lie on the circle. A polygon is circumscribed about a circle if all the sides of the polygon are tangent to the circle.

Square *ABCD* is inscribed in circle *O*. We can also say that circle *O* is circumscribed about square *ABCD*.

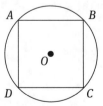

Square *PQRS* is circumscribed about circle *O*. We can also say that circle *O* is inscribed in square *PQRS*.

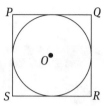

When a triangle is inscribed in a semicircle in such a way that one side of the triangle coincides with the diameter of the semicircle, the triangle is a right triangle.

Example:

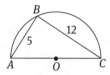

What is the diameter of semicircle *O* above?

AC is a diameter of semicircle *O* because it passes through center point *O*. So triangle *ABC* fits the description given above of a right triangle. Moreover, triangle *ABC* is a special 5:12:13 right triangle with a hypotenuse of 13. Therefore, the length of diameter *AC* is 13.

Example:

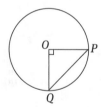

If the length of chord $PQ = 4\sqrt{2}$, what is the circumference of the circle with center *O*?

   Ⓐ 4

   Ⓑ 8

   Ⓒ 4π

   Ⓓ 8π

   Ⓔ $8\pi\sqrt{2}$

To find the circumference, we need the radius, which is either *OP* or *OQ* in this circle. We are given the length of *PQ*. *PQ* is a chord of the circle (it connects two points on the circle), but it's also the hypotenuse of right triangle *OPQ*. Do we know anything else about that triangle? Since *OP* and *OQ* are both radii of the circle, they must have the same length, so the triangle is an isosceles right triangle. Using the ratio of the lengths of sides of a 45:45:90 right triangle, with PQ as the hypotenuse, the length of each radius is 4, making the circumference $2\pi r$ or 8π, answer choice (**D**).

GEOMETRY CONCEPT CHECK

Before you move on, check your understanding of geometry on the GRE by considering a few questions:

· What are the special right triangles that are commonly tested on the GRE?

· The length of one side of an isosceles right triangle is 6. What is the length of the hypotenuse of that triangle?

· If a circle has a radius of 4, what is the area of a sector with an interior angle of 45°?

· What is the height of a cylinder that has a diameter of 10 and a volume of 200π?

If you feel confident in your ability to tackle questions that deal with these concepts, proceed to the practice set that follows.

If you feel like you would like some additional guided practice, head to your online resources. Under **Math Foundations**, click **Geometry Guided Practice**. Try each question on your own first. Then watch a video explanation in which a Kaplan GRE instructor describes a strategic approach.

Geometry Practice Set

Directions: Try answering these questions to practice what you have learned about geometry. Answers and explanations follow at the end of the chapter.

Basic

1. Point m has coordinates $(-2,-10)$, and point n has coordinates $(-8,-6)$. What are the coordinates of the midpoint of the line segment that has endpoints m and n?

2. The hypotenuse of a right triangle is 17, and one of the legs is 8. What is the area of the triangle?

3. The area of a circle is 36. What is the circle's diameter?

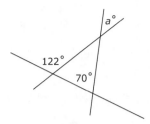

4.   In the diagram above, what is the value of a?

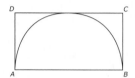

5. $\overline{AB}$ is the diameter of the semicircle above, which is tangent to $\overline{CD}$. If the area of the semicircle is 50π, then what is the area of rectangle $ABCD$?

Intermediate

6.   Each side of an equilateral triangle is 12. What is the area of the triangle?

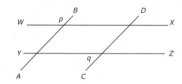

7.   In the diagram above, $\overline{AB} \parallel \overline{CD}$ and $\overline{WX} \parallel \overline{YZ}$. If $p = 125°$, then what does q equal?

8.   How many times does the parabola represented by the function $f(x) = x^2 - 3x + 28$ intersect the parabola represented by the function $g(x) = 2x^2 + 7x + 53$?

9.   A circle and a square have the same area. What is the ratio of the radius of the circle to the length of a side of the square?

10. Darnell leaves his house and walks 25 feet due north, then 42 feet due east, and then stops. Melanie leaves the same house and walks 86 feet due east, then walks in a straight line to where Darnell is standing. What is the area of the region enclosed by the paths Darnell and Melanie walked?

Advanced

11. The perimeter of a rhombus is 44. What is the maximum area the rhombus could have?

12. The area of circle O is one-fourth that of circle P. The circumference of circle O is what fraction of the circumference of circle P?

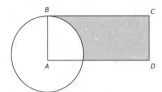

13. In the figure above, rectangle $ABCD$ is tangent to circle A at point B. If the radius of circle A is 12 and the length of rectangle $ABCD$ is three times its height, what is the area of the shaded region?

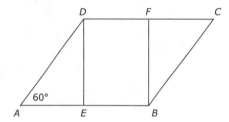

14. In the figure above, $DC = 14$ and the area of parallelogram $ABCD$ is $84\sqrt{3}$. What is the area of rectangle $EDFB$?

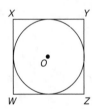

15. In the diagram above, circle O is circumscribed by square $WXYZ$. Circle O is also the base of a right cylindrical container. When this container is filled with 637π cubic centimeters of liquid, the liquid rises 13 centimeters high. What is the area of square $WXYZ$, in square centimeters?

Answers and explanations follow on the next page. ▶ ▶ ▶

Geometry Practice Set Answer Key

1. $(-5, -8)$
2. 60
3. $\dfrac{12}{\sqrt{\pi}}$
4. 52
5. 200

6. $36\sqrt{3}$
7. $55°$
8. 1
9. $\dfrac{1}{\sqrt{\pi}}$
10. 1,600

11. 121
12. $\dfrac{1}{2}$
13. $432 - 36\pi$
14. $48\sqrt{3}$
15. 196

Geometry Practice Set Answers and Explanations

Basic

1. $(-5, -8)$

The midpoint of a line segment is found by taking the average of the x-coordinates of the endpoints and the average of the y-coordinates of the endpoints. For m and n, the average of the x-coordinates is $[-2 + (-8)] \div 2 = (-10) \div 2 = -5$. The average of the y-coordinates is $(-6 + -10) \div 2 = -16 \div 2 = -8$.

2. 60

The area of a triangle equals (base)(height) $\div$ 2. For a right triangle, the base and height are the legs. This is an 8:15:17 right triangle, so the legs are 8 and 15. Thus, the area is $(8)(15) \div 2 = 4(15) = 60$.

Recognizing the 8:15:17 right triangle pattern was helpful, but the missing leg could also have been found via the Pythagorean theorem:

$$8^2 + s^2 = 17^2$$
$$64 + s^2 = 289$$
$$s^2 = 225$$
$$s = 15$$

3. $\dfrac{12}{\sqrt{\pi}}$

The area of a circle equals πr^2. Set this equal to 36 and solve for r:

$$36 = \pi r^2$$
$$r^2 = \frac{36}{\pi}$$
$$r = \frac{6}{\sqrt{\pi}}$$

This is the radius. The diameter is twice that, or $\dfrac{12}{\sqrt{\pi}}$.

4. 52

Angles on one side of a straight line add up to $180°$, so the interior angle of the triangle that is next to the $122°$ angle must equal $180° - 122°$, or $58°$. The angles of a triangle add up to $180°$ as well, so now the final angle of the triangle must be $180° - 70° - 58° = 52°$. Angle a is vertical to this last angle, and vertical angles are always congruent. Thus, angle a is also $52°$.

5. 200

If the area of half a circle is 50π, then the area of the entire circle is twice that, or 100π. For a circle, area $= \pi r^2$, so the radius of the semicircle is 10. ($100\pi = \pi r^2$, so $r^2 = 100$ and $r = 10$.) This is also the height of the rectangle. The diameter of the semicircle is twice that, or 20. This is also the width of the rectangle. The area of a rectangle is width $\times$ height, which is $20 \times 10 = 200$.

Intermediate

6. $36\sqrt{3}$

In an equilateral triangle, all sides are equal and all angles are equal to 60°. The area is equal to $\frac{1}{2}bh$. The base is equal to 12, but the height needs to be calculated. Drawing a height will create two 30°-60°-90° triangles.

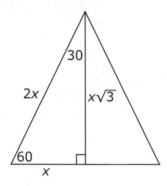

The ratio of sides in a 30°-60°-90° triangle is $x : x\sqrt{3} : 2x$. For each smaller triangle, the side opposite the 30° angle (x) is 6. That means the height (opposite the 60° angle) is equal to $6\sqrt{3}$. With the height determined, the area of the original equilateral triangle is equal to $\frac{1}{2}(12)(6\sqrt{3}) = 36\sqrt{3}$.

7. 55°

Because both pairs of lines are parallel, all of the acute angles are congruent and all of the obtuse angles are congruent. As a result, every obtuse angle is supplementary to every acute angle. Since p is obtuse and q is acute, it must be that $p + q = 180°$. Thus, $q = 180° - 125° = 55°$.

8. 1

To find the point(s) of intersection between two functions in the coordinate plane, set them equal to each other, and solve:

$$2x^2 + 7x + 53 = x^2 - 3x + 28$$
$$x^2 + 10x + 25 = 0$$
$$(x + 5)(x + 5) = 0$$

This equation has only one solution: -5. Thus, there is only one point of intersection between the two parabolas.

9. $\dfrac{1}{\sqrt{\pi}}$

Call the radius r and the length of a side of the square s. The question asks for the ratio of r to s, or $\frac{r}{s}$. The area of the circle is πr^2 and the area of the square is s^2. The question states that these are equal:

$$\pi r^2 = s^2$$

Take the square root of both sides to simplify:

$$\sqrt{\pi}r = s$$

Finally, divide both sides by s and by $\sqrt{\pi}$ to find the ratio of r to s:

$$\frac{r}{s} = \frac{1}{\sqrt{\pi}}$$

10. 1,600

Draw a diagram to visualize the region:

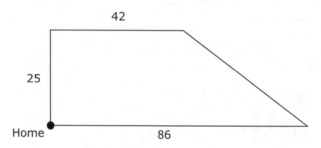

This is a trapezoid. The area of a trapezoid equals the average of the bases times the height:

$$\text{Area} = 25 \times (42 + 86) \div 2$$
$$\text{Area} = 25 \times (128) \div 2$$
$$\text{Area} = 25 \times 64 = 1,600$$

Advanced

11. 121

All four sides of a rhombus have equal length, so the length of each side here is $44 \div 4 = 11$. The area of a rhombus equals base × height, and there's no way that the height (the distance between two opposite sides) could possibly be longer than the base (the length of one side). The height would be maximized when it is equal to the length of one side, which occurs when adjacent sides are perpendicular, i.e., when the rhombus is a square. Thus, a rhombus's area is maximized when the rhombus is a square, and the maximum area of the rhombus in the question is simply 11×11, or 121.

12. $\frac{1}{2}$

Let x be the radius of circle O. In that case, the following is true of circle O:

Circumference of circle O: $2\pi x$
Area of circle O: πx^2

The question says that circle P has an area four times as big, or $4\pi x^2$. That means the following is true of circle P:

Radius of circle P:
$\pi r^2 = 4\pi x^2 \quad r^2 = 4x^2 \quad r = \sqrt{4x^2} = 2x$
Circumference of circle P: $2(2x)\pi = 4\pi x$

The circumference of circle O is $2\pi x$, which is half the circumference of circle P, $4\pi x$.

13. $432 - 36\pi$

The radius of circle A is also the height of rectangle $ABCD$, so $AB = 12$. The length of rectangle $ABCD$ is three times this height, so $BC = 3 \times 12 = 36$. That means the area of rectangle $ABCD$ is $12 \times 36 = 432$.

The sector of the circle that's inside the rectangle is one-fourth of the entire circle. That's because angle A is a 90° angle, and 90° is one-quarter of 360°, the total number of degrees in a circle. The total area of the circle is $\pi r^2 = \pi(12)^2 = 144\pi$. One-fourth of that is $144\pi \div 4 = 36\pi$.

The shaded area is this sector area subtracted from the total area of the rectangle, or $432 - 36\pi$.

14. $48\sqrt{3}$

The area of a parallelogram is base × height, so $84\sqrt{3} = 14DE$ and $DE = 6\sqrt{3}$. By the properties of 30°-60°-90° triangles, $AE = 6$. (We know triangle ADE is a 30°-60°-90° triangle because angle A is 60°, and angle E, formed by altitude DE, is 90°.) It follows that $EB = AB - AE = 14 - 6 = 8$. The area of a rectangle is also base × height, so the area of rectangle $EDFB$ is $EB \times ED = 8 \times 6\sqrt{3} = 48\sqrt{3}$.

15. 196

The volume of a right cylinder is $V = \pi r^2 h$. In this case, the volume is 637π and the height is 13, so plug those values in for V and h, respectively, and solve for r:

$$637\pi = \pi r^2(13)$$
$$r^2 = 637 \div 13 = 49$$
$$r = 7$$

The diameter of the circle is $2r$, or $2(7) = 14$. This is also the length of a side of square $WXYZ$. The area of a square is the length of one side squared, so the area of square $WXYZ$ is 14^2, or 196.

CHAPTER 16

QUANTITATIVE COMPARISON

Introduction to Quantitative Comparison

In each Quantitative Comparison question, you'll see two mathematical expressions. One is Quantity A and the other is Quantity B. You will be asked to compare them. Some questions include additional centered information. This centered information applies to both quantities and is essential to making the comparison. Since this type of question is about the relationship between the two quantities, you usually won't need to calculate a specific value for either quantity. Therefore, you do not want to rely on the onscreen calculator to answer these questions.

The directions for a Quantitative Comparison question will look like this:

Directions: Select the correct answer.

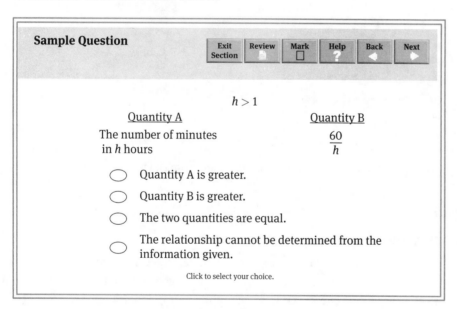

THE KAPLAN METHOD FOR QUANTITATIVE COMPARISON

STEP 1 Analyze the centered information and quantities.

STEP 2 Approach strategically.

How the Kaplan Method for Quantitative Comparison Works

Now let's discuss how the Kaplan Method for Quantitative Comparison works.

[STEP 1]

Analyze the centered information and the quantities.

Notice whether the quantities contain numbers, variables, or both. If there is centered information, decide how it affects the information given in the quantities. Note that a variable has the same value each time it appears within a question.

[STEP 2]

Approach strategically.

Think about a strategy you could use to compare the quantities now that you've determined the information you have and the information you need. There are a variety of approaches to solving a Quantitative Comparison question, and the practice examples will take you through several of these.

How to Apply the Kaplan Method for Quantitative Comparison

Now let's apply the Kaplan Method to a Quantitative Comparison question:

Quantity A	Quantity B
$\dfrac{1}{4} + \dfrac{1}{5} + \dfrac{1}{6} + \dfrac{1}{7}$	$\dfrac{1}{\dfrac{1}{4} + \dfrac{1}{5} + \dfrac{1}{6} + \dfrac{1}{7}}$

- Ⓐ Quantity A is greater.
- Ⓑ Quantity B is greater.
- Ⓒ The two quantities are equal.
- Ⓓ The relationship cannot be determined from the information given.

[STEP 1]

Analyze the centered information and the columns.

This problem would be a nightmare to calculate under timed conditions. But the only thing you need to figure out is whether one quantity is greater than the other. One thing you might notice is that choice (D) is not an option here. Because both quantities contain only numbers, there is a definite value for each quantity, and a relationship can be determined. Answer choice (D) is never correct when the quantities contain only numbers.

Note that the quantity on the left is the same as the quantity in the denominator of the fraction on the right. You can think about this problem as a comparison of x and $\dfrac{1}{x}$ (or the reciprocal of x), where x has a definite value. Your job now is to figure out just how to compare them.

[STEP 2]
Approach strategically.

Before you start to do a long calculation, think about what you already know. While you may not know the sum of the four fractions, you do know two things: $\frac{1}{4} + \frac{1}{4} + \frac{1}{4} + \frac{1}{4} = 1$, and $\frac{1}{5}, \frac{1}{6}$, and $\frac{1}{7}$ are each less than $\frac{1}{4}$. Because the reciprocal of any number between 0 and 1 is greater than 1, and because Quantity A is a positive number less than 1, its reciprocal in Quantity B is greater than 1. So choice **(B)** is correct. Quantitative Comparisons rarely, if ever, ask for exact values, so don't waste time calculating them.

Now let's apply the Kaplan Method to a second Quantitative Comparison question:

$$w > x > 0 > y > z$$

Quantity A	Quantity B
$w + y$	$x + z$

  Ⓐ   Quantity A is greater.

  Ⓑ   Quantity B is greater.

  Ⓒ   The two quantities are equal.

  Ⓓ   The relationship cannot be determined from the information given.

[STEP 1]
Analyze the centered information and the quantities.

In this problem, there are four variables: w, x, y, and z. You are asked to compare the values of the sums of pairs of variables. You know the relative values of the different variables, but you don't know the actual amounts. You do know that two of the variables (w and x) must be positive and two of the variables (y and z) must be negative numbers.

[STEP 2]
Approach strategically.

In this case, think about the different sums as pieces of the whole. If every "piece" in one quantity is greater than a corresponding "piece" in the other quantity and if the only operation involved is addition, then the quantity with the greater individual values will have the greater total value. From the given information, we know the following:

- $w > x$
- $y > z$

The first term, w, in Quantity A is greater than the first term, x, in Quantity B. Similarly, the second term, y, in Quantity A is greater than the second term, z, in Quantity B. Because each piece in Quantity A is greater than the corresponding piece in Quantity B, Quantity A must be greater; the answer is **(A)**.

Now let's apply the Kaplan Method to a third Quantitative Comparison question:

The diameter of circle O is d, and the area is a.

Quantity A	Quantity B
$\dfrac{\pi d^2}{2}$	a

- (A) Quantity A is greater.
- (B) Quantity B is greater.
- (C) The two quantities are equal.
- (D) The relationship cannot be determined from the information given.

[STEP 1]

Analyze the centered information and the quantities.

In this problem, you are given additional information: the sentence that tells you the diameter of circle O is d and the area is a. This is important information because it gives you a key to unlocking this question. Given that information, you can tell that you are comparing the area, a, of circle O and a quantity that includes the diameter of the same circle. If you're thinking about the formula for calculating area given the diameter, you're thinking right!

[STEP 2]

Approach strategically.

Make Quantity B look more like Quantity A by rewriting a, the area of the circle, in terms of the diameter, d. The area of any circle equals πr^2, where r is the radius. Because the radius is half the diameter, you can substitute $\dfrac{d}{2}$ for r in the area formula to get $a = \pi r^2 = \pi\left(\dfrac{d}{2}\right)^2$ in Quantity B. Simplifying, you get $\dfrac{\pi d^2}{4}$.

Because both quantities contain π, we could compare $\dfrac{d^2}{2}$ to $\dfrac{d^2}{4}$. But let's take it one step further. You know that d is a distance and must be a positive number. That makes it possible to divide both quantities, $\dfrac{d^2}{2}$ and $\dfrac{d^2}{4}$, by d^2 and then just compare $\dfrac{1}{2}$ to $\dfrac{1}{4}$. This makes it easy to see that Quantity A is always greater because $\dfrac{1}{2} > \dfrac{1}{4}$. Choice (**A**) is correct.

Kaplan's Additional Tips for Quantitative Comparison Questions

Memorize the answer choices

It is a good idea to memorize what the Quantitative Comparison answer choices mean. This is not as difficult as it sounds. The choices are always the same. The wording and the order never vary. If the choices become second nature to you, you will save lots of time on Test Day.

When there is at least one variable in a problem, try to demonstrate two different relationships between quantities

Here's why demonstrating two different relationships between the quantities is an important strategy: if you can demonstrate two different relationships, then choice (**D**) is correct. There is no need to examine the question further.

But how can this demonstration be done efficiently? A good suggestion is to look at the expression(s) containing a variable and notice the possible values of the variable given the mathematical operation involved. For example, if x can be any real number and you need to compare $(x + 1)^2$ to $(x + 1)$, pick a value for x that will make $(x + 1)$ a fraction between 0 and 1 and then pick a value for x that will make $(x + 1)$ greater than 1. By choosing values for x in this way, you are basing your number choices on mathematical properties you already know: a positive fraction less than 1 becomes smaller when squared, but a number greater than 1 grows larger when squared.

Compare quantities piece by piece

Compare the value of each "piece" in each quantity. If every "piece" in one quantity is greater than a corresponding "piece" in the other quantity and the operation involved is either addition or multiplication, then the quantity with the greater individual values will have the greater total value.

Make one quantity look like the other

When the Quantities A and B are expressed differently, you can often make the comparison easier by changing the format of one quantity so that it looks like the other. This is a great approach when the quantities look so different that you can't compare them directly.

Do the same thing to both quantities

If the quantities you are given seem too complex to compare immediately, look closely to see if there is an addition, subtraction, multiplication, or division operation you can perform on both quantities to make them simpler—provided you do not multiply or divide by zero or a negative number. For example, suppose you have the task of comparing $1 + \dfrac{w}{1 + w}$ to $1 + \dfrac{1}{1 + w}$, where w is greater than 0. To get to the heart of the comparison, subtract 1 from both quantities and you have $\dfrac{w}{1 + w}$ compared to $\dfrac{1}{1 + w}$. To simplify even further, multiply both quantities by $(1 + w)$, and then you can compare w to 1.

Don't be tricked by misleading information

To avoid Quantitative Comparison traps, stay alert and don't assume anything. If you are using a diagram to answer a question, use only information that is given or information that you know must be true based on properties or theorems. For instance, don't assume angles are equal or lines are parallel unless it is stated or can be deduced from other information given. Another common mistake is to assume that variables represent only positive integers. As you saw when using the Picking Numbers strategy, fractions or negative numbers often show a different relationship between the quantities.

Don't forget to consider other possibilities

If an answer looks obvious, it may very well be a trap. Consider this situation: a question requires you to think of two integers whose product is 6. If you jump to the conclusion that 2 and 3 are the integers, you will miss several other possibilities. Not only are 1 and 6 possibilities, but there are also pairs of negative integers to consider: -2 and -3, -1 and -6.

Don't fall for look-alikes

Even if two expressions look similar, they may be mathematically different. Be especially careful with expressions involving parentheses or radicals. If you were asked to compare $\sqrt{5x} + \sqrt{5x}$ to $\sqrt{10x}$, you would not want to fall into the trap of saying the two expressions were equal. Although time is an important factor in taking the GRE, don't rush to the extent that you do not apply your skills correctly. In this case, $\sqrt{5x} + \sqrt{5x} = 2\sqrt{5x}$, which is not the same as $\sqrt{10x}$ unless $x = 0$.

QUANTITATIVE COMPARISON CONCEPT CHECK

Before you move on, check your understanding by considering these questions:

· What are the four answer choices for every Quantitative Comparison question?

· When do you know the correct choice cannot be (D)?

· When you cannot calculate the values of both quantities, or when doing so would be time-consuming, what are four alternative strategies you can use?

· When you pick numbers in Quantitative Comparison, why do you need to pick more than one number or set of numbers?

If you feel like you've got the hang of it, great! Proceed to the practice set that starts on the next page.

If you'd like a quick video review of this chapter, or if you would like some additional guided practice, head to your online resources. Under **Quantitative Comparison**, click **Strategy for Quantitative Comparison** to watch a quick video review of this chapter. Or click **Quantitative Comparison Guided Practice** to apply what you've learned.

Quantitative Comparison Practice Set

Try the following Quantitative Comparison questions using the Kaplan Method for Quantitative Comparison. If you're up to the challenge, time yourself: on Test Day, you'll want to spend roughly one and a half minutes on each question.

For the following questions, select Ⓐ if Quantity A is greater, Ⓑ if Quantity B is greater, Ⓒ if the quantities are equal, and Ⓓ if the relationship cannot be determined from the information given.

1.
Quantity A	Quantity B
$x^2 + 2x - 2$	$x^2 + 2x - 1$

Ⓐ Ⓑ Ⓒ Ⓓ

$x = 2y$; y is a positive integer.

2.
Quantity A	Quantity B
4^y	$\dfrac{1}{2^{-x}}$

Ⓐ Ⓑ Ⓒ Ⓓ

---

q, r, and s are positive numbers; $qrs > 12$.

3.
Quantity A	Quantity B
$\dfrac{qr}{5}$	$\dfrac{3}{s}$

Ⓐ Ⓑ Ⓒ Ⓓ

In triangle XYZ not given, the measure of angle X equals the measure of angle Y.

4.
Quantity A	Quantity B
The degree measure of angle Z	The degree measure of angle X plus the degree measure of angle Y

Ⓐ Ⓑ Ⓒ Ⓓ

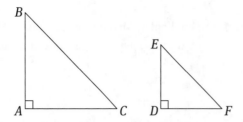

$\angle ABC = 45°$ and $ED = DF$. The area of triangle ABC is 4 times the area of triangle DEF.

5.

Quantity A	Quantity B	
$\dfrac{AC}{EF}$	$\sqrt{2}$	Ⓐ Ⓑ Ⓒ Ⓓ

Set A consists of 35 consecutive integers.

6.

Quantity A	Quantity B	
The probability of selecting an even number less than the median from set A	The probability of selecting an odd number greater than the median from set A	Ⓐ Ⓑ Ⓒ Ⓓ

For all shows, a local theater sells tickets at one price for adults and a reduced price for children. On Sunday afternoons, all tickets are sold at a discount of 20%.

7.

Quantity A	Quantity B	
The amount of money collected for 120 adults and 100 children on a Saturday night.	The amount of money collected for 150 adults and 120 children on a Sunday afternoon.	Ⓐ Ⓑ Ⓒ Ⓓ

8.

Quantity A	Quantity B	
$(x+2)(x-2)$	$\dfrac{-5\left(x^2 - 25\right)(x - 1)}{(x + 5)\left(x^2 - 6x + 5\right)}$	Ⓐ Ⓑ Ⓒ Ⓓ

An apartment building has apartments numbered 2 through 85, consecutively.

9.   Quantity A   Quantity B

The probability that the apartment $\frac{3}{14}$
number of a randomly selected
tenant contains a 4

A car begins at Point A traveling 30 miles per hour. The car decreases its speed
by 5 miles per hour every 10 minutes until the car comes to a complete stop.

10.   Quantity A   Quantity B

The total number of miles traveled   The average speed of the car in miles
between Point A and the final   per hour between Point A and the final
stopping point.   stopping point.

Quantitative Comparison Practice Set Answer Key

1. **B**	6. **D**
2. **C**	7. **A**
3. **D**	8. **A**
4. **D**	9. **D**
5. **C**	10. **C**

Quantitative Comparison Practice Set Answers and Explanations

1. B

Comparing the two quantities piece by piece, you find that the only difference is the third piece: -2 in Quantity A and -1 in Quantity B. You don't know the value of x, but whatever it is, x^2 in Quantity A must have the same value as x^2 in Quantity B, and $2x$ in Quantity A must have the same value as $2x$ in Quantity B. Because any quantity minus 2 must be less than that quantity minus 1, Quantity B is greater than Quantity A. **(B)** is the correct answer.

2. C

Make the quantities look alike. If $x = 2y$, then $-x = -2y$. Replace the exponent $-x$ in Quantity B with $-2y$. Thus, Quantity B becomes $\frac{1}{2^{-2y}}$. A value with a negative exponent in the denominator is equivalent to the same value with a positive exponent in the numerator, so Quantity B can be restated as 2^{2y}. Since $4 = 2^2$, Quantity A can be written as $(2^2)^y = 2^{2y}$. The quantities are identical, and **(C)** is correct.

3. D

Do the same thing to both quantities to make them look like the centered information. When you multiply both quantities by $5s$, you get qrs in Quantity A and 15 in Quantity B. Because qrs could be any integer greater than 12, qrs could be greater than, equal to, or less than 15. **(D)** is correct.

4. D

Because angle $X =$ angle Y, at least two sides of the triangle are equal. You can draw two diagrams with X and Y as the base angles of a triangle. In one diagram, make the triangle tall and narrow so that angle X and

angle Y are very large and angle Z is very small. In this case, Quantity B is greater. In the second diagram, make the triangle short and wide so that angle Z is much larger than angle X and angle Y. In this case, Quantity A is greater. Because more than one relationship between the quantities is possible, the correct answer is **(D)**.

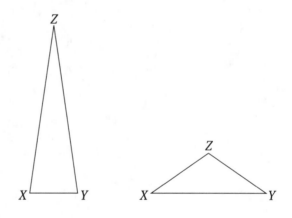

5. C

Since $\angle ABC$ is $45°$, $\angle BCA$ is $180° - 90° - 45° = 45°$, so ABC is an isosceles right triangle. Because $ED = DF$, triangle DEF is also an isosceles right triangle. The formula for the area of a triangle is Area $= \frac{1}{2}$ base $\times$ height. Since the triangles in this question are isosceles right triangles, the formula for the area of a triangle can be restated as $\frac{1}{2}$ base^2 by substituting the base in for the height, since they are the same value. Given that the area of triangle ABC is four times the area of triangle DEF, set up the equation $\left(\frac{1}{2}\right)AC^2 = 4\left(\frac{1}{2}\right)DF^2$. Even though there are two variables but only one equation, you can solve by Picking Numbers because only the ratio matters, not the actual values. Try 2 for the value of AC to get $\frac{1}{2}(2)^2 = 2DF^2$, so $DF^2 = 1$ and $DF = 1$. Given the side ratios of an isosceles right triangle, $1:1:\sqrt{2}$, side $EF = \sqrt{2}$. So Quantity A becomes $\frac{AC}{EF} = \frac{2}{\sqrt{2}}$. Multiply both the numerator and the denominator by $\sqrt{2}$ to get $\frac{(\sqrt{2})2}{(\sqrt{2})\sqrt{2}} = \frac{2\sqrt{2}}{2} = \sqrt{2}$. This is the same as Quantity B, so **(C)** is correct.

6. D

In a set of 35 consecutive integers, the median will be the number in the middle. Of the remaining 34 values, 17 will be less than the median and 17 will be greater.

Imagine that the range of values is 1 through 35. In this case, the first value is odd, and the values 1 through 17 are below the median, 18 is the median, and 19 through 35 are above the median. So there are 9 odd numbers and 8 even numbers below the median, the median itself is even, and there are 9 odd numbers and 8 even numbers above the median.

Now imagine that the range of values is 2 through 36. In this case, the first value is even, the median is 19, there are 9 even numbers and 8 odd numbers below the median, and there are 9 even numbers and 8 odd numbers above the median.

So, if the first integer is odd, there's an 8 in 35 chance of picking an even number less than the median and a 9 in 35 chance of picking an odd number greater than the median. Quantity B would be greater than Quantity A. However, if the first integer is even, the odds are reversed, with a 9 in 35 chance of picking an even number less than the median and an 8 in 35 chance of picking an odd number greater than the median. That would make Quantity A greater than Quantity B. Because more than one relationship is possible, **(D)** is the correct answer.

7. A

The stimulus provides no actual prices for the different tickets, so use A to represent the regular price of an adult's ticket and C to represent the regular price of a child's ticket. The tickets are full price on Saturday, so Quantity A could be calculated as: $120A + 100C$.

On Sunday afternoon, there's a 20% discount on all tickets. That means the tickets will be 80% of their original price. Quantity B would thus be calculated as:

$$150(.8A) + 120(.8C) = 120A + 96C$$

Comparing the two results, both quantities have an equal total in sales from adults, but Quantity A has $100C$ while Quantity B has $96C$. That means Quantity A is larger, making **(A)** the correct answer.

8. A

Using FOIL, Quantity A can be rewritten as $x^2 - 4$. Quantity B needs to be simplified. In the numerator, $x^2 - 25$ can be factored into $(x + 5)(x - 5)$. In the denominator, $x^2 - 6x + 5$ can be factored into $(x - 5)(x - 1)$. The fraction can then be simplified by canceling out common factors in the numerator and denominator:

$$\frac{-5(x^2 - 25)(x - 1)}{(x + 5)(x^2 - 6x + 5)} = \frac{-5(x + 5)(x - 5)(x - 1)}{(x + 5)(x - 5)(x - 1)}$$
$$= \frac{-5}{1} = -5$$

So, Quantity B is equal to -5. Without knowing what x is, it might seem that Quantity A and Quantity B cannot be compared. However, when x is squared, the result cannot be negative. The smallest value it could have is 0. Subtracting 4, the smallest possible value of Quantity A is -4. That means Quantity A must be greater than or equal to -4. Any such number will always be greater than -5, so Quantity A will always be greater than Quantity B, no matter what x is. That makes **(A)** the correct answer.

9. D

It may be tempting to jump straight into the probability formula here:

$$\text{Probability} = \frac{\text{Number of desired outcomes}}{\text{Number of total outcomes}}.$$ Counting each apartment with a 4 in it (those starting with 4 as well as ending in 4) and the number of total apartments would give $\frac{18}{84}$, which, when simplified, equals Quantity B. However, notice that the centered information gives information about apartments, while Quantity A is based on selecting a random *tenant*. There's no

information on how many tenants are in each apart-ment. The above math works if each apartment has an equal number of tenants. However, if each apartment with a 4 in the number has three tenants while other apartments only have one, it would be more likely that a randomly selected tenant lives in an apartment with a 4 in the number. Since more than one relationship is possible, the correct answer is (**D**).

10. C

It's important to realize that the total distance need not be calculated to compare the two quantities. For this question, let d represent the total distance, in miles, traveled. Quantity A will thus be equal to d.

Quantity B is the average speed for the entire trip. The average speed, in miles per hour, is calculated by taking the total mileage (d) and dividing that by the total number of hours. The car starts at 30 miles per hour and slows down 5 miles per hour every 10 minutes. That means it will travel first at 30 miles per hour, then 25 miles per hour, then 20, then 15, then 10, then 5. After that, it will stop. It will travel for 10 minutes at each of those 6 speeds, for a total of 60 minutes, which is 1 hour. That means the average speed will be equal to $\frac{d}{1} = d$. Regardless of the value of d (which could be calculated, but would only take up valuable time for this question), the two quantities are equal. That makes (**C**) the correct answer.

CHAPTER 17

PROBLEM SOLVING

Introduction to Problem Solving

Problem Solving can be broken up into several general mathematics categories: algebra, arithmetic, number properties, and geometry.

In a Problem Solving question, you may be asked to solve a pure math problem or a word problem involving a real-world situation. You will be asked to enter your answer into an onscreen box, select one answer, or select one or more options that correctly answer the problem.

The directions for a Problem Solving question requiring a single answer will look like this:

> **Directions:** Click to select your choice.

A Problem Solving question requiring you to select a single answer will look like this, with ovals next to each answer choice:

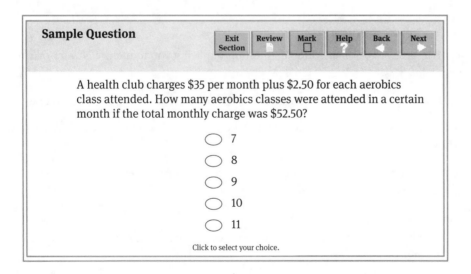

The directions for a Problem Solving question requiring you to select one or more answers will look like this:

> **Directions:** Click to select your choice(s).

If a Problem Solving question asks you to select your choice(s), at least one answer is correct, but as many as all the choices may be correct. You must select all of the correct choices (and none of the incorrect ones) for the question to be counted as correct.

A Problem Solving question requiring you to select one or more answers will look like this, with squares next to each answer choice:

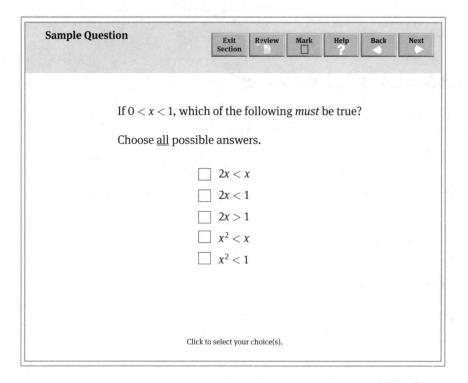

The directions for a Problem Solving question requiring you to make a Numeric Entry will look like this:

Directions: Click in the box and type your numeric answer. Backspace to erase.

Enter your answer as an integer or decimal if there is one box or as a fraction if there are two boxes.

To enter an integer or decimal, type directly in the box or use the Transfer Display button on the calculator.

- Use the backspace key to erase.
- Use a hyphen to enter a negative sign; type a hyphen a second time to remove it. The digits will remain.
- Use a period for a decimal point.
- The Transfer Display button will enter your answer directly from the calculator.
- Equivalent forms of decimals are all correct. (*Example:* $0.14 = 0.140$)
- Enter the exact answer unless the question asks you to round your answer.

To enter a fraction, type the numerator and denominator in the appropriate boxes.

- Use a hyphen to enter a negative sign.
- The Transfer Display button does not work for fractions.
- Equivalent forms of fractions are all correct. (*Example:* $\frac{25}{15} = \frac{5}{3}$.) If numbers are large, reduce fractions to fit in boxes.

A Problem Solving question with Numeric Entry will look like this:

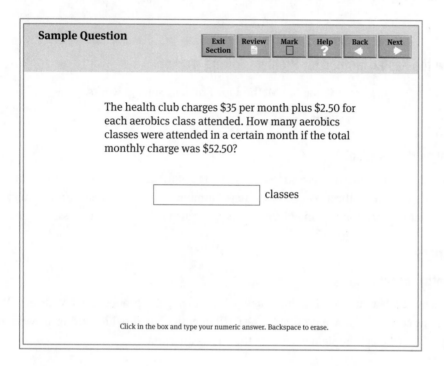

THE KAPLAN METHOD FOR PROBLEM SOLVING

STEP 1   Analyze the question.

STEP 2   Identify the task.

STEP 3   Approach strategically.

STEP 4   Confirm your answer.

How the Kaplan Method for Problem Solving Works

Now let's discuss how the Kaplan Method for Problem Solving works.

[**STEP 1**]
Analyze the question.

Look at what the question is asking and what area of math is being tested. Also note any particular trends in the answer choices (e.g., numbers/variables, integers/non-integers) and what information is being given. Unpack as much information as possible.

[**STEP 2**]
Identify the task.

Determine what question is being asked before solving the problem. Ask yourself, "What does the correct answer represent?" The GRE intentionally provides wrong answers for test takers who get the right answer to the wrong question.

[**STEP 3**]
Approach strategically.

Depending on the type of problem, you may use straightforward math—the textbook approach—to calculate your answer, or you may choose one of the following strategies: Picking Numbers, Backsolving, or Strategic Guessing.

When Picking Numbers to substitute for variables, choose numbers that are manageable and fit the description given in the problem. Backsolving is another form of Picking Numbers; you'll start with one of the answer choices and plug that choice back into the question. Lastly, Strategic Guessing can be a great time-saver on the GRE—being able to make a smart guess on a question is preferable to taking too much time and thus compromising your ability to answer other questions correctly.

[**STEP 4**]
Confirm your answer.

Check that your answer makes sense. Also check that you answered the question that was asked.

How to Apply the Kaplan Method for Problem Solving

Now let's apply the Kaplan Method to a Problem Solving question:

> In a bag of candy, 7 of the candies are cherry flavored, 8 are lemon, and 5 are grape. If a candy is chosen randomly from the bag, what is the probability that the candy is *not* lemon?

[**STEP 1**]

Analyze the question.

You are given the number of candies in a bag and asked to identify the probability that a randomly selected candy is not lemon flavored. You will have to type your answer into the box.

[**STEP 2**]

Identify the task.

The probability of an event is defined as $\dfrac{\text{Number of desired outcomes}}{\text{Number of possible outcomes}}$. You will need to find the number of desired outcomes (those in which you don't choose a lemon candy) and the total number of possible outcomes.

[**STEP 3**]

Approach strategically.

There are 20 candies in the bag, so there are 20 possible outcomes. Of all the candies, 12 are not lemon, so there are 12 desired outcomes. So, the probability of *not* lemon is $\dfrac{12}{20}$. You should avoid reducing fractions for Numeric Entry questions, since all equivalent forms will be counted as correct. Save your time for other questions and limit your risk of committing an error in calculation.

[**STEP 4**]

Confirm your answer.

Although it might be fun to get a bag of candies and check your answer in a real-world way, it's not practical, especially on Test Day. A more practical check would be to find the probability of choosing a lemon candy at random to be certain that $P(\text{lemon}) = 1 - P(\text{not lemon})$. There are 8 lemon candies out of 20, so this check can be done easily.

$$p(\text{lemon}) \overset{?}{=} 1 - p(\text{not lemon})$$

$$\frac{8}{20} \overset{?}{=} 1 - \frac{12}{20}$$

$$\frac{8}{20} \overset{?}{=} \frac{20}{20} - \frac{12}{20}$$

$$\frac{8}{20} = \frac{8}{20}$$

This check is a way to confirm that the correct numbers have been used in the problem and the correct answer has been found.

Now let's apply the Kaplan Method to a second Problem Solving question:

> When n is divided by 14, the remainder is 10. What is the remainder when n is divided by 7?
>
> (A) 2
> (B) 3
> (C) 4
> (D) 5
> (E) 6

[STEP 1]

Analyze the question.

In this question, you are asked to compare the relationship between the numbers 14 and 7 used as divisors.

[STEP 2]

Identify the task.

The task is to use the fact that division of a number, n, by 14 yields a remainder of 10 to identify the remainder when the same number is divided by 7.

[STEP 3]

Approach strategically.

A good strategy for this question is to pick a number for n that satisfies the condition for division by 14 and then see what happens when it is divided by 7.

Any number divided by itself will give a remainder of zero. So if we need a remainder of 10, we want a number that is 10 more than the number we are dividing by. Be careful; you may be thinking of choosing $14 \div 7 = 2$ or $10 \div 2 = 5$. But these are both trap answer choices because the question also involves using a remainder. Therefore, 24 is a great number to pick here, because when we try 24:

$$24 \div 14 = 1 \text{ Remainder } 10$$

Now that we've confirmed that 24 works, we answer the question that's being asked. Divide 24 by 7:

$24 \div 7 = 3$ Remainder 3

Answer choice (**B**) is the correct answer.

[STEP 4]

Confirm your answer.

You can quickly double-check your work, or you can try another number for *n* that results in a remainder of 10 when divided by 14:

$38 \div 14 = 2$ Remainder 10, and $38 \div 7 = 5$ Remainder 3

So the remainder is 3 in each case. The correct answer is (**B**).

Now let's apply the Kaplan Method to a third Problem Solving question:

> The line $4x + 6y = 24$ passes through which of the following points?
>
> Indicate <u>all</u> possible answers.
>
> A   (0,4)
> B   (2,3)
> C   (3,2)
> D   (5,4)
> E   (9,−1)

[STEP 1]

Analyze the question.

This question is about a line on the coordinate plane. The equation is a function that represents a line. The numbers in the parentheses in the answer choices represent points (x,y) that are mentioned in the equation.

[STEP 2]

Identify the task.

Your job is to identify which of the given points lie on the line. A line passes through a point if the coordinates of the point make the equation of the line true, so this is the same as saying that you need to find out which point(s), when plugged into the equation, make the equation true.

[STEP 3]

Approach strategically.

You need to find all correct answers, so test all of them. Substitute the first coordinate for x and the second coordinate for y.

- **(A)** Test (0,4): $4x + 6y = 24 \rightarrow 4(0) + 6(4) = 0 + 24 = 24$. This works.
- **(B)** Test (2,3): $4x + 6y = 24 \rightarrow 4(2) + 6(3) = 8 + 18 \neq 24$. Eliminate.
- **(C)** Test (3,2): $4x + 6y = 24 \rightarrow 4(3) + 6(2) = 12 + 12 = 24$. This works.
- **(D)** Test (5,4): $4x + 6y = 24 \rightarrow 4(5) + 6(4) = 20 + 24 \neq 24$. Eliminate.
- **(E)** Test (9,−1): $4x + 6y = 24 \rightarrow 4(9) + 6(-1) = 36 - 6 \neq 24$. Eliminate.

So choices **(A)** and **(C)** are correct.

[STEP 4]

Confirm your answer.

Double-check your work to make sure you haven't made any careless errors, such as mistakenly plugging in a value for x when dealing with the variable y.

Kaplan's Additional Tips for Problem Solving

Choose an efficient strategy

The GRE is not a traditional math test that requires that you show your work in order to get credit, testing the process as well as the answer. The GRE tests only the answer—not how you found it. Because time is often your biggest concern on the GRE, the best way to each solution is often the quickest way, and the quickest way is often not straightforward math. Through practice, you'll become familiar with approaching each question in a more strategic way.

Rely on Kaplan math strategies

Using Kaplan strategies is a way to use reasoning in conjunction with mathematics to answer a question quickly. There may also be cases in which you can combine approaches: for example, using straightforward math to simplify an equation, then picking manageable numbers for the variables to solve that equation.

Picking Numbers

Problems that seem difficult can be good candidates for the Picking Numbers strategy. They include problems where either the question or the answer choices have variables, the problem tests a number property you don't recall, or the problem and the answer choices deal with percents or fractions without using actual values.

Backsolving

Backsolving is a similar strategy to Picking Numbers, except that you'll use one of the five answer choices as the number to pick. After all, the testmaker gives you the correct answer; it's just mixed in with the wrong answers. Remember, numerical answer choices are always in ascending or descending order. Use that information to your advantage when using Backsolving. Start with either (B) or (D) first, because you'll have a 40 percent chance of finding the correct answer based on your first round of calculations. If you don't happen to pick the correct answer the first time, reason whether the number you started with was too large or too small. If you test choice (B) when the answer choices are in ascending order and (B) turns out to be too large, then (A) is the correct answer. If (B) is too small, then test choice (D). If (D) is too large, then (C) is the correct answer. If (D) is too small, then (E) is correct. The opposite would be true if the choices were in descending order. Backsolving allows you to find the correct answer without ever needing to test more than two of the answer choices.

Use Strategic Guessing

This is a good strategy if you can eliminate choices by applying number property rules or by estimating because gaps between answer choices are wide.

If some of the choices are out of the realm of possibility, eliminate them and move on.

PROBLEM SOLVING CONCEPT CHECK

Before you move on, check your understanding by considering these questions:

- What are the different answer choice formats you might see with a Problem Solving question?

- What is the Kaplan Method for Problem Solving questions?

- In addition to the straightforward math, what are some alternative ways to approach a Problem Solving question strategically?

If you feel like you've got the hang of it, great! Proceed to the practice set that follows.

If you'd like a quick video review of this chapter, or if you would like some additional guided practice, head to your online resources. Under **Problem Solving**, click **Strategy for Problem Solving** to watch a quick video review of this chapter. Or click **Problem Solving Guided Practice** to apply what you've learned.

Problem Solving Practice Set

Try the following Problem Solving questions using the Kaplan Method for Problem Solving. If you're up to the challenge, time yourself; on Test Day, you'll want to spend only about 2 minutes on each question.

1. If $r = 3s$, $s = 5t$, $t = 2u$, and $u \neq 0$, what is the value of $\frac{rst}{u^3}$?

   (A) 30

   (B) 60

   (C) 150

   (D) 300

   (E) 600

2. In the diagram, ℓ_1 is parallel to ℓ_2. The measure of $\angle a$ is 40 degrees. What is the sum of the measures of angles d and w less the sum of the measures of angles y and c?

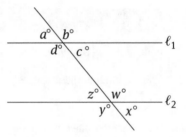

   Note: Figure not drawn to scale.

   [   ] degrees

3. At Central Park Zoo, the ratio of sea lions to penguins is 4:11. If there are 84 more penguins than sea lions, how many sea lions are there?

   (A) 24

   (B) 36

   (C) 48

   (D) 72

   (E) 121

4. Which of the following numbers has more than two distinct prime factors?
    Indicate <u>all</u> such numbers.

    A 20

    B 30

    C 100

    D 200

    E 210

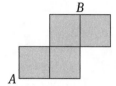

5. The figure above is made up of 4 squares. If a straight line segment were to be
    drawn from A to B, it would have a length of $8\sqrt{2}$ units. What is the perimeter
    of the entire figure in units?

    Ⓐ 20

    Ⓑ 32

    Ⓒ 40

    Ⓓ 64

    Ⓔ 80

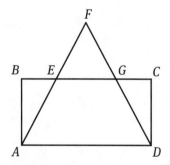

6. The figure above consists of triangle *ADF* and rectangle *ABCD*. *BE* = *CG* = 1.5
    and *EG* = 2. If the area of triangle *EFG* = x, what is the area of rectangle *ABCD*?

    Ⓐ 5x

    Ⓑ $\dfrac{5x}{2}$

    Ⓒ 15x

    Ⓓ $\dfrac{15x}{2}$

    Ⓔ $\dfrac{25x}{2}$

7. Before last night's game, a basketball player had scored an average (arithmetic mean) of 20 points per game. She scored 25 points in last night's game, raising her average to 21 points per game.

    How many games did she play before last night's game?

    (A) 3

    (B) 4

    (C) 5

    (D) 6

    (E) 7

8. Set A consists of the values 1, 2, and 3. Set B consists of the values 5, 6, and 7. One number is selected at random from each set. The two selected numbers are then added together.

    The probability that the sum is even is how much greater than the probability that the sum is a prime number?

    (A) $\dfrac{1}{9}$

    (B) $\dfrac{2}{9}$

    (C) $\dfrac{1}{3}$

    (D) $\dfrac{2}{5}$

    (E) $\dfrac{3}{5}$

9. How many positive odd factors does 768 have?

    (A) 0

    (B) 1

    (C) 2

    (D) 3

    (E) 4

10. Evan trains for running on a circular path with a radius of $\dfrac{5}{6\pi}$ km.

    If Evan starts at one point and runs continuously in one direction for a total of 5 km, how many times does Evan complete a full lap around the entire circle?

    (A) 2

    (B) 3

    (C) 4

    (D) 5

    (E) 6

Answers and explanations follow on the next page. ▶ ▶ ▶

Problem Solving Practice Set Answer Key

1.	E	6.	D
2.	100	7.	B
3.	C	8.	C
4.	B, E	9.	C
5.	C	10.	B

Problem Solving Practice Set Answers and Explanations

1. E

The other variables all build upon u, so use the Picking Numbers strategy: pick a small number for u and find the values for r, s, and t. For instance, if $u = 1$, then $t = 2u$, so $t = 2$; $s = 5t$, so $s = 10$; and $r = 3s$, so $r = 30$. So, $\frac{rst}{u^3} = \frac{30 \times 10 \times 2}{1 \times 1 \times 1} = 600$. The correct answer is **(E)**.

2. 100

Since ℓ_1 and ℓ_2 are parallel, the rules for angles created when parallel lines are cut by a transversal apply. If $\angle a$ has a measure of 40°, then $\angle z$ is also 40°. Because the sum of angles that make up a straight line is 180°, angles d and w are each $180° - 40° = 140°$. Furthermore, since vertical (opposite) angles are equal, $\angle y$ is 140° and $\angle c$ is 40°. Thus, $d + w - (y + c) = 140 + 140 - (140 + 40) = 280 - 180 = \mathbf{100}$.

3. C

The question asks for the number of sea lions, and there are fewer sea lions than penguins, so starting small is a good idea. Backsolving works well here. Start with (B). If there are 36 sea lions, then there are $36 + 84 = 120$ penguins, and the ratio of sea lions to penguins is $\frac{36}{120} = \frac{3}{10}$. This ratio is less than $\frac{4}{11}$, so the answer must be larger. Try (D). If there are 72 sea lions, then there are $72 + 84 = 156$ penguins, and the ratio of sea lions to penguins is $\frac{72}{156} = \frac{6}{13}$. Since this ratio is too large, the correct answer must be **(C)**.

4. B, E

The question asks which numbers have more than two *distinct* prime factors. Start with 20 and break it down into prime factors: $2 \times 2 \times 5$. Since 20 has only 2 *distinct*

prime factors (2 and 5), (A) can be eliminated. Next, notice that 100 is just 20×5, so it has the same two distinct prime factors as 20. (C) can therefore be eliminated. Similarly, 200 is just 100×2, so 200 also has the same two distinct prime factors as 20 and 100. Eliminate (D). Now break down 30 into prime factors: $2 \times 3 \times 5$. There are three distinct prime factors here, so **(B)** is one of the correct answers. Since 210 is 30×7, it has four distinct prime factors ($2 \times 3 \times 5 \times 7$), so **(E)** is also one of the correct answers.

5. C

Each square shares at least one side with another square. That means all of the squares have the same side length. Segment AB would pass through two of the squares, creating two isosceles right triangles in each square. Since each square is the same size, the hypotenuse of each of those triangles would be $\frac{8\sqrt{2}}{2} = 4\sqrt{2}$ units. Recall that with isosceles right triangles, the ratio of the side lengths is $x : x : x\sqrt{2}$, with $x\sqrt{2}$ representing the hypotenuse. That means the actual hypotenuse of $4\sqrt{2}$ corresponds to $x\sqrt{2}$, and x, representing one side of a square, is 4. There are 10 sides around the perimeter of the figure, so the entire figure has a perimeter of $10 \times 4 = 40$ units. **(C)** is the correct answer.

6. D

It helps to mark up the figure as you work, so start by redrawing it on your scratch sheet. The area of a rectangle is length × width. The length is the sum of the three top segments: $BE + EG + CG = 1.5 + 2 + 1.5 = 5$. The width of the rectangle would be the height of triangle AFD less the height of triangle EFG. With an area of x and a base of 2, you can solve for the height of EFG: $\frac{1}{2}(2)(h) = x$. The height of EFG would be x.

The height of *AFD* can be solved by recognizing that triangles *EFG* and *AFD* are similar. They share their top angle, and sides *AF* and *DF* cut through the parallel lines of the rectangle, creating two sets of corresponding angles. Similar triangles have proportional sides. The base of *EFG* is 2 and the base of *AFD* is 5, so the proportion is 2:5. The heights would be in the same proportion: $\frac{2}{5} = \frac{x}{h}$, where *h* is the height of *AFD*. Cross multiply to get $2h = 5x$. Divide by 2 to solve for *h*: $\frac{5x}{2}$. That means the width of the rectangle would be $\frac{5x}{2} - x = \frac{3x}{2}$. That makes the area of the rectangle $5\left(\frac{3x}{2}\right) = \frac{15x}{2}$, making (**D**) the correct answer.

7. B

This question can be deftly handled using the balance approach. The last score was 25, which is 4 points above the final average. That means the previous games must have been a total of 4 points below the final average. The average for each previous game was 20, which is 1 point below the final average. It would take 4 games at 1 point below average to balance out the 4 points above average achieved on the last game. That makes (**B**) the correct answer.

This can also be solved algebraically. Let *g* represent the number of games she played before last night's game. If she averaged 20 points per game by then, she scored a total of 20*g* points. After last night's game, she played one more game for a total of $g + 1$ games. She also scored 25 additional points for a total of $20g + 25$ points. Her new average is 21, which is found by dividing her current total points by the total number of games she has played:

$$21 = \frac{20g + 25}{g + 1}$$

Cross multiply to get $21(g + 1) = 20g + 25$. Distribute the 21 to get $21g + 21 = 20g + 25$. From there, isolate *g* to get $g = 4$. That means she played 4 games before last night's game.

8. C

The total number of possible outcomes is the number of possible outcomes from Set A (3) multiplied by the number of possible outcomes from Set B (3). That's a total of 9 possible outcomes; 5 of those are even:

$(1 + 5 = 6; 1 + 7 = 8; 2 + 6 = 8; 3 + 5 = 8; 3 + 7 = 10)$ and only 2 are prime $(1 + 6 = 7; 2 + 5 = 7)$. So, the probability of getting an even result is $\frac{5}{9}$, while the probability of getting a prime result is $\frac{2}{9}$. Subtract those figures to figure out how much greater the probability is of getting an even result: $\frac{5}{9} - \frac{2}{9} = \frac{3}{9} = \frac{1}{3}$. (**C**) is the correct answer.

Note that (D) is a trap for those who only look at the possible sums. There are five distinct sums that are possible: 6, 7, 8, 9, 10. However, there is only one way that a sum of 6 can result $(1 + 5)$, while there are two ways that a sum of 7 can result $(1 + 6$ and $2 + 5)$. Thus, the probability of getting each sum is not the same. Each individual outcome of selecting a number from each set must be considered.

9. C

With smaller numbers, it would be straightforward to simply list out all of the positive factors and count how many were odd. With 768, however, that would be overly time-consuming. Remember, though, that any non-prime number greater than 1 can be expressed as the product of prime factors, and finding prime factors is more manageable, even with large numbers.

A prime factor tree would show that the prime factorization of 768 consists of eight 2s and a 3. Since multiplying the 3 by any combination of 2s would result in an even factor, 3 itself is the only positive odd factor that can be generated through prime factorization. (B), however, is a trap for those who forget that 1 is a factor of every number. 768 thus has two positive odd factors, 1 and 3, and (**C**) is the correct answer.

10. B

The distance covered in a full lap around the circle would be equal to the circumference of that circle. The circumference of a circle is equal to $2\pi r$. With a radius of $\frac{5}{6\pi}$, the circumference of the circular path is $2\pi\left(\frac{5}{6\pi}\right) = \frac{10}{6} = \frac{5}{3}$.

If Evan ran *t* times around the path, the total distance run would be $\frac{5}{3}t$. Evan ran a total of 5 km, so $\frac{5}{3}t = 5$. Divide both sides by $\frac{5}{3}$ to get $t = 3$, which means Evan ran 3 times around the path. (**B**) is the correct answer.

CHAPTER 18

DATA INTERPRETATION

Introduction to Data Interpretation Questions

Data Interpretation questions are based on information located in tables or graphs, and they test your understanding of statistics. The data may be located in one table or graph, but you might also need to extract data from two or more tables or graphs. There will be a set of questions for you to answer based on each data presentation.

You may be asked to choose one or more answers from a set of answer choices or to enter your answer in a Numeric Entry field.

The directions for Data Interpretation questions will look like this:

Questions 15–17 are based on the following table.

PERCENT OF SALES PER CLIENT FOR CURTAIN FABRIC OVER THREE MONTHS

	MAY	JUNE	JULY
The Home Touch	45%	25%	48%
Curtains Unlimited	30%	23%	23%
Max's Curtain Supply	9%	23%	17%
Valances by Val	13%	20%	8%
Wendy's Windows	3%	9%	4%

A Data Interpretation question that requires you to choose exactly one correct answer will look like this:

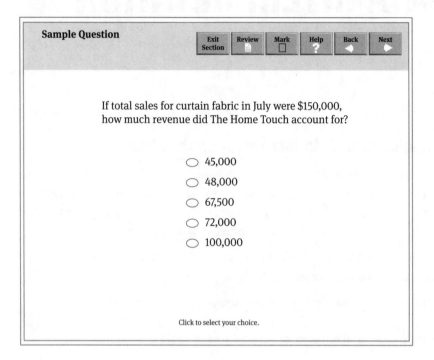

A Data Interpretation question that requires you to select all the answer choices that apply will look like this:

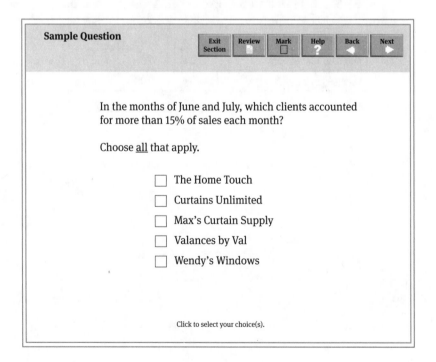

A Data Interpretation question that requires you to enter your numeric answer in a box will look like this:

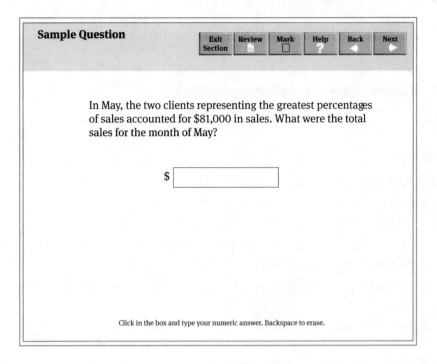

> **THE KAPLAN METHOD FOR DATA INTERPRETATION**
>
> **STEP 1** Analyze the tables and graphs.
>
> **STEP 2** Approach strategically.

How the Kaplan Method for Data Interpretation Works

Now let's discuss how the Kaplan Method for Data Interpretation works.

[STEP 1]

Analyze the tables and graphs.

Tables, graphs, and charts often come in pairs that are linked in some way (for example, a manufacturer's total revenue and its revenue by product line). Familiarize yourself with the information in both graphs (or tables) and with how the two are related before attacking the questions. Scan the figures for these components:

- **Title**. Read the charts' titles to ensure you can get to the right chart or graph quickly.
- **Scale**. Check the units of measurement. Does the graph measure miles per minute or hour? Missing the units can drastically change your answer.
- **Notes**. Read any accompanying notes—the GRE will typically give you information only if it is helpful or even critical to getting the correct answer.
- **Key**. If there are multiple bars or lines on a graph, make sure you understand the key so you can match up the correct quantities with the correct items.

[STEP 2]

Approach strategically.

Data Interpretation questions are designed to test your understanding of fractions and percents and your attention to detail. Taking a split second to make sure you answered the right question can make the difference between a correct answer and the "right" answer to the wrong question.

Questions tend to become more complex as you move through a set. For instance, if a question set contains two graphs, the first question likely refers to just one graph. A later question will usually combine data from both graphs. If you don't use both graphs for this later question, the chances are good you have missed something.

No matter how difficult graph questions appear at first glance, you can usually simplify single-answer multiple-choice questions by taking advantage of their answer choice format. By approximating the answer rather than calculating it wherever possible, you can quickly identify the right one. As we saw with Problem Solving, estimation can be one of the fastest ways to identify the correct answer in math problems. Data Interpretation questions benefit from this strategy, as they tend to be the most time-consuming questions to answer.

How to Apply the Kaplan Method for Data Interpretation

Now let's apply the Kaplan Method to a Data Interpretation question:

CLIMOGRAPH OF CITY S

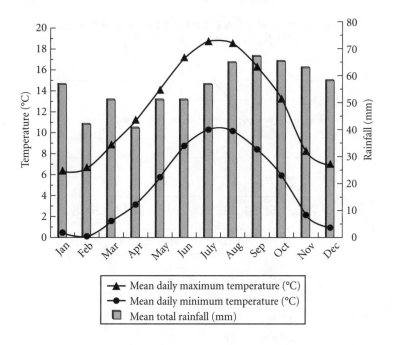

The Tourism Board of City S uses the information provided in the climograph to market the city as a tourist destination. One criterion is that the average monthly rainfall be less than 60 millimeters. What fraction of the months meet this criterion?

[STEP 1]

Analyze the tables and graphs.

Take the analysis of the graph step-by-step. Start with the title of the graph to verify that the data given are for City S. Then take note of the scale for each type of information—degrees Celsius for temperature and millimeters for rainfall. There are data for each month of the year, which means you will not have to convert the units to answer the question that's being asked.

[STEP 2]

Approach strategically.

The question asks only about rainfall; those data are given by the bars on the graph. According to the bars, rainfall is greater than 60 mm in August, September, October, and

November. That's 4 of 12 months that *do not* meet the criterion, so 8 of 12 months *do* meet it. You may enter the fraction $\frac{8}{12}$ directly into the boxes, and your answer will be accepted. It is *not* required that you reduce it.

Now let's apply the Kaplan Method to a second Data Interpretation question:

**CUSTOMERS WHO SWITCHED SERVICE PROVIDERS
(IN MILLIONS OF CUSTOMERS)**

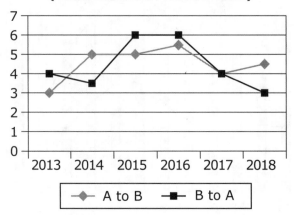

COMPANY A PROFIT 2017

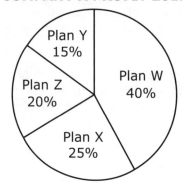

In 2017, Company A had a total profit of $220 million. If half of the customers who switched to Company A were responsible for half of the profit for Plan X, how much did these customers contribute per person toward Company A's profit for the year?

(A) $1.10

(B) $13.75

(C) $20.25

(D) $27.50

(E) $55.00

[STEP 1]

Analyze the tables and graphs.

This question has information about numbers of customers switching service providers for various years. It also has information about one company's profit for the year 2017, so the data in the two graphs are linked by the year 2017.

$\left[\text{ STEP 2 }\right]$

Approach strategically.

Approach the question methodically, starting with identifying the number of customers who switched to Company A. The line chart indicates that 4 million customers switched to Company A. This is the only information needed from the top graph.

The pie chart shows the breakdown of profit from the various plans offered and indicates that 25% of the profit came from Plan X.

The other information you need to get to the correct answer is given in the question stem:

- Profit of $220 million.
- Half of the customers who switched were responsible for half of Plan X's profits.

Now that your information is organized, all you need to do is the calculation. Plan X accounts for 25% of $220 million = $55 million. Half of $55 million is $27.5 million.

If 4 million people switched, then half of the people who switched would be 2 million.

The last step is to divide $27.5 by 2 (you can drop the zeros in the millions because they will cancel out): $27.5 ÷ 2 = $13.75. The correct choice is (**B**).

Now let's apply the Kaplan Method to a third Data Interpretation question:

**CUSTOMERS WHO SWITCHED SERVICE PROVIDERS
(IN MILLIONS OF CUSTOMERS)**

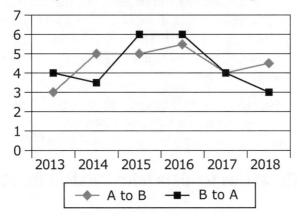

COMPANY A PROFIT 2017

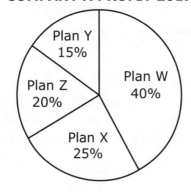

The management of Company B is most interested in the data for the years in which there were at least one million *more* customers who switched from Company A to Company B than switched from Company B to Company A. In which years did this happen?

Choose <u>all</u> that apply.

- [A] 2014
- [B] 2015
- [C] 2016
- [D] 2017
- [E] 2018

[STEP 1]

Analyze the tables and graphs.

This question asks for a comparison of facts between Company A and Company B. Take time to verify which line in the top graph represents customers switching to Company A and which line represents customers switching to Company B. Confirm that the title states that the data are given in millions and then look at the scale on the line graph.

[STEP 2]

Approach strategically.

After examining the line graph carefully, you are ready to gather the information needed to answer the question. The years that satisfy the requirement are those years for which the line representing A to B is at least one full horizontal row above the line representing B to A. Read the graph carefully because you must identify all the correct choices to get credit for a correct answer.

When you are clear what to look for on the graph, start from the left and identify the years 2014 and 2018 as those in which at least one million more customers switched from A to B than switched from B to A. These are choices (**A**) and (**E**).

Kaplan's Additional Tips for Data Interpretation Questions

Slow down

There's always a lot going on in Data Interpretation problems—both in the charts and in the questions themselves. If you slow down the first time through, you can avoid calculation errors and having to reread the questions and charts.

Pace yourself wisely

To ensure that you score as many points on the exam as possible, use the allotted time for a section wisely. Remember that each question type has the same value. If you must miss a few questions in a section, make them the ones that would take you the longest to answer, not the ones at the end of the section that you could have answered correctly but simply didn't get to. Data Interpretation questions are generally some of the more time-consuming ones to answer, and if answering them isn't one of your strong suits, save them for the end.

DATA INTERPRETATION CONCEPT CHECK

Before you move on, check your understanding by considering these questions:

- What types of charts might you see in a Data Interpretation set?

- What math concepts are most frequently tested in Data Interpretation questions?

- How much information in the charts and tables do you need to evaluate before tackling the questions?

If you feel like you've got the hang of it, great! Proceed to the practice set that starts on the next page.

If you'd like a quick video review of this chapter, or if you would like some additional guided practice, head to your online resources. Under **Data Interpretation**, click **Strategy for Data Interpretation** to watch a quick video review of this chapter. Or click **Data Interpretation Guided Practice** to apply what you've learned.

Data Interpretation Practice Set

Try the following Data Interpretation questions using the Kaplan Method for Data Interpretation. If you're up to the challenge, time yourself; on Test Day, you'll want to spend only about 2 minutes on each question.

Questions 1–5 are based on the following graphs.

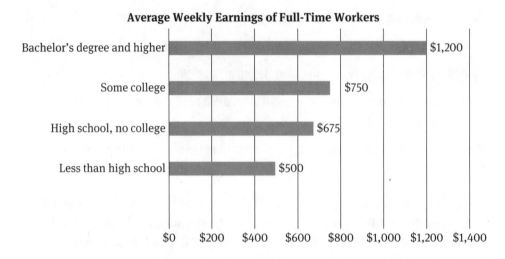

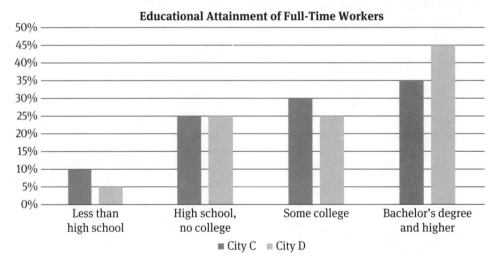

1. On average, a person who graduated from high school but did not attend college earns what percent less than a person whose education included some college but not a bachelor's degree if both are full-time workers?

   Ⓐ 8%

   Ⓑ 10%

   Ⓒ 11%

   Ⓓ 33%

   Ⓔ 90%

2. The population of City C is 200,000, and 40% of the residents are full-time workers. The number of full-time workers in City C who have no college education at all is

   Ⓐ 8,000

   Ⓑ 20,000

   Ⓒ 28,000

   Ⓓ 52,000

   Ⓔ 70,000

3. The total weekly earnings of full-time workers in City D with some college but no degree is $22.5 million. If the wages in each city are consistent with the average weekly earnings in the first graph, what are the total weekly earnings of full-time workers with less than a high school education in City D?

   Ⓐ $500,000

   Ⓑ $1,500,000

   Ⓒ $2,500,000

   Ⓓ $3,000,000

   Ⓔ $4,500,000

4. If the workers in both cities earn the averages shown in the chart, how much greater is the overall weekly earnings average in City D than in City C?

   Ⓐ $55.00

   Ⓑ $57.50

   Ⓒ $275.00

   Ⓓ $5,500.00

   Ⓔ $5,750.00

5. Hannah attended some college and earns 20% more than the average person in her educational category. After she earns her degree, she'll earn the average weekly salary for bachelor's degree holders. Hannah will spend $6,000 in tuition and take a 50% pay cut for 30 weeks to earn the degree. After she gets her degree, for how many weeks will she need to work to recoup her lost wages and tuition using the extra money she will earn weekly?

    ☐ weeks

Questions 6–10 refer to the following stimulus.

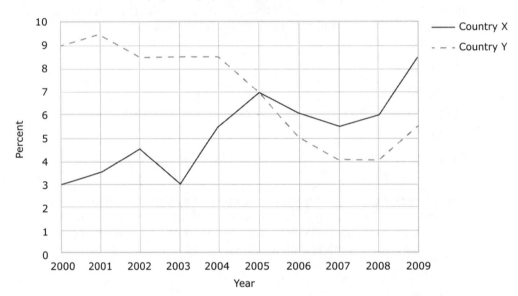

Unemployment (%) in Country X and Country Y

6. For which of the six years from 2000 to 2005 was the unemployment rate in Country Y more than 5 percentage points greater than that of Country X?

    A   2000

    B   2001

    C   2002

    D   2003

    E   2004

    F   2005

7. Which of the following is closest to the average (arithmetic mean) of the 9 changes in the percentage of unemployed workers in Country X between consecutive years from 2000 to 2009?

    A   0.4%

    B   0.5%

    C   0.6%

    D   0.7%

    E   1.3%

8. In 2006, the unemployment rate of Country X was approximately what percent of that of Country Y?

   Ⓐ 16.7%

   Ⓑ 20%

   Ⓒ 60%

   Ⓓ 83.3%

   Ⓔ 120%

9. If it were discovered that the unemployment rate for Country Y shown for 2003 was incorrect and should have been 6% instead, then the average (arithmetic mean) unemployment rate per year for the 10 years shown would have been off by approximately how many percentage points?

   Ⓐ 0.25

   Ⓑ 0.3

   Ⓒ 2.5

   Ⓓ 3

   Ⓔ 25

10. The percent change in unemployment was greatest for which one of the following?

   Ⓐ Country X, from 2000 to 2002

   Ⓑ Country X, from 2003 to 2004

   Ⓒ Country X, from 2008 to 2009

   Ⓓ Country Y, from 2004 to 2006

   Ⓔ Country Y, from 2005 to 2007

Data Interpretation Practice Set Answer Key

1.	B	6.	A, B, D
2.	C	7.	C
3.	D	8.	E
4.	B	9.	A
5.	65	10.	B

Data Interpretation Practice Set Answers and Explanations

1. B

Referring to the first bar chart, the average weekly earnings of a high school graduate are $675 and those of a worker with some college are $750. So the difference in weekly earnings is $750 − $675 = $75. Since the comparison is being made to the worker with some college, the percentage change is $\frac{\$75}{\$750} \times 100\% = 10\%$, which is **(B)**, the correct answer. If you used $675 as the denominator, you would have chosen (C), 11%. Note that (E), 90%, is what percent *of* the earnings of the person with some college is earned by the high school graduate, not what percent *less*.

2. C

The number of full-time workers in City C is 200,000 × 0.40 = 80,000. The two dark gray bars on the left are the percentages of those workers without college degrees in City C; that is, 10% + 25% = 35%. Thus, the number of full-time workers in City C with no college at all is 0.35 × 80,000 = 28,000, which is **(C)**.

3. D

If the total weekly earnings of the workers with some college is $22,500,000 and the average weekly earnings of that cohort are $750, then there are $\frac{22,500,000}{750} = 30,000$ such workers. Refer to the second graph to see that these 30,000 people make up one-quarter of the workforce in City D, so the total workforce there is 4 × 30,000 = 120,000. Full-time workers with less than a high school education are 5% of that total, which is 120,000 × 0.05 = 6,000 people. Since this category of workers earns $500 per week, their total weekly earnings are 6,000 × $500 = $3,000,000. **(D)** is correct.

4. B

This is a weighted average question. Since the numbers of workers in each category are given in percentages, pick 100 as the number of workers in each city. Because you only need to find the *difference* between the two weighted averages, there are shortcuts that greatly simplify the calculations. In the "Less than high school" category, there would be 10% of 100 or 10 workers in C and there would be just 5 in D. Those 5 "extra" workers in C earn 5 × $500 = $2,500 weekly. There are the same number of high school graduates in both cities, so there will be no difference. Move along to the "Some college" group: there are 30 in C and 25 in D. The weekly earnings for 5 such people is 5 × $750 = $3,750. In both of these categories of workers, the total earnings in City D are less than those in City C. Finally, there are 10 *more* of the high-earners in City D. Those people make 10 × $1,200 = $12,000 per week. So, the total weekly earnings in City D are $12,000 − $3,750 − $2,500 = $5,750 greater than in City C. Remember that this comparison was based upon 100 workers, so the difference in the averages is $\frac{\$5,750}{100} = \$57.50$, which is **(B)**. If you didn't use the shortcut and actually computed the weighted averages, they are $921.25 and $863.75, which gives the same $57.50 difference.

5. 65

Hannah's current earnings are 20% greater than the category average, which makes them 1.2 × $750 = $900 per week. If she takes a 50% pay cut for 30 weeks, her lost wages will be $\frac{\$900}{2} \times 30 = \$13,500$. Adding that to the college expenses of $6,000, Hannah needs to make up a total of $19,500. When she gets her degree, Hannah will be making $1,200 per week. If she hadn't cut back her hours to attend school, she would still be making $900 per week, so she is recouping her $19,500 at the rate of $1,200 − $900 = $300 per week. So, it would take Hannah $\frac{\$19,500}{300} = $ **65 weeks** to recoup her costs.

6. A, B, D

Calculate the differences for the years 2000 through 2005:

(A): 2000: 9% − 3% = 6%. Correct.

(B): 2001: 9.5% − 3.5% = 6%. Correct.

(C): 2002: 8.5% − 4.5% = 4%. Incorrect.

(D): 2003: 8.5% − 3% = 5.5%. Correct.

(E): 2004: 8.5% − 5.5% = 3%. Incorrect.

(F): 2005: 7% − 7% = 0%. Incorrect.

Note that precise calculation is not necessary for 2004 and 2005; eyeballing the difference in the graph should be sufficient for these years.

7. C

First, find the changes from year to year. Note that downward changes must be represented by negative values; making all the values positive yields distractor choice (E).

2000 to 2001: 0.5%

2001 to 2002: 1%

2002 to 2003: −1.5%

2003 to 2004: 2.5%

2004 to 2005: 1.5%

2005 to 2006: −1%

2006 to 2007: −0.5%

2007 to 2008: 0.5%

2008 to 2009: 2.5%

Then, calculate the average of these changes:

$$\frac{0.5 + 1 - 1.5 + 2.5 + 1.5 - 1 - 0.5 + 0.5 + 2.5}{9}$$

$$= \frac{5.5}{9} = 0.6\overline{1}$$

The correct answer is **(C)**.

8. E

Look up the unemployment values for 2006:

Country X: 6%

Country Y: 5%

Six is 1.2 times 5, and 1.2 = 120%. Thus, the unemployment rate of Country X (6) is 120% of that of Country Y (5). Critical thinking also leads to **(E)** without having to do any calculations, as the correct answer has to be greater than 100% and the other four choices are less than 100%. Many of the trap choices hinge on a misunderstanding of the question. Five is about 16.7% smaller than 6 (A), and 6 is 20% greater than 5 (B). (D) is backward, giving Y as a percent of X.

9. A

The 2003 unemployment rate for Country Y shown in the graph is 8.5%, so 6% is a decrease of 2.5 percentage points. At this point, you could calculate both averages and compare them directly, but it's much faster to think critically. There are 10 years shown, so each year contributes one tenth of the average. Thus, a decrease of 2.5 percentage points would decrease the overall average by 2.5 ÷ 10, or 0.25 percentage points, **(A)**.

10. B

Recall the percent change formula:

$$\text{Percent Change} = \frac{\text{Change}}{\text{Original}} \times 100\%$$

Strategic elimination is much faster here than precise calculation. For Country X, comparing (A) and **(B)**, 2000 and 2003 had the same rate, but the rate in 2004 was higher than the rate in 2002, so (A) is wrong. Also for Country X, comparing **(B)** and (C), the increase from 2003 to 2004 was the same as the increase from 2008 to 2009 (2.5 percentage points in both cases), but the value in 2003 was much lower, so a 2.5 percentage point change represented a more significant change in 2003 to 2004. (C) is wrong.

For Country Y, (D) and (E) feature decreases that are less than 50%: $\frac{3.5}{8.5}$ and $\frac{3}{7}$, respectively. **(B)** is $\frac{2.5}{3}$, which is much greater than 50% and thus the right answer.

CHAPTER 19

QUANTITATIVE REASONING PRACTICE SETS

In this chapter, you will take three practice sets, composed of 20 questions each. A diagnostic tool is provided after each section to help you learn from your mistakes.

Review of the Kaplan Methods for Quantitative Reasoning

Before starting your practice sets, review the steps and strategies you have studied for answering each type of Quantitative Reasoning question quickly, efficiently, and correctly.

THE KAPLAN METHOD FOR QUANTITATIVE COMPARISON

STEP 1 Analyze the centered information and quantities.

STEP 2 Approach strategically.

THE KAPLAN METHOD FOR PROBLEM SOLVING

STEP 1 Analyze the question.

STEP 2 Identify the task.

STEP 3 Approach strategically.

STEP 4 Confirm your answer.

THE KAPLAN METHOD FOR DATA INTERPRETATION

STEP 1 Analyze the tables and graphs.

STEP 2 Approach strategically.

Quantitative Reasoning Practice Set 1

35 Minutes — 20 Questions

Directions: For each question, indicate the best answer, using the directions given.

You may use a calculator for all the questions in this section.

If a question has answer choices with **ovals**, then the correct answer is a single choice. If a question has answer choices with **squares**, then the correct answer consists of one or more answer choices. Read each question carefully.

Important Facts:

All numbers used are real numbers.

All figures lie in a plane unless otherwise noted.

Geometric figures, such as lines, circles, triangles, and quadrilaterals, **may or may not be drawn to scale**. That is, you should not assume that quantities such as lengths and angle measures are as they appear in a drawing. But you can assume that lines shown as straight are indeed straight, points on a line are in the order shown, and all geometric objects are in the relative positions shown. For questions involving drawn figures, base your answers on geometric reasoning rather than on estimation, measurement, or comparison by sight.

Coordinate systems, such as xy-planes and number lines, **are** drawn to scale. Therefore, you may read, estimate, and compare quantities in these figures by sight or by measurement.

Graphical data presentations, such as bar graphs, line graphs, and pie charts, **are** drawn to scale. Therefore, you may read, estimate, and compare data values by sight or by measurement.

Directions: In questions 1–8, compare the value in Quantity A to the value in Quantity B. Information concerning one or both of the quantities to be compared is centered above the two quantities. Compare the two quantities and select Ⓐ if Quantity A is greater Ⓑ if Quantity B is greater, Ⓒ if the two quantities are equal, and Ⓓ if the relationship cannot be determined from the information given.

1.   Quantity A   Quantity B

The number of distinct ways to form an ordered line of 3 people by choosing from 6 people   The number of distinct ways to form an unordered group of 3 people by choosing from 10 people   Ⓐ Ⓑ Ⓒ Ⓓ

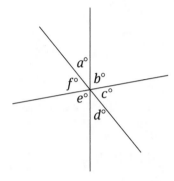

$$a° + b° = 2c° \text{ and } e° = 2d°$$

2.   Quantity A   Quantity B

          $a°$ $2(b° - f°)$ Ⓐ Ⓑ Ⓒ Ⓓ

$$7p + 3 = r$$
$$3p + 7 = s$$

3.   Quantity A   Quantity B

          r s Ⓐ Ⓑ Ⓒ Ⓓ

The original cost of a shirt is x dollars.

4.   Quantity A   Quantity B

          x The cost of the shirt if the original cost is first increased by 10% and then decreased by 10%   Ⓐ Ⓑ Ⓒ Ⓓ

A customer service center had z inbound calls on hold. During the next minute, one-third of those calls were answered but 15 new calls were placed on hold so that 35 callers were then holding.

5.   Quantity A   Quantity B

          z 33   Ⓐ Ⓑ Ⓒ Ⓓ

There are n people in a room. One-third of them leave the room. Four people enter the room. There are now $\frac{5}{6}$ of the original number of people in the room.

6.	Quantity A	Quantity B	
	n	20	

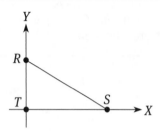

Note: Figure not drawn to scale.

Triangle RST is formed by the intersections of the line $x = 12 - 2y$ with the two axes of the coordinate plane.

7.	Quantity A	Quantity B	Ⓐ Ⓑ Ⓒ Ⓓ
	The measure of angle RST	$30°$	

x is an integer.
$$1 < x < 9$$

8.	Quantity A	Quantity B	Ⓐ Ⓑ Ⓒ Ⓓ
	$\left(\sqrt{x} + \sqrt{x}\right)^2$	$x + x\sqrt{x}$	

Directions: The remaining questions have several different formats. Select one answer if the answer choice letters are inside ovals. If the answer choice letters are inside boxes, select all choices that apply. If there is a rectangular box, enter your response as a numerical value.

9. If $\frac{x}{y} = \frac{2}{3}$ and $x + y = 15$, which of the following is greater than y?

Indicate all possible choices.

- Ⓐ $\sqrt{65}$
- Ⓑ $\sqrt{82}$
- Ⓒ $\sqrt{99}$
- Ⓓ $\sqrt{101}$
- Ⓔ $\sqrt{122}$

10. The product of two integers is 10. Which of the following could be the average (arithmetic mean) of the two numbers?

Indicate all possible choices.

- Ⓐ -5.5
- Ⓑ -3.5
- Ⓒ -1.5
- Ⓓ 1.5
- Ⓔ 3.5

11. For which of the following numbers does the sum of its prime factors equal the sum of the prime factors of 420?

    Indicate <u>all</u> possible choices.

    - [A] 52
    - [B] 104
    - [C] 150
    - [D] 176
    - [E] 450

12. The average (arithmetic mean) bowling score of n bowlers is 160. The average of these n scores together with a score of 170 is 161. What is the number of bowlers, n?

    $\boxed{}$ bowlers

13. Set T consists of five integers: the first five odd prime numbers when counting upward from zero. This gives set T a standard deviation of approximately 3.71. Which of the following values, if added to the set T, would increase the standard deviation of set T?

    - (A) 11
    - (B) 9
    - (C) 7.8
    - (D) 4.15
    - (E) 3.7

14.

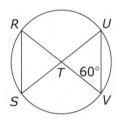

The circle shown has center T. The measure of angle TVU is 60°. If the circle has a radius of 3, what is the length of segment RS?

- (A) 2
- (B) $2\sqrt{2}$
- (C) 3
- (D) $3\sqrt{3}$
- (E) $6\sqrt{2}$

15. What is the probability of rolling a total of 7 with a single roll of two fair six-sided dice, each with the distinct numbers 1–6 on each side?

- (A) $\dfrac{1}{12}$
- (B) $\dfrac{1}{6}$
- (C) $\dfrac{2}{7}$
- (D) $\dfrac{1}{3}$
- (E) $\dfrac{1}{2}$

16. There are 8 fields of exactly the same size that are to be plowed by 7 farmers who work at identical rates. If it takes 5 hours for 4 of the farmers to plow the first 2 fields, how many hours will it take the remaining 3 farmers to plow the remaining 6 fields?

☐ hours

Questions 17–20 are based on the following graph and table.

**WATER USAGE BY YEAR, TOWN W
(IN BILLIONS OF GALLONS)**

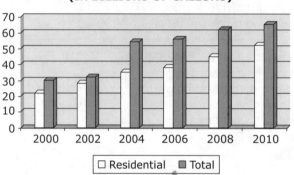

☐ Residential ■ Total

DAILY WATER USAGE STATISTICS
(with efficient appliances and good maintenance)

Use	Gallons per Capita
Showers	9
Clothes washers	10
Toilets	8
Leaks	4
Faucets	11
Other	4

17. Which best describes the range (in billions of gallons) for residential water consumption from 2000 to 2010, inclusive?

Ⓐ 10
Ⓑ 20
Ⓒ 30
Ⓓ 40
Ⓔ 50

18. In the year in which total usage exceeded residential usage by the least number of gallons, approximately what percent of total usage was residential usage?

Ⓐ 68%
Ⓑ 75%
Ⓒ 88%
Ⓓ 95%
Ⓔ 98%

19. In 2004, only 10,000 residents of town W lived in homes with efficient appliances and good maintenance. How many gallons per day were used by these residents for the three daily household purposes requiring the most water?

Ⓐ 110,000

Ⓑ 160,000

Ⓒ 270,000

Ⓓ 300,000

Ⓔ 460,000

20. Households with efficient appliances and good maintenance can reduce water consumption by about 35%. If half of the residential consumption in town W in 2010 was by households with efficient appliances and good maintenance, approximately how many gallons of water (in billions) were saved that year?

Ⓐ 5

Ⓑ 14

Ⓒ 40

Ⓓ 52

Ⓔ 65

Quantitative Reasoning Practice Set 1 Answer Key

1.	C	11.	B, D
2.	C	12.	9
3.	D	13.	E
4.	A	14.	C
5.	B	15.	B
6.	A	16.	20
7.	B	17.	C
8.	A	18.	C
9.	B, C, D, E	19.	D
10.	A, B, E	20.	B

Diagnose Your Results

Diagnostic Tool

Tally up your score and write your results below.

Total

Total Correct: _____ out of 20 correct

By Question Type

Quantitative Comparison (questions 1–8) _____ out of 8 correct

Problem Solving (questions 9–16) _____ out of 8 correct

Data Interpretation (questions 17–20) _____ out of 4 correct

Look back at the questions you got wrong and think about your experience answering them.

[STEP 1]

Find the roadblocks.

If you struggled to answer some questions, then to improve your score, you need to pinpoint exactly what "roadblocks" tripped you up.

To do that, ask yourself the following two questions:

Am I weak in the skills being tested?

This will be very easy for you to judge. Maybe you've forgotten how to calculate an average or what PEMDAS stands for. If you know you need to brush up on your math skills, review the content in chapters 10 through 15 in this book.

Did the question types throw me off?

If the answer is yes, then you need to become more comfortable with them! Quantitative Comparisons have a unique format, and Data Interpretation can be daunting with its charts, graphs, and tables. If you struggled, review chapters 16 through 18 of this book.

Make sure you understand the principles and how to apply the methods. These strategies will help you improve your speed and efficiency on Test Day. Remember, it's not a math test; it's a critical reasoning test.

[STEP 2]

Find the blind spots.

Did you answer some questions quickly and confidently but get them wrong anyway?

When you come across wrong answers like these, you need to figure out what you thought you were doing right, what it turns out you were doing wrong, and why that happened. The best way to do that is to **read the answer explanations!**

The explanations give you a detailed breakdown of why the correct answer is correct and why all the other answers choices are incorrect. This helps to reinforce the Kaplan principles and methods for each question type and helps you figure out what blindsided you so it doesn't happen again.

[STEP 3]

Reinforce your strengths.

Now read through all the answer explanations for the ones you got right. You should check every answer because, if you guessed correctly without actually knowing how to get the right answer, reading the explanations helps you make sure that you learn what you need to. Equally important, on a problem you knew how to do, there may be a faster way to get to the answer than the way you chose or even just a different way. Understanding more than one approach to a given problem will deepen your critical thinking skills. Reading the explanation for a question you got right also helps to reinforce the Kaplan principles and methods for each question type, which in turn helps you work more efficiently so you can get the score you want. Keep your skills sharp with more practice.

Quantitative Reasoning Practice Set 1 Answers and Explanations

1. C

Quantity A is a permutation because order matters. The number of ways 3 people chosen from a group of 6 can be arranged in a line, where order matters, is $6 \times 5 \times 4 = 120$. Quantity B is a combination because order does not matter. The number of ways 3 people can be selected from a group of 10, where order does not matter, is:

$$_{10}C_3 = \frac{10!}{3!(10-3!)} = \frac{10 \times 9 \times 8}{3 \times 2 \times 1} = \frac{720}{6} = 120$$

The two quantities are equal.

2. C

There are three pairs of vertical angles in the figure: a and d, b and e, and c and f, so the values in each pair are equal. The sum of the angles that make up a straight line is $180°$, so $a + b + c = 180$. The centered information states that $a + b = 2c$, so substitute $2c$ for $a + b$ to get $2c + c = 180$. Thus, $3c = 180$ and $c = 60$. Given that $e = 2d$, substitute b for e and a for d to get $b = 2a$. Substituting again, $a + 2a + 60 = 180$, so $3a = 120$, and $a = 40$. So $b = 2a = 80$. Now that the values for all the angles are known, compare the two quantities. Quantity A, $a°$, is $40°$. Quantity B is $2(b° - f°)$. Using the fact that $c = f$, this is $2(80° - 60°) = 2(20°) = 40°$, so the quantities are equal. **(C)** is correct.

3. D

Pick a value for p and see what effect it has on r and s. If $p = 1$, $r = (7 \times 1) + 3 = 10$, and $s = (3 \times 1) + 7 = 10$, and the two quantities are equal. But if $p = 0$, $r = (7 \times 0) + 3 = 3$, and $s = (3 \times 0) + 7 = 7$, and Quantity A is less than Quantity B. Because there are at least two different possible relationships, the answer is **(D)**.

4. A

Use the Picking Numbers strategy to answer this question. Suppose the original selling price of the shirt, x, is $100. After a 10% increase in price, the shirt would sell for 110% of $100, which is $110. If there is a 10% decrease next, the shirt would sell for 90% of the current price. That would be 90% of $110: $0.9 \times \$110 = \$99$.

This price is less than the original amount, x, so Quantity A is greater.

5. B

Since this is a Quantitative Comparison question, you do not need to know the exact value of z, just whether it is less than, equal to, or greater than 33. So, instead of solving for z, just plug in 33 as the initial number of calls on hold. Since $\frac{1}{3}$ were answered, that would have left $33 - \frac{1}{3}(33) = 33 - 11 = 22$ of the original callers on hold. Adding 15 more would bring the total to 37, which is greater than the 35 callers who were actually holding. Thus, the initial number was less than 33 and **(B)** is correct. (For the record, $z = 30$.)

6. A

There are n people in a room. One-third of them leave the room. So, there are $n - \frac{1}{3}n$ people in the room. Four people enter the room, so you have $n - \frac{1}{3}n + 4$ people. There are now $\frac{5}{6}$ of the original number of people in the room, therefore $n - \frac{1}{3}n + 4 = \frac{5}{6}n$. Now solve for n.

$$
\begin{aligned}
n - \tfrac{1}{3}n + 4 &= \tfrac{5}{6}n \\
\tfrac{2}{3}n + 4 &= \tfrac{5}{6}n \\
4 &= \tfrac{5}{6}n - \tfrac{2}{3}n \\
4 &= \tfrac{5}{6}n - \tfrac{4}{6}n \\
4 &= \tfrac{1}{6}n \\
24 &= n
\end{aligned}
$$

So, $n = 24$ and Quantity A is larger.

7. B

Since point R is the intersection of the line with the y-axis, plug $x = 0$ into the equation for the line: $0 = 12 - 2y$, so $y = 6$. The coordinates of point R are $(0,6)$. Similarly, for point S, $x = 12 - 2(0) = 12$. The coordinates of point S are $(12,0)$. For many line questions, you will need to restate the equation in standard $y = mx + b$ form, but that is not necessary here. This is a right triangle because the two legs are on the x- and y-axes.

Quantity B is 30°, so think about the characteristics of a 30°-60°-90° triangle, one of which is that the short leg is half the length of the hypotenuse. With legs of 6 and 12, the hypotenuse of triangle RST is greater than 12. Therefore, since the short leg is 6, which is *less* than half the length of the hypotenuse, triangle RST must be "flatter" than a 30°-60°-90° triangle, and angle RST must be less than 30°. (**B**) is correct.

8. A

Start by simplifying the quantity in Quantity A: $\left(\sqrt{x} + \sqrt{x}\right)^2$ is the same as $\left(2\sqrt{x}\right)^2$, which is $4x$. Subtract x from both quantities, and you're left with $3x$ in Quantity A and $x\sqrt{x}$ in Quantity B. Now divide both sides by x, and you're left with 3 in Quantity A and $\sqrt{x}$ in Quantity B. Square both quantities, and you get 9 in Quantity A and x in Quantity B. Since x is an integer between 1 and 9, exclusive, Quantity A is larger. If the algebra seems too abstract, go ahead and use the Picking Numbers strategy. If x equals 4, then Quantity A equals $(2 + 2)^2 = 16$, and Quantity B equals $4 + 8 = 12$.

9. B, C, D, E

If $\frac{x}{y} = \frac{2}{3}$, then $3x = 2y$ and $y = \frac{3x}{2}$. Substitute $y = \frac{3x}{2}$ into the equation $x + y = 15$: $x + \frac{3x}{2} = 15$, $2x + 3x = 30$, $5x = 30$, $x = 6$. Then, $y = \frac{3x}{2} = \frac{3(6)}{2} = 9$ and $y^2 = 81$. So any answer with greater than 81 under the radical will be greater than y. Therefore, the correct choices are (**B**), (**C**), (**D**), and (**E**).

10. A, B, E

The best place to start here is with pairs of positive integers that have a product of 10. The numbers 5 and 2 have a product of 10, as do 10 and 1. But remember that integers may be negative, so −1 and −10 are possible, as well as −2 and −5. The mean of −1 and −10 is −5.5; the mean of −2 and −5 is −3.5. The mean of 2 and 5 is 3.5. The correct answers are (**A**), (**B**), and (**E**).

11. B, D

The prime factorization of 420 is $2 \times 2 \times 3 \times 5 \times 7$. The sum of these prime factors is $2 + 2 + 3 + 5 + 7 = 19$. Now test each of the choices. The prime factorization of 52 is $2 \times 2 \times 13$, giving a sum of $2 + 2 + 13 = 17$. For 104, note that this is just 52×2. Just add one more 2 to the sum of the prime factors of 52 to get $17 + 2 = 19$. For 150, the prime factorization is $2 \times 3 \times 5 \times 5$, giving a sum of $2 + 3 + 5 + 5 = 15$. For 176, the prime factorization is $2 \times 2 \times 2 \times 2 \times 11$, giving a sum of $2 + 2 + 2 + 2 + 11 = 19$. Finally, note that 450 is 150×3. Since you already did the prime factorization of 150, just add one more 3 to get a sum of $15 + 3 = 18$. Thus, (**B**) and (**D**) are the correct answers.

12. 9

Use the definition of *average* to write the sum of the first n bowlers' scores: $\frac{\text{Sum of scores}}{n} = \text{Average}$ therefore, $n \times \text{average} = \text{sum of scores}$. Substitute the values given in the question and you have $160n = $ sum of scores for the initial set of bowlers. Now write the formula for the average again, using the additional score of 170. Now there are $n + 1$ bowlers.

$$\frac{\text{Sum of scores}}{n} = \text{Average}$$

$$\frac{160n + 170}{n + 1} = 161$$

Cross multiply and use algebra to solve for n.

$$\begin{aligned} 160n + 170 &= 161(n + 1) \\ 160n + 170 &= 161n + 161 \\ 170 - 161 &= 161n - 160n \\ 9 &= n \end{aligned}$$

There were **9** bowlers in the original group.

13. E

First, identify the numbers in set T: 3, 5, 7, 11, 13.
The average of the numbers in set T is
$\frac{3 + 5 + 7 + 11 + 13}{5} = \frac{39}{5} = 7.8$. Its standard deviation is given in the question stem as 3.71. In order to increase the standard deviation of a set of numbers, you must add a value that is more than one standard deviation away from the mean. One standard deviation *below* the mean for set T is $7.8 - 3.71 = 4.09$, and one standard deviation *above* the mean is $7.8 + 3.71 = 11.51$. Any value outside this range $4.09 \leq x \leq 11.51$ would increase set T's standard deviation, since it would make the set more "spread out" from the mean than it currently is. The only choice that does that is choice (**E**).

14. C

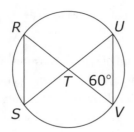

Solving this problem involves several steps, but none is too complicated. The circle has its center at point T. Start with the triangle on the right whose vertices are at T and two points on the circumference of the circle. This makes two of its sides radii of the circle, which we're told each have a length of 3. Because all radii must have equal length, this makes the triangle an isosceles triangle. In addition, you're told one of the base angles of this triangle has a measure of 60°. Thus, the other base angle must also have a measure of 60° (since the base angles in an isosceles triangle have equal measure). The sum of the two base angles is 120°, leaving 180° − 120° or 60° for the other angle, the one at point T (making $\triangle TUV$ an equilateral triangle with sides of 3).

Now, angle RTS is opposite this 60° angle, so its measure must also be 60°. Therefore, $\triangle RST$ is another equilateral triangle, and its sides are 3. Therefore, the length of RS is 3, choice (**C**).

15. B

The probability formula is:

$$\text{Probability} = \frac{\text{Number of desired outcomes}}{\text{Number of possible outcomes}}$$

When one die is rolled, there are six possible outcomes. When two dice are rolled, the number of possible outcomes is 6×6, or 36. Getting a total value of 7 can be achieved in the following ways: (1,6), (2,5), (3,4), (4,3), (5,2), and (6,1). There are six possible ways.

So the probability of rolling a total of 7 is $\frac{6}{36}$, which can be reduced to $\frac{1}{6}$, choice (**B**).

16. 20

First, 2 fields are plowed in 5 hours. But that's with 4 farmers plowing. One farmer would take four times as long, or $5 \times 4 = 20$ hours, to plow 2 fields. At that rate, one farmer would take $20 \times 3 = 60$ hours to plow the remaining 6 fields. Three farmers, then, could do the job in $\frac{1}{3}$ of the time, or **20** hours.

17. C

The residential usage (in billions) in 2000 was about 22; the usage was about 52 in 2010. Since 52 was the highest usage over this time period and 22 was the lowest, the range is the difference between these numbers. Therefore, $52 - 22 = 30$, and the range is about 30 billion gallons. The correct answer is (**C**).

18. C

The two amounts were closest to each other in 2002. The residential amount appears to be about 28; the total appears to be about 32: $28 \div 32 = 0.875$. Choice (**C**) is the closest.

19. D

The three usages with the greatest amounts per person are faucets, washers, and showers, totaling 30 gallons per day. Multiply by 10,000 to get 300,000, choice (**D**).

20. B

The residential consumption (in billions) in 2010 was approximately 52. Take half of that amount, 26, to represent the amount of water used by households with efficient appliances and plumbing. Let W represent the amount of water these households would have used otherwise.

Set up a percent equation to solve for W. Remember, the savings were 35%, so subtract 35 from 100 to find the percent that would have been used.

$$26 = (100\% - 35\%) \times W$$
$$26 = 65\% \times W$$
$$26 = 0.65 \times W$$
$$\frac{26}{0.65} = 40 = W$$

The savings in billions of gallons was $40 - 26 = 14$. The correct answer is **(B)**.

Quantitative Reasoning Practice Set 2

35 Minutes — 20 Questions

Directions: For each question, indicate the best answer, using the directions given.

You may use a calculator for all the questions in this section.

If a question has answer choices with **ovals**, then the correct answer is a single choice. If a question has answer choices with **squares**, then the correct answer consists of one or more answer choices. Read each question carefully.

Important Facts:

All numbers used are real numbers.

All figures lie in a plane unless otherwise noted.

Geometric figures, such as lines, circles, triangles, and quadrilaterals, **may or may not be drawn to scale**. That is, you should not assume that quantities such as lengths and angle measures are as they appear in a drawing. But you can assume that lines shown as straight are indeed straight, points on a line are in the order shown, and all geometric objects are in the relative positions shown. For questions involving drawn figures, base your answers on geometric reasoning rather than on estimation, measurement, or comparison by sight.

Coordinate systems, such as *xy*-planes and number lines, **are** drawn to scale. Therefore, you may read, estimate, and compare quantities in these figures by sight or by measurement.

Graphical data presentations, such as bar graphs, line graphs, and pie charts, **are** drawn to scale. Therefore, you may read, estimate, and compare data values by sight or by measurement.

Directions: In questions 1–10, compare the value in Quantity A to the value in Quantity B. Information concerning one or both of the quantities to be compared is centered above the two quantities. Compare the two quantities and select Ⓐ if Quantity A is greater, Ⓑ if Quantity B is greater, Ⓒ if the two quantities are equal, and Ⓓ if the relationship cannot be determined from the information given.

1.
Quantity A	Quantity B	
The average (arithmetic mean) of 100, 101, and 103	The median of 100, 101, and 103	Ⓐ Ⓑ Ⓒ Ⓓ

A and *B* are points on the circumference of the circle with center *O* (not shown). The length of chord *AB* is 15.

2.
Quantity A	Quantity B	
Circumference of circle *O*	12π	Ⓐ Ⓑ Ⓒ Ⓓ

$$x = \frac{4}{3}r^2h^2$$
$$x = 1$$

r and *h* are positive.

3.
Quantity A	Quantity B	
h	$\dfrac{\sqrt{3}}{2r}$	Ⓐ Ⓑ Ⓒ Ⓓ

$\triangle ABC$ lies in the *xy*-plane with *C* at (0,0), *B* at (6,0), and *A* at (*x,y*), where *x* and *y* are positive. The area of $\triangle ABC$ is 18 square units.

4.
Quantity A	Quantity B	
y	6	Ⓐ Ⓑ Ⓒ Ⓓ

For $x \neq y$, $x \Phi y = \dfrac{x + y}{x - y}$

$p > 0 > q$

5.
Quantity A	Quantity B	
$p \Phi q$	$q \Phi p$	Ⓐ Ⓑ Ⓒ Ⓓ

$$x \neq 0$$

6.

Quantity A	Quantity B	
$\dfrac{1}{x} + \dfrac{1}{x}$	$\dfrac{1}{x} \times \dfrac{1}{x}$	Ⓐ Ⓑ Ⓒ Ⓓ

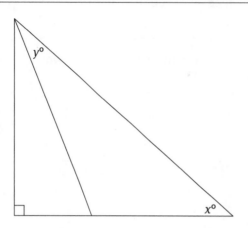

7.

Quantity A	Quantity B	
$x + y$	$90°$	Ⓐ Ⓑ Ⓒ Ⓓ

$$4s - 5t = 10$$
$$t - s = -4$$

8.

Quantity A	Quantity B	
s	t	Ⓐ Ⓑ Ⓒ Ⓓ

$$6(10)^n > 60{,}006$$

9.

Quantity A	Quantity B	
n	6	Ⓐ Ⓑ Ⓒ Ⓓ

In a four-digit positive integer y, the thousands digit is 2.5 times the tens digit.

10.

Quantity A	Quantity B	
The tens digits of y	4	Ⓐ Ⓑ Ⓒ Ⓓ

Directions: The remaining questions have several different formats. Select one answer if the answer choice letters are inside ovals. If the answer choice letters are inside boxes, select all choices that apply. If there is a rectangular box, enter your response as a numerical value.

11. What is the average (arithmetic mean) of $2x + 3$, $5x - 4$, $6x - 6$, and $3x - 1$?

    Ⓐ $2x + 4$
    Ⓑ $3x - 2$
    Ⓒ $3x + 2$
    Ⓓ $4x - 2$
    Ⓔ $4x + 2$

12.

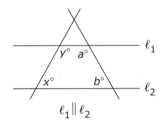

$\ell_1 \parallel \ell_2$

Which of the following statements must be true about the figure shown above?

    Ⓐ $x = a$
    Ⓑ $x = b$
    Ⓒ $a = b$
    Ⓓ $y = b$
    Ⓔ $x + y = a + b$

13.

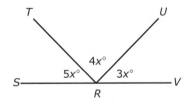

What is the degree measure of angle *SRU*?

    Ⓐ 15
    Ⓑ 45
    Ⓒ 105
    Ⓓ 135
    Ⓔ 180

14. There are at least 200 apples in a grocery store. The ratio of the number of oranges to the number of apples is 9 to 10. How many oranges could there be in the store?

Indicate <u>all</u> possible choices.

    Ⓐ 171
    Ⓑ 180
    Ⓒ 216
    Ⓓ 252
    Ⓔ 315

15.

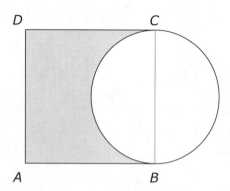

Square *ABCD* has a side length of 4. *BC* is the diameter of the circle. Which of the following is greater than or equal to the area of the shaded region, in square units?

Indicate <u>all</u> possible choices.

- A $16 - 16\pi$
- B $16 - 4\pi$
- C $16 - 2\pi$
- D $16 + \pi$
- E $16 + 4\pi$

$-30 \leq 6x \leq 60$ and $40 \geq 2y + 4 \geq 8$

16. What is the greatest possible value of $x - y$?

[   ]

---

17. A fair, six-sided die is rolled three times. What is the probability that the result of exactly one of the rolls will be an even number?

- Ⓐ 0.167
- Ⓑ 0.250
- Ⓒ 0.333
- Ⓓ 0.375
- Ⓔ 0.500

Questions 18–20 are based on the following graphs.

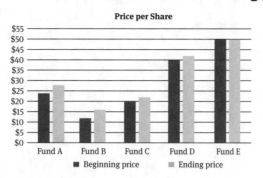

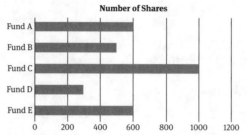

18. Which of the funds had the greatest percent increase in its price from the beginning to the end of the measured period?

    (A) Fund A

    (B) Fund B

    (C) Fund C

    (D) Fund D

    (E) Fund E

19. What was the total value of the investment in Funds C and E at the beginning of the measured period?

    $ ☐

20. In which fund did the total dollar value of the investment have the greatest dollar value increase between the beginning and end of the measured period?

    (A) Fund A

    (B) Fund B

    (C) Fund C

    (D) Fund D

    (E) Fund E

Quantitative Reasoning Practice Set 2 Answer Key

1.	A	11.	D
2.	A	12.	E
3.	C	13.	D
4.	C	14.	B, C, D, E
5.	D	15.	C, D, E
6.	D	16.	8
7.	B	17.	D
8.	A	18.	B
9.	D	19.	50,000
10.	B	20.	A

Diagnose Your Results

Diagnostic Tool

Tally up your score and write your results below.

Total

Total Correct: _____ out of 20 correct

By Question Type

Quantitative Comparison (questions 1–10) _____ out of 10 correct

Problem Solving (questions 11–17) _____ out of 7 correct

Data Interpretation (questions 18–20) _____ out of 3 correct

Repeat the steps outlined in the Diagnose Your Results page that follows the Quantitative Reasoning Practice Set 1 answer key.

Quantitative Reasoning Practice Set 2 Answers and Explanations

1. A

This question requires no computation but only a general understanding of how averages work and what the word "median" means. The median of a group of numbers is the "middle number"; it is the value above which half of the numbers in the group fall and below which the other half fall. If you have an even number of values, the median is the average of the two "middle" numbers; if you have an odd number of values, the median is one of the values. Here, in Quantity B, the median is 101. In Quantity A, if the numbers were 100, 101, and 102, then the average would also be 101, but because the third number, 103, is greater than 102, then the average must be greater than 101. Quantity A is greater than 101, and Quantity B equals 101; Quantity A is larger.

2. A

Start with the information you are given. You know that the length of the chord is 15. What does that mean? Well, because you don't know exactly where A and B are, it doesn't mean too much, but it does tell you that the distance between two points on the circle is 15. That tells you that the diameter must be at least 15. If the diameter were less than 15, then you couldn't have a chord that was equal to 15, because the diameter is always the longest chord in a circle. The diameter of the circle is 15 or greater, so the circumference must be at least 15π. That means that Quantity A must be larger than Quantity B.

3. C

The equation in the centered information looks complicated, but we'll take it one step at a time. Because Quantity A has only h in it, solve the equation for h, leaving h on one side of the equal sign and r on the other side. First, substitute the value for x into the first equation; then solve for h in terms of r.

$$x = \frac{4}{3}r^2h^2 \qquad \text{Substitute 1 for } x.$$

$$1 = \frac{4}{3}r^2h^2 \qquad \text{Divide both sides by } \frac{4}{3}.$$

$$\frac{3}{4} = r^2h^2 \qquad \text{Take the positive square root of both sides, using the information that } r \text{ and } h \text{ are positive.}$$

$$\frac{\sqrt{3}}{2} = rh \qquad \text{Divide both sides by } r \text{ to get } h \text{ alone.}$$

$$h = \frac{\sqrt{3}}{2r} \qquad \text{The two quantities are equal.}$$

4. C

Draw an xy-plane and label the points given to help solve this problem. You know where points B and C are; they're on the x-axis. You don't know where A is, however, which may make you think that the answer is choice (D). But you're given more information: you know that the triangle has an area of 18. The area of any triangle is one-half the product of the base and the height. Make side BC the base of the triangle; you know the coordinates of both points, so you can find their distance apart, which is the length of that side. C is at the origin, the point $(0,0)$; B is at the point $(6,0)$. The distance between them is the distance from 0 to 6 along the x-axis, or just 6. So that's the base. What about the height? Because you know that the area is 18, you can plug what you know into the area formula.

$$\text{Area} = \frac{1}{2} \times \text{base} \times \text{height}$$

$$18 = \frac{1}{2} \times 6 \times \text{height}$$

$$\text{height} = \frac{18}{3}$$

$$\text{height} = 6$$

That's the other dimension of the triangle. The height is the distance between the x-axis and point A. Now you know that A must be somewhere in the first quadrant, since both the x- and y-coordinates are positive. Don't worry about the x-coordinate of the point, because that's not what's being compared; you care only about the value of y. You know that the distance from the x-axis to the point is 6, because that's the height of the triangle and that y must be positive. Therefore, the y-coordinate of the point must be 6. That's what the y-coordinate is: a measure of the point's vertical distance from the x-axis. (Note that if you hadn't been told that y was positive, there would be two possible values for y: 6 and -6. A point that's 6 units below the x-axis would also give a triangle with height 6.) You still don't know the x-coordinate of the point, and in fact you can't figure that out, but you don't care. You know that y is 6; therefore, the two quantities are equal.

5. D

With symbolism problems like this, it sometimes helps to put the definition of the symbol into words. For this symbol, you can say something like "$x \Phi y$ means take the sum of the two numbers and divide that by the difference of the two numbers." One good way to do this problem is to Pick Numbers. You know that p is positive and q is negative. So suppose p is 1 and q is -1. Figure out what $p \Phi q$ is first. You start by taking the sum of the numbers, or $1 + (-1) = 0$. That's the numerator of the fraction, and you don't really need to go any further than that. Whatever their difference is, because the numerator is 0, the whole fraction must equal 0. (The difference can't be 0 also, since $p \neq q$.) So that's $p \Phi q$. Now what about $q \Phi p$? Well, that's going to have the same numerator as $p \Phi q$: 0. The only thing that changes when you reverse the order of the numbers is the denominator of the fraction. So $q \Phi p$ has a numerator of 0, and that fraction must equal 0 as well.

So you've found a case where the quantities are equal. Try another set of values and see whether the quantities are always equal. If $p = 1$ and $q = -2$, then the sum of the numbers is $1 + (-2)$ or -1. So that's the numerator of the fraction in each quantity. Now for the denominator of $p \Phi q$, you need $p - q = 1 - (-2) = 1 + 2 = 3$. Then the value of $p \Phi q$ is $\frac{-1}{3}$. The denominator of $q \Phi p$ is $q - p = -2 - 1 = -3$. In that case, the value of $q \Phi p$ is $\frac{-1}{-3}$ or $\frac{1}{3}$. The relationship between quantities is different; therefore, the answer is (**D**).

6. D

Picking Numbers will help you solve this problem. For $x = 1$, $\frac{1}{x} + \frac{1}{x} = \frac{1}{1} + \frac{1}{1} = 2$ and

$\frac{1}{x} \times \frac{1}{x} = \frac{1}{1} \times \frac{1}{1} = 1$, so Quantity A is larger. For $x = -1$, $\frac{1}{x} + \frac{1}{x} = \frac{1}{-1} + \frac{1}{-1} = -2$ and $\frac{1}{x} \times \frac{1}{x} = \frac{1}{-1} \times \frac{1}{-1} = 1$, so Quantity B is larger. The relationship between quantities is different; therefore, the answer is (**D**).

7. B

The sum of the interior angles of a triangle is $180°$. One of the angles of the large triangle formed by the outside perimeter is a right angle, or $90°$ angle. The remaining $90°$ must come from the sum of x, y, and the angle adjacent to y. Therefore, the sum of x and y alone must be less than $90°$. Quantity B is greater, making the answer (**B**).

8. A

You could solve this system of equations by substitution or combination. To use combination, multiply all the terms of $t - s = -4$ by 4 to get $-4s + 4t = -16$. Now add this result to the other equation:

$$4s - 5t = 10$$
$$\underline{-4s + 4t = -16}$$
$$-t = -6$$

So $t = 6$. Plug this value into the second equation: $6 - s = -4$, to get $s = 10$. Thus, Quantity A is greater, and (**A**) is correct.

9. D

Divide both sides of the inequality by 6. You're left with $(10)^n > 10{,}001$. The number 10,001 can also be written as $10^4 + 1$, so you know that $(10)^n > 10^4 + 1$. Therefore, Quantity A, n, must be 5 or greater. Quantity B is 6. Because n could be less than, equal to, or greater than 6, you need more information.

10. B

Try to set the quantities equal. Could the tens digit of y be 4? If it is, and the thousands digit is 2.5 times the units digit, then the thousands digit must be . . . 10? That can't be right. A digit must be one of the integers 0–9; 10 isn't a digit. Therefore, 4 is too big to be the tens digit of y.

In fact, the only possible value for the tens digit of y is 2. Quantity B is greater than Quantity A.

11. D

To find the average, add the quantities together and divide by 4: $(2x + 3) + (5x - 4) + (6x - 6) + (3x - 1)$ $= 16x - 8$ and $\dfrac{16x - 8}{4} = 4x - 2$. The correct choice is (D).

12. E

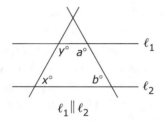

$\ell_1 \parallel \ell_2$

When a transversal cuts a pair of parallel lines, in this case ℓ_1 and ℓ_2, the angles are always supplementary and their sum is 180. So, the sum $(x + y)$ is equal to the sum $(a + b)$. The exact values of the individual angle measures cannot be determined from the figure. The answer is (E).

13. D

First, find the value of x, using the fact that there are 180° in a straight line. Set the sum of the angle measures equal to 180: $5x + 4x + 3x = 180$, $12x = 180$, and $x = 15$. Angle SRU equals $4x + 5x = 9x$, which is 135°. Choice (D) is correct.

14. B, C, D, E

You know that the ratio of oranges to apples is 9 to 10 and that there are at least 200 apples. The ratio tells you that there are more apples than oranges. At the minimum, there must be 180 oranges to satisfy the proportion $\dfrac{9}{10} = \dfrac{180}{200}$. There could be more than 200 apples, so any number of oranges greater than 180 for which the ratio 9:10 applies is also correct. All of the choices are multiples of 9, so the correct choices are (B), (C), (D), and (E).

15. C, D, E

The area of the shaded region is the area of the square minus the area of the portion of the circle that is inside the square. The area of a square is its side squared. The area of square $ABCD$ is $4^2 = 4 \times 4$, which is 16. Now find the area of the portion of the circle that is inside the square. Because the diameter of the circle is a side of the square, you know that exactly one-half of the circle's area is inside the square. Also, because the diameter of the circle is twice the radius, the radius of the circle is $\dfrac{4}{2}$ or 2. The area of a circle with a radius r is πr^2. The area of the complete circle in this question is $\pi(2)^2$, which is 4π. So half the area of this circle is 2π. Thus, the area of the shaded region is $16 - 2\pi$.

That means that $16 - 4\pi$ and $16 - 16\pi$ are less than $16 - 2\pi$, so they cannot be correct choices. However, the sum of 16 and any positive number is greater than 16 and also greater than $16 - 2\pi$. So, the correct choices are (C), (D), and (E).

16. 8

Simplify each inequality to restate them in terms of x and y. Divide all the terms of $-30 \leq 6x \leq 60$ by 6 to get $-5 \leq x \leq 10$. To simplify $40 \geq 2y + 4 \geq 8$, subtract 4 from each term to get $36 \geq 2y \geq 4$. Then, divide through by 2 to see that $18 \geq y \geq 2$. The maximum value of $x - y$ will be the greatest possible value of x minus the least possible value of y. This is $10 - 2$, so the correct answer is 8.

17. D

Although there are 6 numbers on the die, when it comes to evens and odds, there are only two outcomes of a roll. Thus, for three rolls, there are $2 \times 2 \times 2 = 8$ equally possible outcomes: EEE, EEO, EOE, EOO, OOO, OOE, OEO, and OEE. Three of these, EOO, OOE, and OEO, result in exactly one even number. Use the probability formula

$$\text{Probability} = \frac{\text{Number of desired outcomes}}{\text{Number of total possible outcomes}}$$ to

determine the probability, which is $\dfrac{3}{8}$.

The decimal equivalent $\dfrac{3}{8}$ is 0.375, so (D) is correct.

18. B

The first graph shows the beginning and ending prices. Start by "eyeballing" the two bars for each of the five funds. Fund E was flat, so eliminate that one. Fund D had a slight increase, but since the question asks for the greatest *percent* increase and Fund D had a relatively high beginning price, it does not have the greatest percent increase.

You might be able to infer that Fund B had the greatest percent increase since its starting value was less than those of Fund A and Fund C, but here are the calculations to confirm that. Use the percent change formula to compare the increases of these three funds:

$$\text{Percent change} = \frac{\text{New value} - \text{Original value}}{\text{Original value}} \times 100\%.$$

Fund A had an original price of $24 and a new price of $28, so the percent change was

$$\frac{28 - 24}{24} \times 100\% = \frac{4}{24} \times 100\% = \frac{1}{6} \times 100\% = 16.67\%.$$

For Fund B:
$$\frac{16 - 12}{12} \times 100\% = \frac{4}{12} \times 100\% = \frac{1}{3} \times 100\% = 33.33\%.$$

For Fund C:
$$\frac{22 - 20}{20} \times 100\% = \frac{2}{20} \times 100\% = \frac{1}{10} \times 100\% = 10.00\%.$$

So, Fund B had the greatest percentage increase, and (**B**) is correct.

19. 50,000

Extract the per share prices of the two funds from the first chart and multiply each by the number of shares shown on the second chart. For Fund C, that is $20/share × 1,000 shares = $20,000. For Fund E, the value is $50/share × 600 shares = $30,000. Thus, the total is $20,000 + $30,000 = **$50,000**.

20. A

The dollar value increase of each fund is the price increase per share times the number of shares held. For Fund A, that was ($28 − $24)(600) = ($4)(600) = $2,400. Fund B increased by ($16 − $12)(500) = ($4)(500) = $2,000. The increase in Fund C was ($22 − $20)(1,000) = ($2)(1,000) = $2,000. The value of the investment in Fund D increased by ($42 − $40)(300) = ($2)(300) = $600. Fund E's price did not increase, so the correct choice is (**A**).

Quantitative Reasoning Practice Set 3

35 Minutes — 20 Questions

Directions: For each question, indicate the best answer, using the directions given.

You may use a calculator for all the questions in this section.

If a question has answer choices with **ovals**, then the correct answer is a single choice. If a question has answer choices with **squares**, then the correct answer consists of one or more answer choices. Read each question carefully.

Important Facts:

All numbers used are real numbers.

All figures lie in a plane unless otherwise noted.

Geometric figures, such as lines, circles, triangles, and quadrilaterals, **may or may not be drawn to scale**. That is, you should not assume that quantities such as lengths and angle measures are as they appear in a drawing. But you can assume that lines shown as straight are indeed straight, points on a line are in the order shown, and all geometric objects are in the relative positions shown. For questions involving drawn figures, base your answers on geometric reasoning rather than on estimation, measurement, or comparison by sight.

Coordinate systems, such as *xy*-planes and number lines, **are** drawn to scale. Therefore, you may read, estimate, and compare quantities in these figures by sight or by measurement.

Graphical data presentations, such as bar graphs, line graphs, and pie charts, **are** drawn to scale. Therefore, you may read, estimate, and compare data values by sight or by measurement.

Directions: In questions 1–8, compare the value in Quantity A to the value in Quantity B. Information concerning one or both of the quantities to be compared is centered above the two quantities. Compare the two quantities and select Ⓐ if Quantity A is greater, Ⓑ if Quantity B is greater, Ⓒ if the two quantities are equal, and Ⓓ if the relationship cannot be determined from the information given.

The diameter of a circle equals the diagonal of a square whose side length is 4.

1. | Quantity A | Quantity B | |
    | The circumference of the circle | $20\sqrt{2}$ | Ⓐ Ⓑ Ⓒ Ⓓ |

$$a < b < c$$
$$b + c < 0$$

2. | Quantity A | Quantity B | |
    | ac | 0 | Ⓐ Ⓑ Ⓒ Ⓓ |

3. | Quantity A | Quantity B | |
    | The number of distinct positive integer factors of 96 | The number of distinct positive integer factors of 72 | Ⓐ Ⓑ Ⓒ Ⓓ |

$$x > 0$$

4. | Quantity A | Quantity B | |
    | $\dfrac{x+1}{x}$ | $\dfrac{x}{x+1}$ | Ⓐ Ⓑ Ⓒ Ⓓ |

$$2^p = 4^q$$

5. | Quantity A | Quantity B | |
    | p | $2q$ | Ⓐ Ⓑ Ⓒ Ⓓ |

6. | Quantity A | Quantity B | |
    | The number of seconds in 7 hours | The number of hours in 52 weeks | Ⓐ Ⓑ Ⓒ Ⓓ |

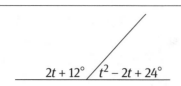

$$2t + 12° \quad / \quad t^2 - 2t + 24°$$

7.

Quantity A	Quantity B	
t	12	

$$x > 2$$

8.

Quantity A	Quantity B	
x^3	$4x$	

Directions: The remaining questions have several different formats. Select one answer if the answer choice letters are inside ovals. If the answer choice letters are inside boxes, select all choices that apply. If there is a rectangular box, enter your response as a numerical value.

9. If $A \blacklozenge B = \dfrac{A + B}{B}$, and $C \clubsuit = C + 3$, what is the value of $(9\clubsuit) \blacklozenge 3$?

10. Rectangle A has a length of 12 inches and a width of 5 inches. Rectangle B has a length of 9 inches and a width of 10 inches. By what number must the area of rectangle A be multiplied in order to get the area of rectangle B?

11.

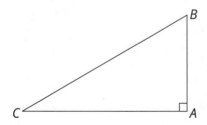

In right triangle ABC above, side AB has a length of x units, side AC has a length of 12 units, and side BC has a length of $x + 8$ units. What is the area of ABC in square units?

 square units

12. If the average test score of four students is 85, which of the following scores could a fifth student receive such that the average of all five scores is greater than 84 and less than 86?

    Indicate __all__ possible choices.

    A 88
    B 86
    C 85
    D 83
    E 80

13. Meg is twice as old as Rolf, but three years ago, she was two years older than Rolf is now. How old is Rolf now?

    [   ] years old

14. The cost, in cents, of manufacturing x crayons is $570 + 0.5x$. The crayons sell for 10 cents each. What is the minimum number of crayons that need to be sold so that the revenue received recoups the manufacturing cost?

    Ⓐ 50
    Ⓑ 57
    Ⓒ 60
    Ⓓ 61
    Ⓔ 95

15. If $xy \neq 0$, $\dfrac{1-x}{xy} =$

    Ⓐ $\dfrac{1}{xy} - \dfrac{1}{y}$

    Ⓑ $\dfrac{x}{y} - \dfrac{1}{x}$

    Ⓒ $\dfrac{1}{xy} - 1$

    Ⓓ $\dfrac{1}{xy} - \dfrac{x^2}{y}$

    Ⓔ $\dfrac{1}{x} - \dfrac{1}{y}$

16. Set J is comprised of all positive integers x such that x^3 is a multiple of both 72 and 216. Which of the following integers are factors of every member of set J?

    Indicate __all__ such integers.

    A 2
    B 3
    C 6
    D 9
    E 12

17. If $x > 0$ and $2x^2 + 6x = 8$, then the average (arithmetic mean) of $x + 2$, $2x - 1$, and $x + 4$ is equal to which of the following?

    Ⓐ -2
    Ⓑ 3
    Ⓒ 3.5
    Ⓓ 5
    Ⓔ 7

Questions 18–20 refer to the following graphs:

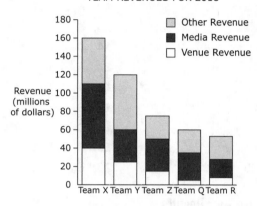

TEAM REVENUES FOR 2018

PERCENTAGES OF VENUE
REVENUES FOR TEAM X, 2018

18. For the team with the median venue revenue in 2018, media revenue represented approximately what percent of that team's total revenue?

    (A) 25%
    (B) 30%
    (C) 45%
    (D) 70%
    (E) 85%

19. If Team Y earned total revenues of at least $150 million in 2019, then Team Y's total revenue could have increased by what percent from 2018 to 2019?

Indicate all such percents.

    [A] 20%
    [B] 25%
    [C] 30%
    [D] 35%
    [E] 40%

20. In 2018, the venue revenues for Team X from merchandise sales and ticket sales were approximately what percent of the venue revenues for Team X from food sales?

    (A) 43%
    (B) 53%
    (C) 67%
    (D) 71%
    (E) 86%

Quantitative Reasoning Practice Set 3 Answer Key

1.	B	11.	30
2.	D	12.	A, B, C, D
3.	C	13.	5
4.	A	14.	C
5.	C	15.	A
6.	A	16.	A, B, C
7.	C	17.	B
8.	A	18.	C
9.	5	19.	B, C, D, E
10.	1.5	20.	E

Diagnose Your Results

Diagnostic Tool

Tally up your score and write your results below.

Total

Total Correct: _____ out of 20 correct

By Question Type

Quantitative Comparison (questions 1–8) _____ out of 8 correct

Problem Solving (questions 9–17) _____ out of 9 correct

Data Interpretation (questions 18–20) _____ out of 3 correct

Repeat the steps outlined in the Diagnose Your Results page that follows the Quantitative Reasoning Practice Set 1 answer key.

Quantitative Reasoning Practice Set 3 Answers and Explanations

1. B

The diagonal of a square of side 4 is $4\sqrt{2}$. The circumference of a circle is π times the diameter. So, the circumference of this circle is $4\sqrt{2}\pi$. Now write Quantity B, $20\sqrt{2}$, as $4(5)\sqrt{2}$ and you can compare the quantities piece by piece. The factors of 4 and $\sqrt{2}$ are the same in both quantities, but π is less than 5. So, Quantity B is larger.

2. D

You could pick numbers here, but using logic would be more efficient. Since $b + c$ is negative, then b, as the smaller of the two, must be negative. Since a is less than b, it must also be negative. But, c could be negative or positive with a smaller absolute value than the absolute value of b, or c could even be zero. The product of a and c will be greater than 0 if both are negative. However, if c is positive, the product of a and c would be negative. And if c is zero, then the two quantities are equal. All three relationships are possible; therefore, (**D**) is correct.

3. C

There are 12 positive integer factors of 96: 1, 2, 3, 4, 6, 8, 12, 16, 24, 32, 48, and 96. There are 12 positive integer factors of 72: 1, 2, 3, 4, 6, 8, 9, 12, 18, 24, 36, and 72. The two quantities are equal.

4. A

If $x > 0$, then $\dfrac{x + 1}{x}$, which also equals $1 + \dfrac{1}{x}$, must be greater than 1. On the other hand, $\dfrac{x}{x + 1}$ must be less than 1. This is because when $x > 0$, the numerator x is smaller than the denominator, so the ratio $\dfrac{x}{x + 1} < 1$. Therefore, $\dfrac{x + 1}{x} > \dfrac{x}{x + 1}$ when $x > 0$, and Quantity A is greater.

5. C

For this question, notice the relationship between the bases, 2 and 4. When comparing exponents, it's easiest to work with equal bases.

You know that $4 = 2^2$. Therefore, $4^q = (2^2)^q = 2^{2q}$. Now you have $2^p = 2^{2q}$, so $p = 2q$. The quantities are equal, choice (**C**).

6. A

Before you go to the trouble of multiplying the terms, let's see if there's a shortcut. For the GRE, make sure you know the common unit conversions for time. There are 60 seconds in a minute and 60 minutes in an hour, so there are $7 \times 60 \times 60$ seconds in 7 hours. There are 24 hours in a day and 7 days in a week, so there are $7 \times 24 \times 52$ hours in 52 weeks. Let's rewrite the quantities:

Quantity A	Quantity B
$7 \times 60 \times 60$	$7 \times 24 \times 52$

Taking away the common values gives you:

Quantity A	Quantity B
60×60	24×52

You still shouldn't do the math, however. The best strategy is to compare piece by piece, which shows that Quantity A is larger than Quantity B.

7. C

The sum of the measures of the angles on one side of a straight line is $180°$. The equation for these angles can be written as $(2t + 12) + (t^2 - 2t + 24) = 180$. Removing the parentheses to combine like terms results in the equation $t^2 + 36 = 180$. This equation simplifies to $t^2 = 144$, which means that t is ± 12. However, since angle measurements on the GRE are always positive, t is 12. (**C**) is correct.

8. A

Since $x > 2$, you know $x > 0$ and you can divide both quantities by x without changing their relationship. Quantity A is then x^2 and Quantity B is 4. Since $x > 2$, the least value for x^2 is greater than $2^2 = 4$. Therefore, (**A**) is correct.

9. 5

Let's first find the value of 9♣. Then we'll find the value of (9♣)♦3.

Since $C♣ = C + 3$, $9♣ = 9 + 3 = 12$.

Therefore, $(9♣)♦3 = 12♦3$.

Since $A♦B = \dfrac{A + B}{B}$, $12♦3 = \dfrac{12 + 3}{3} = \dfrac{15}{3}$.

Therefore, $(9♣)♦3 = 5$.

10. 1.5

The area of a rectangle is its length times its width.

The area of rectangle A is $12 \times 5 = 60$.

The area of rectangle B is $9 \times 10 = 90$.

So the area 60 of rectangle A must be multiplied by a number, which you can call x, to obtain the area 90 of rectangle B.

Then $60x = 90$. So $x = \dfrac{90}{60} = \dfrac{3}{2} = 1.5$.

11. 30

Here's a problem where it really pays to have learned the Pythagorean triplets. The Pythagorean theorem will work because this is a right triangle, but it is much more strategic to see if any of the Pythagorean triplets work first. Start by testing the 3:4:5 and 5:12:13 triplets. The 3:4:5 is not the correct triplet because, while 12 is a multiple of 3 and 4, the other side lengths (either 16 and 20 if 12 is the shorter leg, or 9 and 15 if 12 is the longer leg) do not fit into the expressions given for AB and BC. (Remember that geometric figures on the GRE are not necessarily drawn to scale.) Next check 5:12:13. If AC is 12, then AB must be 5 and BC must be 13. This fits the given information as $5 + 8 = 13$. Now it is time to find the area (be careful to not just answer with the value of x).

The area of a triangle is one-half the base times the height. The area of a right triangle is $\frac{1}{2} \times (\text{leg})_1 \times (\text{leg})_2$, because one leg can be considered to be the base and the other leg can be considered to be the height. So the area of triangle ABC is

$$\frac{1}{2} \times (AC) \times (AB) = \frac{1}{2} \times 12 \times 5 = 6 \times 5 = 30$$

The answer is **30**.

12. A, B, C, D

The average formula is as follows:

$$\text{Average} = \frac{\text{Sum of the terms}}{\text{Number of terms}}$$

Therefore,

$$\text{Sum of the terms} = \text{Average} \times \text{Number of terms}$$

The sum of the scores of the four students whose average was 85 is $85(4) = 340$. Let's call the fifth student's score x. If the new average is to be greater than 84 and less than 86 and the sum of the scores of all five students is $340 + x$, then $84 < \dfrac{340 + x}{5} < 86$. If you multiply all parts of the inequality by 5, you get $420 < 340 + x < 430$. Subtracting 340 from all parts of the inequality, you get $80 < x < 90$, making **(A)**, **(B)**, **(C)**, and **(D)** the correct choices.

13. 5

This question can be broken into two equations with two unknowns, Meg's age now (M) and Rolf's age now (R). Equation (i) shows the relationship now; equation (ii) shows the relationship three years ago.

$$\text{(i) } M = 2 \times R \qquad \text{(ii) } M - 3 = R + 2$$

Substitute $2R$ for M in equation (ii) and solve for R:

$$
\begin{aligned}
M - 3 &= R + 2 \\
2R - 3 &= R + 2 \\
2R - R &= 2 + 3 \\
R &= 5
\end{aligned}
$$

Rolf is **5** years old now.

14. C

The cost of manufacturing x crayons is $(570 + 0.5x)$ cents. Because each crayon sells for 10 cents, x crayons will sell for $10x$ cents. You want the smallest value of x such that $10x$ cents is at least $570 + 0.5x$ cents. So you must solve the equation $10x = 570 + 0.5x$ for the value of x that will recoup the investment.

$$
\begin{aligned}
10x &= 570 + 0.5x \\
9.5x &= 570 \\
x &= 60
\end{aligned}
$$

The minimum number of crayons is 60, choice **(C)**.

Alternatively, you could have avoided setting up an algebraic equation by Backsolving, starting with either (B) or (D).

15. A

You can write that $\dfrac{1-x}{xy} = \dfrac{1}{xy} - \dfrac{x}{xy}$. By canceling a factor of x from the numerator and denominator of $\dfrac{x}{xy}$, you have $\dfrac{x}{xy} = \dfrac{1}{y}$.

So, $\dfrac{1-x}{xy} = \dfrac{1}{xy} - \dfrac{x}{xy} = \dfrac{1}{xy} - \dfrac{1}{y}$. The answer is (A).

16. A, B, C

The first thing to find for this question is the set of integers that will work for set J. You need x^3 to be a multiple of the LCM (least common multiple) of 72 and 216. Since 216 is 72×3, the LCM is 216. If this does not stand out immediately, use prime factorization to find the LCM. The prime factorization of 72 is $(2^3) \times (3^2)$ and the prime factorization of 216 is $(2^3) \times (3^3)$, which confirms that 216 is the LCM for 72 and 216. Setting x^3 equal to 216 means that $x = 6$. This confirms that J is the set of all positive integers that are multiples of 6. The factors of 6 are 1, 2, 3, and 6, so (A), (B), and (C) are the correct choices. Be careful with 12: it is a multiple of 6, not a factor.

17. B

The goal is to find the average of $(x+2)$, $(2x-1)$, and $(x+4)$, which requires finding a value for x. In order to find x, set the equation equal to 0 by subtracting 8 from both sides. The resulting equation, $2x^2 + 6x - 8 = 0$, factors into $(2x-2)(x+4) = 0$. This means that x can be either 1 or -4. However, x was stipulated to be positive, so $x = 1$.

$$
\begin{aligned}
\text{Average} &= \frac{\text{sum of terms}}{\text{number of terms}} \\
&= \frac{(x+2) + (2x-1) + (x+4)}{3} \\
&= \frac{4x+5}{3}
\end{aligned}
$$

When you substitute 1 for x, the equation becomes $\dfrac{(4(1)+5)}{3} = 3$, so (B) is the correct answer.

18. C

Before you answer any graph question, begin by examining the graphs. Here you have two graphs, a segmented bar graph representing team revenue breakdowns for five teams and a pie chart showing the distribution of venue revenues for Team X.

You're now ready to attack the question, which asks you to find the team with the median venue revenue for 2018 and to determine what percent of that team's total revenue is media revenue. This question must refer to the first graph, and the first part of the question—finding the team with the median venue revenue—is straightforward. *Median* refers to the number in the middle. By looking at the white portions of the bars in the top graph, you see that Team Z has the median venue revenue. The fastest approach to the answer here (and throughout graph questions generally) is to approximate. The downside to bar graphs is that it's often very hard to get a read on the values. The upside is that if you approximate, often you don't have to read the values. Here you need to determine what percent of Team Z's bar is represented by media revenue (the segment in the middle—always be especially careful to isolate the correct piece of data). By approximating, you can see that the middle segment is about half of the entire bar. Thus the correct answer has to be close to 50%. The only answer choice that works is (C), 45%.

19. B, C, D, E

Percent change problems are extremely popular graph questions, and as long as you set them up correctly, they are a great opportunity. This question asks for the approximate percent increase in Team Y's total revenue from 2018 to 2019, so you need to figure out (roughly) the amount of increase, place that over the original amount, and then convert the fraction into a percent. You are given the total revenue for 2019 as at least $150 million, so you need to locate the total revenue for 2018 from the bar graph. It looks to be approximately $120 million, so the amount of increase is $30 million (or more), and the original amount is $120 million. Now let's apply the formula:

$$\text{Percent increase} = \frac{\$30 \text{ million}}{\$120 \text{ million}} \times 100\%$$

$$= \frac{1}{4} \times 100\%$$

$$= 25\%$$

So, any percent greater than or equal to 25% is the answer. The answers are **(B)**, **(C)**, **(D)**, and **(E)**.

20. E

When looking at the bar graph, you see from the lowest portion of the bar for Team X that venue revenues of Team X were approximately $40 million (call it 40m, for short). From the pie chart, the venue revenues of Team X from merchandise sales were approximately 20% of 40 million dollars, the venue revenues from ticket sales were approximately 10%, and the venue revenues from food sales were approximately 35%. The venue revenues of Team X from merchandise, in dollars, were approximately $0.2(40m) = 8m$. The venue revenues of Team X from ticket sales, in dollars, were approximately $0.1(40m) = 4m$. So the venue revenues of Team X from merchandise sales and ticket sales, in dollars, were approximately $8m + 4m = 12m$. The venue revenues of Team X from food sales, in dollars, were approximately $0.35(40m) = 14m$. The percent of the venue revenues of Team X that were from merchandise sales and ticket sales, out of the venue revenues of Team X that were from food sales, is approximately $\frac{12m}{14m} \times 100\% = \frac{6}{7} \times 100\% \approx 85.7\%$.

To the nearest percent, 85.7% is 86%. Choice **(E)** is correct.

PART FOUR

ANALYTICAL WRITING

CHAPTER 20

INTRODUCTION TO ANALYTICAL WRITING

Overview

The Analytical Writing Measure tests your ability to analyze a complex proposition and formulate a response. Your critical thinking skills will be tested by tasks that ask you to construct an argument and to evaluate someone else's argument. Your writing skills will be measured by how well you organize your essay and how well you express your ideas in formal written English. These skills are exactly those you will need to perform well as a student at the graduate level.

Specifically, this portion of the test evaluates your ability to do the following:

- Articulate and defend a position by developing a cogent argument in which you support your conclusion by providing relevant evidence
- Deconstruct and evaluate an argument, identifying its flaws and considering how the argument might be strengthened
- Identify and focus on ideas that are important and relevant to your thesis rather than minor or irrelevant ideas
- Write articulately and effectively, using a variety of sentence structures and varied vocabulary

In this section of the book, we'll take you through the two Analytical Writing tasks you'll see on the GRE and give you the strategies you need to efficiently compose a high-scoring essay for each. Also, because your Analytical Writing score depends in part on your ability to use the rules of standard written English grammar and usage, these are reviewed in the Analytical Writing Foundations and Content Review chapter.

Analytical Writing Essay Types

The Analytical Writing section of the GRE allows the test to evaluate your ability to plan and compose a logical, well-reasoned essay under timed conditions. You will complete two different essay tasks, and you'll have 30 minutes for each essay.

- The Analyze an Issue task will provide a brief statement on an issue of general interest and instructions on how to respond to the issue. You can discuss the issue from any perspective, making use of your own educational and personal background, examples from current or historical events, material that you've read, or even hypothetical situations. For this essay, you will develop your own argument.

- The Analyze an Argument task will present a short argument and instructions on how to respond to it. You will assess the cogency of the argument, analyzing the author's chain of reasoning and evaluating the use of evidence. For this essay, you will not develop your own argument but, instead, will critique the argument presented in the prompt.

For each task, you'll be given one topic and specific instructions. The instructions are not the same for each Issue essay or for each Argument essay, so be sure to read them carefully.

Scoring

The scoring for the Analytical Writing Measure is *holistic*, which means that the graders base your score on an overall impression of each essay, rather than adding a specific point value for each idea you express or deducting points for errors. A holistic score emphasizes the interrelationship of content, organization, and syntax and represents the unified effect of these combined elements.

One human grader and one computer program score each essay, and their scores are averaged. If their scores differ by a certain margin, a second human grader will also score the essay, and the two human scores will be averaged. Keep in mind that because your essay is being scored by a human who is reading fairly quickly and by a computer algorithm, it is important to write in a clear and well-organized way, staying on topic, constructing each paragraph around a main point, and using language correctly.

You will receive your essay score, along with your official score report, within 10 to 15 days of your test date. The schools to which you apply will receive the same score report plus the essays themselves.

The scoring scale is from 0 to 6, with 6 being the highest score. Although the Analytical Writing Measure comprises two separate essays, ETS reports a single score that represents the average of your scores for the two essays, rounded up to the nearest half point. As you can see from the table, about three-fourths of test takers (76%) score between a 3.0 and 5.0, meaning that scores above and below this range are uncommon.

SCORE	PERCENT OF TEST TAKERS WITH A LOWER SCORE
6.0	99
5.5	98
5.0	92
4.5	81
4.0	57
3.5	39
3.0	15
2.5	7
2.0	2
1.5	1
1.0	–
0.5	–
0	–

Analytical Writing Measure: Percentiles

Based on performance of test takers July 1, 2015 to June 30, 2018

The Scoring Rubric

Each of the two essays requires different reasoning and presentation, so each has slightly different scoring criteria. However, the following rubric will give you a general idea of the guidelines graders have in mind when they score Analytical Writing essays.

6: "Outstanding" Essay

- Throughout the essay, presents and convincingly supports an insightful opinion on the issue or a critique of the argument.
- Communicates complex ideas clearly and develops them in depth with very persuasive reasoning and/or examples.
- Is well organized, grouping and connecting ideas logically.
- Demonstrates superior command of language, showing variety of sentence structure and vocabulary and using accepted conventions of formal writing; any flaws are minor and do not detract from the essay's meaning.

5: "Strong" Essay

- Generally presents and supports a thoughtful opinion on the issue or critique of the argument.
- Communicates complex ideas clearly and develops them with logical reasons and/or well-chosen examples.
- Is generally well organized, grouping and connecting ideas logically.
- Demonstrates solid control of language, showing variety of sentence structure and vocabulary and using accepted conventions of formal writing; any flaws are minor and do not detract from the essay's meaning.

4: "Adequate" Essay

- Presents and supports an opinion on the issue or a critique of the argument.
- Communicates ideas clearly and develops them with reasons and/or examples.
- Is adequately organized, using satisfactory logical connections.
- Demonstrates good control of language, generally using correct grammar and usage; some errors may affect clarity.

3: "Limited" Essay

- Succeeds only partially in presenting and supporting an opinion on the issue or a critique of the argument.
- May communicate ideas unclearly; analysis and development of ideas may be superficial.
- Is poorly organized, with little logical connection between ideas.
- Demonstrates weak control of language, making errors that affect meaning and clarity.

2: "Weak" Essay

- Attempts but does not succeed in presenting and supporting an opinion on the issue or a critique of the argument.
- Struggles to communicate ideas.
- Mostly lacks organization.
- Meaning is impeded by many serious mistakes in sentence structure and usage.

1: "Fundamentally Deficient" Essay

- Does not present or support a coherent opinion on the issue or a critique of the argument.
- Fails to communicate ideas.
- Is disorganized.
- Lacks meaning due to widespread and severe mistakes in sentence structure and usage.

0: "Unscorable" Essay

- Completely ignores topic, simply copies the prompt, or is written in a language other than English or contains undecipherable text.

How the Computer-Based Essays are Administered

To be scored, your essay must be typed into the computer before time is up. You may outline your essay on the scratch paper you will be given, or you may outline it on the computer. If you use the computer to type your outline, be sure to delete every part of the outline before submitting the essay.

Before the Analytical Writing Measure, you will be given a brief tutorial on how to use the word processing program. Don't worry. The GRE's word processor is simple and easy to use; the only functions are *insert text*, *delete text*, *cut text*, *paste text*, and *undo*. You'll be well acquainted with these commands by the time you start writing. Do *not* write anything on your scratch paper during the tutorial, as doing so is against test policy and can result in disciplinary action. You may start writing on the scratch paper once the timed Writing section begins.

When you practice writing essays, turn off any auto-edit functions your word processor or browser has, including spell check, grammar check, and autocorrect/autocomplete. The GRE's word processor doesn't have these functions, so you will get more realistic practice if you do not use them.

Pacing Strategy

You'll have a limited amount of time to show the essay graders that you can analyze the stimulus critically, put together your own thoughts logically, and express yourself clearly. Consequently, you'll need to know ahead of time how you're going to approach each essay.

	ANALYZE AN ISSUE	ANALYZE AN ARGUMENT
Number of Questions	1	1
Time per Question	30 minutes	30 minutes

The Kaplan Method for Analytical Writing will help you plan and execute a clear, organized essay in the amount of time allotted. Note that the timing guidelines below are suggestions for how you should most effectively divide the 30 minutes you'll have for each of the essays. Different writers go through the different steps at their own pace, so don't feel chained to the breakdown below. As you practice, you will get a better sense of the amount of time you need to spend on each step to produce the best essay possible.

[STEP 1]

Take the Issue/Argument Apart: 2 minutes

[STEP 2]

Select the Points You'll Make: 5 minutes

[STEP 3]

Organize Your Thoughts: 1 minute

[STEP 4]

Write Your Essay: 20 minutes

[STEP 5]

Proofread: 2 minutes

Keep these guidelines in mind as you prepare for the test. If you use them as you write practice essays, you will be comfortable working within the 30-minute time frame on Test Day.

Navigating the Analytical Writing Section of This Book

The chapter immediately following this one, "Analytical Writing Foundations and Content Review," will review correct sentence structure, punctuation, and usage as well as effective writing style.

After that, you will find separate chapters on the Issue essay and the Argument essay. Each of these chapters includes an introduction to the particular essay task and an explanation of the strategies that will help you address the task efficiently and effectively. You'll also have opportunities to practice writing essays yourself and review examples of essays that would earn different scores.

Finally, at the end of this section, you'll find the Analytical Writing Practice Sets. Each practice set consists of two tasks, one Issue essay and one Argument essay, just like you'll see on Test Day. After you use the prompts to practice writing essays, compare your work to the example essays at the end of the chapter to evaluate your thinking and writing skills and to pinpoint areas for improvement. When you are finished with this section of the book, you should be thoroughly prepared for both essay tasks you will encounter in the Analytical Writing Measure on the GRE.

CHAPTER 21

ANALYTICAL WRITING FOUNDATIONS AND CONTENT REVIEW

Introduction to Analytical Writing Foundations and Content Review

The GRE tests your ability to construct a coherent, logical, and well-developed response to a writing prompt. This requires a mastery of the elements of formal standard English, including grammar, usage, and punctuation. It also means writing in an effective style that communicates ideas in an engaging and readable way. To sum up, you want to write *correctly*, *clearly*, and *concisely*. Here are the important concepts you need to know:

- Writing Correctly
  - Avoiding sentence fragments and run-ons
  - Ensuring subject-verb agreement
  - Using pronouns to refer to nouns
  - Using modifiers correctly
  - Using parallel structure effectively
  - Using commas correctly
  - Using semicolons and colons correctly
  - Using apostrophes correctly

- Writing Clearly
  - Using a variety of sentence structures
  - Using active voice rather than passive voice
  - Opening sentences strongly

- Writing Concisely
  - Removing unnecessary sentences
  - Avoiding needless self-reference
  - Streamlining wordy phrases
  - Eliminating redundancy
  - Avoiding excessive qualification

This chapter will cover all of these writing concepts, providing practice sets for each. At the end of the chapter, you'll find more tips for practicing and proofreading your writing to help you craft the most effective essays possible on the GRE Analytical Writing Measure.

Writing Correctly

Avoiding Sentence Fragments and Run-Ons

Every sentence in formal expository writing must have an independent clause: a clause that contains a subject and a predicate. A sentence fragment has no independent clause; a run-on sentence has two or more independent clauses that are improperly connected. As you edit your practice essays, check your sentence constructions, noting any tendency toward fragments or run-on sentences.

FRAGMENTS: Global warming. That is what the scientists and journalists are worried about these days.

CORRECT: Global warming is causing concern among scientists and journalists these days.

FRAGMENTS: Mountains, ocean, and forests, all within easy driving distance of Seattle, a wonderful place to live. If you can ignore the rain.

CORRECT: Seattle is a wonderful place to live, with mountains, ocean, and forests all within easy driving distance. However, it certainly does rain often there.

FRAGMENT: Why is the author's position preposterous? Because he makes generalizations that go beyond the facts.

CORRECT: The author's position is preposterous because he makes generalizations that go beyond the facts.

Beginning sentences with coordinating conjunctions—*for, and, nor, but, or, yet,* and *so*—is acceptable in moderation and is sometimes an effective stylistic choice to emphasize an idea. Nonetheless, check whether joining sentences with the conjunction or using an adverb, such as *moreover* or *however*, would be more effective.

CORRECT: Most people would agree that indigent patients should receive excellent health care. But every treatment has a price.

CORRECT: Most people would agree that indigent patients should receive excellent health care. However, every treatment has a price.

Time pressure may cause you to write two or more sentences as one. When you proofread your essays, watch out for independent clauses that are not joined properly.

RUN-ON: Current insurance practices are unfair they discriminate against the people who need insurance most.

You can repair run-on sentences in any one of three ways. First, you could use a period to make separate sentences of the independent clauses.

CORRECT: Current insurance practices are unfair. They discriminate against the people who need insurance most.

You could also use a semicolon. A semicolon functions like a weak period; it separates independent clauses but signals to the reader that the ideas in the clauses are related.

CORRECT: Current insurance practices are unfair; they discriminate against the people who need insurance most.

Yet another method of connecting clauses is to use a conjunction, which makes explicit how the clauses are related. If you use one of the FANBOYS (**F**or, **A**nd, **N**or, **B**ut, **O**r, **Y**et, **S**o) coordinating conjunctions to connect independent clauses, you must also insert a comma before the conjunction.

CORRECT: Current insurance practices are unfair because they discriminate against the people who need insurance most.

CORRECT: Current insurance practices are unfair, for they discriminate against the people who need insurance most.

A common cause of run-on sentences is the misuse of adverbs like *however, nevertheless, furthermore, likewise*, and *therefore*. These words may not be used to connect clauses.

RUN-ON: Current insurance practices are discriminatory, furthermore, they make insurance too expensive for the poor.

CORRECT: Current insurance practices are discriminatory. Furthermore, they make insurance too expensive for the poor.

Avoiding Sentence Fragments and Run-ons Practice Set

Read the sentences below and make revisions to correct fragments and run-ons.

1. The writer of this letter lays out an incoherent argument about why Adams Realty is superior it is disorganized, has weak points and with unclear examples, and so is unconvincing.

   _____

   _____

2. Leadership ability. That is the elusive quality that our current government employees have yet to capture.

   _____

   _____

Answers and Explanations

1. **In this disorganized letter, the writer lays out an incoherent and ultimately unconvincing argument, raising weak points and using unclear examples in an attempt to illustrate the superiority of Adams Realty.**

We have two choices to amend this run-on sentence: rearrange it or break it into two different sentences. We've gone with rearrangement for this example. We have put the adjectives describing the letter and argument before those nouns and explained what the argument does in a modifying phrase set off by a comma.

2. **Leadership ability is the elusive quality that our current government employees have yet to capture.**

The first "sentence" here is a fragment. Fortunately, it can easily be incorporated into the following complete sentence, as the pronoun "that" refers to "Leadership ability."

Ensuring Subject-Verb Agreement

A verb must agree with its subject in number (singular or plural). Do not let any words that come between the subject and the verb confuse you as to the number of the subject.

INCORRECT: The joy of undertaking risky pursuits, especially if one has dependents, are selfish.

CORRECT: The *joy* of undertaking risky pursuits, especially if one has dependents, *is* selfish.

Watch out for collective nouns like *group*, *audience*, *committee*, or *majority*. These take a singular verb unless you are emphasizing the independent actions of the individuals forming the group.

CORRECT: If a *majority* of the jury *thinks* that the defendant is guilty, then the public should have faith in the verdict. (The collective decision-making body is being emphasized.)

CORRECT: If a *majority* of the committee *have signed* their names to the report, then donors should have confidence in the report's conclusions. (The individual members of the committee, each of whom has signed his or her own name, are being emphasized.)

A subject that consists of two or more nouns connected by the conjunction *and* takes a plural verb.

CORRECT: Imagine, for example, that *Karl*, an expert in cooking Hunan chicken, *and George*, an expert in preparing Hunan spicy duck, *have started* a new restaurant.

However, when the subject consists of two or more nouns connected by *or* or *nor*, the verb agrees with the CLOSER noun.

CORRECT: If either the president's advisers or the *president* himself *is* misinformed, a poor decision will result.

CORRECT: If either the president or *his advisers are* misinformed, a poor decision will result.

Some connecting phrases look as though they should make a group of words into a plural subject but actually do not. The only connecting word that can make two or more singular nouns into a plural subject is *and*. In particular, the following connecting words and phrases do NOT result in a plural subject:

along with, as well as, besides, in addition to, together with, in combination with

INCORRECT: The president, along with the secretary of state and the director of the CIA, are sometimes misinformed.

CORRECT: The *president*, along with the secretary of state and the director of the CIA, *is* sometimes misinformed.

Ensuring Subject-Verb Agreement Practice Set

Read the sentences below and revise to ensure subject-verb agreement.

1. The arts is a very important topic to discuss at this point in history.

   _____

   _____

2. The organization's membership, consisting of a number of interest groups and many vocal individuals, reside in over twenty countries.

   _____

   _____

Answers and Explanations

1. **The arts are a very important topic to discuss at this point in history.**

The verb is plural because the sentence is referring to more than one type of art, even though they collectively form a single topic of discussion.

2. **The organization's membership, consisting of a number of interest groups and many vocal individuals, resides in over twenty countries.**

The verb must be singular because the subject is the singular "membership." Don't allow the intervening nouns "interest groups" and "individuals" to distract from the subject-verb pair.

Using Pronouns to Refer to Nouns

A pronoun is a word that replaces a noun in a sentence. Every time you write a pronoun—such as *he, him, his, she, her, hers, it, its, they, their, that,* or *which*—it must refer unambiguously to a particular noun, called the pronoun's antecedent. Pronouns that do not refer clearly to an antecedent can obscure your intended meaning.

UNCLEAR: An effective teacher tells a student she is talented. (Does *she* refer to *teacher* or *student*?)

CLEAR: If students are talented, an effective teacher tells them so.

UNCLEAR: Civil servants know more about how to run a government agency than do political appointees because they have learned from experience.

(Does *they* refer to *civil servants* or *political appointees*?)

CLEAR: Because civil servants have learned from experience, they know more about how to run a government agency than do political appointees.

Don't be afraid to repeat the antecedent if necessary to make your meaning clear.

UNCLEAR: Many people would rather settle in Albuquerque than in Phoenix, although it has a higher crime rate.

CLEAR: Many people would rather settle in Albuquerque than in Phoenix, although Albuquerque has a higher crime rate.

Pronouns cannot refer to implied nouns. Even if you think the reader will know what you mean, do not use a pronoun without a clear and appropriate antecedent. Instead, rewrite the sentence so that there is no doubt.

INCORRECT: When scientists are reviewing the literature, they must be sure it is thorough.

(*It* could refer only to the scientists' review, but the noun *review* does not appear in the sentence.)

CORRECT: When scientists are reviewing the literature, they must be sure their review is thorough.

Sometimes in your essays, you may want to refer to people in general or society at large. Whichever option you choose, be consistent.

- If you are referring to a group of which you, and likely your reader, are a part, then the first-person plural *we*, *us*, and *our* are appropriate.
- If you are referring to a group you are not a member of, then the third-person plural *they*, *them*, and *their* are appropriate.
- Another option is to use the impersonal *one* and *one's*.

INCONSISTENT: Not all wilderness areas are similar to the glorious Ansel Adams landscapes that we hold in our imaginations. If you've seen pictures of the Arctic National Wildlife Refuge, one would be unimpressed by the "natural beauty" of that massive swamp.

CONSISTENT: Not all wilderness areas are similar to the glorious Ansel Adams landscapes that many people hold in their imaginations. If they were to see pictures of ANWR, they would be unimpressed by the "natural beauty" of that massive swamp.

Using Pronouns to Refer to Nouns Practice Set

Revise the following sentences to correct unclear pronoun references.

1. Sports enthusiasts' desires should not trump the needs of the river and the quiet enjoyment of the people who live near the river. Their opinions should be taken into account.

_____

_____

2. During finals week, students might study all night, which they have not done the rest of the semester.

_____

_____

Answers and Explanations

1. **Sports enthusiasts' desires should not trump the needs of the river and the quiet enjoyment of the people who live near the river, whose opinions should be taken into account.**

In the original sentences, it is unclear whether the pronoun "their" refers to the people who live near the river or the sports enthusiasts. Combining the sentences and replacing "their" with "whose" clarifies matters.

2. **During finals week, students might study all night, even though they have followed a less grueling schedule the rest of the semester.**

In the original sentence, the pronoun "which" means "studying all night," but "studying," a noun form of the verb "study," does not appear in the sentence. The revision corrects the problem by using "even though" to connect the clauses and stating clearly what the students have done the rest of the semester.

Using Modifiers Correctly

In English, the position of a word within a sentence often establishes the word's relationship to other words in the sentence. In particular, modifiers should be placed as close as possible to what they modify. If a modifier is placed too far from the word it modifies, the meaning may be lost or obscured. Notice, in the following sentences, the ambiguity that results when the modifying phrases are misplaced:

UNCLEAR: Workers meet to discuss the problem of inefficiency in the office.

CLEAR: Workers meet in the office to talk about the problem of inefficiency.

UNCLEAR: Even a great athlete might only practice a little during the off-season.

CLEAR: Even a great athlete might practice only a little during the off-season.

In addition to misplaced modifiers, watch for dangling modifiers: modifiers whose intended referents are not even present.

INCORRECT: Coming out of context, Peter was startled by Julia's perceptiveness.

CORRECT: Julia's remark, coming out of context, startled Peter with its perceptiveness.

Using Modifiers Correctly Practice Set

Read the following sentences and revise to correct the faulty modification.

1. Inspired by Zelda Sayre, excerpts of her diaries ended up in F. Scott Fitzgerald's novels.

   _____

   _____

2. Having been an avid lifelong reader, a bookstore with a café seems like heaven on earth to me.

   _____

   _____

Answers and Explanations

1. **Inspired by Zelda Sayre, F. Scott Fitzgerald used excepts of her diaries in his novels.**

The original sentence says that excerpts of Sayre's diaries felt inspired by Sayre and this feeling of inspiration caused them to enter Fitzgerald's novels. The revision makes much more sense, saying that Fitzgerald felt inspired by Sayre and used her writing in his own works.

2. **A bookstore with a café seems like heaven on earth to an avid lifelong reader like me.**

As originally written, the sentence says the bookstore has been an enthusiastic reader. The revised sentence makes clear that the author has been an avid reader.

Using Parallel Structure Effectively

It can be rhetorically effective to use a particular construction more than once to provide emphasis. The technique is called _parallel construction_, because each part of the construction must be in the same grammatical form.

CORRECT: As a leader, Lincoln inspired a nation to throw off the chains of slavery; as a philosopher, he proclaimed the greatness of the little man; as a human being, he served as a timeless example of humility.

The repetition of clauses, each with the same structure, provides the sentence with a strong sense of rhythm and organization and alerts the reader to the multiple aspects of Lincoln's character.

One common type of parallel construction is a list.

INCORRECT: They are sturdy, attractive, and cost very little. (The phrase _They are_ makes sense preceding the adjectives _sturdy_ and _attractive_, but it cannot be understood before _cost very little_.)

CORRECT: They are sturdy and attractive, and they cost very little.

CORRECT: They are sturdy, attractive, and inexpensive.

INCORRECT: All business students should learn word processing, accounting, and how to program computers.

CORRECT: All business students should learn word processing, accounting, and computer programming.

This principle applies to any words that might precede items in a series: either repeat the word before every element in the series or include it only before the first item.

INCORRECT: People can invest their money in stocks, real estate, and in gold.

CORRECT: People can invest their money in stocks, in real estate, and in gold.

CORRECT: People can invest their money in stocks, real estate, and gold.

Besides lists, a number of other constructions require parallel form. These constructions include the following:

> X is as _____ as Y.
>
> X is more _____ than Y.
>
> X is less _____ than Y.
>
> Both X and Y . . .
>
> Either X or Y . . .
>
> Neither X nor Y . . .
>
> Not only X but also Y . . .
>
> Between X and Y . . .

X and Y can stand for as little as one word or as much as a whole clause, but in any case, the grammatical structure of X and Y must be identical.

INCORRECT: The view from a humble cottage may be as spectacular as from a lavish penthouse.

CORRECT: The view from a humble cottage may be as spectacular as the view from a lavish penthouse.

Using Parallel Structure Effectively Practice Set

Read these sentences and revise to correct parallelism.

1. Scientists should not only use a sample that is representative of the population at large but also they should ask questions that are germane to the problem under study.

   _____

   _____

2. The health care providers are well trained, highly motivated, and are given the supplies necessary to diagnose and treat patients.

   _____

   _____

Answers and Explanations

1. **Scientists should not only use a sample that is representative of the population at large but also ask questions that are germane to the problem under study.**

For the parallel construction *not only . . . but also* to work in this sentence, the two thoughts must have identical grammatical form. Therefore, the repetition of "they [scientists] should" is incorrect: the construction now reads "not only use a sample that . . . but also ask questions that . . . " and is in parallel form.

2. **The health care providers are well trained and highly motivated, and they have the supplies necessary to diagnose and treat patients.**

In this example, the list was not in parallel form. One solution is to place the third item in the series in a separate clause.

Using Commas Correctly

Commas have several uses. One use of commas is to separate items in a series when there are more than two items. The final comma—the one that precedes the word *and*— is optional (but be consistent throughout your essays).

CORRECT: A robust economy is indicated by low inflation, high employment and healthy consumer confidence.

CORRECT: A robust economy is indicated by low inflation, high employment, and healthy consumer confidence.

Use commas to separate two or more adjectives before a noun, but do not use a comma after the last adjective in the series.

INCORRECT: The manatee is a round, blubbery, bewhiskered, creature whose continued presence in American waters is endangered by careless boaters.

CORRECT: The manatee is a round, blubbery, bewhiskered creature whose continued presence in American waters is endangered by careless boaters.

Another use of commas is to set off clauses and phrases that are not necessary to the main idea of the sentence. In other words, if you could remove a phrase or clause from a sentence and the sentence would still make sense, then enclose those words in commas.

CORRECT: Leonardo da Vinci, who is known primarily as an artist, was also an accomplished scientist.

The main idea is that da Vinci was an accomplished scientist. The intervening clause serves to provide additional information about da Vinci and, while interesting, could be removed from the sentence. Thus, it should be set off with commas.

Also use commas after introductory words and phrases.

CORRECT: Having been told for many years to conserve water, California residents were disappointed to learn the drought was likely to continue.

CORRECT: During the long drought, many Californians became impatient with pleas to conserve water.

CORRECT: Finally, some Californians dealt with chronic water restrictions by replacing their lawns with artificial turf.

One more use of commas is to separate independent clauses (clauses that could stand alone as complete sentences) connected by the FANBOYS coordinating conjunctions (For, And, Nor, But, Or, Yet, So).

INCORRECT: Some nations have struggled to maintain a democratic form of government for many decades, yet have not experienced a breakdown in the rule of law.

CORRECT: Some nations have struggled to maintain a democratic form of government for many decades, yet they have not experienced a breakdown in the rule of law.

CORRECT: Some nations have struggled to maintain a democratic form of government for many decades yet have not experienced a breakdown in the rule of law.

Using Commas Correctly Practice Set

Correct the punctuation errors in the following sentences.

1. Judges, teachers, and parents, should not be trying to win a popularity contest.

   _____

   _____

2. Hesitating interminably before taking action Hamlet is an indecisive and thus tragically flawed character.

   _____

   _____

Answers and Explanations

1. **Judges, teachers, and parents should not be trying to win a popularity contest.**

The series of three items, which is the compound subject of this sentence, properly has commas between items but should not be set off with a comma from the rest of the sentence.

2. **Hesitating interminably before taking action, Hamlet is an indecisive and thus tragically flawed character.**

The phrase "Hesitating interminably before taking action" is not necessary to the main idea of the sentence and should therefore be set off with a comma.

Using Semicolons and Colons Correctly

Semicolons have two uses. One is to join two closely related independent clauses without using a coordinating conjunction (such as *and, or*, or *but*). The text on each side of the semicolon must be a complete sentence.

INCORRECT: Because whooping cranes are an endangered species; wildlife conservationists are working hard to breed the birds in captivity.

CORRECT: Whooping cranes are an endangered species; they are unlikely to survive if wildlife conservationists cannot successfully establish them in new habitats.

Note that if you use an adverb such as *therefore, nevertheless*, or *moreover* to establish the relationship between ideas, then you must either start a new sentence or use a semicolon; you may not use a comma to connect the clauses.

CORRECT: The whooping crane population has recovered somewhat from its low of only a few hundred individuals; however, the species is still in danger of extinction.

CORRECT: Prices for certain agricultural commodities have fallen rapidly in recent years; nevertheless, the traditional American farm is not in danger of disappearing.

Another use for semicolons is to separate items in a series when the items themselves contain commas.

CORRECT: Three important dates in the history of China are 1368, when the Ming Dynasty overthrew the Mongols; 1644, when China annexed Mongolia and Tibet; and 1949, when Mao Zedong defeated the Nationalists and established the People's Republic of China.

A colon may be used to introduce a series, but what precedes the colon must be a complete sentence.

INCORRECT: At an ideal high school, students would study: English, another modern language, and Latin; biology, chemistry, and physics; and the visual and performing arts.

CORRECT: At an ideal high school, students would study the following: English, another modern language, and Latin; biology, chemistry, and physics; and the visual and performing arts.

Using Semicolons and Colons Correctly Practice Set

Correct the punctuation errors in the following sentences.

1. Very few students would voluntarily take Latin, therefore, requiring this subject for graduation will convince students to enroll in Latin classes.

   _____

   _____

2. A town that pursued such a policy would experience: a decrease in population, an increase in abandoned homes, and a rapid rise in the crime rate.

   _____

   _____

Answers and Explanations

1. **Very few students would voluntarily take Latin; therefore, requiring this subject for graduation will convince students to enroll in Latin classes.**

The two independent clauses in the sentence cannot be separated by a comma without a coordinating conjunction. Replacing the first comma with a semicolon makes the sentence grammatically correct. A period could also have been used to create two sentences. Yet another option would have been to change "therefore," to "so" because *so* is one of the conjunctions that can be used with a comma.

2. **A town that pursued such a policy would experience a decrease in population, an increase in abandoned homes, and a rapid rise in the crime rate.**

A colon may not be interposed between a verb and the verb's object. Here, simply removing the colon solves the problem. Another solution would have been to insert "the following" or "these consequences" or some other words to create a complete sentence before the colon.

Using Apostrophes Correctly

Use the apostrophe to indicate the possessive form of a noun. Singular nouns are made possessive by adding an apostrophe and an *s*. If a plural noun already ends in *s*, add only an apostrophe; if a plural noun does not end in *s*, then follow the rule for singular nouns.

NOUN	POSSESSIVE
the student	the student's laptop
Saint Francis	Saint Francis's life
the bass	the bass's music
the students	the students' teacher
the children	the children's well-being

CORRECT: The nation's young people are pessimistic. (The author is discussing the youth of one nation.)

CORRECT: These nations' young people hold many values in common. (The author is discussing the young people of more than one country. First form the plural and then add the apostrophe to indicate possession.)

Possessive pronouns do not use an apostrophe (with the exception of the neutral *one*, which forms its possessive by adding '*s*).

INCORRECT: Great respect had been their's for many years.

CORRECT: Great respect had been *theirs* for many years.

One of the most common errors involving the apostrophe is using it in the contraction *you're* or *it's* to indicate the possessive form of *you* or *it*, respectively.

INCORRECT: By taking this stance on the issue, the institution will harm it's reputation.

CORRECT: By taking this stance on the issue, the institution will harm *its* reputation.

INCORRECT: Telling a customer, "You're product cannot be delivered," might be difficult.

CORRECT: Telling a customer, "*Your* product cannot be delivered," might be difficult.

In general, contractions are not appropriate in formal writing. However, you will be writing quickly on the GRE, and your natural writing style may include using some contractions. Fortunately, their occasional use will not hurt your GRE Analytical Writing Measure score. If you use a contraction, be sure to place the apostrophe where the omitted letter would go.

CONTRACTED: They'd intended to address the question of equal rights, but they couldn't get on the meeting's agenda.

FULL FORM: They *had intended* to address the question of equal rights, but they *could not* get on the meeting's agenda.

Using Apostrophes Correctly Practice Set

Read the sentences below and revise for appropriate apostrophe use.

1. People should be allowed to keep their money and use it for the thing's they want.

   _____

   _____

2. Worker's incomes will rise only if employees improve their skills through further training.

   _____

   _____

Answers and Explanations

1. **People should be allowed to keep their money and use it for the things they want.**

The word "things" in this sentence is used as a plural direct object and not as a possessive.

2. **Workers' incomes will rise only if employees improve their skills through further training.**

The apostrophe should follow the "s" in "Workers," as the word refers to more than one employee.

Writing Clearly

Using a Variety of Sentence Structures

Using the same sentence structure to express your ideas over and over leads to a monotonous reading experience. Moreover, using a mix of sentence structures is an effective way to give some ideas more emphasis than others and to establish specific relationships among various ideas. Thus, varying your sentences helps you communicate more clearly, and the GRE essay scorers look for this feature in your writing.

Here are four common sentence structures:

TYPE	DESCRIPTION	EXAMPLE
Simple sentence	One independent clause (one subject, one predicate)	The new product is unlikely to be profitable.
Compound sentence	Two independent clauses (joined by a coordinating conjunction)	The new product is unlikely to be profitable, *and* management should not invest in its development.
Complex sentence	One independent clause, one dependent clause (joined by a subordinating conjunction)	*Because* the new product is unlikely to be profitable, management should not invest in its development.
Compound-complex sentence	Two independent clauses, one with an associated dependent clause	*Because* the new product is unlikely to be profitable, management should not invest in its development, *but* other new products may show more promise.

MONOTONOUS: The government should take care of all its citizens. The poorest citizens should be guaranteed a basic standard of living. They should receive food and shelter. Children should be given an education.

INTERESTING: The government should take care of all its citizens, guaranteeing even the poorest a basic standard of living. They should receive food and shelter, and children should be given an education as well.

Note that when you use non-simple sentences, your choice of connecting words is very important because it tells the reader the direction of your thinking: Are you continuing your thought with a discussion of a closely related idea or a consequence of the first idea? Or are you turning toward a new or contrasting idea? The road signs you look for as a reader in the Verbal section of the test, where they are clues to the author's meaning, are the same road signs you will use as a writer of GRE essays to help readers understand your meaning.

EXAMPLE: Although the government should take care of all its citizens, it should guarantee the poorest no more than a basic standard of living. While children should be given an education, adults should receive only food and shelter.

Even though most of the words are the same, by rearranging sentence structures and using different connecting words, the writer in this example is making a different point than the writer in the "interesting" example above.

Using a Variety of Sentence Structures Practice Set

Revise the passages to vary the sentence structure.

3. Many plant and animal species benefit humans directly. Some as-yet undiscovered species may benefit us in unknown ways. Every species should be saved from extinction if possible.

   _____

   _____

4. The bread riots of medieval Europe were not political in nature. Hungry peasants ransacked their lords' grain silos to get food. The peasants did not envision overthrowing the feudal order.

   _____

   _____

Answers and Explanations

1. **Because many species benefit humans directly and some as-yet undiscovered species may benefit us in unknown ways, every species should be saved from extinction if possible.**

This example revision uses "Because" to establish the benefits that plants and animals offer humans as evidence for the conclusion that as many species as possible should be saved.

2. **During the bread riots of medieval Europe, hungry peasants ransacked their lords' grain silos to get food, but they did not envision overthrowing the feudal order. Thus, these outbreaks of violence were not political in nature.**

In this example of revision, the author has used "but" to establish a contrast between ransacking silos and overthrowing the feudal lords. Then with "Thus," this contrast is used to support the conclusion that the riots were not political acts.

Using Active Voice Rather Than Passive Voice

In the active voice, the subject performs the action (e.g., "we write essays"). In the passive voice, the subject is the receiver of the action and is often only implied (e.g., "essays are written by us" or simply "essays are written").

PASSIVE: The estimate of this year's tax revenues was prepared by the city manager.

ACTIVE: The city manager prepared the estimate of this year's tax revenues.

The passive voice is useful when you want to emphasize the receiver of the action, such as in the following cases:

- The response to the action is more interesting than the doing of it: *Earth's axis would be shifted by the impact of the asteroid.* (The focus of your essay might be on the fate of Earth rather than on the asteroid.)
- You do not know who or what performed the action: *The letter was opened before I received it.*
- You prefer not to refer directly to the person who performs the action: *An error has been made in computing these data.* (Passive voice is sometimes referred to as the "politician's voice" because it helps the narrator avoid accountability.)

However, in your essays for the GRE's Analytical Writing Measure, you will usually want to emphasize the person or thing doing the action. Also, repeated use of the passive voice can create anemic, soggy prose that is less lively and engaging than sentences written in the active voice.

To change from the passive to the active voice, ask *who* or *what* is performing the action.

ACTIVE: The asteroid's impact would shift Earth's axis.

ACTIVE: Someone opened the letter before I received it.

ACTIVE: I made an error in computing these data.

Using Active Voice Rather Than Passive Voice Practice Set

In the sentences below, replace instances of passive voice with active voice wherever possible.

1. The faulty wiring in the walls might go unnoticed by safety officials until a fire breaks out.

   _____

   _____

2. The end of Spain's conception of itself as a global power was marked by that country's defeat in the Spanish-American War.

   _____

   _____

Answers and Explanations

1. **Safety officials might not notice the faulty wiring in the walls until a fire breaks out.**

The safety officials are the ones doing (or not doing) the action, so in active voice, they are the subject of the sentence.

2. **Defeat in the Spanish-American War marked the end of Spain's conception of itself as a global power.**

In active voice, "Defeat" is the subject of the sentence.

Opening Sentences Strongly

Try not to begin a sentence with *There is, There are*, or *It is.* These roundabout expressions lack a subject or an active verb and are essentially devoid of content.

Opening Sentences Strongly Practice Set

Revise the following sentences to improve the openings.

1. There isn't much wilderness left, so we should protect what we have.

   _____

   _____

2. There are several reasons why this plane is obsolete.

   _____

   _____

Answers and Explanations

1. **We should protect what little wilderness we have left.**

This statement expresses a position in a direct, forceful manner.

2. **This plane is obsolete for several reasons.**

The revised sentence immediately puts the plane at the center of the discussion, and by ending with "for several reasons," it leads naturally toward a sentence stating what the reasons are.

Writing Concisely

Removing Unnecessary Sentences

The GRE essay scorers will reward your effective expression of relevant ideas. Sentences that don't say anything substantive or that repeat things you have already said detract from your essay. Plus, these sentences take time to write, and you want to make every one of your 30 minutes count. Therefore, follow these guidelines:

- Don't write a sentence that strays from the thesis. Using Steps 1 through 3 of the Kaplan Method for Analytical Writing, plan your essay carefully. No matter how interesting the idea that just popped into your head is, if it does not fit in the plan for your essay, leave it out.

- Don't ask a question only to answer it. Rhetorical questions just mean the reader has to spend more time getting to your point.

- Don't merely copy the essay's prompt. The essay graders will look for your thoughts in your words. When you refer to information or an idea in the prompt, paraphrasing it will demonstrate that you understand it whereas merely copying it leaves your understanding in doubt.

- Don't write a whole sentence only to announce that you are changing the subject. You can signal a shift to another aspect of the topic or another point you want to make with a transitional word or phrase.

WORDY: Which idea of the author's is more in line with what I believe? This is a very interesting question. In fact, the author's ideas about consciousness being a uniquely human attribute are similar to my own.

CONCISE: Consciousness is a uniquely human attribute.

The author of the wordy example above is just wasting words and time. Get to the point quickly and stay there.

Removing Unnecessary Sentences Practice Set

Rewrite each pair of sentences as one concise statement.

1. What's the purpose of getting rid of the chemical pollutants in water? People cannot safely consume water that contains chemical pollutants.

   _____

   _____

2. I do not believe it is necessary to include the telemetry data in this study. The telemetry data add little of value to the understanding of stellar drift.

   _____

   _____

Answers and Explanations

1. **People cannot safely consume water that contains chemical pollutants.**

The first sentence is an unnecessary rhetorical question.

2. **The telemetry data are unnecessary to this study as they add little to the understanding of stellar drift.**

The author expresses two different but related thoughts: the merits of the data and whether to include them. Combining the sentences allows the elegant expression of both ideas and the relationship between them.

Avoiding Needless Self-Reference

Avoid using such unnecessary phrases as *I believe*, *I feel*, and *in my opinion*. There is no need to remind your reader that what you are writing is your opinion. Such phrases add nothing of substance to your essay and make you sound insecure. Moreover, they take time to write.

WEAK: I am of the opinion that air pollution is a more serious problem than most people realize.

FORCEFUL: Air pollution is a more serious problem than most people realize.

On the other hand, if you describe something that happened to you—for instance, if you use an example from personal experience to illustrate a point you make in your Issue essay—then refer to yourself with first-person pronouns (*I*, *me*, *my*, *mine*). Doing so is perfectly acceptable and much more comfortable than discussing yourself in the third person ("The author had an inspirational teacher in third grade"; "One's guilty conscience taught one never to steal again").

APPROPRIATE: My family had to emigrate because the authorities were abusing their power, and I will never forget the terror we felt when soldiers stopped us at the border.

Avoiding Needless Self-Reference Practice Set

Eliminate unnecessary self-reference in these sentences.

1. It seems to me that nuclear energy is safer and cleaner than burning fossil fuels. I think we should build more nuclear power plants.

   _____

   _____

2. The author, in my personal opinion, has outdated ideas.

   _____

   _____

Answers and Explanations

1. **Nuclear energy is safer and cleaner than burning fossil fuels, so we should build more nuclear power plants.**

"It seems to me" and "I think" hedge unnecessarily and intrude on the argument. Also note that combining these statements with "so" makes the argument flow better from evidence to conclusion.

2. **The author has outdated ideas.**

Your readers will always assume that what you write is your opinion.

Streamlining Wordy Phrases

Using several words when one would do can be tempting. You may have been taught that more elaborate phrasing makes your prose more scholarly or more formal. However, it actually just means you are taking longer to say what you are saying, wasting your time and the reader's.

WORDY: I am of the opinion that the aforementioned salespeople should be advised that they will be evaluated with regard to the utilization of responsive organizational software for the purpose of devising a dynamic network of customers.

CONCISE: Managers should tell the salespeople that sales staff will be evaluated on their use of flexible computerized databases to develop a customer network.

Streamlining Wordy Phrases Practice Set

Revise the wordy phrases in the following sentences.

1. Government funding cripples the natural relationship of arts enthusiasts and artists by subsidizing work and makes artists less creative and forces the taxpayer to take on the burden of paying for art they don't like.

    _____

    _____

2. There are many reasons why some may believe that the services of one real estate agent are superior in quality to the services of another competing real estate agent or group of agents, including the personal service they provide, the care and quality of the work they do, and the communication lines they set up and keep open.

    _____

    _____

Answers and Explanations

1. **The government should not subsidize artists because doing so makes them less creative and forces taxpayers to pay for art they do not like.**

The original sentence contains unnecessary repetition. It does not need to include both "funding" and "subsidizing," as both words refer to the same thing. The phrase "cripples the natural relationship" is also redundant, as that idea is implied by the list of the negative effects government funding has on both artists and taxpayers.

2. **Reasons for choosing one real estate agent over another include personal service, care, communication, and quality of work.**

The revised sentence condenses the two main clauses: the main idea (choosing one real estate agent over another) and the subsequent list. It also pares down the unnecessary repetition. There is no need to explain that communication lines are both set up and kept open, for example.

Eliminating Redundancy

Redundancy means that the writer needlessly repeats an idea. For example, it is redundant to speak of _a beginner lacking experience_. The word _beginner_ itself implies a lack of experience. You can eliminate redundant words or phrases without changing the meaning of the sentence.

Here are some common redundancies:

REDUNDANT	CONCISE
refer back	refer
few in number	few
small-sized	small
grouped together	grouped
from their own personal viewpoint	from their viewpoint
end result	result
serious crisis	crisis
new initiatives	initiatives

REDUNDANT: It is wise to plan ahead for unexpected problems.

CONCISE: It is wise to plan for unexpected problems.

In this example, "plan ahead" is redundant. In what situation would you "plan behind"? "Unexpected problems" is acceptable because, while some problems are unexpected, others are readily anticipated.

Eliminating Redundancy Practice Set

Revise the following sentences to eliminate redundancy.

1. All of these problems have combined together to create a serious crisis.

   _____

   _____

2. That monument continues to remain a significant tourist attraction.

   _____

   _____

Answers and Explanations

1. **All of these problems have combined to create a crisis.**

Crises are inherently serious, and things cannot combine apart. The adverb and adjective are redundant.

2. **That monument remains a significant tourist attraction.**

There is no need to reinforce "remain" with "continues." The verb "remain" implies continuation.

Avoiding Excessive Qualification

Because the object of your essay is to convince your reader of your point of view, you will want to adopt a reasonable tone. The occasional use of such qualifiers as *fairly*, *rather*, *somewhat*, and *relatively* and of such expressions as *seems to be*, *a little*, and a *certain amount of* will let the reader know you are not overstating your case. Excessive use of such modifiers, however, will make you sound unsure of yourself and weaken your argument.

WEAK: A fairly minor breach of etiquette can possibly disrupt a relationship, bringing negotiations pretty much to a standstill.

STRONG: A minor breach of etiquette can disrupt a relationship, bringing negotiations to a standstill.

Other qualifiers, such as *very*, *really*, *extremely*, *drastically*, and *a lot*, can be used sparingly for emphasis, but their overuse will make your writing sound unconsidered and lacking in nuance. To state your idea more forcefully, think of a more precise word.

WEAK: Yuja Wang is a very good pianist. Her interpretations are really expressive.

STRONG: Yuja Wang is a virtuoso pianist. Her interpretations express a range of tones from delicate to abrasive.

Finally, don't qualify words that are already absolute, as the qualifier is redundant.

WRONG	CORRECT
more unique	unique
the very worst	the worst
completely full	full

Avoiding Excessive Qualification Practice Set

Revise the following sentences to repair excessive qualification.

1. She was a fairly excellent teacher.

   _____

   _____

2. It is possible that we might overcome these obstacles.

   _____

   _____

Answers and Explanations

1. **She was an excellent teacher.**

You are asserting that this teacher was excellent, so say so! The use of the adverb "fairly" unnecessarily weakens the point of the sentence.

2. **We might overcome these obstacles.**

The word "might" implies that overcoming the obstacles is possible but not certain, so saying "it is possible" is unnecessary. The original sentence is also an example of the weak "It is" opening.

Kaplan's Additional Tips for Writing Foundations

Practicing Your Writing

You should practice writing Issue essays and Argument essays by using the practice prompts in Chapters 22, 23, and 24 of this book. You can get more practice by going to the testmaker's website (**www.ets.org**), finding the pools of Issue and Argument topics published there, and writing responses to a few of them. However, you might want to practice other aspects of writing without worrying about constructing an Analytical Writing Measure essay. If so, here are a couple of ways you can become a more fluent writer of formal academic English.

Break Down Writer's Block

Worried you'll freeze up on Test Day and be unable to make the words and sentences come out? A feeling of being blocked is not unusual. Even professional writers, such as journalists and novelists, sometimes feel this way. You can't write correctly, clearly, and concisely if you can't write at all.

An effective way to overcome this barrier is to engage regularly in freewriting. Set a timer for a short period, perhaps as little as two minutes to begin with. When the timer starts, you start writing. The only rule is that you cannot stop to think, to cross out or delete, or to fix anything; you must keep your pen moving across the paper or your fingers tapping on the keyboard, even if all you can think of to write is your name over and over. Some people find it helpful to use a prompt as a starting point, such as by opening a book at random and reading the first sentence on the page or reading the headline of a news website. As you become more comfortable producing words without stopping, extend the time of your freewriting. Oh, and there's one more rule: you don't have to show your freewriting output to anyone—it can go straight into the trash if you want. You'll have plenty of opportunities to judge your work and have it evaluated by others, but the point of freewriting is to free yourself from inhibitions.

Refine Your "Ear" for Correct Writing

Do you struggle to know whether you've broken a grammar rule or not? To mitigate your self-doubt, use style imitation to train your mental ear to detect correct and incorrect writing. Choose a piece of expository writing, an opinion or analysis piece of the same sort you will write on Test Day, from a reputable publication (see Chapter 4: Verbal Foundations and Content Review for some suggestions). Using a paragraph or two as a model, imitate the author's sentence structures exactly but write about another topic so that you are using the author's grammar but substituting different nouns, verbs, modifiers, and so forth. If the author has written about a serious subject, you can do so as well or write on a lighthearted or trivial topic. If adapting someone else's language to your own ideas is too difficult at first, then even just copying the advanced writer's work word for word will be helpful. By following in the footsteps of a sophisticated writer, you will practice writing correct and varied sentences and develop a keen awareness of what's right and what's not.

Proofreading Your Writing

The last step of the Kaplan Method for Analytical Writing is to proofread your essay. Naturally, you will look for the errors of grammar, punctuation, and style highlighted in this chapter. You will also look for misspelled words. Here are some tips for other ways to polish your writing in the final minutes before you submit your essay.

Vary Your Vocabulary

If you are writing about education and you've used the term "educational system" over and over, plug in some different words here and there such as *schools*, *school system*, and *the way we teach our children*. If you've said with regard to a certain situation that X will be "challenging," Y will be "challenging," and Z will be "challenging," try using more precise language: X will force government to be innovative, Y will require finding the money to fund the program, and Z will necessitate persuading the public to relinquish a long-held belief. Note that varying your vocabulary does not necessarily mean using long or unusual words. In fact, if you try to use words you're not comfortable with, you are likely to misuse them, and misused words, no matter how fancy they are, will detract from your essay's quality. Just scan for repetition of words that could irritate the reader and find other ways of expressing the idea.

Use Transition Words

During proofreading is a great time to look for opportunities to add some "road signs" to help the reader move easily from one sentence to the next. Just as in the Verbal section of the test, words such as *also*, *moreover*, and *in addition* signal the continuation of a line of thinking, while words such as *however*, *nevertheless*, and *despite* indicate a contrasting thought.

Rephrase Awkward Sentences

Maybe you realize as you review your essay that a sentence is correct but nonetheless reads awkwardly. Revising it to flow more smoothly is not as high a priority as fixing clear errors, but it is still worthwhile if you have time. A quick fix for much stylistic awkwardness, as well as many outright errors, is to break a longer sentence into two shorter ones.

In the chapters that follow, you will learn how to approach the two basic types of Analytical Writing tasks on the GRE. The Argument task will ask you to analyze an incomplete argument, while the Issue task will oblige you to come up with one of your own. Although each type of task requires you to approach an argument in distinctly different ways, both are built on the foundations you studied in this chapter.

CHAPTER 22

THE ISSUE ESSAY

Introduction to the Issue Essay

The first of the Analytical Writing essay tasks is the Issue essay. For this essay, you will be given a point of view on a topic. The directions will ask you to take a position on the issue, and they'll instruct you to explain your position convincingly. You will therefore need to express an opinion and write an argument in support of it. In constructing your argument, you will provide evidence in the form of reasons and/or examples to support your position.

For the topic, expect about one to two sentences that discuss a broad, general issue. The prompt may state one point of view, one point of view along with a reason for that opinion, or opposing points of view. Regardless of the prompt format, the test will present a statement that could reasonably be either supported or argued against. Your job is to form an opinion on the topic and make a case for that opinion.

The directions for the Issue essay will begin like this:

> You will be given a brief quotation that states or implies an issue of general interest and specific instructions on how to respond to that issue. You will then have 30 minutes to plan and compose a response according to the specific instructions. A response to any other issue will receive a score of zero.

> Make sure that you respond according to the specific instructions and support your position on the issue with reasons and examples drawn from such areas as your reading, experience, observations, and/or academic studies.

The directions will go on to explain the criteria the scorers will use to evaluate your essay, and they will encourage you to plan your response before you write it and to leave time for revision. If you are well acquainted with the essay directions before Test Day, then you will not have to spend any of your 30 minutes reading them.

The next screen will present the topic you will write on, followed by specific instructions for your essay. The topic will look like this:

> Pursuing a financially secure career tends to inhibit creativity and innovation.

The specific instructions for how to approach the Issue essay task will look something like this:

> Write a response in which you discuss the extent to which you agree or disagree with the statement and explain your reasoning for the position you take. In developing and supporting your position, you should consider ways in which the statement might or might not hold true and explain how these considerations shape your position.

The Issue essay instructions vary from one topic to another, so make sure to read them carefully. Other instructions you may see for the Issue essay look like this:

- Write a response in which you discuss the extent to which you agree or disagree with the recommendation and explain your reasoning for the position you take. In developing and supporting your position, describe specific circumstances in which adopting the recommendation would or would not be advantageous and explain how these examples shape your position.
- Write a response in which you discuss the extent to which you agree or disagree with the claim. In developing and supporting your position, be sure to address the most compelling reasons and/or examples that could be used to challenge your position.
- Write a response in which you discuss which view more closely aligns with your own position and explain your reasoning for the position you take. In developing and supporting your position, you should address both of the views presented.
- Write a response in which you discuss the extent to which you agree or disagree with the claim and the reason on which that claim is based.
- Write a response in which you discuss your views on the policy and explain your reasoning for the position you take. In developing and supporting your position, you should consider the possible consequences of implementing the policy and explain how these consequences shape your position.

THE KAPLAN METHOD FOR ANALYTICAL WRITING

STEP 1   Take the issue/argument apart.

STEP 2   Select the points you will make.

STEP 3   Organize, using Kaplan's essay templates.

STEP 4   Type your essay.

STEP 5   Proofread your work.

How the Kaplan Method for Analytical Writing Works

Now let's discuss how the Kaplan Method for Analytical Writing works for the Issue essay.

[**STEP 1**]

Take the issue apart.

Read the topic and consider both sides of the issue. Restate the issue in your own words. Consider the other side of the issue and put that into your own words as well. Note: Use your scratch paper to capture your thoughts throughout Steps 1–3.

[**STEP 2**]

Select the points you will make.

After you consider what both sides of the issue mean, think of reasons and examples for both sides. After coming up with at least two reasons in support of one side and one reason for the other, decide which side you will support or the extent to which you agree or disagree with the stated position. The side you choose to write in favor of should be the side you believe you can write the more compelling essay on; this does not need to be the position with which you personally agree. There is no "right" or "wrong" position.

[**STEP 3**]

Organize, using Kaplan's Issue essay template.

Now plan the body of your essay so that when you start writing, you can proceed confidently and focus on expressing your ideas. Review the ideas you brainstormed in Step 2. If some of the ideas are closely related, consider discussing them both in the same body paragraph. You may find that you don't actually have much to say about one or more of the points you jotted down—cross these out. Once any weak points are crossed out and related ideas grouped, decide what order you'll discuss your ideas in; write ①, ②, ③, etc. next to them on your scratch paper to indicate the order of paragraphs. Be sure to lead with your best argument. Then organize the remaining paragraph(s) by considering how the essay as a whole will flow. Like any good debater, you want to be prepared for an argument that the other side could make. Make sure to acknowledge at least one point the other side might bring up, but also rebut it; this is where you'll use one or more of the reasons you thought of in Step 2 for the other side of the issue.

- **Paragraph 1:** Paraphrase the issue (the statement, claim, recommendation, or policy) and state your position. You might begin by explaining why the issue is important or worthy of discussion, and you may choose to summarize the points you will make in your essay. However, your most important task here is to inform the reader of your position on the issue.

- **Paragraph 2:** State and elaborate upon the strongest point in support of your position, within the scope of the specific instructions.

- **Paragraph 3:** State and elaborate upon another point in support of your position, within the scope of the specific instructions.

- **Additional paragraphs, as time permits:** If you have time and have more strong points to make, you may write additional paragraphs in which you state and elaborate upon other points in support of your position. Note that a few well-developed paragraphs will earn a higher score than many superficial paragraphs. (Time valve #1: skip if need be.)
- **Next-to-last paragraph:** Address an opposing point to your position; then refute it with relevant detailed support. Another option is to raise and rebut counterarguments with your own arguments in each body paragraph, instead of devoting a paragraph to this purpose. Just make sure your essay acknowledges at least one argument someone on the other side would make. (Time valve #2: combine with conclusion if need be.)
- **Last paragraph:** Conclude by summarizing your position in a way that addresses the specific instructions.

[STEP 4]

Type your essay.

You shouldn't proceed with this step until you've completed the three preceding ones. You'll save time and energy by preparing your essay before you start typing it. Graders have a limited amount of time in which to read your essay, so start and conclude with strong statements. Be forceful and concise with your prose and link related ideas with transition words and phrases. When you write crisply and give clear indicators of how one idea connects to the next, you will make your writing flow and make the grader's job easier.

[STEP 5]

Proofread your work.

Save enough time (at least a couple of minutes) to skim the entire essay. Look for errors you can address quickly: capitalization, paragraph divisions, double-typed words, miscellaneous typos, and small grammatical errors.

How to Apply the Kaplan Method for Analytical Writing to the Issue Essay

Now let's apply the Kaplan Method for Analytical Writing to a sample Issue task:

The drawbacks of traditional energy sources mean that they are not a long-term solution to the problem of meeting ever-increasing energy needs.

Write a response in which you discuss the extent to which you agree or disagree with the statement and explain your reasoning for the position you take. In developing and supporting your position, you should consider ways in which the statement might or might not hold true and explain how these considerations shape your position.

[STEP 1]

Take the issue apart.

Your first step is to dissect the issue. Begin taking notes on your scratch paper. Start by restating the issue in your own words: "Although we will need more energy, we cannot count on conventional energy sources as a solution because of their serious disadvantages."

Now, consider the other side of the issue—in your own words, this might be "The power sources we mostly rely on today have proven themselves reliable and cost-effective, and their disadvantages do not outweigh their usefulness for meeting our energy needs."

[STEP 2]

Select the points you will make.

Your job, as stated in the directions, is to decide whether or not you agree with the statement and then to explain your decision. Some would argue that the use of power sources such as oil, coal, and nuclear power put the health of humans and the environment at risk, while others would say that we can't afford not to use them. Which side do you take?

Remember, this isn't about showing the graders what your deep-seated beliefs about energy policy are—it's about showing that you can formulate an argument and communicate it clearly. The position you choose to take for the Issue essay does not have to be one you actually believe.

Quickly jot down on your scratch paper the pros and cons of each side and choose the side for which you have more relevant things to say. For this topic, that process might go something like this:

Arguments *for* the use of traditional power sources:

- They are inexpensive compared to newer ways of generating energy, such as solar power, wind power, and biofuels.
- New ways of extracting oil, coal, and natural gas have been discovered, and hydroelectric and nuclear power are inexhaustible.
- Industries are set up to use current energy sources and would have to be adapted to new ones.

Arguments *against* the use of traditional power sources:

- All such sources are harmful to the environment, and some are dangerous to people. Even the newest and cleanest of these, nuclear power, creates radioactive waste. Examples: Three Mile Island, Chernobyl, Fukushima.
- There are other, more environmentally friendly energy sources. Examples: solar, wind, biofuels.
- Investment in these industries limits development of other options. Examples: utility rates that don't take environmental damage into account, while other industries struggle to get subsidies, investment; regulations that are not as strict or whose enforcement is delayed.

Again, it doesn't matter which side you take. There is no *right* answer as far as the testmaker is concerned. Let's say that in this case, you decide that you can write a more compelling essay about the disadvantages of conventional power. You would choose to argue in favor of the prompt, irrespective of what your own beliefs might be. You may choose not to include in your essay all the points you come up with, depending on how strong you think they are and how much you have time to write.

[STEP 3]

Organize, using Kaplan's Issue essay template.

You have already begun to think out your arguments—that's how you picked the side you did in the first place. Now's the time to determine which point you'll make in which paragraph, including those that weaken the opposing side. The only person who needs to understand your notes is you, so feel free to use abbreviations. In this case, your scratch-work might look something like the following:

Paragraph 1: Traditional power sources (oil, coal, natural gas, hydroelectric, nuclear) are not a viable option for the long term.

Paragraph 2: All such sources are harmful to the environment, and some are dangerous to people. Even the newest and cleanest of these, nuclear power, creates radioactive waste. Examples: Three Mile Island, Chernobyl, Fukushima.

Paragraph 3: Investment in these industries limits development of other options. Examples: utility rates that don't take environmental damage into account, while other industries struggle to get subsidies, investment; regulations that are not as strict or whose enforcement is delayed.

Paragraph 4: Other, more environmentally friendly energy sources are more expensive now, but need not be. Examples: solar, wind, biofuels.

Paragraph 5: Focusing on cheapness of old technologies and current drawbacks of newer ones is shortsighted. Further investment in traditional energy generation damages our environment and delays the development of the energy sources we will inevitably need.

[STEP 4]

Type your essay.

Remember, open with a general statement indicating that you understand the issue and then assert your position. From there, make your main points. Note: As a basis for comparison, we've included an outstanding essay that deserves a score of 6. The second prompt will include an adequate essay that deserves a score of 4.

Sample Issue Essay 1

A range of well-developed energy technologies are currently available to industries and individual consumers: oil, coal, natural gas, hydroelectric, and nuclear power each contribute to our economy and our lifestyle, enabling us to live with one of the largest "environmental footprints" in human history. Despite each of these energy sources' benefits, each also has drawbacks that make it unsustainable for the long term. Therefore, it is imperative that alternative power-generating technologies be developed.

Despite extensive regulation and efforts to make our predominant energy sources environmentally safe, all have negative effects on the environment and thus on human safety. Burning coal and oil causes air pollution. Drilling for oil and transporting it via pipelines raises the specter of oil spills. Increasingly, extracting oil and natural gas is being accomplished through hydraulic fracturing ("fracking"), a process associated with contamination of water supplies and increased incidence of earthquakes. Hydroelectric power depends on damming rivers, exacting a tremendous cost on the wildlife that depend on these freshwater lifelines; moreover, climate change will put increasing pressure on rivers and lakes. The most recently developed of these technologies, nuclear energy, is inexpensive in the short term, causes no air or water pollution under normal operating conditions, and uses a virtually inexhaustible fuel supply. However, even this solution has long-term consequences that render it unacceptable, as it creates radioactive waste that requires storage for thousands of years, and the plants themselves can suffer accidents that release radiation, as witnessed at Three Mile Island in Pennsylvania, Chernobyl in Ukraine, and Fukushima in Japan. Because no energy source we currently rely on can be trusted not to irreparably harm the planet we live on, these technologies need to be phased out in favor of better alternatives.

Beyond the enormous long-term environmental problems and short-term health risks, current energy sources impose economic costs on consumers. By being relatively inexpensive in the short term, they make other alternatives seem too costly. Thus, for example, electric utilities maintain coal-burning and nuclear plants, their costs underwritten by rates that fail to cover the externality of environmental damage. Power companies also save money whenever regulations are not written as strictly as needed to protect the environment or when regulatory enforcement is postponed. In the meantime, companies trying to develop innovative energy supplies struggle to find reliable funding. If the true costs of power generation were being levied, consumers would feel much more motivated to switch to other types of energy. Currently, however, artificially low costs are prolonging usage of unsustainable technologies.

Indeed, the companies that produce power often claim they cannot make more environmentally friendly alternatives affordable. Yet there already exist homes heated by the sun, cars fueled by corn, and cities lit up in no small part by the wind. If the limited resources devoted to such energy alternatives have already produced such consequential results, more intensive investment would likely make these alternatives less expensive, perhaps even more cost-effective than the forms of energy now offered as the most economical solution. Another argument against sustainable energy is that it is unreliable, for example, that solar works only when the sun is shining and wind works only when a breeze is blowing. It must be remembered, though, that older power technologies were unreliable early in their development, but successive engineering refinements made them the seemingly indispensable mainstays of a developed economy they are today. Set against whatever inconvenience they may engender is the fact that sunlight, air, and plants are in virtually limitless supply and do not inherently create harmful environmental impacts.

Thus, those who argue that alternative energy sources are too expensive and unreliable are being shortsighted. In fact, the current energy supply imposes tremendous indirect costs in its threat to the health of humans and the environment at large, and engineers have barely begun to tap the potential of other energy sources. Not only are the drawbacks to conventional energy too great to justify its continuing use, but the long-term benefits of renewable resources will likely reward investment in their development. If these alternatives are explored more seriously than they have been, they have the potential to be transformative technologies in the same way that the refinement of petroleum revolutionized transportation and manufacturing and massive hydroelectric projects powered development of the western United States. With limited resources at our disposal and a burgeoning global population to consider, we should not delay in diverting resources from traditional to innovative energy sources.

[STEP 5]
Proofread your work.

Be sure to allot a few minutes after you have finished writing to review your essay. Though you do not have to write a grammatically flawless essay to score well, mistakes that interfere with readability will reduce your score. You can practice your writing skills in Chapter 21: Analytical Writing Foundations and Content Review.

Assessment of Sample Issue Essay 1: "Outstanding," Score of 6

This essay is carefully constructed throughout, enabling the reader to move effortlessly from point to point as the writer examines the multifaceted implications of the issue. The writer begins with a strong thesis statement ("it is imperative that alternative power-generating technologies be developed") to introduce his own position on the issue. He proceeds to provide compelling reasons and examples to support the premise. Along the way, he acknowledges arguments for the other side (the energy industry is regulated, current energy sources are inexpensive, and the "claim" that alternative sources are not affordable), thus "consider[ing] ways in which the statement might or might not hold true," but also effectively rebuts these arguments. The final paragraph takes the argument to an effective conclusion. The writing is clear, concise, and correct. Sentence structure is varied, and diction and vocabulary are strong and expressive.

How to Apply the Kaplan Method for Analytical Writing to Another Issue Essay

Now let's apply the Kaplan Method for Analytical Writing to a second Issue essay task:

> People who hold high expectations for others are rewarded with high performance and respect.
>
> > Write a response in which you discuss the extent to which you agree or disagree with the claim. In developing and supporting your position, be sure to address the most compelling reasons and/or examples that could be used to challenge your position.

[STEP 1]

Take the issue apart.

Begin by putting the issue in your own words: "If you expect people to do well, they will, and they will respect you for it." Next, consider the other side of the issue and do the same: "If you expect too much of people, they may get frustrated and perform at a lower level, or you may lose their respect."

[STEP 2]

Select the points you will make.

Your job, as stated in the directions, is to decide whether or not you agree with the statement and then to explain your decision in light of the arguments someone could use on the other side of the issue. Some would argue that high expectations yield high results, while others may think that unrealistically high expectations destroy confidence. Which side do you take?

Think through the pros and cons of each side and choose the side for which you have more relevant things to say.

For this topic, that process might go something like this:

Arguments *for* holding people to high expectations:

- Striving to meet high expectations improves people's skills, and when these individuals succeed, their success leads to increased confidence and higher performance. Example: challenge office interns.
- Without expectations, people don't know how they will be measured or to what level they should perform. Examples: 2nd graders design skyscrapers; retirees train for Olympics.
- High expectations convey confidence and trust. Example: challenges from teachers.

Arguments *against* holding people to high expectations:

- People could lose confidence or even give up if they are unable to meet the expectations.
- You may be thought of as someone who is unyielding or only concerned with performance.

Remember, it doesn't matter which side you take since there is no *right* answer. Say that in this case, you decide to argue in favor of having high expectations for others.

[STEP 3]

Organize, using Kaplan's Issue essay template.

Now's the time to decide in what order you'll make your points, including counterarguments that weaken the opposing side. Your scratchwork for this essay might look something like this:

Paragraph 1: High expectations often yield high performance and respect, whether or not the expectations are met.

Paragraph 2: Without expectations, people don't know how they will be measured or to what level they should perform. Examples: 2nd graders design skyscrapers; retirees train for Olympics.

Paragraph 3: High expectations convey confidence and trust. Example: challenges from teachers.

Paragraph 4: Striving to meet high expectations improves people's skills, and when these individuals succeed, their success leads to increased confidence and higher performance. Example: challenge office interns.

Paragraph 5: A leader might try to be sensitive to people's feelings and preserve their self-esteem. However, people feel bad and fail when others do not value them enough and believe they are capable of less than they actually are.

Paragraph 6: In all cases, high expectations are worth the risk.

[STEP 4]

Type your essay.

Sample Issue Essay 2

High expectations yield high performance and respect in every case, whether the expectations are met or unmet. Setting expectations allows people to know how they will be measured and to what level they should perform. They also convey confidence and a sense of trust. Once the expectations are met, people feel bolstered by their achievement and have a much stronger sense of self-confidence, leading to even higher performance. These results hold up in a variety of contexts, including in educational, business, and political realms.

The purpose of expectations is often lost in the assignment of a task. The expectations themselves may take the form of the actual tasks to be done, but really, the expectation is the ownership, resourcefulness, and skill of the person assigned the task. Expecting someone to do something overly challenging, such as asking second-graders to design a skyscraper or challenging a retiree to train for the Olympics, may seem egregious, but the stories that intrigue us most are usually about people rising to the challenge. Our own expectations are recalibrated when we learn of people exceeding the expectations we set ourselves to. We look to where the bar is set to see how we measure up. Given a bar, people will usually do what it takes to measure up.

Good teachers are often described as "hard, but fair." This is a good description of someone who holds high expectations for his or her students, and is rewarded by that assessment. A hard but fair teacher is one who challenges the students to exceed their own expectations of themselves, and often others' expectations of them. These are the teachers who assign fourth-grade students research papers or ask eighth graders to take a 100-question math test in 100 minutes. Students take up the challenge because it feels good to succeed. They gain confidence and look at tasks unrelated to the classroom in new ways.

High performance breeds higher performance. Once someone has been resourceful or learned a new skill to achieve a task, the person feels empowered to be similarly resourceful achieving different tasks. In fact, a high performer may take on more challenges without prompting. This bears out in business: the neophyte office intern who pulls together a critical report through resourcefulness, skill, and a little luck is a familiar story, but for good reason. This intern with his or her fresh ideas stands out among the drones and is challenged further, rocketing to the proverbial top of the company. If the same expectations were put on the rest of the workforce, would other employees be as resourceful to achieve the expectations? Most likely, as long as the employee is motivated enough by the challenge.

Some people may be frustrated by high expectations, and some may simply ignore those expectations, but being presented with a challenge ultimately builds a person's confidence. No one ever failed because he or she was fairly challenged by a daunting task and supported while tackling it. People fail because others do not value them enough and believe they are capable of less than they actually are. In fact, just being challenged is often enough to shake up people's self-expectations and make them reconsider what they are actually capable of.

In all cases, high expectations are worth the risk. The challenge bolsters self-esteem and self-confidence, and yields high performance. It improves performance in classrooms, on the job, and in other areas where challenges present themselves.

[STEP 5]
Proofread your work.

Take the last couple of minutes to catch any serious errors.

Assessment of Sample Issue Essay 2: "Adequate," Score of 4

This essay is, on the whole, well constructed and laid out. The reader can systematically move from point to point as the writer examines the implications of the issue. The writer begins by agreeing with the statement and presenting specific reasons for agreeing. She gives examples to illustrate her point and organizes her essay well. The author's analysis is generally cogent. She asks the reader to take a bit of a leap with some of her claims. For example, claiming that "people will usually do what it takes to measure up" when given a bar is a conclusion not really supported by the paragraph leading us to that conclusion. She asserts that people are inherently encouraged, rather than discouraged, by daunting challenges but never really justifies that assertion. However, the writing is clean and concise and includes only a few errors. Sentence structure is varied, and the author's diction is strong and expressive. For all these reasons, this essay receives a score of 4.

Kaplan's Additional Tips for the Issue Essay

You Will Know Enough to Respond to the Task

The types of issues in the pool of Issue essay tasks are intentionally designed to be accessible to any reasonably well-informed, thoughtful person. They won't require esoteric knowledge. Don't worry if you're not very familiar with a subject or haven't thought about the issue before. By giving yourself permission to brainstorm freely in Step 2, you will come up with a few good points to make, and that is all you need to write a high-scoring essay. If you are concerned that you won't be able to think of good reasons or examples under pressure, prepare for this part of the test by regularly reading about current and historical events, which are excellent sources of ideas.

Don't Succumb to "Analysis Paralysis"

Usually when test takers have difficulty thinking of much to say, it is because they are holding themselves to too high a standard. In Step 2, you just need to come up with points that are reasonable and relevant. The essay scorers do not expect you to be earth-shatteringly brilliant as you address a topic you've never seen before in 30 minutes. Therefore, don't allow yourself to freeze up because your ideas don't seem insightful enough. Just let whatever comes to mind flow out onto your scratch paper, and you will find enough there to build a solid essay.

Don't Worry About Whether Your Position Is "Correct"

The purpose of the Issue essay is to develop an argument and defend it. You're going to be scored on how well supported your position is, not on whether it is the "right answer." Indeed, by design the topics chosen for this task are not black-and-white issues; they can be argued successfully from very different points of view.

Use Each Step of the Method, One Step at a Time

Your goal is to express a position on the issue and support your position with evidence. You can't do that unless you've thought of reasons and examples to support your stance on the topic, and you can't think of relevant reasons and examples unless you know what your stance is, and you can't have a clear idea of your stance unless you've thought about how one could be for or against the position in the prompt. So start at the beginning, with Step 1: Take the Issue Apart, and proceed step-by-step.

Don't Overcomplicate Your Prose

Some people believe that writing in a convoluted manner makes their ideas sound more intelligent, but this is not true. In the Analytical Writing section, be as clear and linear in your writing as possible. Bombastic rhetorical flourishes may seem impressive when you first write them, but they tend to fall flat with graders who have read many hundreds of essays. The point here is to assert and defend a position, not impress the graders with your wit. Substantive thinking and a direct writing style will easily outweigh complexity for the sake of complexity.

Make Sure Your Conclusion Is Strong

It's important to end your essay with a statement that puts a capstone on your argument. If you are concerned about running out of time before you have a chance to write a strong conclusion, consider writing a concluding sentence after you finish your first paragraph. After all, you know how your essay will end—with a restatement of your thesis—so you can write the ending now. Try to use different words than you used to state your position in the first paragraph. Ideally, you will finish typing your essay (Step 4) with a few minutes to spare for proofreading, and then you can elaborate on your conclusion if you wish. However, you can write your body paragraphs in a more relaxed frame of mind, knowing that your essay has a solid ending.

Issue Essay Practice Set

Issue Essay 1

30 Minutes
Length: 1 essay

Directions: You will be given a brief quotation that states or implies an issue of general interest and specific instructions on how to respond to that issue. You will then have 30 minutes to plan and compose a response according to the specific instructions. A response to any other issue will receive a score of zero.

Make sure that you respond according to the specific instructions and support your position on the issue with reasons and examples drawn from such areas as your reading, experience, observations, and/or academic studies.

Before you begin writing, you may want to think for a few minutes about the issue and the specific task instructions and then plan your response. Be sure to develop your position fully and organize it coherently, but leave time to reread what you have written and make any revisions you think are necessary.

> The perceived greatness of any political leader has more to do with the challenges faced by that leader than with any of his or her inherent skills and abilities.

Write a response in which you discuss the extent to which you either agree or disagree with the statement and explain your reasoning for the position you take. In developing and supporting your position, you should consider ways in which the statement might or might not be true and explain how these considerations shape your position.

Issue Essay 2

30 Minutes
Length: 1 essay

Directions: You will be given a brief quotation that states or implies an issue of general interest and specific instructions on how to respond to that issue. You will then have 30 minutes to plan and compose a response according to the specific instructions. A response to any other issue will receive a score of zero.

Make sure that you respond according to the specific instructions and support your position on the issue with reasons and examples drawn from such areas as your reading, experience, observations, and/or academic studies.

Before you begin writing, you may want to think for a few minutes about the issue and the specific task instructions and then plan your response. Be sure to develop your position fully and organize it coherently, but leave time to reread what you have written and make any revisions you think are necessary.

> Progress should be the aim of any great society. People too often cling unnecessarily to obsolete ways of thinking and acting because they enjoy feeling comfortable and fear the unknown.

Write a response in which you discuss the extent to which you either agree or disagree with the statement and explain your reasoning for the position you take. In developing and supporting your position, you should consider ways in which the statement might or might not be true and explain how these considerations shape your position.

Issue Essay Practice Set Answers and Explanations

Issue Essay Sample Essays and Assessments Issue Essay 1

What follows are top-scoring sample essays for each of the practice tasks. Note how the authors adhere to the Kaplan Method for Analytical Writing.

Essay 1: "Outstanding," Score of 6

Perceptions of greatness in national and political leaders are largely determined by the seriousness of the problems that they face during their terms in office. Most national histories principally highlight individuals in the context of significant events in which the leaders played important roles. Most political leaders need to have large stores of inherent skill and ability just in order to become a political leader. However, history remembers those who lived in great times more fondly than those who did not. Examples of this are numerous and include the histories of Abraham Lincoln, Woodrow Wilson, and Winston Churchill—all people who are perceived as great leaders largely because of the times in which they lived.

Abraham Lincoln is often considered the greatest of all the American presidents. His image graces two units of the currency, and he has one of the largest monuments built in his honor in Washington, D.C. However, Lincoln is considered great largely because he faced a great challenge—the civil war between the North and the South in the 1860s. Lincoln led the United States to victory over the rebels and reunited the country and is therefore considered an impressive leader. This is not to say that Lincoln was not skilled. Many know that he was born in a log cabin and progressed to law school and eventually to the presidency. He was also a skilled orator. However, another man, James Buchanan, also was born in a log cabin, went to law school, gave good speeches, and ascended to the presidency, yet there are no monuments to Buchanan in the capital or pictures of his face on the five-dollar bill.

Woodrow Wilson was another talented person who ascended to the presidency of the United States. However his talents are not what make his perceived greatness. In this age, few remember whether Wilson was particularly smart, a very good speech maker, or a good arbitrator. Most remember that he led the United States to victory in the first World War and therefore perceive him as an effective leader. At the time, however, Wilson was rather unpopular. In fact, he had so little sway with Congress that he was unable to get the United States to join the League of Nations—a fact that many claim helped lead to the second World War.

Winston Churchill was another person whom history views favorably because of the incredible challenges that he faced. However, Churchill was not very popular with the British public before World War II, nor did he impress a future US president. When Franklin Roosevelt first met Churchill, before either was the leader of his respective country, Roosevelt wrote in his diary that the Englishman was full of himself and far too talkative. Early in his term as prime minister, Churchill even faced a no-confidence vote in Parliament. However, the events of World War II accorded him the perception of greatness in the eyes of history.

Many might argue that these individuals and other men and women were already great before history gave them great challenges. While it is impossible to definitely disprove this assertion and they must in fact have had certain skills and abilities—otherwise, they would not have been political leaders—most examples point to the fact that the times make the man or woman. If the presidencies of Buchanan and Lincoln were switched, we would very likely have the Buchanan memorial instead. In summary, it is true that the perceived greatness of a political leader is more due to great challenges than superior inherent ability. The historical examples of Lincoln, Wilson, and Churchill bear this out. All were talented, but so too are all political leaders. Only the leaders that live in eventful times are remembered as great.

Assessment of Essay 1

This essay is particularly well constructed; the author begins by discussing the qualities of political leaders and how they are presented in history books. He asserts his position, "people . . . are perceived as great leaders largely because of the times in which they lived" clearly and effectively and previews the three examples he will use to support this idea. He proceeds to support his position with compelling evidence, drawing on his knowledge of three historical figures who are, by consensus, regarded as great. He is particularly effective in contrasting the example of Lincoln with that of Buchanan, who had a similar background but served as president under less trying circumstances. The writing is largely clear and direct, with skillful use of diction and few errors. For all these reasons, this essay receives a score of 6.

Issue Essay 2

Essay 2: "Outstanding," Score of 6

Keeping up with global progress is, doubtless, a desirable attribute of any society. However, to purport that the reasons certain societies may not progress at the same rate as "great" societies are their reluctance to break out of their comfort zone and their fear of the unknown is to present an overly simplistic view. Such a view does not take into consideration the set of economic, political, and cultural constraints that affect every society's ability to progress on a global scale.

Before exploring these constraints, it would be useful to examine the use of the word "great" in the above context. The concept of what makes a society great is highly subjective; some may equate greatness with military might or economic dominance, while others would emphasize cultural achievement or progress in care for less privileged citizens. Whatever one's definition of greatness, however, it is ludicrous to suggest that any society actively rejects the desire to be great. Many societies face the seemingly insurmountable struggle to maintain societal structure in the face of economic need or political upheaval; the desire for greatness can emerge only when a society's basic structure is intact.

Societies facing severe economic challenges are virtually unable to progress in areas such as medicine, military power, and agriculture even if they want to do so. Countries like Bolivia use a majority of their limited resources to maintain the status quo of their largely agrarian society. Bolivian farmers are not afraid of the unknown or passively content with their current situation, but are using all of their resources to sustain their families and maintain the social structure of their villages. Given this situation, the luxury of advancements in medicine, technology, and military power is simply not possible.

Also, societies embroiled in political upheaval, such as South Sudan, are unable to send their young and talented members to university where they can spearhead progress; the most vigorous segments of the population are required to serve in the military or to care for their families through difficult economic and political times. Maintaining societal coherence amid chaotic conditions engenders a lack of progress, as it is generally measured, but as we have seen throughout time, episodes of great drama in any given society can yield important works of art. One such example is Albert Camus' *The Stranger*, written during the French Resistance. Another, more current example is *They Poured Fire on Us from the Sky*, Benjamin Ajak's autobiographical novel about Sudanese boys fleeing that country's civil war.

Another point to consider is that, in some cases, an entire society's cultural history, including its artistic contributions, is preserved only through its living members' rich oral tradition and their active rejection of change in the realms of technology and science. This is evident when considering the Amish, whose motivation for using horse-drawn buggies and refusing access to the Internet lies, not in fear or discomfort, but in a conscious desire to sustain a traditional way of life that they find sometimes difficult but always valuable.

In conclusion, to devalue a society that is not among the most progressive in the world is to discount the contributions a so-called "unprogressive" society can make, such as artistic and cultural expression unique to that society. Progress is a valuable tool for the advancement of a society, but blindly reaching for greatness can lead to a society's downfall just as much as ignoring it altogether can. The balance between accepting a society's constraints and highlighting its strengths is what will ultimately lead to a society's greatness.

Assessment of Essay 2

This is a particularly insightful essay. The argument developed in this essay asks the reader to question certain presuppositions about what constitutes "greatness" as the term is applied to a society. Instead of merely answering the question of whether the progress of society is hindered by clinging to traditional views and obsolete ways of thinking, the essay forces the reader to reconsider what progress actually entails. Thus, the essay has the potential to elicit the cultural bias of the reader and force him to confront it. The author challenges the received notions of "great" and "progress" as "an overly simplistic view." From there, she proceeds to defend her position by examining different cultural contexts and how we might understand "greatness" within those contexts. The essay is well constructed; the author begins by providing examples of how greatness must be understood contextually. She then adds several examples, such as French and Sudanese novels, to illustrate greatness produced under conditions that would seem to block progress of any sort. The writing is clear and direct, contains few errors, and reveals skillful use of diction. For all these reasons, this essay receives a score of 6.

CHAPTER 23

THE ARGUMENT ESSAY

Introduction to the Argument Essay

The second Analytical Writing task is the Argument essay. In the Argument essay passage, the author will try to persuade you of something—the author's conclusion—by citing some evidence. The directions will ask you to decide how convincing you find the argument. Thus, you will need to analyze the argument and evaluate its use of evidence. You will also explain how a different approach or more information could make the argument stronger or weaker.

Know that every argument prompt presented on the GRE is flawed. Therefore, always read the argument with a critical eye. Look carefully for unstated *assumptions* the writer makes in order to move from evidence to conclusion. Note that unlike for the Issue essay, you are not being asked to agree or disagree with the author's *position*; instead, you must analyze the *chain of reasoning* used in the argument.

The directions for the Argument essay will begin like this:

> You will be given a short passage that presents an argument and specific instructions on how to respond to that passage. You will then have 30 minutes to plan and compose a response in which you evaluate the passage according to the specific instructions. A response to any other argument will receive a score of zero.

> Note that you are NOT being asked to present your own views on the subject. Make sure that you respond according to the specific instructions and support your evaluation with relevant reasons and/or examples.

As with the Issue essay, the directions will go on to explain the scoring criteria, and they will encourage you to plan your response before you write it and to leave time for revision. If you are familiar with these directions before Test Day, you will not have to spend any time reading them.

The next screen will present the argument you will analyze, followed by specific instructions for your essay. The argument will look like this:

> The following is a memorandum from the business manager of a television station.

> "Over the past year, our late-night news program has devoted increased time to national news and less time to weather and local news. During this time period, most of the complaints received from viewers were concerned with our station's coverage of weather and local news. In addition, local businesses that used to advertise during our late-night news program have just canceled their advertising contracts with us. Therefore, in order to attract more viewers to the program and to avoid losing any further advertising revenues, we should restore the time devoted to weather and local news to its former level."

The specific instructions for how to approach the Argument essay task will look something like this:

> Write a response in which you discuss what specific evidence is needed to evaluate the argument and explain how the evidence would weaken or strengthen the argument.

The Argument essay instructions vary from one argument to another, so make sure to read them carefully. Other instructions you may see for the Argument essay look like this:

- Write a response in which you examine the stated and/or unstated assumptions of the argument. Be sure to explain how the argument depends on these assumptions and what the implications are for the argument if the assumptions prove unwarranted.

- Write a response in which you discuss what questions would need to be answered in order to decide whether the recommendation/advice/prediction/conclusion and the argument on which it is based are reasonable. Be sure to explain how the answers to these questions would help to evaluate the recommendation/advice/prediction/conclusion.

- Write a response in which you discuss what questions would need to be answered in order to decide whether the recommendation is likely to have the predicted result. Be sure to explain how the answers to these questions would help to evaluate the recommendation.

- Write a response in which you discuss one or more alternative explanations that could rival the proposed explanation and explain how your explanation(s) can plausibly account for the facts presented in the argument.

> **THE KAPLAN METHOD FOR ANALYTICAL WRITING**
>
> **STEP 1**   Take the issue/argument apart.
>
> **STEP 2**   Select the points you will make.
>
> **STEP 3**   Organize, using Kaplan's essay templates.
>
> **STEP 4**   Type your essay.
>
> **STEP 5**   Proofread your work.

How the Kaplan Method for Analytical Writing Works

Now let's discuss how the Kaplan Method for Analytical Writing works for the Argument essay.

[STEP 1]

Take the argument apart.

The first step in analyzing an argument is to identify the conclusion, that is, the author's main point. After you've nailed down the conclusion, your next step is to characterize the evidence used to support it.

[STEP 2]

Select the points you will make.

Now that you clearly understand the argument, proceed to analyze it. The focus of your thinking will vary depending on the specific instructions for your essay, but in general, you will be addressing the assumptions, or gaps, in the author's argument. You might do this by directly identifying the assumptions, by determining what type of evidence would fill in the gaps, or by discussing whether the possibilities the author has overlooked could be better accounted for by another argument. Note, too, any terms that are ambiguous and would need definition for the argument to be clear. Finally, think of additional evidence that might be found that could strengthen or weaken the argument. Regardless of the variation in your approach, the argument will always be weak, and you will always conclude your essay by saying, in your own words, that without additional evidence, the intended audience for the argument should be skeptical of its claim.

[STEP 3]

Organize, using Kaplan's Argument essay template.

Now plan the body of your essay so that when you start writing, you can proceed confidently to deliver a well-organized critique. Review the assumptions you brainstormed in Step 2. If some of the potential flaws in the argument are closely related, consider discussing them both in the same body paragraph. You may find that you don't feel very confident discussing one or more of the points you jotted down—cross these out. Once any weak points are crossed out and related ideas grouped, decide what order you'll discuss your ideas in. Organize your body paragraph(s) by considering how the essay as a whole will flow, and write ①, ②, ③, etc. next to them on your scratch paper to indicate the order of paragraphs. Of course, you don't just want to find fault with the argument. Make sure to discuss the evidence that, if included by the author, would make the argument more convincing.

- **Paragraph 1:** Paraphrase the argument (the author's conclusion and evidence). Summarize the goal of your essay, according to the specific instructions. State your thesis, which is that the argument is unconvincing.
- **Paragraph 2:** State and evaluate an important assumption the author makes, question to be answered, or possible alternative explanation (depending on the specific instructions).
- **Paragraph 3:** State and evaluate another assumption the author makes, question to be answered, or possible alternative explanation.
- **Additional paragraphs, as time permits:** State and evaluate additional assumptions the author makes, questions to be answered, or possible alternative explanations. (Time valve #1: skip if need be.)
- **Next-to-last paragraph:** Do not stop at pointing out the flaws in the author's reasoning. Show what evidence, if it were true, would strengthen the argument. Another option is to discuss this evidence in each body paragraph, instead of devoting a paragraph to this purpose; just make sure your essay includes consideration of how the argument could be improved. (Time valve #2: combine with conclusion if need be.)
- **Last paragraph:** Conclude by summarizing your main points in a way that addresses the specific instructions. State that unless additional evidence is provided, the audience for the argument should find it unpersuasive.

[STEP 4]

Type your essay.

You shouldn't proceed with this step until you've completed the three preceding ones. Graders can give your essay a limited amount of time, so start and conclude with strong statements. Be forceful and concise with your prose and link related ideas with transition words and phrases. When you write crisply and give clear indicators of how one idea connects to the next, you will make your writing flow and earn a higher score.

[STEP 5]

Proofread your work.

Save enough time (at least a couple of minutes) to skim the entire essay, looking for small errors that are easy to fix. Having a sense of the errors you tend to make will help you identify and repair them.

How to Apply the Kaplan Method for Analytical Writing to the Argument Essay

Now let's apply the Kaplan Method for Analytical Writing to a sample Argument task:

> The problem of poor teacher performance that has plagued the state's public school systems is bound to become a good deal less serious in the future. The state has initiated comprehensive guidelines that oblige teachers to complete a number of required credits in education and educational psychology at the graduate level before being certified.

Write a response in which you examine the stated and/or unstated assumptions of the argument. Be sure to explain how the argument depends on these assumptions and what the implications are for the argument if the assumptions prove unwarranted.

[**STEP 1**]

Take the argument apart.

Conclusion (the point the argument is trying to make): In the state's public school system, poorly trained teachers will become much better trained.

Evidence (facts offered to support the conclusion): New guidelines require these teachers to complete graduate courses in education and educational psychology to be certified.

[**STEP 2**]

Select the points you will make.

Analyze the gaps between the evidence offered and the conclusion drawn. These unspoken conditions or beliefs, necessary for the conclusion to make sense in light of the evidence, are the author's assumptions.

Assumptions:

- Classroom instruction in education will improve teachers' classroom performance—this is the knowledge teachers need and the way they should learn it.
- Poor teachers haven't already had these courses.
- The teachers who get certified will be the teachers in the classroom. So already-certified poor teachers will not still be teaching in the future, and not-yet-certified teachers will be hired in public schools.
- This requirement has no unintended negative consequences, such as dissuading excellent teaching candidates from getting certified or taking resources away from existing teacher-training programs.
- The terms "poor performance," "good deal less serious," and "in the future" are unambiguous.

You may choose not to discuss all the assumptions you identify, depending on how strong you think your analysis of a given assumption would be and how much time you have to write.

Also determine what types of evidence would make the argument stronger or more logically sound. Here is evidence that would address each of the assumptions listed above:

- Evidence demonstrating that these courses will make teachers better
- Evidence that poor teachers haven't already taken these courses
- Evidence that poor teachers won't still be teaching in the future (or why they'll be better trained); evidence suggesting that teachers who get certified under the new requirement will be offered jobs
- Evidence that teachers want this training and that their tuition will be paid, without curtailing existing valuable training programs
- Explanations of what is meant by the vague terms used—how improvement will be measured and when it can be expected

[STEP 3]

Organize, using Kaplan's Argument essay template.

You have already done quite a bit of thinking about "the assumptions of the argument" and "the implications . . . if the assumptions prove unwarranted." Now you will decide in what order you'll discuss the assumptions so that your essay flows well. The only person who needs to understand your notes is you, so feel free to use abbreviations. Your scratchwork might look similar to this example:

Paragraph 1: The argument is that improved academic training, specifically graduate-level credits in education and psychology, will substantially alleviate the problem of poorly performing teachers.

Paragraph 2: The author assumes that classroom instruction in education will improve teachers' classroom performance—that this is the knowledge teachers need and/or the way they should learn it. However, classroom courses in education and educational psychology may or may not address the cause of the problem. Indeed, perhaps the poor teachers have already taken the specified courses yet are still ineffective.

Paragraph 3: The author assumes some connection exists between certification under the new guidelines and actually teaching in the classroom. However, already-certified poor teachers may still be teaching in the future (without the training), and not-yet-certified teachers may not be hired in the public schools.

Paragraph 4: If a similar state has instituted similar guidelines and seen improvement in teacher performance, then the argument would be stronger. Evidence that certification equates to actual teaching (there is a plan to remove uncertified teachers, and there's a budget to hire new teachers) would also strengthen the argument.

Paragraph 5: The author relies upon unsupported assumptions, and people who care about the public schools should doubt that teachers will soon be more effective as a result of this plan.

Now use your notes as an outline to write from.

[STEP 4]

Type your essay.

You have your ideas and a plan, so begin typing out your essay. Remember to open by showing that you understand the author's argument by paraphrasing the conclusion and evidence in the prompt. Your essay for this assignment might look like one of the following sample essays. Note: As bases for comparison, we've included one outstanding essay that deserves a score of 6 and—later in this chapter—one adequate essay that deserves a score of 4.

Sample Argument Essay 1

The argument that improved academic training, in the form of required credits in education and psychology, will substantially alleviate the problem of poorly performing teachers may seem logical at first glance. However, the author relies on unsupported assumptions about what kind of development teachers need and mechanisms for replacing poor teachers with newly certified teachers. Therefore, the argument is fundamentally flawed and unconvincing.

First, the writer assumes that the required courses will produce better teachers. In fact, the courses might be entirely irrelevant to the teachers' failings. Suppose, for example, that the main problem lies in cultural and linguistic misunderstandings between teachers and students; graduate-level courses that do not address these issues would be of little use in bridging these gaps and improving educational outcomes. Furthermore, the writer assumes that poorly performing teachers have not already taken these courses. If the state's teachers have already undergone such training but still fail to serve their students, then requiring them to take the classes again is unlikely to address the problem. In fact, the writer establishes no correlation between the teachers' classroom performance and their academic coursework.

Additionally, the writer provides no evidence that poorly performing teachers who are already certified will either stop teaching or will undergo additional training. In its current form, the argument implies that only teachers seeking certification, who may or may not be teachers already in the system, will receive the specified training. Furthermore, the author fails to establish a link between becoming certified and actually being hired in the public school system. If school systems have budget shortfalls and institute a hiring freeze, then newly certified teachers may not enter classrooms for quite some time. Unless there is a way to transition poor teachers out of the classroom and ensure teachers with proper training are soon hired, the bright future the writer envisions may be decades away.

The notion that the specified coursework will create better teachers would be strengthened by evidence that the training will address barriers to educating students. For example, if a state with similar demographics had implemented similar guidelines and then seen either improved learning as measured by standardized tests or improved teaching as documented by teacher observations, then one could conclude with more confidence that the guidelines should be implemented in this state. Also, the author would be considerably more persuasive if she showed that a plan is in place to either require all teachers to gain this certification or terminate poor performers without the certification. The author should also demonstrate that the public schools have the budgets to hire newly certified teachers so they can begin to have an effect on students.

In conclusion, the writer is not necessarily mistaken in stating that the state's comprehensive guidelines will lead to improvement in educational outcomes in public schools. After all, the additional training would probably not adversely affect classroom performance. However, to support the assertion that the guidelines will effectively solve the state's problem, the writer must first define the scope of the problem more clearly and submit more conclusive evidence that the new requirements will, in fact, improve overall teaching performance. Without such evidence, stakeholders in the public school system, including parents, administrators, and legislators, should be skeptical that education will improve anytime soon.

[STEP 5]
Proofread your work.

Be sure to allot some time after you have finished writing to review your essay. While a few grammatical and spelling errors here and there won't harm your score, having so many mistakes that the clarity of your essay suffers will prevent it from getting a high score. After all, neither the human grader nor the computer algorithm will spend extra time struggling to understand your thoughts if they're not expressed clearly. You can practice your writing skills in Chapter 21: Analytical Writing Foundations and Content Review.

Assessment of Sample Argument Essay 1: "Outstanding," Score of 6

This outstanding response demonstrates the writer's insightful analytical skills. The introduction recaps the argument and clearly states that it is flawed, noting two of the prompt's unsupported assumptions. The writer follows up with a one-paragraph examination of these two serious flaws in the argument. Specifically, the author exposes these points:

- The assumption that the required courses will produce better teachers, including the assumption that the proposed training is what teachers need and that poor teachers have not already had this training
- The lack of evidence that ineffective teachers currently working will stop teaching and be replaced by newly certified, and presumably more effective, teachers

Before wrapping up, the author details what kind of evidence would address these assumptions, bolstering the argument. Each point receives thorough and cogent development (given the time constraints) in a smooth and logically organized discourse. This essay's language is economical and error-free, with sentences that vary in length and complexity, while the diction and vocabulary stand out as both precise and expressive.

How to Apply the Kaplan Method for Analytical Writing to Another Argument Essay

Now let's apply the Kaplan Method for Analytical Writing to a second Argument task:

> The commercial airline industry in the country of Freedonia has experienced impressive growth in the past three years. This trend will surely continue in the years to come, since the airline industry will benefit from recent changes in Freedonian society: incomes are rising; most employees now receive more vacation time; and interest in travel is rising, as shown by an increase in media attention devoted to foreign cultures and tourist attractions.

Write a response in which you discuss what questions would need to be answered in order to decide whether the prediction and the argument on which it is based are reasonable. Be sure to explain how the answers to these questions would help to evaluate the prediction.

[STEP 1]

Take the argument apart.

Conclusion (the point the argument's trying to make): The growth in Freedonia's airline industry will continue.

Evidence (facts offered to support the conclusion): Incomes are up. People have more vacation time. There's more interest in travel, indicated by media coverage of foreign lands.

[**STEP 2**]

Select the points you will make.

Analyze the gaps between the evidence offered and the conclusion drawn. These unspoken conditions or beliefs, necessary for the conclusion to make sense in light of the evidence, are the author's assumptions.

Assumptions:

- Incomes will continue to rise.
- Consumers will put their money toward airline travel instead of other goods/services.
- Those who wish to travel will want to go somewhere requiring air travel.
- The increased media attention to foreign cultures and tourist attractions is due to public interest in travel or is stimulating this interest.
- The airline industry will benefit from the above changes—there is enough space at airports and available capital/labor, plus a regulatory/legal environment conducive to travel.

You may choose not to discuss all the assumptions you identify, depending on how strong you think your analysis of a given assumption would be and how much time you have to write.

Also determine what types of evidence would make the argument stronger or more logically sound. Here is evidence that would address each of the assumptions listed above:

- Evidence that the positive economic trends will continue
- Evidence that people like to travel on vacation and, specifically, that they want to go places by air
- Evidence suggesting the cause of the increased media coverage of foreign cultures is in fact due to an interest in travel or that people exposed to such content then want to travel
- If all of the above are true, evidence that the Freedonian airline industry will grow as a result

[**STEP 3**]

Organize, using Kaplan's Argument essay template.

You have already done quite a bit of thinking about "what questions would need to be answered" to "evaluate the prediction" that Freedonia's airline industry will continue to grow. Now you will decide in what order you'll discuss the author's assumptions and the evidence that would fill in these gaps so that your essay flows well. The following text models a test taker's thought process in outlining an Argument essay. Your notes will likely be much shorter than this. The only person who needs to understand your notes is you, so feel free to use abbreviations.

Paragraph 1: The conclusion is that the positive growth in Freedonia's commercial airline industry will continue. The evidence is that income, vacation time, and interest in travel are all on the rise. However, a good deal more evidence is required before one can accept the conclusion.

Paragraph 2: The author assumes that positive economic conditions will continue. However, the cause of these conditions is not explained, so we need to ask whether the factors generating economic growth are stable or likely to subside. The author also assumes that consumers will put their money toward airline travel instead of other goods/services, so we need to know more about what people are likely to do with their discretionary income.

Paragraph 3: The author assumes that the increased media attention to foreign cultures and tourist attractions is either a response to public interest in travel or is stimulating this interest. However, no connection between the topics of media coverage and a desire to travel is established. A question worth asking is whether the media are covering foreign cultures more because media executives have evidence of the public's increased interest in traveling to other countries or for some other reason. It's also worth asking whether people who see such content are more likely to travel by air.

Paragraph 4: The author assumes that the airline industry will benefit from a better economy and more interest in foreign travel. However, Freedonia's airline industry is not necessarily positioned to expand. We must ask whether the industry has the capacity to grow further—the supply of labor and capital and adequate infrastructure in the form of airport runways and terminals must be in place. Or is the better economy a result of conditions that would inhibit air travel?

Paragraph 5: If inquiries turn up evidence that contradicts the author's assumptions, then Freedonia's airline industry might not experience further growth or may even suffer a downturn in the future.

Now use your notes as an outline to write from.

[STEP 4]

Type your essay.

Sample Argument Essay 2

The author concludes that the positive growth in Freedonia's commercial airline industry will continue for years to come. The evidence is that incomes, vacation time, and interest in travel are all on the rise. While this argument may seem tenable at first glance, the conclusion relies on assumptions for which there is no clear evidence.

First, the writer assumes that the favorable economic conditions in Freedonia will continue. It is entirely possible that they will not, and that employees will have neither the money nor the vacation time necessary to pay for expensive foreign vacations. Suppose, for example, that incomes do not continue to rise. People would not have the money to spend on expensive vacations. Also, people may choose to spend their money on other luxuries besides travel. Airline industry analysts should ask whether economic factors are likely to stay positive.

Secondly, do we really know that the citizens of Freedonia will want to spend their money on vacations? Also, how do we know they will want to visit places that necessitate air travel? True, there is more media attention on foreign cultures and tourist attractions, but the argument would be stronger if the author provided evidence of a direct relationship between this media content and a desire to spend disposable income and vacation time traveling. The author does not explain where this interest comes from. Also, even if people are interested, it does not necessarily follow that they will be either willing or able to indulge that interest with extravagant holidays, since there could be an economic downturn.

Furthermore, the writer does not explain what relation, if any, these economic conditions have to the airline industry. What if the changes in Freedonian society that have led to higher incomes and more vacation time do not help the airline industry? Perhaps the economic changes are the result of protective tariffs and trade policies that make it harder for Freedonians to conduct business internationally. Perhaps the government is limiting imports and exports. Or maybe all the airports are as big as cities will allow them to be, so airlines can have no more planes. We need this information because if these possibilities could shrink the growth of the airline industry.

If the writer has made wrong assumptions regarding Freedonian society, the prospects of the commercial airline industry in Freedonia are less rosy. It would mean that there will be less income and less interest in foreign travel.

[STEP 5]
Proofread your work.

Take the last couple of minutes to catch any serious errors.

Assessment of Sample Argument Essay 2: "Adequate," Score of 4

This essay is reasonably well constructed throughout, enabling the reader to move from point to point as the writer examines the multifaceted implications of the issue. The writer correctly identifies and articulates several assumptions that the argument makes and does an adequate job of pointing out what questions need to be asked (what additional evidence is needed) to enhance the argument's cogency. The essay suffers because the writer jumps around a little bit, mixing the points about economic trends and consumer choices between the second and third paragraphs. Also, the explanation of the economic climate of Freedonia and its implications for foreign travel is slight. Finally, the author's conclusion does not do a particularly good job of restating the author's position effectively. The writing itself is direct and includes relatively few errors. Sentence structure is not particularly varied, and the word choice and vocabulary are adequate. For these reasons, the essay earns an "Adequate" score of 4.

Kaplan's Additional Tips for the Argument Essay

Be Able to Identify Any Subsidiary Conclusions

If an argument has a number of statements in it, deciding what the author's ultimate point is can be challenging. It is not unusual for a GRE Argument essay task to have subsidiary conclusions. A subsidiary conclusion is a claim supported by evidence that, in turn, is used as evidence to support a further claim. Here's an example:

> Carrying a wider selection of products will help our store attract more customers, because a recent survey of our town's residents showed they prefer to do all their shopping in one place. Therefore, stocking a greater variety of goods will make us more competitive with the store next door.

A survey is given as evidence of customer preference, and the conclusion is drawn that offering more products will attract more customers. This conclusion is then used as evidence for the main conclusion—that the proposed plan will make this store more competitive with the one next door. You can analyze the assumptions linking the survey results with the prediction that more customers will shop at the store, and you can analyze the assumptions linking the idea that attracting more customers will make the store more competitive.

If you're having trouble figuring out which conclusion is the main one, try paraphrasing each of them as "X because Y." Is this argument saying, "More competitive because more customers" or "More customers because more competitive"? It is saying the store will be more competitive (main conclusion) because it will have more customers (subsidiary conclusion).

Don't Attack the Evidence

This is important. Your task is not to agree or disagree with the author's evidence. Accept whatever evidence is presented as true, but take aim at the logical linkages between that evidence and the conclusion drawn. That means pointing out the argument's assumptions, that is, where the author makes a logical leap by assuming, rather than supporting with evidence, a connection between ideas.

Don't Attack the Conclusion

While your thesis will be that the argument is unconvincing, meaning that the conclusion is not supported by the evidence given, do not assert that the author's conclusion is untrue. After all, it is a deeply flawed argument to say the moon is far away because it looks small, since other things look small (e.g., the letters on this page) but aren't far away. Nonetheless, the moon *is* far away. The conclusion to a flawed argument may still be correct.

Use Each Step of the Method, One Step at a Time

Your goal is to identify the argument's assumptions, explain why they make the argument weak, and discuss evidence that would strengthen the argument. You can't do that unless you've figured out what the argument's assumptions are, and you can't determine the assumptions unless you know what the author's conclusion and evidence are. So start at the beginning, with Step 1: Take the Argument Apart, and proceed step-by-step.

Don't Overcomplicate Your Prose

Some people believe that writing in an unnecessarily complicated way makes their analysis sound more complex, but this is not true. In the Analytical Writing section, be as clear and direct in your writing as possible. Using overly long sentences puts you at risk of losing control of the sentence and making a grammatical error, not to mention confusing the reader. And using big words for the sake of using big words puts you at risk of using the vocabulary incorrectly. Do write in a formal academic style, but use a style that is natural for you; don't contort your prose to conform to some imaginary ideal.

Make Sure Your Conclusion Is Strong

It's important to end your essay with a strong statement about the inadequacy of the author's argument. If you are concerned about running out of time before you have a chance to write a strong conclusion, consider writing a concluding sentence after you finish your first paragraph. After all, you know how your essay will end—with a restatement of your thesis about how the argument rests on unsupported assumptions and is thus unpersuasive—so you can write the ending now. Try to use different words than you used to state your position in the first paragraph. Ideally, you will finish typing your essay (Step 4) with a few minutes to spare for proofreading, and then you can elaborate on your conclusion if you wish. However, you can write your body paragraphs in a more relaxed frame of mind, knowing that your essay has a solid ending.

Argument Essay Practice Set

Argument Essay 1

30 Minutes

Length: 1 essay

Directions: You will be given a short passage that presents an argument and specific instructions on how to respond to that passage. You will then have 30 minutes to plan and compose a response in which you evaluate the passage according to the specific instructions. A response to any other argument will receive a score of zero.

Note that you are NOT being asked to present your own views on the subject. Make sure that you respond according to the specific instructions and support your evaluation with relevant reasons and/or examples.

Before you begin writing, you may want to think for a few minutes about the argument passage and the specific task instructions and then plan your response. Be sure to develop your response fully and organize it coherently, but leave time to reread what you have written and make any revisions you think are necessary.

> The following appeared in the City Council Proceedings section of the local newspaper in Smithville.
>
> "The city council of Smithville has recommended making changes to police procedures to improve the visibility of the police force. These changes include hiring more police officers, budgeting more funds for police overtime, and directing officers to patrol significantly more often on foot rather than from their patrol cars. These improvements in visibility would significantly lower the crime rate in Smithville and make its citizens feel safer."

Write a response in which you discuss what questions would need to be answered in order to decide whether the recommendation is likely to have the predicted result. Be sure to explain how the answers to these questions would help to evaluate the recommendation.

Argument Essay 2

30 Minutes

Length: 1 essay

Directions: You will be given a short passage that presents an argument and specific instructions on how to respond to that passage. You will then have 30 minutes to plan and compose a response in which you evaluate the passage according to the specific instructions. A response to any other argument will receive a score of zero.

Note that you are NOT being asked to present your own views on the subject. Make sure that you respond according to the specific instructions and support your evaluation with relevant reasons and/or examples.

Before you begin writing, you may want to think for a few minutes about the argument passage and the specific task instructions and then plan your response. Be sure to develop your response fully and organize it coherently, but leave time to reread what you have written and make any revisions you think are necessary.

> Tusk University should build a new recreational facility, both to attract new students and to better serve the needs of our current student body. Tusk projects that enrollment will double over the next 10 years, based on current trends. The new student body is expected to reflect a much higher percentage of commuter students than we currently enroll. This will make the existing facilities inadequate. Moreover, the cost of health and recreation club membership in our community has increased rapidly in recent years. Thus, students will find it much more advantageous to make use of the facilities on campus. Finally, an attractive new recreation center would make prospective students, especially athletically gifted ones, more likely to enroll at Tusk.

Write a response in which you examine the stated and/or unstated assumptions of the argument. Be sure to explain how the argument depends on these assumptions and what the implications are for the argument if the assumptions prove unwarranted.

Argument Essay Practice Set Answers and Explanations

Argument Essay Sample Essays and Assessments

What follows are top-scoring sample essays for each of the practice prompts. Note how the authors adhere to the Kaplan Method for Analytical Writing.

Essay 1 : "Outstanding," Score of 6

The city council of Smithville believes that increasing the visibility of its police force will reduce crime and increase the safety of its citizens. However, the memo provides no evidence to support this argument, and the city council may not be taking other variables, alternative solutions, or the citizens' desires into consideration.

The Smithville city council assumes that crime persists because the city's police force has too low a profile, but the memo never cites evidence to support this position. The council could do something as simple yet effective as asking the town librarian to review published studies to see whether a parallel exists between a high police presence and reduced crime rates. It could also hire an independent research firm to determine whether a correlation exists between Smithville crime scenes and a lack of police activity.

The council should consider other factors that might account for the current crime rate. The police force may be undertrained or poorly managed. If so, adding more officers or encouraging officers to work longer hours could actually compound the problem. Here again, research could be a vital ally in the council's case: What have other towns with similar problems identified as causal factors? What training do their police forces receive? How are they deployed, on foot or in patrol cars? Answering questions like these might help clarify a solution to the town's problem. The council should also research historic solutions to the problem: How have towns like theirs reduced a growing crime rate? This research could bolster the council's position or uncover alternative, less costly solutions to crime-fighting.

The council also assumes that a higher police presence automatically reduces citizen concerns over crime, but it doesn't take into consideration the relationship between the residents and the police. Some communities regard police officers with a great deal of distrust, and that attitude may be pronounced in a community where the police force is perceived as unable to cope with crime. Has the community itself, through its elected leaders, the police chief, op-ed pieces in the newspaper, or community groups, expressed a need for a stronger police force? The memo never says.

As it currently stands, the Smithville city council's memo announces a recommendation that appears to have been made in a vacuum. To convince citizens that bolstering the police force and changing patrol procedures is the way to fight crime, the memo needs to state how the council arrived at this decision. Only then can citizens feel that the council is taking the right course of action.

Assessment of Essay 1

The author successfully identifies and analyzes this argument's recommendation: that the way for Smithville to lower its crime rate and improve citizen safety is to increase police visibility.

In the opening paragraph, the essay restates the argument and then cites its unsupported assumptions. In the following four paragraphs, the author insightfully discusses the assumptions and perceptively suggests what information would help in evaluating the recommendation.

Specifically, the author cites these points undermining the argument:

- The assumption that a higher police profile will lower the crime rate
- The assumption that no other cause exists for the high crime rate but low police visibility
- The lack of research into historically successful alternative solutions (the assumption that no such alternatives exist)
- The assumption that the town's citizens will agree that the council's solution is the right one and thus "feel safer"

Throughout the essay, the author uses well-organized paragraphs—each starts with a broad statement followed by supporting statements—and her ideas logically flow from one sentence to the next. She uses succinct diction and alternates complex and simple sentences.

The essay concludes strongly by summarizing the evidence necessary for the council to authoritatively recommend that higher police visibility will reduce crime and increase citizen safety. The essay remains focused and clear throughout, earning a score of 6.

Argument Essay 2

Argument Essay 2 : "Strong," Score of 5

The author contends that Tusk University should build a new recreational facility to attract new students, and to better serve the needs of its current students. The argument also asserts that this will lead to greater enrollment over the next ten years. While it may prove to be a worthy project, the argument appears to rely on assumptions that lack conclusive supporting evidence. The writer would be well advised to address these issues to make the point of the argument more cogent and convincing.

First and foremost, the writer assumes, without providing any evidence, that recreational facilities will be a significant factor in attracting and serving students interested in Tusk.

This begs the question of the role of recreation and/or athletic facilities in the matriculation and retention of students in institutions of higher learning. In the absence of any reference to the academic mission of the University, or even of the role that the facility might have in attracting, retaining, or helping to fund areas more central to that mission, the writer's conclusion appears unsupported.

Secondly, the writer assumes, again without citing specific evidence, that the projected doubling of enrollment will by itself lead to an increase in demand for the new recreational facilities proposed. Even if the facilities would indeed be attractive relative to those available off campus, the author has provided no proof that a substantial part of the increased or even current enrollment would be inclined to consider the new facilities an asset to their education. Suppose for a moment that this enlarged commuter-based enrollment turns out to be largely made up of part-time students with jobs and family demands away from the campus. Would such a student body see the new facility as a priority? Would the schedules of such students allow them to take advantage of the improvement?

Finally, the author fails to describe what specific services, programs, and amenities the proposed new facility will provide, how and at what cost relative to facilities available elsewhere these will be made available to the university community, and how the financial burden of both building and operating the new center will be offset. Beyond these issues endemic to the campus setting, the writer presents no overview of the environmental, social, and public relations aspects of the project in a larger context, either intra- or extra-collegiate.

The issues raised here could easily be addressed by providing evidence that backs up the author's claim. By assembling sufficient and specific demographic and economic evidence to support the argument's questionable assumptions, the writer may not only be able to overcome the limitations of the current argument, but provide a rationale for the proposal beyond the terms offered here.

Assessment of Essay 2

This essay adequately targets the argument's unstated assumptions and inadequate evidence. The essay identifies and critiques the gaps in the author's chain of logic and reasoning that result from assuming the following:

- That recreational facilities will be a significant factor in attracting and serving students interested in Tusk
- That doubling enrollment will by itself lead to an increase in demand for, and presumably in use of, the new recreational facilities

The writer clearly grasps the argument's central weaknesses. But although the ideas are clear, the essay lacks transitional phrases and is not well organized. The writing feels rushed and lacks proofreading. While the writer demonstrates a better-than-adequate control of language and ably conforms to the conventions of written English, this 5 essay suffers from turgid prose and a lack of the more thorough development of a typical 6 response.

CHAPTER 24

ANALYTICAL WRITING PRACTICE SETS

In this chapter, you will find two pairs of Analytical Writing prompts to practice on. Each pair consists of an Analyze an Issue task and an Analyze an Argument task. For a test-like experience, write your essays on a computer with spell check and grammar check turned off.

When you complete the essays, read and analyze the sample essays to gauge whether your essays are similarly strong and would earn a high score.

Review of the Kaplan Method for Analytical Writing

Before starting your practice essays, review the steps and strategies you have studied for responding to each type of Analytical Writing task efficiently, thoughtfully, and coherently.

STEP 1   Take the issue/argument apart.

STEP 2   Select the points you will make.

STEP 3   Organize, using Kaplan's essay templates.

STEP 4   Type your essay.

STEP 5   Proofread your work.

Applying the Kaplan Method to Each Essay Task

	ISSUE ESSAY	ARGUMENT ESSAY
1. Take the issue/ argument apart. **2 minutes**	Identify the pro and con sides of the issue and what the thesis statement would be for each.	Identify the argument's conclusion and evidence.
2. Select the points you will make. **5 minutes**	Brainstorm reasons to support each side of the issue. Think of an example that illustrates each reason. Pick the side you will argue.	Identify the assumptions the argument's author has made. Why might the conclusion not follow from the evidence? Brainstorm the evidence that, if true, would strengthen the argument.
3. Organize, using Kaplan's essay templates. **1 minute**	For the side you will argue, combine any points that are very similar. Eliminate any weak ideas. Number your remaining points from strongest to weakest. Pick one point from the other side, which you will rebut.	Combine points that are very similar. Eliminate any weak ideas. Number your remaining points from strongest to weakest.
4. Type your essay. **20 minutes**	¶ **1:** Paraphrase the issue in terms of your thesis, which is your position on the issue. ¶ **2:** Explain one reason for your position. Use logic and illustrate with example(s). ¶ **3:** Explain another argument for your position, using logic and example(s). . . . Repeat as you have points to make and time to make them. ¶ **Next-to-last:** Acknowledge a point for the other side, but rebut it. ¶ **Last:** Conclude that your position is the correct one. Recap the points made above in fresh language if you have time.	¶ **1:** Paraphrase the argument's conclusion and evidence. State your thesis, which is that the argument is unconvincing. ¶ **2:** Explain one flaw in the argument. Use logic and illustrate the implications of the flaw with example(s). ¶ **3:** Explain another flaw in the argument. Use logic and example(s). . . . Repeat as you have points to make and time to make them. ¶ **Next-to-last:** Explain what evidence would strengthen the argument, if the author used it. ¶ **Last:** Conclude that the argument is not persuasive. Recap the points above in fresh language if you have time.
5. Proofread your work. **2 minutes**	Look for and fix errors of grammar, usage, spelling, and punctuation. Add transition words where helpful. Replace imprecise or wordy language with specific, concise language.	Look for and fix errors of grammar, usage, spelling, and punctuation. Add transition words where helpful. Replace imprecise or wordy language with specific, concise language.

Analytical Writing Practice Set 1

Analyze an Issue Instructions

You will be given a brief quotation that states or implies an issue of general interest and specific instructions on how to respond to that issue. You will then have 30 minutes to plan and compose a response according to the specific instructions. A response to any other issue will receive a score of zero.

Make sure that you respond according to the specific instructions and support your position on the issue with reasons and examples drawn from such areas as your reading, experience, observations, and/or academic studies.

Keep in mind that your response will be evaluated based on how well you:

- Respond to the specific task instructions
- Consider the complexities of the issue
- Organize, develop, and express your ideas
- Support your ideas with relevant reasons and/or examples
- Control the elements of standard written English

Before you begin writing, you may want to think for a few minutes about the issue and the specific task instructions and then plan your response. Be sure to develop your position fully and organize it coherently, but leave time to reread what you have written and make any revisions you think are necessary.

Issue Topic

Claim: Restaurants should be required to display nutritional information about the food they serve.

Reason: This knowledge will help diners make healthy choices and reduce their risk of diet-related health problems.

Write a response in which you discuss the extent to which you agree or disagree with the claim and the reason on which that claim is based.

Analyze an Argument Instructions

You will be given a short passage that presents an argument and specific instructions on how to respond to that passage. You will then have 30 minutes to plan and compose a response in which you evaluate the passage according to the specific instructions. A response to any other argument will receive a score of zero.

Note that you are NOT being asked to present your own views on the subject. Make sure that you respond according to the specific instructions and support your evaluation with relevant reasons and/or examples.

Keep in mind that your response will be evaluated based on how well you:

- Respond to the specific task instructions
- Identify and analyze features of the argument relevant to the assigned task
- Organize, develop, and express your ideas
- Support your ideas with relevant reasons and/or examples
- Control the elements of standard written English

Before you begin writing, you may want to think for a few minutes about the argument passage and the specific task instructions and then plan your response. Be sure to develop your response fully and organize it coherently, but leave time to reread what you have written and make any revisions you think are necessary.

Argument Topic

The following appeared as part of a promotional campaign to sell advertising on channels provided by the local cable television company.

> "Advertising with Cable Communications Corp. is the most effective way to increase a company's profits. Recently, Adams Car Dealership began advertising with Cable Communications, and over a subsequent 30-day period, the dealership's sales rose 15% over sales the previous month. In addition, the company's customer ratings show that people who purchase new cars from Adams are more satisfied with the quality and performance of their vehicles than are car dealership customers on average. Customer satisfaction has been found to be a key factor in positive word-of-mouth publicity."

Write a response in which you examine the stated and/or unstated assumptions of the argument. Be sure to explain how the argument depends on these assumptions and what the implications are for the argument if the assumptions prove unwarranted.

Analytical Writing Practice Set 2

Analyze an Issue Instructions

You will be given a brief quotation that states or implies an issue of general interest and specific instructions on how to respond to that issue. You will then have 30 minutes to plan and compose a response according to the specific instructions. A response to any other issue will receive a score of zero.

Make sure that you respond according to the specific instructions and support your position on the issue with reasons and examples drawn from such areas as your reading, experience, observations, and/or academic studies.

Keep in mind that your response will be evaluated based on how well you:

- Respond to the specific task instructions
- Consider the complexities of the issue
- Organize, develop, and express your ideas
- Support your ideas with relevant reasons and/or examples
- Control the elements of standard written English

Before you begin writing, you may want to think for a few minutes about the issue and the specific task instructions and then plan your response. Be sure to develop your position fully and organize it coherently, but leave time to reread what you have written and make any revisions you think are necessary.

Issue Topic

> Some people believe that all results of publicly funded scientific studies should be made available to the general public free of charge. Others believe the scientific journals that publish such studies have a right to make money by charging for access to their content.

Write a response in which you discuss which view more closely aligns with your own position and explain your reasoning for the position you take. In developing and supporting your position, you should address both of the views presented.

Analyze an Argument Instructions

You will be given a short passage that presents an argument and specific instructions on how to respond to that passage. You will then have 30 minutes to plan and compose a response in which you evaluate the passage according to the specific instructions. A response to any other argument will receive a score of zero.

Note that you are NOT being asked to present your own views on the subject. Make sure that you respond according to the specific instructions and support your evaluation with relevant reasons and/or examples.

Keep in mind that your response will be evaluated based on how well you:

- Respond to the specific task instructions
- Identify and analyze features of the argument relevant to the assigned task
- Organize, develop, and express your ideas
- Support your ideas with relevant reasons and/or examples
- Control the elements of standard written English

Before you begin writing, you may want to think for a few minutes about the argument passage and the specific task instructions and then plan your response. Be sure to develop your response fully and organize it coherently, but leave time to reread what you have written and make any revisions you think are necessary.

Argument Topic

The following appeared in *Ram*, the Altamonte High School student newspaper.

> "Of Altamonte students polled, 65% say they participate in an intramural, a varsity, or a community sports team. Being a member of a sports team keeps one fit and healthy and promotes an active lifestyle. Since the majority of students are taking care of their physical fitness after or outside of school, Altamonte High should eliminate physical education classes and put more resources into the development of its intramural and varsity sports teams."

Write a response in which you discuss what specific evidence is needed to evaluate the argument and explain how the evidence would weaken or strengthen the argument.

Analytical Writing Practice Set 1 Answers and Explanations

Analytical Writing Practice Set 1: Sample Essays and Assessments

Issue Essay

"Outstanding" Essay (score of 6)

Requiring restaurants to publish nutritional information about their meals, such as fat and calorie content, has its detractors. They say that disclosing the makeup of meals may alarm diners, driving them away and reducing the restaurants' income. They also balk at the cost of determining these data for every item on the menu. However, the benefits of such a program far outweigh its drawbacks. As noted by the author, such disclosure would let restaurant patrons make informed eating choices, an important consideration given what we know about the significant effects of unhealthy diet on chronic illness and premature death. In addition, providing this information may actually benefit the restaurants in terms of both revenue and public relations.

A healthy diet has been found to contribute to better overall health; studies show, for example, that a healthy diet lowers cholesterol and reduces the risk of heart disease. In contrast, a poor diet, one rich in fat and calories, contributes to obesity and thus to diabetes, heart attack, and stroke. Even some cancers have been linked to obesity. All of these illnesses can be disabling or even fatal to the individual, and all contribute to high health care costs. Because people are eating out with increasing frequency, it makes sense to provide information to guide their food choices in restaurants. People already choose their meals on the basis of whether they want steak or seafood, soup or salad, and mashed potatoes or french fries. Now they will also be able to choose whether to eat healthily or not.

Restaurant owners are understandably concerned that disclosing information perceived as negative could deter people from patronizing their establishment. After all, people go to a restaurant to enjoy themselves, not to read a lecture about grams of saturated fat. If this occurred, not only would these businesses suffer financially, but also people would not benefit from the nutritional information on the menus. This concern is unfounded, however. First, if all restaurants have to comply with the law, no single business will suffer. Second, restaurants would not be at a disadvantage with respect to grocery stores, where almost all the food already has nutritional information on the label; indeed, the law would simply bring restaurants into parity with food stores. Finally, knowing that high calorie counts may reduce their food's popularity, restaurants may figure out healthier ways to prepare meals, thus attracting more diners and benefiting those same diners.

Determining the fat and calorie content of meals will cost restaurants money initially, but disclosing this information will yield returns over the long term as people will feel confident that they are in charge of their fat and calorie intake. Thus, consumers will have a sense of control and be more likely, rather than less so, to eat at a restaurant. When restaurants become places where people can make informed choices about their health, these businesses will reap the benefit of public good will.

Requiring restaurants to post nutrition information would benefit both owners and patrons. It would have immediate and lasting positive effects on diners who choose to eat healthily. Furthermore, it would instill a sense of control and confidence in diners, who would appreciate knowing what they are eating, thus helping to sustain the trend of dining out more often.

Analyze an Issue Essay Assessment

This essay addresses the task and is well constructed. The essay writer begins by acknowledging arguments against requiring restaurants to disclose nutritional information and then states a clear opinion, expressing support for the stated position and the evidence given in support of it. ("As noted by the author, such disclosure would let restaurant patrons make informed eating choices, an important consideration given what we know about the significant effects of unhealthy diet on chronic illness and premature death.") The writer proceeds to support that position with compelling evidence about health, business operations, and public relations. The reasons given are logical and supported by relevant examples. The essay addresses the arguments against adopting the proposed regulation throughout, rather than in one paragraph near the end, and that is a perfectly acceptable approach. The writing is clear and direct, with a variety of sentence structure and vocabulary. For all these reasons, this essay receives a score of 6.

Argument Essay

"Outstanding" Essay (score of 6)

Cable Communications Corporation argues that all businesses would realize increased profits from advertising with the cable television company. As evidence for this assertion, the cable company cites the experience of Adams Car Dealership, a recent advertiser. After beginning to advertise with Cable Communications, Adams saw a 15% increase in sales over the previous month. In addition, the car dealership's customers are more satisfied than average.

Although Adams is experiencing some success, the argument for advertising with the cable company is unconvincing because it makes unwarranted assumptions.

To begin with, the argument presupposes that the example of Adams Car Dealership is relevant for other businesses. Car dealerships may enjoy a particular advantage from advertising because car buyers are willing to shop around to make such a major purchase. The same may not be said, for example, of a drugstore. In general, people will pick up aspirin and shampoo at the nearest store, regardless of which stores they have seen advertised, because these products are commodities and cost relatively little. Thus, advertising might be much more effective for a car dealership than for a drugstore or many other businesses. The argument would be more persuasive if it provided examples of different kinds of businesses—those selling big-ticket items and inexpensive items, marketing to retail and wholesale customers, and representing diverse industries.

Moreover, the author assumes a link between Adams Car Dealership's success and its decision to advertise with Cable Communications, but this linkage is poorly established. Adams' improved sales could have been due to a seasonal increase in car sales that always happens during that month. Alternatively, perhaps Adams put its cars on sale that month and attracted many customers with lower prices. Or maybe Adams benefited from the great word-of-mouth publicity it garners from its satisfied customers. In addition, the time frame is not definitive: Adams had higher sales in some later 30-day period but not necessarily immediately after it began advertising on the cable channels. Perhaps the company placed ads for some time before any sales increase occurred; it is even possible that the company began advertising, saw a steep sales decline, and then had a 15 percent sales increase that did not bring revenues back to their pre-advertising level. Without more definitive evidence showing that advertising with Cable Communications led to increased sales, and that the sales increase was not due to some other reason, a business owner should be skeptical of the cable company's claim. Moreover, the claim is that advertising will lead to greater profits, but the evidence is only about Adams' sales, as though one can assume sales translate into profits. If the cost of advertising exceeded the additional revenues earned, then Adams did not have increased profits.

The promotional text also presupposes that business owners do not have a better option for advertising. The argument is that advertising on these cable channels is "the most effective," but such a judgment does not hold up if advertising in other media would have been more effective. Perhaps Adams would have experienced even better sales had it advertised in print or online. For business owners to make an informed decision regarding their advertising expenditures, they need to see a comparison between results from advertising with Cable Communications and other marketing activities.

To convince business owners that they should advertise with Cable Communications, the promotional campaign should show that a wide variety of businesses have benefited by advertising with the company. Furthermore, it should show that the success was due to the ads and not to unrelated factors and that profits would not have been even greater had the companies invested their marketing dollars elsewhere. For example, Cable Communications could present data showing that an advertiser had higher sales the 30 days immediately after beginning to advertise and that these sales were higher than for the same period one year earlier. The cable company could also compare its clients' sales trends to those of other businesses in the same industries. Finally, the data should not be about sales but about the bottom line: profits. After all, advertising costs money, so the return needs to justify the investment.

To conclude, the promotional campaign by Cable Communications turns upon unstated presuppositions. Unless the company provides additional evidence regarding the superior ability of cable advertising to boost profits for companies of different sorts, business owners should find this pitch to advertise with Cable Communications unconvincing.

Analyze an Argument Essay Assessment

The author successfully identifies and analyzes this argument's main contention: that advertising with Cable Communications will increase the profits of every business.

In the opening paragraph, the essay restates the argument's conclusion and evidence and then cites its unsupported assumptions. In the following four paragraphs, the author insightfully explains the implications of these assumptions for the argument and perceptively suggests evidence that would strengthen the cable company's case.

Specifically, the author cites these points undermining the argument:

1. The one-size-fits-all fallacy that all businesses would benefit from cable advertising based on the example of one company
2. The assumption that a 15 percent increase in sales was caused by the advertising and not merely correlated with it
3. The assumption that an increase in sales is equivalent to an increase in profits
4. The assumption that, even if advertising here works well, it is the best marketing strategy

Throughout the essay, the author uses well-organized paragraphs—each starts with a broad statement followed by supporting details—and the ideas logically flow from one sentence to the next. An appropriate use of key words helps the reader follow transitions within and between points. The writing is correct, clear, and concise, using a variety of sentence structures and vocabulary.

The essay concludes strongly by making specific suggestions that would improve the cable company's argument and then stating that, without such evidence, the argument is unconvincing. The essay remains focused and clear throughout, earning a score of 6.

Analytical Writing Practice Set 2 Answers and Explanations

Analytical Writing Practice Set 2: Sample Essays and Assessments

Issue Essay

"Outstanding" Essay (score of 6)

Scientific journals that charge a subscription or newsstand price should amend this practice to avail the public of results of publicly funded research. The reasoning here is twofold: first, the public's taxes have paid for all or a part of the research, and second, scientific results should always be readily accessible to all interested parties.

A publicly funded project means, in effect, that the taxpayers own the research and therefore have a right to the results free of charge. Granted, many research projects are funded by a combination of private contributions, institutional grants, and public monies. Even when this is the case, the public should not be punished for being one part of a coalition that may include profit-making groups. Perhaps the research committee will need to include in its duties finding venues to make research results readily available at no charge. The mere fact of public financial support of research, in whole or in part, entitles taxpayers to access to the fruits of that research.

Another reason to let the public see results at no charge is that from a broad philosophical standpoint, people should be allowed access to scientific information. Innovation in the private sector necessitates access to the latest research and technological developments. A result of making such research widely available is that the process of innovation becomes self-sustaining. New discoveries feed new developments in the industry or service sector, which in turn fuel further research. Publishers of scientific journals may respond to such an argument by saying that they need to charge a fee in order to cover their expenses of editing and formatting articles, maintaining the websites where they appear, and printing and mailing hard copies of the journals. With that said, the government and private sponsors of a project should cover these expenses, including them in their budgeted overhead, in the same proportion as their support of the research. Additionally, popular science magazines, using their revenues from advertisers and subscribers, might pay journals for the right to reprint the research for their lay audience, who would appreciate getting a look at academic studies curated for their significance and relevance.

In addition, science is by and large an international endeavor, with new discoveries fueled by cooperation among far-flung researchers, yet scientists in certain oppressive countries are not able to participate in this productive exchange of ideas. For example, scientists in the former Soviet Union were not allowed to read about scientific endeavors outside of the USSR. This enforced ignorance led to decades of wasted money, effort, and time as researchers were unable to learn from others' mistakes and successes. Scientists in fields from aeronautics to zoology need access to professional journals to stay abreast of cutting-edge information. Ethically speaking, every scientist is charged with nurturing scientific debate and furthering knowledge that will help people. Wider availability of published research will promote more scientific advancement in every corner of the world, helping scientists fulfill their charge.

Some scientists and government officials will undoubtedly refuse to allow sensitive or secret scientific information to be available to the public for free. Indeed, governments should not disseminate research publicly if doing so would compromise national security. However, the research under discussion is what is already published in scientific journals and available, at a price, for public consumption.

In conclusion, scientific journals that charge a subscription or newsstand price are profiting unjustifiably when they publish wholly or partially publicly funded research results. These journals need to adjust this practice for the benefit of the public and other professionals. The public's taxes have paid for all or a part of the research, and for ethical reasons, research results must be readily accessible to all interested parties.

Analyze an Issue Essay Assessment

From the beginning, the author takes a specific position on the issue and supports it, using strong examples and reasons. The author includes counterarguments, including the potential cost of publication that the scientific journals must foot, thereby addressing both views presented in the prompt. However, the author provides clear rebuttals with powerful supporting evidence. The inclusion of the Soviet example gives a vivid illustration of the consequences of not freely sharing information, and it appeals to the reader's sense of justice and ethics. Paragraphs are well organized and well developed, and the writer demonstrates a mastery of formal standard English. For all these reasons, this essay receives a score of 6.

Argument Essay

"Outstanding" Essay (score of 6)

The student newspaper article falls short of presenting a convincing argument for eliminating all physical education classes at Altamonte High School and putting more resources into the development of intramural and varsity sports. First, the article's author relies on a statistic that may not represent the population of students under consideration. Second, the article goes beyond what is supported by the evidence, reaching the drastic recommendation that "Altamonte High should eliminate all physical education classes."

The author's primary evidence is a survey in which 65 percent of Altamonte students polled said they participate in sports outside of physical education classes. However, maybe only 100 out of 2,400 students were polled; such a small sample can lead to biased results. Maybe mostly athletes responded to the poll since they were the students most interested in the topic. Or maybe only seniors, who tend to have more intramural and varsity members than freshmen, answered the questions. Notwithstanding these potential problems with the data, the author assumes that the poll respondents reflect the sports participation of the student body.

The author also overlooks the extent to which the 65 percent of polled students participate in intramural, varsity, and community teams, assuming that "participate" equates to getting all the exercise one needs. In fact, some students might be on multiple teams, while others might be on the roster of a team but rarely be selected by the coach to play. Moreover, some positions in some sports require little physical exertion. If the students are soccer forwards or football running backs, they are getting plenty of exercise, but if they are goalies or place kickers, they are getting much less. Sometimes a player is injured and cannot play for a period of time, getting no exercise. Finally, many sports are seasonal, but fitness requires regular exercise year-round.

The article also bases its conclusion in part on an unfounded opinion: Just because some members of sports teams are fit and healthy does not mean that all are. Even if everyone on a team is physically active, there are other dimensions of fitness. The sport might not promote all three of cardiovascular endurance, strength, and flexibility. It is possible that none of these out-of-school activities teach nutrition, personal safety, how to avoid drug abuse and eating disorders, and other physical education goals beyond competition and teamwork.

In addition, the argument assumes that if a majority of people are getting some benefit from a program, then that program is working well enough. Even if 65 percent of all Altamonte students, and not just those who responded to the poll, are participating in extracurricular sports, that may not be satisfactory. After all, physical fitness in youth is highly correlated with an active lifestyle throughout life, and being active is in turn related to a wide range of positive health outcomes. Eliminating physical education classes, as the author suggests, would leave over a third of students without an exercise option, and if they currently eschew sports teams for whatever reason, they may well continue to do so.

In conclusion, the Ram article would be more convincing if more data from the poll were provided to show that the result accurately represents the student body. The argument would also be stronger if more details were given about how active the members of the intramural, varsity, and community teams are ("They stretch for 15 minutes and run for 30 minutes during warm-up") and whether health and fitness are addressed comprehensively by the coaches in these programs. The author of the article also needs to justify why 65 percent, if this is indeed a valid statistic, is a sufficient proportion of students to justify eliminating the physical education classes on which the other 35 percent rely.

In the absence of such evidence, the school administration should maintain the physical education curriculum rather than eliminate it. However, given students' potentially broad participation in other activities, research into how those activities could supplement or replace classes during the school day should be conducted. If extracurricular sports teams are in fact sufficient to promote physical well-being in teenagers and if enough students could participate regularly, then the article's conclusion would warrant serious consideration.

Analyze an Argument Essay Assessment

The author successfully addresses several flaws of the argument in this response, including the potentially faulty or misused statistic and various unsupported assumptions.

The author cites the following evidence as potentially flawed:

- The reliance on poll data that may be biased because the polled students could be a small and/or unrepresentative sample
- The generalization that students who participate in sports teams are healthier and fitter than those who do not
- The illogical conclusion that if something is good for a majority of students, it is sufficiently beneficial for all students

Throughout the essay, the paragraphs are well constructed and support the author's contention that the argument is flawed.

The essay concludes by suggesting evidence that would improve the article and evaluating the article in terms of the absence or presence of such evidence, thus fulfilling the task stated in the prompt. The suggestions for additional evidence would definitely address the flaws noted and strengthen the argument. The essay maintains focus and clarity throughout, earning a score of 6.

PART FIVE

PRACTICE TEST

CHAPTER 25

PRACTICE TEST

Before taking this practice test, find a quiet place where you can work without interruption for 3 hours and 45 minutes. Make sure you have a comfortable desk, several pencils, and scratch paper. Time yourself according to the time limits shown at the beginning of each section. For the most accurate results, you should go through all five sections in one sitting. When you're finished, consult the answer key and explanations found in the next chapter to see how you performed. We've also provided a scoring scale that will give you an approximation of your scoring ability. Good luck!

While the practice test you are about to take will provide you with a rough idea of the kind of questions you'll face on your official GRE, keep in mind that nearly all GRE examinations are administered on a computer. As you learned in Chapter 2, that means that based on your performance in the first section of both Quantitative and Verbal Reasoning, the computer-based GRE will produce a low, medium, or high difficulty second section. Since the printed practice test you are about to take does not adapt based on your performance, it is different in kind and degree than the actual computer-based GRE you will likely see on Test Day. For a more accurate representation of the GRE, and to see a more accurate reflection of your scoring abilities, we recommend that you take your Kaplan online practice test.

In general, the way you approach this printed practice test will be very similar to the way you approach the official computer-based GRE. On the actual test, you will be given scrap paper that you can use to jot down important words or phrases or to calculate mathematical problems. We recommend you do that here. Also, on the official GRE you will have the ability to mark questions within a section to return to them later if time allows. It would be a good idea to use that same approach in this practice test. Finally, we suggest that you write your essays if you're going to take the paper-based GRE, and type your essays if you plan to take the computer-based GRE, to better simulate the Test Day experience. You should type your essays with spell-check and grammar-check off.

Analytical Writing 1: Analyze an Issue

30 Minutes — 1 Question

Directions: You will be given a brief quotation that states or implies a topic of general interest, along with explicit instructions on how to respond to that topic. Your response will be evaluated according to how well you do the following:

- Respond to the specific directions the task gives you
- Reflect on the complexities of the issue
- Organize and develop your thoughts
- Support your reasoning with relevant examples
- Express yourself in standard written English

  Scientific theories, which most people consider as 'fact,' almost invariably prove to be inaccurate. Thus, one should look upon any information described as 'factual' with skepticism since it may well be proven false in the future.

Write an essay in which you take a position on the statement above. In developing and supporting your viewpoint, consider ways in which the statement might or might not hold true.

Analytical Writing 2: Analyze an Argument

30 Minutes — 1 Question

Directions: You will be presented with a short passage that asserts an argument or position, along with explicit instructions on how to respond to the passage. Your response will be evaluated according to how well you do the following:

- Respond to the specific directions the task gives you
- Analyze and interpret important elements of the passage
- Organize and develop your analysis
- Support your reasoning with relevant examples
- Express yourself in standard written English

The following appeared in a memorandum from the owner of the Juniper Café, a small, local coffee shop in the downtown area of a small American city:

"We must reduce overhead here at the café. Instead of opening at 6 a.m. weekdays, we will now open at 8 a.m. On weekends, we will only be open from 9 a.m. until 4 p.m. The decrease in hours of operations will help save money because we won't be paying for utilities, employee wages, or other operating costs during the hours we are closed. This is the best strategy for us to save money and remain in business without having to eliminate jobs."

Write a response in which you discuss what questions would need to be answered in order to assess the reasonableness of both the prediction and the argument upon which it is based. Be sure to explain how the answers to these questions would help to evaluate the prediction.

**You have finished this section and now will begin
the next section.**

Verbal Reasoning 1

30 Minutes — 20 Questions

Directions: For each item, select the best answer choice using the directions given.

If a question has answer choices with **ovals**, then the correct answer will be a single choice. If a question's answer choices have **squares**, the correct answer may have more than one choice. Be sure to read all directions carefully.

For each blank, select an answer choice from the corresponding column of choices. Fill in the blank in such a way that it best completes the text.

1. The oppressive regime, having taken control of the country's military and mass media, sought to _____ the fledgling rebellion that aimed to restore individual freedoms.

    Ⓐ produce

    Ⓑ facilitate

    Ⓒ stymie

    Ⓓ elucidate

    Ⓔ redress

2. According to Norse mythology, the mischievous god Loki, a shape-shifting deity known for his _____, would often transform into animals in order to interfere with the other gods' plans and alliances.

    Ⓐ avarice

    Ⓑ chicanery

    Ⓒ pragmatism

    Ⓓ diffidence

    Ⓔ apathy

3. The Dewey Decimal System, a numerical method devised by Melvil Dewey in 1876 for categorizing nonfiction books according to topic, may seem (i) _____ when compared to the advanced technologies found today in most modern libraries, but it continues to be a valuable organizational tool. The system has developed dramatically since its inception, and it is likely to continue to evolve in perpetuity as the accumulation of the knowledge it catalogs is (ii) _____ pursuit.

Blank (i)		Blank (ii)	
A	abstruse	D	a vacuous
B	archaic	E	an illuminating
C	misguided	F	an inexhaustible

4. The intrepid group of veteran hikers chose to advance along a mountain path that was notoriously (i) _____, while the (ii) _____ team of inexperienced hikers took a decidedly more circuitous, though less challenging, trail.

Blank (i)		Blank (ii)	
A	facile	D	circumspect
B	scenic	E	bewildered
C	treacherous	F	reckless

5. The 1918 influenza pandemic initially drew (i) _____ attention, principally due to the fact that most regions experienced (ii) _____ fatalities among the enormous numbers of people infected. Yet, there were warnings: those who did expire from influenza were often young adults who, prior to their infection, had been of (iii) _____ health.

Blank (i)		Blank (ii)		Blank (iii)	
A	widespread	D	myriad	G	unpredictable
B	adverse	E	infrequent	H	vulnerable
C	scant	F	innumerable	I	sound

6. The replacement of human steelworkers with robots has not only made the steel production process involving molten metal less (i) _____ but has also (ii) _____ production quality due to the robots' ability to make very precise measurements, each at the same exact place and under the same conditions as the others.

Blank (i)		Blank (ii)	
A	humane	D	hampered
B	perilous	E	sterilized
C	compassionate	F	enhanced

For the following questions, select the **two** answer choices that, when inserted into the sentence, fit the meaning of the sentence as a whole **and** yield complete sentences that are similar in meaning.

7. Johnson's colleagues were _____ when he was awarded tenure by the university; his ideas were seldom acknowledged or discussed by other scholars, and when they were discussed, they were usually dismissed outright.

- [A] irate
- [B] unsurprised
- [C] perplexed
- [D] envious
- [E] bewildered
- [F] gratified

8. For many professionals, the promise that mobile communication will improve peace of mind has collided with the reality that the ability to be reached by superiors during times intended to be devoted to family can lead to _____.

   A flexibility

   B serenity

   C perturbation

   D productivity

   E vexation

   F tranquility

9. During the 16th century, many food plants native to the Americas, including specimens as _____ as potatoes and chocolate, were transported to Europe, where they reshaped people's diets and revolutionized traditional cuisines.

   A distributed

   B varied

   C regarded

   D diverse

   E unexpected

   F reviled

10. Historically, soap has been _____ by treating animal or vegetable oils with a strong base, such as sodium hydroxide, to create a form of lipid with hydrophobic "tails," which surround oil and other particles, and hydrophilic "heads," which attract water molecules.

    A manufactured

    B enhanced

    C improved

    D produced

    E ameliorated

    F undermined

Questions 11 and 12 are based on the passage below.

Most literature is written such that the order of reading is unambiguous. Indeed, most Western prose is intended to be read from left to right and top to bottom. This is not the only system, however; texts written in Arabic or Hebrew are read from right to left, and hieroglyphics, which can seem involved to modern eyes, were understood by ancient readers to be read vertically, down columns arranged from left to right. There exist, on the other hand, works of literature that require effort on the part of the reader to determine an appropriate order for reading the text on the page or even an appropriate order of the pages themselves. These works of ergodic literature (from the Greek *ergon*, meaning "work," and *hodos*, meaning "path") challenge the reader to be an active participant in experiencing the prose. The *I Ching*, for example, instructs the reader to pick random numbers and use them to look up passages to read. Mark Z. Danielewski's *House of Leaves* is a modern illustration of ergodic literature. One chapter in which a group of characters traverses a maze is presented in a similarly labyrinthine manner: the reader must navigate text that winds back and forth, upside-down and right-side-up, and across and between pages to follow the episode.

Consider each of the choices separately and select all that apply.

11. Which of the following would the author of the passage most likely consider an example of ergodic literature?

    [A] Guillaume Apollinaire's *Calligrammes*, a book of poetry in which the text is arranged into complicated shapes and images that carry as much meaning as the text itself

    [B] James Joyce's *Finnegans Wake*, a novel written in a stream of consciousness style, which lacks a clear plot and includes a large number of made-up words

    [C] Marc Saporta's *Composition No. 1*, a work of literature presented as a box of 150 loose pages intended to be shuffled and read in a random order

12. In the context in which it appears, "involved" most nearly means

    (A) participatory

    (B) troubling

    (C) intelligible

    (D) archaic

    (E) complex

Question 13 is based on the passage below.

When people today recall Hannibal Barca, the Carthaginian general who lived from 247 to circa 181 BCE, they typically focus on the one fact that is commonly taught in history classes: during the Second Punic War against Rome, Hannibal marched across the Alps with a team of war elephants, nearly all of which were lost due to the harsh conditions of the region. Historians and students of history alike regard this decision as a blunder. Of course, were this the only notable event in Hannibal's military career, it would be correct to look upon him with disfavor.

No one would disagree that Hannibal underestimated the number of souls that would be lost on the perilous march through France and incorrectly believed that the elephants would be hardier than they turned out to be for the trek. Nonetheless, it is abundantly clear from historical accounts that he was aware of the danger and planned well ahead of time to reinforce his numbers by using both his charisma and his military might to convince the Gauls and other tribes native to the Alpine foothills to join him in fighting the Romans, and was largely successful in doing so. He was also a master tactician, able to take advantage of the diversity of his fighting forces, the local terrain, and the single-minded regimentation of the Roman forces to win skirmishes in which his own troops were vastly outnumbered.

13. The two highlighted sentences play which of the following roles in the passage?

   (A) The first states the main thesis of the passage; the second is a fact that seems at odds with this thesis.

   (B) The first is a position that the author intends to refute; the second is a justification for this refutation.

   (C) The first is a position the author regards as legitimate but incomplete; the second is support for the author's thesis.

   (D) The first provides a reason for doubting the position maintained by the author; the second is the author's main conclusion.

   (E) The first states an outside position that the author reluctantly concedes; the second is part of an explanation for this reluctance.

Questions 14–16 are based on the passage below.

The first recorded example of what we would recognize as organized religion was that of the Mesopotamians, a civilization located in what would become modern-day Iraq. The two rivers that defined the region, the Tigris and Euphrates, flooded violently and unpredictably. As a result, the Mesopotamians viewed their pantheon of gods as capricious and vengeful, and the citizens were thus burdened with carrying out what they believed to be the will of the gods and providing lavish offerings in order to keep the gods appeased and prevent disaster. Different circumstances existed in Egypt: The Egyptians lived along the Nile, a river that, prior to the completion of the Aswan High Dam in 1970, would flood gently every four months, depositing silt that provided nutrients vital to agriculture in the region. The Egyptian people thus saw themselves as beloved by their gods and considered themselves the favored civilization, a bastion of order in an otherwise chaotic world.

14. The author is primarily concerned with

   (A) describing the origins of organized religion in two ancient civilizations

   (B) arguing that living along the Nile was far less stressful than living between the Tigris and the Euphrates

   (C) distinguishing between two civilizations by noting the ways in which individual gods in their pantheons represented different natural phenomena

   (D) persuading readers that modern religions reflect the geopolitical characteristics of their places of origin

   (E) contrasting the environmental features of two regions as an explanation of differences between their endemic religions

Consider each of the choices separately and select all that apply.

15. Based on the information in the passage, which of the following cultures could be reasonably expected to have religious beliefs similar to those of the Mesopotamians?

   [A] A coastal civilization that is hit by a typhoon during the first week of summer each year

   [B] A plains culture that endures tornadoes that can level structures without warning throughout the spring

   [C] A society that lives along a fault line and experiences random mild tremors

16. Select the sentence that best describes a reason for a civilization to view itself as favored by its gods.

Questions 17–19 are based on the passage below.

It is a scientific fact that water is among the few substances that expand when they freeze. This explains why ice floats in liquid water; because it is less dense than the water around it, the buoyant force pushes it to the surface. Larger differences in density create stronger buoyant forces. This fact also accounts for the observation that melting ice does not cause the level of the surface of the water in which it is floating to change. While some of the ice protrudes above the surface, melting causes the volume of what was the ice cube to decrease so that the newly melted water exactly fills the space that the frozen ice cube occupied under the surface.

There are those who would use these facts to declare that the melting of the polar ice caps would not contribute to sea level rise, but this is an example of the saying that "a little knowledge is a dangerous thing." First, the southern polar cap is not floating on the surface of the ocean, but rather is supported by the Antarctic land mass. As a result, the portions of this ice cap that are submerged displace far less ocean water than would be displaced by a floating cap. Additionally, the ocean water is salty while the ice caps are fresh. Consequently, ocean water is more dense than fresh water, which means that it generates larger buoyant forces and so can support a larger ice cap than fresh water would. For both of these reasons, melting of the polar ice caps would in fact cause nontrivial sea level rise.

17. Which of the following statements presents a situation most analogous to that described in the highlighted sentence?

     (A) Receiving advance payment to write an original score for a musical, but failing to listen to the music from other contemporary productions in an effort to avoid being influenced by current trends in musical theater

     (B) Obtaining an undergraduate degree in economics, but failing to use any of the principles taught by professors and instead relying upon instinct and intuition about human behavior to build a successful company

     (C) Spending the time to learn a large number of programming languages in great detail, but failing to recognize that employers in a certain job market require use of only a single programming language

     (D) Studying the Italian language well enough to pass a final exam in a college course, but failing to be fluent enough to converse with native speakers on a trip to Italy

     (E) Being aware that hydrogen peroxide and vinegar are perfectly safe to handle on their own, but failing to understand that mixing them together creates peracetic acid, a highly caustic substance

Consider each of the choices separately and select all that apply.

18. Which of the following statements is supported by this passage?

     A   The solid state of most substances can be expected to sink when placed into the liquid state of the same substance.

     B   Hydrazine, a colorless liquid with a density less than that of water, can be expected to float when placed into liquid water.

     C   If the southern polar ice caps were not supported by a land mass, their melting would not cause rising sea levels.

19. The passage cites each of the following as contributing to a complete explanation for melting ice caps causing a rise in sea levels EXCEPT:

     (A) a physical property of water that sets it apart from most other substances

     (B) a geological feature that calls into question the applicability of a known scientific phenomenon in a specific instance

     (C) a description of an event that provides context for the use of scientific principles in a specific case

     (D) a difference between the phenomenon in question and another phenomenon that exaggerates the described effect

     (E) a general property of liquids that is applicable to at least some of the specific instances of the phenomenon in question

Question 20 is based on the passage below.

The Arnolfini Portrait, painted by Dutch artist Jan van Eyck in 1434, depicts two richly dressed figures, a man and a woman, standing hand-in-hand in an upstairs room which most likely functioned as a place to receive visitors. A common interpretation of the painting is that it is meant to serve as a marriage contract of sorts. The artist's signature is both elaborate and central to the painting, appearing to be drawn on the wall behind the couple. The reflection in a mirror beneath the signature shows two additional figures just inside the door, one of whom is presumably van Eyck himself. It is argued that these two individuals constitute the two witnesses required to make a wedding legal, and that van Eyck's signature acts as a testament to this role. Additionally, the female subject appears pregnant, which many interpret as a sign that this is a marriage of necessity.

More recent and informed scholarship, on the other hand, questions the legitimacy of this analysis. An unmarried woman would have worn her hair down, while the female figure is wearing her hair up in a headdress. Furthermore, the female may not be pregnant after all, as female virgin saints were often depicted similarly, and her size may be a symbol of fertility rather than of pregnancy.

20. In this passage, the author is primarily concerned with

    (A) describing the creation and details of a portrait

    (B) condemning a critic's faulty reasoning in evaluating a painting

    (C) presenting an alternative interpretation of a work of art

    (D) demonstrating that an interpretation of an artwork may be incorrect

    (E) discussing a depiction of historical marriage customs

You have finished this section and now will begin

the next section.

Quantitative Reasoning 1

35 Minutes — 20 Questions

Directions: For each question, indicate the best answer, using the directions given.

You may use a calculator for all the questions in this section.

If a question has answer choices with **ovals**, then the correct answer is a single choice. If a question has answer choices with **squares**, then the correct answer consists of one or more answer choices. Read each question carefully.

Important Facts:

All numbers used are real numbers.

All figures lie in a plane unless otherwise noted.

Geometric figures, such as lines, circles, triangles, and quadrilaterals, **may or may not be drawn to scale**. That is, you should not assume that quantities such as lengths and angle measures are as they appear in a drawing. But you can assume that lines shown as straight are indeed straight, points on a line are in the order shown, and all geometric objects are in the relative positions shown. For questions involving drawn figures, base your answers on geometric reasoning rather than on estimation, measurement, or comparison by sight.

Coordinate systems, such as xy-planes and number lines, **are** drawn to scale. Therefore, you may read, estimate, and compare quantities in these figures by sight or by measurement.

Graphical data presentations, such as bar graphs, line graphs, and pie charts, **are** drawn to scale. Therefore, you may read, estimate, and compare data values by sight or by measurement.

Directions: In questions 1–8, compare the value in Quantity A to the value in Quantity B. Information concerning one or both of the quantities to be compared is centered above the two quantities. Compare the two quantities and select Ⓐ if Quantity A is greater, Ⓑ if Quantity B is greater, Ⓒ if the two quantities are equal, and Ⓓ if the relationship cannot be determined from the information given.

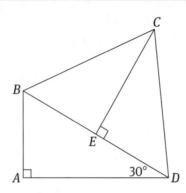

$\triangle BCD$ is an equilateral triangle and $AB = 1$.

1.	Quantity A	Quantity B	
	The length of CE	$\sqrt{3}$	Ⓐ Ⓑ Ⓒ Ⓓ

$$3a - 2b = 9$$
$$5a = 34 - 3b$$

2.	Quantity A	Quantity B	
	a	b	Ⓐ Ⓑ Ⓒ Ⓓ

A box contains only red, white, and blue marbles. Twenty percent of the marbles are blue. Of the remaining marbles, one-quarter are red.

3.	Quantity A	Quantity B	
	The number of red marbles	One-third the number of white marbles	Ⓐ Ⓑ Ⓒ Ⓓ

4.	Quantity A	Quantity B	
	$(r + 3)(s + 2)$	$rs + 12$	Ⓐ Ⓑ Ⓒ Ⓓ

$$X = (86)(47)(94)(123)(64)(56)(72)$$

5.	Quantity A	Quantity B	
	The units digit of X	5	Ⓐ Ⓑ Ⓒ Ⓓ

Diego drinks 50% more coffee per year than Pablo does. Lilly drinks the same amount of coffee in the first half of each year as she does in the second, and she drinks twice as much coffee in one of these periods as Pablo does in a whole year.

6. Quantity A   Quantity B

The amount of coffee Diego drinks in 5 years   The amount of coffee Lilly and Pablo combined drink in 2 years

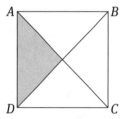

ABCD is a square with a perimeter of 20 units. *AC* and *BD* are diagonals.

7. Quantity A   Quantity B

The length of side *BC* in units   The number of square units shaded in the figure

a and *b* are positive integers such that $4 < a + b < 6$ and $|a - b| = 1$

8. Quantity A   Quantity B

The volume of a cylinder with radius *a* and height *b*   The volume of a cylinder with radius *b* and height *a*   Ⓐ Ⓑ Ⓒ Ⓓ

Directions: The remaining questions have several different formats. Select one answer if the answer choice letters are inside ovals. If the answer choice letters are inside boxes, select all choices that apply. If there is a rectangular box, enter your response as a numerical value.

9.

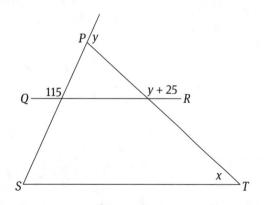

In the figure above, *QR* is parallel to *ST*. What is the measure of angle *x*?

Ⓐ 35
Ⓑ 45
Ⓒ 65
Ⓓ 70
Ⓔ 110

10. A particular natural history museum has three rooms where fossilized dinosaur skeletons are displayed. Nine dinosaur skeletons have recently been donated to the museum. If each room will have exactly one of these skeletons added to its exhibits, how many ways are there to arrange the new skeletons?

$$\boxed{}$$

11. A film production company must submit 5 of its movies released this year for consideration for an awards ceremony. This year, the company released 14 movies; 8 of these were horror movies and 6 were romantic comedies. If it submits at least 3 romantic comedies, how many groups of 5 movies can be submitted?

- (A) 276
- (B) 432
- (C) 560
- (D) 681
- (E) 686

12. Last year, a coffee roasting company purchased new roasting machines to bring their total number of machines to 10. These 10 machines can roast 210 lbs of coffee beans in 3 hours. Before purchasing the new machines, the company could roast 84 lbs of beans in 2 hours. If all of the machines work at the same constant rate, how many machines did the company buy last year?

$$\boxed{}$$ machines

13. Given a positive integer p, how many integers are greater than $2p$ and less than $4p - 1$?

- (A) $\dfrac{p}{2}$
- (B) p
- (C) $p + 1$
- (D) $2p - 2$
- (E) $3p - 3$

14. If $a = bx$, $1 < x < 4$, and $c = \dfrac{b}{3}$, then $\dfrac{a}{c}$ could be which of the following? Indicate all possible choices.

- [A] 1
- [B] 3
- [C] 5
- [D] 10
- [E] 12
- [F] 15

15.

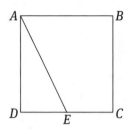

In the figure above, the perimeter of square *ABCD* is 32 and the area of △*ADE* is 12. What is the length of *EC*?

16. Both x and y are positive integers. If $x^2 + 2xy + y^2 = 49$ and $x^2 - y^2 = -7$, then $y =$

Ⓐ 2

Ⓑ 3

Ⓒ 4

Ⓓ 5

Ⓔ 7

17. If $3 < x < 7$ and $4 > y > -2$, which of the following must be true?

Indicate <u>all</u> possible choices.

Ⓐ $x - y > 0$

Ⓑ $x + y > 0$

Ⓒ $x > y$

Ⓓ $2y - x > 0$

Ⓔ $2x - y > 1$

Questions 18–20 are based on the following graphs.

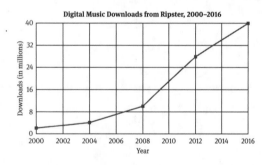

18. During the year when the combined percent downloads of Latin and Dance exceeded Pop, what was the approximate combined number of Latin and Dance downloads?

Ⓐ 0.5 million

Ⓑ 2.5 million

Ⓒ 8.5 million

Ⓓ 10 million

Ⓔ 12 million

19. By what percent did Pop downloads increase
     from 2008 to 2012?

     Ⓐ 43%

     Ⓑ 57%

     Ⓒ 75%

     Ⓓ 86%

     Ⓔ 133%

---

20. In 2016, which of the following genres had
     between 6 million and 11 million downloads,
     inclusive?

     Choose <u>all</u> that apply.

     Ⓐ Pop

     Ⓑ Country

     Ⓒ R&B/Hip-Hop

     Ⓓ Latin

     Ⓔ Dance

     Ⓕ Other

**You have finished this section and now will begin
the next section.**

Verbal Reasoning 2

30 Minutes — 20 Questions

Directions: For each item, select the best answer choice using the directions given.

If a question has answer choices with **ovals**, then the correct answer will be a single choice. If a question's answer choices have **squares**, the correct answer may be more than one choice. Be sure to read all directions carefully.

For each blank, select an answer choice from the corresponding column of choices. Fill all blanks in such a way that they best complete the text.

1. As technology grows increasingly sophisticated and _____, parents should consider the potentially negative consequences of its constant use: a child who can retrieve the answer to any question merely by asking her digital assistant may lose her ability to think for herself.

   Ⓐ feckless

   Ⓑ unreliable

   Ⓒ irksome

   Ⓓ pervasive

   Ⓔ repetitious

2. All languages evolve by (i) _____ new words, abandoning old words, and changing other words significantly. For this reason, it may seem as though modern English has little connection with the language of William Shakespeare, since most current speakers (ii) _____ archaic words such as "thou" and "bethink." Nevertheless, modern English (iii) _____ phrases to Shakespeare, including "wild goose chase" and "forever and a day."

Blank (i)		Blank (ii)		Blank (iii)	
A	auguring	D	eschew	G	owes many familiar
B	embracing	E	appropriate	H	portends several disconcerting
C	obscuring	F	mitigate	I	attributes few impeccable

3. Certain species of cephalopod, such as squid, octopus, and nautilus, found exclusively in marine environments, use a form of jet propulsion to move through the water as they search for prey and (i) _____ predators. Although animals have used this mechanism, which draws on the principles of Newton's third law of physics, for thousands of years, humans did not (ii) _____ jet propulsion for transportation until the invention of the internal combustion engine, which made a somewhat inefficient method of locomotion (iii) _____ for many modern applications, including turbines and turbojets.

Blank (i)		Blank (ii)		Blank (iii)	
A	evade	D	fortuitously analyze	G	commensurate
B	bifurcate	E	effectively harness	H	feasible
C	dissemble	F	rampantly augment	I	sporadic

4. Though seemingly axiomatic, the principle of "finders keepers" causes (i) _____ debate when applied to antiquities. Looters who prize a quick payoff above archaeological scholarship frequently raid graves and other ancient sites, seeking anything they can sell on the international market; this (ii) _____ the country's claim to ownership of its cultural treasures and destroys the historical record.

Blank (i)		Blank (ii)	
A	dispassionate	D	stabilizes
B	perfunctory	E	flouts
C	contentious	F	demotes

5. Many avant-garde artists struggle to gain acceptance as (i) _____ work often produces confusion or even rage when it debuts. Even so, history holds numerous examples of works that (ii) _____ riots when they premiered but (iii) _____ enormous sums when sold.

Blank (i)		Blank (ii)		Blank (iii)	
A	complacent	D	suppressed	G	expended
B	decorous	E	engendered	H	underscored
C	provocative	F	belied	I	garnered

6. Philosophers have long debated the true meaning of love, and perhaps the diverse uses of the word have made its definition _____, but genuine love always arises from a mutual sense of understanding and respect—needs that are truly universal.

- (A) benign
- (B) nebulous
- (C) pernicious
- (D) seditious
- (E) specious

For the following questions, select the two answer choices that, when inserted into the sentence, fit the meaning of the sentence as a whole and yield complete sentences that are similar in meaning.

7. There are many conflicting studies regarding the health effects of caffeine; while many emphasize the unpleasant results of its consumption, others focus on its _____ properties.

   A addictive
   B lackadaisical
   C salubrious
   D adventitious
   E beneficent
   F innocuous

8. The critic maintained that the researcher's _____ was not in question but argued that her conclusion was not sufficiently supported by the available evidence.

   A discomfiture
   B integrity
   C egoism
   D mortification
   E rectitude
   F ineptitude

9. Upon reading an incendiary article questioning the merits of his college in the local newspaper, the class president felt compelled to harangue the editor in a _____ that voiced his objections in the strongest possible terms.

   A missive
   B screed
   C tome
   D quandary
   E diatribe
   F hypothesis

10. Though all birds of prey share certain features, including excellent eyesight and sharp talons, which make these birds excellent hunters by equipping them to find and catch prey, some species display _____ characteristics, such as the high-speed dive of the peregrine falcon.

    A voracious
    B unique
    C fleeting
    D rapid
    E advantageous
    F distinctive

Question 11 is based on the passage below.

Some educators endorse the "look and say" method for teaching elementary school children how to read. This approach is also known as the "whole language method" because it trains students to recognize each word as a single entity. For this reason, it affords a degree of fluency with known words: when a student has memorized a word, she will be able to recognize and read it in future encounters. This method fails, however, to prepare students to decipher new words: a student who has not previously encountered and learned a word will not be able to read it and will therefore be limited to her range of known "word patterns." Given the significant deficiency of this method, teachers should use a phonics-based approach, which trains students to decode or "sound out" words from the letters that comprise them. It offers a major advantage over the "look and say" method by allowing a student to read and understand words that she has not encountered in print before.

11. In the argument above, the two highlighted sentences play which of the following roles?

    (A) The first summarizes a position that the author opposes; the second supports the author's recommendation.

    (B) The first states the main point of the argument; the second provides evidence for that conclusion.

    (C) The first provides support for a position that the author ultimately rejects; the second serves as evidence for the author's recommendation.

    (D) The first supports the conclusion for the position with which the author disagrees; the second states the overall conclusion of the argument.

    (E) The first states the conclusion of the argument; the second provides support for that conclusion.

Question 12 is based on the passage below.

Realism in painting and sculpture often indicates an advanced degree of civilization. For example, the artists of ancient Greece produced their most famous and recognizable statues during the so-called "Golden Age," which marked the maturation of Greek culture after centuries of gradual advancement. The ancient Romans later adopted realistic forms in their art but failed to maintain them in the face of barbarian invasions and social disintegration. It took nearly a millennium for Europeans to redevelop the skill of creating realistic painting and sculpture, the earliest post-Classical examples of which date to 13th-century Italy.

12. It can be inferred from the passage that which of the following is true about realistic painting and sculpture?

  - (A) Societies with an advanced degree of civilization invariably reject unrealistic art forms in favor of realistic art forms.

  - (B) The artists of ancient Egypt who embraced realism ushered in a new era of cultural advancement.

  - (C) An advanced culture is more likely to produce realistic art than it is to produce any other type of art.

  - (D) In some societies, realism in painting and sculpture can take decades, or even centuries, to develop.

  - (E) Modern abstract art resulted from the deterioration of European and American culture after the end of the 19th century.

Questions 13 and 14 are based on the passage below.

The Battle of Trafalgar in 1805 was, perhaps, the most important British naval victory of the Napoleonic Wars. Before the battle, the people of England lived under constant threat of invasion by Napoleon's troops, but after the decisive victory of the British fleet under Admiral Nelson, French naval forces were never again strong enough to invade. As the battle loomed, however, such a victory may not have seemed such a foregone conclusion to the British. Their fleet was outnumbered and outgunned by the combined French and Spanish fleet; indeed, one Spanish ship, the *Santísima Trinidad*, was the most heavily armed ship in the world at the time. Furthermore, Nelson took a risk by employing an unorthodox battle plan. By approaching the opposing line of battle head-on, the British ships would be open to enemy broadsides without being able to return fire. The risk paid off, and the British were victorious, capturing or destroying twenty-two enemy ships without losing a single ship of their own. There was one significant loss for the British, though. During the battle, a French marksman shot Admiral Nelson, who died three hours later; upon learning this, King George III is said to have exclaimed, "We have lost more than we have gained."

Consider each of the choices separately and select all that apply.

13. Which of the following statements would the author of the passage likely agree with?

  - [A] Acting contrary to conventional military wisdom may contribute to a victory in battle.

  - [B] The loss of Admiral Nelson outweighed any strategic benefits gained by the British victory.

  - [C] The British would have lost the Battle of Trafalgar had Admiral Nelson used more conventional tactics.

14. The author mentions the *Santísima Trinidad* in order to

    (A) suggest that it was the main target of Admiral Nelson's plan of attack

    (B) give an example of a common ship design of the era

    (C) show why the Spanish felt confident that they would be victorious

    (D) explain why Admiral Nelson thought that the British fleet would lose the battle

    (E) point out one difficulty the British fleet would need to overcome to win the battle

Questions 15–20 are based on the passage below.

Scandals involving authors of memoirs have raised questions about how much artistic license should be allowed in a purported work of nonfiction. By definition, nonfiction works are about facts and real events, but perception of real events can vary greatly depending on the point of view of the writer, especially an author recounting personal experience in the form of a memoir. Consideration of the reaction to two specific incidents involving narrative memoirs that were later proven to be largely, or wholly, untrue shows how much the repercussions can vary when the fallacies are revealed.

In 2008, writer Margaret Seltzer decided that the story of a mixed ethnicity, Native American foster child trying to survive the gang culture of South Central Los Angeles was a story that needed to be told. Unfortunately, she chose to recount that story in the form of a memoir, adopting the pseudonym Margaret B. Jones so that she could not readily be identified, to tell the tale in her book *Love and Consequences*. When it was revealed, by her sister, that she was actually white and grew up in a wealthy suburb of Los Angeles, Seltzer claimed that her desire was to give voice to legitimate concerns that were going unheard. This claim, though, ran counter to the persona she adopted for radio interviews while promoting the memoir, during which she chose to use a vernacular and carry herself in a way that she thought would lend authenticity to her story. In doing so, she did a disservice to those whose experiences she had appropriated, and within a week she suffered the consequences: all copies of the book were recalled by the publisher, and Seltzer has not had any published works since that time.

Prior to Seltzer, author James Frey had also experienced the highs and lows of writing a successful memoir that was not completely based in fact. Before his tale of the dark depths of addiction and the winding road to recovery, *A Million Little Pieces*, landed him at the top of *The New York Times* best-seller list for fifteen weeks in 2005, Frey and his editor's notions of what should be considered a memoir were quite loose. Everything came tumbling down when Frey's book was exposed as containing a number of fabrications, and just as quickly as Frey rose to prominence, he became a media pariah. Frey claimed that he had never represented *A Million Little Pieces* as anything other than a memoir and that his embellishment of events was within the bounds of what is considered acceptable as a memoir within the literary world. His time in the media spotlight tends to belie his claim, as it saw him embrace the fraudulent persona he had created for himself in his book. In recent years, the view of the publishing world and the media toward Frey has softened, and he later returned to the best-seller list with his fictional work, *Bright Shiny Morning*.

15. While discussing memoirs, the author specifically chooses to refer to Frey in order to

    (A) argue that the media's response to Frey was too harsh

    (B) present an example of an author who experienced literary success after a significant scandal

    (C) focus on one of the more obscure memoir hoaxes in modern history

    (D) point out the malicious intent when an author decides to lie in a memoir

    (E) highlight the permanent damage that comes from going beyond the accepted bounds of the memoir genre

16. The primary purpose of the passage is to

    (A) criticize the consequences of the memoir genre being defined so loosely

    (B) cast doubt on the effectiveness of the repercussions faced by Seltzer and Frey

    (C) argue that both Seltzer and Frey were treated unfairly by the media

    (D) discuss the consequences to authors when memoirs are proven to be false

    (E) debate whether artistic license outweighs commitment to facts within the memoir genre

17. According to the passage, Seltzer's book can best be characterized as

    (A) self-serving

    (B) unpremeditated

    (C) authentic

    (D) spontaneous

    (E) authoritative

18. It can reasonably be inferred from the author's recounting of what happened to Seltzer and Frey that

    (A) they did not consciously seek to deceive their readers

    (B) both authors were at least partially responsible for the negative consequences that they faced

    (C) neither author ever experienced positive press after releasing their respective memoirs

    (D) authors in the memoir genre are more prone to deception than authors in other genres

    (E) they valued long-term financial success over journalistic integrity

19. According to the passage, Seltzer took all of the following steps to lend to the credibility of her memoir EXCEPT:

   (A) adopting a persona for her on-air interviews

   (B) setting the memoir in South Central Los Angeles

   (C) eliciting her family's cooperation

   (D) using the pseudonym Margaret B. Jones

   (E) changing the way she spoke during interviews

20. In the author's opinion, one major difference between the experiences of Seltzer and Frey is that

   (A) Seltzer lied with good intentions, while Frey lied purely for financial gain

   (B) Seltzer's bad press was less damaging than Frey's bad press

   (C) Seltzer deserved to never have another work published and Frey deserved his later success

   (D) Seltzer's family sought to damage her career, but Frey's family was very supportive

   (E) Seltzer's fabrication was quickly discovered and penalized, while Frey's fabrications took longer to be addressed

You have finished this section and now will begin

the next section.

Quantitative Reasoning 2

35 Minutes — 20 Questions

Directions: For each question, indicate the best answer, using the directions given.

You may use a calculator for all the questions in this section.

If a question has answer choices with **ovals**, then the correct answer is a single choice. If a question has answer choices with **squares**, then the correct answer consists of one or more answer choices. Read each question carefully.

Important Facts:

All numbers used are real numbers.

All figures lie in a plane unless otherwise noted.

Geometric figures, such as lines, circles, triangles, and quadrilaterals, **may or may not be drawn to scale**. That is, you should not assume that quantities such as lengths and angle measures are as they appear in a drawing. But you can assume that lines shown as straight are indeed straight, points on a line are in the order shown, and all geometric objects are in the relative positions shown. For questions involving drawn figures, base your answers on geometric reasoning, rather than on estimation, measurement, or comparison by sight.

Coordinate systems, such as *xy*-planes and number lines, **are** drawn to scale. Therefore, you may read, estimate, and compare quantities in these figures by sight or by measurement.

Graphical data presentations, such as bar graphs, line graphs, and pie charts, **are** drawn to scale. Therefore, you may read, estimate, and compare data values by sight or by measurement.

Directions: In questions 1–8, compare the value in Quantity A to the value in Quantity B. Information concerning one or both of the quantities to be compared is centered above the two quantities. Compare the two quantities and select Ⓐ if Quantity A is greater, Ⓑ if Quantity B is greater, Ⓒ if the two quantities are equal, and Ⓓ if the relationship cannot be determined from the information given.

The perimeter of isosceles $\triangle ABC$ is 32, and the length of one side is 10. The height, measured from the vertex where the two equal sides meet, is 8.

1.

Quantity A	Quantity B	
The length of the longest side of $\triangle ABC$	12	Ⓐ Ⓑ Ⓒ Ⓓ

$$g(z) = \frac{1}{(z-1)^2}$$

$$z \neq 1$$

2.

Quantity A	Quantity B	
$g\left(\frac{1}{3}\right)$	2	Ⓐ Ⓑ Ⓒ Ⓓ

Cities A and B are 400 miles apart. Eugene can travel from A to B by plane at an average speed of 300 miles per hour or by train at an average speed of 60 miles per hour.

3.

Quantity A	Quantity B	
The number of minutes later Eugene could leave A traveling by plane and arrive at B at the same time that he would have arrived if he had traveled by train	330 minutes	Ⓐ Ⓑ Ⓒ Ⓓ

In 2015, Navid's annual salary increased from $50,000 to $60,000. In 2017, his annual salary increased from $60,000 to $70,800.

4.

Quantity A	Quantity B	
The percent increase in Navid's salary in 2015	The percent increase in Navid's salary in 2017	Ⓐ Ⓑ Ⓒ Ⓓ

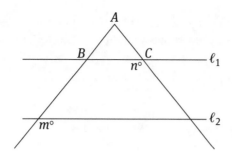

In the above figure, ℓ_1 and ℓ_2 are parallel. $m = 150$ and $n = 120$.

5.	Quantity A	Quantity B	
	The length of AB	The length of AC	

$3y - z = 8$ and the length of RT is 4.

6.	Quantity A	Quantity B	
	The length of segment RS	2.5	

$$x + y < z$$

7.	Quantity A	Quantity B	
	$2x - z$	$-y$	

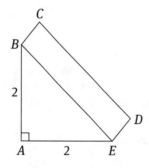

The area of $\triangle ABE$ = the area of rectangle $BCDE$

8.	Quantity A	Quantity B	
	The ratio of side BE to side DE	4:1	

Directions: The remaining questions have several different formats. Select one answer if the answer choice letters are inside ovals. If the answer choice letters are inside boxes, select all choices that apply. If there is a rectangular box, enter your response as a numerical value.

9.

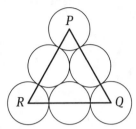

The sides of triangle PQR touch or pass through the center points of each of the six circles. Each of the circles has the same circumference of 8π. What is the perimeter of triangle PQR?

- (A) 16
- (B) 36
- (C) 48
- (D) 56
- (E) 72

10. If $\dfrac{14}{6^{-2}} \times 45 = 2^x \times 3^4 \times 35$, what is the value of x?

- (A) −2
- (B) 1
- (C) 2
- (D) 3
- (E) 4

11. If $\dfrac{w-z}{w} = 3 - 5\dfrac{2}{5}$ and neither w nor z is equal to zero, then $\dfrac{w}{z} =$

- (A) $-\dfrac{5}{12}$
- (B) $-\dfrac{5}{17}$
- (C) $\dfrac{5}{17}$
- (D) $\dfrac{5}{12}$
- (E) $\dfrac{12}{17}$

12.

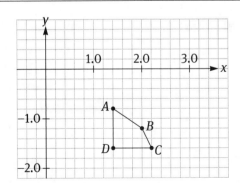

What is the area of the figure above determined by points A, B, C, and D?

[ ] square units

13. Which of the following is 40% less than 1.25×10^4?

    Ⓐ 7.5×10^2

    Ⓑ 5.0×10^3

    Ⓒ 7.5×10^3

    Ⓓ 1.0×10^4

    Ⓔ 1.75×10^4

14. Which of the following is divisible by an odd number of different positive integers?

    Indicate <u>all</u> possible numbers.

    Ⓐ 9

    Ⓑ 17

    Ⓒ 24

    Ⓓ 36

    Ⓔ 42

15.

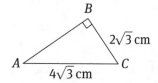

What is the length of a line segment drawn from point B to a point on side AC such that the line segment is perpendicular to side AC?

    ☐ centimeters

16. If the average of three numbers is $5a - 2$ and the average of two of the numbers is $4a + 2b + 1$, which of the following is the other number in terms of a and b?

    Ⓐ $a - 2b - 3$

    Ⓑ $5a + 2b + 3$

    Ⓒ $7a - 4b - 8$

    Ⓓ $9a + 2b - 1$

    Ⓔ $11a - 2b - 5$

17. Which points lie on the graph of $y = \dfrac{3x^2 + 2}{x - 1}$?

    Indicate <u>all</u> possible choices.

    Ⓐ $(-5, -13)$

    Ⓑ $(-4, -10)$

    Ⓒ $(0, 2)$

    Ⓓ $\left(3, 14\frac{1}{2}\right)$

    Ⓔ $\left(5, 19\frac{1}{2}\right)$

Questions 18–20 refer to the chart below.

**Members of a National Legal Association
by Practice Area, 2015**

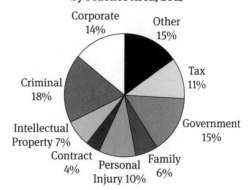

18. If 20,000 members of the national legal association were family law attorneys in 2015, how many members were criminal law attorneys?

   - (A) 6,500
   - (B) 12,000
   - (C) 22,400
   - (D) 40,000
   - (E) 60,000

19. In the same national legal association in 2016, criminal law attorneys still represented 18% of all lawyers, but there were 4,500 fewer criminal law attorneys in 2016 than there were in 2015. If there were 28,000 corporate law members in 2015, how many total members did the legal association have in 2016?

   - (A) 160,000
   - (B) 175,000
   - (C) 180,000
   - (D) 200,000
   - (E) 220,000

20. Assuming that the number of personal injury lawyers stays constant from 2015 to 2016, by approximately what percent would the number of intellectual property lawyers have to increase from 2015 to 2016 to reach the number of personal injury lawyers?

   - (A) 3%
   - (B) 7%
   - (C) 10%
   - (D) 30%
   - (E) 43%

You have finished this section and there are no more sections.

CHAPTER 26

PRACTICE TEST ANSWERS

Verbal Reasoning 1

1. C
2. B
3. B, F
4. C, D
5. C, E, I
6. B, F
7. C, E
8. C, E
9. B, D
10. A, D
11. A, C
12. E
13. C
14. E
15. B
16. See Answers and Explanations
17. E
18. A, B
19. C
20. D

Quantitative Reasoning 1

1. C
2. A
3. C
4. D
5. B
6. B
7. B
8. D
9. B
10. 504
11. E
12. 4
13. D
14. C, D
15. 5
16. C
17. B, E
18. D
19. C
20. B, D, F

Verbal Reasoning 2

1. D
2. B, D, G
3. A, E, H
4. C, E
5. C, E, I
6. B
7. C, E
8. B, E
9. B, E
10. B, F
11. C
12. D
13. A
14. E
15. B
16. D
17. A
18. B
19. C
20. E

Quantitative Reasoning 2

1. C
2. A
3. B
4. A
5. A
6. A
7. D
8. C
9. C
10. D
11. C
12. 0.4
13. C
14. A, D
15. 3
16. C
17. B, D
18. E
19. B
20. E

Practice Results

Add up the number of correct questions in each section and write the results below.

Verbal Reasoning: _____ out of 40

Quantitative Reasoning: _____ out of 40

Verbal Reasoning		
Raw Verbal Score	**Verbal Scaled Score Range**	**Percentile Rank**
40	165–170	96–99
39	162–170	92–99
38	160–170	87–99
37	159–169	84–99
36	158–168	81–98
35	157–167	77–98
34	157–167	77–98
33	154–164	66–94
32	154–164	66–94
31	153–163	62–92
30	151–161	53–87
29	151–161	53–87
28	150–160	48–85
27	150–160	48–85
26	149–159	43–82
25	148–158	39–79
24	147–157	35–75
23	146–156	32–72
22	146–156	32–72
21	145–155	28–68
20	145–155	28–68
19	144–154	24–64
18	143–153	21–60
17	142–152	18–55
16	141–151	15–51
15	140–150	12–46
14	139–149	10–40
13	138–148	8–37
12	137–147	7–33
11	136–146	5–30
10	136–146	5–30
9	135–145	3–26
8	134–144	2–22
7	133–143	2–19
6	132–142	1–16
5	130–140	1–10
4	130–139	1–9
3	130–138	1–7
2	130–137	1–5
1	130–136	1–4
0	130–135	1–3

Quantitative Reasoning		
Raw Quant Score	**Quant Scaled Score Range**	**Percentile Rank**
40	166–170	90–99
39	162–170	80–96
38	160–168	74–94
37	158–166	68–90
36	156–164	61–86
35	153–161	50–77
34	152–160	46–74
33	151–159	42–72
32	150–158	38–68
31	149–157	34–65
30	148–156	30–61
29	148–156	30–61
28	147–155	26–58
27	147–155	26–58
26	146–154	23–54
25	146–154	23–54
24	145–153	20–50
23	145–153	20–50
22	144–152	16–46
21	144–152	16–46
20	143–151	14–42
19	143–151	14–42
18	142–150	12–38
17	142–150	12–38
16	141–149	10–34
15	141–149	10–34
14	140–148	8–30
13	140–148	8–30
12	139–147	6–26
11	138–146	4–23
10	137–145	3–20
9	136–144	2–16
8	135–143	2–14
7	134–142	1–12
6	133–141	1–10
5	132–140	1–8
4	131–139	1–6
3	130–138	1–4
2	130–137	1–3
1	130–136	1–2
0	130–134	0–1

Understanding Scaled Scores and Percentiles

As mentioned at the beginning of Chapter 25, the printed practice test you just took is different from the GRE that you will encounter on Test Day. While this paper-and-pencil version gives you a general idea of what is on the GRE, the computer-based version is a multi-stage test that adapts after the first section, and such adaptation obviously does not occur during a paper-based test.

Because of these limiting factors with the paper-and-pencil format, we can only provide a general approximation of possible score outcomes based on your performance on the test you just took. Thus, in the tables on previous pages, you'll notice that the number of correct answers you earn in each section (your "Raw Score") corresponds to a range of possible scaled scores and percentiles. For a closer test-like experience, and for a more precise score, we suggest taking one of your Kaplan online practice tests.

On the GRE, and on your Kaplan online practice test, you'll receive one Verbal and one Quantitative **scaled score**, based on the standard 130–170 GRE score range. As you research different graduate schools, it is important to determine the scaled score you need in order to gain entry into the school and program of your choice. While one school might ask for a 155 score in each section, another might require scores of 145. Or a school might set a standard of 150 in Quant but 155 in Verbal. Knowing the scores you need will help you prepare more effectively and set a realistic target for improvement.

The **percentile** associated with your Verbal and Quantitative scaled score tells you how well you performed compared to other typical GRE students. Scoring in the 99th percentile indicates that you scored as well as or better than 99% of all other test takers. A 30th percentile score, on the other hand, indicates that you scored as well as or better than just 30% of test takers.

Analytical Writing 1: Analyze an Issue Answers and Explanations

Sample Essay Responses

Issue Essay Sample Response: Score of 6

Note that your essay need not be perfect to receive a very high score. It just needs to be a very strong rough draft.

At face value, the belief that "one should look upon any information described as 'factual' with skepticism since it may well be proven false in the future," seems ludicrous almost to the point of threatening anarchy. Yet not only does this belief prove well justified, it is also the linchpin around which our complex, highly technical society creates and consolidates its advances.

Science itself provides the best evidence and examples in support of this statement. One need look no further than contemporary medicine to see how far we have come from the days when illness was perceived as a sign of moral weakness or as a punishment from on high. In fact, the most outstanding characteristic of what we call "the scientific method" amounts to endless questioning of received theory in search of a more comprehensive explanation of what we perceive to be true. This iterative style of inquiry (and re-inquiry) perpetuates an ongoing scientific dialogue that catalyzes further breakthroughs in the developed world.

Furthermore, advances made through constant questioning are not limited to the scientific arena: the skeptical attitudes of ancient Greek philosophers, as well as those of Renaissance mariners, 19th century suffragists, and 20th century civil rights activists, have left the world a richer and more hopeful place. By refusing to accept the world as explained by contemporary "fact," these doubters helped give birth to societies and cultures in which human potential and accomplishment have been enabled to an unprecedented degree.

In contrast, those societies that cultivate adherence to received belief and a traditional non-skeptical approach have advanced very little over the centuries. In Tibet, for instance, the prayer wheels spin endlessly around a belief system as secure and unquestioning as the Himalayas themselves. While there may very well be things worth learning from such a society, Tibet has proven to lack adaptability and expansiveness and prefers to turn inward, away from the modern world. Such introspection has given Tibet neither immunity nor an array of defenses in the face of contemporary medical, social, and political problems. Thus, cultural inflexibility regarding received wisdom and convention comes with a price.

To conclude, it seems clear from the above discussion that a healthy skepticism remains the hallmark of Western epistemology as we face the future. A close look at the statement reveals that it is not advocating the wholesale rejection of orthodox thinking, but rather that we be open to redefining our assumptions. As the basis of our resiliency and creativity, this attitude offers the most positive prognosis for a society that revels in the solution of conundrums that its own constant questioning brings continually into view.

Analytical Writing 2: Analyze an Argument Answers and Explanations

Argument Essay Sample Response: Score of 6

Again, note that an essay need not be perfect (this one contains quite a few typos) in order to achieve a very high score.

In this memo, the owner of the Juniper Café concludes that cutting hours is the "best strategy for us to save money and remain in business without having to eliminate jobs." While the café's employees are undoubtedly grateful for the intent of the memo, they may see that its logic is flawed. First, the memo does not provide enough supporting evidence to prove that the money saved by cutting hours would exceed the money lost by losing early-morning and weekend clients. Second, the owner does not seem to evaluate other options that would either cut back on overhead or change the café's operation to bring in more revenue.

First, the owner relies on an unproven assumption about the cause of the overhead. He concludes, without justifying, that being open too many hours is causing too much overhead expense. There may be other causes, however, such as waste in other areas of management. While it is true that reducing café hours would save money spent on utilities, employee wages, and other operating costs, there is no evidence that those savings would outweigh the café's loss of business. The owner's message fails to give details of operating costs, wages, and utilities saved if the café is closed for the hours suggested by the memo. Perhaps the highest utility expenses are actually incurred between noon and 3 p.m., when the sun is the hottest and the café's air conditioning and refrigeration are most in use. The owner needs to do more research, including the habits and demography of the town. For example, since the café is located in the downtown area, perhaps *increasing* the number of hours the café is open would be a better solution.

Yes, it would cost more in overhead, but doing so might, in fact, make much more money for the café. Say, for instance, the Juniper becomes the only restaurant open on Friday and Saturday date nights, after the football games and movies let out. Second, the owner of the Juniper Café is not considering that the café serves a small American city. Cutting early-morning hours at a café, in a downtown area, where businesspeople and city workers most likely stop for coffee or breakfast on their way to work, seems very short-sighted and ill-informed. Are there one or more other cafés that will gladly steal business from 6 a.m. to 8 a.m. weekdays and that will perhaps win the permanent loyalty of those customers for lunch and dinner?

Furthermore, the owner does not seem to have evaluated other options to save the café. There are other places where overhead costs could potentially be cut. Certainly the owner would benefit from a brainstorming session with all employees, to get other ideas on the table. Maybe a new, lower-rent freezer storage facility is nearby. Maybe employees can suggest cutting waste in the purchasing department or dropping services the café doesn't need. It stands to reason that there is a plurality of ways to decrease overhead, aside from simply cutting hours.

In conclusion, the memo as it stands now does not logically prove that reduction in those particular hours will result in financial and future success for the café. There are several unstated assumptions upon which the argument turns, principally the assertion that simply being open for a certain number of hours is causing crippling overhead expenses. The owner's argument would profit enormously from further research, which may affect the hours he chooses to cut. Customer polling could show that few people eat or want coffee in that part of town between 2 p.m. and 5 p.m., and the café could be closed between lunch and dinner, adding flex hours or overlapping shifts for the staff. The memo lacks outlining what other restaurant services are available in the area and how or if they affect the 6 a.m. to 8 a.m. block and weekend hours. Once the marketing research and brainstorming is complete, the owner of the Juniper Café will make a better informed choice for his café's operating hours.

Analytical Writing Scoring Rubric

6: "Outstanding" Essay

- Insightfully presents and convincingly supports an opinion on the issue or a critique of the argument
- Communicates ideas clearly and is generally well organized; connections are logical
- Demonstrates superior control of language: grammar, stylistic variety, and accepted conventions of writing; minor flaws may occur

5: "Strong" Essay

- Presents well-chosen examples and strongly supports an opinion on the issue or a critique of the argument
- Communicates ideas clearly and is generally well organized; connections are logical
- Demonstrates solid control of language: grammar, stylistic variety, and accepted conventions of writing; minor flaws may occur

4: "Adequate" Essay

- Presents and adequately supports an opinion on the issue or a critique of the argument
- Communicates ideas fairly clearly and is adequately organized; logical connections are satisfactory
- Demonstrates satisfactory control of language: grammar, stylistic variety, and accepted conventions of writing; some flaws may occur

3: "Limited" Essay

- Succeeds only partially in presenting and supporting an opinion on the issue or a critique of the argument
- Communicates ideas unclearly and is poorly organized
- Demonstrates less than satisfactory control of language: contains significant mistakes in grammar, usage, and sentence structure

2: "Weak" Essay

- Shows little success in presenting and supporting an opinion on the issue or a critique of the argument
- Struggles to communicate ideas; essay shows a lack of clarity and organization
- Meaning is impeded by many serious mistakes in grammar, usage, and sentence structure

1: **"Fundamentally Deficient" Essay**
- Fails to present a coherent opinion and/or evidence on the issue or a critique of the argument
- Fails to communicate ideas; essay is seriously unclear and disorganized
- Lacks meaning due to widespread and severe mistakes in grammar, usage, and sentence structure

0: **"Unscorable" Essay**
- Completely ignores topic
- Attempts to copy the assignment
- Written in a foreign language or contains undecipherable text

Verbal Reasoning 1 Answers and Explanations

1. C

The regime is described as "oppressive" and has been consolidating power by taking over the military and the press. You can predict that an oppressive regime would want to "stop" a group that wished to promote individual freedoms. Choice **(C)** *stymie*, which means "to hinder," correctly matches this prediction. Eliminate (A) *produce*, which means "to make happen," and (B) *facilitate*, which means "to enable," since each is the opposite of the prediction. (D) *elucidate*, which means "to clarify," and (E) *redress*, which means "to make right," do not make sense in context.

2. B

Since this sentence does not contain any detour road signs, you can expect that the meaning of the missing word will align with the context clues given in the sentence. The Norse god Loki is described as "mischievous" and as one who "interferes" by changing his form. You can predict that the missing word means something like "trickery." There is a match for this prediction in **(B)** *chicanery*, which means "deceptive behavior." Eliminate (A) *avarice* ("greed"), (C) *pragmatism* ("practicality"), (D) *diffidence* ("shyness"), and (E) *apathy* ("indifference") because they do not fit the sentence's context clues.

3. B, F

The detour road sign "but" in the first sentence indicates that there is a contrast between how the Dewey Decimal System is perceived in light of new technology and the fact that it "continues to be a valuable organizational tool." You can predict that the Dewey Decimal System may seem "outdated." This prediction matches **(B)** *archaic*, which means "old-fashioned." Eliminate (A) *abstruse*, which means "difficult to understand," and (C) *misguided*, which means "foolish," as neither is supported by the context clues.

For the second blank, the context clues "continue" and "in perpetuity" (meaning "forever") indicate that the accumulation of knowledge is a pursuit that never ends.

You can predict the phrase "an infinite" to complete the sentence. Choice **(F)** *an inexhaustible* means "an endless" and is correct. Eliminate (D) *a vacuous*, as *vacuous* means "foolish," and (E) *an illuminating*, as *illuminating* means "enlightening," since neither meaning is supported by the context clues.

4. C, D

The detour road sign "while" indicates that the situation described in the first half of this sentence will contrast with the situation described in the second half. The context clues "intrepid" and "notoriously" in the first half of the sentence imply that the path chosen by the veteran hikers was difficult. Predict "dangerous" for the first blank. Choice **(C)** *treacherous*, which means "hazardous," matches this prediction and is correct. Eliminate (A) *facile*, which means "easy," since this is the opposite of the prediction, and (B) *scenic*, which means "pretty," since this meaning is not supported by any context clues.

The second blank describes the other group of hikers. These hikers were "inexperienced" and opted to take a "less challenging" trail. You can predict that this group is "cautious." Choice **(D)** *circumspect*, which means "careful," is a match and is correct. Eliminate (E) *bewildered*, which means "confused," as this is not supported by the context, and (F) *reckless*, which means "careless," as this is the opposite of what the sentence calls for.

5. C, E, I

The key to this question is the detour road sign "yet." Without that road sign and the rest of the sentence, one could predict a number of words for the first two blanks, even some that are opposite others. Was there *little* attention because of *few* fatalities? Was there a *great deal* of attention due to a *large number* of fatalities? "Yet, there were warnings" provides the answer. "Yet" hints that the warnings were not heeded. So predict that the pandemic initially drew "little" attention (for the first blank) due to the fact that even though many people were infected, there was a "lack" of deaths (for the second blank). This reasoning leads to **(C)** *scant*, or "having a small or insufficient supply," as the correct answer for the first blank, and **(E)** *infrequent*, or "rare," for the second blank. (A) *widespread* is the opposite of what is needed for the first blank, while (D) *myriad* and (F) *innumerable*, both of which mean "very many," are the opposite of what is needed for the second blank. Additionally, (D) and (F) are close in meaning to each other, which is a sign that neither is correct. Note that (B) *adverse*, which means "hostile," "harmful," or "acting in a contrary direction," doesn't fit here, as there is nothing in the sentence that suggests the type of attention the pandemic received, just the amount it received.

For the third blank, if the young adults who died had been in poor health to begin with, their deaths wouldn't have raised warning flags. It must be, then, that they were young adults of otherwise "good" or "stable" health. This prediction leads to **(I)** *sound*, or "free from injury or disease," as the correct answer for the third blank. Similarly, if the young adults' health had been (G) *unpredictable*, their deaths wouldn't be expected to attract attention or serve as a warning. (H) *vulnerable*, or "capable of being attacked or wounded," is the opposite of what this sentence requires.

6. B, F

Replacing human workers with robots could be considered a good thing or a bad thing, depending on whom you ask. The second part of the sentence mentions an "ability" of the robots. That's a positive statement about the robots, so predict that the second blank will describe how the robots have "improved" production quality. **(F)** *enhanced* is a great match for the prediction and is the correct answer for the second blank. (D) *hampered*, or "created difficulties for," is the opposite of what is needed here. (E) *sterilized* can mean "made incapable of reproducing," "made free of living microorganisms," or even "made powerless or useless," none of which makes sense in this sentence.

For the first blank, note the straight-ahead road sign "not only...but...also" in the sentence. This phrase means that the first part of the sentence should mention something positive about using robots just as the second part of the sentence did. Additionally, note that the production process involves molten metal. Distancing humans from very hot, liquid metal sounds like a safety improvement, so predict that the change has made steel production less "dangerous." **(B)** *perilous*, or "hazardous," is a

perfect match. (A) *humane* and (C) *compassionate*, both of which basically mean "sympathetic," are tempting traps for those who miss the sentence's clues and focus on how human workers might be losing their jobs rather than on the benefits of using robots.

7. C, E

Note the contrast between the first part of the sentence and the second. According to the second part of the sentence, scholars don't view Johnson's ideas favorably. They reject them without much consideration. Yet, as the first part of the sentence says, Johnson was awarded tenure. Based on the second part of the sentence, you can predict that Johnson's colleagues—that is, other scholars—would be "surprised" or "puzzled" by the fact that he was awarded tenure. **(C)** *perplexed* and **(E)** *bewildered*, both of which mean "confused," match the prediction and are correct. The sentence does not imply that Johnson's colleagues were (A) *irate*, which means "angry," at his being granted tenure; and even if they were, there is no second choice to give the sentence the same meaning. (D) *envious*, or "jealous," can be eliminated for the same reason. (F) *gratified*, or "pleased," doesn't make sense in light of the fact that Johnson's colleagues reject his ideas. Finally, (B) *unsurprised* is the opposite of what the sentence calls for.

8. C, E

The phrase "collided with" serves as a detour road sign in this sentence. The "promise" that mobile communication is supposed to improve "peace of mind" contrasts with the fact that it allows the professionals' supervisors to reach them when they are trying to spend time with their families. Thus, the word in the blank should contrast with "peace of mind." "Stress" or "anxiety" would be fine predictions. **(C)** *perturbation*, which means "agitation," and **(E)** *vexation*, which means "frustration," are great matches and are correct. (B) *serenity* and (F) *tranquility* both mean "calmness" and are the opposite of what is needed. Be careful: you might think that the ability to be reached by superiors at any time would lead to (A) *flexibility* or (D) *productivity*, but neither of these contrasts with the promised "peace of mind."

9. B, D

The structure of this sentence is challenging: the blank is part of an example, so you should use the content of the example to predict. One type of food is "potatoes," while the other is "chocolate." Predict the answer: "specimens as 'different' as potatoes and chocolate." **(B)** and **(D)** match that prediction nicely and create sentences with equivalent meanings. (A) *distributed* does not work well with the syntax of the sentence and does not have a match among the answer choices. (C) *regarded* and (E) *unexpected* are wrong for a similar reason: they have no synonyms among the other answer choices. Finally, (F) *reviled* has a strongly negative connotation that the sentence does not support.

10. A, D

Perhaps you weren't expecting a chemistry lesson, but this question provides it. Don't let the unfamiliar content distract you; instead, focus on the clues. You need a verb in the blank: what have people historically done to soap? The best clues are "treating" and "to create." These words indicate that people made soap with this process. Both **(A)** *manufactured* and **(D)** *produced* match this meaning and are the correct answers. (B) *enhanced* and (C) *improved* are synonyms but do not match the clues in the sentence: there is nothing to indicate that soap was once an inferior product and needed improving. (E) *ameliorated* means "to make a bad situation more tolerable" and is not supported by the clues in the sentence. Finally, there's no suggestion in this sentence that people (F) *undermined* soap; instead, they used this process to create it.

11. A, C

The passage defines ergodic literature as works that present the text, pages, or chapters without a prescribed order. Both **(A)** and **(C)** fit this definition, as *Calligrammes* presents the text such that it is not to be read "left to right and top to bottom," and *Composition No. 1* does not have a prescribed order to its pages. If matching these answer choices to the definition alone is difficult, compare them to the texts mentioned in the passage; *Calligrammes* is similar to *House of Leaves* in its arrangement of text on the page, and *Composition No. 1* is similar to the *I Ching* in the randomness involved in determining its order of reading.

(B) does not match this definition. While *Finnegans Wake* might be difficult to understand or interpret, there is nothing in the description of the novel that suggests that determining the order of reading requires effort on the part of the reader.

12. E

Hieroglyphics are described in the passage as having a prescribed order of reading that is different from that of many modern forms of writing, and the passage states that this order was "understood" by ancient readers. By contrast, modern readers might find them difficult to understand or excessively complicated, and this is exactly what "involved" means in this context. **(E)** *complex* is a close match for this definition and is the correct answer.

(A) *participatory* is a common definition of "involved," but the sentence does not specify anything that the hieroglyphics are participating in. There is nothing in the passage to suggest that hieroglyphics are (B) *troubling*, and (C) *intelligible* or "easily read or understood" is the opposite of the meaning expressed in the sentence. Finally, hieroglyphics are described as (D) *archaic* or "ancient," but this answer choice misses the contrast between the difficulty modern readers may have in reading hieroglyphics and the ease with which contemporary readers understood their arrangement.

13. C

In this Logic question, you have to characterize the relationship between the two highlighted phrases. One of the difficulties in doing so is that the author's thesis is not stated outright but merely implied: though Hannibal made a mistake in marching elephants across the Alps, it would be incorrect to consider only this incident when evaluating Hannibal's military prowess. As a result, the first highlighted sentence is a position that the author believes is an accurate evaluation of Hannibal but isn't the only thing we should remember about him. The second highlighted sentence provides evidence for the idea that Hannibal was actually a better general than many believe him to be based on the single story discussed in the first paragraph. The only answer choice that correctly matches both of these roles is **(C)**.

(A) is incorrect because it misrepresents the author's position; the author argues that this blunder isn't the whole story, so the first highlighted sentence cannot be the author's main point. (B) might seem tempting, but recall that the author agrees in the second paragraph that Hannibal "did incorrectly believe that the elephants would be hardier" than they were. Since the author concedes that this was a blunder, the author is not attempting to refute the first highlighted statement. (D) is a reasonable interpretation of the first highlighted statement, but since the second highlighted statement is evidence for a position rather than the position itself, this choice can be eliminated. Finally, (E) distorts the author's tone; while the author concedes that Hannibal made a mistake, there is no language to suggest that this concession is difficult for the author.

14. E

This Global question asks for a summary of the author's purpose. The passage focuses on the ways in which the geography of the Mesopotamian and Egyptian civilizations influenced their religious beliefs. The author's tone is one of explanation rather than argument, so (B) "*arguing that…*" and (D) "*persuading readers…*" can be immediately eliminated. Looking at the remaining choices, (**E**) is a match. (A) is too broad; the author is interested in more than just a general explanation of the origin of the two religions, so this choice misses the major role of geography in the author's explanation. (C) distorts the point of the passage, as the author does not drill all the way down to what "individual gods" in each pantheon represent, nor does the author use "different natural phenomena," as both of the examined religions were influenced by the same phenomenon, flooding rivers.

15. B

The author claims that the cause for the specific features of the Mesopotamian religious beliefs is the "violent and unpredictable" nature of the region's natural disasters. While the typhoons described in (A) are certainly violent, they are predictable, occurring once during a specific week of the year. This means that (A) can be eliminated. (**B**) describes a phenomenon that has both of these qualities: the tornadoes are highly destructive

and occur "without warning," so (**B**) is a correct answer. Finally, (C) misses the mark because while the tremors are unpredictable, they are described as "mild." Eliminate (C).

16. Different circumstances existed in Egypt: The Egyptians lived along the Nile, a river that, prior to the completion of the Aswan High Dam in 1970, would flood gently every four months, depositing silt that provided nutrients vital to agriculture in the region.

The question stem references a civilization that sees itself as favored by the gods, so the correct answer should be a sentence that can be associated with the Egyptians. Specifically, the question is asking for a cause for this view. Since the author's position in the passage is that geography influenced the religious beliefs of the Mesopotamian and Egyptian cultures, look for the sentence that describes the environmental feature that led to this belief for the Egyptians. The second-to-last sentence is the one that describes the flooding of the Nile as gentle, predictable, and beneficial for the Egyptians, and the final sentence says that this results in the attitude described in the question stem. The second-to-last sentence, "Different circumstances existed in Egypt…," is the correct answer.

17. E

This question asks for a situation analogous to the first sentence of the second paragraph, which contains the aphorism "a little knowledge is a dangerous thing." The passage provides some context for this idea, saying that someone who has a cursory understanding of the basic scientific principles discussed in the first paragraph might be led to incorrect and harmful conclusions about the ideas discussed in the second paragraph. The correct answer will share this structure.

(A) describes a situation in which restricting knowledge actually produces a desired effect, since this person is attempting to limit exposure to musical ideas that might influence his or her own writing, so this choice can be eliminated. (B) can likewise be eliminated since this person presumably has a great deal of knowledge but is not using it, instead benefiting from skills and intuition. Eliminate (C) because it describes someone who gains too much information rather than too little. Eliminate (D) because, while it describes an example of too little knowledge, there is no indication that this lack of knowledge will lead the student to come to an incorrect conclusion.

This leaves **(E)**, which is correct. The individual described, similar to the critics described in the passage, has a little bit of knowledge about these two chemicals, but lacks an understanding about their reaction when mixed, and expects that their mixture would likewise be harmless. It turns out that the opposite is true, just as the critics in the passage expect the sea level to stay the same, when in reality it would rise.

18. A, B

Because there is no research clue given in the question stem, the best strategy for this all-that-apply Inference question is to check each choice against the information presented in the passage. **(A)** is supported by the first two sentences; ice floats on water because it is less dense than water, which results from the property that water expands when it freezes. The first sentence describes water as being "among the few substances" that do this, so it can be reasonably inferred that most substances do not. **(B)** is also supported by the second sentence; the lower density of ice directly causes it to float, so anything with a lower density can likewise be expected to float. (C), on the other hand, is contradicted by the second paragraph. The passage cites two reasons why the melting of ice caps would cause sea level rise: the land mass described in (C) and the difference in density between sea water and fresh water. Even if the Antarctic ice were not supported by land, the difference in density would still be sufficient to cause a rise in sea level. (C), therefore, is incorrect.

19. C

The passage provides four facts to fully explain the phenomenon in question, each of which corresponds to one of the four incorrect answers. The fact that water is rare among compounds in that it expands when it freezes corresponds to choice (A). The notion that the southern ice cap rests on a land mass, indicating that the scientific principles mentioned in the first paragraph do not apply in this case, matches up with (B). **(C)** is not present in

the passage, as there is no mention of a specific event in the passage. Thus, it is the correct answer. The difference between salty ocean water and fresh water causing greater buoyancy allows elimination of (D). Finally, the description of differences in density causing the buoyant force is represented by (E).

20. D

The author begins by describing the Arnolfini Portrait and discusses some evidence for a common interpretation: The painting is a "marriage contract of sorts." The author goes on to say that other art historians have reasons to doubt this interpretation. As a result, **(D)** is the best description of the author's purpose.

Both (A) and (E) are too specific; the author does describe the painting and makes mention of marriage customs as evidence, but neither of these is the focus of the passage. (B) and (C) are extreme; the author doesn't go as far as to condemn the interpretation or say that it is faulty, nor is the author interested in presenting her own interpretation of the painting.

Quantitative Reasoning 1 Answers and Explanations

1. C

The question shows a figure with an equilateral triangle that shares a side with the hypotenuse of a 30°-60°-90° triangle. You are asked to compare the height of the equilateral triangle to $\sqrt{3}$. Because triangle ABD is a 30°-60°-90° triangle, the length of the hypotenuse is twice that of the shortest side. Given that $AB = 1$, it follows that $BD = 2$. Since triangle BCD is equilateral, sides BC and CD are also 2 units long, and all three of its angles are 60°. A perpendicular line dropped from a vertex of an equilateral triangle to the opposite side bisects both the angle at the vertex and the opposite side. So, angle ECD is 30°, side DE is 1, and side CD is 2. You can use the Pythagorean theorem to calculate the length of CE: $1^2 + CE^2 = 2^2$, so $CE^2 = 4 - 1 = 3$ and $CE = \sqrt{3}$. Alternatively, you could have used the ratios of the sides of the 30°-60°-90° triangle CED to get the same result. Since Quantity A and B are both $\sqrt{3}$, **(C)** is correct.

2. A

If you tried to solve the system of equations by substitution, because of the coefficients of a and b, you would wind up with fractions, so use combination instead. Start by rearranging the second equation to get $5a + 3b = 34$. Make the coefficients of b the same in both equations by multiplying the first equation by 3 to get $9a - 6b = 27$ and the second equation by 2 to yield $10a + 6b = 68$. Now, add the two equations to eliminate b:

$$9a - 6b = 27$$
$$\underline{10a + 6b = 68}$$
$$19a = 95$$

So $a = 5$. Plug this into the first equation to get $3(5) - 2b = 9$, so $15 - 9 = 2b$ and $b = 3$. Thus $a > b$, so (**A**) is correct.

3. C

The centered information provides information about percents and fractions of different-colored marbles in a box. Since the problem involves percents of unknown values, pick 100 as the total number of marbles.

If 20% of the marbles are blue, then 20 out of the 100 are blue, and 80 are either red or white. Since one-quarter of those 80 are red, there are $80 \times 0.25 = 20$ red marbles; the other $80 - 20 = 60$ are white. Thus, Quantity A is 20 and Quantity B is one-third of 60, which is also 20. Therefore, (**C**) is correct.

4. D

To make the quantities easier to compare, make them look more alike. Use FOIL to multiply out Quantity A: $(r + 3)(s + 2) = rs + 2r + 3s + 6$. Now, both quantities have terms rs and a number, so you can subtract Quantity B, $rs + 12$, from both quantities to make Quantity A $2r + 3s - 6$. After the subtraction, Quantity B is zero. If $2r + 3s - 6$ is positive, Quantity A is greater than Quantity B; if $2r + 3s - 6$ is negative, Quantity B is greater than Quantity A. Since there are no restrictions on the values of r and s, either case could be true and (**D**) is correct.

You could also use Picking Numbers. For example, let $r = 2$ and $s = 3$. Then Quantity A is $(2 + 3)(3 + 2) = 25$ and Quantity B is $(2 \times 3) + 12 = 18$. In this case,

Quantity A is greater. But if you let $r = -3$ and $s = -2$, Quantity A will be 0 while Quantity B will still be 18, making Quantity B greater. Once again, you have demonstrated that a definite relationship cannot be determined.

5. B

The units digit (or ones digit) is the last digit before the decimal point; in this case, it will be the right-most digit. To compare the units digit of X to 5, you don't actually need to do the entire multiplication; you need to pay attention only to the last digit. So, multiply the last digit in each of the individual numbers and drop the tens digit if applicable. The first two numbers, 86 and 47, become $6 \times 7 = 42$; and then, 42×94 becomes $2 \times 4 = 8$; and so on: $8 \times 3 = 24$; $4 \times 4 = 16$; $6 \times 6 = 36$; and $6 \times 2 = 12$. Thus, the last digit is 2, which is less than 5. Choice (**B**) is correct.

6. B

First express the relationships described in the centered information algebraically. Diego drinks 50% *more* coffee than Pablo drinks. That means Diego drinks 150% of whatever amount Pablo drinks. Using P for the amount of coffee Pablo drinks in a year and D for the amount of coffee Diego drinks in a year, this relationship can be expressed as $D = 1.5P$. Lilly is also compared to Pablo. She, however, drinks twice as much in *half* a year as Pablo does in a whole year. So in one year, Lilly drinks four times as much as Pablo does. That equation can be written as $L = 4P$. Now consider Quantity A. If Diego drinks $1.5P$ in one year, then in 5 years, he drinks $5(1.5P) = 7.5P$. For Quantity B, the amount of coffee Lilly and Pablo combined drink in 2 years would be $2(L + P) = 2(4P + P) = 2(5P) = 10P$. Thus, Quantity B is greater than Quantity A, regardless of the value of P (i.e., how much coffee Pablo drinks per year), and the answer is (**B**).

You could also have picked numbers. Say Pablo drinks 100 ounces of coffee per year. Then, Diego drinks 150 ounces per year and Lilly drinks 400 ounces per year. Using these numbers, Quantity A is $150(5) = 750$, while Quantity B is $2(400 + 100) = 1,000$. Again, (**B**) is correct.

7. B

The figure shows a square with a perimeter of 20 units. Since all four sides of a square have the same length, each side of this square has a length of $20 \div 4 = 5$ units; this is Quantity A. The area of a square is equal to the square of one of its sides, so the area of the square is $(5 \text{ units})^2 = 25 \text{ units}^2$. Since each side of a square is the same length, the four triangles created by the two diagonals in the figure have the same area, which means that Quantity B, the area of the shaded region, is one-fourth the area of the square, or $25 \text{ units}^2 \div 4$. This is clearly greater than Quantity A, which is $20 \text{ units} \div 4$, so there is no need to do any further calculation. **(B)** is the correct answer.

8. D

Since a and b are integers, the sum of a and b will be an integer. The only way that sum can be greater than 4 and less than 6 is if it is equal to 5. Thus $a + b = 5$. Think of the possible integer values for a and b that would make this true. One of them could be 1 and the other 4, or one could be 2 and the other 3. However, the centered information also says that the absolute value of $a - b$ is 1. This means a and b are one apart. Thus, either $a = 2$ and $b = 3$ or $a = 3$ and $b = 2$. Both Quantity A and Quantity B deal with the volume of a cylinder, which can be found by squaring the radius and multiplying by π and the height of the cylinder. Thus, Quantity A is $a^2(\pi)(b)$, while Quantity B is $b^2(\pi)(a)$. Since a, b, and π are all positive, both Quantities can be divided by all three of those values to end up with a for Quantity A and b for Quantity B. Since it's impossible to know which of a or b is 2 and which is 3, the correct answer is **(D)**.

9. B

Start with the most concrete information given. The angle to the right of the 115° angle is supplementary to it and therefore measures $180 - 115 = 65$. Since QR is parallel to ST, SP and TP are transversals, and therefore angle PST is 65°, and the angle to the left of the $y + 25$ angle is equal to x. Finally, angle SPT is supplementary to y, and therefore measures $180 - y$. At this point, the figure with information added looks like this:

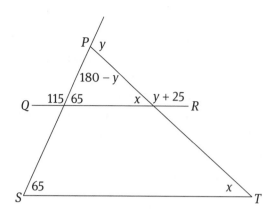

The angles of triangle SPT add up to 180, so $(180 - y) + 65 + x = 180$. This simplifies to $x - y = -65$. (Note that the same equation could have been set up for the small triangle at the top of the figure with the portion of QR that crosses triangle SPT as its base.) Now make use of the $y + 25$ angle. Since it is supplementary to x, $(y + 25) + x = 180$. This simplifies to $x + y = 155$. At this point, you have two equations involving x and y: $x - y = -65$ and $x + y = 155$. Add the two equations together to get $2x = 90$, which means $x = 45$ and the correct answer is **(B)**.

10. 504

This is a permutation problem because the order in which the fossils are chosen matters; each room is a slot that will be filled with one fossilized dinosaur skeleton. For the first room, there are 9 skeletons to choose from. Because one of the nine has already been chosen, for the second room there will be 8 possible skeletons, leaving 7 possibilities for the third room. Thus, the number of possible displays is $9 \times 8 \times 7 = $ **504**.

11. E

The question asks for the number of groups of movies a production company can submit for awards consideration. This is a combinations problem, as the order of the movies doesn't matter. Since there must be at least 3 romantic comedies, the possible groups are 3 romantic comedies and 2 horror movies, 4 romantic comedies and 1 horror movie, or 5 romantic comedies. To find the total number of possible groups, find out how many ways there are to make each type of group and add them up.

If all 5 submitted movies are romantic comedies, then there are $_6C_5$ ways to select such a group. It's possible to use the combinations formula to find this number, but some critical thinking will likely be faster. For each group of five movies, there's one that's not picked. There are 6 ways to choose the movie that will be left out, so there are 6 ways to pick a group of 5 movies.

If 4 of the submitted movies are romantic comedies, there are $_6C_4$ ways to select these 4:

$$_6C_4 = \frac{6!}{4!(6-4)!} = \frac{6!}{4! \times 2!}$$

$$= \frac{6 \times 5 \times \cancel{4 \times 3 \times 2 \times 1}}{\cancel{4 \times 3 \times 2 \times 1} \times 2 \times 1}$$

$$= \frac{30}{2} = 15$$

Each of these 15 groups of 4 could be submitted along with any of the 8 horror movies as the fifth in the set, so there are $8 \times 15 = 120$ ways to submit 4 romantic comedies and 1 horror movie.

The last case to consider is 3 romantic comedies and 2 horror movies. First, count the romantic comedies:

$$_6C_3 = \frac{6!}{3!(6-3)!} = \frac{6!}{3! \times 3!}$$

$$= \frac{\cancel{6} \times 5 \times 4 \times \cancel{3 \times 2 \times 1}}{\cancel{3 \times 2} \times 1 \times \cancel{3 \times 2 \times 1}}$$

$$= 20$$

Now, count the horror movies:

$$_8C_2 = \frac{8!}{2!(8-2)!} = \frac{8!}{2! \times 6!}$$

$$= \frac{8 \times 7 \times \cancel{6 \times 5 \times 4 \times 3 \times 2 \times 1}}{2 \times 1 \times \cancel{6 \times 5 \times 4 \times 3 \times 2 \times 1}}$$

$$= \frac{8 \times 7}{2} = 4 \times 7 = 28$$

Each of these 28 sets of horror movies can be submitted along with any of the 20 sets of romantic comedies, so there are $20 \times 28 = 560$ possible sets of 3 romantic comedies and 2 horror movies. To find the total number of possible 5 movie sets, add up the three possibilities: $560 + 120 + 6 = 686$. **(E)** is correct.

12. 4

Since you need to determine how many machines are needed to roast 84 lbs of coffee beans in 2 hours, start by finding out how much an individual machine can roast in 2 hours. If 10 machines can roast 210 lbs of coffee beans in 3 hours, they can roast 70 lbs in 1 hour. This means that 1 machine can roast 7 lbs in 1 hour, or 14 lbs in 2 hours. $\frac{84}{14} = 6$, so the company originally had 6 roasting machines. Be careful, though; the question asks for the number of new machines purchased, not the original number of roasting machines. If they started with 6 and now have 10, they bought **4** machines.

13. D

Picking Numbers is the best strategy here. If $p = 2$, then $2p = 4$ and $4p - 1 = 7$. The integers 5 and 6 fall between 4 and 7, so plug $p = 2$ into the answer choices to see which is equal to 2, the number of integers.

(A) $\frac{2}{2} \neq 2$

(B) $2 = 2$

(C) $2 + 1 \neq 2$

(D) $2(2) - 2 = 2$

(E) $3(2) - 3 \neq 2$

Both (B) and **(D)** equal 2, so try $p = 3$. In this case $2p = 6$ and $4p - 1 = 11$. There are 4 integers in between: 7, 8, 9, and 10. Since $p = 3$, eliminate (B). Double-check **(D)**: $2(3) - 2 = 6 - 2 = 4$; **(D)** is correct.

14. C, D

The question states that a is a multiple of b, but that multiple is given as a range. The equation $c = \frac{b}{3}$ is also provided, and you're asked to find what $\frac{a}{c}$ could be. Since x, the multiplier for b, could be any value between (but not including) 1 and 4, there are infinite possible values for $\frac{a}{c}$. Plug in the limits for x, 1 and 4, to find the range of allowable values for that fraction.

Simplifying a bit makes this task easier. Rewrite $c = \frac{b}{3}$ as $b = 3c$ so that you can rewrite $a = bx$ as $a = 3cx$. Divide both sides of this equation by c to get $\frac{a}{c} = 3x$. If $x = 1$, then $3x = 3$. If $x = 4$, then $3x = 12$. So the allowable range is $3 < \frac{a}{c} < 12$. Choices (C) and (D) fall within this range. Choices (B) and (E) do not because the endpoints are not included: $1 < x < 4$, not $1 \leq x \leq 4$.

15. 5

Since the perimeter of a square is 4 times the length of a side, the length of each side of $ABCD$ is $32 \div 4 = 8$. The area of a triangle is $\frac{1}{2} \times$ base $\times$ height. The base of the triangle in the figure is DE, the height is AD, and the area is 12. Thus, $12 = \frac{1}{2} \times DE \times 8$, $12 = 4DE$, and $DE = 3$. Since $DE + EC = 8$, $EC = 8 - DE$. Plug in 3 for DE to get $EC = 8 - 3 = $ **5**.

16. C

The question provides two quadratic equations for the positive integers x and y and asks for the value of y. Notice that the first equation is the pattern quadratic, $(a + b)^2 = a^2 + 2ab + b^2$. So, $x^2 + 2xy + y^2 = (x + y)^2 = 49$. Thus, since x and y are positive, $x + y = \sqrt{49} = 7$, but this is not enough information to solve for either x or y. The second equation is another pattern quadratic. Factor $x^2 - y^2$ to $(x + y)(x - y) = -7$. From the other equation, you know that $x + y = 7$, so substitute to get $7(x - y) = -7$, which means that $x - y = -1$. Combine the two equations to isolate one of the variables. You can get y to drop out simply by adding them: $x + y + x - y = 7 + (-1)$. Thus, $2x = 6$ and $x = 3$. Substitute 3 for x in the equation $x + y = 7$ to find that $y = 4$. Choice (C) is correct.

Some critical thinking could save time on this question. Once you find out that $x - y = -1$, which means that y is 1 greater than x and that the two must add up to 7, you could easily determine that x and y have to be 3 and 4, respectively.

17. B, E

The problem gives ranges for both x and y and asks which of the inequalities in the choices *must* be true. Therefore, any choice that could be false can be eliminated. For range questions such as this one, examine the extreme values of the variables as limited by the given ranges. For instance, > 3 could be as small as 3.0000001 or even less. (Note that this problem does not specify that x and y must be integers.)

(A) Incorrect. While a value of x close to 7 minus a value of y close to -2 is positive, a value of x close to 3 less a value of y close to 4 is negative. Since the question asks for statements that *must* be true rather than those that merely *could* be true, this choice is incorrect.

(B) Correct. You only need to examine the minimum values. Since $-2 + 3 > 0$, this inequality will be valid for all permitted values of x and y.

(C) Incorrect. Since the maximum value of y is almost 4 and the minimum value of x is just greater than 3, it is possible for y to be greater than x.

(D) Incorrect. Use the lower limit for y and the upper limit for x: $2(-2) - 7 = -11$, which is much less than 0.

(E) Correct. Use the lower limit for x and the upper limit for y: $2(3) - 4 = 2$, which is greater than 1.

The correct answers are (B) and (E).

18. D

First, determine the year when the combined percent downloads for Latin and Dance was greater than the percent downloads for Pop. In 2012, Pop was 25% and Latin and Dance combined were 35%, which means 2012 is the year in question. The line graph shows that the total number of downloads in 2012 was 28 million. Rounding 28 million up to 30 million and recognizing that 35% is a little more than one-third leads to about 10 million downloads. (D) is the correct choice.

19. C

To find the percent increase in Pop downloads, first find the actual number of Pop downloads for 2008 and for 2012. In 2008, the line graph shows the total number of downloads was 10 million, and the bar graph shows that 40% of those were Pop downloads. That means that the number of Pop downloads in 2008 was 0.40×10 million $= 4$ million. In 2012, the total number of downloads was 28 million, and 25% of those were Pop downloads; so, there were 0.25×28 million $= 7$ million Pop downloads. Applying the percent increase formula to those values results in:

$$\text{Percent increase} = \frac{\text{Amount of increase}}{\text{Original whole}} \times 100\%$$

$$\frac{7 \text{ million} - 4 \text{ million}}{4 \text{ million}} \times 100\%$$

$$= \frac{3 \text{ million}}{4 \text{ million}} \times 100\% = 75\%$$

(C) is the correct answer.

20. B, D, F

Since the bar graph is based on percentages, determine what percent 6 million and 11 million downloads fall between in 2016 and check those against the answer choices. In 2016, there were 40 million total downloads, so the percents that the correct answers need to fall between are 6 million $\div$ 40 million $= 15\%$ and 11 million $\div$ 40 million $= 27.5\%$. Now, go through the choices systematically.

(A): Pop represented 30% of downloads in 2016. That's outside the range because it is greater than 27.5%.

(B): Country represented 20% of downloads in 2016, which does fall between 15% and 27.5%. **(B)** is a correct choice.

(C): R&B/Hip-Hop represented 10% of downloads in 2016. That's less than 15% and is thus outside the range.

(D): Latin represented 15% of downloads in 2016, and since the range is inclusive, **(D)** is correct.

(E): Dance represented 10% of downloads in 2016. That's less than 15% and is thus outside the range.

(F): Other represented 15% of downloads in 2016. Like **(D)**, this choice works because the range is inclusive. **(F)** is correct.

(B), **(D)**, and **(F)** are the correct choices.

Verbal Reasoning 2
Answers and Explanations

1. D

The clues "as technology grows" and "its constant use" allow for a prediction here: the word in the blank should match the phrase "its constant use," so a word like "prevalent" or "widespread" would work well. **(D)** fits that prediction well and is correct. (A) *feckless* means "useless," which does not match the example of "a child who can retrieve the answer to any question." (B) *unreliable* is wrong for the same reason. (C) *irksome* means "annoying," but the sentence does not provide any clues that technology is annoying. Finally, (E) *repetitious* is incorrect because the sentence does not suggest that technology repeats itself; indeed, the phrase "increasingly sophisticated" indicates change.

2. B, D, G

Blank (i) offers a strong clue, so it's a good place to start: languages do something to "new words" while "abandoning old" and "changing others." Predict "adopting" or "creating." **(B)** is a clear match, since *embracing* means "accepting." (A) *auguring* means "predicting." This is a tempting trap, but it does not match the word "evolve," which appears earlier in the sentence. Languages would not "change" merely by predicting new words. Lastly, (C) *obscuring* means "hiding," but nothing in the sentence suggests that a language would hide new words.

The next easiest blank is likely blank (iii), since the sentence gives examples of modern phrases that came from Shakespeare. Use those examples to predict "credits," but be flexible with these phrasal answer choices. **(G)** matches well: the clues in the sentence indicate that these modern English phrases came from Shakespeare. (H) *portends several disconcerting* means "predicts several disturbing" phrases, but the sentence does not suggest that these phrases are disturbing. The verb in (I), *attributes*, could work in the context of the sentence, but the other words in the answer choice, *few impeccable*, make this incorrect, since the sentence does not indicate that Shakespeare made few or "perfect" contributions to modern English.

Finally, predict for blank (ii). The sentence claims that modern English seems to have "little connection" with Shakespeare's language, and the structural keyword "since" offers the explanation. Speakers of modern English "avoid" or "don't use" these archaic words. (D) means "shun" and is correct. (E) *appropriate* means "take for one's own use," but that is the opposite of the sentence's meaning, while (F) *mitigate* means "reduce" or "alleviate," but current speakers do not reduce these words.

3. A, E, H

Begin with blank (i): these animals use jet propulsion to search for prey and *avoid* or *try to get away from* predators. (**A**) works nicely here and is correct. (B) *bifurcate* means "to divide into two branches," but that does not describe getting away from predators. (C) *dissemble* means "to disguise a true feeling," but cephalopods use jet propulsion to move, not to disguise anything.

The word "although" sets up a contrast between animals, which have used jet propulsion for millennia, and humans. The implication is that humans were not able to use jet propulsion to get around until the internal combustion engine was invented. That can serve as your prediction: "did not 'use' jet propulsion." (**E**) is a great match for this prediction. (D) *fortuitously analyze* means "examine by a lucky chance." There is no suggestion of chance playing a role. Moreover, the sentence indicates that the invention of the internal combustion engine allowed humans to *use* jet propulsion, not just to examine it. (F) *rampantly augment* means "add to without restraint." This is incorrect because the sentence does not imply that the invention happened "without restraint" or that people "added to" jet propulsion.

The final blank follows from the contrast keyword "although," as well. Animals have used jet propulsion for a long time, and humans were able to use it after the invention of the internal combustion engine. This development of jet propulsion "made a somewhat inefficient method of locomotion 'workable' for many modern applications." (**H**) matches that prediction. (G) *commensurate* means "in proportion" and does not match the context of the sentence. (I) *sporadic* means "scattered," but the sentence does not imply that the internal combustion engine made jet propulsion "scattered."

4. C, E

"Axiomatic" means "self-evident or beyond question." The detour road sign "though" sets up a contrast between the apparent truth of the phrase and the debate that it causes. Anticipate the right answer to be a word like "difficult" or "major" debate. (**C**) means "causing argument" and matches the prediction perfectly. (A) *dispassionate* means "not influenced by strong feelings," but a major debate would cause strong feelings. (B) *perfunctory* means "involving a minimum of effort." This is incorrect because nothing in the sentence indicates that the debaters are not trying.

Blank (ii) describes the effect that looters who steal artifacts from archaeological sites have on "the country's claim of ownership." Since these looters are taking antiquities without regard for the country's claim, you should predict "ignores" or "undermines." (**E**) means "disregards" and describes the actions of the looters well. (D) *stabilizes* has a positive connotation and does not match the negative implication of the sentence. (F) *demotes* means "makes something less important." The looters may view the country's claim as unimportant, but the act of looting itself ("this" in the original sentence) does not make the country's claim less important.

5. C, E, I

The first part of sentence one makes a claim about "avant-garde," or radical, artists. The straight-ahead road sign "as" shows that the second part of this sentence provides a reason for that claim. Why would radical artists have a hard time gaining acceptance? Because their work confuses and enrages people. Even if the word "avant-garde" is unfamiliar, you can use "produces confusion or even rage" to understand the negative connotation for blank (i). "Controversial" work would have this effect. (**C**) *provocative* matches that prediction perfectly and is correct. (A) *complacent* means "satisfied with things as they are; lacking a desire to change things," but this is the opposite of "avant-garde." (B) *decorous* is wrong for a similar reason: it means "proper," which is the opposite of the blank's intended meaning.

For blank (ii), use clues in the previous sentence: "often produces confusion or even rage." The same works that enraged people might easily have "caused" riots.

Process of elimination may help here. (D) *suppressed* means "restrained," but these works "often" caused confusion, even rage. (E) *engendered* means "caused or gave rise to." This is exactly the effect you'd expect controversial works to have, so (E) is correct. (F) *belied* means "shown to be false," but riots cannot be shown to be false. The riot may have been based on something false or otherwise incorrect, but this blank refers to the riot itself.

There are two detour road signs in the second sentence that help with blank (iii). The phrase "even so" indicates that you should expect an outcome that contrasts with the fact that avant-garde artists struggle for acceptance. The word "but" signals a contrast between the immediate result of the works (riots) with a subsequent result (enormous sums when sold). A good prediction for blank (iii) would be "earned." (I) is correct, since *garnered* means "acquired." (G) *expended* means "used up," which is the opposite of the intended meaning. (H) *underscored* means "emphasized," but the artworks do not merely emphasize the amount of money; they are sold for enormous sums.

6. B

The word "but" creates a contrast between the first and second parts of this sentence. Philosophers have debated about what love really means, but there is one common thread: real love comes from shared understanding and respect. The author entertains the idea that the "diverse uses" of the word "love" have made it harder to achieve a clear definition. Predict "unclear." (B) works well, since *nebulous* means "cloudlike, hazy." (A) *benign* means "harmless," but this does not match the sentence's implication that love is hard to define. (C) *pernicious*, meaning "destructive," (D) *seditious*, or "tending to incite rebellion," and (E) *specious*, or "false," have negative connotations that are too strong for this sentence.

7. C, E

The blank is at the end of the sentence, but the main clue comes toward the beginning; "conflicting" indicates a contrast between the results of the studies. The sentence describes "unpleasant results," so the missing word must describe results that contrast with this. You are looking for a pair of synonyms that have a positive tone and mean something like "pleasant" or "healthy."

(C) *salubrious* means "healthful," and (E) *beneficent* means "advantageous," so that's the correct pair. (A) *addictive* may catch your eye because caffeine can in fact be habit-forming, but the missing word refers to its positive properties. (B) *lackadaisical* means "without enthusiasm," which doesn't fit the context. (D) *adventitious* may be tempting as it looks similar to "advantageous," but it actually means "extrinsic" or "not inherent." Finally, (F) *innocuous*, or "harmless," is not strong enough to contrast with "unpleasant;" furthermore, no other word gives the sentence a similar meaning.

8. B, E

This sentence features the detour road sign "but." On the one hand, the critic does not question something about the researcher; on the other hand, the critic argues that her conclusion isn't supported. The critic finds fault with the researcher's conclusion, so the missing word will be something with which the critic does not find fault. It may be difficult to formulate a specific prediction, so use process of elimination in the answer choices. Start by eliminating anything with a negative charge: (A) *discomfiture* ("embarrassment"); (D) *mortification* (also "embarrassment," which makes these choices a trap pair of synonyms); and (F) *ineptitude* ("lack of skill or ability"). (C) *egoism* ("self-interest") does not fit the context of the sentence, since the critic does not suggest that the researcher is selfish. The correct answers, then, must be (B) *integrity* and (E) *rectitude*, both of which mean "moral correctness" or "honesty." The idea of honesty fits the context of the sentence: the critic is not suggesting that the researcher lied, just that her evidence was not strong enough to prove her conclusion.

9. B, E

The straight-ahead road sign "upon" reveals how the class president reacted to the "incendiary" article. The word "incendiary" literally means "designed to cause fires." When used metaphorically, however, it means "tending to cause conflict." After reading the conflict-causing article, the class president "felt compelled" to respond and "voice his objections." Predict something that follows from the adjective "incendiary": what would someone write to "voice his objections" in response to such an article? It could be something neutral like "response" or something more charged, like "protest" or "complaint." There is an additional clue in the word "harangue," which means "rant," so "protest" is a good prediction. (**B**) and (**E**) match nicely and are correct: they both mean "a verbal attack."

(A) *missive* means "letter." A person could certainly write a letter to an editor, but this has no match among the answer choices, nor is it as charged as the word "harangue" would lead you to expect. (C) *tome* ("a book, especially a long one") is not supported by the clues in the sentence. It's possible the response was long, but the sentence does not indicate that. Additionally, *tome* has no match among the other choices. A *quandary* (D) is a "dilemma," and while a protest or complaint might create a quandary, they are not the same thing. Finally, (F) *hypothesis*, "an explanation proposed for a given phenomenon," does not match the context of the sentence, which gives no hint that the class president seeks to explain anything.

10. B, F

The subordinate clauses in this sentence may make it difficult to analyze. Break the sentence apart to simplify its meaning. The sentence begins with a contrast word, "though," which means that the second half of the sentence, "some species display..." will discuss some features that not all birds of prey share. The other parts of the sentence that mention "excellent eyesight," "excellent hunters," and "high-speed dive" are examples and elaborations that you can ignore unless you need to fine tune your prediction. At this point, however, look for two words that mean "different." (**B**) *unique* and (**F**) *distinctive* fit well, since they both draw on the contrast between "all birds of prey" and "some species." (A) *voracious* means "wanting a great deal of food." This may be true of some birds of prey, but it does not follow from the contrast in the sentence. (C) *fleeting*, "lasting for only a little while," is incorrect because the sentence does not suggest that the characteristics are only temporary. Given the example of the peregrine falcon, (D) *rapid* might be tempting. This choice, however, is incorrect because it misses the contrast in the sentence and lacks a match among the other choices. (E) *advantageous* means "helpful" and is incorrect because it does not create a contrast: all of the characteristics cited in

the sentence ("excellent eyesight," "sharp talons") could be described as helpful. Moreover, there is no match among the remaining choices.

11. C

This argument begins with a discussion of the "look and say" method for teaching children how to read. Though the author describes one benefit of that method, she ultimately rejects the approach and recommends a phonics-based method. The first highlighted sentence offers a benefit of the whole language method. Eliminate (A), since this sentence does not "summarize" the position. Eliminate (B) and (E) since the first highlighted sentence does not state the author's main point or conclusion. The second highlighted sentence offers an advantage of the phonics-based approach. From the remaining choices, eliminate (D) because this sentence is not the conclusion of the argument. (The author's conclusion is that "teachers should use a phonics-based approach.") (**C**) is correct.

12. D

The correct answer to this Inference question must be supported by the passage. The passage discusses the correlation between advanced cultures and realistic art. According to the author, realistic art "often" shows an "advanced" civilization. The author does not claim that this is a perfect correlation, but she cites examples of advanced civilizations that produced realistic art (ancient Greeks and Romans). Analyze each answer to find the choice that is supported by the passage, but be careful to avoid anything that is too extreme to be supported or that goes beyond the scope of the paragraph. (A) goes wrong in two ways: "invariably" is too extreme to follow from the author's tentative claims, and "reject unrealistic art forms" goes beyond the scope of the passage. Perhaps advanced civilizations embrace both realistic and unrealistic art forms. (B) is incorrect because the author does not make a clear causal claim in the passage. Additionally, since the passage makes a qualified assertion ("often"), it's impossible to extend that claim to other civilizations. (C) compares the likelihood that an advanced culture would produce realistic art instead of "any other type of art." The paragraph does not include information about the relative frequency of realistic art and "any other type," so this choice is incorrect. **(D)** makes a tentative claim, "in some...can take...," that is easy to support from the passage. The author claims that Europeans took "nearly a millennium" to develop realistic painting and sculpture after the ancient Romans lost the ability to create them. Tentative or "soft" claims are easier to support than absolute claims. This choice is correct. **(E)** is incorrect because the author does not discuss modern abstract art.

13. A

According to the passage, Nelson's tactics were unorthodox, so they could be described as "contrary to conventional military wisdom." They're also described as a risk that "paid off," so the author must think that they contributed, at least in part, to the British victory. **(A)** is correct. **(B)** may seem tempting because it lines up with what King George III said in regard to Nelson's death, but there is no way to know whether the author agrees with it, so it's incorrect. **(C)** is incorrect because it's too extreme; the author thinks that the unconventional tactics contributed to the victory, but again, there is no way to know whether she believes they were essential to the victory.

14. E

This Logic question asks why a particular detail was used. The *Santísima Trinidad* was mentioned in the middle of the passage as an example to support the point that the British fleet was outgunned and that victory did not seem certain. **(E)** is a good match for this prediction; the British may not have been confident of victory because of the more powerful enemy fleet. **(A)** is incorrect; all that was said about Nelson's battle plan is that it was "unorthodox." **(B)** is contradicted by the passage; if this ship was a common design, then it wouldn't be "the most heavily armed ship in the world." **(C)** may seem tempting, since the ship is used in support of the idea that the British weren't certain that they'd be victorious; however, there's no discussion of what the Spanish thought about their chances in the battle. **(D)** is too extreme; the British may not have been entirely confident that they'd win, but that doesn't mean Nelson thought that they would lose.

15. B

This Logic question requires researching the last paragraph of the passage. The example of Frey differs from that of Seltzer in that he experienced more success before his downfall and was able to write a successful novel later in his career. **(B)** is the choice that captures the later literary success and is the correct answer. The last sentence says that the media's view softened later, but that does not mean that their initial reaction was too harsh, which makes **(A)** incorrect. **(C)** is incorrect because there is no support in the passage that Frey was an obscure example. The phrase "malicious intent" is too extreme based on the passage and makes **(D)** incorrect. Frey did not experience permanent damage to his literary career, so **(E)** is incorrect.

16. D

The main point of the passage is to discuss the experiences of two authors whose memoirs were later shown to be untrue. The choice that most closely matches this understanding is **(D)**. The incorrect answer choices are either too narrow or misrepresent the purpose of the passage with strong negative language. **(A)** speaks to a direct criticism that does not occur anywhere within the passage. **(B)** refers to the repercussions, but their effectiveness is never directly addressed in the passage. **(C)** is incorrect because the author never explicitly takes a side on whether the two authors were treated unfairly. **(E)** is addressed within the passage, but the debate between the two views is not the main point of the passage.

17. A

The author notes that Seltzer claimed to write the book to give a voice to those ignored by society, but the author goes on to say that this claim was not substantiated by the persona Seltzer adopted when promoting her book. The author implies that Seltzer was looking out for her own interests and states that she did a disservice to the people who actually experienced the events she wrote about. This matches **(A)** *self-serving*, which means "to put one's own welfare and interests before those of others." **(B)** *unpremeditated* and **(D)** *spontaneous* both mean "without forethought," but Seltzer knew that her memoir was a fabrication, so these choices are both incorrect. Seltzer's book is the opposite of *authentic* since it never actually happened, so (C) is incorrect. (E) *authoritative*, or "accurate," is incorrect for the same reason.

18. B

This Inference question is too broad to make a prediction, so it is best to work through the choices and look for proof in the passage. (A) is not true for either author. Seltzer's work was a complete fabrication, and Frey's memoir included many embellishments.
(B) has support in the passage because the falsehoods and exaggerations the two authors included in their memoirs were intentional and led to their respective downfalls. (C) is incorrect because it is too sweeping a statement to make, especially considering that Frey wrote another best seller. The passage does not speak on the level of deception in other genres, so (D) is incorrect. (E) is incorrect because the passage never states Frey's motivations, and while the author implies that Seltzer's reason for writing was self-serving, there is no explicit mention of a financial motive. The correct answer is **(B)**.

19. C

This is a Detail EXCEPT question, so find the detail that is not mentioned in the passage. Also, keep in mind that Seltzer's experience is discussed in the second paragraph, so that is where your research should be focused. (A) and (E) are mentioned in the penultimate sentence of the second paragraph as something Seltzer felt she needed to do to lend authenticity to her story, so both choices are incorrect. Seltzer grew up in the suburbs of Los Angeles but changed the setting of her memoir to South Central Los Angeles to lend it credence, so (B) is incorrect. Seltzer's sister revealed her true identity, so it is reasonable to infer that Seltzer did not elicit her family's cooperation; thus, **(C)** is the correct answer. The second sentence in the second paragraph states that Seltzer used the pseudonym Margaret B. Jones so that she could not be readily identified. It can be inferred that this step was taken to add authenticity to a story that could otherwise easily be proved untrue, so (D) is incorrect.

20. E

This Inference question asks for one of the differences in Seltzer's and Frey's experiences as described in the passage. A few key differences stand out: Seltzer never had another work published while Frey wrote another best seller, Seltzer's memoir was wholly untrue while Frey's was only partly untrue, and Frey experienced more success with *A Million Little Pieces* than Seltzer did with *Love and Consequences*. **(E)** is the best match because Seltzer's memoir was recalled shortly after it was discovered to have been fabricated, while Frey remained on the best-seller list for fifteen weeks before his fabrications were exposed. (A) is incorrect because the passage never states that Frey's *only* motivation was financial gain. Seltzer had her book recalled and never published another, so the negative media attention she received was at least as damaging as that received by Frey, making (B) incorrect. (C) is incorrect because the author never addresses whether the respective consequences to either author were deserved. Frey's family is never mentioned in the passage, so (D) is incorrect.

Quantitative Reasoning 2 Answers and Explanations

1. C

The perimeter of isosceles triangle *ABC* is 32, the length of one side is 10, and the height is 8. Your job is to compare the longest side of the triangle to 12. There are two ways to create an isosceles triangle with perimeter 32 and one side of length 10. In one scenario, there are two sides, each 10 units long. In this case, the remaining side will be $32 - 10 - 10 = 12$ units long, and the triangle will look like this sketch:

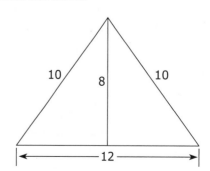

In this instance, the height bisects the base of $\triangle ABC$ to create two right triangles, each with a short leg of 6 and a hypotenuse of 10. So these are $3:4:5$ right triangles with sides of 6, 8, and 10. Thus, the height of $\triangle ABC$, as stated in the centered information, is 8, and it follows that sides of 10, 10, and 12 are allowable for $\triangle ABC$ under the constraints provided. The length of the longest side of $\triangle ABC$ is 12, and the two Quantities are equal.

In the second scenario, the side with length 10 is the side that does *not* match another side. In this case, the total length of the two equal sides must be $32 - 10 = 22$, which means each of the matching sides is half that, 11. So this time, $\triangle ABC$ would be divided into right triangles with one side equal to 5 and a hypotenuse of 11.

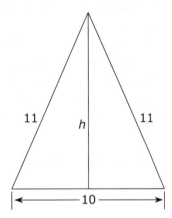

Using the Pythagorean theorem, $h^2 + 5^2 = 11^2$. So, $h^2 = 121 - 25 = 96$. Thus, the height of this triangle is $\sqrt{96}$. However, the centered information states that the height is 8; therefore, the equal sides can't be 11. Instead, the equal sides of $\triangle ABC$ are 10, and the longest side is 12, as shown in the first sketch; **(C)** is correct.

2. A

The centered information is a function of the variable z. The comparison is between the value of the function when z is $\frac{1}{3}$ and the number 2. Plug $\frac{1}{3}$ in for z and evaluate the function: $g\left(\frac{1}{3}\right) = \dfrac{1}{\left(\frac{1}{3}-1\right)^2} = \dfrac{1}{\left(-\frac{2}{3}\right)^2} = \dfrac{1}{\frac{4}{9}}$. When dividing by a fraction, invert the fraction and multiply. So, $g\left(\frac{1}{3}\right) = 1 \times \frac{9}{4} = 2\frac{1}{4}$. Since this is greater than 2, **(A)** is correct.

3. B

The centered information provides the distance between two cities and the average speeds between the two cities when traveling by plane and by train. Quantity A is just a way of saying how much longer it takes to travel from A to B by train than by plane. Quantity B is 330 minutes.

Use the basic formula Rate $\times$ Time $=$ Distance rearranged to Time $= \dfrac{\text{Distance}}{\text{Rate}}$. For the plane, that is $\frac{400}{300} = 1\frac{1}{3}$ hours. For the train, the time is $\frac{400}{60} = 6\frac{2}{3}$ hours. The difference is $6\frac{2}{3} - 1\frac{1}{3} = 5\frac{1}{3}$ hours. When converted to minutes, that is $5 \times 60 + \frac{1}{3} \times 60 = 300 + 20 = 320$ minutes. **(B)** is correct.

Alternatively, you could have converted the two speeds to miles per minute by dividing the speeds in miles per hour by 60. The plane's speed was $300 \div 60 = 5$ miles per minute, and the train's speed was 1 mile per minute. Thus, the plane took $400 \div 5 = 80$ minutes, and the train made the journey in $400 \div 1 = 400$ minutes. The difference between the two is 320 minutes.

4. A

The centered information describes two raises that Navid received in two separate years. The first raise was $10,000 and the second was $10,800. Quantity A represents the percent increase of the first raise and Quantity B the percent increase of the second. Be careful here. While the second raise may have a greater dollar amount, it may not have been a greater percent increase, since each percent increase is based on a different starting value.

The percent increase formula is

$$\text{Percent increase} = \frac{\text{Amount}}{\text{Original whole}} \times 100\%$$

Start by finding the percent increase in 2015:

$$\text{Percent increase} = \frac{\$10,000}{\$50,000} \times 100\% = 0.2 \times 100\% = 20\%$$

Now, find the percent increase for 2017:

$$\text{Percent increase} = \frac{\$10,800}{\$60,000} \times 100\% = 0.18 \times 100\% = 18\%$$

Thus, despite the fact that the dollar value of the 2017 raise was greater, the 2015 raise was actually a bigger percent increase. Quantity A is greater, so the answer is (**A**).

5. A

Remember that geometry figures need not be drawn to scale on the GRE, so avoid the temptation to answer the question based on the appearance of the diagram. Since angle ACB makes a straight line along with n and $n = 120°$, angle ACB must be $60°$. Since ℓ_1 and ℓ_2 are parallel, all acute angles formed by a transversal are equal as well as all obtuse angles. Notice that angle ABC makes a straight line along with one of these obtuse angles; this obtuse angle must therefore be equal to m, so it's also $150°$. Thus, angle ABC is $30°$. This means that triangle ABC is a $30°$-$60°$-$90°$ triangle, and its side lengths have the ratio $x : x\sqrt{3} : 2x$, where x is the side opposite the $30°$ angle. In this triangle, that's AC. So $AC = x$ and $AB = x\sqrt{3}$. Although there's no way to find out the value of x, AB must be bigger; (**A**) is correct. It's also possible to get to this answer without using the $30°$-$60°$-$90°$ side ratio because in a triangle, a side opposite a larger angle is longer than a side opposite a smaller angle.

6. A

The centered information shows line segment RT with a total length of 4 divided into segments y and z where $3y - z = 8$. The comparison is between the length of segment RS, which is y, and 2.5. Since the total length of the line segment is 4, you can write the equation $y + z = 4$. Now, you have two variables and two distinct linear equations. Add the two equations:

$$3y - z = 8$$
$$\underline{y + z = 4}$$
$$4y = 12$$
$$y = 3$$

Since $3 > 2.5$, (**A**) is correct.

7. D

To make the comparison easier to work with, manipulate the given inequality so that x and z are on the left side and $-y$ is on the right, just as it is in Quantity A on the left and Quantity B on the right. Subtract z and y from both sides of the centered inequality: $x + y - z - y < z - z - y$ simplifies to $x - z < -y$. If x is negative, then $2x - z$ is even less than $x - z$, so Quantity B would be greater. However, if, for instance, $x = 2, y = 1$, and $z = 4$, then $x - z < -y$, so these values are permissible, but $2x - z > -y$. So, for those values, Quantity A is greater. (**D**) is correct.

8. C

The area of a triangle equals $\frac{1}{2} \times$ base $\times$ height, which for $\triangle ABE$ is $\frac{1}{2} \times 2 \times 2 = 2$. Furthermore, since $\triangle ABE$ is a right isosceles, the ratio of the sides is $1 : 1 : \sqrt{2}$. Because the equal sides are 2, the hypotenuse, BE, is $2\sqrt{2}$. The area of a rectangle is base $\times$ height. In this case, that is $BE \times DE$. Plug in the known values: $2 = 2\sqrt{2} \times DE$. Divide both sides by $2\sqrt{2}$ to get $\frac{2}{2\sqrt{2}} = DE$, which simplifies to $\frac{1}{\sqrt{2}} = DE$. Thus, the ratio of BE to DE is $\frac{2\sqrt{2}}{\frac{1}{\sqrt{2}}} = 2\sqrt{2} \times \frac{\sqrt{2}}{1} = \frac{4}{1}$. This is equivalent to $4 : 1$, so (**C**) is correct.

9. C

The formula for the circumference of a circle is $\pi \times$ diameter. If the circumference of each circle in the figure is 8π, the diameter of each circle is 8, and the radius is 4. Each side of triangle PQR consists of the full diameter of the circle in the middle plus the radii of the two circles on the ends. For example, side RP consists of the radius of the circle with center R, the diameter of the middle circle above that, and the radius of the circle with center P. Thus, side RP has a length of $4 + 8 + 4 = 16$. Since each side of the triangle passes through the same number of radii, each side has the same length. The perimeter of the entire triangle is therefore $16 \times 3 = 48$. The correct answer is (**C**).

10. D

Begin by dealing with the negative exponent in the fraction. To handle a negative exponent, take the reciprocal of the base to the positive value of the exponent. In other words, $6^{-2} = \dfrac{1}{6^2}$. That means $\dfrac{14}{6^{-2}} = \dfrac{14}{\frac{1}{6^2}} = 14 \times \dfrac{6^2}{1} = 14 \times 6^2$. The equation then becomes $14 \times 6^2 \times 45 = 2^x \times 3^4 \times 35$. At this point, rather than multiplying and dividing with the calculator, break the numbers down into their prime factors. This will keep the numbers small and make it easier to see how the exponents fit in. The result is $2 \times 7 \times (2 \times 3)^2 \times 3 \times 3 \times 5 = 2^x \times 3^4 \times 5 \times 7$. Expand the exponents to get $2 \times 7 \times 2 \times 3 \times 2 \times 3 \times 3 \times 3 \times 5 = 2^x \times 3 \times 3 \times 3 \times 3 \times 5 \times 7$. Now divide both sides by all of the common prime factors. Do this simply by crossing off the prime factors that appear on both sides, as follows: $2 \times \cancel{7} \times 2 \times \cancel{3} \times 2 \times \cancel{3} \times \cancel{3} \times \cancel{3} \times \cancel{5} = 2^x \times \cancel{3} \times \cancel{3} \times \cancel{3} \times \cancel{3} \times \cancel{5} \times \cancel{7}$. What remains is $2 \times 2 \times 2 = 2^x$. Thus $x = 3$, and (**D**) is the correct answer.

11. C

The question provides only one equation with two variables, but it asks for the value of the ratio of those two variables rather than the values of the variables themselves. This question could not ask for the value of each variable since it provides only one distinct equation with two variables. It is possible, however, to solve for the ratio of the variables. Start by simplifying the right side: $3 - 5\dfrac{2}{5} = \dfrac{15}{5} - \dfrac{27}{5} = -\dfrac{12}{5} = \dfrac{w - z}{w}$. Cross multiply to get rid of the fractions: $5(w - z) = -12w$. Distribute: $5w - 5z = -12w$. Then, add $12w$ and $5z$ to both sides to get $17w = 5z$. Finally, divide both sides by z and by 17: $\dfrac{w}{z} = \dfrac{5}{17}$. (**C**) is correct.

12. 0.4

The figure can be divided into a right triangle on top of a trapezoid. Use the numbers on the grid to calculate the dimensions of the triangle and the trapezoid. The base of the triangle extends to the left from point B $(2.0, -1.2)$ to the point where a horizontal line would intersect line AB at $(1.4, -1.2)$. The height of the triangle is the distance from this point to point A $(1.4, -0.8)$. So the length of

the base is $|2.0 - 1.4| = 0.6$ and the height is $|-0.8 - (-1.2)| = 0.4$. Use the equation for the area of a triangle: $A = \dfrac{1}{2}bh = \dfrac{1}{2} \times 0.6 \times 0.4 = 0.12$.

The upper parallel side of the trapezoid is the base of the triangle, which is 0.6 long. The lower parallel side is line DC, so the length of that side is $|2.2 - 1.4| = 0.8$. The height of the trapezoid is $|-1.2 - (-1.6)| = 0.4$. Use the formula for the area of a trapezoid:

$\text{Area} = \dfrac{b_1 + b_2}{2} \times h = \dfrac{0.6 + 0.8}{2} \times 0.4 = 0.28$. So the total area of the figure is $0.12 + 0.28 = \mathbf{0.4}$ square units.

13. C

The question asks for the number that is 40% less than 1.25×10^4, which is 12,500. To minimize calculation, find $100\% - 40\% = 60\%$ of 12,500: $0.60 \times 12,500 = 7,500$. In scientific notation, this is 7.5×10^3, which is (**C**).

14. A, D

The right answer(s) for this question must have an odd number of factors in order to be divisible by an odd number of different positive integers. First, eliminate any prime numbers since they are divisible only by themselves and 1. (B) 17 is a prime number. Now check the remaining choices. The factors of 9 are 1, 3, and 9, so (**A**) is a correct choice. The positive factors of 24 are 1, 2, 3, 4, 6, 8, 12, and 24 for a total of 8, so eliminate (C). The distinct positive factors of 36 are 1, 2, 3, 4, 6, 9, 12, 18, and 36 for a total of 9, so (D) is a correct choice. Finally, the positive factors of 42 are 1, 2, 3, 6, 7, 14, 21, and 42. Since there are 8 factors, (**E**) is incorrect. The correct choices are (**A**) and (**D**).

Perhaps you noticed that both correct answers are perfect squares. That is because the numbers that are not perfect squares have pairs of factors and thus an even number of factors. However, a perfect square has one single factor that is the square root, thereby creating an odd number of factors. If you make this connection initially, you can quickly identify the correct choices.

15. 3

Triangle ABC is a right triangle with a short side of $2\sqrt{3}$ cm and a hypotenuse of $4\sqrt{3}$ cm. Because the short side is half the hypotenuse, this is a 30°-60°-90° triangle with the 30° angle at vertex A. The ratio of the sides of this triangle are $1:\sqrt{3}:2$, so side AB is $\sqrt{3} \times 2\sqrt{3} = 2 \times 3 = 6$.

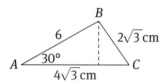

A perpendicular line from B to line AC creates two more 30°-60°-90° triangles. In the triangle on the left, the perpendicular is the short side and the hypotenuse is 6. The length of the perpendicular is half the length of the hypotenuse, or **3**.

16. C

Rearrange the formula $\text{Average} = \dfrac{\text{Sum of terms}}{\text{Number of terms}}$ to Sum of terms = Average × Number of terms. The sum of all three numbers is $3(5a - 2) = 15a - 6$. The average of the other two numbers is $4a + 2b + 1$, so their total is twice that, or $8a + 4b + 2$. The remaining number must be the difference between these totals: $15a - 6 - (8a + 4b + 2) = 15a - 6 - 8a - 4b - 2 = 7a - 4b - 8$. **(C)** is correct.

17. B, D

Test each point. Substitute a value for x and compare the result to the given value for y in the ordered pair.

(A) Let $x = -5$.
$$y = \frac{3x^2 + 2}{x - 1} = \frac{3(-5)^2 + 2}{-5 - 1} = \frac{77}{-6} \neq -13$$

(B) Let $x = -4$.
$$y = \frac{3x^2 + 2}{x - 1} = \frac{3(-4)^2 + 2}{-4 - 1} = \frac{50}{-5} = -10$$

(C) Let $x = 0$.
$$y = \frac{3x^2 + 2}{x - 1} = \frac{3(0)^2 + 2}{0 - 1} = \frac{2}{-1} \neq 2$$

(D) Let $x = 3$.
$$y = \frac{3x^2 + 2}{x - 1} = \frac{3(3)^2 + 2}{3 - 1} = \frac{29}{2} = 14\frac{1}{2}$$

(E) Let $x = 5$.
$$y = \frac{3x^2 + 2}{x - 1} = \frac{3(5)^2 + 2}{5 - 1} = \frac{77}{4} \neq 19\frac{1}{2}$$

The correct answers are **(B)** and **(D)**.

18. E

An efficient way to solve this question is to consider that the number of criminal law attorneys (18%) is three times as large as the number of family law attorneys (6%). Simply multiply the 20,000 family law attorneys by 3 to find that there are 60,000, **(E)**, criminal law attorneys.

19. B

Start by finding the total number of lawyers in 2015. Since there were 28,000 corporate law members representing 14% of all lawyers in 2015, divide 28,000 by 14% to get 200,000 total. Use this to find the number of criminal law attorneys in 2015: 18% of 200,000 is 36,000. Once you know this, you can calculate the number of criminal law attorneys in 2016. First, 4,500 fewer than 36,000 is 31,500. And since criminal law attorneys still make up 18% of all attorneys in 2016, divide 31,500 by 18%. That gives you **(B)**, 175,000.

20. E

The question asks for the percent increase from one value to the next. Use the percent change formula: first find the amount of change between values and then divide that amount by the original value. In 2015, the difference between intellectual property lawyers and personal injury lawyers is 3%. But that's not the correct answer, because you are looking for the *percent increase*. The amount of change (3%) divided by the original amount (7%) is roughly 43%, **(E)**.

Perhaps an easier way to think about this would be to pick a real number for total lawyers. Here, because the question deals with percents, a good number to pick would be 100. In that case, out of 100 lawyers in 2015, 7 are intellectual property and 10 are personal injury. For the number of intellectual property lawyers to increase to match the number of personal injury lawyers, there would need to be 3 more intellectual property lawyers. So, the increase from 7 to 10 would be 3, and 3 divided by 7 is roughly 43%.

PART SIX

TEST DAY AND BEYOND

CHAPTER 27

TAKE CONTROL OF THE TEST

Now that you're familiar with the content that makes up each section of the GRE and are armed with the strategies and techniques you'll need to tackle all of the question types, you're ready to turn your attention to building the right mentality and attitude that will help you succeed on Test Day. Let's first go over the basic principles of good test mentality.

Kaplan's Four Basic Principles of Good Test Mentality

You are already armed with the weapons that you need to do well on the GRE. But you must wield those weapons with the right frame of mind and in the right spirit. This involves taking a certain stance toward the entire test and bolstering your stamina, confidence, and attitude.

Test Awareness

To do your best on the GRE, keep in mind that the test is different from other tests you've taken before, both in terms of its content and in terms of its scoring system. If you took a test in high school or college and got a quarter of the questions wrong, you probably received a mediocre grade. But this is not necessarily true with the GRE. The test is geared so that even the very best test takers don't necessarily get every question right.

What does this mean for you? Well, just as you shouldn't let one tough Reading Comprehension passage ruin an entire section, you shouldn't let what you consider to be a subpar performance on one section ruin your performance on the entire test. If you allow that subpar section to rattle you, it sets in motion a downward spiral that could do serious damage to your score. Losing a few extra points won't do you in, but losing your head will. Keeping your composure is an important test-taking skill.

Also, you should remember that if you feel you've done poorly on a section, it could very well have been the experimental section. You'll have the opportunity immediately after you've taken the test to think about whether you want to cancel your score. You might underestimate your performance, since you're more likely to remember the questions you thought were more difficult. The major takeaway is to stay confident throughout the test.

Stamina

Overall, the GRE is a grueling experience. Remember, you'll be completing six full-length sections on Test Day (one Analytical Writing, two Verbal Reasoning, two Quantitative Reasoning, and one Experimental or Research). It is a true test of endurance, and some test takers run out of gas on the final few sections.

To avoid this, you must build up your test-taking stamina by taking as many full-length practice tests as possible several weeks before the test. If you do this, by Test Day, completing this test won't seem like such a daunting task.

You can download a free copy of the POWERPREP II software, including two multi-stage practice tests, directly from **www.gre.org**.

Another option, if you haven't already done so, would be to take a Kaplan course, either classroom-based or online. You could also set up special one-on-one tutoring sessions with Kaplan faculty. If you decide to go this route, visit **www.kaptest.com/GRE** or call 1-800-KAP-TEST for information on a Kaplan classroom or tutoring program.

Confidence

Confidence is self-sustaining, and unfortunately, so is its opposite—self-doubt. Confidence in your ability leads to quick, sure answers and an ease of concentration that translates into more points. If you lack confidence, you might lose concentration and end up reading sentences and answer choices two, three, or four times. This leads to timing difficulties, which only continue the downward spiral, causing anxiety and a tendency to rush. If you subscribe to the test-prep mindset that we've described, however, you'll be ready and able to take control of the test. Learn our techniques and then practice them over and over again. That's the way to score your best on the test.

Attitude

Those who fear the test or consider it an extra hurdle in the long race toward graduate school usually don't fare as well as those who see the GRE as an opportunity to show off the reading and reasoning skills that graduate schools are looking for. In fact, consider this: the test is designed to reward you. Those who look forward to the GRE as a challenge—or, at least, who enjoy the opportunity to distinguish themselves from the rest of the applicant pack—tend to score better than do those who resent it.

It may sound a little dubious, but take our word for it: altering your approach is proven to raise scores. Here are a few steps you can take to make sure you develop the right GRE attitude:

- Recognize that the GRE is a challenge but also an opportunity. Focus on the skills you've learned and remember that these will set you apart from your competition.
- Remember that, yes, the GRE is obviously important, but contrary to what some people think, this one test will not single-handedly determine the outcome of your life. In many cases, it's not even the most important piece of your graduate application.

- Since the test is predictable, think of the GRE as a reward for understanding the same core skills that show up all the time.
- Remember that you're more prepared than most people. You've trained with Kaplan. You have the tools you need plus the know-how to use those tools.

Kaplan's basic principles of good test mentality are as follows:

- Be aware of the test and keep your composure even when you are struggling with a difficult question; missing one question won't ruin your score for a section.
- Build your stamina by taking as many practice tests as you can.
- Be confident; you are already well on your way to a great score!
- Stay positive; consider the GRE an opportunity rather than an obstacle.

The Kaplan Stress-Management System

Is it starting to feel as if your whole life is a buildup to the GRE? You've known about it for years, worried about it for months, and now spent at least a few weeks in solid preparation for it. As the test gets closer, you may find that your anxiety is on the rise. You shouldn't worry. Armed with the preparation strategies that you've learned from this book, you're in good shape for Test Day. To calm any pretest jitters that you may have, however, let's go over a few strategies for the couple of days before the test.

Tips for the Days Just Before the Exam

- The best test takers do less and less as the test approaches. Taper off your study schedule and take it easy on yourself. Give yourself time off, especially the evening before the exam. By that time, if you've studied well, everything you need to know is firmly stored in your memory bank. In fact, it's in your best interest to marshal your physical and psychological resources for the last 24 hours or so before the test. Keep the test out of your consciousness; go to a movie, take a pleasant walk, or just relax. Eat healthy meals and steer clear of sugar and caffeine. And, of course, get plenty of rest that night and also the night before. It's hard to fall asleep earlier than you're used to, and you don't want to lie there worrying about the test.
- Most importantly, make sure you know where the test will be held and the easiest, quickest way to get there. You'll have great peace of mind by knowing that all the little details are set before Test Day.
- Visit the test site a few days in advance, particularly if you are especially anxious.

Handling Stress During the Test

The biggest source of stress will be the test itself. Fear not! The following are methods to relieve your stress during the test:

- Keep moving forward instead of getting bogged down in a difficult question. You don't have to get everything right to achieve a solid score. So don't linger out of desperation on a question that is going nowhere even after you've spent considerable time on it.
- Breathe! Weak test takers tend to share one major trait: they don't breathe properly as the test proceeds. They might hold their breath without realizing it or breathe irregularly. Improper breathing hurts confidence and accuracy. Just as importantly, it interferes with clear thinking.

Test Day

The night before Test Day, gather the following things together:

- ID
- admission ticket
- a watch
- a bottle of water
- aspirin or other painkiller, in case you get a headache
- a snack, such as fruit or an energy bar, to keep your energy up for the later sections of the test
- names of schools you'd like to receive your scores

Test Day should start with a moderate, high-energy breakfast. Cereal, fruit, bagels, or eggs are good. Avoid doughnuts, pastries, or anything else with a lot of sugar. Also, unless you are utterly catatonic without it, it's a good idea to stay away from coffee.

Yes, perhaps you drink two cups every morning and don't even notice it. But it's different during the test. Coffee won't make you alert (your adrenaline will do that much more effectively); it will just give you the jitters. Kaplan has done experiments in which test takers go into one exam having drunk various amounts of coffee and another exam without having drunk coffee. The results indicate that even the most caffeine-addicted test takers will lose their focus midway through the second section if they've had coffee, but they report no alertness problems without it.

When you get to the test center, you will be seated at a computer station. Some administrative questions will be asked before the test begins and, once you're done with those, you're set to go. While you're taking the test, a small clock will count down the time you have left in each section. The computer will tell you when you're done with each section and when you've completed the test.

Here are some last-minute reminders to help guide your work on the test:

- Take a few minutes now to look back over your preparation and give yourself credit for all the work you put into it. Confidence is far more useful than distress.

- Don't bother trying to figure out which section is the experimental section. It can't help you, and you might make a tragic mistake if you guess wrong. Instead, just do your best on every section.

- Dress in layers for maximum comfort. This way, you can adjust to the room's temperature accordingly.

- During the exam, try not to fixate on what your score is or how you're doing so far. It's counterproductive to continue to think about questions you've already answered or ones you haven't gotten to yet. If you worry about the next section, or the one you've just completed, you'll just feel overwhelmed. Instead, focus on the question-by-question task of picking the correct answer choice. Try to take things one step at a time. Concentrate on each question, each passage, and each essay prompt—on the mechanics, in other words—and you'll avoid cognitive confusion.

After all the hard work that you've put in preparing for and taking the GRE, make sure you take time to celebrate afterward. Plan to get together with friends the evening after the test. You prepared for the test ahead of time. You did your best. You're going to get a great score.

CHAPTER 28

WHERE AND WHEN TO APPLY

You probably know what you want to study as a graduate student, but where should you apply? The answer to this question is dependent on two main factors: which programs would be best for you and which of these programs you can actually get into. This chapter will help you answer these questions—and many more you may have about the process of choosing a school for postgraduate study.

What Programs You Should Consider

Once you have made the decision to pursue graduate studies, you should take the decision about where to go to school seriously—it will have a major influence on your daily life for the next several years and will influence your academic and career paths for years to come. Many students allow themselves to be influenced by a professor, a mentor, or school rankings and then find they're unhappy in a certain program because of its location, its workload, its cost, or some other unforeseen factor. If you complete your own research, even if it takes time and hard work, you will be happier with your own choice. Let's take a look at some of the factors you'll need to consider when choosing a school.

Your Goals

Keep your goals in mind when evaluating graduate programs. Before you take the leap, it's important that you have a pretty clear idea where your interests lie, what grad school life is like, and whether you're compatible with a particular program and its professors. Armed with this information, you should be able to successfully apply to the right programs, get accepted, and use your time in graduate school to help you get a head start on the post-graduation job search.

Students decide to enter master's and doctoral degree programs for a variety of reasons. Some want to pursue a career in academia. To teach at two-year colleges, you'll need at least a master's degree; to teach and do research at four-year colleges, universities, and graduate programs, you'll need a doctorate. Other people need graduate education to meet national and state licensing requirements in fields such as social work, engineering, and architecture. Some students want to change careers, while others expect an advanced degree to open up new opportunities in their current field.

Most master's programs are two years long. Master's students are generally one of two types: those on an academic track, where the degree program focuses on classical research and scholarship, and those on a practical track, where the degree program is actually a professional training course that qualifies people to enter or advance in a field such as social work or education.

Other options to consider if you're pursuing a master's degree are cooperative, joint, and interdisciplinary programs. In cooperative programs, you apply to, answer to, and graduate from one school, but you have access to classes, professors, and facilities at one or more cooperating schools. In joint- or dual-degree programs, you work toward two degrees simultaneously, either within the same school or at two neighboring schools. Interdisciplinary programs are generally run by a committee consisting of faculty from a number of different departments. You apply to, register with, and are graduated by only one of the departments; you and your faculty committee design your curriculum.

Doctoral programs are designed to create scholars capable of independent research that will add new and significant knowledge to their fields. At first, you'll be regarded as an apprentice in your field. Your first year or two in the program will be spent on coursework, followed by "field" or "qualifying" exams. Once you have passed those exams, demonstrating that you have the basic factual and theoretical knowledge of your field down cold, you'll be permitted to move on to independent research in the form of your doctoral dissertation. During most of this time, you can get financial aid in the form of stipends through teaching or research.

If you want to get a doctoral degree, you can get a master's and then apply to PhD programs, or you may enter directly into the doctoral program. The first method gives you flexibility but generally takes longer, costs more in the long run, and means reliving the application process. However, some doctoral programs in certain fields of study require a full master's degree for acceptance.

Program Reputation

Although you should not place too much stock in school and program rankings, you should consider a program's overall reputation. When you assess a program's reputation, don't just consider its national ranking, but think about whether it fits your goals and interests. You can get information from a variety of sources, formal and informal.

Each year, various groups publish rankings of graduate programs: *U.S. News and World Report* on American graduate programs, *Maclean's* on Canadian programs, and many others. These rankings can give you a general sense of the programs in your field and may include profiles of distinguished professors, but they tell you nothing about departmental politics, job placement records, or financial aid possibilities.

You should find out which programs are highly regarded in the areas that interest you. You can learn these details through professional associations (such as the American Psychological Association for programs in psychology fields), comprehensive commercial directories of graduate programs (available through school or local libraries), and the Internet.

Don't forget to contact schools and departments directly. Most departments have a chairperson who is also the admissions contact; she can put you in touch with current students and alumni who are willing to discuss the program with you. The chair is usually willing to answer questions as well.

Try to speak to at least one current student and one alum from each program you're seriously considering. You'll find that many graduate students are quite outspoken about the strengths and weaknesses of professors, programs, and the state of the job market in their field.

If you're an undergraduate, or still have contacts from your undergraduate experience, ask your professors for their take on the various graduate programs. You'll often find that they have a great deal of inside information on academic and research trends, impending retirements, intellectual rivalries, and rising stars.

Remember, a program's reputation isn't everything. However, the higher your school is regarded in the marketplace, the better your job prospects are likely to be upon graduation.

Location

Two key questions you should consider regarding a school's location are: How will it affect the overall quality of your graduate school experience, and how will it affect your ability to be employed once you are done with your studies? Some students prefer an urban setting. Others prefer a more rustic environment. Cost of living can also be a factor.

Geography may be an important criterion for you. Perhaps your geographical choices are limited by a spouse's job or other family obligations. Perhaps you already know where you want to live after graduation. If you're planning on a career in academia, you'll probably want to choose a nationally known program, regardless of where it's located. If, on the other hand, your program involves a practice component (physician's assistant, social work, education, or some interdisciplinary programs), you may want to concentrate your school search on the area in which you hope to live and work, at least initially.

Curriculum

To maximize the value of your graduate school experience, be sure that a department's areas of concentration match up with your own interests. Knowing a program's particular theoretical bent and practical selling points can help ensure that you choose a school that reflects your own needs and academic leanings. Does one school of thought or one style of research predominate? If so, is there anyone else working in the department with a different theoretical framework? Will you have opportunities to work within a variety of theories and orientations? What special opportunities are available? How well are research programs funded? Do the professors have good records at rounding up grants? In field or clinical work, what are the options? Are programs available in your area of interest?

Find the environment that works best for you. Don't put yourself in a situation in which you don't have access to the courses or training you're seeking. It's your education. Your time. Your energy. Your investment in your future. By being proactive, you can help guarantee that you maximize your graduate school experience.

Faculty

One of the most important decisions you make in your graduate school career will be your choice of adviser. This one person will help you with course selection as well as clinical, research, or field education opportunities; he can make or break the thesis/ dissertation process. So when you investigate a department, look for a faculty member whose interests and personality are compatible with yours. Since this single person (your "dream adviser") may not be available, be sure to look for a couple of other professors with whom you might be able to work.

If one of your prime motivations in attending a certain program is to take classes from specific professors, make sure you'll have that opportunity. At the master's level, access to prominent professors is often limited to large, foundation-level lecture courses, where papers and exams are graded by the professor's graduate assistants or tutors. At the doctoral level, professors are generally much more accessible.

Is the department stable or changing? Find out whether the faculty is nearing retirement age. Impending retirements may not affect you in a two-year master's program, but this is a serious consideration in doctoral programs, which can (and often do) stretch on for over five years. If you have hopes of working with a distinguished professor, will she even be available for that time—or longer, if you get delayed? Will the department be large and stable enough to allow you to put together a good thesis or dissertation committee? Also, try to find out whether younger members of the department are established. Do they get sufficient funding? Have they settled in to the institution enough that there are not likely to be political controversies?

Placement

Although some people attend graduate school for the love of knowledge, most want to enhance their career prospects in some way. When you graduate with your hard-won degree, what are your chances of getting your desired job?

You'll want to ask what kind of track record a given program has in placing its alumni. With a highly competitive job market, it's especially important to find out when and where graduates have found work. If you're considering work in business, industry, local agencies, schools, health care facilities, or the government, find out whether these employers visit the campus to recruit. Major industries may visit science programs to interview prospective graduates. Some will even employ graduate students over the summer or part-time. If you're going into academia, find out whether recent grads have been able to find academic posts, how long the search took, and where they're working. Are they getting tenure-track positions, or are they shifting from temporary appointment to temporary appointment with little hope of finding a stable position? Don't just look at the first jobs that a school's graduates take. Where are they in 5, 10, or even 25 years?

Your career is more like a marathon than a sprint. So take the long view. A strong indicator of a program's strength is the accomplishments of its alumni.

Student Body

Some graduate catalogs contain profiles of or statements by current master's and PhD students. Sometimes this is an informal blurb on a few students—it's really marketing material—and sometimes it's a full listing of graduate students. Use this as a resource both to find out what everyone else in the program is up to and to find current students you can interview about the school and the program.

Because much of your learning will come from your classmates, consider the makeup of your class. A school with a geographically, professionally, and ethnically diverse student body will expose you to far more viewpoints than will a school with a more homogeneous group. If you're an older applicant, ask yourself how you'll fit in with a predominantly younger group of students. For many, the fit is terrific, but for others, the transition can be tougher. The answer depends on you, but it's something to consider.

The student body, as well as the faculty, will have varied philosophical and political orientations. The theories and perspectives considered liberal in one program can be deemed conservative in another, and where you fit among your peers can have a lot of influence on your image and your opportunities. If you plan on an academic career, remember that your student colleagues will someday likely be your professional colleagues.

Networking

Forging relationships—with your classmates, your professors, and, in a larger sense, all the alumni—is a big part of the graduate school experience. One of the things you'll take with you when you graduate, aside from an education, a diploma, and debt, is that network. And whether you thrive on networking or tend to shy away from it, it's a necessity. At some point, it may help you advance your career, in academia or outside.

Quality of Life

Your graduate school experience will extend far beyond your classroom learning, particularly for full-time students. That's why it's so important to find out as much as you can about the schools that interest you. For example, what activities would you like to participate in? Perhaps convenient recreational facilities or an intramural sports program is appealing. If you'd like to be involved in community activities, perhaps there's a school volunteer organization. Regardless of your interests, your ability to maintain balance in your life in the face of a rigorous academic challenge will help you keep a healthy outlook.

Housing is another quality-of-life issue to consider. Is campus housing available? Is off-campus housing convenient? Is it affordable? Where do most of the students live?

Quality of life is another important consideration for significant others, especially if your school choice requires a move to a new city. When graduate school takes over your life, your partner may feel left out. Find out what kind of groups and activities there are for families and partners. For example, are there any services to help your spouse find employment? Is child care available? What sort of public transportation is available?

Full-Time versus Part-Time

In a full-time program, you can focus your energy on your studies to maximize your learning. You're also likely to meet more people and forge closer relationships with your classmates. Many programs are oriented toward the full-time student, and many top-tier programs don't offer part-time options. A part-time schedule may also make it difficult for you to take classes with the best professors.

There are, however, many compelling reasons for attending part-time. It may not be economically feasible for you to attend full-time. Or you may wish to continue gaining professional experience while earning the degree that will allow you to move on to the next level. If there's a possibility that you'll have to work while you're in school, particularly while you're in the coursework stage, check out the flexibility of any program that interests you. Are there night or weekend classes? When is the library open? What about the lab? Talk to students currently in the program, especially those who work. Part-time programs often take a long time to complete, which can be discouraging, especially when licensure or salary increases are at stake. However, there are some programs, especially master's programs, that are specifically designed for part-time students (for example, many business school and physical therapy programs). In such programs, classes can be taken on weekends or specific nights of the week. It can be worth seeking out these sorts of options.

Although many students in full-time graduate programs support themselves with part-time work, their primary allegiance is to the graduate program. Many students who must work during graduate school are employed by their schools. This is an option worth exploring. Since graduate studies tend to become the focus of your life, if you can manage full-time or nearly full-time studies at the higher levels, do it. You can graduate earlier and start picking up the financial pieces that much sooner—often with a more secure base for your job search in the form of good support from your adviser.

Most master's programs are flexible about part-time studies, but doctoral programs are less so. Many doctoral programs expect a minimum amount of time "in residence"—that is, enrolled as a full-time student for a certain number of consecutive semesters. This requirement is usually listed in the catalog.

Program Costs

Some graduate programs charge per credit or per hour, meaning that your tuition bill is calculated by the number of credits you take each semester. Other programs charge per semester or per year with a minimum and maximum number of credits you can take per semester for that flat fee. In general, per-credit tuition makes sense for part-time students, while per-semester tuition makes sense for full-time students. Generally speaking, the most expensive kind of graduate program (per semester) will be a master's degree at a private school. Loans are available to master's-level students, but grants, scholarships, and other forms of "free" financial assistance are harder to find. Furthermore, most private schools apply the same tuition rate to in-state and out-of-state residents. State colleges and universities usually give in-state residents a tuition break. Other forms of savings can come from finding the cheapest living and housing expenses and from working your way through the program as quickly as possible.

At the doctoral level, tuition remission (you don't pay any of it) and grants or stipends (they pay you) are common. Percentages of doctoral students in a program receiving full tuition remission plus stipend/grant money can range anywhere from 0 percent to 100 percent—every student in the program pays no tuition and receives some grant or stipend. In these programs, the major financial burden will be your living expenses over the years of coursework, language requirements, qualifying and field exams, research, and the dissertation.

Where You Can Get In

Once you've developed a list of schools that meet your needs, take an objective look at your chances of getting into them.

A good way to get a sense of how graduate schools will perceive you is to make up a fact sheet with your GRE scores (or projected scores), your overall grade point average (GPA), your GPA in your major, and your work experience. Outside activities and your personal statement will contribute to the overall "score" that admissions officers will use to evaluate you, but let's stick with the raw data for now.

The next step is to find a current source of information about graduate school programs. There are several guides published every year that provide data about acceptance rates for given years, as well as median GPA and GRE scores. You can also request this information directly from a given department. The school of your dreams may not care very much about your GPA, but it might be very interested in your GRE scores. Make sure you find out what your target school prioritizes in its search for worthy applicants.

One of the best ways to gauge whether you're in contention for a certain program is to compare your numbers to theirs. And remember that you needn't hit the nail on the head. Median is similar to average, so some applicants do better or worse than the GRE scores or GPA cited. And remember all the other factors that add up to make you a desirable applicant. Comparing numbers is merely a good way to get a preliminary estimate of your compatibility with the schools of your choice.

"Safety" Schools

Once you have some idea of where you fall in the applicant pool, you can begin to make decisions about your application strategy. No matter what your circumstances, it's wise to choose at least one school that is likely to accept you, a "safety" school. Make sure it's one that fits your academic goals and your economic circumstances. If your GRE scores and GPA are well above a school's median scores and you don't anticipate any problems with other parts of your record or application, you've probably found your safety school.

"Wishful Thinking" Schools

If your ideal program is one that you don't seem qualified for, apply to your "dream school" anyway. You may be surprised! GPA and GRE scores aren't the only criteria by which applicants are judged, and you may discover that you're admitted in spite of your academic background on the merits of your personal statement, work samples, or other criteria. It's always worth a try. Some people underestimate their potential and apply only to safety schools. This can often lead to disappointment when they end up at one of these schools and discover that it doesn't provide the rigorous training they want.

When to Apply

With the number of graduate school applications received by institutions of higher learning on the rise, the issue of when to apply for admission has become very important. There are perfect times to begin and end the application process. You should begin at least a year before you plan to enter school (sooner if you're a nontraditional candidate or are changing fields). Find out the following essential dates as early as possible and incorporate them into your own personal application schedule:

- standardized test registration deadlines
- transcript deadlines (some schools send out transcripts only on particular dates)
- letters-of-recommendation due dates
- application deadlines (submit your application as early as possible to ensure that you get a fair and comprehensive review)
- financial aid forms deadlines (federal/state programs, universities, and independent sources of aid all have definite deadlines)

Setting Up an Application Schedule

We've organized the following "seasonal" schedule to help you understand how to proceed through the admissions process.

Winter (18–20 months prior to start date)

- If you're a nontraditional applicant or plan to switch fields, begin investigating program requirements. Take courses to make up any missing portion of your background.

Spring (16–18 months prior to start date)

- Browse through program catalogs and collect information on different grants and loans. Create your own graduate school library.

Summer

- Request applications from schools. If they're not available yet, ask for last year's so you can get a feel for the questions you'll have to answer.
- Write a draft of your personal statement and show it to trusted friends and/or colleagues for feedback.
- Consider registering for the GRE in the fall. This will give you plenty of time to submit your scores with your application.
- Research your options for test preparation. Take the test included in this book to give you a good idea of where you stand with regard to the GRE.

Early Fall

- Ask for recommendations. Make sure that your recommenders know enough about you to write a meaningful letter. Ask them first if they would be willing to write you recommendations and then ask how much lead time they would need. Once your recommenders have agreed to write recommendations, make sure to give them clear deadlines so you can avoid any timing conflicts.

Late Fall

- Take the GRE.
- Request applications from schools, if you haven't already done so.
- Request institutional, state, and federal financial aid materials from school aid offices.
- Request information on independent grants and loans.
- Order transcripts from your undergraduate (and any graduate) institution(s).
- Follow up with your recommenders, sending a thank-you note to those who have sent their recommendations in already.

Winter

- Fill out applications. Mail them as early as possible.
- Fill out financial aid applications. Mail these early as well.
- Make sure your recommendation writers have the appropriate forms and directions for mailing. Remind them of deadline dates.

Spring

- Sit back and relax (if you can). Most schools indicate how long it will take to inform you of their decision. This is also a crucial time to solidify your financial plans as you begin to receive offers of aid (with any luck).

The timing described here is approximate, and you needn't follow it exactly. The most important thing for you to do is make yourself aware of strict deadlines well in advance so that you'll be able to devote plenty of quality time to your application. In the next chapter, we'll go over the application process in detail.

CHAPTER 29

HOW TO APPLY TO GRADUATE SCHOOL

You've taken the GRE, and you've researched schools that offer programs you want. Your next step in the application process is to get the application forms from the various schools you've selected. Some schools will require you to complete an online application, some will have PDF downloads of the application documents, and yet others will require that you request applications that will then be sent to you. Once you get the applications, you'll notice one thing quickly: no two applications are exactly alike. Some ask you to write one essay or personal statement, and others ask for three or more essays on various subjects. Some have very detailed forms requiring extensive background information; others are satisfied with your name and address and little else.

Despite these differences, most applications follow a general pattern with variations on the same kinds of questions. So read this section with the understanding that, although not all of it is relevant to every application, these guidelines will be valuable for just about any graduate school application you'll encounter.

How Schools Evaluate Applicants

Each graduate school has its own admissions policies and practices, but all programs evaluate your application based on a range of objective and subjective criteria. Regardless of which schools you are pursuing, understanding how admissions officers judge your candidacy can give you a leg up on the competition.

Generally, all admissions officers use the application process to measure your intellectual abilities, aptitude in your field of study, and personal characteristics. When you submit your application, admissions officers will evaluate the total package. Most admissions officers look for reasons to admit candidates, not reject them. Your challenge, therefore, is to distinguish yourself positively from the other candidates.

Intellectual Ability

To assess your intellectual ability, admissions officers look at two key factors: your academic record and your GRE scores.

Academic Record

Your grade point average (GPA) is important, but it's just part of your academic profile. Admissions officers will consider the reputation of your undergraduate institution and the difficulty of your courses. Admissions officers are well aware that comparing GPAs from different schools and even different majors from the same school is like comparing apples and oranges. So they'll look closely at your transcript. Do your grades show an upward trend? How did you perform in your major? How did you fare in courses related to the program you're applying to?

Admissions officers focus primarily on your undergraduate performance, but they will consider all graduate studies and nondegree coursework that you have completed. Be sure to submit those transcripts. Generally, the undergraduate GPA of an applicant who is about to complete or has recently completed an undergraduate degree is given much more weight than that of an applicant returning to school after several years.

If you have a poor academic record, it will be tougher to get into a top school, but it is by no means impossible. Your challenge is to find other ways to demonstrate your intellectual horsepower. High GRE scores, an intelligently written personal statement, and strong recommendations will help.

The GRE

You are already familiar with the GRE and are armed with strategies to score higher on the test. An integral part of the admissions process at virtually all schools, the GRE measures general verbal, quantitative, and analytical writing skills. Some programs, particularly in psychology and the sciences, require you to take one or more GRE Subject Tests as well. In addition to or instead of the GRE, some programs require the Miller Analogies Test (MAT). Be sure to check with the programs you're considering to see which tests they require.

When admissions officers review your GRE scores, they'll look at your Verbal Reasoning, Quantitative Reasoning, and Analytical Writing scores separately, particularly if they have any questions about your abilities in a certain area. Different programs give varying weight to each score. If you've taken the GRE more than once, schools will generally credit you with your highest score for each section, though some may average the scores or take the most recent.

If used by itself, the GRE may not be a perfect predictor of academic performance, but it is the single best one available. The GRE does not measure your intelligence, nor does it measure the likelihood of your success in your field. The revised GRE has been designed to predict with more certainty your success in graduate school. As with any standardized test, by preparing properly for the GRE, you can boost your score significantly. The strategies you practice and learn will also help you decipher difficult academic text you may encounter in your future studies.

One thing to note is that your essays from the Analytical Writing section are now sent to the schools to which you send a score report. Previously, schools would only receive your score report. Schools will know that these are GRE essays, completed under time limits. Still, it makes the Analytical Writing section even more important to complete well.

Fellowships and Assistantships

Some graduate programs award fellowships and assistantships partly on the basis of GRE scores. Because most programs have limited funds and therefore limited positions to offer, the awards process can be quite competitive. Not only should you take your scores seriously, you should also confirm the submission deadline with your department. The financial aid deadline is usually earlier than the application deadline.

Relevant Experience and Skills

When evaluating your application, admissions officers look at work experience and other activities related to the program in question. In fields like psychology, social work, and health, your research and practical experience will play a role in the admissions decision. If you're applying to film, writing, or other arts programs, you'll be asked to submit samples of your work. And if you're planning on an academic career, your research and publications will be of particular interest to the admissions committee. The way you present yourself and your achievements should be tailored to the programs you're applying to.

You can communicate some of your abilities through the straightforward "data" part of your application. Be sure to describe your job and internship responsibilities. Be aware that your job title alone will not necessarily communicate enough about what you do or the level of your responsibilities. If you are asked to submit a resume or CV, make sure you illustrate your experience and on-the-job training in a way that highlights skills you already have and those you think will serve you well in your future field of study.

If you are working and applying to a graduate program in the same field, admissions officers will look at your overall career record. How have you progressed? Have you been an outstanding performer? What do your recommendation writers say about your performance? Have you progressed to increasingly higher levels of responsibility? If you have limited work experience, you will not be expected to match the accomplishments of an applicant with 10 years' experience, but you will be expected to demonstrate your abilities.

Extracurricular activities and community involvement also present opportunities for you to highlight your skills. For younger applicants, college activities play a more significant role than for more seasoned applicants. Your activities say a lot about who you are and what's important to you. Were you a campus leader? Did your activities require discipline and commitment? Did you work with a team? What did you learn from your involvement?

Active community involvement provides a way for you to demonstrate your skills and to impress admissions officers with your personal character. In fact, many applications ask directly about community activities. Getting involved in your community is a chance to do something worthwhile and enhance your application in the process.

Personal Characteristics

The third, and most subjective, criterion on which schools evaluate you is your personal character. Admissions officers judge you in this area primarily through your personal statement (and essays, if applicable), recommendations, and personal interview (if applicable). Although different schools emphasize different qualities, most seek candidates who demonstrate maturity, integrity, responsibility, and a clear sense of how they fit into their chosen field. The more competitive programs place special emphasis on these criteria because they have many qualified applicants for each available spot in the class.

Who Evaluates Applicants

At most schools, the admissions board includes professional admissions officers and/or faculty from the department to which you're applying. At some schools, the authority to make admissions decisions lies with the graduate school itself—that is, with the central administration. At others, it lies with individual departments.

What Decisions Do They Make?

Upon reviewing your application, the admissions board may make any number of decisions, including the following:

- *Admit:* Congratulations, you're in! But read the letter carefully. The board may recommend or, in some cases, require you to do some preparatory coursework to ensure that your quantitative or language skills are up to speed.

- *Reject:* At the top schools, there are far more qualified applicants than spaces in the class. Even though you were rejected, you can reapply at a later date. However, if you are considering reapplying, you need to understand why you were rejected and whether you have a reasonable chance of being admitted the next time around. Some schools will speak with you about your application, but they often wait until the end of the admissions season, by which time you may have accepted another offer.

- *Waiting list:* Schools use the waiting list to manage class size, leaving the applicant with a mixed message. The good news is that you are a strong enough candidate to have made the list. The bad news is there is no way to know with certainty whether you'll be accepted. Take heart, though, that schools do tend to look kindly upon wait-listed candidates who reapply in a subsequent year. Similar to the waiting list is the *provisional admit.* You may be asked to retake the GRE or resend another part of your application in order to gain admission to your desired school.

- *Request for an interview:* Schools at which an interview is not required may request that you interview prior to making their final decision. Your application may have raised some specific issues that you can address in an interview, or perhaps the board feels your personal statement did not give them a complete enough picture to render a decision. Look at this as a positive opportunity to strengthen your case.

Preparing Your Application

A key part of getting into the graduate school of your choice is to develop a basic application strategy so you can present yourself in the best light.

Your Application as a Marketing Tool

When it comes to applying to graduate school, you are the product. Your application is your marketing document. Of course, marketing yourself doesn't mean that you should lie or even embellish; it just means that you need to make a tight presentation of the facts. Everything in your application should add up to a coherent whole and underscore the fact that not only are you qualified to be in the program but you should be in it.

Many application forms have a comforting and accepting tone. *Why would you like to come to our program?* they ask. They do want an answer to that question, but what's even more important—the subtext for the whole application process—is the question: *Why should we accept you?* This is the question that your application will answer. And with some effective marketing strategies, your answer will be clear, concise, coherent, and strong.

Maximizing the Various Parts of Your Application

Let's take a close look at how you should approach the specific parts of your application.

Personal Statement

Your personal statement is a critical part of your application. The personal statement is where you can explain why you're applying to graduate school, what interests you about this program, and what your future goals are. The situations you choose to write about and the manner in which you present them can have a major bearing on the strength of your candidacy.

Writing an effective personal statement requires serious self-examination and sound strategic planning. What major personal and professional events have shaped you? What accomplishments best demonstrate your abilities? Remember, admissions officers are interested in getting to know you as a complete person. What you choose to write about sends clear signals about what's important to you and what your values are. You want the readers to put your essay down and think, "Wow! That was really interesting and memorable," and, "Wow! This person really knows why he's going into this program and has real contributions to make to the field."

Creating Your Statement

Your statement should demonstrate the patterns in your life that have led you to apply to the program. Part of demonstrating why you are right for the program involves demonstrating that you understand what the program is and where it will lead you. A personal statement requires honesty and distinctiveness. If you are heading to graduate school straight from undergraduate school, what has made you so certain that you know what you want to do with your life? If you are returning to school, particularly if you are changing fields, what has led you to this decision? You can use vignettes from your personal history, academic life, work life, and extracurricular activities to explain. If you are applying to a doctoral program, indicate which ideas, fields of research, or problems intrigue you. It's always a good idea to demonstrate familiarity with the field you want to enter.

You should start compiling information for your statement three or four months before you fill out your application. Write a draft once you've narrowed your list of potential topics. Have it edited by someone who knows you well. After rewriting, have someone whose opinion and writing skills you trust read your final draft, make suggestions, and, above all, help you proofread.

General Personal Statement Tips

Once you've determined what you plan to write for your statement, keep the following tips in mind:

- *Length:* Schools are pretty specific about how long they want your statement to be. Adhere to their guidelines.

- *Spelling/typos/grammar:* Remember, your application is your marketing document. What would you think of a product that's promoted with sloppy materials containing typos, spelling errors, and grammatical mistakes?

- *Write in the active voice:* Candidates who write well have an advantage in the application process because they can state their case in a concise, compelling manner. Sentences in the passive voice tend to be unnecessarily wordy. For example:

  > Passive voice: *The essays were written by me.*
  > Active voice: *I wrote the essays.*

  Strong writing will not compensate for a lack of substance, but poor writing can torpedo an otherwise impressive candidate.

- *Tone:* On the one hand, you want to tout your achievements and present yourself as a poised, self-confident applicant. On the other hand, arrogance and self-importance do not go over well with admissions officers. Before you submit your application, be sure that you're comfortable with the tone as well as the content.

- *Creative approaches:* If you choose to submit a humorous or creative application, you are employing a high-risk, high-reward strategy. If you're confident you can pull it off, go for it. Be aware, though, that what may work for one admissions officer may fall flat with another. Admissions officers who review thousands of essays every year may consider your approach gimmicky or simply find it distracting. Remember, your challenge is to stand out in the applicant pool in a positive way. Don't let your creativity obscure the substance of your application.

- *Answer the question asked:* Schools do not want to receive a personal statement or other essay that seems to have been written generically or perhaps even for another school.

Making Your Statement Distinctive

Depending on the amount of time you have and the amount of effort you're willing to put in, you can write a personal statement that will stand out from the crowd. One of the first mistakes that some applicants make is in thinking that "thorough" and "comprehensive" are sufficient qualities for their personal statement. They try to include as much information as possible, without regard for length limitations or strategic intent. Application readers dread reading these bloated personal statements. So how do you decide what to include? There are usually clear length guidelines, and admissions officers prefer that you adhere to them. So get rid of the idea of "comprehensive" and focus more on "distinctive."

Unless they ask for it, don't dwell on your weak points. A strong personal statement, for example, about how much you learned in your current position and how the experience and knowledge you've gained inspired you to apply to graduate school will give readers what they want—a quick image of who you are, how you got that way, and why you want to go to their school. One of the best ways to be distinctive is to sell your image briefly and accurately, including real-life examples to back up your points.

The admissions team wants to know about you, but there is the potential for including too much personal information. Beware of sharing reasons for applying that include furthering personal relationships, improving finances, or proving someone wrong.

"Distinctive" means that your statement should answer the questions that admissions officers think about while reading personal statements: What's different about this applicant? Why should we pick this applicant over others? Authentic enthusiasm can be a plus, and writing about parts of your life or career that are interesting and relevant helps grab a reader's attention.

The Interview

In some programs, an interview with the department is conducted at the applicant's discretion: if you want one, you're welcome to ask. In other programs, only the most promising applicants are invited to interview. Whether or not a department can pay your travel expenses depends on its financial circumstances. If you have the opportunity, definitely go to interview at your first-choice departments. There's no substitute for face-to-face contact with your potential colleagues, and by visiting the school, you can check out the city or town where it is located. You should investigate cost-of-living and transportation options during your visit.

As you prepare for an interview, here are some tips:

- *Review your application:* If you've submitted your application prior to the interview, your interviewer is likely to use it as a guide and may ask specific questions about it. Be sure you remember what you wrote.
- *Be ready to provide examples and specifics:* Professionally trained interviewers are more likely to ask you about specific situations than to ask broad, open-ended questions. They can learn more by asking what you've done in situations than by asking what you think you'd do. Here are a few situations an interviewer may ask you to

discuss: "Tell me about a recent accomplishment." "Discuss a recent situation in which you demonstrated leadership." "Give me an example of a situation where you overcame difficult circumstances." As you think about these situations, be prepared to discuss specifics—what you did and why you did it that way. You do not need to "script" or over-rehearse your responses, but you should go into the interview confident that you can field any question.

- *Be open and honest*: Don't struggle to think of "right" answers. The only right answers are those that are right for you. By responding openly and honestly, you'll find the interview less stressful, and you'll come across as a more genuine, attractive candidate.

- *Ask questions*: The interview is as much an opportunity for you to learn about the school as for the school to learn about you. Good questions demonstrate your knowledge about a particular program and your thoughtfulness about the entire process.

- *Follow proper professional decorum*: Be on time, dress appropriately, and follow up with thank-you letters. Treat the process as you would a job interview, which in many respects it is.

- *Watch your nonverbal cues*: Nonverbal communication is much more important than people realize. Maintain eye contact, keep good posture, sustain positive energy, and avoid nervous fidgeting. It will help you come across as confident, poised, and mature.

- *Be courteous to the administrative staff*: These people are colleagues of the board members, and how you treat them can have an impact, either positive or negative.

- *Relax and have fun*: Interviews are inherently stressful. But by being well prepared, you can enhance your prospects for admission, learn about the school, and enjoy yourself in the process.

Recommendations

Graduate schools will require at least three recommendations. Choose recommenders who can write meaningfully about your strengths. One of the more common mistakes is to sacrifice an insightful recommendation from someone who knows you well for a generic recommendation from a celebrity or a prominent professor. Admissions officers are not impressed by famous names. So unless that individual knows you and can write convincingly on your behalf, it's not a strategy worth pursuing. Good choices for recommenders include current and past supervisors, professors, academic and nonacademic advisers, and people you work with in community activities.

Many schools will specifically request an academic recommendation. Professors in your major are ideal recommenders, as they can vouch for your ability to study at the graduate level. If you don't have a professor who can recommend you, use a TA who knows your work well. Similarly, if requesting a recommendation from your employer would create an awkward situation, look for someone else who can comment on your skills. Your recommendations will confirm your strengths and, in some cases, help you overcome perceived weaknesses in your application.

If you wish to submit an extra recommendation, it's generally not a problem. Most schools will include the letter in your file, and those that don't will not penalize you for it. You should, however, send a note explaining why you have requested an additional recommendation so it does not appear that you disregarded the instructions. It's also a good idea to check with the admissions department before submitting an extra recommendation.

Asking for Recommendations

There are two fundamental rules of requesting recommendations: ask early and ask nicely. As soon as you decide to go to graduate school, you should start sizing up potential recommendation writers and let them know that you may ask them for a recommendation. This will give them plenty of time to think about what to say. Once they've agreed, let them know about deadlines well in advance to avoid potential scheduling conflicts. The more time they have, the better the job they'll do recommending you. As for asking nicely, you should let these people know you think highly of their opinion and you'd be happy and honored if they would consider writing you a letter of recommendation. You can help your recommenders by scheduling brief appointments with them to discuss your background; providing a list of due dates for each application; providing any forms required by the program; listing which recommendations will be submitted in hard copy and which will be submitted online; providing any forms required by the program; supplying stamped, addressed envelopes for hard-copy submissions; and following up with the recommenders.

Before You Submit Your Application

When you've completed your personal statement and you're ready to submit your application, take two more steps to ensure that your application is as strong as it can be.

1. Be sure to read your personal statement in the context of your entire application.
   - Does the total package make sense? Does it represent you favorably? Is everything consistent?
   - Have you demonstrated your intellectual ability, relevant experience and skills, and personal characteristics?
   - Most importantly, do you feel good about the application? After all, you don't want to be rejected on the basis of an application that you don't believe represents the real you.

2. Have someone you trust and respect review your application. Someone who has not been involved in writing the application may pick up spelling or grammatical errors that you've overlooked. In addition, because your application is an intensely personal document that requires significant self-examination, you may not be able to remain objective. Someone who knows you and can be frank will tell you whether your application has "captured" you most favorably. Note, however, that some schools prohibit you from using any outside help on your application. A last-minute once-over from a friend or family member is probably within reason, but you may want to directly ask the school what is permissible.

Putting It All Together

There are no magic formulas that automatically admit you to, or reject you from, the school of your choice. Rather, your application is like a jigsaw puzzle. Each component—GPA, GRE scores, professional experience, school activities, recommendations—is a different piece of the puzzle.

Outstanding professional experience and personal characteristics may enable you to overcome a mediocre academic record. Conversely, outstanding academic credentials will not ensure your admission to a top-tier program if you do not demonstrate strong relevant skills and experience, as well as solid personal character. Your challenge in preparing your application is to convince the admissions board that all of the pieces in your background fit together to form a substantial and unique puzzle.

Congratulations!

You have all of the tools you need to put together a stand-out application package, including a top GRE score. Best of luck, and remember, your Kaplan training will be with you each step of the way.

A Special Note for International Students

About a quarter of a million international students pursue advanced academic degrees at the master's or PhD level at US universities each year. This trend of pursuing higher education in the United States, particularly at the graduate level, is expected to continue. Business, management, engineering, and the physical and life sciences are popular areas of study for students coming to the United States from other countries. Along with these academic options, international students are also taking advantage of opportunities for research grants, teaching assistantships, and practical training or work experience in US graduate departments.

If you are not from the United States but are considering attending a graduate program at a university in the United States, here is what you'll need to get started.

- If English is not your first language, you will probably need to take the Test of English as a Foreign Language (TOEFL) or show some other evidence that you're proficient in English prior to gaining admission to a graduate program. Graduate programs will vary on what is an acceptable TOEFL score. For degrees in business, journalism, management, or the humanities, a minimum TOEFL score of 100 (600 on the paper-based TOEFL) or better is expected. For the hard sciences and computer technology, a TOEFL score of 79 (550 on the paper-based TOEFL) is a common minimum requirement.

- You may also need to take the GRE. The strategies in this book are designed to help you maximize your score on the computer-based GRE. However, many sites outside the United States and Canada offer only the paper-based version of the GRE. Fortunately, most strategies can be applied to the paper-based version as well. For additional paper-based GRE strategies, see chapter 2.

- Because admission to many graduate programs is quite competitive, you may want to select three or four programs you would like to attend and complete applications for each program.

- Selecting the correct graduate school is very different from selecting a suitable undergraduate institution. You should research the qualifications and interests of faculty members teaching and doing research in your chosen field. Look for professors who share your specialty.

- You need to begin the application process at least a year in advance. Be aware that many programs offer only August or September start dates. Find out application deadlines and plan accordingly.

- Finally, you will need to obtain an I-20 Certificate of Eligibility in order to obtain an F-1 student visa to study in the United States.

Kaplan English International Centers*

If you need more help with the complex process of graduate school admissions, assistance preparing for the TOEFL or GRE, or help building your English language skills in general, you may be interested in Kaplan's English language and test preparation for international students, available at Kaplan's International Centers/Colleges around the world.

Kaplan's English courses have been designed to help students and professionals from outside the United States meet their educational and career goals. At locations throughout the United States, international students take advantage of Kaplan's programs to help them improve their academic and conversational English skills; to raise their scores on the TOEFL, GRE, and other standardized exams; and to gain admission to the schools of their choice. Our staff and instructors give international students the individualized instruction they need to succeed. Here is a brief description of some of Kaplan's programs for international students.

General Intensive English

Kaplan's General Intensive English course is the fastest and most effective way for students to improve their English. This full-time program integrates the four key elements of language learning—listening, speaking, reading, and writing. The challenging curriculum and intensive schedule are designed for both the general language learner and the academically bound student.

TOEFL and Academic English (TAE)

Our world-famous TOEFL course prepares you for the TOEFL and teaches you the academic language and skills needed to succeed in a university. Designed for high-intermediate to proficiency-level English speakers, our course includes TOEFL-focused reading, writing, listening, speaking, vocabulary, and grammar instruction.

General English

Our General English course is a semi-intensive program designed for students who want to improve their listening and speaking skills without the time commitment of an intensive program. With morning or afternoon class times and flexible Structured Study hours throughout the week, our General English course is perfect for every schedule.

GRE for International Students

The GRE is required for admission to many graduate programs in the United States. Nearly a half-million people take the GRE each year. A high score can help you stand out from other test takers. This course, designed especially for nonnative English speakers, includes the skills you need to succeed on each section of the GRE as well as access to Kaplan's exclusive computer-based practice materials and extra Verbal practice.

Other Kaplan Programs

Since 1938, more than three million students have come to Kaplan to advance their studies, prepare for entry to American universities, and further their careers. In addition to the above programs, Kaplan offers courses to prepare for the SAT, GMAT, LSAT, MCAT, DAT, OAT, PCAT, USMLE, NCLEX, and other standardized exams at locations throughout the United States.

Applying to Kaplan English Programs

To get more information, or to apply for admission to any of Kaplan's programs for international students and professionals, please visit our website at **www.kaplaninternational.com**.

PART SEVEN

GRE RESOURCES

KAPLAN'S WORD GROUPS

The following lists contain a lot of common GRE words grouped together by meaning. Make flashcards from these lists and look over your cards a few times a week from now until the day of the test. Look over the word group lists once or twice a week every week until the test. If you don't have much time until the exam date, look over your lists more frequently. Then, by the day of the test, you should have a rough idea of what most of the words on your lists mean.

Note: The categories in which these words are listed are *general* and should *not* be interpreted as the exact definitions of the words.

A

Abbreviated Communication
abridge
compendium
cursory
curtail
syllabus
synopsis
terse

Act Quickly
abrupt
apace
headlong
impetuous
precipitate

Assist
abet
advocate
ancillary
bolster
corroborate
countenance
espouse
mainstay
munificent
proponent
stalwart
sustenance

B

Bad Mood
bilious
dudgeon
irascible
pettish
petulant
pique
querulous
umbrage
waspish

Beginner/Amateur
dilettante
fledgling
neophyte
novitiate
proselyte
tyro

Beginning/Young
burgeoning
callow
engender
inchoate
incipient
nascent

Biting (as in wit or temperament)
acerbic
acidulous
acrimonious
asperity
caustic
mordacious
mordant
trenchant

Bold
audacious
courageous
dauntless

Boring
banal
hackneyed
insipid
mundane
pedestrian
platitude
prosaic
quotidian
trite

C

Carousal
bacchanalian
debauchery
depraved
dissipated
iniquity
libertine
libidinous
licentious
reprobate
ribald
salacious
sordid
turpitude

Changing Quickly

capricious

mercurial

volatile

Copy

counterpart

emulate

facsimile

factitious

paradigm

precursor

simulate

vicarious

Criticize/Criticism

aspersion

belittle

berate

calumny

castigate

decry

defame/defamation

denounce

deride/derisive

diatribe

disparage

excoriate

gainsay

harangue

impugn

inveigh

lambaste

objurgate

obloquy

opprobrium

pillory

rebuke

remonstrate

reprehend

reprove

revile

tirade

vituperate

D

Death/Mourning

bereave

cadaver

defunct

demise

dolorous

elegy

knell

lament

macabre

moribund

obsequies

sepulchral

wraith

Denying of Self

abnegate

abstain

ascetic

spartan

stoic

temperate

Dictatorial

authoritarian

despotic

dogmatic

hegemonic/hegemony

imperious

peremptory

tyrannical

Difficult to Understand

abstruse

ambiguous

arcane

bemusing

cryptic

enigmatic

esoteric

inscrutable

obscure

opaque

paradoxical

perplexing

recondite

turbid

Disgusting/Offensive

defile

fetid

invidious

noisome

odious

putrid

rebarbative

E

Easy to Understand

articulate

cogent

eloquent

evident

limpid

lucid

pellucid

Eccentric/Dissimilar

aberrant

anachronism

anomalous

discrete

eclectic

esoteric

iconoclast

Embarrass

abash

chagrin

compunction

contrition

diffidence

expiate

foible

gaucherie

rue

Equal

equitable

equity

tantamount

F

Falsehood

apocryphal

canard

chicanery

dissemble

duplicity

equivocate

erroneous

ersatz

fallacious

feigned

guile

mendacious/mendacity

perfidy

prevaricate

specious

spurious

Family

conjugal

consanguine

distaff

endogamous

filial

fraternal

fratricide

progenitor

scion

sorority

Favoring/Not Impartial

ardent/ardor

doctrinaire

fervid

partisan

tendentious

zealot

Forgive/Make Amends

absolve

acquit

exculpate

exonerate

expiate

palliate

redress

vindicate

Funny

chortle

droll

facetious

flippant

gibe

jocular

levity

ludicrous

raillery

riposte

simper

G

Gaps/Openings

abatement

aperture

fissure

hiatus

interregnum

interstice

lull

orifice

rent

respite

rift

Generous/Kind

altruistic

beneficent

clement

largess

magnanimous

munificent

philanthropic

unstinting

Greedy

avaricious

covetous

mercenary

miserly

penurious

rapacious

venal

H

Hard-Hearted

asperity

baleful

dour

fell

malevolent

mordant

sardonic

scathing

truculent

vitriolic

vituperation

Harmful

baleful

baneful

deleterious

inimical

injurious

insidious

minatory

perfidious

pernicious

Harsh-Sounding

cacophony

din

dissonant

raucous

strident

Hatred

abhorrence

anathema

antagonism

antipathy

detestation

enmity

loathing

malice

odium

rancor

Healthy

beneficial

salubrious

salutary

Hesitate

dither

oscillate

teeter

vacillate

waver

Hostile

antithetic

churlish

curmudgeon

irascible

malevolent

misanthropic

truculent

vindictive

I

Innocent/Inexperienced

credulous

gullible

ingenuous

naive

novitiate

tyro

Insincere

disingenuous

dissemble

fulsome

ostensible

unctuous

Investigate

appraise

ascertain

assay

descry

peruse

L

Lazy/Sluggish

indolent

inert

lackadaisical

languid

lassitude

lethargic

phlegmatic

quiescent

slothful

torpid

Luck

amulet

auspicious

fortuitous

kismet

optimum

portentous

propitiate

propitious

providential

serendipity

talisman

N

Nag

admonish

belabor

cavil

enjoin

exhort

harangue

hector

martinet
remonstrate
reproof

Nasty

fetid
noisome
noxious

Not a Straight Line

askance
awry
careen
carom
circuitous
circumvent
gyrate
labyrinth
meander
oblique
serrated
sidle
sinuous
undulating
vortex

O

Overblown/Wordy

bombastic
circumlocution
garrulous
grandiloquent
loquacious
periphrastic
prolix
rhetoric
turgid
verbose

P

Pacify/Satisfy

ameliorate
appease
assuage

defer
mitigate
mollify
placate
propitiate
satiate
slake
soothe

Pleasant-Sounding

euphonious
harmonious
melodious
sonorous

Poor

destitute
esurient
impecunious
indigent

Praise

acclaim
accolade
aggrandize
encomium
eulogize
extol
fawn
laud/laudatory
venerate/veneration

Predict

augur
auspice
fey
harbinger
portentous
precursor
presage
prescient
prognosticate

Prevent/Obstruct

discomfit
encumber

fetter
forfend
hinder
impede
inhibit
occlude

S

Smart/Learned

astute
canny
erudite
perspicacious

Sorrow

disconsolate
doleful
dolor
elegiac
forlorn
lament
lugubrious
melancholy
morose
plaintive
threnody

Stubborn

implacable
inexorable
intractable
intransigent
obdurate
obstinate
recalcitrant
refractory
renitent
untoward
vexing

T

Terse

compendious
curt

laconic
pithy
succinct
taciturn

Time/Order/Duration

anachronism
antecede
antedate
anterior
archaic
diurnal
eon
ephemeral
epoch
fortnight
millennium
penultimate
synchronous
temporal

Timid/Timidity

craven
diffident
pusillanimous
recreant
timorous
trepidation

Truth

candor/candid
fealty
frankness
indisputable
indubitable
legitimate
probity
sincere
veracious
verity

U

Unusual

aberration

anomaly
iconoclast
idiosyncrasy

W

Walking About

ambulatory
itinerant
meander
peripatetic

Wandering

discursive
expatiate
forage
itinerant

peregrination
peripatetic
sojourn

Weaken

adulterate
enervate
exacerbate
inhibit
obviate
stultify
undermine
vitiate

Wisdom

adage

aphorism
apothegm
axiom
bromide
dictum
epigram
platitude
sententious
truism

Withdrawal/Retreat

abeyance
abjure
abnegation
abortive

abrogate
decamp
demur
recant
recidivism
remission
renege
rescind
retrograde

KAPLAN'S ROOT LIST

Kaplan's Root List can boost your knowledge of GRE-level words, and that can help you get more questions right. No one can predict exactly which words will show up on your test, but the testmakers favor certain words. The Root List gives you the component parts of many typical GRE words. Knowing these words can help you because you may run across them on your GRE. Also, becoming comfortable with the types of words that pop up will reduce your anxiety about the test.

Knowing roots can help you in two more ways. First, instead of learning one word at a time, you can learn a whole group of words that contain a certain root. They'll be related in meaning, so if you remember one, it will be easier for you to remember others. Second, roots can often help you decode an unknown GRE word. If you recognize a familiar root, you could get a good enough grasp of the word to answer the question.

This list is a starting point and a quick review, not an exhaustive guide. Roots are given in their most common forms, with their most common or broadest definitions; often, other forms and meanings exist. Similarly, the definitions for the words given as examples may be incomplete, and other senses of those words may exist. Get into the habit of looking up unfamiliar words in a good, current dictionary—whether on paper or on the Internet—and be sure to check their etymologies while you're there.

A

A/AN: not, without

agnostic: one who believes the existence of God is not provable

amoral: neither moral nor immoral; having no relation to morality

anomaly: an irregularity

anonymous: of unknown authorship or origin

apathy: lack of interest or emotion

atheist: one who does not believe in God

atrophy: the wasting away of body tissue

atypical: not typical

AB: off, away from, apart, down

abdicate: to renounce or relinquish a throne

abduct: to take away by force

abhor: to hate, detest

abject: cast down; degraded

abnormal: deviating from a standard

abolish: to do away with, make void

abstinence: forbearance from any indulgence of appetite

abstract: conceived apart from concrete realities, specific objects, or actual instances

abstruse: hard to understand; secret, hidden

ABLE/IBLE: capable of, worthy of

changeable: able to be changed

combustible: capable of being burned; easily inflamed

inevitable: impossible to be avoided; certain to happen

presentable: suitable for being presented

AC/ACR: sharp, bitter, sour

acerbic: sour or astringent in taste; harsh in temper

acid: something that is sharp, sour, or ill-natured

acrimonious: caustic, stinging, or bitter in nature

acumen: mental sharpness; quickness of wit

acute: sharp at the end; ending in a point

exacerbate: to increase bitterness or violence; aggravate

ACOU: hearing

acoustic: pertaining to hearing; sound made through mechanical, not electronic, means

ACT/AG: to do, to drive, to force, to lead

agile: quick and well-coordinated in movement; active, lively

agitate: to move or force into violent, irregular action

pedagogue: a teacher

prodigal: wastefully or recklessly extravagant

synagogue: a gathering or congregation of Jews for the purpose of religious worship

AD: to, toward, near

(Often the *d* is dropped and the first letter to which *a* is prefixed is doubled.)

accede: to yield to a demand; to enter office

adapt: adjust or modify fittingly

addict: to give oneself over, as to a habit or pursuit

address: to direct a speech or written statement to

adhere: to stick fast; cleave; cling

adjacent: near, close, or contiguous; adjoining

adjoin: to be close or in contact with

admire: to regard with wonder, pleasure, and approval

advocate: to plead in favor of

attract: to draw either by physical force or by an appeal to emotions or senses

AL/ALI/ALTER: other, another

alias: an assumed name; another name

alibi: the defense by an accused person that he was verifiably elsewhere at the time of the crime with which he is charged

alien: one born in another country; a foreigner

allegory: figurative treatment of one subject under the guise of another

alter ego: the second self; a substitute or deputy

alternative: a possible choice

altruist: a person unselfishly concerned for the welfare of others

AM: love

amateur: a person who engages in an activity for pleasure rather than financial or professional gain

amatory: of or pertaining to lovers or lovemaking

amiable: having or showing agreeable personal qualities

amicable: characterized by exhibiting good will

amity: friendship; peaceful harmony

amorous: inclined to love, esp. sexual love

enamored: inflamed with love; charmed; captivated

inamorata: a female lover

AMBI/AMPHI: both, on both sides, around

ambidextrous: able to use both hands equally well

ambient: moving around freely; circulating

ambiguous: open to various interpretations

amphibian: any cold-blooded vertebrate, the larva of which is aquatic and the adult of which is terrestrial; a person or thing having a twofold nature

AMBL/AMBUL: to go, to walk

ambulance: a vehicle equipped for carrying sick people (from a phrase meaning "walking hospital")

ambulatory: of, pertaining to, or capable of walking

perambulator: one who makes a tour of inspection on foot; a baby stroller

preamble: an introductory statement (originally: to walk in front)

ANIM: of the life, mind, soul, breath

animal: a living being

animosity: a feeling of ill will or enmity

equanimity: mental or emotional stability, especially under tension

magnanimous: generous in forgiving an insult or injury

unanimous: of one mind; in complete accord

ANNUI/ENNI: year

annals: a record of events, esp. a yearly record

anniversary: the yearly recurrence of the date of a past event

annual: of, for, or pertaining to a year; yearly

annuity: a specified income payable at stated intervals

perennial: lasting for an indefinite amount of time

ANT/ANTE: before

antebellum: before the war (especially the American Civil War)

antecedent: existing, being, or going before

antedate: precede in time

antediluvian: belonging to the period before the biblical flood; very old or old-fashioned

anterior: placed before

ANTHRO/ANDR: man, human

androgen: any substance that promotes masculine characteristics

androgynous: being both male and female

android: a robot; a mechanical man

anthropocentric: regarding humanity as the central fact of the universe

anthropology: the science that deals with the origins of humankind

misanthrope: one who hates humans or humanity

philanderer: one who carries on flirtations

ANTI: against, opposite

antibody: a protein naturally existing in blood serum that reacts to overcome an antigen

antidote: a remedy for counteracting the effects of poison, disease, etc.

antipathy: aversion

antipodal: on the opposite side of the globe

antiseptic: free from germs; particularly clean or neat

APO: away

apocalypse: revelation; discovery; disclosure

apocryphal: of doubtful authorship or authenticity

apogee: the highest or most distant point

apology: an expression of one's regret or sorrow for having wronged another

apostasy: a total desertion of one's religion, principles, party, cause, etc.

apostle: one of the 12 disciples sent forth by Jesus to preach the Gospel

AQUA/AQUE: water

aquamarine: a bluish-green color

aquarium: a tank for keeping fish and other underwater creatures

aquatic: having to do with water

aqueduct: a channel for transporting water

subaqueous: underwater

ARCH/ARCHI/ARCHY: chief, principal, ruler

anarchy: a state or society without government or law

archenemy: chief enemy

architect: the devisor, maker, or planner of anything

monarchy: a government in which the supreme power is lodged in a sovereign

oligarchy: a state or society ruled by a select group

ARD: to burn

ardent: burning; fierce; passionate

ardor: flame; passion

arson: the crime of setting property on fire

AUTO: self

autocrat: an absolute ruler

automatic: self-moving or self-acting

autonomy: independence or freedom

B

BE: about, to make, to surround, to affect (often used to transform words into transitive verbs)

belie: to misrepresent; to contradict

belittle: to make small; to make something appear smaller

bemoan: to moan for; to lament

bewilder: to confuse completely (that is, to make one mentally wander)

BEL/BELL: beautiful

belle: a beautiful woman

embellish: to make beautiful; to ornament

BELL: war

antebellum: before the war (especially the American Civil War)

belligerent: warlike, given to waging war

rebel: a person who resists authority, control, or tradition

BEN/BENE: good

benediction: act of uttering a blessing

benefit: anything advantageous to a person or thing

benevolent: desiring to do good to others

benign: having a kindly disposition

BI/BIN: two

biennial: happening every two years

bilateral: pertaining to or affecting two or both sides

bilingual: able to speak one's native language and another with equal facility

binocular: involving two eyes

bipartisan: representing two parties

combination: the joining of two or more things into a whole

BON/BOUN: good, generous

bona fide: in good faith; without fraud

bonus: something given over and above what is due

bountiful: generous

BREV/BRID: short, small

abbreviate: to shorten

abridge: to shorten

brevet: an honorary promotion with no additional pay

breviloquent: laconic; concise in one's speech

brevity: shortness

brief: short

BURS: purse, money

bursar: treasurer

bursary: treasury

disburse: to pay

reimburse: to pay back

C

CAD/CID: to fall, to happen by chance

accident: happening by chance; unexpected

cascade: a waterfall descending over a steep surface

coincidence: a striking occurrence of two or more events at one time, apparently by chance

decadent: decaying; deteriorating

recidivist: one who repeatedly relapses, as into crime

CANT/CENT/CHANT: to sing

accent: prominence of a syllable in terms of pronunciation

chant: a song; singing

enchant: to subject to magical influence; bewitch

incantation: the chanting of words purporting to have magical power

incentive: that which incites action

recant: to withdraw or disavow a statement

CAP/CIP/CEPT: to take, to get

anticipate: to realize beforehand; foretaste or foresee

capture: to take by force or stratagem

emancipate: to free from restraint

percipient: having perception; discerning; discriminating

precept: a commandment or direction given as a rule of conduct

susceptible: capable of receiving, admitting, undergoing, or being affected by something

CAP/CAPIT/CIPIT: head, headlong

capital: the city or town that is the official seat of government

capitulate: to surrender unconditionally or on stipulated terms

caption: a heading or title

disciple: one who is a pupil of the doctrines of another

precipice: a cliff with a vertical face

precipitate: to hasten the occurrence of; to bring about prematurely

CARD/CORD/COUR: heart

cardiac: pertaining to the heart

concord: agreement; peace, amity

concordance: agreement, concord, harmony

discord: lack of harmony between persons or things

encourage: to inspire with spirit or confidence

CARN: flesh

carnage: the slaughter of a great number of people

carnival: a traveling amusement show

carnivorous: eating flesh

incarnation: a being invested with a bodily form

reincarnation: rebirth of a soul in a new body

CAST/CHAST: to cut

cast: to throw or hurl; fling

caste: a hereditary social group, limited to people of the same rank

castigate: to punish in order to correct

chaste: free from obscenity; decent

chastise: to discipline, esp. by corporal punishment

CAUS/CAUT: to burn

caustic: burning or corrosive

cauterize: to burn or deaden

cautery: an instrument used for branding; branding

holocaust: a burnt offering; complete destruction by fire or other means

CED/CEED/CESS: to go, to yield, to stop

accede: to yield to a demand; to enter office

antecedent: existing, being, or going before

cessation: a temporary or complete discontinuance

concede: to acknowledge as true, just, or proper; admit

incessant: without stop

predecessor: one who comes before another in an office, position, etc.

CELER: speed

accelerant: something used to speed up a process

accelerate: to increase in speed

celerity: speed; quickness

decelerate: to decrease in speed

CENT: hundred, hundredth

bicentennial: two-hundredth anniversary

cent: a hundredth of a dollar

centigrade: a temperature system with one hundred degrees between the freezing and boiling points of water

centimeter: one-hundredth of a meter

centipede: a creature with many legs

century: one hundred years

percent: in every hundred

CENTR: center

centrifuge: an apparatus that rotates at high speed and separates substances of different densities using centrifugal force

centrist: of or pertaining to moderate political or social ideas

concentrate: to bring to a common center; to converge, to direct toward one point

concentric: having a common center, as in circles or spheres

eccentric: off-center

CERN/CERT/CRET/CRIM/CRIT: to separate, to judge, to distinguish, to decide

ascertain: to make sure of; to determine

certitude: freedom from doubt

criterion: a standard of judgment or criticism

discreet: judicious in one's conduct of speech, esp. with regard to maintaining silence about something of a delicate nature

discrete: detached from others, separate

hypocrite: a person who pretends to have beliefs that she does not

CHROM: color

chromatic: having to do with color

chrome: a metallic element (chromium) used to make vivid colors or something plated with chromium

chromosome: genetic material that can be studied by coloring it with dyes

monochromatic: having only one color

CHRON: time

anachronism: something that is out-of-date or belonging to the wrong time

chronic: constant, habitual

chronology: the sequential order in which past events occurred

chronometer: a highly accurate clock or watch

synchronize: to occur at the same time or agree in time

CIRCU/CIRCUM: around

circuit: a line around an area; a racecourse; the path traveled by electrical current

circuitous: roundabout, indirect

circumference: the outer boundary of a circular area

circumspect: cautious; watching all sides

circumstances: the existing conditions or state of affairs surrounding and affecting an agent

CIS: to cut

exorcise: to seek to expel an evil spirit by ceremony

incision: a cut, gash, or notch

incisive: penetrating, cutting

precise: definitely stated or defined

scissors: cutting instrument for paper

CLA/CLO/CLU: to shut, to close

claustrophobia: an abnormal fear of enclosed places

cloister: a courtyard bordered with covered walks, esp. in a religious institution

conclude: to bring to an end; finish; to terminate

disclose: to make known, reveal, or uncover

exclusive: not admitting of something else; shutting out others

preclude: to prevent the presence, existence, or occurrence of

CLAIM/CLAM: to shout, to cry out

clamor: a loud uproar

disclaim: to deny interest in or connection with

exclaim: to cry out or speak suddenly and vehemently

proclaim: to announce or declare in an official way

reclaim: to claim or demand the return of a right or possession

CLI: to lean toward

climax: the most intense point in the development of something

decline: to cause to slope or incline downward

disinclination: aversion, distaste

proclivity: inclination, bias

recline: to lean back

CO/COL/COM/CON: with, together

coerce: to compel by force, intimidation, or authority

collaborate: to work with another, cooperate

collide: to strike one another with a forceful impact

commensurate: suitable in measure, proportionate

compatible: capable of existing together in harmony

conciliate: to placate, win over

connect: to bind or fasten together

COGN/CONN: to know

cognition: the process of knowing

incognito: with one's name or identity concealed

recognize: to identify as already known

CONTRA/CONTRO/COUNTER: against

contradict: to oppose; to speak against

contrary: opposed to; opposite

controversy: a disputation; a quarrel

counterfeit: fake; a false imitation

countermand: to retract an order

encounter: a meeting, often with an opponent

CORP/CORS: body

corporation: a company legally treated as an individual

corps: a body (an organized group) of troops

corpse: a dead body

corpulent: obese; having a lot of flesh

corset: a garment used to give shape and support to the body

incorporation: combining into a single body

COSM: order, universe, world

cosmetic: improving the appearance (making it look better ordered)

cosmic: relating to the universe

cosmology: a theory of the universe as a whole

cosmonaut: an astronaut; an explorer of outer space

cosmopolitan: worldly

cosmos: the universe; an orderly system; order

microcosm: a small system that reflects a larger whole

COUR/CUR: running, a course

concur: to accord in opinion; agree

courier: a messenger traveling in haste who bears news

curriculum: the regular course of study

cursive: handwriting in flowing strokes with the letters joined together

cursory: going rapidly over something; hasty; superficial

excursion: a short journey or trip

incursion: a hostile entrance into a place, esp. suddenly

recur: to happen again

CRE/CRESC/CRET: to grow

accretion: an increase by natural growth

accrue: to be added as a matter of periodic gain

creation: the act of producing or causing to exist

excrescence: an outgrowth

increase: to make greater in any respect

increment: something added or gained; an addition or increase

CRED: to believe, to trust

credentials: anything that provides the basis for belief

credit: trustworthiness

credo: any formula of belief

credulity: willingness to believe or trust too readily

incredible: unbelievable

CRYPT: hidden

apocryphal: of doubtful authorship or authenticity

crypt: a subterranean chamber or vault

cryptography: procedures of making and using secret writing

cryptology: the science of interpreting secret writings, codes, ciphers, and the like

CUB/CUMB: to lie down

cubicle: any small space or compartment that is partitioned off

incubate: to sit upon for the purpose of hatching

incumbent: holding an indicated position

recumbent: lying down; reclining; leaning

succumb: to give away to superior force; yield

CULP: fault, blame

culpable: deserving blame or censure

culprit: a person guilty of an offense

inculpate: to charge with fault

mea culpa: through my fault; my fault

D

DAC/DOC: to teach

didactic: intended for instruction

docile: easily managed or handled; tractable

doctor: someone licensed to practice medicine; a learned person

doctrine: a particular principle advocated, as of a government or religion

indoctrinate: to imbue a person with learning

DE: away, off, down, completely, reversal

decipher: to make out the meaning; to interpret

defame: to attack the good name or reputation of

deferential: respectful; to yield to judgment

defile: to make foul, dirty, or unclean

delineate: to trace the outline of; sketch or trace in outline

descend: to move from a higher to a lower place

DELE: to erase

delete: erase; blot out; remove

indelible: impossible to erase; lasting

DEM: people

democracy: government by the people

demographics: vital and social statistics of populations

endemic: peculiar to a particular people or locality

epidemic: affecting a large number of people at the same time and spreading from person to person

pandemic: general, universal

DEXT: right hand, right side, deft

ambidextrous: equally able to use both hands

dexter: on the right

dexterity: deftness; adroitness

DI: day

dial: a device for seeing the hour of the day; a clock face; rotatable disks or knobs used as a control input

diary: a record of one's days

dismal: gloomy (from "bad days")

diurnal: daily

meridian: a direct line from the North Pole to the South Pole; the highest point reached by the sun; noon

quotidian: everyday; ordinary

DI/DIA: in two, through, across

diagnose: to identify disease or fault from symptoms

dialogue: a conversation between two or more persons

diameter: a line going through a circle, dividing it in two

dichotomy: division into two parts, kinds, etc.

DI/DIF/DIS: away from, apart, reversal, not

diffuse: to pour out and spread, as in a fluid

dilate: to make wider or larger; to cause to expand

dilatory: inclined to delay or procrastinate

disperse: to drive or send off in various directions

disseminate: to scatter or spread widely; promulgate

dissipate: to scatter wastefully

dissuade: to deter by advice or persuasion

DIC/DICT/DIT: to say, to tell, to use words

dictionary: a book containing a selection of the words of a language

interdict: to forbid; prohibit

predict: to tell in advance

verdict: a judgment or decision

DIGN: worth

condign: well deserved; fitting; adequate

deign: to think fit or in accordance with one's dignity

dignitary: a person who holds a high rank or office

dignity: nobility or elevation of character; worthiness

disdain: to look upon or treat with contempt

DOG/DOX: opinion

dogma: a system of tenets, as of a church

orthodox: sound or correct in opinion or doctrine

paradox: an opinion or statement contrary to accepted opinion

DOL: to suffer, to pain, to grieve

condolence: expression of sympathy with one who is suffering

doleful: sorrowful, mournful

dolorous: full of pain or sorrow, grievous

indolence: a state of being lazy or slothful

DON/DOT/DOW: to give

anecdote: a short narrative about an interesting event

antidote: something that prevents or counteracts ill effects

donate: to present as a gift or contribution

endow: to provide with a permanent fund

pardon: kind indulgence, forgiveness

DORM: sleep

dormant: sleeping; inactive

dormitory: a place for sleeping; a residence hall

DORS: back

dorsal: having to do with the back

endorse: to sign on the back; to vouch for

DUB: doubt

dubiety: doubtfulness

dubious: doubtful

indubitable: unquestionable

DUC/DUCT: to lead

abduct: to carry off or lead away

conducive: contributive, helpful

conduct: personal behavior, way of acting

induce: to lead or move by influence

induct: to install in a position with formal ceremonies

produce: to bring into existence; give cause to

DULC: sweet

dulcet: sweet; pleasing

dulcified: sweetened; softened

dulcimer: a musical instrument

DUR: hard, lasting

dour: sullen, gloomy (originally: hard, obstinate)

durable: able to resist decay

duration: the length of time something exists

duress: compulsion by threat, coercion

endure: to hold out against; to sustain without yielding

obdurate: stubborn, resistant to persuasion

DYS: faulty, abnormal

dysfunctional: poorly functioning

dyslexia: difficulty in learning to read and interpret symbols

dyspepsia: impaired digestion

dystrophy: faulty or inadequate nutrition or development

E

E/EX: out, out of, from, former, completely

efface: to rub or wipe out; surpass, eclipse

evade: to escape from, avoid

exclude: to shut out; to leave out

exonerate: to free or declare free from blame

expire: to breathe out; to breathe one's last; to end

extricate: to disentangle, release

EGO: self

ego: oneself; the part of oneself that is self-aware

egocentric: focused on oneself

egoism/egotism: selfishness; self-absorption

EM/EN: in, into

embrace: to clasp in the arms; to include or contain

enclose: to close in on all sides

EPI: upon

epidemic: affecting a large number of people at the same time and spreading from person to person

epidermis: the outer layer of the skin

epigram: a witty or pointed saying tersely expressed

epilogue: a concluding part added to a literary work

epithet: a word or phrase, used invectively as a term of abuse

EQU: equal, even

adequate: equal to the requirement or occasion

equation: the act of making equal

equidistant: equally distant

iniquity: gross injustice; wickedness

ERR: to wander

err: to go astray in thought or belief, to be mistaken

errant: wandering or traveling, especially in search of adventure

erratic: deviating from the proper or usual course in conduct

error: a deviation from accuracy or correctness

ESCE: becoming

adolescent: between childhood and adulthood

convalescent: recovering from illness

incandescent: glowing with heat, shining

obsolescent: becoming obsolete

reminiscent: reminding or suggestive of

EU: good, well

eugenics: improvement of qualities of race by control of inherited characteristics

eulogy: speech or writing in praise or commendation

euphemism: pleasant-sounding term for something unpleasant

euphony: pleasantness of sound

euthanasia: killing a person painlessly, usually one who has an incurable, painful disease

EXTRA: outside, beyond

extract: to take out, obtain against a person's will

extradite: to hand over (person accused of crime) to state where crime was committed

extraordinary: beyond the ordinary

extrapolate: to estimate (unknown facts or values) from known data

extrasensory: derived by means other than known senses

F

FAB/FAM: to speak

affable: friendly, courteous

defame: to attack the good name of

fable: fictional tale, esp. legendary

famous: well-known, celebrated

ineffable: too great for description in words; that which must not be uttered

FAC/FIC/FIG/FAIT/FEIT/FY: to do, to make

configuration: manner of arrangement, shape

counterfeit: imitation, forgery

deficient: incomplete or insufficient

effigy: sculpture or model of person

faction: small dissenting group within larger one, esp. in politics

factory: building for manufacture of goods

prolific: producing many offspring or much output

ratify: to confirm or accept by formal consent

FAL: to err, to deceive

default: to fail

fail: to be insufficient; to be unsuccessful; to die out

fallacy: a flawed argument

false: not true; erroneous; lying

faux pas: a false step; a social gaffe

infallible: incapable of being wrong or being deceived

FATU: foolish

fatuity: foolishness; stupidity

fatuous: foolish; stupid

infatuated: swept up in a fit of passion, impairing one's reason

FER: to bring, to carry, to bear

confer: to grant, bestow

offer: to present for acceptance, refusal, or consideration

proffer: to offer

proliferate: to reproduce; produce rapidly

referendum: a vote on a political question open to the entire electorate

FERV: to boil, to bubble

effervescent: with the quality of giving off bubbles of gas

fervid: ardent, intense

fervor: passion, zeal

FI/FID: faith, trust

affidavit: a written statement on oath

confide: to entrust with a secret

fidelity: faithfulness, loyalty

fiduciary: of a trust; held or given in trust

infidel: disbeliever in the supposed true religion

FIN: end

confine: to keep or restrict within certain limits; imprison

definitive: decisive, unconditional, final

final: at the end; coming last

infinite: boundless; endless

infinitesimal: infinitely or very small

FLAGR/FLAM: to burn

conflagration: a large, destructive fire

flagrant: blatant, scandalous

flambeau: a lighted torch

inflame: to set on fire

FLECT/FLEX: to bend, to turn

deflect: to bend or turn aside from a purpose

flexible: able to bend without breaking

genuflect: to bend knee, esp. in worship

inflect: to change or vary pitch of

reflect: to throw back

FLU/FLUX: to flow

confluence: merging into one

effluence: flowing out of (light, electricity, etc.)

fluctuation: something that varies, rising and falling

fluid: a substance, esp. gas or liquid, capable of flowing freely

mellifluous: pleasing, musical

FORE: before

foreshadow: be warning or indication of (future event)

foresight: care or provision for future

forestall: to prevent by advance action

forthright: straightforward, outspoken, decisive

FORT: chance

fortuitous: happening by luck

fortunate: lucky, auspicious

fortune: chance or luck in human affairs

FORT: strength

forte: strong point; something a person does well

fortify: to provide with fortifications; strengthen

fortissimo: very loud

FRA/FRAC/FRAG/FRING: to break

fractious: irritable, peevish

fracture: breakage, esp. of a bone

fragment: a part broken off

infringe: to break or violate (a law, etc.)

refractory: stubborn, unmanageable, rebellious

FUG: to flee, to fly

centrifugal: flying off from the center

fugitive: on the run; someone who flees

fugue: a musical composition in which subsequent parts imitate or pursue the first part; a psychological state in which one flies from one's own identity

refuge: a haven for those fleeing

refugee: a fleeing person who seeks refuge

subterfuge: a deception used to avoid a confrontation

FULG: to shine

effulgent: shining forth

refulgent: radiant; shining

FUM: smoke

fume: smoke; scented vapor; to emit smoke or vapors

fumigate: to treat with smoke or vapors

perfume: scents, from burning incense or other sources of fragrance

FUS: to pour

diffuse: to spread widely or thinly

fusillade: continuous discharge of firearms or outburst of criticism

infusion: the act of permeating or steeping; liquid extract so obtained

profuse: lavish, extravagant, copious

suffuse: to spread throughout or over from within

G

GEN: birth, creation, race, kind

carcinogenic: producing cancer

congenital: existing or as such from birth

gender: classification roughly corresponding to the two sexes and sexlessness

generous: giving or given freely

genetics: the study of heredity and variation among animals and plants

progeny: offspring, descendants

GNI/GNO: to know

agnostic: one who believes that the existence of God is not provable

diagnose: to identify disease or fault from symptoms

ignoramus: a person lacking knowledge, uninformed

ignore: to refuse to take notice of

prognosis: to forecast, especially of disease

GRAD/GRESS: to step

aggressive: given to hostile acts or feelings

degrade: to humiliate, dishonor, reduce to lower rank

digress: to depart from the main subject

egress: going out; way out

progress: forward movement

regress: to move backward, revert to an earlier state

GRAM/GRAPH: to write, to draw

diagram: a figure made by drawing lines; an illustration

epigram: a short poem; a pointed statement

grammar: a system of language and its rules

graph: a diagram used to convey mathematical information

graphite: mineral used for writing, as the "lead" in pencils

photograph: a picture, originally made by exposing chemically treated film to light

GRAT: pleasing

gracious: kindly, esp. to inferiors; merciful

grateful: thankful

gratuity: money given for good service

ingratiate: to bring oneself into favor

GREG: flock

aggregate: a number of things considered as a collective whole

congregate: to come together in a group

egregious: remarkably bad; standing out from the crowd

gregarious: sociable; enjoying spending time with others

segregate: to separate from the crowd

H

HAP: by chance

haphazard: at random

hapless: without luck

happen: occur (originally: to occur by chance)

happily: through good fortune

happy: pleased, as by good fortune

mishap: an unlucky accident

perhaps: a qualifier suggesting something might (or might not) take place

HEMI: half

hemisphere: half a sphere; half of the Earth

hemistich: half a line of poetry

HER/HES: to stick

adherent: able to adhere; believer or advocate of a particular thing

adhesive: tending to remain in memory; sticky; an adhesive substance

coherent: logically consistent; having waves in phase and of one wavelength

inherent: involved in the constitution or essential character of something

(H)ETERO: different, other

heterodox: different from acknowledged standard; holding unorthodox opinions or doctrines

heterogeneous: of other origin; not originating in the body

heterosexual: of or pertaining to sexual orientation toward members of the opposite sex; relating to different sexes

HOL: whole

catholic: universal

holocaust: a burnt offering; complete destruction by fire or other means

hologram: a sort of three-dimensional image

holograph: a document written entirely by the person whose name it's in

holistic: considering something as a unified whole

(H)OM: same

anomaly: deviation from the common rule

homeostasis: a relatively stable state of equilibrium

homogeneous: of the same or a similar kind of nature; of uniform structure of composition throughout

homonym: one of two or more words spelled and pronounced alike but different in meaning

homosexual: of, relating to, or exhibiting sexual desire toward a member of one's own sex

HUM: earth

exhume: unearth

humble: down-to-earth

humility: the state of being humble

HYPER: over, excessive

hyperactive: excessively active

hyperbole: purposeful exaggeration for effect

hyperglycemia: an abnormally high concentration of sugar in the blood

HYPO: under, beneath, less than

hypochondriac: one affected by extreme depression of mind or spirits, often centered on imaginary physical ailments

hypocritical: pretending to have beliefs one does not

hypodermic: relating to the parts beneath the skin

hypothesis: assumption subject to proof

I

ICON: image, idol

icon: a symbolic picture; a statue; something seen as representative of a culture or movement

iconic: being representative of a culture or movement

iconoclast: one who attacks established beliefs; one who tears down images

iconology: symbolism

IDIO: one's own

idiom: a language, dialect, or style of speaking particular to a people

idiosyncrasy: peculiarity of temperament; eccentricity

idiot: an utterly stupid person

IN/IM: in, into

(Often the *m* is dropped and the first letter to which *i* is prefixed is doubled.)

implicit: not expressly stated; implied

incarnate: given a bodily, esp. a human, form

indigenous: native; innate, natural

influx: the act of flowing in; inflow

intrinsic: belonging to a thing by its very nature

IN/IM: not, without

(Often the *m* is dropped and the first letter to which *i* is prefixed is doubled.)

immoral: not moral; evil

impartial: not partial or biased; just

inactive: not active

indigent: poor, needy, lacking in what is needed

indolence: showing a disposition to avoid exertion; slothful

innocuous: not harmful or injurious

INTER: between, among

interim: a temporary or provisional arrangement; meantime

interloper: one who intrudes in the domain of others

intermittent: stopping or ceasing for a time

intersperse: to scatter here and there

interstate: connecting or jointly involving states

INTRA: inside, within

intramural: within a school; inside a city

intrastate: within a state

intravenous: inside the veins

IT/ITER: way, journey

ambition: strong desire to achieve (from "going around" for votes)

circuit: a line around an area; a racecourse; the path traveled by electrical current

itinerant: traveling

itinerary: travel plans

reiterate: to repeat

transit: traveling; means of transportation

J

JECT: to throw, to throw down

abject: utterly hopeless, humiliating, or wretched

conjecture: formation of opinion on incomplete information

dejected: sad, depressed

eject: to throw out, expel

inject: to place (quality, etc.) where needed in something

JOC: joke

jocose: given to joking; playful

jocular: in a joking manner; funny

jocund: merry; cheerful

joke: a witticism; a humorous anecdote; something funny

JOIN/JUG/JUNCT: to meet, to join

adjoin: to be next to and joined with

conjugal: related to marriage

conjunction: joining; occurring together; a connecting word

injunction: a command; an act of enjoining

junction: the act of joining; combining; a place where multiple paths join

junta: a group of military officers who join together to run a country; a council

rejoinder: to reply, retort

subjugate: to make subservient; to place under a yoke

JOUR: day

adjourn: to close a meeting; to put off further proceedings for another day

journal: a record of one's days

journey: a trip (originally: a day's travel)

JUD: to judge

adjudicate: to act as a judge

judiciary: a system of courts; members of a court system

judicious: having good judgment

prejudice: a previous or premature judgment; bias

JUR: law, to swear

abjure: to renounce on oath

adjure: to beg or command

jurisprudence: a system of law; knowledge of law

perjury: willful lying while on oath

JUV: young

juvenile: young; immature

juvenilia: writings or art produced in one's youth

rejuvenate: to refresh; to make young again

L

LANG/LING: tongue

bilingual: speaking two languages

language: a system of (usually spoken) communication

linguistics: the study of language

LAUD: praise, honor

cum laude: with honors

laudable: praiseworthy

laudatory: expressing praise

LAV/LAU/LU: to wash

ablution: act of cleansing

antediluvian: before the biblical flood; extremely old

deluge: a great flood of water

dilute: to make thinner or weaker by the addition of water

laundry: items to be, or that have been, washed

lavatory: a room with equipment for washing hands and face

LAX/LEAS/LES: loose

lax: loose; undisciplined

laxative: medicine or food that loosens the bowels

lease: to rent out (that is, to let something loose for others' use)

leash: a cord used to hold an animal while giving it some freedom to run loose

relax: loosen; be less strict; calm down

release: let go; set free

LEC/LEG/LEX: to read, to speak

dialect: a manner of speaking; a regional variety of a language

lectern: a reading desk

lecture: an instructional speech

legend: a story; a written explanation of a map or illustration

legible: readable

lesson: instruction (originally: part of a book or an oral instruction to be studied and repeated to a teacher)

lexicographer: a writer of dictionaries

lexicon: a dictionary

LECT/LEG: to select, to choose

collect: to gather together or assemble

eclectic: selecting ideas, etc. from various sources

elect: to choose; to decide

predilection: preference, liking

select: to choose with care

LEV: to lift, to rise, light (weight)

alleviate: to make easier to endure, lessen

levee: an embankment against river flooding

levitate: to rise in the air or cause to rise

levity: humor, frivolity, gaiety

relevant: bearing on or pertinent to information at hand

relieve: to mitigate; to free from a burden

LI/LIG: to tie, to bind

ally: to unite; one in an alliance

league: an association; a group of nations, teams, etc. that have agreed to work for a common cause

liable: legally responsible; bound by law

liaison: a connection; one who serves to connect

lien: the right to hold a property due to an outstanding debt

ligament: a band holding bones together; a bond

ligature: a connection between two letters; a bond

oblige: to obligate; to make indebted or form personal bonds by doing a favor

rely: to depend upon (originally: to come together; to rally)

LIBER: free

deliver: to set free; to save; to hand over

liberal: generous; giving away freely

liberality: generosity

liberate: set free

libertine: one who follows one's own path, without regard for morals or other restrictions

liberty: freedom

livery: a uniform; an emblem indicating an owner or a manufacturer (originally: an allowance of food or other provisions given to servants)

LITH: stone

acrolith: a statue with a stone head and limbs (but a wooden body)

lithography: a printing process that originally involved writing on a flat stone

lithology: the study of rocks and stones

lithotomy: an operation to remove stones from the body

megalith: a very big stone

monolith: a single block of stone, often shaped into a monument

LOC/LOG/LOQU: word, speech, thought

colloquial: of ordinary or familiar conversation

dialogue: a conversation, esp. in a literary work

elocution: art of clear and expressive speaking

eulogy: a speech or writing in praise of someone

grandiloquent: pompous or inflated in language

loquacious: talkative

prologue: introduction to a poem, play, etc.

LUC/LUM/LUS: light (brightness)

illuminate: to supply or brighten with light

illustrate: to make intelligible with examples or analogies

illustrious: highly distinguished

lackluster: lacking brilliance or radiance

lucid: easily understood, intelligible

luminous: bright, brilliant, glowing

translucent: permitting light to pass through

LUD/LUS: to play

allude: to refer casually or indirectly

delude: to mislead the mind or judgment of, deceive

elude: to avoid capture or escape defection by

illusion: something that deceives by producing a false impression of reality

ludicrous: ridiculous, laughable

prelude: a preliminary to an action, event, etc.

M

MACRO: great, long

macro: broad; large; a single computer command that executes a longer set of commands

macrobiotics: a system intended to prolong life

macrocephalous: having a large head

macrocosm: the universe; a large system that is reflected in at least one of its subsets

macroscopic: large enough to be visible to the naked eye

MAG/MAJ/MAX: big, great

magnanimous: generous in forgiving an insult or injury

magnate: a powerful or influential person

magnify: to increase the apparent size of

magnitude: greatness of size, extent, or dimensions

maxim: an expression of general truth or principle

maximum: the highest amount, value, or degree attained

MAL/MALE: bad, ill, evil, wrong

maladroit: clumsy; tactless

malady: a disorder or disease of the body

malapropism: humorous misuse of a word

malediction: a curse

malfeasance: misconduct or wrongdoing often committed by a public official

malfunction: failure to function properly

malicious: full of or showing malice

malign: to speak harmful untruths about, to slander

MAN/MANU: hand

emancipate: to free from bondage

manifest: readily perceived by the eye or the understanding

manual: operated by hand

manufacture: to make by hand or machinery

MAND/MEND: to command, to order, to entrust

command: to order; an order; control

commend: to give something over to the care of another; to praise

countermand: to retract an order

demand: to strongly ask for; to claim; to require

mandatory: commanded; required

recommend: to praise and suggest the use of; to advise

remand: to send back

MEDI: middle

immediate: nearest; having nothing in between

intermediate: in the middle

mean: average; in the middle

mediate: to serve as a go-between; to try to settle an argument

medieval: related to the Middle Ages

mediocre: neither good nor bad; so-so

medium: size between small and large; a substance or agency that things travel through (as, for example, light travels through air, and news is conveyed by television and newspapers)

MEGA: large, great

megalith: a very big stone

megalomania: a mental condition involving delusions of greatness; an obsession with doing great things

megalopolis: a very large city

megaphone: a device for magnifying the sound of one's voice

megaton: explosive power equal to 1,000 tons of TNT

MICRO: very small

microbe: a very small organism

microcosm: a small system that reflects a larger whole

micron: a millionth of a meter

microorganism: a very small organism

microscope: a device that magnifies very small things for viewing

MIN: small

diminish: to lessen

diminution: the act or process of diminishing

miniature: a copy or model that represents something in greatly reduced size

minute: a unit of time equal to one-sixtieth of an hour

minutiae: small or trivial details

MIN: to project, to hang over

eminent: towering above others; projecting

imminent: about to occur; impending

preeminent: superior to or notable above all others

prominent: projecting outward

MIS: bad, wrong, to hate

misadventure: bad luck; an unlucky accident

misanthrope: one who hates people or humanity

misapply: to use something incorrectly

mischance: bad luck; an unlucky accident

mischief: bad or annoying behavior

misconstrue: to take something in a way that wasn't intended; to understand something incorrectly

misfit: somebody or something that doesn't fit in

MIS/MIT: to send

emissary: a messenger or an agent sent to represent the interests of another

intermittent: stopping and starting at intervals

remission: a lessening of intensity or degree

remit: to send money

transmit: to send from one person, thing, or place to another

MISC: mixed

miscellaneous: made up of a variety of parts or ingredients

promiscuous: consisting of diverse and unrelated parts or individuals; indiscriminate

MOB/MOM/MOT/MOV: to move

automobile: a vehicle that moves under its own power; a motorized car

demote: to move downward in an organization

immovable: incapable of being moved; unyielding

locomotion: moving from place to place; the ability to do so

mob: the rabble; a disorderly group of people (from the Latin *mobile vulgus*, meaning "the fickle crowd")

mobile: movable

mobilize: to make ready for movement; to assemble

moment: an instant; importance

momentous: of great importance (originally: having the power to move)

momentum: the force driving a moving object to keep moving; a growing force

motion: movement

motive: a reason for action; what moves a person to do something

motor: a device that makes something move

mutiny: rebellion against authority, esp. by sailors

promote: to move to a higher rank in an organization

remove: to take away; to move away

MOLL: soft

emollient: something that softens or soothes (e.g., a lotion)

mild: gentle; kind

mollify: soothe; soften; calm

mollusk: a phylum of invertebrate animals—including octopuses, squids, oysters, clams, and slugs—with soft bodies

MON/MONIT: to remind, to warn

admonish: to counsel against something; caution

monitor: one that admonishes, cautions, or reminds

monument: a structure, such as a building, tower, or sculpture, erected as a memorial

premonition: forewarning, presentiment

remonstrate: to say or plead in protest, objection, or reproof

summon: to call together; convene

MON/MONO: one

monarchy: rule by a single person

monk: a man in a religious order living apart from society (originally: a religious hermit)

monochord: a musical instrument with a single string

monogram: a design combining multiple letters into one

monograph: a scholarly study of a single subject

monologue: a speech or other dramatic composition recited by one person

monomania: an obsession with a single subject

monotonous: boring; spoken using only one tone

MOR/MORT: death

immortal: not subject to death

morbid: susceptible to preoccupation with unwholesome matters

moribund: dying, decaying

MORPH: shape

amorphous: without definite form; lacking a specific shape

anthropomorphism: attribution of human characteristics to inanimate objects, animals, or natural phenomena

metamorphosis: a transformation, as by magic or sorcery

MULT: many

multiple: many, having many parts; a number containing some quantity of a smaller number without remainder

multiplex: having many parts; a movie theater or other building with many separate units

multiply: to increase; to become many

multitudinous: very many; containing very many; having very many forms

MUT: to change

commute: to substitute; exchange; interchange

immutable: unchangeable, invariable

mutation: the process of being changed

permutation: a complete change; transformation

transmute: to change from one form into another

N

NAT/NAS/NAI/GNA: birth

cognate: related by blood; having a common ancestor

naive: lacking worldliness and sophistication; artless

nascent: starting to develop

native: belonging to one by nature; inborn; innate

natural: present due to nature, not to artificial or man-made means

renaissance: rebirth, esp. referring to culture

NAU/NAV: ship, sailor

astronaut: one who travels in outer space

circumnavigate: to sail all the way around

cosmonaut: one who travels in outer space

nauseous: causing a squeamish feeling (originally: seasickness)

nautical: related to sailing or sailors

naval: related to the navy

nave: the central portion of a church (which resembles the shape of a ship)

navy: a military force consisting of ships and sailors

NIHIL: nothing, none

annihilate: wipe out; reduce to nothing

nihilism: denial of all moral beliefs; denial that existence has any meaning

NOC/NOX: harm

innocent: uncorrupted by evil, malice, or wrongdoing

innocuous: not harmful or injurious

noxious: injurious or harmful to health or morals

obnoxious: highly disagreeable or offensive

NOCT/NOX: night

equinox: one of two times in a year when day and night are equal in length

noctambulant: walking at night; sleepwalking

nocturnal: related to the night; active at night

nocturne: a dreamlike piece of music; a painting set at night

NOM: rule, order

astronomy: the scientific study of the universe beyond the Earth

autonomy: independence, self-governance

economy: the careful or thrifty use of resources, as of income, materials, or labor

gastronomy: the art or science of good eating

taxonomy: the science, laws, or principles of classification

NOM/NYM/NOUN/NOWN: name

acronym: a word formed from the initial letters of a name

anonymous: having an unknown or unacknowledged name

nomenclature: a system of names; systematic naming

nominal: existing in name only; negligible

nominate: to propose by name as a candidate

noun: a word that names a person, place, or thing

renown: fame; reputation

synonym: a word having a meaning similar to that of another word of the same language

NON: not

nonconformist: one who does not conform to a church or other societal institution

nonentity: something that doesn't exist; something that is unimportant

nonpareil: something with no equal

nonpartisan: not affiliated with a political party

NOUNC/NUNC: to announce

announce: to proclaim

pronounce: to articulate

renounce: to give up, especially by formal announcement

NOV/NEO/NOU: new

innovate: to begin or introduce something new

neologism: a newly coined word, phrase, or expression

neophyte: a beginner; a new convert; a new worker

neoplasm: a new growth in the body; a tumor

nouveau riche: one who has lately become rich

novice: a person new to any field or activity

renovate: to restore to an earlier condition

NULL: nothing

annul: to cancel; to make into nothing

nullify: to cancel; to make into nothing

nullity: the condition of being nothing

O

OB: toward, to, against, over

obese: extremely fat, corpulent

obfuscate: to render indistinct or dim; darken

oblique: having a slanting or sloping direction

obsequious: overly submissive

obstinate: stubbornly adhering to an idea, inflexible

obstreperous: noisily defiant, unruly

obstruct: to block or fill with obstacles

obtuse: not sharp, pointed, or acute in any form

OMNI: all

omnibus: an anthology of the works of one author or of writings on related subjects

omnipotent: all powerful

omnipresent: everywhere at one time

omniscient: having infinite knowledge

ONER: burden

exonerate: to free from blame (originally: to relieve of a burden)

onerous: burdensome; difficult

onus: a burden; a responsibility

OSS/OSTE: bone

ossify: to become bone; to harden; to become callous

ossuary: a place where bones are kept; a charnel house

osteopathy: a medical system based on the belief that many illnesses can be traced to issues in the skeletal system

P

PAC/PEAC: peace

appease: to bring peace to

pacifier: something or someone that eases the anger or agitation of

pacify: to ease the anger or agitation of

pact: a formal agreement, as between nations

PALP: to feel

palpable: capable of being felt; tangible

palpate: to feel; to examine by feeling

palpitate: to beat quickly, as the heart; to throb

PAN/PANT: all, everyone

pandemic: widespread, general, universal

panegyric: formal or elaborate praise at an assembly

panoply: a wide-ranging and impressive array or display

panorama: an unobstructed and wide view of an extensive area

pantheon: a public building containing tombs or memorials of the illustrious dead of a nation

PAR: equal

apartheid: any system or caste that separates people according to race, etc.

disparage: to belittle, speak disrespectfully about

disparate: essentially different

par: an equality in value or standing

parity: equally, as in amount, status, or character

PARA: next to, beside

parable: a short, allegorical story designed to illustrate a moral lesson or religious principle

paragon: a model of excellence

parallel: extending in the same direction

paranoid: suffering from a baseless distrust of others

parasite: an organism that lives on or within a plant or an animal of another species, from which it obtains nutrients

parody: to imitate for purposes of satire

PAS/PAT/PATH: feeling, suffering, disease

compassion: a feeling of deep sympathy for someone struck by misfortune, accompanied by a desire to alleviate suffering

dispassionate: devoid of personal feeling or bias

empathy: the identification with the feelings or thoughts of others

impassive: showing or feeling no emotion

pathogenic: causing disease

sociopath: a person whose behavior is antisocial and who lacks a sense of moral responsibility

sympathy: harmony or agreement in feeling

PAU/PO/POV/PU: few, little, poor

impoverish: to deplete

paucity: smallness of quantity; scarcity; scantiness

pauper: a person without any personal means of support

poverty: the condition of being poor

puerile: childish, immature

pusillanimous: lacking courage or resolution

PEC: money

impecunious: having no money; penniless

peculation: embezzlement

pecuniary: relating to money

PED: child, education

encyclopedia: book or set of books containing articles on various topics, covering all branches of knowledge or of one particular subject

pedagogue: a teacher

pedant: one who displays learning ostentatiously

pediatrician: a doctor who primarily has children as patients

PED/POD: foot

antipodes: places that are diametrically opposite each other on the globe

expedite: to speed up the progress of

impede: to slow or prevent progress by means of obstacles or hindrances

pedal: a foot-operated lever or part used to control

pedestrian: a person who travels on foot

podium: a small platform for an orchestra conductor, speaker, etc.

PEL: to drive, to push

compel: to force; to command

dispel: to drive away; to disperse

expel: to drive out; to banish; to eject

impel: to force; to drive forward

propel: to drive forward

PEN/PENE: almost

peninsula: a landmass that is mostly surrounded by water, making it almost an island

penultimate: second-to-last

penumbra: a shaded area between pure shadow and pure light

PEN/PUN: to pay, to compensate

penal: of or pertaining to punishment, as for crimes

penalty: a punishment imposed for a violation of law or rule

penance: a punishment undergone to express regret for a sin

penitent: contrite

punitive: serving for, concerned with, or inflicting punishment

PEND/PENS: to hang, to weight, to pay

appendage: a limb or other subsidiary part that diverges from the central structure

appendix: supplementary material at the end of a text

compensate: to counterbalance, offset

depend: to rely; to place trust in

indispensable: absolutely necessary, essential, or requisite

stipend: a periodic payment; fixed or regular pay

PER: completely

perforate: to make a way through or into something

perfunctory: performed merely as routine duty

perplex: to cause to be puzzled or bewildered over what is not understood

persistent: lasting or enduring tenaciously

perspicacious: shrewd, astute

pertinacious: resolute, persistent

peruse: to read with thoroughness or care

PERI: around

perimeter: the border or outer boundary of a two-dimensional figure

peripatetic: walking or traveling about; itinerant

periscope: an optical instrument for seeing objects in an obstructed field of vision

PET/PIT: to go, to seek, to strive

appetite: a desire for food or drink

centripetal: moving toward the center

compete: to strive to outdo another

impetuous: characterized by sudden or rash action or emotion

petition: a formally drawn request soliciting some benefit

petulant: showing sudden irritation, esp. over some annoyance

PHIL: love

bibliophile: one who loves or collects books

philatelist: one who loves or collects postage stamps

philology: the study of literary texts to establish their authenticity and determine their meaning

philosopher: one who investigates the truths and principles of being, knowledge, or conduct (originally: lover of wisdom)

PHOB: fear

claustrophobia: fear of enclosed places

hydrophobia: fear of water, which is a symptom of rabies; rabies

phobia: fear; an irrational fear

xenophobia: fear of foreigners; hatred of foreigners

PHON: sound

euphony: the quality of sounding good

megaphone: a device for magnifying the sound of one's voice

phonetics: the study of the sounds used in speech

polyphony: the use of simultaneous melodic lines to produce harmonies in musical compositions

telephone: a device for transmitting sound at a distance

PHOTO: light

photograph: a picture, originally made by exposing chemically treated film to light

photon: a packet of light or other electromagnetic radiation

photosynthesis: a process by which plants create carbohydrates when under light

PLAC: to please

complacent: self-satisfied, unconcerned

complaisant: inclined or disposed to please

implacable: unable to be pleased

placebo: a substance with no pharmacological effect that acts to placate a patient who believes it to be a medicine

placid: pleasantly calm or peaceful

PLE/PLEN: to fill, full

complete: having all parts or elements

deplete: to decrease seriously or exhaust the supply of

implement: an instrument, tool, or utensil for accomplishing work

plenitude: fullness

plethora: excess, overabundance

replete: abundantly supplied

supplement: something added to supply a deficiency

PLEX/PLIC/PLY: to fold, twist, tangle, or bend

complex: composed of many interconnected parts

duplicity: deceitfulness in speech or conduct, double-dealing

implicate: to show to be involved, usually in an incriminating manner

implicit: not expressly stated, implied

replica: any close copy or reproduction

supplicate: to make humble and earnest entreaty

POLY: many

polyandry: the practice of having multiple husbands

polygamy: the practice of having multiple wives

polyglot: someone who speaks many languages

polygon: a figure with many sides

polytheism: belief in many gods

PON/POS/POUND: to put, to place

component: a constituent part, elemental ingredient

expose: to lay open to danger, attack, or harm

expound: to set forth in detail

juxtapose: to place close together or side by side

repository: a receptacle or place where things are deposited

PORT: to carry

deportment: conduct, behavior

disport: to divert or amuse oneself

export: to transmit abroad

import: to bring in from a foreign country

importune: to urge or press with excessive persistence

portable: easily carried

POST: behind, after

post facto: after the fact

posterior: situated at the rear

posterity: future generations

posthumous: after death

POT: to drink

potable: drinkable; safe to drink; a drink

potation: drinking; a drink

potion: a drinkable medicine, poison, or other concoction

PRE: before, in front

precarious: dependent on circumstances beyond one's control

precedent: an act that serves as an example for subsequent situations

precept: a commandment given as a rule of action or conduct

precocious: unusually advanced or mature in mental development or talent

premonition: a feeling of anticipation over a future event

presentiment: foreboding

PREHEND/PRISE: to take, to get, to seize

apprehend: to take into custody

comprise: to include or contain

enterprise: a project undertaken

reprehensible: deserving rebuke or censure

reprisals: retaliation against an enemy

surprise: to strike with an unexpected feeling of wonder or astonishment

PRI/PRIM: first

primal: original; most important

primary: first; most important

prime: first in quality; best

primeval: ancient; going back to the first age of the world

pristine: original; like new; unspoiled; pure

PRO: in front, before, much, for

problem: a difficult question (originally: one put before another for solution)

proceed: to go forward

profuse: spending or giving freely

prolific: highly fruitful

propound: to set forth for consideration

proselytize: to convert or attempt to recruit

provident: having or showing foresight

PROB: to prove, to test

approbation: praise, consideration

opprobrium: the disgrace incurred by shameful conduct

probe: to search or examine thoroughly

probity: honesty, high-mindedness

reprobate: a depraved or wicked person

PROP/PROX: near

approximate: very near; close to being accurate

proximate: nearby; coming just before or just after

proximity: nearness; distance

PROT/PROTO: first

protagonist: the main character in a play or story

protocol: diplomatic etiquette; a system of proper conduct; the original record of a treaty or other negotiation

prototype: the first version of an invention, on which later models are based

protozoan: belonging to a group of single-celled animals, which came before more complex animals

PSEUD/PSEUDO: false

pseudonym: a false name; a pen name

pseudopod: part of a single-celled organism that can be stuck out (like a foot) and used to move around

pseudoscience: false science; something believed to be based on the scientific method but that actually is not

PUG: to fight

impugn: to challenge as false

pugilist: a fighter or boxer

pugnacious: to quarrel or fight readily

repugnant: objectionable or offensive

PUNC/PUNG/POIGN: to point, to prick, to pierce

compunction: a feeling of uneasiness for doing wrong

expunge: to erase, eliminate completely

point: a sharp or tapering end

punctilious: strict or exact in the observance of formalities

puncture: the act of piercing

pungent: caustic or sharply expressive

PYR: fire

pyre: a bonfire, usually for burning a dead body

pyromania: an urge to start fires

pyrosis: heartburn

pyrotechnics: fireworks

Q

QUAD/QUAR/QUAT: four

quadrant: a quarter of a circle; a 90-degree arc

quadrille: a square dance involving four couples

quadruple: four times as many

quadruplets: four children born in one birth

quart: one-fourth of a gallon

quaternary: the number four; the fourth in a series

QUE/QUIS: to seek

acquire: to come into possession of

conquest: the act gaining control by force

exquisite: of special beauty or charm

inquisitive: given to research, eager for knowledge

perquisite: a gratuity, tip

querulous: full of complaints

query: a question, an inquiry

QUIE/QUIT: quiet, rest

acquiesce: to comply, give in

disquiet: lack of calm or peace

quiescence: the condition of being at rest, still, inactive

quiet: making little or no sound

tranquil: free from commotion or tumult

QUIN/QUINT: five

quinquennial: a five-year period; a fifth anniversary

quintessence: the essential part of something (originally: the "fifth essence," which was believed to permeate everything and be what stars and planets were made of)

quintuple: five times as many

R

RACI/RADI: root

deracinate: to uproot

eradicate: to uproot; to wipe out

radical: pertaining to roots; questioning everything, even basic beliefs; going to root causes; thorough

radish: a root vegetable

RAMI: branch

ramification: a branch; an offshoot; a collection of branches; a consequence

ramiform: branchlike

RE: back, again

recline: to lean back; to lie down

regain: to gain again; to take back

remain: to stay behind; to be left; to continue to be

reorganize: to organize again

request: to ask (originally: to seek again)

RECT: straight, right

correct: to set right

direct: to guide; to put straight

erect: upright; starting up straight

rectangle: a four-sided figure in which every angle is a right angle

rectitude: moral uprightness; moral straightness

REG: king, rule

interregnum: a period between kings

realm: a kingdom; a domain

regal: kingly; royal

regent: one who serves on behalf of a king; one who rules

regicide: killing a king; one who kills a king

regiment: a body of troops in an army; to form into such a body; to subject to strict rule

regular: having a structure following some rule; orderly; normally used; average

RETRO: backward

retroactive: extending to things that happened in the past

retrofit: to install newer parts into an older device or structure

retrograde: moving backward; appearing to move backward

retrospective: looking back at the past

RID/RIS: to laugh

derision: the act of mockery

risible: causing laughter

ROG: to ask

abrogate: to abolish by formal means

arrogant: making claims to superior importance or rights

arrogate: to claim unwarrantably or presumptuously

derogatory: belittling, disparaging

interrogate: to ask questions of, esp. formally

surrogate: a person appointed to act for another

RUB/RUD: red

rouge: a red powder used as makeup

rubella: German measles; a disease marked by red spots

rubicund: reddish; rosy-cheeked

rubric: a rule; a guide for scoring tests; a heading in a book set in red letters

russet: reddish-brown; a coarse cloth, usually reddish-brown; a type of apple or pear, typically reddish-brown

RUD: crude

erudite: scholarly; learned (that is, trained out of crudeness)

rude: uncivilized; impolite

rudimentary: undeveloped; related to rudiments

rudiments: first principles; imperfect first step of one's training

S

SACR/SANCT: holy

execrable: abominable

sacrament: something regarded as possessing sacred character

sacred: devoted or dedicated to a deity or religious purpose

sacrifice: the offering of some living or inanimate thing to a deity in homage

sacrilege: the violation of anything sacred

sanctify: to make holy

sanction: authoritative permission or approval

SAG/SAP/SAV: taste, thinking, discerning

insipid: tasteless

sagacious: perceptive; discerning; insightful

sage: wise

sapient: wise

savant: a learned person

savor: taste; to enjoy flavors

SAL: salt

salary: payment for services (originally: money for Roman soldiers to buy salt)

saline: containing salt; salty

SAL/SIL/SAULT/SULT: to leap, to jump

assault: a sudden or violent attack

desultory: at random, unmethodical

exult: to show or feel triumphant joy

insolent: boldly rude or disrespectful

insult: to treat with contemptuous rudeness

resilient: able to spring back to an original form after compression

salient: prominent or conspicuous

somersault: to roll the body end over end, making a complete revolution

SALU: health

salubrious: healthful

salutary: healthful

salute: to greet; a gesture of greeting (originally: to wish good health)

SALV: to save

salvage: to save; something saved or recovered

salvation: being saved

savior: one who saves

SAN: healthy

sane: mentally healthy

sanitarium: a place of healing

sanitary: promoting health; related to conditions that affect health, such as cleanliness

SANG: blood

consanguinity: being related by blood

sanguinary: bloody; bloodthirsty

sanguine: hopeful; confident (from the "sanguine humor," which was believed to be associated with those traits)

SAT: enough

assets: property; possessions (originally: enough property to cover one's debts)

dissatisfied: feeling that one does not have enough

sate: to fill

satisfy: to meet one's desires; to meet an obligation; to provide with enough

saturate: to fill completely; to entirely satisfy

SCI: to know

conscience: the inner sense of what is right or wrong, impelling one toward right action

conscious: aware of one's own existence

omniscient: knowing everything

prescient: having knowledge of things before they happen

unconscionable: unscrupulous

SCRIBE/SCRIPT: to write

ascribe: to credit or assign, as to a cause or course

circumscribe: to draw a line around

conscription: draft

describe: to tell or depict in words

postscript: any addition or supplement

proscribe: to condemn as harmful or odious

scribble: to write hastily or carelessly

script: handwriting

transcript: a written or typed copy

SE: apart, away

secede: to withdraw formally from an association

sedition: incitement of discontent or rebellion against a government

seduce: to lead astray

segregate: to separate or set apart from others

select: to choose in preference to another

separate: to keep apart, divide

sequester: to remove or withdraw into solitude or retirement

SEC/SEQU/SUE/SUI: to follow

non sequitur: an inference or a conclusion that does not follow from the premises

obsequious: fawning

prosecute: to seek to enforce by legal process

pursue: to chase after

second: next after the first

sequence: the following of one thing after another

suite: a series; a set (originally: a train of followers)

SED/SESS/SID: to sit, to settle

assiduous: diligent, persistent, hardworking (literally, "sitting down" to business)

dissident: disagreeing, as in opinion or attitude (literally, "sitting apart")

insidious: intended to entrap or beguile; lying in wait to entrap

preside: to exercise management or control; to sit in the leader's chair

resident: a person who lives in a place

residual: remaining, leftover

sediment: the matter that settles to the bottom of a liquid

session: a meeting at which people sit together in discussion

SEM: seed, to sow

disseminate: to spread; to scatter around

semen: seed (of male animals)

seminary: a school, esp. for religious training (originally: a place for raising plants)

SEMI: half

semicircle: half a circle

semiconscious: only partly conscious; half awake

SEN: old

senate: the highest legislative body (from "council of elders")

senescent: getting old

senile: relating to old age; experiencing memory loss or other age-related mental impairments

sire: a title for a king; a father (originally: an important person, an old man)

SENS/SENT: to feel, to be aware

dissent: to differ in opinion, esp. from the majority

insensate: without feeling or sensitivity

presentiment: a feeling that something is about to happen

resent: to feel or show displeasure

sense: any of the faculties by which humans and animals perceive stimuli originating outside the body

sensory: of or pertaining to the senses or sensation

sentiment: an attitude or feeling toward something

sentinel: a person or thing that stands watch

SIN/SINU: bend, fold, curve

insinuate: to introduce in sneaky or winding ways

sinuous: moving in a bending or wavy manner

sinus: a curved or irregularly shaped cavity in the body, such as those related to the nostrils

SOL: alone

desolate: deserted; laid waste; left alone

isolate: to set apart from others

soliloquize: talk to oneself; talk onstage as if to oneself

solipsism: the belief that the only thing that really exists, or can really be known, is oneself

solitude: the state of being alone

SOL: to loosen, to free

absolution: forgiveness for wrongdoing

dissolute: indifferent to moral restraints

dissolution: the act or process of dissolving into parts or elements

dissolve: to make a solution of, as by mixing in a liquid

resolution: a formal expression of opinion or intention made

soluble: capable of being dissolved or liquefied

SOL: sun

parasol: an umbrella that protects from the sun

solar: related to the sun

solarium: a sunroom; a room with windows for taking in the sun

solstice: one of two days when the sun reaches its highest point at noon and seems to stand still

SOMN: sleep

insomnia: inability to sleep

somnambulist: a sleepwalker

somniferous: sleep-inducing

somniloquist: one who talks while asleep

somnolent: sleep-inducing; sleepy; drowsy

SOPH: wisdom

philosopher: one who studies logic, beauty, truth, etc.; one who seeks wisdom

sophism: a superficially appealing but fallacious argument

sophisticated: complex; worldly; experienced

SOURC/SURG/SURRECT: to rise

insurgent: rising up in revolution; rushing in

insurrection: rising up in armed rebellion

resurrection: coming back to life; rising again

source: where something comes from (such as spring water rising out of the ground)

surge: to rise up forcefully, as ocean waves

SPEC/SPIC: to look, to see

circumspect: watchful and discreet, cautious

conspicuous: easily seen or noticed; readily observable

perspective: one's mental view of facts, ideas, and their interrelationships

perspicacious: having keen mental perception and understanding

retrospective: contemplative of past situations

specious: deceptively attractive

spectrum: a broad range of related things that form a continuous series

speculation: the contemplation or consideration of some subject

SPIR: breath

aspire: to desire; to pant for (originally: to breathe on)

expire: to breathe out; to breathe one's last; to come to an end

spirit: the breath of life; the soul; an incorporeal supernatural being; an outlook; a lively quality

STA/STI: to stand, to be in place

apostasy: renunciation of an object of one's previous loyalty

constitute: to make up

destitute: without means of subsistence

obstinate: stubbornly adhering to a purpose, opinion, or course of action

stasis: the state of equilibrium or inactivity caused by opposing equal forces

static: of bodies or forces at rest or in equilibrium

STRICT/STRING/STRAN: to tighten, to bind

astringent: causing to tighten

constrain: to confine; to bind within certain limits

restriction: a limitation

strangle: to kill by suffocation, usually by tightening a cord or one's hand around the throat

SUA: sweet, pleasing, to urge

assuage: to make less severe, ease, relieve

dissuade: to deter; to advise against

persuade: to encourage; to convince

suave: smoothly agreeable or polite; sweet

SUB/SUP: below, under

subliminal: existing or operating below the threshold of consciousness

submissive: inclined or ready to submit

subsidiary: serving to assist or supplement

subterfuge: an artifice or expedient used to evade a rule

subtle: thin, tenuous, or rarefied

suppose: to put down as a hypothesis; to use as the underlying basis of an argument; to assume

SUMM: highest, total

consummate: highly qualified; complete; perfect

sum: total; amount of money

summary: concise statement of the total findings on a subject; comprehensive

summit: highest point

SUPER/SUR: over, above

supercilious: arrogant, haughty, condescending

superfluous: extra, more than necessary

superlative: the highest kind or order

supersede: to replace in power, as by another person or thing

surmount: to get over or across, to prevail

surpass: to go beyond in amount, extent, or degree

surveillance: a watch kept over someone or something

SYM/SYN: together

symbiosis: living together in a mutually beneficial relationship

symmetry: balanced proportions; having opposite parts that mirror one another

sympathy: affinity; feeling affected by what happens to another

symposium: a meeting at which ideas are discussed (originally: a party at which people drink together)

synonym: a word that means the same thing as another

synthesis: combining things to create a new whole

T

TAC/TIC: to be silent

reticent: disposed to be silent or not to speak freely

tacit: unspoken understanding

taciturn: uncommunicative

TACT/TAG/TAM/TANG: to touch

contact: to touch; to get in touch

contagious: able to spread by contact, as disease

contaminate: to corrupt, taint, or otherwise damage the integrity of something by contact or mixture

contiguous: directly touching; sharing a boundary

intact: untouched; whole

intangible: unable to be touched

tactile: pertaining to touch; touchable

TAIN/TEN/TENT/TIN: to hold

abstention: the act of refraining voluntarily

detain: to keep from proceeding

pertain: to have reference or relation

pertinacious: persistent, stubborn

sustenance: nourishment, means of livelihood

tenable: capable of being held, maintained, or defended

tenacious: holding fast

tenure: the holding or possessing of anything

TEND/TENS/TENT/TENU: to stretch, to thin

attenuate: to weaken or reduce in force

contentious: quarrelsome, disagreeable, belligerent

distend: to expand by stretching

extenuating: making less serious by offering excuses

tendentious: having a predisposition toward a point of view

tension: the act of stretching or straining

tentative: of the nature of, or done as a trial, attempt

TEST: to bear witness

attest: bear witness

contest: to dispute (from bringing a lawsuit by calling witnesses)

detest: to despise; to hate (originally: to curse something by calling upon God to witness it)

protest: a dissent; a declaration, esp. of disagreement

testament: a statement of a person's wishes for the disposal of his or her property after death; a will

testify: bear witness

THEO: god

apotheosis: glorification, glorified ideal

atheist: one who does not believe in a deity or divine system

theocracy: a form of government in which a deity is recognized as the supreme ruler

theology: the study of divine things and the divine faith

THERM: heat

thermal: relating to heat; retaining heat

thermometer: a device for measuring heat

thermonuclear: relating to a nuclear reaction that takes place at high temperatures

thermostat: a device for regulating heat

TIM: fear

intimidate: to strike fear into; to make fearful

timid: fearful; shy

TOR/TORQ/TORT: to twist

contort: to twist; to distort

distort: to pull out of shape, often by twisting; to twist or misrepresent facts

extort: to wring money, property, or services out of somebody using threats or force

torch: a portable flame used for light (perhaps derived from hemp twisted around sticks, then dipped in pitch)

torque: twisting force; a force that creates rotation

tort: a wrongful act (other than breach of contract) that legally entitles one to damages

torture: to inflict pain (including by twisting instruments like the rack or wheel)

TORP: stiff, numb

torpedo: a explosive weapon used to sink ships (originally: a fish—the electric ray—that could shock victims to numbness)

torpid: numbed; sluggish

torpor: numbness; listlessness; apathy

TOX: poison

antitoxin: an antibody that counteracts a given poison

intoxication: being poisoned; drunkenness

toxic: poisonous

TRACT: to drag, to pull, to draw

abstract: to draw or pull away, remove

attract: to draw either by physical force or by an appeal to emotions or senses

contract: a legally binding document

detract: to take away from, esp. a positive thing

protract: to prolong, draw out, extend

tractable: easily managed or controlled

tractor: a powerful vehicle used to pull farm machinery

TRANS: across, beyond

intransigent: refusing to agree or compromise

transaction: the act of carrying on or conduct to a conclusion or settlement

transcendent: going beyond ordinary limits

transgress: to violate a law, command, or moral code

transition: a change from one way of being to another

transparent: easily seen through, recognized, or detected

U

ULT: last, beyond

penultimate: second-to-last

ulterior: beyond what is immediately present; future; beyond what is stated; hidden

ultimate: last; final

ultimatum: final offer; final terms

ultraviolet: beyond the violet end of the spectrum

UMBR: shadow

adumbrate: to foreshadow; to sketch; to overshadow

penumbra: a shaded area between pure shadow and pure light

somber: gloomy; darkened

umbrage: shade; shadow; displeasure; resentment

umbrella: a device providing shade from the sun or protection from rain

UN: not

unseen: not seen

unusual: not usual; exceptional; strange

UND: wave

abound: to be plentiful; to overflow (from water flowing in waves)

inundate: to flood

undulate: to move in a wavelike way

UNI/UN: one

reunion: a meeting that brings people back together

unanimous: of one mind; in complete accord

unicorn: a mythical animal with a single horn

uniform: of one kind; consistent

universe: all things considered as one whole

URB: city

suburb: a residential area just outside a city; an outlying area of a city

urban: relating to a city

urbane: polite; refined; polished (considered characteristic of those in cities)

urbanization: the process of an area becoming more like a city

US/UT: to use

abuse: to use wrongly or improperly

usage: a customary way of doing something

usurp: to seize and hold

utilitarian: efficient, functional, useful

V

VAIL/VAL: strength, use, worth

ambivalent: being caught between contradictory feelings of equal power or worth

avail: to have force; to be useful; to be of value

convalescent: recovering strength; healing

equivalent: of equal worth, strength, or use

evaluate: to determine the worth of

invalid: having no force or strength; void

valediction: a farewell (from wishing that someone be well; i.e., that someone have strength)

valid: having force; legally binding; effective; useful

value: worth

VEN/VENT: to come or to move toward

adventitious: accidental

contravene: to come into conflict with

convene: to assemble for some public purpose

intervene: to come between disputing factions, mediate

venturesome: showing a disposition to undertake risks

VER: truth

aver: to affirm, to declare to be true

veracious: habitually truthful

verdict: a judgment or decision

verisimilitude: the appearance or semblance of truth

verity: truthfulness

VERB: word

proverb: an adage; a byword; a short, commonly known saying

verbatim: exactly as stated; word-for-word

verbose: wordy

verbiage: excessive use of words; diction

VERD: green

verdant: green with vegetation; inexperienced

verdure: fresh, rich vegetation

VERS/VERT: to turn

aversion: dislike

avert: to turn away from

controversy: a public dispute involving a matter of opinion

diverse: of a different kind, form, character

extrovert: an outgoing person

inadvertent: unintentional

introvert: a person concerned primarily with inner thoughts and feelings

revert: to return to a former habit

VI: life

convivial: sociable

joie de vivre: joy of life (French expression)

viable: capable of living

vivacity: the quality of being lively, animated, spirited

vivid: strikingly bright or intense

VID/VIS: to see

adviser: one who gives counsel

evident: plain or clear to the sight or understanding

survey: to view in a general or comprehensive way

video: elements pertaining to the transmission or reception of an image

vista: a view or prospect

VIL: base, mean

revile: to criticize with harsh language

vile: loathsome, unpleasant

vilify: to slander, to defame

VIRU: poison

virulent: acrimonious; very bitter; very poisonous

viruliferous: containing a virus

virus: a submicroscopic agent that infects an organism and causes disease

VOC/VOK: call, word

advocate: to support or urge by argument

avocation: something one does in addition to a principle occupation

convoke: to call together

equivocate: to use ambiguous or unclear expressions

invoke: to call on a deity

vocabulary: the stock of words used by or known to a particular person or group

vocation: a particular occupation

vociferous: crying out noisily

VOL: wish

benevolent: characterized by or expressing goodwill

malevolent: characterized by or expressing bad will

volition: free choice, free will; act of choosing

voluntary: undertaken of one's own accord or by free choice

VOLU/VOLV: to roll, to turn

convolution: a twisting or folding

evolve: to develop naturally; literally, to unfold or unroll

revolt: to rebel; to turn against those in authority

revolve: to rotate; to turn around

voluble: easily turning; fluent; changeable

volume: a book (originally: a scroll); size or dimensions (originally: of a book)

VOR: to eat

carnivorous: meat-eating

omnivorous: eating or absorbing everything

voracious: having a great appetite

COMMON GRE-LEVEL WORDS IN CONTEXT

The GRE tests the same kinds of words over and over again. Here you will find some common GRE-level words with their definitions in context to help you to remember them. If you see a word that's unfamiliar to you, take a moment to study the definition and, most importantly, reread the sentence with the word's definition in mind.

Remember: learning vocabulary words in context is one of the best ways for your brain to retain the words' meanings. A broader vocabulary will serve you well on all four GRE Verbal question types and will also be extremely helpful in the Analytical Writing section.

A

ABATE: to reduce in amount, degree, or severity

As the hurricane's force ABATED, the winds dropped and the sea became calm.

ABSCOND: to leave secretly

The patron ABSCONDED from the restaurant without paying his bill by sneaking out the back door.

ABSTAIN: to choose not to do something

She ABSTAINED from choosing a mouthwatering dessert from the tray.

ABYSS: an extremely deep hole

The submarine dove into the ABYSS to chart the previously unseen depths.

ADULTERATE: to make impure

The chef made his ketchup last longer by ADULTER-ATING it with water.

ADVOCATE: to speak in favor of

The vegetarian ADVOCATED a diet containing no meat.

AESTHETIC: concerning the appreciation of beauty

Followers of the AESTHETIC movement regarded the pursuit of beauty as the only true purpose of art.

AGGRANDIZE: to increase in power, influence, and reputation

The supervisor sought to AGGRANDIZE herself by claiming that the achievements of her staff were actually her own.

ALLEVIATE: to make more bearable

Taking aspirin helps to ALLEVIATE a headache.

AMALGAMATE: to combine; to mix together

Giant Industries AMALGAMATED with Mega Products to form Giant-Mega Products Incorporated.

AMBIGUOUS: doubtful or uncertain; able to be interpreted several ways

The directions she gave were so AMBIGUOUS that we disagreed on which way to turn.

AMELIORATE: to make better; to improve

The doctor was able to AMELIORATE the patient's suffering using painkillers.

ANACHRONISM: something out of place in time

The aged hippie used ANACHRONISTIC phrases, like "groovy" and "far out," that had not been popular for years.

ANALOGOUS: similar or alike in some way; equivalent to

In the Newtonian construct for explaining the existence of God, the universe is ANALOGOUS to a mechanical timepiece, the creation of a divinely intelligent "clockmaker."

ANOMALY: deviation from what is normal

The near-boiling river in Peru called Shanay-Timpishka is a geological ANOMALY: it is the only naturally heated body of water that is not heated by its proximity to a volcano.

ANTAGONIZE: to annoy or provoke to anger

The child discovered that he could ANTAGONIZE the cat by pulling its tail.

ANTIPATHY: extreme dislike

The ANTIPATHY between the French and the English regularly erupted into open warfare.

APATHY: lack of interest or emotion

The APATHY of voters is so great that less than half the people who are eligible to vote actually bother to do so.

ARBITRATE: to judge a dispute between two opposing parties

Since the couple could not come to an agreement, a judge was forced to ARBITRATE their divorce proceedings.

ARCHAIC: ancient, old-fashioned

Her ARCHAIC Commodore computer could not run the latest software.

ARDOR: intense and passionate feeling

Bishop's ARDOR for the landscape was evident when he passionately described the beauty of the scenic Hudson Valley.

ARTICULATE: able to speak clearly and expressively

She is such an ARTICULATE defender of labor that unions are among her strongest supporters.

ASSUAGE: to make something unpleasant less severe

Serena used aspirin to ASSUAGE her pounding headache.

ATTENUATE: to reduce in force or degree; to weaken

The Bill of Rights ATTENUATED the traditional power of governments to change laws at will.

AUDACIOUS: fearless and daring

Her AUDACIOUS nature allowed her to fulfill her dream of skydiving.

AUSTERE: severe or stern in appearance; undecorated

The lack of decoration makes military barracks seem AUSTERE to the civilian eye.

B

BANAL: predictable, clichéd, boring

He used BANAL phrases like "have a nice day" and "another day, another dollar."

BOLSTER: to support; to prop up

The presence of giant footprints BOLSTERED the argument that Sasquatch was in the area.

BOMBASTIC: pompous in speech and manner

The ranting of the radio talk-show host was mostly BOMBASTIC; his boasting and outrageous claims had no basis in fact.

C

CACOPHONY: harsh, jarring noise

The junior high orchestra created an almost unbearable CACOPHONY as they tried to tune their instruments.

CANDID: impartial and honest in speech

The observations of a child can be charming since they are CANDID and unpretentious.

CAPRICIOUS: changing one's mind quickly and often

Queen Elizabeth I was quite CAPRICIOUS; her courtiers could never be sure which of their number would catch her fancy.

CASTIGATE: to punish or criticize harshly

Many Americans are amazed at how harshly the authorities in Singapore CASTIGATE perpetrators of what would be considered minor crimes in the United States.

CATALYST: something that brings about a change in something else

The imposition of harsh taxes was the CATALYST that finally brought on the revolution.

CAUSTIC: biting in wit

Dorothy Parker gained her reputation for CAUSTIC wit from her cutting, yet clever, insults.

CHAOS: great disorder or confusion

In many religious traditions, God created an ordered universe from CHAOS.

CHAUVINIST: someone prejudiced in favor of a group to which he or she belongs

The attitude that men are inherently superior to women and therefore must be obeyed is common among male CHAUVINISTS.

CHICANERY: deception by means of craft or guile

Dishonest used car salespeople often use CHICANERY to sell their beat-up old cars.

COGENT: convincing and well-reasoned

Swayed by the COGENT argument of the defense, the jury had no choice but to acquit the defendant.

CONDONE: to overlook, pardon, or disregard

Some theorists believe that failing to prosecute minor crimes is the same as CONDONING an air of lawlessness.

CONVOLUTED: intricate and complicated

Although many people bought *A Brief History of Time*, few could follow its CONVOLUTED ideas and theories.

CORROBORATE: to provide supporting evidence

Fingerprints CORROBORATED the witness's testimony that he saw the defendant in the victim's apartment.

CREDULOUS: too trusting; gullible

Although some four-year-olds believe in the Easter Bunny, only the most CREDULOUS nine-year-olds still believe in him.

CRESCENDO: steadily increasing volume or force

The CRESCENDO of tension became unbearable as Evel Knievel prepared to jump his motorcycle over the school buses.

D

DECORUM: appropriateness of behavior or conduct; propriety

The countess complained that the vulgar peasants lacked the DECORUM appropriate for a visit to the palace.

DEFERENCE: respect, courtesy

The respectful young law clerk treated the Supreme Court justice with the utmost DEFERENCE.

DERIDE: to speak of or treat with contempt; to mock

The awkward child was often DERIDED by his "cooler" peers.

DESICCATE: to dry out thoroughly

After a few weeks of lying on the desert's baking sands, the cow's carcass became completely DESICCATED.

DESULTORY: jumping from one thing to another; disconnected

Diane had a DESULTORY academic record; she had changed majors 12 times in three years.

DIATRIBE: an abusive, condemnatory speech

The trucker bellowed a DIATRIBE at the driver who had cut him off.

DIFFIDENT: lacking self-confidence

Steve's DIFFIDENT manner during the job interview stemmed from his nervous nature and lack of experience in the field.

DILATE: to make larger; to expand

When you enter a darkened room, the pupils of your eyes DILATE to let in more light.

DILATORY: intended to delay

The congressman used DILATORY measures to delay the passage of the bill.

DILETTANTE: someone with an amateurish and superficial interest in a topic

Jerry's friends were such DILETTANTES that they seemed to have new jobs and hobbies every week.

DIRGE: a funeral hymn or mournful speech

Melville wrote the poem "A DIRGE for James McPherson" for the funeral of a Union general who was killed in 1864.

DISABUSE: to set right; to free from error

Galileo's observations DISABUSED scholars of the notion that the Sun revolved around the Earth.

DISCERN: to perceive; to recognize

It is easy to DISCERN the difference between butter and butter-flavored topping.

DISPARATE: fundamentally different; entirely unlike

Although the twins appear to be identical physically, their personalities are DISPARATE.

DISSEMBLE: to present a false appearance; to disguise one's real intentions or character

The villain could DISSEMBLE to the police no longer—he admitted the deed and tore up the floor to reveal the body of the old man.

DISSONANCE: a harsh and disagreeable combination, often of sounds

Cognitive DISSONANCE is the inner conflict produced when long-standing beliefs are contradicted by new evidence.

DOGMA: a firmly held opinion, often a religious belief

Linus's central DOGMA was that children who believed in the Great Pumpkin would be rewarded.

DOGMATIC: dictatorial in one's opinions

The dictator was DOGMATIC—he, and only he, was right.

DUPE: to deceive; a person who is easily deceived

Bugs Bunny was able to DUPE Elmer Fudd by dressing up as a lady rabbit.

E

ECLECTIC: selecting from or made up from a variety of sources

Budapest's architecture is an ECLECTIC mix of Eastern and Western styles.

EFFICACY: effectiveness

The EFFICACY of penicillin was unsurpassed when it was first introduced; the drug completely eliminated almost all bacterial infections for which it was administered.

ELEGY: a sorrowful poem or speech

Although Thomas Gray's "ELEGY Written in a Country Churchyard" is about death and loss, it urges its readers to endure this life and to trust in spirituality.

ELOQUENT: persuasive and moving, especially in speech

The Gettysburg Address is moving not only because of its lofty sentiments but also because of its ELOQUENT words.

EMULATE: to copy; to try to equal or excel

The graduate student sought to EMULATE his professor in every way, copying not only how she taught but also how she conducted herself outside of class.

ENERVATE: to reduce in strength

The guerrillas hoped that a series of surprise attacks would ENERVATE the regular army.

ENGENDER: to produce, cause, or bring about

His fear and hatred of clowns was ENGENDERED when he witnessed the death of his father at the hands of a clown.

ENIGMA: a puzzle; a mystery

By speaking in riddles and dressing in old robes, the artist gained a reputation as something of an ENIGMA.

ENUMERATE: to count, list, or itemize

Moses returned from the mountain with tablets on which the commandments were ENUMERATED.

EPHEMERAL: lasting a short time

The lives of mayflies seem EPHEMERAL to us, since the flies' average life span is a matter of hours.

EQUIVOCAL: open to more than one interpretation; misleading

Asked a pointed question, the politician nevertheless gave an EQUIVOCAL answer.

EQUIVOCATE: to use expressions of double meaning in order to mislead

When faced with criticism of her policies, the politician EQUIVOCATED and left all parties thinking she agreed with them.

ERRATIC: wandering and unpredictable

The plot seemed predictable until it suddenly took a series of ERRATIC turns that surprised the audience.

ERUDITE: learned, scholarly, bookish

The annual meeting of philosophy professors was a gathering of the most ERUDITE, well-published individuals in the field.

ESOTERIC: known or understood by only a few

Only a handful of experts are knowledgeable about the ESOTERIC world of particle physics.

ESTIMABLE: admirable

Most people consider it ESTIMABLE that Mother Teresa spent her life helping the poor of India.

EULOGY: speech in praise of someone

His best friend gave the EULOGY, outlining his many achievements and talents.

EUPHEMISM: use of an inoffensive word or phrase in place of a more distasteful one

The funeral director preferred to use the EUPHEMISM "sleeping" instead of the word "dead."

EXACERBATE: to make worse

It is unwise to take aspirin to try to relieve heartburn; instead of providing relief, the drug will only EXACERBATE the problem.

EXCULPATE: to clear from blame; prove innocent

The adversarial legal system is intended to convict those who are guilty and to EXCULPATE those who are innocent.

EXIGENT: urgent; requiring immediate action

The patient was losing blood so rapidly that it was EXIGENT to stop the source of the bleeding.

EXONERATE: to clear of blame

The fugitive was EXONERATED when another criminal confessed to committing the crime.

EXPLICIT: clearly stated or shown; forthright in expression

The owners of the house left a list of EXPLICIT instructions detailing their house sitter's duties, including a schedule for watering the house plants.

F

FANATICAL: acting excessively enthusiastic; filled with extreme, unquestioned devotion

The stormtroopers were FANATICAL in their devotion to the emperor, readily sacrificing their lives for him.

FAWN: to grovel

The understudy FAWNED over the director in hopes of being cast in the part on a permanent basis.

FERVID: intensely emotional; feverish

The fans of Maria Callas were unusually FERVID, doing anything to catch a glimpse of the great opera singer.

FLORID: excessively decorated or embellished

The palace had been decorated in a FLORID style; every surface had been carved and gilded.

FOMENT: to arouse or incite

The protesters tried to FOMENT feeling against the war through their speeches and demonstrations.

FRUGALITY: a tendency to be thrifty or cheap

Scrooge McDuck's FRUGALITY was so great that he accumulated enough wealth to fill a giant storehouse with money.

G

GARRULOUS: tending to talk a lot

The GARRULOUS parakeet distracted its owner with its continuous talking.

GREGARIOUS: outgoing, sociable

She was so GREGARIOUS that when she found herself alone, she felt quite sad.

GUILE: deceit or trickery

Since he was not fast enough to catch the roadrunner on foot, the coyote resorted to GUILE in an effort to trap his enemy.

GULLIBLE: easily deceived

The con man pretended to be a bank officer so as to fool GULLIBLE bank customers into giving him their account information.

H

HOMOGENEOUS (or HOMOGENOUS): of a similar kind

The class was fairly HOMOGENEOUS, since almost all of the students were senior journalism majors.

I

ICONOCLAST: one who opposes established beliefs, customs, and institutions

His lack of regard for traditional beliefs soon established him as an ICONOCLAST.

IMPERTURBABLE: not capable of being disturbed

The counselor had so much experience dealing with distraught children that she seemed IMPERTURBABLE, even when faced with the wildest tantrums.

IMPERVIOUS: impossible to penetrate; incapable of being affected

A good raincoat will be IMPERVIOUS to moisture.

IMPETUOUS: quick to act without thinking

It is not good for an investment broker to be IMPETUOUS, since much thought should be given to all the possible options.

IMPLACABLE: unable to be calmed down or made peaceful

His rage at the betrayal was so great that he remained IMPLACABLE for weeks.

INCHOATE: not fully formed; disorganized

The ideas expressed in Nietzsche's mature work also appear in an INCHOATE form in his earliest writing.

INGENUOUS: showing innocence or childlike simplicity

She was so INGENUOUS that her friends feared that her innocence and trustfulness would be exploited when she visited the big city.

INIMICAL: hostile, unfriendly

Even though the children had grown up together, they were INIMICAL to each other at school.

INNOCUOUS: harmless

Some snakes are poisonous, but most species are INNOCUOUS and pose no danger to humans.

INSIPID: lacking interest or flavor

The critic claimed that the painting was INSIPID, containing no interesting qualities at all.

INTRANSIGENT: uncompromising; refusing to be reconciled

The professor was INTRANSIGENT on the deadline, insisting that everyone turn the assignment in at the same time.

INUNDATE: to overwhelm; to cover with water

The tidal wave INUNDATED Atlantis, which was lost beneath the water.

IRASCIBLE: easily made angry

Attila the Hun's IRASCIBLE and violent nature made all who dealt with him fear for their lives.

L

LACONIC: using few words

She was a LACONIC poet who built her reputation on using words as sparingly as possible.

LAMENT: to express sorrow; to grieve

The children continued to LAMENT the death of the goldfish weeks after its demise.

LAUD: to give praise; to glorify

Parades and fireworks were staged to LAUD the success of the rebels.

LAVISH: to give unsparingly (v.); extremely generous or extravagant (adj.)

She LAVISHED the puppy with so many treats that it soon became overweight and spoiled.

LETHARGIC: acting in an indifferent or slow, sluggish manner

The clerk was so LETHARGIC that, even when the store was slow, he always had a long line in front of him.

LOQUACIOUS: talkative

She was naturally LOQUACIOUS, which was a problem in situations in which listening was more important than talking.

LUCID: clear and easily understood

The explanations were written in a simple and LUCID manner so that students were immediately able to apply what they learned.

LUMINOUS: bright, brilliant, glowing

The park was bathed in LUMINOUS sunshine, which warmed the bodies and the souls of the visitors.

M

MALINGER: to evade responsibility by pretending to be ill

A common way to avoid the draft was by MALINGERING—pretending to be mentally or physically ill so as to avoid being enlisted by the army.

MALLEABLE: capable of being shaped

Gold is the most MALLEABLE of precious metals; it can easily be formed into almost any shape.

METAPHOR: a figure of speech comparing two different things; a symbol

The METAPHOR "a sea of troubles" suggests a lot of troubles by comparing their number to the vastness of the sea.

METICULOUS: extremely careful about details

To find all the clues at the crime scene, the investigators METICULOUSLY examined every inch of the area.

MISANTHROPE: a person who dislikes others

The character Scrooge in *A Christmas Carol* is such a MISANTHROPE that even the sight of children singing makes him angry.

MITIGATE: to soften; to lessen

A judge may MITIGATE a sentence if she decides that a person committed a crime out of need.

MOLLIFY: to calm or make less severe

Their argument was so intense that it was difficult to believe any compromise would MOLLIFY them.

MONOTONY: lack of variation

The MONOTONY of the sound of the dripping faucet almost drove the research assistant crazy.

N

NAIVE: lacking sophistication or experience

Having never traveled before, the elementary school students were more NAIVE than their high school counterparts on the field trip.

O

OBDURATE: hardened in feeling; resistant to persuasion

The president was completely OBDURATE on the issue, and no amount of persuasion would change his mind.

OBSEQUIOUS: overly submissive and eager to please

The OBSEQUIOUS new associate made sure to compliment her supervisor's tie and agree with him on every issue.

OBSTINATE: stubborn, unyielding

The OBSTINATE child could not be made to eat any food that he disliked.

OBVIATE: to prevent; to make unnecessary

The river was shallow enough to wade across at many points, which OBVIATED the need for a bridge.

OCCLUDE: to stop up; to prevent the passage of

A shadow is thrown across the earth's surface during a solar eclipse, when the light from the sun is OCCLUDED by the moon.

ONEROUS: troublesome and oppressive; burdensome

The assignment was so extensive and difficult to manage that it proved ONEROUS to the team in charge of it.

OPAQUE: impossible to see through; preventing the passage of light

The heavy buildup of dirt and grime on the windows almost made them OPAQUE.

OPPROBRIUM: public disgrace

After the scheme to embezzle the elderly was made public, the treasurer resigned in utter OPPROBRIUM.

OSTENTATION: excessive showiness

The OSTENTATION of the Sun King's court is evident in the lavish decoration and luxuriousness of his palace at Versailles.

P

PARADOX: a contradiction or dilemma

It is a PARADOX that those most in need of medical attention are often those least able to obtain it.

PARAGON: model of excellence or perfection

She is the PARAGON of what a judge should be: honest, intelligent, hardworking, and just.

PEDANT: someone who shows off learning

The graduate instructor's tedious and excessive commentary on the subject soon gained her a reputation as a PEDANT.

PERFIDIOUS: willing to betray one's trust

The actress's PERFIDIOUS companion revealed all of her intimate secrets to the gossip columnist.

PERFUNCTORY: done in a routine way; indifferent

The machinelike bank teller processed the transaction and gave the waiting customer a PERFUNCTORY smile.

PERMEATE: to penetrate

This miraculous new cleaning fluid is able to PERMEATE stains and dissolve them in minutes!

PHILANTHROPY: charity; a desire or an effort to promote goodness

New York's Metropolitan Museum of Art owes much of its collection to the PHILANTHROPY of private collectors who willed their estates to the museum.

PLACATE: to soothe or pacify

The burglar tried to PLACATE the snarling dog by saying, "Nice doggy," and offering it a treat.

PLASTIC: able to be molded, altered, or bent

The new material was very PLASTIC and could be formed into products of vastly different shapes.

PLETHORA: excess

Assuming that more was better, the defendant offered the judge a PLETHORA of excuses.

PRAGMATIC: practical as opposed to idealistic

While daydreaming gamblers think they can get rich by frequenting casinos, PRAGMATIC gamblers realize that the odds are heavily stacked against them.

PRECIPITATE: to throw violently or bring about abruptly; lacking deliberation

Upon learning that the couple married after knowing each other only two months, friends and family members expected such a PRECIPITATE marriage to end in divorce.

PREVARICATE: to lie or deviate from the truth

Rather than admit that he had overslept again, the employee PREVARICATED and claimed that heavy traffic had prevented him from arriving at work on time.

PRISTINE: fresh and clean; uncorrupted

Since concerted measures had been taken to prevent looting, the archeological site was still PRISTINE when researchers arrived.

PRODIGAL: lavish, wasteful

The PRODIGAL son quickly wasted all of his inheritance on a lavish lifestyle devoted to pleasure.

PROLIFERATE: to increase in number quickly

Although she only kept two guinea pigs initially, they PROLIFERATED to such an extent that she soon had dozens.

PROPITIATE: to conciliate; to appease

The management PROPITIATED the irate union by agreeing to raise wages for its members.

PROPRIETY: correct behavior; obedience to rules and customs

The aristocracy maintained a high level of PROPRIETY, adhering to even the most minor social rules.

PRUDENCE: wisdom, caution, or restraint

The college student exhibited PRUDENCE by obtaining practical experience along with her studies, which greatly strengthened her resume.

PUNGENT: sharp and irritating to the senses

The smoke from the burning tires was extremely PUNGENT.

Q

QUIESCENT: motionless

Many animals are QUIESCENT over the winter months, minimizing activity in order to conserve energy.

R

RAREFY: to make thinner or sparser

Since the atmosphere RAREFIES as altitudes increase, the air at the top of very tall mountains is too thin to breathe.

REPUDIATE: to reject the validity of

The old woman's claim that she was Russian royalty was REPUDIATED when DNA tests showed she was of no relation to them.

RETICENT: silent, reserved

Physically small and RETICENT in her speech, Joan Didion often went unnoticed by those upon whom she was reporting.

RHETORIC: effective writing or speaking

Lincoln's talent for RHETORIC was evident in his beautifully expressed Gettysburg Address.

S

SATIATE: to satisfy fully or overindulge

His desire for power was so great that nothing less than complete control of the country could SATIATE it.

SOPORIFIC: causing sleep or lethargy

The movie proved to be so SOPORIFIC that soon loud snores were heard throughout the theater.

SPECIOUS: deceptively attractive; seemingly plausible but fallacious

The student's SPECIOUS excuse for being late sounded legitimate but was proved otherwise when her teacher called her home.

STIGMA: a mark of shame or discredit

In *The Scarlet Letter*, Hester Prynne was required to wear the letter *A* on her clothes as a public STIGMA for her adultery.

STOLID: unemotional; lacking sensitivity

The prisoner appeared STOLID and unaffected by the judge's harsh sentence.

SUBLIME: lofty or grand

The music was so SUBLIME that it transformed the rude surroundings into a special place.

T

TACIT: done without using words

Although not a word had been said, everyone in the room knew that a TACIT agreement had been made about which course of action to take.

TACITURN: silent, not talkative

The clerk's TACITURN nature earned him the nickname "Silent Bob."

TIRADE: long, harsh speech or verbal attack

Observers were shocked at the manager's TIRADE over such a minor mistake.

TORPOR: extreme mental and physical sluggishness

After surgery, the patient experienced TORPOR until the anesthesia wore off.

TRANSITORY: temporary, lasting a brief time

The reporter lived a TRANSITORY life, staying in one place only long enough to cover the current story.

V

VACILLATE: to sway physically; to be indecisive

The customer held up the line as he VACILLATED between ordering chocolate chip or rocky road ice cream.

VENERATE: to respect deeply

In a traditional Confucian society, the young VENERATE their elders, deferring to the elders' wisdom and experience.

VERACITY: truthfulness; accuracy

She had a reputation for VERACITY, so everyone trusted her description of events.

VERBOSE: wordy

The professor's answer was so VERBOSE that his student forgot what the original question had been.

VEX: to annoy

The old man who loved his peace and quiet was VEXED by his neighbor's loud music.

VOLATILE: easily aroused or changeable; lively or explosive

His VOLATILE personality made it difficult to predict his reaction to anything.

W

WAVER: to fluctuate between choices

If you WAVER too long before making a decision about which testing site to register for, you may not get your first choice.

WHIMSICAL: acting in a fanciful or capricious manner; unpredictable

The ballet was WHIMSICAL, delighting the children with its imaginative characters and unpredictable sets.

Z

ZEAL: passion, excitement

She brought her typical ZEAL to the project, sparking enthusiasm in the other team members.

Commonly Confused Words

ALREADY: by this or that time, previously

He already completed his work.

ALL READY: completely prepared

The students were all ready to take their exam.

ALTOGETHER: entirely, completely

I am altogether certain that I turned in my homework.

ALL TOGETHER: in the same place

She kept the figurines all together on her mantle.

CAPITAL: a city containing the seat of government; the wealth or funds owned by a business or individual; resources

Atlanta is the capital of Georgia.

The company's capital gains have diminished in recent years.

CAPITOL: the building in which a legislative body meets

Our trip included a visit to the Capitol building in Washington, D.C.

COARSE: rough, not smooth; lacking refinement

The truck's large wheels enabled it to navigate the coarse, rough terrain.

His coarse language prevented him from getting hired for the job.

COURSE: path, series of classes or studies

James's favorite course is biology.

The doctor suggested that Amy rest and let the disease run its course.

HERE: in this location

George Washington used to live here.

HEAR: to listen to or to perceive by the ear

Did you hear the question?

ITS: a personal pronoun that shows possession

Please put the book back in its place.

IT'S: the contraction of "it is" or "it has"

It's snowing outside.

It's been too long.

LEAD: to act as a leader, to go first, or to take a superior position

The guide will lead us through the forest.

LED: past tense of "lead"

The guide led us through the forest.

LEAD: a metal

It is dangerous to inhale fumes from paint containing lead.

LOOSE: free, to set free, not tight

She always wears loose clothing when she does yoga.

LOSE: to become without

Use a bookmark so you don't lose your place in your book.

PASSED: the past tense of pass; a euphemism for someone dying

We passed by her house on Sunday.

PAST: that which has gone by or elapsed in time

In the past, Abby never used to study.

We drove past her house.

PRINCIPAL: the head of a school; main or important

The quarterback's injury is the principal reason the team lost.

The principal of the school meets with parents regularly.

PRINCIPLE: a fundamental law or truth

The laws of motion are among the most important principles in physics.

STATIONARY: fixed, not moving

Thomas rode a stationary bicycle at the gym.

STATIONERY: paper used for letter writing

The principal's stationery has the school's logo on the top.

THEIR: possessive of "they"

Paul and Ben studied for their test together.

THERE: a place; in that matter or respect

There are several question types on the GRE.

Please hang up your jacket over there.

THEY'RE: contraction of "they are"

Be careful of the bushes, as they're filled with thorns.

MATH REFERENCE

The math on the GRE covers a lot of ground—from number properties and arithmetic to basic algebra and symbol problems to geometry and statistics. Don't let yourself be intimidated.

We've highlighted the 100 most important concepts that you need to know and divided them into three levels. The GRE Quantitative sections test your understanding of a relatively limited number of mathematical concepts, all of which you will be able to master.

Level 1 consists of foundational math topics. Though these topics may seem basic, review this list so that you are aware that these skills may play a part in the questions you will answer on the GRE. Look over the Level 1 list to make sure you're comfortable with the basics.

Level 2 is where most people start their review of math. Level 2 skills and formulas come into play quite frequently on the GRE. If the skills needed to handle Level 1 or 2 topics are keeping you from feeling up to the tasks expected on the GRE Quantitative section, you might consider taking the Kaplan GRE Math Refresher course.

Level 3 represents the most challenging math concepts you'll find on the GRE. Don't spend a lot of time on Level 3 if you still have gaps in Level 2, but once you've mastered Level 2, tackling Level 3 can put you over the top.

LEVEL 1

1. How to add, subtract, multiply, and divide WHOLE NUMBERS

You can check addition with subtraction.

$$17 + 5 = 22 \qquad 22 - 5 = 17$$

You can check multiplication with division.

$$5 \times 28 = 140 \qquad 140 \div 5 = 28$$

2. How to add, subtract, multiply, and divide FRACTIONS

Find a common denominator before adding or subtracting fractions.

$$\frac{4}{5} + \frac{3}{10} = \frac{8}{10} + \frac{3}{10} = \frac{11}{10} \text{ or } 1\frac{1}{10}$$

$$2 - \frac{3}{8} = \frac{16}{8} - \frac{3}{8} = \frac{13}{8} \text{ or } 1\frac{5}{8}$$

To multiply fractions, multiply the numerators first and then multiply the denominators. Simplify if necessary.

$$\frac{3}{4} \times \frac{1}{6} = \frac{3}{24} = \frac{1}{8}$$

You can also reduce before multiplying numerators and denominators. This keeps the products small.

$$\frac{5}{8} \times \frac{2}{15} = \frac{\overset{1}{\cancel{5}}}{\underset{4}{\cancel{8}}} \times \frac{\overset{1}{\cancel{2}}}{\underset{3}{\cancel{15}}} = \frac{1}{12}$$

To divide by a fraction, multiply by its reciprocal. To write the reciprocal of a fraction, flip the numerator and the denominator.

$$5 \div \frac{1}{3} = \frac{5}{1} \times \frac{3}{1} = 15 \qquad \frac{1}{3} \div \frac{4}{5} = \frac{1}{3} \times \frac{5}{4} = \frac{5}{12}$$

3. How to add, subtract, multiply, and divide DECIMALS

To add or subtract, align the decimal points and then add or subtract normally. Place the decimal point in the answer directly below existing decimal points.

$$\begin{array}{r} 3.25 \\ + 4.4 \\ \hline 7.65 \end{array} \qquad \begin{array}{r} 7.65 \\ - 4.4 \\ \hline 3.25 \end{array}$$

To multiply with decimals, multiply the digits normally and count off decimal places (equal to the total number of places in the factors) from the right.

$$2.5 \times 2.5 = 6.25$$
$$0.06 \times 2,000 = 120.00 = 120$$

To divide by a decimal, move the decimal point in the divisor to the right to form a whole number; move the decimal point in the dividend the same number of places. Divide as though there were no decimals and then place the decimal point in the quotient.

$$6.25 \div 2.5$$
$$= 62.5 \div 25 = 2.5$$

4. How to convert FRACTIONS TO DECIMALS and DECIMALS TO FRACTIONS

To convert a fraction to a decimal, divide the numerator by the denominator.

$$\frac{4}{5} = 0.8 \qquad \frac{4}{50} = 0.08 \qquad \frac{4}{500} = 0.008$$

To convert a decimal to a fraction, write the digits in the numerator and use the decimal name in the denominator.

$$0.003 = \frac{3}{1,000} \qquad 0.03 = \frac{3}{100} \qquad 0.3 = \frac{3}{10}$$

5. How to add, subtract, multiply, and divide POSITIVE AND NEGATIVE NUMBERS

When addends (the numbers being added) have the same sign, add their absolute values; the sum has the same sign as the addends. But when addends have different signs, subtract the absolute values; the sum has the sign of the greater absolute value.

$$3 + 9 = 12, \text{ but } -3 + (-9) = -12$$
$$3 + (-9) = -6, \text{ but } -3 + 9 = 6$$

In multiplication and division, when the signs are the same, the product/quotient is positive. When the signs are different, the product/quotient is negative.

$$6 \times 7 = 42 \text{ and } -6 \times (-7) = 42$$
$$-6 \times 7 = -42 \text{ and } 6 \times (-7) = -42$$
$$96 \div 8 = 12 \text{ and } -96 \div (-8) = 12$$
$$-96 \div 8 = -12 \text{ and } 96 \div (-8) = -12$$

6. How to plot points on the NUMBER LINE

To plot the point 4.5 on the number line, start at 0, go right to 4.5, halfway between 4 and 5.

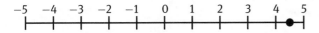

To plot the point -2.5 on the number line, start at 0, go left to -2.5, halfway between -2 and -3.

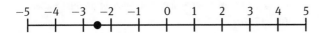

7. How to plug a number into an ALGEBRAIC EXPRESSION

To evaluate an algebraic expression, choose numbers for the variables or use the numbers assigned to the variables.

Evaluate $4np + 1$ when $n = -4$ and $p = 3$.

$4np + 1 = 4(-4)(3) + 1 = -48 + 1 = -47$

8. How to SOLVE a simple LINEAR EQUATION

Use algebra to isolate the variable. Do the same steps to both sides of the equation.

$$
\begin{aligned}
28 &= -3x - 5 \\
28 + 5 &= -3x - 5 + 5 \quad \text{Add 5.} \\
33 &= -3x \\
\frac{33}{-3} &= \frac{-3x}{-3} \quad \text{Divide by } -3. \\
-11 &= x
\end{aligned}
$$

9. How to add and subtract LINE SEGMENTS

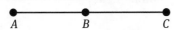

If $AB = 6$ and $BC = 8$, then $AC = 6 + 8 = 14$.
If $AC = 14$ and $BC = 8$, then $AB = 14 - 8 = 6$.

10. How to find the THIRD ANGLE of a TRIANGLE, given the other two angles

Use the fact that the sum of the measures of the interior angles of a triangle always equals 180°.

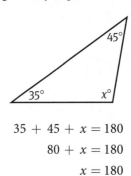

$$
\begin{aligned}
35 + 45 + x &= 180 \\
80 + x &= 180 \\
x &= 180
\end{aligned}
$$

LEVEL 2

11. How to use PEMDAS

When you're given a complex arithmetic expression, it's important to know the order of operations. Just remember PEMDAS (as in "Please Excuse My Dear Aunt Sally"). What PEMDAS means is this: Clean up **Parentheses** first (nested sets of parentheses are worked from the innermost set to the outermost set); then deal with **Exponents** (or **Radicals**); then do the **Multiplication** and **Division** together, going from left to right; and finally do the **Addition** and **Subtraction** together, again going from left to right.

Example:

$$9 - 2 \times (5 - 3)^2 + 6 \div 3 =$$

Begin with the parentheses:

$$9 - 2 \times (2)^2 + 6 \div 3 =$$

Then do the exponent:

$$9 - 2 \times 4 + 6 \div 3 =$$

Now do multiplication and division from left to right:

$$9 - 8 + 2 =$$

Finally, do addition and subtraction from left to right:

$$1 + 2 = 3$$

12. How to use the PERCENT FORMULA

Identify the part, the percent, and the whole.

$$Part = Percent \times Whole$$

Find the part.

Example:

What is 12 percent of 25?

Setup:

$$Part = \frac{12}{100} \times 25 = \frac{300}{100} = 3$$

Find the percent.

Example:

45 is what percent of 9?

Setup:

$$45 = \frac{Percent}{100} \times 9$$
$$4{,}500 = Percent \times 9$$
$$500 = Percent$$

Find the whole.

Example:

15 is $\frac{3}{5}$ percent of what number?

Setup:

$$15 = \frac{3}{5}\left(\frac{1}{100}\right) \times Whole$$
$$15 = \frac{3}{500} \times Whole$$
$$Whole = 15\left(\frac{500}{3}\right) = \frac{7{,}500}{3} = 2{,}500$$

13. How to use the PERCENT INCREASE/DECREASE FORMULAS

Identify the original whole and the amount of increase/decrease.

$$Percent\ increase = \frac{Amount\ of\ increase}{Original\ whole} \times 100\%$$

$$Percent\ decrease = \frac{Amount\ of\ decrease}{Original\ whole} \times 100\%$$

Example:

The price goes up from \$80 to \$100. What is the percent increase?

Setup:

$$Percent\ increase = \frac{20}{80} \times 100\%$$
$$= 0.25 \times 100\% = 25\%$$

14. How to predict whether a sum, difference, or product will be ODD or EVEN

Don't bother memorizing the rules. Just take simple numbers such as 2 for even numbers and 3 for odd numbers and see what happens.

Example:

If m is even and n is odd, is the product mn odd or even?

Setup:

Say $m = 2$ and $n = 3$.
$2 \times 3 = 6$, which is even, so mn is even.

15. How to recognize MULTIPLES OF 2, 3, 4, 5, 6, 9, 10, and 12

2: Last digit is even.

3: Sum of digits is a multiple of 3.

4: Last two digits are a multiple of 4.

5: Last digit is 5 or 0.

6: Sum of digits is a multiple of 3, and last digit is even.

9: Sum of digits is a multiple of 9.

10: Last digit is 0.

12: Sum of digits is a multiple of 3, and last two digits are a multiple of 4.

16. How to find a COMMON FACTOR of two numbers

Break both numbers down to their prime factors to see which they have in common. Then multiply the shared prime factors to find all common factors.

Example:

What factors greater than 1 do 135 and 225 have in common?

Setup:

First find the prime factors of 135 and 225;
$135 = 3 \times 3 \times 3 \times 5$, and $225 = 3 \times 3 \times 5 \times 5$. The numbers share $3 \times 3 \times 5$ in common. Thus, aside from 3 and 5, the remaining common factors can be found by multiplying 3, 3, and 5 in every possible combination: $3 \times 3 = 9$, $3 \times 5 = 15$, and $3 \times 3 \times 5 = 45$. Therefore, the common factors of 135 and 225 are 3, 5, 9, 15, and 45.

17. How to find a COMMON MULTIPLE of two numbers

The product of two numbers is the easiest common multiple to find, but it is not always the least common multiple (LCM).

Example:

What is the least common multiple of 28 and 42?

Setup:

$$28 = 2 \times 2 \times 7$$
$$42 = 2 \times 3 \times 7$$

The LCM can be found by finding the prime factorization of each number, then seeing the greatest number of times each factor is used. Multiply each prime factor the greatest number of times it appears.

In 28, 2 is used twice. In 42, 2 is used once. In 28, 7 is used once. In 42, 7 is used once, and 3 is used once.

So you multiply each factor the greatest number of times it appears in a prime factorization:

$$\text{LCM} = 2 \times 2 \times 3 \times 7 = 84$$

18. How to find the AVERAGE or ARITHMETIC MEAN

$$Average = \frac{Sum\ of\ terms}{Number\ of\ terms}$$

Example:

What is the average of 3, 4, and 8?

Setup:

$$Average = \frac{3 + 4 + 8}{3} = \frac{15}{3} = 5$$

19. How to use the AVERAGE to find the SUM

$$Sum = (Average) \times (Number\ of\ terms)$$

Example:

17.5 is the average (arithmetic mean) of 24 numbers.

What is the sum of the 24 numbers?

Setup:

$$Sum = 17.5 \times 24 = 420$$

20. How to find the AVERAGE of CONSECUTIVE NUMBERS

The average of evenly spaced numbers is simply the average of the smallest number and the largest number. The average of all the integers from 13 to 77, for example, is the same as the average of 13 and 77:

$$\frac{13 + 77}{2} = \frac{90}{2} = 45$$

21. How to COUNT CONSECUTIVE NUMBERS

The number of integers from A to B inclusive is $B - A + 1$.

Example:

How many integers are there from 73 through 419, inclusive?

Setup:

$$419 - 73 + 1 = 347$$

22. How to find the SUM OF CONSECUTIVE NUMBERS

$$Sum = (Average) \times (Number\ of\ terms)$$

Example:

What is the sum of the integers from 10 through 50, inclusive?

Setup:

Average: $\frac{10 + 50}{2} = 30$

Number of terms: $50 - 10 + 1 = 41$
Sum: $30 \times 41 = 1,230$

23. How to find the MEDIAN

Put the numbers in numerical order and take the middle number.

Example:

What is the median of 88, 86, 57, 94, and 73?

Setup:

First, put the numbers in numerical order. Then, take the middle number:

$$57, 73, 86, 88, 94$$

The median is 86.

In a set with an even number of numbers, take the average of the two in the middle.

Example:

What is the median of 88, 86, 57, 73, 94, and 100?

Setup:

First, put the numbers in numerical order.

$$57, 73, 86, 88, 94, 100$$

Because 86 and 88 are the two numbers in the middle:

$$\frac{86 + 88}{2} = \frac{174}{2} = 87$$

The median is 87.

24. How to find the MODE

Take the number that appears most often. For example, if your test scores were 88, 57, 68, 85, 98, 93, 93, 84, and 81, the mode of the scores would be 93 because it appears more often than any other score. (If there's a tie for most often, then there's more than one mode. If each number in a set is used equally often, there is no mode.)

25. How to find the RANGE

Take the positive difference between the greatest and least values. Using the example under "How to find the MODE" above, if your test scores were 88, 57, 68, 85, 98, 93, 93, 84, and 81, the range of the scores would be 41, the greatest value minus the least value ($98 - 57 = 41$).

26. How to use actual numbers to determine a RATIO

To find a ratio, put the number associated with *of* on the top and the number associated with *to* on the bottom.

$$Ratio = \frac{of}{to}$$

The ratio of 20 oranges to 12 apples is $\frac{20}{12}$, or $\frac{5}{3}$. Ratios should always be reduced to lowest terms.

Ratios can also be expressed in linear form, such as 5:3.

27. How to use a ratio to determine an ACTUAL NUMBER

Set up a proportion using the given ratio.

Example:

The ratio of boys to girls is 3 to 4. If there are 135 boys, how many girls are there?

Setup:

$$\frac{3}{4} = \frac{135}{g}$$
$$3 \times g = 4 \times 135$$
$$3g = 540$$
$$g = 180$$

28. How to use actual numbers to determine a RATE

Identify the quantities and the units to be compared. Keep the units straight.

Example:

Anders typed 9,450 words in $3\frac{1}{2}$ hours. What was his rate in words per minute?

Setup:

First convert $3\frac{1}{2}$ hours to 210 minutes. Then set up the rate with words on top and minutes on bottom (because "per" means "divided by"):

$$\frac{9,450 \text{ words}}{210 \text{ minutes}} = 45 \text{ words per minute}$$

29. How to deal with TABLES, GRAPHS, AND CHARTS

Read the question and all labels carefully. Ignore extraneous information and zero in on what the question asks for. Take advantage of the spread in the answer choices by approximating the answer whenever possible and choosing the answer choice closest to your approximation.

30. How to count the NUMBER OF POSSIBILITIES

You can use multiplication to find the number of possibilities when items can be arranged in various ways.

Example:

How many three-digit numbers can be formed with the digits 1, 3, and 5 each used only once?

Setup:

Look at each digit individually. The first digit (or, the hundreds digit) has three possible numbers to plug in: 1, 3, or 5. The second digit (or, the tens digit) has two possible numbers, since one has already been plugged in. The last digit (or, the ones digit) has only one remaining possible number. Multiply the possibilities together: $3 \times 2 \times 1 = 6$.

31. How to calculate a simple PROBABILITY

$$Probability = \frac{Number\ of\ desired\ outcomes}{Number\ of\ total\ possible\ outcomes}$$

Example:

What is the probability of throwing a 5 on a fair six-sided die?

Setup:

There is one desired outcome—throwing a 5. There are 6 possible outcomes—one for each side of the die.

$$Probability = \frac{1}{6}$$

32. How to work with new SYMBOLS

If you see a symbol you've never seen before, don't be alarmed. It's just a made-up symbol whose operation is uniquely defined by the problem. Everything you need to know is in the question stem. Just follow the instructions.

33. How to SIMPLIFY BINOMIALS

A binomial is a sum or difference of two terms. To simplify two binomials that are multiplied together, use the **FOIL** method. Multiply the **F**irst terms, then the **O**uter terms, followed by the **I**nner terms and the **L**ast terms. Lastly, combine like terms.

Example:

$$(3x + 5)(x - 1) =$$
$$3x^2 - 3x + 5x - 5 =$$
$$3x^2 + 2x - 5$$

34. How to FACTOR certain POLYNOMIALS

A polynomial is an expression consisting of the sum of two or more terms, where at least one of the terms is a variable.

Learn to spot these classic polynomial equations.

$$ab + ac = a(b + c)$$
$$a^2 + 2ab + b^2 = (a + b)^2$$
$$a^2 - 2ab + b^2 = (a - b)^2$$
$$a^2 - b^2 = (a - b)(a + b)$$

35. How to solve for one variable IN TERMS OF ANOTHER

To find x "in terms of" y, isolate x on one side, leaving y as the only variable on the other.

36. How to solve an INEQUALITY

Treat it much like an equation—adding, subtracting, multiplying, and dividing both sides by the same thing. Just remember to reverse the inequality sign if you multiply or divide by a negative quantity.

Example:

Rewrite $7 - 3x > 2$ in its simplest form.

Setup:

$$7 - 3x > 2$$

First, subtract 7 from both sides:

$$7 - 3x - 7 > 2 - 7$$
$$-3x > -5$$

Now divide both sides by -3, remembering to reverse the inequality sign:

$$x < \frac{5}{3}$$

37. How to handle ABSOLUTE VALUES

The *absolute value* of a number n, denoted by $|n|$, is defined as n if $n \geq 0$ and $-n$ if $n < 0$. The absolute value of a number is the distance from zero to the number on the number line. The absolute value of a number or an expression is always positive.

$$|-5| = 5$$

If $|x| = 3$, then x could be 3 or -3.

Example:

If $|x - 3| < 2$, what is the range of possible values for x?

Setup:

Represent the possible range for $x - 3$ on a number line.

```
 -5  -4  -3  -2  -1   0   1   2   3   4   5
 ├───┼───┼───○───┼───┼───┼───○───┼───┤
```

$|x - 3| < 2$, so $(x - 3) < 2$ and $(x - 3) > -2$
$x - 3 < 2$ and $x - 3 > -2$
$x < 2 + 3$ and $x > -2 + 3$
$x < 5$ and $x > 1$
So, $1 < x < 5$.

38. How to TRANSLATE ENGLISH INTO ALGEBRA

Look for the key words and systematically turn phrases into algebraic expressions and sentences into equations.

Here's a table of key words that you may have to translate into mathematical terms:

Operation	Key Words
Addition	sum, plus, and, added to, more than, increased by, combined with, exceeds, total, greater than
Subtraction	difference between, minus, subtracted from, decreased by, diminished by, less than, reduced by
Multiplication	of, product, times, multiplied by, twice, double, triple

Operation	Key Words
Division	quotient, divided by, per, out of, half, ratio of _ to _
Equals	equals, is, was, will be, the result is, adds up to, costs, is the same as

39. How to find an ANGLE formed by INTERSECTING LINES

Vertical angles are equal. Angles along a line add up to 180°.

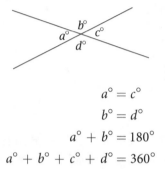

$$a° = c°$$
$$b° = d°$$
$$a° + b° = 180°$$
$$a° + b° + c° + d° = 360°$$

40. How to find an angle formed by a TRANSVERSAL across PARALLEL LINES

When a transversal crosses parallel lines, all the acute angles formed are equal, and all the obtuse angles formed are equal. Any acute angle plus any obtuse angle equals 180°.

Example:

$$e° = g° = p° = r°$$
$$f° = h° = q° = s°$$
$$e° + q° = g° + s° = 180°$$

41. How to find the AREA of a TRIANGLE

$$Area = \frac{1}{2}(Base)(Height)$$

Base and height must be perpendicular to each other. Height is measured by drawing a perpendicular line segment from the base—which can be any side of the triangle—to the angle opposite the base.

Example:

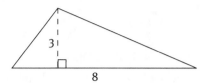

Setup:

$$Area = \frac{1}{2}(8)(3) = 12$$

42. How to work with ISOSCELES TRIANGLES

Isosceles triangles have at least two equal sides and two equal angles. If a GRE question tells you that a triangle is isosceles, you can bet that you'll need to use that information to find the length of a side or a measure of an angle.

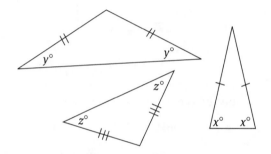

43. How to work with EQUILATERAL TRIANGLES

Equilateral triangles have three equal sides and three 60° angles. If a GRE question tells you that a triangle is equilateral, you can bet that you'll need to use that information to find the length of a side or the measure of an angle.

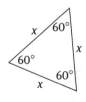
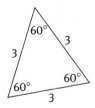

44. How to work with SIMILAR TRIANGLES

In similar triangles, corresponding angles are equal and corresponding sides are proportional. If a GRE question tells you that triangles are similar, use the properties of similar triangles to find the length of a side or the measure of an angle.

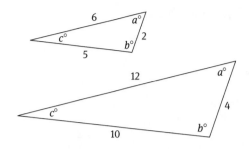

45. How to find the HYPOTENUSE or a LEG of a RIGHT TRIANGLE

For all right triangles, the Pythagorean theorem is $a^2 + b^2 = c^2$, where a and b are the legs and c is the hypotenuse.

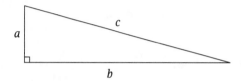

46. How to spot SPECIAL RIGHT TRIANGLES

Special right triangles are seen on the GRE with frequency. Recognizing them can streamline your problem solving.

3:4:5

5:12:13

These numbers (3, 4, 5 and 5, 12, 13) represent the ratio of the side lengths of these triangles.

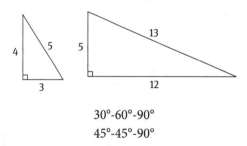

30°-60°-90°

45°-45°-90°

In a 30°-60°-90° triangle, the side lengths are multiples of 1, $\sqrt{3}$, and 2, respectively. In a 45°-45°-90° triangle, the side lengths are multiples of 1, 1, and $\sqrt{2}$, respectfully.

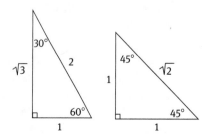

47. How to find the PERIMETER of a RECTANGLE

$$Perimeter = 2(Length + Width)$$

Example:

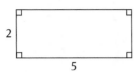

Setup:

$$Perimeter = 2(2 + 5) = 14$$

48. How to find the AREA of a RECTANGLE

$$Area = (Length)(Width)$$

Example:

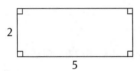

Setup:

$$Area = 2 \times 5 = 10$$

49. How to find the AREA of a SQUARE

$$Area = (Side)^2$$

Example:

Setup:

$$Area = 3^2 = 9$$

50. How to find the AREA of a PARALLELOGRAM

$$Area = (Base)(Height)$$

Example:

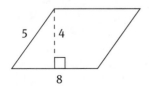

Setup:

$$Area = 8 \times 4 = 32$$

51. How to find the AREA of a TRAPEZOID

A trapezoid is a quadrilateral having only two parallel sides. You can always drop a perpendicular line or two to break the figure into a rectangle and a triangle or two triangles. Use the area formulas for those familiar shapes. Alternatively, you could apply the general formula for the area of a trapezoid:

$$Area = (Average\ of\ parallel\ sides) \times (Height)$$

Example:

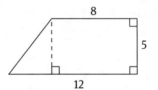

Setup:

$$Area\ of\ rectangle = 8 \times 5 = 40$$
$$Area\ of\ triangle = \frac{1}{2}(4 \times 5) = 10$$
$$Area\ of\ trapezoid = 40 + 10 = 50$$
$$Area\ of\ trapezoid = \left(\frac{8+12}{2}\right) \times 5 = 50$$

52. How to find the CIRCUMFERENCE of a CIRCLE

$$Circumference = 2\pi r,\ where\ r\ is\ the\ radius$$
$$Circumference = \pi d,\ where\ d\ is\ the\ diameter$$

Example:

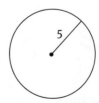

Setup:

$$Circumference = 2\pi(5) = 10\pi$$

53. How to find the AREA of a CIRCLE

$$Area = \pi r^2, \text{ where } r \text{ is the radius}$$

Example:

Setup:

$$Area = \pi \times 5^2 = 25\pi$$

54. How to find the DISTANCE BETWEEN POINTS on the coordinate plane

If two points have the same x-coordinates or the same y-coordinates—that is, they make a line segment that is parallel to an axis—all you have to do is subtract the numbers that are different. Just remember that distance is always positive.

Example:

What is the distance from $(2,3)$ to $(-7,3)$?

Setup:

The ys are the same, so just subtract the xs: $2 - (-7) = 9$.

If the points have different x-coordinates and different y-coordinates, make a right triangle and use the Pythagorean theorem or apply the special right triangle attributes if applicable.

Example:

What is the distance from $(2,3)$ to $(-1,-1)$?

Setup:

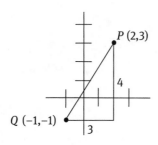

It's a 3:4:5 triangle!
$PQ = 5$

55. How to find the SLOPE of a LINE

$$Slope = \frac{Rise}{Run} = \frac{Change\ in\ y}{Change\ in\ x}$$

Example:

What is the slope of the line that contains the points $(1,2)$ and $(4,-5)$?

Setup:

$$Slope = \frac{-5-2}{4-1} = \frac{-7}{3} = -\frac{7}{3}$$

LEVEL 3

56. How to determine COMBINED PERCENT INCREASE/DECREASE when no original value is specified

Start with 100 as a starting value.

Example:

A price rises by 10% one year and by 20% the next. What's the combined percent increase?

Setup:

Say the original price is $100.

Year one:
$100 + (10\% \text{ of } 100) = 100 + 10 = 110$

Year two:
$110 + (20\% \text{ of } 110) = 110 + 22 = 132$

From 100 to 132 is a 32 percent increase.

57. How to find the ORIGINAL WHOLE before percent increase/decrease

Think of a 15% increase over x as $1.15x$ and set up an equation.

Example:

After decreasing by 5%, the population is now 57,000. What was the original population?

Setup:

$0.95 \times (Original\ population) = 57,000$

Divide both sides by 0.95.

$Original\ population = 57,000 \div 0.95 = 60,000$

58. How to solve a SIMPLE INTEREST problem

With simple interest, the interest is computed on the principal only and is given by

$$Interest = Principle \times rt$$

In this formula, r is defined as the interest rate per payment period and t is defined as the number of payment periods.

Example:

If \$12,000 is invested at 6 percent simple annual interest, how much interest is earned after 9 months?

Setup:

Since the interest rate is annual and we are calculating how much interest accrues after 9 months, we will express the payment period as $\frac{9}{12}$.

$$(12,000) \times (0.06) \times \frac{9}{12} = 540$$

59. How to solve a COMPOUND INTEREST problem

If interest is compounded, the interest is computed on the principal as well as on any interest earned. To compute compound interest:

$$(Final\ balance) = (Principal) \times \left(1 + \frac{interest\ rate}{c}\right)^{(time)(c)}$$

where $c =$ the number of times the interest is compounded annually.

Example:

If \$10,000 is invested at 8 percent annual interest, compounded semiannually, what is the balance after 1 year?

Setup:

Final balance

$$= (10,000) \times \left(1 + \frac{0.08}{2}\right)^{(1)(2)}$$

$$= (10,000) \times (1.04)^2$$

$$= 10,816$$

Semiannual interest is interest that is distributed twice a year. When an interest rate is given as an annual rate, divide by 2 to find the semiannual interest rate.

60. How to solve a REMAINDERS problem

Pick a number that fits the given conditions and see what happens.

Example:

When n is divided by 7, the remainder is 5. What is the remainder when $2n$ is divided by 7?

Setup:

Find a number that leaves a remainder of 5 when divided by 7. You can find such a number by taking any multiple of 7 and adding 5 to it. A good choice would be 12. If $n = 12$, then $2n = 24$, which when divided by 7 leaves a remainder of 3.

61. How to solve a DIGITS problem

Use a little logic—and some trial and error.

Example:

If A, B, C, and D represent distinct digits in the addition problem below, what is the value of D?

$$\begin{array}{r} AB \\ + BA \\ \hline CDC \end{array}$$

Setup:

Two 2-digit numbers will add up to at most something in the 100s, so $C = 1$. B plus A in the units column gives a 1, and since A and B in the tens column don't add up to C, it can't simply be that $B + A = 1$. It must be that $B + A = 11$, and a 1 gets carried. In fact, A and B can be any pair of digits that add up to 11 (3 and 8, 4 and 7, etc.), but it doesn't matter what they are: they always give you the same value for D, which is 2:

$$\begin{array}{r} 47 \\ +74 \\ \hline 121 \end{array} \qquad \begin{array}{r} 83 \\ +38 \\ \hline 121 \end{array}$$

62. How to find a WEIGHTED AVERAGE

Give each term the appropriate "weight."

Example:

The girls' average score is 30. The boys' average score is 24. If there are twice as many boys as girls, what is the overall average?

Setup:

$$Weighted\ avg. = \frac{(1 \times 30) + (2 \times 24)}{3} = \frac{78}{3} = 26$$

HINT: Don't just average the averages.

63. How to find the NEW AVERAGE when a number is added or deleted

Use the sum of the terms of the old average to help you find the new average.

Example:

Michael's average score after four tests is 80. If he scores 100 on the fifth test, what's his new average?

Setup:

Find the original sum from the original average:

$$Original\ sum = 4 \times 80 = 320$$

Add the fifth score to make the new sum:

$$New\ sum = 320 + 100 = 420$$

Find the new average from the new sum:

$$New\ average = \frac{420}{5} = 84$$

64. How to use the ORIGINAL AVERAGE and NEW AVERAGE to figure out WHAT WAS ADDED OR DELETED

Use the sums.

$Number\ added = (New\ sum) - (Original\ sum)$
$Number\ deleted = (Original\ sum) - (New\ sum)$

Example:

The average of five numbers is 2. After one number is deleted, the new average is −3. What number was deleted?

Setup:

Find the original sum from the original average:

$$Original\ sum = 5 \times 2 = 10$$

Find the new sum from the new average:

$$New\ sum = 4 \times (-3) = -12$$

The difference between the original sum and the new sum is the answer.

$$Number\ deleted = 10 - (-12) = 22$$

65. How to find an AVERAGE RATE

Convert to totals.

$$Average\ A\ per\ B = \frac{Total\ A}{Total\ B}$$

Example:

If the first 500 pages have an average of 150 words per page, and the remaining 100 pages have an average of 450 words per page, what is the average number of words per page for the entire 600 pages?

Setup:

$$
\begin{aligned}
Total\ pages &= 500 + 100 = 600 \\
Total\ words &= (500 \times 150) + (100 \times 450) \\
&= 75{,}000 + 45{,}000 \\
&= 120{,}000
\end{aligned}
$$

$$Average\ words\ per\ page = \frac{120{,}000}{600} = 200$$

To find an average speed, you also convert to totals.

$$Average\ speed = \frac{Total\ distance}{Total\ time}$$

Example:

Rosa drove 120 miles one way at an average speed of 40 miles per hour and returned by the same 120-mile route at an average speed of 60 miles per hour. What was Rosa's average speed for the entire 240-mile round trip?

Setup:

To drive 120 miles at 40 mph takes 3 hours. To return at 60 mph takes 2 hours. The total time, then, is 5 hours.

$$Average\ speed\ =\ \frac{240\ miles}{5\ hours}\ =\ 48\ mph$$

66. How to solve a COMBINED WORK PROBLEM

In a combined work problem, you are given the rate at which people or machines perform work individually and you are asked to compute the rate at which they work together (or vice versa). The work formula states: *The inverse of the time it would take everyone working together equals the sum of the inverses of the times it would take each working individually.*

In other words:

$$\frac{1}{r}\ +\ \frac{1}{s}\ =\ \frac{1}{t}$$

where r and s are, for example, the number of hours it would take Rebecca and Sam, respectively, to complete a job working by themselves, and t is the number of hours it would take the two of them working together. Remember that all these variables must stand for units of *time* and must all refer to the amount of time it takes to do the same task.

Example:

If it takes Joe 4 hours to paint a room and Pete twice as long to paint the same room, how long would it take the two of them, working together, to paint the same room, if each of them works at his respective individual rate?

Setup:

Joe takes 4 hours, so Pete takes 8 hours; thus:

$$\frac{1}{4}+\frac{1}{8}=\frac{1}{t}$$

$$\frac{2}{8}+\frac{1}{8}=\frac{1}{t}$$

$$\frac{3}{8}=\frac{1}{t}$$

$$t=\frac{1}{\left(\frac{3}{8}\right)}=\frac{8}{3}$$

So it would take them $\frac{8}{3}$ hours, or 2 hours and 40 minutes, to paint the room together.

67. How to determine a COMBINED RATIO

Multiply one or both ratios by whatever you need in order to get the terms they have in common to match.

Example:

The ratio of a to b is 7:3. The ratio of b to c is 2:5. What is the ratio of a to c?

Setup:

Multiply each member of $a{:}b$ by 2 and multiply each member of $b{:}c$ by 3, and you get $a{:}b = 14{:}6$ and $b{:}c = 6{:}15$. Now that the values of b match, you can write $a{:}b{:}c = 14{:}6{:}15$ and then say $a{:}c = 14{:}15$.

68. How to solve a DILUTION or MIXTURE problem

In dilution or mixture problems, you have to determine the characteristics of a resulting mixture when different substances are combined. Or, alternatively, you have to determine how to combine different substances to produce a desired mixture. There are two approaches to such problems—the straightforward setup and the balancing method.

Example:

If 5 pounds of raisins that cost $1 per pound are mixed with 2 pounds of almonds that cost $2.40 per pound, what is the cost per pound of the resulting mixture?

Setup:

The straightforward setup:

($1)(5) + ($2.40)(2) = $9.80 = total cost for 7 pounds of the mixture

The cost per pound is $\frac{\$9.80}{7}\ =\ \$1.40$.

Example:

How many liters of a solution that is 10% alcohol by volume must be added to 2 liters of a solution that is 50% alcohol by volume to create a solution that is 15% alcohol by volume?

Setup:

The balancing method: Make the weaker and stronger (or cheaper and more expensive, etc.) substances balance. That is, (percent difference between the weaker solution and the desired solution) × (amount of weaker solution) = (percent difference between the stronger solution and the desired solution) × (amount of stronger solution). Make n the amount, in liters, of the weaker solution.

$$n(15 - 10) = 2(50 - 15)$$
$$5n = 2(35)$$
$$n = \frac{70}{5} = 14$$

So 14 liters of the 10% solution must be added to the original, stronger solution.

69. How to solve an OVERLAPPING SETS problem involving BOTH/NEITHER

Some GRE word problems involve two groups with overlapping members and possibly elements that belong to neither group. It's easy to identify this type of question because the words *both* and/or *neither* appear in the question. These problems are quite workable if you just memorize the following formula:

Group 1 + Group 2 + Neither − Both = Total

Example:

Of the 120 students at a certain language school, 65 are studying French, 51 are studying Spanish, and 53 are studying neither language. How many are studying both French and Spanish?

Setup:

$$65 + 51 + 53 - Both = 120$$
$$169 - Both = 120$$
$$Both = 120$$

70. How to solve an OVERLAPPING SETS problem involving EITHER/OR CATEGORIES

Other GRE word problems involve groups with distinct "either/or" categories (male/female, blue-collar/white-collar, etc.). The key to solving this type of problem is to organize the information in a grid.

Example:

At a certain professional conference with 130 attendees, 94 of the attendees are doctors, and the rest are dentists. If 48 of the attendees are women and $\frac{1}{4}$ of the dentists in attendance are women, how many of the attendees are male doctors?

Setup:

To complete the grid, use the information in the problem, making each row and column add up to the corresponding total:

	Doctors	Dentists	Total
Male	55	27	82
Female	39	9	48
Total	94	36	130

After you've filled in the information from the question, use simple arithmetic to fill in the remaining boxes until you get the number you are looking for—in this case, that 55 of the attendees are male doctors.

71. How to work with FACTORIALS

You may see a problem involving factorial notation, which is indicated by the ! symbol. If n is an integer greater than 1, then n factorial, denoted by $n!$, is defined as the product of all the integers from 1 to n. For example:

$$2! = 2 \times 1 = 2$$
$$3! = 3 \times 2 \times 1 = 6$$
$$4! = 4 \times 3 \times 2 \times 1 = 24$$

By definition, $0! = 1$.

Also note: $6! = 6 \times 5! = 6 \times 5 \times 4!$, etc. Most GRE factorial problems test your ability to factor and/or cancel.

Example:

$$\frac{8!}{6! \times 2!} = \frac{8 \times 7 \times 6!}{6! \times 2 \times 1} = 28$$

72. How to solve a PERMUTATION problem

Factorials are useful for solving questions about permutations (i.e., the number of ways to arrange elements sequentially). For instance, to figure out how many ways there are to arrange 7 items along a shelf, you would multiply the number of possibilities for the first position times the number of possibilities remaining for the second position, and so on—in other words: $7 \times 6 \times 5 \times 4 \times 3 \times 2 \times 1$, or $7!$.

If you're asked to find the number of ways to arrange a smaller group that's being drawn from a larger group, you can either apply logic, or you can use the permutation formula:

$$_nP_k = \frac{n!}{(n-k)!}$$

where n = (the number in the larger group) and
k = (the number you're arranging).

Example:

Five runners run in a race. The runners who come in first, second, and third place will win gold, silver, and bronze medals, respectively. How many possible outcomes for gold, silver, and bronze medal winners are there?

Setup:

Any of the 5 runners could come in first place, leaving 4 runners who could come in second place, leaving 3 runners who could come in third place, for a total of $5 \times 4 \times 3 = 60$ possible outcomes for gold, silver, and bronze medal winners. Or, using the formula:

$$_5P_3 = \frac{5!}{(5-3)!} = \frac{5!}{2!} = \frac{5 \times 4 \times 3 \times \cancel{2} \times \cancel{1}}{\cancel{2} \times \cancel{1}}$$
$$= 5 \times 4 \times 3 = 60$$

73. How to solve a COMBINATION problem

If the order or arrangement of the smaller group that's being drawn from the larger group does *not* matter, you are looking for the numbers of combinations, and a different formula is called for:

$$_nC_k = \frac{n!}{k!(n-k)!}$$

where n = (the number in the larger group) and
k = (the number you're choosing).

Example:

How many different ways are there to choose 3 delegates from 8 possible candidates?

Setup:

$$_nC_k = \frac{8!}{3!(8-3)!} = \frac{8!}{3! \times 5!}$$
$$= \frac{8 \times 7 \times \cancel{6} \times \cancel{5} \times \cancel{4} \times \cancel{3} \times \cancel{2} \times \cancel{1}}{\cancel{3} \times \cancel{2} \times 1 \times \cancel{5} \times \cancel{4} \times \cancel{3} \times \cancel{2} \times \cancel{1}}$$
$$= 8 \times 7 = 56$$

So there are 56 different possible combinations.

74. How to solve PROBABILITY problems where probabilities must be multiplied

Suppose that a random process is performed. Then there is a set of possible outcomes that can occur. An event is a set of possible outcomes. We are concerned with the probability of events.

When all the outcomes are all equally likely, the basic probability formula is this:

$$Probability = \frac{Number\ of\ desired\ outcomes}{Number\ of\ total\ possible\ outcomes}$$

Many more difficult probability questions involve finding the probability that several events occur. Let's consider first the case of the probability that two events occur. Call these two events A and B. The probability that both events occur is the probability that event A occurs multiplied by the probability that event B occurs given that event A occurred. The probability that B occurs given that A occurs is called the conditional probability that B occurs given that A occurs. Except when events A and B do not depend on one another, the probability that B occurs given that A occurs is not the same as the probability that B occurs.

The probability that three events A, B, and C occur is the probability that A occurs multiplied by the conditional probability that B occurs given that A occurred multiplied by the conditional probability that C occurs given that both A and B have occurred.

This can be generalized to any number of events.

Example:

If 2 students are chosen at random to run an errand from a class with 5 girls and 5 boys, what is the probability that both students chosen will be girls?

Setup:

The probability that the first student chosen will be a girl is $\frac{5}{10} = \frac{1}{2}$, and since there would be 4 girls and 5 boys left out of 9 students, the probability that the second student chosen will be a girl (given that the first student chosen is a girl) is $\frac{4}{9}$. Thus, the probability that both students chosen will be girls is $\frac{1}{2} \times \frac{4}{9} = \frac{2}{9}$. There was conditional probability here because the probability of choosing the second girl was affected by another girl being chosen first. Now let's consider another example where a random process is repeated.

Example:

If a fair coin is tossed 4 times, what's the probability that at least 3 of the 4 tosses will be heads?

Setup:

There are 2 possible outcomes for each toss, so after 4 tosses, there are $2 \times 2 \times 2 \times 2 = 16$ possible outcomes.

We can list the different possible sequences where at least 3 of the 4 tosses are heads. These sequences are

HHHT
HHTH
HTHH
THHH
HHHH

Thus, the probability that at least 3 of the 4 tosses will come up heads is:

$$\frac{\textit{Number of desired outcomes}}{\textit{Number of total possible outcomes}} = \frac{5}{16}$$

We could have also solved this question using the combinations formula. The probability of a head is $\frac{1}{2}$ and the probability of a tail is $\frac{1}{2}$. The probability of any particular sequence of heads and tails resulting from 4 tosses is $\frac{1}{2} \times \frac{1}{2} \times \frac{1}{2} \times \frac{1}{2}$, which is $\frac{1}{16}$.

Suppose that the result of each of the four tosses is recorded in each of the four spaces.

———   ———   ———   ———

Thus, we would record an H for head or a T for tails in each of the 4 spaces.

The number of ways of having exactly 3 heads among the 4 tosses is the number of ways of choosing 3 of the 4 spaces above to record an H for heads.

The number of ways of choosing 3 of the 4 spaces is

$$_4C_3 = \frac{4!}{3!(4-3)!} = \frac{4!}{3!(1)!} = \frac{4 \times 3 \times 2 \times 1}{3 \times 2 \times 1 \times 1} = 4$$

The number of ways of having exactly 4 heads among the 4 tosses is 1.

If we use the combinations formula, using the definition that $0! = 1$, then

$$_4C_4 = \frac{4!}{4!(4-4)!} = \frac{4!}{4!(0)!}$$
$$= \frac{4 \times 3 \times 2 \times 1}{4 \times 3 \times 2 \times 1 \times 1} = 1$$

Thus, $_4C_3 = 4$ and $_4C_4 = 1$. So the number of different sequences containing at least 3 heads is $4 + 1 = 5$.

The probability of having at least 3 heads is $\frac{5}{16}$.

75. How to deal with STANDARD DEVIATION

Like the terms *mean*, *mode*, *median*, and *range*, *standard deviation* is a term used to describe sets of numbers. Standard deviation is a measure of how spread out a set of numbers is (how much the numbers deviate from the mean). The greater the spread, the higher the standard deviation. You'll rarely have to calculate the standard deviation on Test Day (although this skill may be necessary for some high-difficulty questions). Here's how standard deviation is calculated:

- Find the average (arithmetic mean) of the set.
- Find the differences between the mean and each value in the set.
- Square each of the differences.
- Find the average of the squared differences.
- Take the positive square root of the average.

In addition to the occasional question that asks you to calculate standard deviation, you may also be asked to compare standard deviations between sets of data or otherwise demonstrate that you understand what standard deviation means. You can often handle these questions using estimation.

Example:

The table shows high temperatures, in degrees Fahrenheit, in two cities over five days:

September	1	2	3	4	5
City A	54	61	70	49	56
City B	62	56	60	67	65

For the five-day period listed, which city had the greater standard deviation in high temperatures?

Setup:

Even without trying to calculate them out, one can see that City A has the greater spread in temperatures and, therefore, the greater standard deviation in high temperatures. If you were to go ahead and calculate the standard deviations following the steps described above, you would find that the standard deviation in high temperatures for

City A $= \sqrt{\dfrac{254}{5}} \approx 7.1$ while the standard

deviation for City B $= \sqrt{\dfrac{74}{5}} \approx 3.8$.

76. How to MULTIPLY/DIVIDE VALUES WITH EXPONENTS

Add/subtract the exponents.

Example:

$$x^a \times x^b = x^{a+b}$$
$$2^3 \times 2^4 = 2^7$$

Example:

$$\frac{x^a}{x^b} = x^{a-b}$$
$$\frac{2^8}{2^2} = 2^{8-2} = 2^6$$

77. How to handle a value with an EXPONENT RAISED TO AN EXPONENT

Multiply the exponents.

Example:

$$\left(x^a\right)^b = x^{ab}$$
$$\left(3^4\right)^5 = 3^{20}$$

78. How to handle EXPONENTS with a base of ZERO and BASES with an EXPONENT of ZERO

Zero raised to any nonzero exponent equals zero.

Example:

$$0^4 = 0^{12} = 0^1 = 0$$

Any nonzero number raised to the exponent 0 equals 1.

Example:

$$3^0 = 15^0 = (0.34)^0 = (-345)^0 = \pi^0 = 1$$

The lone exception is 0 raised to the 0 power, which is *undefined*.

79. How to handle NEGATIVE POWERS

A number raised to the exponent $-x$ is the reciprocal of that number raised to the exponent x.

Example:

$$n^{-1} = \frac{1}{n}, \ n^{-2} = \frac{1}{n^2}, \text{ and so on}$$

$$5^{-3} = \frac{1}{5^3} = \frac{1}{5 \times 5 \times 5} = \frac{1}{125}$$

80. How to handle FRACTIONAL POWERS

Fractional exponents relate to roots. For instance, $x^{\frac{1}{2}} = \sqrt{x}$.

Likewise, $x^{\frac{1}{3}} = \sqrt[3]{x}$, $x^{\frac{2}{3}} = \sqrt[3]{x^2}$, and so on.

Example:

$$\sqrt{x^{-2}} = \left(x^{-2}\right)^{\frac{1}{2}} = x^{(-2)\left(\frac{1}{2}\right)} = x^{-1} = \frac{1}{x}$$

$$4^{\frac{1}{2}} = \sqrt{4} = 2$$

81. How to handle CUBE ROOTS

The cube root of x is just the number that, when used as a factor 3 times (i.e., cubed), gives you x. Both positive and negative numbers have one and only one cube root, denoted by the symbol $\sqrt[3]{\ }$, and the cube root of a number is always the same sign as the number itself.

Example:

$$(-5) \times (-5) \times (-5) = -125, \text{ so } \sqrt[3]{-125}$$
$$= -5$$
$$\frac{1}{2} \times \frac{1}{2} \times \frac{1}{2} = \frac{1}{8}, \text{ so } \sqrt[3]{\frac{1}{8}} = \frac{1}{2}$$

82. How to ADD, SUBTRACT, MULTIPLY, and DIVIDE ROOTS

You can add/subtract roots only when the parts inside the $\sqrt{\ }$ are identical.

Example:

$$\sqrt{2} + 3\sqrt{2} = 4\sqrt{2}$$
$$\sqrt{2} - 3\sqrt{2} = -2\sqrt{2}$$
$$\sqrt{2} + \sqrt{3} \qquad \text{cannot be combined.}$$

To multiply/divide roots, deal with what's inside the $\sqrt{\ }$ and outside the $\sqrt{\ }$ separately.

Example:

$$\left(2\sqrt{3}\right)\left(7\sqrt{5}\right) = \left(2 \times 7\right)\left(\sqrt{3 \times 5}\right) = 14\sqrt{15}$$
$$\frac{10\sqrt{21}}{5\sqrt{3}} = \frac{10}{5}\sqrt{\frac{21}{3}} = 2\sqrt{7}$$

83. How to SIMPLIFY A RADICAL

Look for factors of the number under the radical sign that are perfect squares; then find the square root of those perfect squares. Keep simplifying until the term with the square root sign is as simplified as possible, that is, when there are no other perfect square factors (4, 9, 16, 25, 36, …) inside the $\sqrt{\ }$. Write the perfect squares as separate factors and "unsquare" them.

Example:

$$\sqrt{48} = \sqrt{16} \times \sqrt{3} = 4\sqrt{3}$$
$$\sqrt{180} = \sqrt{36} \times \sqrt{5} = 6\sqrt{5}$$

84. How to solve certain QUADRATIC EQUATIONS

Manipulate the equation (if necessary) so that it is equal to 0, factor the left side (reverse FOIL by finding two numbers whose product is the constant and whose sum is the coefficient of the term without the exponent), and break the quadratic into two simple expressions. Then find the value(s) for the variable that make either expression = 0.

Example:

$$x^2 + 6 = 5x$$
$$x^2 - 5x + 6 = 0$$
$$(x - 2)(x - 3) = 0$$
$$x - 2 = 0 \text{ or } x - 3 = 0$$
$$x = 2 \text{ or } 3$$

Example:

$$x^2 = 9$$
$$x = 3 \text{ or } -3$$

85. How to solve MULTIPLE EQUATIONS

When you see two equations with two variables on the GRE, they're probably easy to combine in such a way that you get something closer to what you're looking for.

Example:

If $5x - 2y = -9$ and $3y - 4x = 6$, what is the value of $x + y$?

Setup:

The question doesn't ask for x and y separately, so don't solve for them separately if you don't have to. Look what happens if you just rearrange a little and "add" the equations:

$$
\begin{array}{rcl}
5x - 2y & = & -9 \\
+(-4x + 3y & = & 6) \\
\hline
x + y & = & -3
\end{array}
$$

86. How to solve a SEQUENCE problem

The notation used in sequence problems scares many test takers, but these problems aren't as bad as they look. In a sequence problem, the nth term in the sequence is generated by performing an operation, which will be defined for you, on either n or on the previous term in the sequence. The term itself is expressed as a_n. For instance, if you are referring to the fourth term in a sequence, it is called a_4 in sequence notation. Familiarize yourself with sequence notation, and you should have no problem.

Example:

What is the positive difference between the fifth and fourth terms in the sequence 0, 4, 18, . . . whose nth term is $n^2(n - 1)$?

Setup:

Use the definition given to come up with the values for your terms:

$$
\begin{array}{rclclcl}
a_5 & = & 5^2(5 - 1) & = & 25(4) & = & 100 \\
a_4 & = & 4^2(4 - 1) & = & 16(3) & = & 48
\end{array}
$$

So the positive difference between the fifth and fourth terms is $100 - 48 = 52$.

87. How to solve a FUNCTION problem

You may see function notation on the GRE. An algebraic expression of only one variable may be defined as a function, usually symbolized by f or g, of that variable.

Example:

What is the minimum value of x in the function $f(x) = x^2 - 1$?

Setup:

In the function $f(x) = x^2 - 1$, if x is 1, then $f(1) = 1^2 - 1 = 0$. In other words, by inputting 1 into the function, the output $f(x) = 0$. Every number inputted has one and only one output (although the reverse is not necessarily true). You're asked to find the minimum value, so how would you minimize the expression $f(x) = x^2 - 1$? Since x^2 cannot be negative, in this case $f(x)$ is minimized by making $x = 0$: $f(0) = 0^2 - 1 = -1$, so the minimum value of the function is -1.

88. How to handle GRAPHS of FUNCTIONS

You may see a problem that involves a function graphed onto the xy-coordinate plane, often called a "rectangular coordinate system" on the GRE. When graphing a function, the output, $f(x)$, becomes the y-coordinate. For example, in the previous example, $f(x) = x^2 - 1$, you've already determined 2 points, $(1,0)$ and $(0,-1)$. If you were to keep plugging in numbers to determine more points and then plotted those points on the *xy*-coordinate plane, you would come up with something like this:

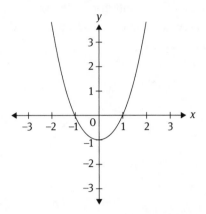

This curved line is called a *parabola*. In the event that you should see a parabola on the GRE (it could be upside down or narrower or wider than the one shown), you will most likely be asked to choose which equation the parabola is describing. These questions can be surprisingly easy to answer. Pick out obvious points on the graph, such as $(1,0)$ and $(0,-1)$ above, plug these values into the answer choices, and eliminate answer choices that don't work with those values until only one answer choice is left.

89. How to handle LINEAR EQUATIONS

You may also encounter linear equations on the GRE. A linear equation is often expressed in the form

$$y = mx + b, \text{ where}$$

$$m = \text{the slope of the line} = \frac{rise}{run}$$

$$b = \text{the } y\text{-intercept (the point where the line crosses the } y\text{-axis)}$$

Example:

The graph of the linear equation

$$y = -\frac{3}{4}x + 3 \text{ is this:}$$

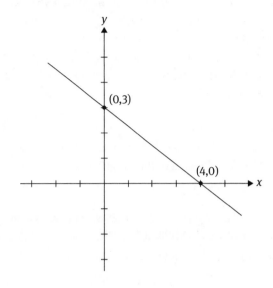

Note:

The equation could also be written in the form $3x + 4y = 12$, but this form does not readily describe the slope and *y*-intercept of the line.

To get a better handle on an equation written in this form, you can solve for *y* to write it in its more familiar form. Or, if you're asked to choose which equation the line is describing, you can pick obvious points, such as $(0,3)$ and $(4,0)$ in this example, and use these values to eliminate answer choices until only one answer is left.

90. How to find the *x*- and *y*-INTERCEPTS of a line

The *x*-intercept of a line is the value of *x* where the line crosses the *x*-axis. In other words, it's the value of *x* when $y = 0$. Likewise, the *y*-intercept is the value of *y* where the line crosses the *y*-axis (i.e., the value of *y* when $x = 0$). The *y*-intercept is also the value *b* when the equation is in the form $y = mx + b$. For instance, in the line shown in the previous example, the *x*-intercept is 4 and the *y*-intercept is 3.

91. How to find the MAXIMUM and MINIMUM lengths for a SIDE of a TRIANGLE

If you know the lengths of two sides of a triangle, you know that the third side is somewhere between the positive difference and the sum of the other two sides.

Example:

The length of one side of a triangle is 7. The length of another side is 3. What is the range of possible lengths for the third side?

Setup:

The third side is greater than the positive difference $(7 - 3 = 4)$ and less than the sum $(7 + 3 = 10)$ of the other two sides.

92. How to find the sum of all the ANGLES of a POLYGON and one angle measure of a REGULAR POLYGON

Sum of the interior angles in a polygon with n sides:

$$(n - 2) \times 180$$

The term *regular* means all angles in the polygon are of equal measure.

Degree measure of one angle in a regular polygon with n sides:

$$\frac{(n - 2) \times 180}{n}$$

Example:

What is the measure of one angle of a regular pentagon?

Setup:

Since a pentagon is a five-sided figure, plug $n = 5$ into the formula:

Degree measure of one angle:

$$\frac{(5 - 2) \times 180}{5} = \frac{540}{5} = 108$$

93. How to find the LENGTH of an ARC

Think of an arc as a fraction of the circle's circumference. Use the measure of an interior angle of a circle, which has 360 degrees around the central point, to determine the length of an arc.

$$Length\ of\ arc = \frac{n}{360} \times 2\pi r$$

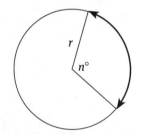

94. How to find the AREA of a SECTOR

Think of a sector as a fraction of the circle's area. Again, set up the interior angle measure as a fraction of 360, which is the degree measure of a circle around the central point.

$$Area\ of\ sector = \frac{n}{360} \times \pi r^2$$

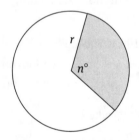

95. How to find the dimensions or area of an INSCRIBED or CIRCUMSCRIBED FIGURE

Look for the connection. Is the diameter the same as a side or a diagonal?

Example:

If the area of the square is 36, what is the circumference of the circle?

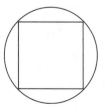

Setup:

To get the circumference, you need the diameter or radius. The circle's diameter is also the square's diagonal. The diagonal of the square is $6\sqrt{2}$. This is because the diagonal of the square transforms it into two separate 45°-45°-90° triangles (see #46). So, the diameter of the circle is $6\sqrt{2}$.

$$Circumference = \pi(Diameter) = 6\pi\sqrt{2}$$

96. How to find the VOLUME of a RECTANGULAR SOLID

$$Volume = Length \times Width \times Height$$

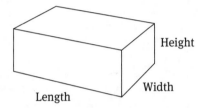

97. How to find the SURFACE AREA of a RECTANGULAR SOLID

To find the surface area of a rectangular solid, you have to find the area of each face and add the areas together. Here's the formula:

Let l = length, w = width, h = height:

$$Surface\ area = 2(lw) + 2(wh) + 2(lh)$$

98. How to find the DIAGONAL of a RECTANGULAR SOLID

Use the Pythagorean theorem twice, unless you spot "special" triangles.

Example:

What is the length of AG?

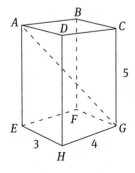

Setup:

Draw diagonal AC.

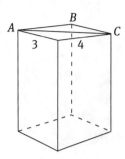

ABC is a 3:4:5 triangle, so $AC = 5$. Now look at triangle ACG:

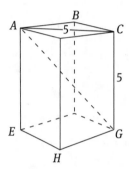

ACG is another special triangle, so you don't need to use the Pythagorean theorem. ACG is a 45°-45°-90° triangle, so $AG = 5\sqrt{2}$.

99. How to find the VOLUME of a CYLINDER

$$Volume = Area\ of\ the\ base \times Height = \pi r^2 h$$

Example:

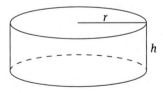

Let $r = 6$ and $h = 3$.

Setup:

$$Volume = \pi r^2 h = \pi(6^2)(3) = 108\pi$$

100. How to find the SURFACE AREA of a CYLINDER

$$Surface\ area = 2\pi r^2 + 2\pi rh$$

Example:

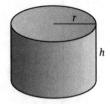

Let $r = 3$ and $h = 4$.

Setup:

$$
\begin{aligned}
Surface\ area &= 2\pi r^2 + 2\pi rh \\
&= 2\pi(3)^2 + 2\pi(3)(4) \\
&= 18\pi + 24\pi = 42\pi
\end{aligned}
$$